ISBN 978-0-428-81956-9
PIBN 10035777

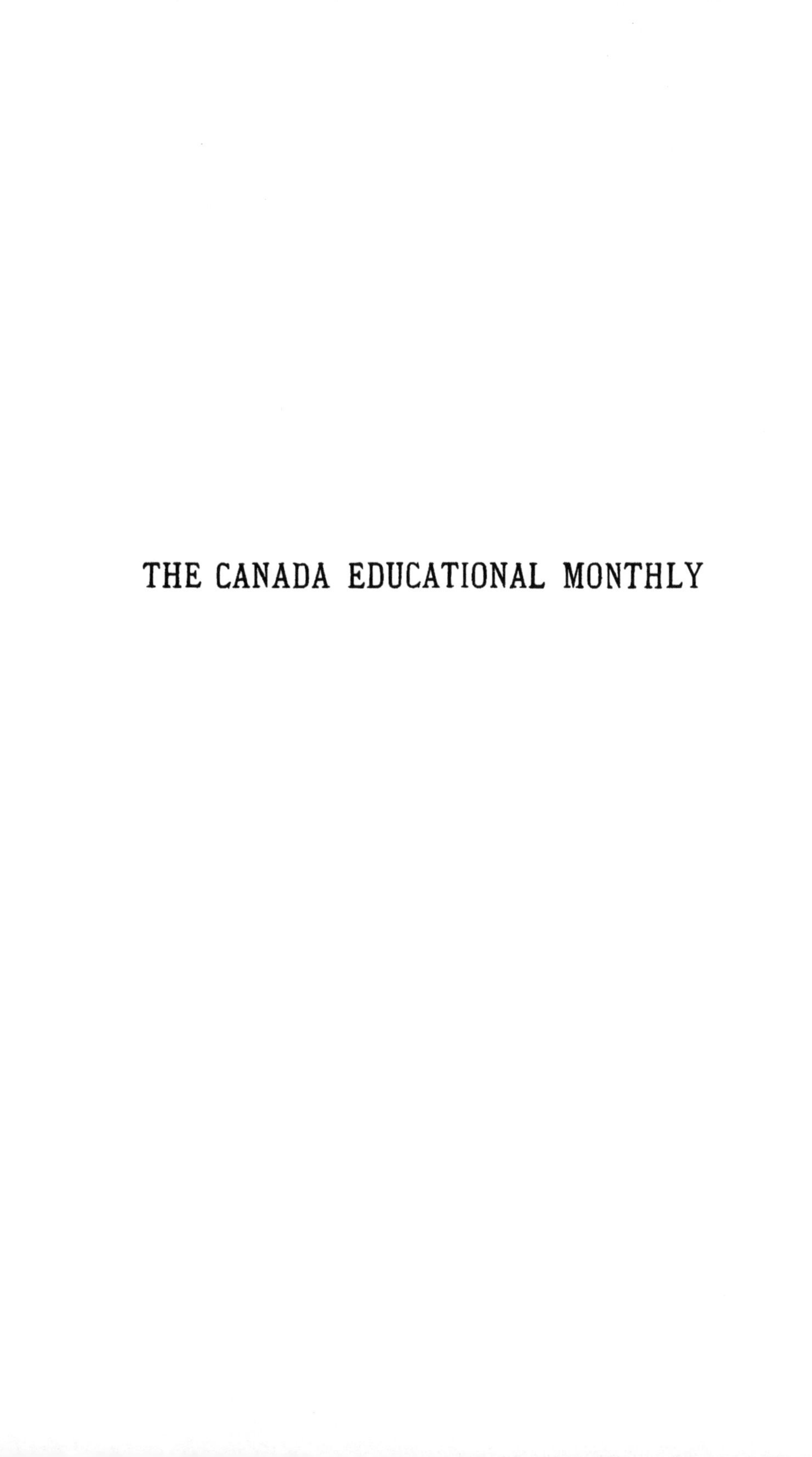

THE CANADA EDUCATIONAL MONTHLY

THE CANADA

EDUCATIONAL

MONTHLY

EDITED BY ARCHIBALD MacMURCHY, M.A

VOL. XIX.

JANUARY TO DECEMBER,

1897.

TORONTO:

THE CANADA EDUCATIONAL MONTHLY PUBLISHING COMPANY.

CONTENTS.

PAGE

Aims and Management of High School Literary Societies............ 123
Dr. Purslow.

Address of Welcome, An.................................... 281
Dr. J. M. Harper.

Bible, The.. 51
Mail and Empire.

Boston School Administration 334
A. S. Witmore.

Brotherhood of Teachers and Educational Reform, The............ 361
Dr. J. M. Harper.

Business of the Teacher, The................................ 321
F. E. Findlay, M.A.

Cambridge School for Girls, The 92
The School Journal.

Canada's Development...................................... 295
The Mail and Empire.

Canadian Unity and a National Bureau of Education............. 209
Dr. J. M. Harper.

Civic Training in Public Schools.............................. 90
W. C. Jacobs.

Claims of Individuality in Education.......................... 241
R. Wormell.

Contemporary Literature..38, 77, 115, 157, 197, 239, 279, 319, 359, 393

Correlation of Studies......................................84, 129
Dr. W. T. Harris.

Correspondence..........................25, 191, 230, 316, 357, 391

Current Events and Comments........62, 104, 143, 182, 224, 349, 390

Editorial Notes 26, 60, 97, 137, 218, 269, 298, 346, 385

Educational Essay... 212
S. Moore.

Education from a Publisher's Standpoint 254, 291
G. H. Tucker.

PAGE

Effect of High School Regulations on Teachers.................... 201
H. J. Strang, B.A.

Elementary Education in Quebec.............................. 45
R. F. Hewton, M.A.

Ethics of Expression, The.................................. 257
Education.

Further Word on Canadian Literature, A....................... 121
Evelyn Durand.

Good Discipline.. 16
Growth of Crime.. 174
Fidelis.

Herbartian Steps of Instruction............................ 45
High School Teacher of Mathematics.......................... 329
P. H. Hanus.

History in the School...................................... 12
S. S. Laurie.

Literature Studies in Public Schools........................ 81
A. L. Carruthers.

Little Things.. 58
Canadian Churchman.

Learning Together.. 378
Ellen E. Kenyon Warner.

Moral Training in Public Schools.......................... 161, 248
D. Fotheringham, B.A.

Modern College Education................................... 342
Grant Allen

Nature Study in Public Schools............................. 167
N. MacMurchy, B.A.

New Woman and the Problems of the Day, The.................. 132
Popular Science Monthly.

Natural Science, Study of.................................. 367
Alex. H. D. Ross, M.A.

PAGE

On Being Human 286, 372
Woodrow Wilson.
Our Great North 297
Outside Influence 176

Pedagogy of the Hat-Taker 267
S. S. Times.
Princeton Celebration 18
N. Y. Evening Post.
Professional Hints and Correspondence 103
Professional Opinion 233
Public School System of Education in Nova Scotia 87
A. H. McKay, LL.D.
Prayer, A 387
Charles Edwin Markham.

Queen's English 214

Recessional 277
Rudyard Kipling.
Reforma ion Schools 171
Religious Instruction 57, 135
Rest from Fear 41
Rev. Hugh Black.

School of Practical Agriculture, A 216
School Work 31, 70, 109, 152, 194, 235, 277, 315, 355
Scope of Science 163
A. H. W. Ross, M.A.
Simplicity in Poetry 126
Educational Times.
Slouch 339
Evening Post.
Solidarity of Town and Farm 266
Arena.
Some Notes on Poetry for Children 7, 48
E. V. Lucas.
Snobbery of Education 174
Spelling Question, The 55
Edward R. Shaw.

PAGE

Teaching Children to Talk 95
P. S. Journal.

Technical Education 59

Temperature of Arid Regions 268
Portland Oregonian.

Theological Life of a Californian Child 53
Prof. Earle Barnes.

To Medical Students 1
Prof. W. Clark.

Value of Psychology 260
Prof. J. G. Hume.

Wages 60
Tennyson.

THE CANADA

EDUCATIONAL MONTHLY

AND SCHOOL MAGAZINE.

JANUARY, 1897.

TO MEDICAL STUDENTS.*

Rev. Prof. William Clark, M.A., LL.D., Trinity College, Toronto.

YOU are here, gentlemen, to be educated for the great and honorable work to which, by God's help, you intend to dedicate the remainder of your lives. With more or less of previous education and preparation, you have come up here to gain that special knowledge and skill which are necessary for the due performance of your duties as surgeons and physicians. And here a remark may be offered which might seem more appropriate at an earlier moment in your educational history, but which is never really out of place. It is, that every professional man should do his best to have under his special training, and as its foundation and basis, a *sound and good general education.* Without this we are not only likely to be narrow and contracted in our views and sympathies, but we shall fail to gain that firm grasp of the facts and principles of our own special subject of which only an educated mind is capable. It is our business not only to learn and to know certain things. This is good and necessary. But it is our business also to be educated men, with minds cultivated and disciplined so as to have keenness of perception and discrimination. Without this much of our labor will be aimless and unprofitable. And although it is desirable that this foundation should be well laid before we raise the superstructure of special instruction, yet much may be done by an earnest and diligent man to repair the omissions and defects of an earlier education. Let us only try to feel the importance of this qualification, and we shall find ways and means of supplying much, at least, of that which is lacking. And the time which is expended for this purpose will certainly not be wasted.

Along with this general education it is most important to foster *a knowledge and love of literature*, first and chiefly, of course, the literature of our own language, but also, if possible, that of some other or others. On this subject it were possible to say much; but it would never be possible for one man, or for many men, to say all that might be said. For a man to use books merely to learn all that may be acquired on the special business of his life would be to condemn his mind to perpetual sterility. Literature humanizes, elevates, refines, enriches, strengthens. The companion-

* Delivered to Trinity College Medical Students.

ship of good books is fellowship with the best and noblest men and women of our race. They bring us the choice thoughts of the choicest minds. The lines in our old Latin Grammar, which taught us that the faithful learning of literature softens the manners, and prevents them from being coarse, are as true as ever they were. Nor is such learning useless even in regard to the special work of our life. It brings to us a knowledge of men more intimate and profound than we could otherwise attain; and such knowledge will always be no inconsiderable element in our equipment for our work. The physician needs to know more than the phenomena of health and disease, more than the particular constitution of the individual man. He needs to know humanity; and although this knowledge must largely be gained by actual intercourse with his fellow-men, it will be greatly supplemented by acquaintance with those great types of manhood and womanhood which are presented to us in the pages of our poets and dramatists, of our historians and writers of fiction.

Of even greater importance, to men of any profession, than the possession of literary tastes and habits is that subtle, profound, all-pervading power which we call *character;* by which, of course, we do not mean merely reputation, or history merely, although history has a chief hand in its formation; but that *Ethos*, that disposition in which we seem to find the unity of the individual, in which we recognize him as a whole. Character is the greatest power in the world for good and for evil. Mere ability, even when supplemented with great knowledge, will have comparatively little power or influence, unless they are reinforced by character; for this is, after all, the organ of the highest and best knowledge, and the guide to the best and most perfect work. Truthfulness, uprightness, purity, kindliness, gentleness, resoluteness in the fulfilment of duty—these form a manifold cord which cannot easily be broken.

And if these remarks, brief as they necessarily are, may be charged with vagueness, we may supplement them by a few words on a point more tangible, the subject of *habits* and their formation. Habits are the outcome of character, and they constitute character. A man's habits, regarded not merely in their outward form, but also in their inward principle, and in the motive which animates them—these are his character. Hence the importance of watching over ourselves, especially in our earlier years, when we take in impressions with ease, and of seeing to it that those habits are formed, the retention of which will be no injury to ourselves or to others.

With regard to some of these you will receive safe and valuable guidance from your studies in this place. You will learn that the laws of our physical constitution cannot be violated with impunity. You will learn that whilst the Author of our being has connected pleasure with all the exercises of our powers, yet the seeking for pleasure by unlawful means, or any form of excess will ever be followed by a retribution of pain and woe; and the "end of these things is death." And you will learn, by many sorrowful examples, and some of them even in your own profession, that a very complete knowledge of the body and its parts and its functions, and of the dangers to which it is exposed, will not always be a safeguard against the evils of which we have been forewarned. It is well that we should early learn to look to a power greater than our own. "Remember now thy Creator in the days of thy youth."

But there are other aspects of this subject less solemn indeed, yet not unimportant, on which something should here be said. We might, for example, point to the importance of *method*, of doing all our work in a well-organized, systematic manner. It is only by such means that our work can be done in any satisfactory manner, or with any approach to completeness. Under the head of method we might place regularity, punctuality, the strict and prompt performance of duty. How easily do such words and phrases drop from our lips, and yet how much they mean, and how hard they are to practise! But we may safely say that if the formation of such habits is arduous; when formed, they are well worth all that they have cost. They are worth it in the mere struggle for existence; but they have a higher value than this. How is it that one man gets to be trusted with the performance of any duty which he deliberately undertakes, and another receives no confidence at all, however strongly he may assure us of his readiness and care to discharge the office entrusted to him? It is because the one is known as possessed of those qualities, as having formed those habits which will ensure the desired result, and another has not.

How many men there are in this world and in this city who complain that all their efforts have come to nothing, that they have tried one employment after another, and all has been in vain! What is the explanation? Let us grant that some are unfortunate, that circumstances beyond their control have so hampered and hindered them that failure was inevitable. But these are exceptional cases. Generally speaking the explanation is only too simple. These people have made engagements and they have not kept them. They have entered into contracts and they have not carried them out. They have undertaken duties and they have not fulfilled them, or they have not done this at the right time, and in the right way. And so men have ceased to trust them, or to employ them, or to count upon them in any way. And the misery of it all is, that such cases soon become well-nigh hopeless. The chain of habit is too strong to be snapped. And everyone, except the wretched man himself, knows that his sloth or his falseness or his conceit has brought him this evil through many years, and that it is now irreparable.

On this point, let me speak one earnest word before I pass on. Young men, your life is still to a large extent before you, to make of it what you will. Doubtless, you have already formed habits which have a considerable power and influence over you. But you can hardly have so far formed them that you are incapable of making a dispassionate estimate of their nature and tendencies; and you have not so formed them that it is no longer possible to change them. Soon you will go forth from these halls and many of you will probably take up your abode in places which will be your homes so long as you live. Try to use the interval of time in such a manner as to form those habits by which you will wish to be distinguished throughout your whole personal and professional career. Remember, this is now possible to you. Every day that you live you may make some progress in one or the other direction. Every day the light of reason and conscience grows clearer or dimmer. Every false word darkens and distorts the sense of truth. Every act of procrastination helps to destroy the habit of prompt recognition of duty and to efface the sense of duty.

A great physician, a native of Canada, Dr. Osler, now of Baltimore, in an address delivered three years ago, in the University of Minneapolis, among many words of wisdom adorned with eloquence, told the students of that place that there was one grace which alone could give permanence to human powers — the *grace of Humility.* The great Spinoza said that the two fertile sources of all evil and hindrances to all good were sloth and conceit; and the great Bacon reminds us emphatically that we can enter the Kingdom of Knowledge only as we enter the Kingdom of heaven—by becoming as little children. And such a quality is of peenliar necessity and excellence in respect to the special point we have been considering of the formation and transformation of our habits. If we are self-satisfied, confident of our own powers and our own attainments, it is but little likely that we shall acquire those habits and dispositions which will fit us for the work of our life; whilst, on the other hand, if we carry about with us a habitual sense of the infinite nature of knowledge, of the difficulty of life, together with a humble estimate of our own powers, we shall be watchful against temptation, we shall resist the beginnings of evil, we shall be careful to fulfil every duty as it arises, never hesitating, never debating or questioning, but only acting with decision and promptitude when the duty has become clear to us. Here is the secret of the formation of habit, and the formation of character.

So far our remarks have been almost equally applicable to men of any profession; and now we come to one, which, while it applies to all men and is the characteristic of him whom we style a gentleman, yet has a special application to the medical man. The physician should be *a man of honour.* There are three classes of men who, beyond all others, have access to the families of other men, and who become, of necessity, acquainted with their condition and circumstances—the lawyer, the clergyman, and the physician; and, if one of these can be dispensed with in time of need, it is not the physician. He is admitted to an intimacy which is accorded to no one else beyond the family circle; and therefore his relation to the family partakes of a sacred character; and the knowledge which he gains of the family is as sacred to him as the privacy of his own home. He will no more discuss his patients with his neighbor than he will discuss his wife.

On these points, gentlemen, you will receive counsel and guidance from the experienced and honorable men who are here set over you; and experience and observation will enforce these lessons. But we who are outside the faculty may sometimes hear and know of circumstances which are not in quite the same manner brought under the notice of medical men themselves; and we know that there is nothing which the ordinary man, and still more the ordinary woman, more indignantly resents than being made the subject of discussion by her medical attendant. Such things seldom occur; but when they do occur, they are fatal, and they ought to be fatal to the reputation and influence of the medical man, however great his ability.

I have dwelt the longer upon subjects not specially medical for obvious reasons; but perhaps I may be allowed to touch upon certain aspects of your work here which may be set forth without special knowledge.

You come here to be qualified for one of the most useful and beneficent kinds of work in which any human being can engage. You come to gain knowledge of man, of his structure and functions, and of those agencies by which disease may be banished and health restored to the bodies of men. You come to have your power and habits of observation rendered more acute and vigorous. You are here that you may become acquainted with the past history of medicine and surgery, and that you may see the experience of the past illustrated in the skilful treatment of the present. You come that you may yourselves gain, by practice, that skill and dexterity which will stand you in stead when you go forth on your work of mercy in the midst of suffering humanity.

When the Apostle of the Gentiles thought of the work on which he had been sent forth to evangelize the world, he exclaimed: "Who is sufficient for these things?" And the same question may well occur to yourselves. One thing at least is certain, that the knowledge and skill which you require will not fall from heaven upon you. At a great price you must obtain this power—at the price of long and arduous labor carried on through many hours and weeks and years—of labor long and arduous, yet most joyful and most sweet in the sense of right and duty which it stimulates, in the exercise of the energies of body and mind, and in the results which flow from it. We are not good for much if we are not willing to work. A slothful man is seldom useful to himself or to others. It is difficult to know what to suggest to a man who is confirmed in sloth. *Perhaps* he might succeed best as a beggar. But begging is not a recognized or even a tolerated profession in this country.

But we must not only be workers, we must *work wisely*, deeply, widely, not being narrow or one-sided. For example, we must avoid the two extremes into which men are apt to fall, of being mere theorists on the one hand, or mere empirics on the other. We must have science. We must know all that can be known, all that we are capable of knowing about the human constitution and its ailments and their cures. But a man might have a quite prodigious knowledge of all the principles and theories of medicine. and yet fail to succeed in his profession because he had not carefully noted the actual operation of these principles in practice. The merely *a priori* method is not good anywhere, but is very bad indeed in medicine. Yet the empiric is no better and no safer. If we must descend from the skies and touch mother earth, in order to gain strength, we must also rise up from the toil and dust of terrestrial labor and gain fresh life and inspiration in the region of principles.

But I am reminded here that I am addressing many different men with different powers and endowments—men who are now qualified, and will hereafter be more fully qualified for different kinds of work.

And first, we may assume that there are here a certain number of men of superior and distinguished ability. Such there have always been in past years. Some such we know to be here with us now, and we may assume that there are others who will speedily be tested and proved, as their predecessors have been. Such men are a gift of God to humanity, for which we ought to be thankful. Perhaps men of this kind stand less in need of exhortations to earnest work than other men do. It is the man of one talent who is under the strongest temptation to hide that one in a napkin. Yet there have been too many cases of splendid gifts neglected and wasted—sometimes even turned to evil instead of good. Men thus highly endowed, then, should be reminded that to whom much is given, of them will much be required, that the talents with which they have been entrusted are not their own to waste or to apply for selfish purposes. They possess them as stewards and they are bound to see that they are expended in such a manner as to fulfil the purpose of the Giver. A great responsibility is laid upon those who are thus endowed. They have a duty to themselves, to see that they make the most and the best of those powers with which they have been endowed. They have a duty to this institution in which they are receiving their education, to maintain its high character and reputation, to see that it suffers no diminution of usefulness or influence through any laxity on their part. They have, moreover, a duty to their country and to mankind, who have perpetual need of the best services of their best men.

But there are others besides those who stand in the first rank, who may here claim a word of counsel and encouragement. It must often have occurred to us, as we have seen gold and silver medals and other marks of distinction conferred upon the men of the first rank. that something like despondency must come over those who belong to what we may call the rank and file of the army. But there is, in fact, no justification for such despondency. It is not in medicine alone, but in all the professions, in the Christian ministry, in law,and in business as well, that the men of distinction are the minority. But besides, whilst we must freely admit that there are certain walks in every profession which can be trodden only by the few, the great body of the work is done, and well and successfully done by the men who do not belong to those few. These men may not make startling discoveries in the science of medicine or invent new methods of treatment. But there is no necessity for their doing any thing of this kind. They can do and they are doing the kind of work which the world needs, and they are doing that work well and faithfully and successfully. And just as there are many able, careful, conscientious, skilful and successful practitioners who have not been gold or silver medalists, so there are now many here who may reach the same results by following the same methods.

To you, gentlemen, of whom I am now thinking, I will say with all earnestness—never despair of yourselves, respect yourselves, stir up the gift that is in you, do your work honestly, conscientiously, devotedly, and you will not fail of your reward.

Think of the generations of students who have passed through these lecture halls. There is not one of them who grudges or regrets the toil he bestowed upon that noble science to which you are giving yourselves. There is not one who does not lament whatever hours he may have wasted, or any duty which he may have neglected. Let it be your endeavour so to live and work in this College that you may have few regrets in the future.

Think, too, of the distinguished men who have given to this College the proud position which it now occupies. They cannot be here forever; yet their hearts will never forget the men or the work of this institution. See that your work here is such as to give them the hope, the confident expectation that when they leave their places vacant, men of their own training will be found to carry on the traditions of the past, and to add fresh lustre to the name of the Trinity Medical College in the future.

Mutual education, in a large sense of the word, is one of the great and incessant occupations of human society, carried on partly with set purpose, and partly not. One generation forms another; and the existing generation is ever acting and reacting upon itself in the persons of its individual members.—*John Henry Newman.*

The man that bids for a smaller salary than his predecessor, and the pettifogging offiee-holder or preferment seeker, is to have no place in New Brunswick after this.

SOME NOTES ON POETRY FOR CHILDREN.

(*Continued from November.*)

I CANNOT find anywhere else such intimate treatment of this side of child life.[1] In Lady Lindsay's "String of Beads" there is a little poem called "A Child's Dream," which takes us part of the way, and which, there can be little doubt, was inspired by Mr. Stevenson's book. Indeed he has had many imitators, but none of them have succeeded in capturing anything but the form. And among other writers of verse, who preceded him, or have made no conscious attempts to work on similar lines, none impresses and convinces as he.

Taking them altogether, the poets have not shown themselves to be closely in touch with children; the great ones have tried and failed, and left it to humbler singers—such as Mary Lamb—to give us the true note. But these humble singers are few and far between, as the editor of the adult volume will quickly discover. We might cite Mrs. Piatt as one example of an author who, with a wide, comprehending love for children, has captured in a hundred efforts little of the genius of childhood. Perhaps in all her poems nothing is so characteristic and illuminating as the triumphal boast, in "Child's World Ballads," of the little girl who had visited Edinburgh:

> I put my hand on every chair
> That said "Don't touch," at Holyrood.

Another good example of an author who wished to produce sympathetic child-poems, but has always broken down, is Mr. Bret Harte. The "Miss Edith" poems are failures, and though he certainly was visited by inspiration when he began "On the Landing," the mood passed before the piece was completed. Two little boys, Bobby, aged three and a half, and Johnny, a year older, are peeping over the balusters at night when they ought to be in bed, watching the guests on the floor below. Here are the best lines:—

BOBBY.

"Do you know why they've put us in that back room,
Up in the attic, close against the sky,
And made believe our nursery's a cloak room?
Do you know why?"

JOHNNY.

"No more I don't, nor why that Sammy's mother,
That ma thinks horrid, 'cause he bunged my eye,
Eats an ice-cream down there like any other.
No more don't I!"

BOBBY.

"Do you know why nurse says it isn't manners
For you and me to ask folks twice for pie,
And no one hits that man with two bananas?
Do you know why?"

JOHNNY.

"No more I don't, nor why that girl, whose dress is
Off of her shoulders, don't catch cold and die,
When you and me gets croup when *we* undresses!
No more don't I!"

BOBBY.

"Perhaps she ain't as good as you and I is,
And God don't want her up there in the sky,
And lets her live—to come in just when pie is—
Perhaps that's why."

IOHNNY.

"Do you know why that man that's got a cropped head,
Rubbed it just now as if he felt a fly?
Could it be, Bobby, something that I dropped?
And is that why?"

[1] There is a little poem in Mrs. Woods' recent volume, "Aeromancy," of much the same character.

BOBBY.

"Good boys behaves, and so they don't get scolded,
Nor drop hot milk on folks as they pass by."

JOHNNY (*piously*).

"Marbles would bounce on Mr. Jones's bald head,
But *I* shan't try."

To this stage the piece is admirable. Then a discordant note is struck. The next remark of Bobby (aged three and a half) is to this effect :—

"Do you know why Aunt Jane is always snarling
At you and me because we tells a lie,
But she don't slap that man that called her darling?
Do you know why?"

In his desire to make a point the author transgresses fatally. And in the next stanza the Seventh Commandment is jeopardized, just as in the modern novel, and we throw away the book.

Looking forward is a childish amusement akin to making believe. "When I am grown up" is a form of words constantly on the child's tongue :—

When I am grown to man's estate
I shall be very proud and great,
And tell the other girls and boys
Not to meddle with my toys.

So says the child in Mr. Stevenson's book. Elsewhere he descends to particulars, and decides that of all professions his choice would be the lamplighter's. But you must have the exquisite little poem in full :—

My tea is nearly ready, and the sun has left the sky,
'Tis time to take the window to see Leerie going by;
For every night at tea-time, and before you take your seat,
With lantern and with ladder he comes posting up the street.

Now Tom would be a driver, and Maria go to sea,
And my papa's a banker, and as rich as he can be,
But I, when I am stronger and can choose what I'm to do,
Oh, Leerie, I'll go round at nights and light the lamps with you.

For we are very lucky, with a lamp before the door,
And Leerie stops to light it, as he lights so many more;
And oh, before you hurry by with ladder and with light,
Oh, Leerie, see a little child and nod to him to-night.

If I had to forget all the poems in the "Child's Garden" and retain but one, I should, I think, choose "The Lamplighter." The last line wanders through the passages of the mind like a gentle musical phrase.

In "Poems Written for a Child" (1868), a volume in which the late Menella Bute Smedley, and an anonymous writer known as "A," collaborated, there are some good "Looking forward" verses called "A Boy's Aspirations," from Miss Smedley's pen. Here are three stanzas out of the ten :—

I was four yesterday, when I'm quite old
I'll have a cricket-ball made of pure gold;
I'll carve the roast meat and help soup and fish;
I'll get my feet wet whenever I wish.

. . . . .

I'll spend a hundred pounds every day;
I'll have the alphabet quite done away;
I'll have a parrot without a sharp beak;
I'll see a pantomime six times a week.

I'll have a rose-tree always in bloom;
I'll keep a dancing bear in mamma's room;
I'll spoil my best clothes and not care a pin;
I'll have no visitors ever let in.

These lines are good, although now and then erroneous. The mistakes are due to ignorance of boy-nature. A boy, for example, neither wants a cricket-ball made of gold—it would be against the laws—nor a rose-tree always in bloom. Nor would it strike him as peculiar ecstasy to keep a dancing-bear in his mother's room; he would prefer it in his own. But readers of our Grown-up's Anthology will like to have it. It will take them back to old days.

In the volume "Poems Written for a Child," from the pen of "A," is a very quaint little anecdote in the same kind, entitled "Wooden Legs." A girl and boy are telling each other what they would like to be :—

Then he said, "I'll be a soldier,
With a delightful gun,
And I'll come home with a wooden leg,
As heroes have often done."

This is a new and acceptable ambition, but some questionable love sentiment is then introduced and the interest evaporates. Indeed, in this variety of story writers are liable to go astray. Sentiment, a steed more apt than any other to get the bit between its teeth, runs away with them. In a desire to attain a dramatic effect dramatic propriety is lost sight of. Children are too near the savage state for symmetrical sentiment. Still, there are instances. Whittier's poem "In School-days" tells of one. He is describing the schoolhouse, through whose windows the sun is shining :—

It touched the tangled golden curls,
And brown eyes full of grieving,
Of one who still her steps delayed,
When all the school were leaving.

For near her stood the little boy,
Her childish favor singled,
His cap pulled low upon a face
Where pride and shame were mingled.

He saw her lift her eyes, he felt
The soft hand's light caressing,
And heard the tremble of her voice,
As if a fault confessing.

"I'm sorry that I spelt the word;
I hate to go above you,
Because," the brown eyes lower fell,
"Because, you see, I love you."

It is prettily conceivable; but that kind of thing may well be postponed. Children who love each other in this way are not making the most of their opportunities as privileged barbarians. To the same family belongs Mr. Dobson's "Drama of the Doctor's Window."

The best poetical expression of the love of girl and boy that I know is to be found in the two sonnets of George Eliot, called "Brother and Sister," which might well be our sole representatives of this class. Such love is always worship, always based on admiration; it is almost always one-sided. Affection, as we understand it—friendship on equal ground—being a civilized growth, comes later. Children are not of civilization as we are. In this connection I should like to quote the lines entitled "Dry Bread," from Victor Hugo's "L'Art d'être Grandpère," which enshrines for us a charming incident, where the actors are not, to the casual eye at least, girl and boy, but girl and old man. The translation is by the Rev. Henry Carrington :—

Jeanne to dry bread and the dark room consigned
For some misdeed; I, to my duty blind,
Visit the prisoner, traitor that I am!
And in the dark slip her a pot of jam.
Those in my realm, on whose authority
Depends the welfare of Society,
Were outraged. Jeanne's soft little voice arose—
"I'll put no more my thumb up to my nose;
No more I'll let the puss my fingers tear."
But they all cry, "That child is well aware
How weak and mean you are. She knows of old
You always take to laughing when we scold;
No government can stand; at every hour
Rule you upset. There is an end of power.
No laws exist. Naught keeps the child in bound;
You ruin all." I bow my head to ground,
And say, "Your grievous charge I can't oppose,
I'm wrong. Yes, by indulgences like those,
The people's ruin has been always wrought.
Put me upon dry bread." "I'm sure we ought
And will." Then Jeanne from her dark corner cries,
But low to me, raising her beauteous eyes
(Love gives the lion's courage to the lamb!)
"And I will go and bring you pots of jam!"

Landor's "Rosina" is somewhat akin.

Another class of poetry, which only the adult should possess, is that which describes particular children. Many poets—Wordsworth pre-eminently—have attempted this kind, but, for the most part, so rapt has been their admiring—almost worshipping—gaze, that in the finished poem the child has been only faintly visible through a golden mist. In other cases the poet has made the child a mere peg upon which to hang a thought of his own. But simple, unaffected descriptions do exist. In "Lays for the Nursery" (bound up with "Whistle Binkie," that charming collection of Scotch poems by minor writers) will be found the history of "Wee Joukydaidles," by James Smith, a very human poem which, probably unconsciously, Mr. William Canton, the author of "The Invisible Playmate," who has for children a love that sometimes becomes adoration, reduces to a couplet when of a certain notable "Little Woman" he says :—

She is my pride, my plague, my rest, my rack, my bliss, my bane,
She brings me sunshine of the heart and softening of the brain.

From Mr. Canton's last volume, "W. V., Her Book, and Various Verses," I should take the poems entitled "Wings and Hands" and "Making Pansies." But enough of the Grown-up's Anthology.

It is time now to explain whence the contents of the Child's Anthology should be drawn. The names that come most naturally to mind are those of "Lewis Carroll" and Edward Lear; and I would add Dr. Hoffman, but that it is a mistake to separate his verses and pictures. These twain would yield many pages; I need not stop to particularize since every one knows them so well. The "Percy Reliques" would be a rich source; and I should include such modern ballads as "John Gilpin," one or two of the Ingoldsby Legends, and a few to be found in the works of less-known experimentalists. Among these is "A," the lady from whom a quotation has already been made. In "Poems Written for a Child," in "Child World" and in "Child Nature," are several capital pieces of humorous narrative. There is, for instance, Fred's story in "Child Nature," entitled "John's Sin." It tells of a giant who, since conscience makes cowards of us all, became a cowherd for conscience' sake, but is baulked at the outset by an inability to milk :—

He could not milk her ; he was skilled
In abstruse science ; was renown'd
In mathematics ; he had Mill'd,
Bain'd, Maurice'd, Hamilton'd, and Brown'd.

. . . .

Herodotus and Mr. Bright
He knew—but could not a milk a cow !

(The deleted lines, it may be mentioned in passing, are remarkable for containing a new rhyme to cow. The ingenious "A" presses the author of "The Bothie of Tober na Vuolich" into that service.) While the giant was bemoaning this incapacity, a dwarf came by, milked the cow, boxed the giant's ears, and led him as prisoner to a farm, where his size became a serious embarrassment. Shortly afterwards he died. The author remarks sententiously :—

A giant in a little room
Alive, is an uncommon bore ;
A giant dead, besides the gloom,
Is such a trouble on the floor.

In the same class are several of the pieces in "Lilliput Levee," by "Matthew Browne," notably the introductory verses, which tell of the revolution, the "Ballad of Frodgedobbulum's Fancy," "Shockheaded

Cicely and the Bears," and "Clean Clara." Frodgedobbulum was

A vulgar giant, who wore no gloves,
And very pig-headed in his loves!

Cleanliness was Clean Clara's passion. She cleaned "a hundred thousand things:"—

She cleaned the mirror, she cleaned the cupboard,
All the books she Indian-rubbered.

. . . .

She cleaned the tent-stich and the sampler,
She cleaned the tapestry, which was ampler,
Joseph going down into the pit,
And the Shunamite woman with the boy in a fit.

There is, of course, fun and fun. I should, for example, omit Hood's comic ballads—"Faithless Sally Brown" and cognate pieces—where I should include Goldsmith's "Elegy on the Death of a Mad Dog" and "Madame Blaize," although superficially they are akin. Hood is for the agile adult brain. He crackles rather than ripples, and children want to be rippled. Moreover, punning is a dissolute habit; and of all distressing developments none equals paronomasia in a child. I should also omit nursery rhymes, because, unlike little boys, they should be heard and not seen. Only antiquarians and folklorists should ever *read* nursery rhymes. A great part of the pleasure with which in after days we greet the nursery rhymes dear to us in the Golden Age (as Mr. Kenneth Grahame calls it), consists in recalling the kind lips by which they were orally transmitted. The voice, the look, the laugh—all hold us again for one rich flashing moment.

Among poets who can with knowledge describe for us child life, both subjective and objective, we are fortunate in possessing Mr. James Whitcomb Riley. Mr. Riley is a New Englander, and the boy to whom he introduces us is a New Englander too, speaking the Hoosier dialect, but none the less boy for that. Let Mr. Riley's right to speak for children be found in these two Hoosier stanzas called "Uncle Sidney,"—it is established there:—

Sometimes, when I bin bad,
An' pa "correcks" me nen,
An' Uncle Sidney he comes here,
I'm allus good again;

'Cause Uncle Sidney says,
An' takes me up an' smiles—
"The goodest mens they is ain't good
As baddest little childs!"

These lines are of course too incendiary in tone to be included in our children's book—every parent and nurse in the country would be up in arms—but they might well be placed on the title page of the other volume. Mr. Riley, however, has written well for both our anthologists. The child, happily undiscriminative of social grade, is always a hero-worshipper, always, but innocently, envious. His hero is the handy man, the postman, the lamplighter, the gamekeeper. To be with the great man is his ambition and joy, to hear him speak, to watch him make things. Mr. Riley expresses in racy musical verse this young passion. Every boy who has known boyhood at all was once envious of a good-natured Jack-of-all-trades, the Raggedy Man's correlative. Look at Mr. Riley's description of the hero:

O! the Raggedy Man! He works for pa;
An' he's the goodest man ever you saw!
He comes to our house every day,
An' waters the horses, and feeds 'em hay;
An' he opens the shed—an' we all 'ist laugh
When he drives out our little old wobble-ly calf;
An' nen—ef our hired girl says he car—
He milks the cow fer 'Lizibuth Ann.
Ain't he a awful good Raggedy Man?
Raggedy! Raggedy! Raggedy Man!

W'y the Raggedy Man—he's ist so good,
He splits the kindlin' and chops the wood;
An' nen he spades in our garden too,
An' does most things 'at boys can't do.
He climbed clean up in our big tree
An' shooked a apple down fer me—
An' nother'n, too, fer 'Lizibuth Ann—
An' nother'n, too, fer the Raggedy Man!
Ain't he a awful good Raggedy Man?
Raggedy! Raggedy! Raggedy Man!

—*Littell's Living Age.*

(*To be continued.*)

HISTORY IN THE SCHOOL.

By S. S. Laurie, University of Edinburgh.

(*Concluded.*)

HAVING defined our aim how are we to proceed? The great principle, "Adapt to the mental growth of the pupil," must govern all we attempt in this as in other subjects. But in obedience to this principle can we not find some general rule of procedure which shall govern all school history from infancy to the eighteenth year—the age which marks the termination of secondary instruction. I think we can, if we consider for a moment the form in which history necessarily presents itself to us.

History externally viewed is a series of related events in time connected with certain communities of persons and localities, the even tenor of events being occasionally disturbed by outbursts of passion and emotion. That is to say, it presents itself to us as an epic made up of dramatic situations with interludes of lyrical raptures—all connected with persons and the aims or ideas which they represent. Or perhaps we should say it is a prosaic epic every now and then passing into drama and accompanied by a lyrical chorus. History cannot be *reasoned* history to a boy; even at the age of seventeen it is only partially so, but it can always be an epic, a drama and a song. The *general* principle of procedure in education is thus revealed. We must teach history to the young as an epic, a drama and a song. A certain number of dates connected with great crises of national history, or with great characters, must of course, be known for the sake of time sequence; and certain prosaic facts must enter as connecting links of the epic as the pupils increase in years. But the younger our pupils are the more must the epic and dramatic and lyric idea of history be kept in view, and the more indifferent must we remain to casual explanations. Thus the history of the school will be full of humanity and so be a humane study; thus will it connect itself with literature, thus will it stir ethical emotion—thus, in short, will it be true history; and when history, in the larger philosophic conception of it, comes within the range of the cultured adult mind, this epic view of it will contribute to a *true* reasoned comprehension.

Thus it is that history shows itself to be, above all other studies, a humane study, and to be rich in all those elements which go to the ethical culture of the young. All subjects when properly taught contribute, it is true, to this ethical culture, for even science can be humanized; but language (in its larger significance) and history contribute most of all, and these two play into each other's hands. Together they constitute the humanistic in education and furnish the best instruments for the moral and religious growth of mind.

When I say that an event or group of events must be enriched with all the elements of humanity, I mean this, for example: Let the period be the Scots' wars of independence.[1] Round Wallace and Bruce this story chiefly gathers. The boy must have conveyed to him a conception of the *conditions* physical, social and political of the period in so far as these

1 The reader will excuse my taking Scotland for my illustration.

are intelligible at the age which he has reached. The story should be *told* to him: and only thereafter read to him. He should then read it himself. This is the epic; the dramatic and the lyrical enters by reading to him, or with him, all the national poetry and song that has gathered round this period. He then, as in every other subject, is invited to *express himself* in the construction of a narrative of the period.

So in the history of England the period of the Spanish Armada, for example, is to be treated in like manner. The boy must strike his roots deep into the national soil or he will never come to much. It matters nothing that the poetry you give contains much that is legendary. A national legend is a far truer element in the inner history of a people than a bald fact.

So much for the method of school history in general. As for the rest, method is the arrangement of instruction in accordance with the principle of mind-growth and the rules which flow from it.[2]

A few words, however, by way of illustration may be added, although they may now be regarded by the intelligent reader as almost superfluous. With these I do not encumber this short paper.

As to method in its *more detailed* applications, we are met at the threshold by this principle, viz., new knowledge must rest on knowledge already acquired if it is to be a living and intelligible growth. In other words we must begin from a child's own mind-centre if we wish to extend his area of knowledge effectively.

Consequently if he is to learn intelligently about past men and events he must have some knowledge of existing men and events. He must have seen enough and talked enough and read enough about things present to his own experience before he can have the imaginative material at his service for comprehending the past and remote. This he gradually acquires from the general course of instruction in the school, and from the reading of simple fables, stories and narratives in his text-books and the school library. His arithmetic, meanwhile, is teaching him to stretch his conception of time, and his geography to localize his own and other countries and to become alive to the fact that he belongs to a distinct nationality. The only historical imaginative material which I would *directly* give before the age of ten complete is the learning by heart of national ballads.

At ten complete I may begin history, and I ask guidance of my principles of method. I am confronted with "Turn everything to use"—that is to say, what intellectual or moral purpose have I in view in teaching history at all? The end must determine the way. I have already spoken of the end; but I may say further:

Geography I teach with a view to extensiveness of mind, arithmetic and geometry with a view to intensiveness of faculty, history with a view to lengthening the brief span of man's life into the past and so explaining the present. I wish the boy as he grows into a youth to be so taught that the national life and character in so far as it is worthy of admiration, and achievements of his fathers shall form part of himself, enter into his judgments on present affairs, and stimulate him to maintain and advance society by the memory of what has been done in the past. It was as citizens of a particular nation, and by a high sense of the duties of citizenship, that our ancestors accomplished all that has made the present desirable as an advance on

2 See Institutes of Education.

the past. My object, then, is to lead the boy to consider himself as a continuation of the past, as handing on, during his lifetime of activity, a tradition of life and character, while aiming to make things better than he found them by keeping before him the highest ideal of the duties of a citizen recognizing the need of self-sacrifice.

If this is not our aim, what is? Why do I not give him the chronology and annals of Peru instead of England and Scotland and the United States?

Thus the general method of teaching history to the young already indicated is confirmed when we begin to apply a principle of all method: "Turn to use." What use? Having settled this, we see that the early teaching of the story of our nation must have, as far as the materials admit, the characteristics of a national Iliad.

In applying a second principle of method we have found that even this epic teaching cannot profitably begin till the boy is in his eleventh year or ten complete.

Let us further consider the different stages in history instruction in accordance with the governing principle that all teachings must be adapted to the mind-growth and the mind-material already possessed.

FROM TENTH TO TWELFTH YEAR.

It is a story to be told, and the wandering minstrel of old is our model teacher. The childhood of history is the history for children. Text-books are out of place—at least till the story has been narrated by the teacher, just as these old minstrels used to sing the deeds of heroes at the courts of princes. The teacher's mind must be very full, and he must cultivate dramatic and graphic narration. Preserve the human interest of the narrative and point the morals as you go without *impressing* them. Narrations should always be given in the presence of a map, and geographical references constantly made.

FROM TWELFTH TO FIFTEENTH YEAR.

Even at this period history cannot be made interesting in any other way than that which I have explained; and if it is not made interesting, it is quite useless in the school. History can be of moral and intellectual value to a boy only in so far as it gathers round persons and dramatic incidents, thereby enriching his moral nature and furnishing food for his imagination. In the thirteenth year a text-book may be put into the pupil's hands *for the first time.*

I do not think that children should be questioned much in history, except with a view to the *language* of the book they may have been reading, after they have been allowed a text-book. The ends of examination in *narrative*, except where words demand explanation, are always best attained by requiring the pupils to reproduce in their own words, orally or on slate or paper, what they have read in their books or heard from their teacher.

A text-book may be allowed when a boy is twelve complete, but it should not be an epitome of history, but a historical reading book. Chronological connections will be furnished by the teacher orally and written on the blackboard, and the poets will be largely utilized, and if not read by the boys, then read *to* them. Portraits of great men and pictures of great historical scenes or monuments should be shown. Lantern slides might be effectively used.

The two first stages of history teaching are thus, as will be seen, annalistic, epic, pictorial—not rational.

FROM FIFTEENTH TO EIGHTEENTH YEAR.

During this period of secondary instruction the pupil may begin his history over again as a reasoned or rational history in some such book as Green's "Short History of England." In the course of these years he will be much exercised in writing historical narratives. Every advantage will continue to be taken of the general literature of the country, the master reading prose and poetical pieces to the pupils, substituting such readings for the ordinary lesson. When speaking of the Wars of the Roses, stop and read Shakespeare's dramas. When reading of the time of Charles I., stop and read Browning's "Strafford," etc. Historical novels, if good, should be in the school library and freely given out. In the last year of his course the pupil should read along with the master (not as lessons in the technical sense) a book on the "Making of England." The occasional acting of great historical events would do much to give life and meaning to the past.

Before the boys leave school a course of *conversational* lectures should be given on the history of the world, with constant reference to a large wall map. Pictorial illustrations of distant countries and of their great works of art should be available in every school.

In classical schools the boys will have meanwhile read the histories of Greece and Rome. These histories should be short and full, that is to say full in their treatment of a few things, and always free from details not essential to the comprehending of the general course of the story of these nations. Such books as Smith's school histories are models of what a school history ought not to be. (Read Smith's England, p. 29 for example.)

The conversational lectures to which I have alluded will connect the civilization of the ancient with the modern world.

You will see from the above that I look on history as contributing in a very direct way to the ethical purpose of the school, and as also constituting an essential part of the humanistic and literary training.

But this is not all. In the secondary stage, and to some extent even in the primary stage, history must be made to teach Citizenship, and as much of the Constitution as may be thought necessary to the equipment of a citizen politician.

The civil relations and the forms of our constitutional polity, including local or municipal organization, should be taught in all secondary schools. The duty of subjects to the state ought to be impressed. But it is quite useless to do this in a formal and text-book way, until the seventeenth year at earliest. Prior to this all that can be taught with effect must arise out of the history teaching from day to day, and be in close association with it and given orally. Such teachings, if incidental and associated with persons and events, take effect; if formal and detached they are wholly ineffectual for their purpose. Their great value is not the knowledge they give, but their effect in deepening that sense of national continuity and the duty of the citizen which history itself is designed to foster.

I have said that a "text-book" of citizenship is not necessary during the school period.

For the masses who do not go to secondary schools, the more formal instruction must be given in evening continuation schools, but not disjoined from general historical reading. If formal and technical, I repeat, it loses its effect. Even the adult mind learns best from the concrete. There is only one interest that is universal, and that is Life.

I would next direct attention to the Economic teaching that may be given in connection with history and which is best so given.

As in instruction in civil relations, there is to be here no text-book if the subject is to be effectively taught. As all effective instruction in civil relations hangs on the history teaching, so all effective school instruction in economics hangs on other subjects, viz., history, the sense-realistic object lesson and geography.

If these are properly understood and adequately taught, they bring about gradually a knowledge of the whole foundation of economics. Production as determined by climatic conditions, industrial production, industrial interchange of products, the nature of commerce, labor, and the organization of labor have all been inevitably taught. What is still wanted, and this only in the secondary period of education, is a fuller explanation of the relation of tools and machinery to production, and to material civilization, and an explanation of capital in its relation to wages and industrial enterprises generally. An explanation of money may also be given. But beyond these things you cannot go without rousing public antagonism. It is not necessary to go further; you have given a solid foundation for future reading and for sound judgment on affairs.

The moral relations of economics—the necessity of *honest* labor, of justice, integrity, truthfulness, and mutual confidence to the existence even for a single week of industrial relations—all arise in connection with historical study and fortify the moral instruction which it gives.

I would connect, as will be seen, the study both of civil relations and of economics with the history of the school. Geographical knowledge is also confirmed and extended in connection with the historical lessons, while the prose and poetical readings illustrative of history are component parts of the literary education. It has been often urged against educational reformers, and with some truth, that they desire to teach too much during the school period. But the moment we begin to get a glimpse of method and of the organization and inter-relation of studies, we see that much may be taught with ease and simplicity if only the teacher himself is properly equipped and understands the scope and purpose of his vocation. We may seem to demand much of the teacher; but not more than the future will demand of him, if he is to be educator as well as instructor.—*School Review.*

GOOD DISCIPLINE.

WE have recently been told that "the good disciplinarian is only too often a person without any sympathy with children." In this modern age we are told many things, some hard of belief, by the thousand and one educational prophets of our time. But in the matter of discipline there does indeed appear to be cherished a superstition which has already survived too long, and which needs to be rooted out. The superstition survives in the ideas which the young teachers bring to the class-room, and in the phrase "thorough disciplinarian" so familiar in testimonials.

The first and foremost fact impressed upon the tiro is that he must at all costs keep order; and it is, of course, true that no work can be done without order. The boys themselves are quick to see this. The mischief lies in the false idea as to what order implies. An experienced teacher has been known to say to a young friend going into a class-room for the first time: "Never mind what you teach them; only keep them quiet and it will be all right." A younger master, exasperated after a long morning's struggle, has been known to say to his form: "I don't care whether you do any work or not; but I will have order." Another man, with his scanty stock of patience expended, made use of almost identical words, and added that there should be absolute quiet for ten minutes before the lesson continued. To obey such an order was clearly impossible, and fresh explosions on both sides followed. There is no need to exaggerate or to take an isolated case as typical. It seems difficult to deny that a false notion of what is meant by discipline widely prevails, and is a source of much trouble to the untrained beginner.

Discipline cannot be dissociated from work, and orders, to be obeyed, must be reasonable. It is a common theory, and one which, though not quite true, is sufficiently accurate for our purpose, that boys are sent to school in order to work. Here is the basis of the teacher's discipline. A certain amount of work imposed by the authorities or by examinations has to be got through in a given time. Without order and method this is impossible. And it may be repeated that the class is no whit behind the teacher in recognizing this truth. Consequently, if Jones *major* will persist in talking, or giggling, or asking irrelevant questions, he is not to be punished for disobeying orders or for offending against the dignity of the cap and gown He only needs to be made to feel that he is interrupting and delaying the work, or that he is becoming bored when a closer attention to the lesson would give him an interest in what he is doing. This may sound like vague advice, but such a course is easier than the alternative of setting Jones a punishment for talking—easier, that is, in the long run. For, if you give him a hundred lines on Monday, he will inevitably be tortured on Tuesday with curiosity to find out how far he may go before you give him five hundred. When the work is made the first thing, and when the boys feel that the master is really wishful to teach them, and does not presume upon his authority, then the difficulty is almost over. For the enthusiastic worker, even if he be a "poor disciplinarian," succeeds in gaining the respect of his form. The new master often goes into his room on the first day thinking it is going to be a tussle between him and the boys, and he is armed at all points. He forgets, or perhaps he has never been told, that on the first day there will be no revolt. The boys "lie low" till they have taken his measure. This is his opportunity. He has plenty of time to show them that he is sympathetic, has some sense of humour, means to work, and will not too greatly stand upon his dignity. If he does that, the boys at once lose their desire to "try it on with old X."; the victory is won, and things go as smoothly as they ever do in form room life.

Sympathy is the first and main desideratum. For children it is a trying ordeal to sit still and be talked to for four or five hours a day. There are even adults who would revolt under such circumstances. But once arouse a fair interest in getting through the work, and, with short interludes for "standing at ease," the time passes quickly. Sympathy means the ability to look at the lesson from the point of view of the class. Consequently, there is a danger of over-emphasizing the need of work. When Mr. X. comes in for his hour's construe-lesson, feeling that he must get through so many pages before the bell rings, he is so absorbed in this idea that he quite misses the humorous point that makes Jones *minor* laugh. Instead of permitting, nay encouraging, the laugh, he pulls up short, and mentally accuses the boy of a desire to interrupt the work and play the fool. The truth is that there is nothing healthier than a good laugh. After it you may rely on keen attention for at least ten minutes.

The power of keeping order, then, implies the lively sympathy with the class, and an understanding of the important fact that boys want to get on, and delight in exercising their minds. The man who is known as a thorough disciplinarian often fails altogether here. As he stalks into his room, every boy subsides into a state of frigid immobility, mental as well as physical. There was a man of this character at a certain school. At his approach two hundred boys, big and little, became so many statues. He was feared; his work was done; his orders were obeyed. But, in the subject for which he was responsible, no boy was ever known to rise above mediocrity. Fear paralyzes: the "pin dropping silence" denotes mental stagnation. Boys are reasonable creatures. They understand the value of order and method. Discipline in the class-room is a means to an end. No one would make the same regulations for a single pupil as he would for a form of thirty boys. The class readily grasp the idea that in order to enjoy the lesson it must be done in an orderly fashion. There is no moral virtue in the blind obedience that carries out an order because it is an order. Obedience should spring from confidence that the giver of the order would not make any unreasonable demand. Disobedience is often a healthier sign than obedience, just because many a master is ignorant of, or indifferent to, what is reasonable. For instance, nothing could be more unreasonable than for an irritated master, who has worked his class into a state of nervous tension, to tell them to sit absolutely quiet. Dickens, with his wonderful insight into child-mind, puts an interesting saying into the mouth of the poor schoolmaster in "The Old Curiosity Shop." When the boys are dismissed for an extra half-holiday in the June sunshine, with the caution to avoid noise for the sake of a sick school-fellow, they break into a joyous shout as soon as they are outside the building. "It's very natural, thank Heaven!" said the poor schoolmaster; "I'm very glad they didn't mind me!"

PRINCETON CELEBRATION.*

The College in Nation's Service.

HERE, then, if you will but look, you have the law of conservatism disclosed; it is a law of progress. But not all change is progress, not all growth is the manifestation of life. Let one part of the body be in haste to outgrow the rest and you have malignant disease, the threat of death. The growth that is a manifestation of life is equitable, draws its springs gently out of the old fountains of strength, builds upon old tissue, covets the old airs that have blown upon it time out of mind in the past. Colleges ought surely to be the best nurseries of such life, the best schools of the progress which conserves. Unschooled men have only their habits to remind them of the past, only their desires and their distinctive judgments of what is to guide them into the future; the college should

* Prof. Woodrow Wilson, Princeton Celebration.

serve the state as its organ of recollection, its seat of vital memory. It should give the countrymen who know the probabilities of failure and success, who can separate the tendencies which are permanent from the tendencies which are of the moment merely, who can distinguish promises from threats, knowing the life men have lived, the hopes they have tested, and the principles they have proved.

This college gave the country at least a handful of such men, in its infancy, and its President for leader. The blood of John Knox ran in Witherspoon's veins. The great drift and movement of English liberty, from Magna Charta down, was in all his teachings; his pupils knew as well as Burke did that to argue the Americans out of their liberties would be to falsify their pedigree. "In order to prove that the Americans have no right to their liberties," Burke cried, "we are every day endeavoring to subvert the maxims which preserve the whole spirit of our own"; the very antiquarians of the law stood ready with their proof that the colonies could not be taxed by Parliament. This revolution, at any rate, was a keeping of faith with the past. To stand for it was to be like Hampden, a champion of law, though he withstood the king. It was to emulate the example of the very men who had founded the Government, then for a little while grown so tyrannous and forgetful of its great traditions. This was the compulsion of life, not of passion, and college halls were a better school of revolution than colonial assemblies, provided, of course, they were guided by such a spirit as Witherspoon's.

Nothing is easier than to falsify the past; lifeless instruction will do it. If you rob it of vitality, stiffen it with pedantry, sophisticate it with argument, chill it with unsympathetic comment, you render it as dead as any academic exercise. The safest way in all ordinary seasons is to let it speak for itself; resort to its records, listen to its poets and to its masters in the humbler art of prose. Your real and proper object, after all, is not to expound, but to realize it, consort with it, and make your spirit kin with it, so that you may never shake the sense of obligation off. In short, I believe that the catholic study of the world's literature as a record of spirit is the right preparation for leadership in the world's affairs, if you undertake it like a man and not like a pedant.

Age is marked in the case of every people just as it is marked in the case of every work of art, into which enters the example of the masters, the taste of long generations of men, the thought that has matured, the achievement that has come with assurance. The child's crude drawing shares the primitive youth of the first hieroglyphies; but a little reading, a few lessons from some modern master, a little time in the old world's galleries set the lad forward a thousand years and more, make his drawing as old as art itself.

The art of thinking is as old, and it is the university's function to impart it in all its length; the stiff and difficult stuffs of fact and experience, of prejudice and affection, in which the hard art is to work its will and the long and tedious combinations of cause and effect out of which it is to build up its results. How else will you avoid a ceaseless round of error? The world's memory must be kept alive, or we shall never see an end of its old mistakes. We are in danger to lose our identity and become infantile in every generation. That is the real menace under which we cower everywhere in this age of change. The old world trembles to see its proletariat in the saddle; we stand dismayed to find ourselves growing no older, always as young as the information of our most numerous voters. The danger does not lie in the fact that the masses whom we have enfranchised seek to work any iniquity upon us, for their aim, take it in the large, is to make a righteous polity. The peril lies in this, that the past is discredited among them, because they played no choosing part in it. It was their enemy, they say, and they will not learn of it. They wish to break with it for ever; its lessons are tainted to their taste.

In America, especially, we run perpetually this risk of newness. Righteously enough, it is in part a consequence of boasting. To enhance our credit for originality we boasted for long that our institutions were one and all our own inventions, and the pleasing error was so got into the common air by persistent discharges of oratory, that every man's atmosphere became surcharged with it, and it seems now quite too late to dislodge it. Three thousand miles of sea, moreover, roll between us and the elder past of the world. We are isolated here. We cannot see other nations in detail, and looked at in the large they do not seem like ourselves. Our problems, we say, are our own, and we will take our own way of solving them. Nothing seems audacious among us, for our case seems to us to stand singular and without parallel. We run in a free field, without recollection of failure, without heed of example.

It is plain that it is the duty of an institution of learning set in the midst of a free population and amid signs of social change, not merely to implant a sense of duty, but to illuminate duty by every lesson that can be drawn out of the past. It is not a dogmatic process. I know of no book in which the lessons of the past are set down. I do not know of any man whom the world could trust to write such a book. But it somehow comes about that the man who has travelled in the realms of thought brings lessons home with him which make him grave and wise beyond his fellows, and thoughtful with the thoughtfulness of a true man of the world.

This, it seems to me, is the real, the prevalent argument for holding every man we can to the intimate study of the ancient classics. All literature that has lasted has this claim upon us—that it is not dead; but we cannot be quite so sure of any as we are of the ancient literature that still lives, because none has lived so long. It holds a sort of leadership in the aristocracy of natural selection.

Read it, moreover, and you shall find another proof of vitality in it, more significant still. You shall recognize its thoughts, and even its fancies, as your long-time familiars—shall recognize them as the thoughts that have begotten a vast deal of your own literature. It is the general air of the world a man gets when he reads the classics, the thinking which depends upon no time, but only upon human nature, which seems full of the voices of the human spirit, quick with the power which moves ever upon the face of affairs. "What Plato has thought he may think; what a saint has felt he may feel; what at any time has befallen any man he can understand."

I believe, of course, that there is another way of preparing young men to be wise. I need not tell you that I believe in the full, explicit instruction in history and in politics, in the experiences of peoples and the fortunes of governments, in the whole story of what men have attempted and what they have accomplished through all the changes both of form and purpose in their organization of their common life. Many minds will receive and heed this systematic instruction which have no ears for the voice that is in the printed page of literature.

It used to be taken for granted—did it not?—that colleges would be found always on the conservative side of politics (except on the question of free trade), but in this latter day a great deal has taken place which goes far towards discrediting the presumption. The college in our day lives very near indeed to the affairs of the world. It is a place of the latest experiments; its laboratories are brisk with the spirit of discovery; its lecture-rooms resound with the discussion of new theories of life and novel programmes of reform. There is no radical like your learned radical, bred in the schools; and thoughts of revolution have in our time been harbored in universities as naturally as they were once nourished among the encyclopædists. It is the scientific spirit of the age that has wrought the change. I stand with my hat off at very mention of the great men who have made our age an age of knowledge. No man more heartily admires, more gladly welcomes, more approvingly reckons, the gain and the enlightenment that have come to the world through the extraordinary advances in physical science which this age has witnessed. He would be a barbarian and a lover of darkness who should grudge that great study any part of its triumph. But I am a student of society and should deem myself unworthy of the comradeship of great men of science should I not speak the plain truth with regard to what I see happening under my own eyes. I have no laboratory but the world of books and men in which I live; but I am much mistaken if the scientific spirit of the age is not doing us a great disservice, working in us a certain great degeneracy. Science has bred in us a spirit of experiment and a contempt for the past. It has made us credulous of quick improvement, hopeful of discovering panaceas, confident of success in every new thing.

Let me say, this is not the fault of the scientist; he has done his work with an intelligence and success which cannot be too much admired. It is the work of the noxious, intoxicating gas which has somehow got into the lungs of the rest of us from out the crevices of his workshop—a gas, it would seem, which forms only in the outer air, and where men do not know the right use of their lungs. I should tremble to see social reform led by men who had breathed it; I should fear nothing better than utter destruction from a revolution conceived and led in the scientific spirit.

Do you wonder, then, that I ask for the old drill, the old memory of times gone by, the old schooling in precedent and tradition, the old keeping of faith with the past as a preparation for leadership in days of social change? We have not given science too big a place in our education; but we have made a perilous mistake in giving it too great a preponderance in method and every other branch of study. We must make the humanities human again, must recall what manner of men we are, must turn back once more to the region of practical ideas.

Of course, when all is said, it is not learning but the spirit of service that will give a college place in the public annals of the nation. It is indispensable, it seems to me, if it is to do its right service, that the air of affairs should be admitted to all its classrooms. I do not mean the air of party politics, but the air of the world's transactions, the consciousness of the solidarity of the race, the sense of the duty of man towards man, of the presence of men in every problem, of the significance of truth for guidance as well as for knowledge, of the potency of ideas, of the promise and the hope that shine in the face of all knowledge. There is laid upon us the compulsion of the national life. We dare not keep aloof and closet ourselves while a nation comes to its maturity. The days of glad expansion are gone, our life grows tense and difficult; our resources for the future lie in careful thought, providence, and a wise economy; and the school must be of the nation. I have had sight of the perfect place of learning in my thought; a free place, and a various, where no man could be and not know with how great a destiny knowledge had come into the world—itself a little world; but not perplexed, living with a singleness of aim not known without; the home of sagacious men, hard-headed, and with a will to know, debaters of the world's questions every day and used to the rough ways of democracy; and yet a place removed, calm Science seated there, recluse, ascetic, like a nun, not knowing that the world passes, not caring if the truth but come in answer to her prayer; and Literature, walking within her open doors in quiet chambers with men of olden time, storied walls about her and calm voices infinitely sweet; here "magic casements opening on the foam of perilous seas in fairy lands forlorn," to which you may withdraw and use your youth for pleasure: there windows open straight upon the street where many stand and talk intent upon the world of men and business. A place where ideals are kept in heart in an air they can breathe, but no fools' paradise. A place where to hear the truth about the past and hold debate upon the affairs of the present, with knowledge and without passion; like the world in having all men's life at heart, a place for men and all that concerns them; but unlike the world in its self-possession, its thorough way of talk, its care to know more than the moment brings to light; slow to take excitement, its air pure and wholesome with a breath of faith; every eye within it bright in the clear day and quick to look towards heaven for the confirmation of its hope. Who shall show us the way to this place? —*Prof. Woodrow Wilson.*

The address by Mr. Cleveland, President of the United States, followed. He was received with unbounded enthusiasm. He said:

MR. PRESIDENT AND LADIES AND GENTLEMEN:

As those in different occupations and with different training each see most plainly in the same landscape view those features which are the most nearly related to their several habitual environments; so, in our contemplation of an event or an occasion, each individual especially observes and appreciates, in the light his mode of thought supplies, such of its features and incidents as are most in harmony with his mental situation.

To-day, while all of us warmly share the general enthusiasm and felicitation which pervade this assemblage, I am sure its various suggestions and meanings assume a prominence in our respective fields of mental vision, dependent upon their relation to our experience and condition. Those charged with the management and direction of the educational advantages of this noble institution most plainly see, with well-earned satisfaction, proofs of its growth and usefulness and its enhanced opportunities for doing good. The graduate of Princeton sees first the evidence of a greater glory and prestige that have come to his Alma Mater and the added honor thence reflected upon himself, while those still within her student halls see most prominently the promise of an increased dignity which awaits their graduation from Princeton University.

But there are others here, not of the family of Princeton, who see, with an interest not to be outdone, the signs of her triumphs on the fields of higher education, and the part she has taken during her long and glorious career in the elevation and betterment of a great people.

Among these I take an humble place; and as I yield to the influences of this occasion, I cannot resist the train of thought which especially reminds me of the promise of national safety and the guarantee of the permanence of our free institutions which may and ought to radiate from the universities and colleges scattered throughout our land.

Obviously a government resting upon the will and universal suffrage of the people has no anchorage except in the people's intelligence. While the advantages of a collegiate education are by no means necessary to good citizenship, yet the college graduate, found everywhere, cannot smother his opportunities to teach his fellow-countrymen and influence them for good, nor hide his talents in a napkin, without recreancy to a trust.

In a nation like ours, charged with the care of numerous and widely varied interests, a spirit of conservatism and toleration is absolutely essential. A collegiate training, the study of principles unvexed by distracting and misleading influences, and a correct apprehension of the theories upon which our republic is established, ought to constitute the college graduate a constant monitor, warning against popular rashness and excess.

The character of our institutions and our national self-interest require that a feeling of sincere brotherhood and a disposition to unite in mutual endeavor should pervade our people. Our scheme of government in its beginning was based upon this sentiment, and its interruption has never failed and can never fail to grievously menace our national health. Who can better caution against passion and bitterness than those who know by thought and study their baneful consequences and who are themselves within the noble brotherhood of higher education?

There are natural laws and economic truths which command implicit obedience, and which should unalterably fix the bounds of wholesome popular discussion and the limits of political strife. The knowledge gained in our universities and colleges would be sadly deficient if its beneficiaries were unable to recognize and point out to their fellow-citizens these truths and natural laws, and to teach the mischievous futility of their non-observance or attempted violation.

The activity of our people and their restless desire to gather to themselves especial benefits and advantages lead to the growth of an unconfessed tendency to regard their government as the giver of private gifts, and to look upon the agencies for its administration as the distributors of official places and preferment. Those who in university or college have had an opportunity to study the mission of our institutions, and who in the light of history have learned the danger to a people of their neglect of the patriotic care they owe the national life intrusted to their keeping, should be well fitted to constantly admonish their fellow-citizens that the usefulness and beneficence of their plan of government can only be preserved through their unselfish and loving support and their contented willingness to accept in full return the peace, protection, and opportunity which it impartially bestows.

Not more surely do the rules of honesty and good faith fix the standard of individual character in a community than do these same rules determine the character and standing of a nation in the world of civilization. Neither the glitter of its power, nor the tinsel of its commercial prosperity, nor the gaudy show of its people's wealth can conceal the cankering rust of national dishonesty, and cover the meanness of national bad faith. A constant stream of thoughtful, educated men should come from our universities and colleges preaching national honor and integrity, and teaching that a belief in the necessity of national obedience to the laws of God is not born of superstition.

I do not forget the practical necessity of political parties, nor do I deny their desirability. I recognize wholesome differences of opinion touching legitimate governmental policies, and would by no means control or limit the utmost freedom in their discussion. I have only attempted to suggest the important patriotic service which our institutions of higher education and their graduates are fitted to render to our people, in the enforcement of those immutable truths and fundamental principles which are related to our national condition, but should never be dragged into the field of political strife nor impressed into the service of partisan contention.

When the excitement of party warfare presses dangerously near our national safeguards, I would have the intelligent conservatism of our universities and colleges warn the contestants in impressive tones against the perils of a breach impossible to repair.

. . . . . .

When the attempt is made to delude the people into the belief that their suffrages can change the operation of natural laws, I would have our universities and colleges proclaim that those laws are inexorable and far removed from political control.

When selfish interest seeks undue private benefits through governmental aid, and public places are claimed as rewards of party service, I would have our universities and colleges persuade the people to a relinquishment of the demand for party spoils and exhort them to a disinterested and patriotic love of their government for its own sake, and because in its true adjustment and unperverted operation it secures to every citizen his just share of the safety and prosperity it holds in store for all.

When a design is apparent to lure the people from their honest thoughts and to blind their eyes to the sad plight of national dishonor and bad faith, I would have Princeton University, panoplied in her patriotic traditions and glorious memories, and joined by all the other universities and colleges of our land, cry out against the infliction of this treacherous and fatal wound.

I would have the influence of these institutions on the side of religion and morality. I would have those they send out among the people not ashamed to acknowledge God, and to proclaim His interposition in the affairs of men, enjoining such obedience to His laws as makes manifest the path of national perpetuity and prosperity.

I hasten to concede the good already accomplished by our educated men in purifying and steadying political sentiment; but I hope I may be allowed to intimate my belief that their work in these directions would be easier and more useful if it were less spasmodic and occasional. The disposition of our people is such that while they may be inclined to distrust those who only on rare occasions come among them from an exclusiveness savoring of assumed superiority, they readily listen to those who exhibit a real fellowship and a friendly and habitual interest in all that concerns the common welfare. Such a condition of intimacy would, I believe, not only improve the general political atmosphere, but would vastly increase the influence of our universities and colleges in their efforts to prevent popular delusions or correct them before they reach an acute and dangerous stage.

I am certain, therefore, that a more constant and active participation in political affairs on the part of our men of education would be of the greatest possible value to our country.

It is exceedingly unfortunate that politics should be regarded in any quarter as an unclean thing, to be avoided by those claiming to be educated or respectable. It would be strange indeed if anything related to the administration of our government or the welfare of our nation should be essentially degrading. I believe it is not a superstituous sentiment that leads to the conviction that God has watched over our national life from its beginning. Who will say that the things worthy of God's regard and fostering care are unworthy of the touch of the wisest and best of men?

I would have those sent out by our universities and colleges, not only the counsellors of their fellow-countrymen, but the tribunes of the people—fully appreciating every condition that presses upon their daily life, sympathetic in every untoward situation, quick and earnest in every effort to advance their happiness and welfare, and prompt and sturdy in the defence of all their rights.

I have but imperfectly expressed the thoughts to which I have not been able to deny utterance on an occasion so full of glad significance, and so pervaded by the atmosphere of patriotic aspiration. Born of these surroundings, the hope cannot be vain that the time is at hand when all our countrymen will more deeply appreciate the blessings of American citizenship, when their disinterested love of their government will be quickened, when fanaticism and passion shall be banished from the field of politics, and when all our people, discarding every difference of condition or opportunity, will be seen under the banner of American brotherhood, marching steadily and unfalteringly on towards the bright heights of our national destiny.—*New York Evening Post.*

CORRESPONDENCE.

To the Editor of THE CANADA EDUCATIONAL MONTHLY:

SIR,—Very much of the illiteracy of matriculants, so greatly complained of on both sides of the line, is due to the plans employed in teaching reading in primary schools. The letters should be taught and "spell and pronounce" should be insisted on from the beginning.

The characters used as letters are: a, b, c, d, e, f, g, h, i, j, k, l, m, n, o, p, q, r, s, t, u, v, w, x, y, z, oo, au and aw, ou and ow, oi and oy, ch, ck, gh, ph, qu, sh, tch, th and wh. The names which should be given to these characters are:—a, be, ke (and se), de, e, ef, ge (and je), he, i, ja, ka, el, em, en, o, pe, koo, ar, es, te, u, v, wou, eks, yi, ze, oo, au, ou, oi, che, ek, af, fe, kwe, she the (and the sharp) and hwe.

If this plan be adopted the result will be better reading, better spelling, and a great saving of time. The difference in time will in many cases be three or more years. Teachers try it. EXPERIENCE.

December 12, 1896.

EDITORIAL NOTES.

THE year has come and gone, and we send to all our teachers the heartiest of greetings as they enter upon the prospect of another year of honest work in a cause which is now confessed by all to be the most important of all professional work. The improvement of the teacher's position is a theme which every teacher is interested in, and the best means of bringing about this improvement is one which is very much in the teacher's own hands. The teacher makes his own environment; and the beginning of a new year, the season when the best of good resolutions are being made on every hand, is surely not an inopportune time to plead with our teachers to co-operate in bearing one another's burdens, and in making that environment the very best of environments. It has always been the duty of the EDUCATIONAL MONTHLY to foster this spirit of co-operation, and in bidding our readers A Happy New Year, we give them an assurance that it is no intention of ours to relax any effort in that direction. Our prospectus indicates the programme we have arranged for the coming year, and it is to be hoped that our readers will assist us to the utmost of their power in extending the usefulness of our periodical.

The reference made in our last issue to the "still small voice" that comes from a remote corner of the Dominion urging an improved professional relationship among teachers is well worth the consideration of every teacher in the land. The ills that flesh is heir to are hardly less frequently expatiated upon than the ills which seem to be the lot of the teacher. And yet when some of the teachers' ills are traced to their origin the teachers themselves are hardly able to free their skirts altogether from blame. For example, in the matter of salaries the teachers' small and precarious emoluments are often traced to the lack of funds in the public chest, or to the poverty of the country districts, whereas it may be too often traced to the unprofessional conduct of the teachers themselves towards one another. In a word, if teachers were only to become true to themselves, they would command not only a higher respect but a higher salary from those who require their services. An instance will illustrate this readily enough. A teacher was once pleading with a school commissioner to support an application he was about to make to the board for an increase of salary.

"Your salary is just what you asked for when you made application for the position you hold, is it not?" asked the commissioner.

"Yes," answered the teacher, "that is true, but I find I cannot live on it. Besides, the teacher that was here last received more money for just the work I am doing."

"Then why did you offer to take the position at a less salary than your predecessor?"

"Because I wanted the place, and being told that there was a very large number of applicants, I asked for a very low salary, thinking that if I gave satisfaction, the board could be induced to give me the amount paid to my predecessor."

"In other words, you expected the board to break their bargain with you. That is a new kind of a way in carrying out a business contract. The fact is, sir, you should never have offered to take the position at a less salary than your predecessor's. You have made your bed and so must lie in it. In my opinion the salary should be given to the position and not to the teacher. But will you tell me who have encouraged the districts to ask candidates to state in their applications the amount of salary required, but the teachers themselves. If I were a teacher I would refrain from applying for a position when such a humiliating request is made in any advertisement, and if all teachers would do the same, the huckstering spirit among trustees and commissioners would soon disappear."

TEACHERS' SALARIES.

WHILE the teachers of Ontario have not yet been reduced to that condition of impecunious serfdom that the letters of Mr. St. Pierre, in the Montreal *Herald*, prove to be so common in Quebec, it is evident that the tendency is steadily downward. An important factor in producing this regrettable result is the crowding of the profession. The excess of the supply of teachers over the demand for their services has resulted, as of necessity it must result, in the reduction of the remuneration to a point at which, if averaged, it would probably not exceed that of the day laborer. Teachers who discuss the matter point to another cause of the decline of salaries that is even more potent than the law of supply and demand, that is, the increasing disposition of School Boards to award a contract for teaching to the lowest tenderer, leaving the question of comparative merit out of consideration. "State salary expected" is a phrase bitterly resented by the teachers of the Province, but which under present conditions they see no hope of having withdrawn from advertisements for teachers.

A young fellow who recently passed his final examinations at the Normal asserts that a large proportion of his classmates, after spending years in study and becoming in a measure cultured and wideawake educationists, are compelled under the tendering system to offer their services to School Boards for from $300 to $400 a year. They know that after the few available prizes are picked up there must be a scramble for the state-salary-expected places, and that the lower their bid the better their chance. As many of them finish their course of study in debt to friends at home, a condition not at all to the liking of a self-respecting young man or woman, they are prepared to make a bargain-day price for their labor that defies competition.

The tendering system seems to have a firm grip of School Trustees and it will not be readily abandoned. We find on looking over our issue of the 14th that of eleven advertisements for teachers eight distinctly require applicants to state salary expected, one leaves this to be inferred, while only two announce the salaries to be paid. These are meagre enough in all conscience, $900 for a mathematical master who must be an honor graduate, and $225 for a Model School assistant. We are left to imagine what will be the salary of the eight teachers who are to be selected, partly, let us hope, because of their abilities, but chiefly it is to be feared because they succeed in underbidding their competitors. A more reasonable and humane method of appointment, we submit, would be to fix upon a salary that would afford a decent living and be in some measure equivalent to the duties to be performed, and select the best teacher offering at the salary. Very many of the School Trustees throughout the Province only require to have their attention directed to the demoralizing effect of the tendering system to agree to its abandonment.—*Globe.*

We quote the above extract from a late issue of *The Daily Globe.* Many teachers in Ontario will vouch for the accuracy of its statements. Nothing is more certain than that a poorly paid teaching staff in our schools—all classes of schools—will inflict a very serious loss on Ontario.

In such circumstances the intelligent, well-trained and capable teacher will seek other spheres of labor where his abilities will be more adequately appreciated. The schools require the services of the ablest—in every sense of the word—the ablest men and women in the country. Men and women of the highest ability, carefully prepared for teaching, non-professionally and professionally, men and women of experience in our schools, for such teachers the country cannot pay too high a salary. But for teachers not so equipped in every respect as above, the country will be compelled to pay in the loss sustained by the children of our Province. As always, so now, we plead for generous treatment of our teachers in the matter of salary and also in every other helpful way. It will pay Ontario a hundred-fold.

PRINCIPAL PETERSON, of McGill University, does not intend that the Classical Department of the Arts Faculty shall fail to mark a progress commensurate with the strides that have been taken by the other Faculties. Through his recommendation, Professor Frank Carter, M.A., has been appointed classical professor, and Mr. S. B. Slack, M.A., classical lecturer. Among the late appointments in this institution may be noted those of Professor S. H. Caffer, M.A., to the chair of architecture; Dr. J. B. Porter, to the chair of mining and metallurgy; Mr. H. W. Urmey, assistant professor of civil engineering; and Mr. Armstrong, assistant professor of drawing. We will be glad in future to receive notices of new appointments that are being made from time to time in all our institutions of learning; colleges, collegiate institutes, high schools and academies.

Chief Superintendent Dr. Inch, in his address before the teachers of Northumberland last month, emphasized the importance of self-culture, especially of those who are cut off from communication with other teachers. In order to be a success in his profession the teacher must be a student all his life. He ought to be a lover of good books, and let no day pass without devoting a certain time to study, so that he may keep up with the intellectual march of progress. He should be methodical in his studies, and have a certain plan to follow, and in this way derive more benefit from his reading.—*Ed. News.*

Does the efficiency of the school enhance the value of the property in its neighborhood? The school commissioner of Georgia has proved that it does, and at the present moment he is vigorously pursuing his campaign for educational progress. He will ask the Legislature to levy a school-tax in each county. He estimates that a tax of one-quarter per cent. would furnish sufficient funds to carry on good schools in all the rural counties for nine months in the year, and build good school-houses as well. In several counties where such a tax has been voluntarily tried, the schools have improved very rapidly, and the market price of land in counties where the schools are good has risen considerably.

The installation of the Rev. Dr. Macrae, late pastor of St. Stephen's Church, St. John, as Principal of Morrin College, Quebec, took place on Thursday evening, Oct. 29th. The cordial welcome extended to Dr. Macrae, and his eloquent and scholarly address in reply, are indications that Quebec has secured one who will be an ornament, not only to his academic halls, but also to the cultured society of that historic city.

Dr. J. M. Harper, Inspector of Superior Schools, has sent in his award in the competition among the colleges, academies and model schools of the Province of Quebec for the best kept grounds and outer environment. The regulation inaugurating this competition is to the effect that three prizes be offered for competition among the Superior Schools of the Province for the school premises most neatly maintained; a first prize of one hundred dollars, a second of fifty dollars, and a third of twenty-five dollars; adjudication to be made by the Inspector of Superior Schools, and the amount of the prize, when awarded, to be paid to the commissioners under whose control the successful school is maintained; no school obtaining a prize to be allowed to compete again for five years, and then only on condition that the school premises have been properly maintained in the interval. This year the competition takes place for the first time, and the award gave Stansted College the first prize; the Gault Institute, of Valleyfield, the second prize; and Freligsburg Model School the third prize. This is an excellent means of inaugurating village improvements.

Can any good educational advice come to us from Japan? Here is a reference to the report of its Minister of Education made by a correspondent of the *School Journal* of England:

In the old days archery, horsemanship, fencing, and throwing the spear occupied the leisure of the people; when the Empire was restored and methods of warfare were revolutionized, the practice of these arts fell into disuse, and military drill became the only substitute for the freer exercises which had preceded it. Regulations have now been issued with the object of promoting the health of the young. In gymnastics every part of the muscular system, including hands and feet, must be brought into play; mere routine is to be avoided, and drill is to be accompanied by military songs. The garments worn should not, as a rule, have tight sleeves, so that the movements of the arms may not be cramped. So far from being rewarded for keeping quiet when out of school, pupils should be encouraged to activity in the open air. Tasks which involve memorizing or the taking of notes impose an undue strain, and should not be given except in case of special necessity. Rewards and punishments by changing the seats of the children or awarding marks tend to unhealthy excitement of the brain, and therefore should not be employed. Boys in elementary schools must be forbidden "to smoke or to keep tobacco pipes." We quote the last of the rules *verbatim*: "Luxury and ease naturally tend to imbecility; in cities and towns, pupils are sometimes to ride in *jinrikisha* or other conveyances in going to and returning from schools; and, though such practice is beyond reach of school discipline, directors and teachers should be very attentive to this matter, and induce the pupils to walk as much as possible." What would the boys in our London day schools say to this conjunction of omnibus, ease and imbecility?

The people of New Zealand are objecting to the policeman as a competent official to take truants in charge. The Minister of Education of that colony has issued a circular stating that in future he will not allow any policeman to be appointed as truant officer; but that instructions have been issued to the police to render all possible assistance to school committees in inducing parents to comply with the provisions of the Attendance Act. Thus constables may not now be truant officers, but must help those who are. Unless the help is confined to moral influence, the grievance still remains. And policemen are not trained to exercise moral influence.

Cape Colony is not seeking reprisal against President Kruger in a novel way. They have lately been doing him a service of which the newspapers have taken no cognisance, but a service, nevertheless, for which he should show due gratitude. They have been endeavoring to supply him with an University, or at least with a share in one. The Amended University of the Cape of Good Hope Incorporation Act contains a provision empowering the Governor to appoint additional members to the Council from the Colony of Natal, the Orange Free State, and the Transvaal Republic, should the Governments of any or all of them undertake to make a sufficient annual contribution towards the funds of the University. The Colony of Natal has already given evidence of a desire for union; and the hope is expressed that the two independent States will avail themselves of this offer, so that the University may become a beneficent institution for the whole of South Africa. It would, indeed, be a healthy sign if the Boers came in as "friendlies" to this educational camp.

The French movement for assisting the young through the years of adolescence is having a sort of reflex action in Germany. Thus a society has been established at Berlin to further the welfare of orphans, that is to say, children who have lost father or mother or both parents, when the school years are over. Advice is to be given them, so that they may choose a calling suited to their power; material aid will be afforded during apprenticeship, if the need for it exists; and every effort will be made to supply by counsel and moral influence the want of the natural guardians. Legal and medical advisers will give their services to the association, which has been established on a voluntary basis; that is, it receives neither support nor express sanction from the State. The project was initiated by Herr Lehrer Pagel, and the first outline of the scheme was published, fitly enough, on Pestalozzi's birthday. It is pleasant to hear that other towns are following the example of Berlin.

The "Babble of the Books' in Chicago between Superintendent Lane and his colleagues is likely to have a quieter ending than the "Babble of the Books" between the Educational Book Company of Toronto and the two leading members of the text-book committee of one section of the Council of Public Instruction of Quebec. The following is what the *Montreal Daily Star* says about it:

"Action is about being taken by Mr. William P. Gundy, of the Educational Book Company, Toronto, against Rev. Mr. Rexford and Prof. A. W. Kneeland, of this city, who, it is alleged, as members of the Text Book Committee of the Protestant Committee of the Council of Public Instruction, sought by unfair means to exclude a series of books published by him, and which for some years had been the authorized series in the Protestant common schools."

The Province of Quebec, we hear, has taken a step in the right direction. In our report of the late Montreal Convention, there was pointed out the three reforms which the educationalists of Quebec were demanding in connection with elementary education, and one of these must have astonished some of our readers, involving as it did the advocacy in favor of having trained teachers provided for all the schools of that Province. This, as the first necessity of any progressive system of public instruction, has happily been secured for the Protestant schools of Quebec. The Committee of which Dr. Harper was convener, has seen its labors end in success, and we have no doubt that in the near future, the provision will be extended to all sections of the Province. Hereafter all teachers under the supervision of the Protestant Committee of the Council of Public Instruction will have to take a course at the McGill Normal School before being eligible to take a position in any of the schools under the same supervision.

SCHOOL WORK.

EDUCATION DEPARTMENT.

ANNUAL EXAMINATIONS, 1896.

SCIENCE.

Editor.—J. B. TURNER, B.A.

THE HIGH SCHOOL AND UNIVERSITY EXAMINATIONS.

FORM IV.

CHEMISTRY.

1. "Hydrogen is an inflammable gas; . . . . it does not support ordinary combustion."

Explain clearly what these statements mean, and describe an experiment so conditioned as to show oxygen as the *inflammable gas*, and hydrogen the *supporter of combustion.*

2. (*a*) Describe any two practical methods of preparing carbon monoxide.

(*b*) Give an account of the properties of this substance.

(*c*) Calculate the weight of carbon monoxide required to fill a right cylindrical vessel 0.5 metre high, and 0.25 metre diameter, the temperature being 25°C. and the pressure 600 mm. mercury.

3. (*a*) Define Specific Heat.

(*b*) State the so-called law of Dulong and Petit.

(*c*) 200 grammes ice at —40° C. is added to 400 grammes water at 95°C. When equilibrum of temperature is attained 200 grammes of zinc at 100° C. is added and a final equilibrium of temperature is reached at 32.5°C. Assuming that no loss of heat by radiation or otherwise takes place, calculate the specific heat of zinc from the data given.

NOTE—*The specific heat of ice is 0.5.*

4. Describe what occurs under the following conditions, giving equations when possible:—

(*a*) Finely divided iron, contained in an iron tube, is strongly heated, and a current of steam is passed over it.

(*b*) Chloride of sodium is treated with strong sulphuric acid, and the gaseous products are passed through a hot porcelain tube containing lumps of manganese dioxide. Finally, the gaseous products from this reaction are passed into a cold and dilute solution of potash.

(*c*) A piece of paper saturated with turpentine ($C_{10}H_{16}$) is dipped into a jar of gaseous chlorine.

5. State Avogadro's Law, and give as complete an account as you can of the facts which justify it.

6. Describe fully the reasons for believing that in the case of the hydrogen molecule (H_n), n is even.

7. With what other elements are Barium, Phosphorus and Bromine re-

spectively grouped? Give a short account of the properties which justify such grouping.

8. Ascertain what acid and what base are present in the salt given you.

FORM IV.

PHYSICS.

---

1. A falling body passes two points 10 feet apart in ½ second; it subsequently passes two other points 10 feet apart in $\frac{1}{10}$ second. Find the difference between the first and the last of these four points. ($g=32$).

2. (*a*) Explain *coefficient of friction*, and give a method of finding it.

(*b*) The base of an inclined plane is 4 feet and the height is 3 feet; a force of 8 pounds acting parallel to the plane will just prevent a 20-lb, weight from sliding down. Find the coefficient of friction between the weight and the plane.

3. How would you show that the height of the mercury in a barometer depends on the pressure of the air?

4. A spherical balloon, 10 metres in diameter, is filled with coal gas (specific gravity, relative to air, .496) at a pressure of 76 cms. of mercury. What is the weight of the balloon and its appendages if it will just not float in air?

5. Show that for strongest current it is best to arrange the cells of a battery so that the internal and external resistances are equal.

6. (*a*) Explain, with diagram, the relation between the polarity of an electro-magnet and the direction of the current.

(*b*) You want to use the current from a dynamo, which delivers electricity at 110 volts, to excite an electro-magnet; how would you construct your electro-magnet that there may be no unnecessary loss of energy. Give full reasons.

7. (*a*) Give a method of finding the velocity of sound in air. How does the velocity depend on the temperature?

(*b*) If the velocity in air at zero is 331 metres per second, what will it be at 20°C.?

8. (*a*) State the laws for transverse vibrations of strings.

(*b*) A vibrating string gives a note *f* when stretched by a weight of 16 lbs. What weight must be used to get the note *a* in the same octave? What weight for *c* of the octave next above?

9. (*a*) Give a simple optical method of measuring the angle of a prism.

(*b*) Give a practicable method for finding the index of refraction of either water or glass.

10. How would you proceed to find the radius of curvature of a concave mirror, not using a distant source of light? Prove formula used, and describe a suitable experimental arrangement.

FORM III.

PHYSICS.

---

1. Describe a two-fluid cell; explain how you would set it up; and show the utility of the two fluids. Also, give the chief uses of the cell you describe, with reasons therefor.

2. Explain the action of the electric bell; give a clear diagram and trace the current through the entire circuit.

3. Describe a simple galvanometer. In what different ways can you increase its sensibility? Give full reasons.

4. Explain, with diagram, the dynamo, giving as full details as possible of the armature.

5. What is an *interval?* Three tuning-forks have frequencies 512, 640, 768 respectively. Compare the intervals between the first and the

second with that between the second and third.

6. Explain the harmonic scale, the diatonic scale and the equally-tempered scale; and give reasons for the wide use of the last.

7. Describe how the air in an open organ tube vibrates, and give a method of investigating it.

8. What is meant by saying that the index of refraction from air to water is 4/3?

Explain, with diagram, total reflexion.

9. An object is placed between two plane mirrors which are at right angles. Draw rays to show how the eye sees the different images.

10. A standard candle and a 4-candle power gas flame are placed 6 feet apart; where must a screen be placed on the line joining the candle and the gas flame so that it may be equally illuminated by each of them?

FORM II.

PHYSICS.

NOTE — Experiments must be adapted for performance in an ordinary school.

1. A body moves from rest under a constant acceleration. Give an experimental method of investigating the distances passed over in each of the first three seconds of its motion; also find the average speed during each of these seconds; and describe, as clearly as you can, the manner in which the motion takes place.

2. (*a*) State, as fully as you can, the various forms of energy, giving illustrations in each case.

(*b*) A piece of lead on an anvil is given a vigorous blow. What transformations of energy take place here?

3. (*a*) A few drops of water are sprinkled on a plate of glass, which is then held in a horizontal plane with the wet side downwards. What inferences can you draw from this simple experiment?

(*b*) Give simple experiments to illustrate *ductility*, *plasticity*, *tenacity*.

4. (*a*) Give three distinct experiments which illustrate the phenomena of *surface tension*.

(*b*) How would you determine the amount of the buoyant force which a liquid exerts on a body?

5 (*a*) How would you find the specific gravity of a piece of cork, using a lead sinker? Give a numerical example.

(*b*) Explain the method of finding the specific gravity by balancing columns of liquids.

6. (*a*) Give three experiments which show that a solid body expands when heated.

(*b*) A bar of iron is riveted to a bar of brass and then held in a strong flame. Describe what happens and deduce any conclusions.

7. Describe fully an experiment to determine at what temperature water has the greatest density.

8. (*a*) Give an experiment to show that the boiling point of water depends on its pressure.

(*b*) How would you find the specific heat of some shot?

TECHNICAL EDUCATION.

In view of the agitation that is now in progress with regard to technical instruction in our public schools the following extract from a recent number of the *Scientific American Supplement* is of especial interest:

A very interesting feature of primary education in Russia, says *Nature*, is the establishment and rapid development of small farms, orchards and kitchen gardens in connection with many primary schools, especially in the villages. The land for such model gardens, or farms on a small scale, was mostly obtained through free grants from the village communes, and, occasionally, from the neighboring landlords; while the expenses are covered by very small money grants from the county and district councils (zemstvos). To take one province in South Russia, namely, Ekaterinoslav, we see from the biennial report just issued, that not only has almost every school an orchard and kitchen garden for the use of the schoolmaster, but that nearly one-half of the schools in the province (227 out of 504) are already in possession of small model kitchen gardens, orchards, tree plantations, or farms, at which gardening, sylviculture and sericulture are regularly taught. The teaching is mostly given by the schoolmasters, who themselves receive instruction in these branches at courses voluntarily attended in the summer, or occasionally by some practical specialist in the neighborhood. The Province of Ekaterinoslav being mostly treeless, special attention is given to tree plantations, and next to silkworm culture. The aggregate area of the 227 school farms or gardens, attains 283 acres, and they contained in 1895, 111,000 fruit trees and 238,300 planted forest trees, nearly 14,000 of the former and 42,000 of the latter having been distributed free among the pupils during the same year. The money grants for these 227 gardens was very small, *i.e.*, a little over three hundred pounds (£314). Besides, over a thousand beehives are kept, partly by the schoolmasters and partly by the children; and some schools had vineyards in connection with them. This movement has widely spread over different provinces of Central Russia, where the culture of cereals dominates at the school farms; while in Caucasia attention is especially given to the silkworm culture and the culture of the vine.

CLASSICAL DEPARTMENT.

PRINCIPAL STRANG, GODERICH.

Questions Based on Cæsar, Book II., Chapters 20 28.

I.

Translate chap. 22 into good idiomatic English.

1. Construction of *natura, legionibus, opus, eventus.*

2. *ut ante demonstravimus.* What word is more commonly used than *ante* in this connection?

3. *impediretur, esset.* Account for the mood in each case.

4. Point out if you can the difference in the force of *et, que,* and *atque* as used in the first three lines.

5. *Hostibus resisterent.* Mention at least six other verbs that you have met with in Cæsar governing a dative instead of an accusative.

II.

Translate into good English the first sentence of Chap. 25, making at least six English sentences of it.

1. *urgeri, confertos, occisis, detracto.* Conjugate each verb.

2. *Signis collatis.* Mention any other military phrases in which *signa* is used, and give the meaning of each.

3. Construction of *impedimento, viro, nonnullos, uni.*

4 *quo* —— *possent.* Why *quo* rather than *ut?*

5. Point out some of the special qualifications Cæsar displayed as a commander in the battle as described in the passage.

III.

Translate idiomatically:

1. Superioribus proeliis exercitati quid fieri oporteret non minus commode ipsi sibi praescribere quam ab aliis doceri poterant.

2. Quaeque prima signa quisque conspexit ad haec constitit, ne in quaerendis suis pugnandi tempus dimitteret.

3. Tantam virtutem praestiterunt ut cum primi cecidissent proximi jacentibus insisterent, atque ex corum corporibus pugnarent.

4. Quae facilia ex difficillimis animi magnitudo redegerat.

5. Qui cum quo in loco res esset quantoque periculo castra versaretur cognovissent, nihil ad celeritatem sibi reliqui fecerunt.

IV.

1. Give abl. sing. and gen. pl. of *quae audax manus, id grave vulnus.*

2. Write down all the active forms of *progredior.*

3. Write the pres. inf. pass. of *conspexit, collatis, fecerunt, redacto, jussit, subeuntes.*

4. Write all the participles of *orior, cognovisset.*

5. Give the Latin for 5, 15, 50, 500, 5000, 5th, 5 times, 5 at a time.

6. Give the nom. genit. and gend. of *scutis, ripis, collis, calonis, lateris, salutis.*

7. Compare *novus, vetus, facilius, magis, inferiore.*

8. Give simpler words from which the following are derived : *funditores, iniquus, agmen, redintegro, tumulo.*

9. Write two Latin sentences rendering " and not " correctly by *neque* and *neve* respectively.

10. Write two Latin sentences rendering " that nothing " correctly by *ne quid* and *ut nihil* respectively.

V.

Translate into idiomatic Latin, after Cæsar :

1. When the enemy were not more than a stone's throw from the camp our men, throwing open all the gates, sallied forth and soon put them to flight.

2. It was a very great advantage to our men that the officers who were in charge of the legions had been trained in the former war, and were thoroughly skilled in this mode of fighting.

3. These, seeing there wasn't time to seek their own ranks, and not knowing what ought to be done, were very easily thrown into confusion.

4. Hearing these shouts in their rear, and believing that reinforcements had arrived from the neighboring winter quarters, the enemy threw down their arms and fled.

5. He hesitated to cross this valley for fear the Gauls might attack his army on the open flanks while on the march.

6. Don't waste time in seeking your comrades, but fall in by the first standard that you see.

7. Finding that they could not escape, and that their only hope of safety lay in valor, they faced about and renewed the fight.

8. This victory made such a change in the feelings of the neighboring tribes that several of them sent ambassadors to Cæsar to beg for peace.

9. Having heard that they had a great reputation for valor, he wished before joining battle to find out the size of their force.

10. We had not time to draw our swords. They were eager to fight. Matters were in a critical condition. Their arrival inspired hope in our men. He is not aware of their dangerous position. They besought him to spare them.

ENGLISH DEPARTMENT.

For Primary.

I.

And, as the finder of some unknown
 realm,
Mounting a summit *whence* he thinks
 to see
On either side of him the imprisoning
 sea,

Beholds, above the clouds that overwhelm
The valley-land, peak after snowy peak
Stretch out of sight, each *like* a silver *helm*
Beneath its plume of smoke, *sublime* and bleak,
And *what* he thought an island finds to be
A continent to him first *oped*,—so we
Can from our height of Freedom look along
A boundless future, *ours* if we be strong.

1. Write out in full each of the subordinate clauses, except the one beginning with *that*; classify them and give their relation.

2. Parse the italicised words.

3. Justify the form *be* in the last line.

II.

1. Write out in full the subordinate clauses in the following: classify them and give their relation.

(*a*) Go where you will you may be sure that you will find some specimens.

(*b*) What's the reason that you did not paint this one the same color as the other one?

(*c*) Had we known that we would have behaved better than usual.

2. Classify the infinitive phrases in the following sentence and give their relation.

It is easy to see that we shall not be able to reach the hall in time to hear him explain to the class how to perform the experiment.

3. Give the relation of the italicized words in the following:

She is just my *age*. No *wonder* that you are tired. He left off *visiting* them. Another *day* and I shall be free. The *rascal*, to think of his doing that! He looked the very *picture* of misery.

4. Show in the case of verbs, pronouns, and adjectives that the tendency of modern English is to drop inflections.

5. Discuss which is the correct form. It is I that am (is) to blame for that result.

6. Explain clearly what is meant by speaking of the *composite* character of the English language.

7. What reasons can you give for thinking that the English language will not undergo nearly so much change during the next six centuries as it did during the last six?

8. Give (*a*) adjectives corresponding to *clergy*, *parish*, *giant*, *monk*, *bishop*, *epistle*, *apostle*.

(*b*) doublets of *pity*, *balm*, *diamond*, *sever*, *survey*, *abridge*, *blame*.

9. Mention (*a*) common errors in the pronunciation of the following words: *covetous*, *grievous*, *insidious*, *presumptuous*, *unctuous*.

(*b*) Common errors in the use of the following words: *affect*, *apt*, *inside*, *dry*, *alternative*.

For Public School Leaving.

" Bright was the summer's noon when quickening steps
Followed each other till a dreary moor
Was crossed, a bare ridge *clomb*, upon whose top
Standing alone, as from a rampart's edge,
I overlooked the bed of Windermere,
Like a vast *river*, *stretching* in the sun."

1. Parse the italicised words.

2. Write out in full the clauses to which *ridge* and *edge* belong respectively, classify each and give its relation.

3. Write out in full the subordinate clauses in the following, classify each and give its relation.

(*a*) I hold it true, whate'er befall;
'Tis better to have loved and lost
Than never to have loved at all.

(*b*) Man 'tis true,
Smit with the beauty of so fair a scene,
Might well suppose the artificer divine
Meant it eternal, had he not himself
Pronounced it transient, glorious as it is,
And still designing a more glorious fair,
Doomed it as insufficient for his praise.

4. Exemplify :

(*a*) *down*, *off*, *over* used (1) as prepositions, (2) as adverbs.

(*b*) *close*, *even*, *well* used (1) as adjectives, (2) as adverbs.

(*c*) *all*, *last*, *much* used (1) as nouns, (2) as adverbs.

5. (*a*) Form adjectives from *clerk*, *grief*, *system*, *occasion*, *explain*, *clay*.

(*b*) Form nouns from *accurate*, *reside*, *prove*, *real*, *art*, *provoke*.

(*c*) Form verbs from *verse*, *large*, *habit*, *write*, *civil*, *bright*.

6. Which of the following is correct ?

(*a*) I am afraid it will have a bad affect (effect).

(*b*) He took the prescription (perscription) to a druggist.

(*c*) I had just as leave (lief) do it as not.

(*d*) A little boy fell off (into) the dock.

(*e*) He turned deathly (deadly) pale when he heard it.

7. Correct any grammatical errors you see in the following sentences, giving your reasons.

(*a*) We will have to be very careful who we admit as members.

(*b*) There don't seem to be any likelihood of him passing the next examination.

(*c*) We are anxious to know whom it could have been that has written it.

(*d*) Neither he nor his father were members of the Society.

For Entrance.

I.

Analyze the following simple sentences :

1. On the coasts of our Maritime Provinces, there are evidences of changes *somewhat* like *those* of the lakes.

2. On the other hand the Chigneeto ship railway excavations have disclosed peat beds *buried* in the sand many *feet* below the present tide level.

3. Of course the diverting of a considerable amount of water *by* the Chicago drainage canal would have its effect on all the lakes and rivers *below*.

4. *Thus* up the margin of the lake
Between the precipice and brake,
O'er stock and rock their race they take,
Then through the dell his horn resounds,
From vain pursuit *to call* the hounds.

II.

Write out in full the subordinate clauses in the following sentences and tell the kind and relation of each :

1. It should be remembered that these changes *that* we have spoken of took place *long* before this continent was discovered.

2. When his attention was called to *what* had been written on the blackboard he was angrier than *ever*.

3. Now it happended that the poet, though he dwelt so far away, had heard of Ernest, and had meditated *much* on his character, until he deemed nothing so *desirable* as to meet him.

4. Thy churlish courtesy for those
Reserve who fear to be thy foes.
As *safe* to me the *mountain* way
At midnight as in blaze of day.

5. Nor breathed he *full* till far *behind*
The pass was left, for then they
wind
Along a wide and level green
Where neither tree nor tuft was
seen

III.

1. Parse the italicised words in the foregoing sentences.

2. Write out the 3rd sing. of each tense of the indic. act. of *was seen.*

3. Write out all the participles of the verb *take,* telling which are active and which passive.

4. Write the superlative of *little, much, far, happy, big,* and the plural of *money, volcano, thief, turf, fisherman, German.*

5. Name at least four uses of the nominative case, and give in sentences an example of each.

6. Write two sentences illustrating the correct use of "You and me," and "You and I."

7. What is the difference in meaning between "It *will* be finished before night," and "It *shall* be finished before night"?

CONTEMPORARY LITERATURE.

"The First Greek Book," by Prof. J. W. White, of Harvard. Ginn & Co., Boston. A text-book prepared to meet the need of junior classes who require a shorter course than the one covered by the same author's "Beginner's Greek Book."

"The Golden Readers, Standard I." Moffatt & Paige, London. This reader consists of short and simple fairy tales and other stories for the young.

"Isaiah in the Cambridge Bible Series, Chapters 1-39," edited by Dr. Skinner. There is no need to add any words of praise to what has already been said as to this most noteworthy undertaking of the Cambridge University Press.

"The Beginners of a Nation," by Edward Eggleston. D. Appleton & Company, New York. This history of a certain aspect of the United States, by a well and favorably known literary man, has been brought out in a fitting and remarkably attractive manner by Appletons. In a dedication of the book to the Hon. James Bryce, M.P., the author speaks of the settlement of the United States in a way which cannot but give pleasure to all British subjects.

From Allyn and Bacon, Boston, have been received two Latin text-books, both of which promise to be of substantial help in the class room. "Virgil's Æneid," Books 1-6, 8 and 9, edited by Principal Comstock, and Bennett's "Latin Composition for Secondary Schools," edited by Prof. Bennett, of Cornell.

In W. C. Heath's well-known Modern Language Series, we have received Goethe's "Iphigenie auf Tauris," edited by Prof. Lewis A. Rhoades, of the University of Illinois, and Scribe and Legouvé's "Bataille De Dames," edited by Prof. Wells, of the University of the South.

"Short Stories of Our Shy Neighbors," by Mrs. M. A. B. Kelly. American Book Company, New York. The author has achieved a charming success in bringing out the various characteristics of the creatures who are given to man for his use and care. Children are sure to be interested in what she tells them.

We have also received from the American Book Company, "The

First Year in German," by I. Keller, and "The Mastery of Books," by the Librarian of Brown University, H. L. Koopman, a book which would be of the greatest use to any boy or girl who has an inclination towards reading. Such advice and guidance cannot be too urgently pressed upon them.

From Macmillan & Company, through their Toronto agents The Copp, Clark Company, we have received the Fourth Book of "Murché's Domestic Science Readers," "French Plays for Schools," by Mrs. J. G. Frazer, "Physiography for Beginners," by A. T. Simmons, B.Sc., also Mrs. J. G. Frazer's "Scenes of Familiar Life in Colloquial French."

Selections from "Chaucer's Canterbury Tales," edited by Dr. Carson, Cornell, and the second book of "Palgrave's Golden Treasury of Songs and Lyrics," edited by Principal Bell, of Government College, Lahore. These have also been received from the New York house of the Macmillan Company through the Copp, Clark Company. The notes and information given in each are particularly full, and make the editions of special value for the school-room.

"The Gases of the Atmosphere," by Prof. Ramsay, of University College, London. The Macmillan Co., London; The Copp, Clark Co., Toronto. This admirable popular treatise has been to a large extent occasioned by the discovery of the new element Argon. All those who take an intelligent interest in science will experience pleasure in reading the present account by Prof. Ramsay.

In the English Men of Action Series, published and distributed by the same firms, we have received the lives of Nelson and Wolfe, the former by John Knox Laughton and the latter by A. G. Bradley. Both are admirably written and possess that quality of interest which engages at once the reader's attention. Too much cannot be said of the wholesome encouragement which the reading of such books relating to what is highest and best in the history of our empire gives to young students.

In the Foreign Statesmen Series, by the same firms, have been recently issued "Philip Augustus," by W. H. Hutton, and "Richelieu," by Richard Lodge. The names of these eminent men of letters are sufficient to guarantee the quality of the books. The series is an admirable extension of the work already done in the Men of Letters and Men of Action.

"Kate Carnegie," by Ian Maclaren. Fleming Revell and Company, Toronto. The peculiar genius of the author has again attained felicitious expression in a charming book, which may rather be called a series of character studies than a novel. Although the "Bonnie Brier Bush" cannot be repeated there are scenes and characters in "Kate Carnegie," which one would be reluctant to forego,—such as Carmichael's relations to and conversations with the purest and most humble of Scottish clerics, the Rabbi. A word must be added on behalf of the Clerk of Presbytery and his resolution, too inspired to be forgotten or foregone.

(1) "A Primer of Spoken English," (2) "A Primer of Phonetics," by Henry Sweet, M.A., Oxford. At the Clarendon Press. These text-books on the study of Phonetics are of great value as contributions to the practical study of spoken English. Both are new and revised editions.

"Paragraph Writing." By Prof. Scott, of Michigan University, and Prof. Denney, of Ohio University. Boston: Allyn and Bacon. This book will be found of service by teachers of English, especially in their classes for Rhetoric and Composition. The plan of the book is good and well carried out.

Quackenbos's "Practical Rhetoric." New York: The American Book Co. This book will take its place among the best recent text-books in English Literature. It is interesting and fresh, full of good examples and satisfactory both in regard to the work of the author and of the publisher. There is a good index.

Monographs on Education.—"How to Teach Reading," by G. Stanley Hall, Ph D. Boston: D. C. Heath & Co. What children should read and how to teach them to read it are the two main topics of this masterly essay, which was issued some time since in a neat pamphlet by Messrs. D. C. Heath & Co. Many valuable hints to teachers are found here, and the whole essay will be found suggestive and helpful.

Sincere congratulations are owing to *Scribner's Magazine* on the beauty and success of their Christmas number. Kenneth Graham, who has done much for the world this year in "The Golden Age," contributes a delightful embodiment of the circus entitled "The Magic Ring." We cannot refrain from mentioning Miss Repplier's "Little Pharisees in Fiction," nor "A Law-Latin Love Story," by F. J. Stimson.

The *Century Magazine* has caught the best and truest Christmas spirit in Thomas A. Janvier's "The Christmas Calends of Provence," and not far away may be found "In Bethlehem of Judea," by Richard Watson Gilder, who, we hope, has safely recovered from the assault of being mentioned as the handsomest man in America. "Breaking His Own Will" is a most successful humorous story by Elizabeth Eggleston Seelye, with good illustrations by Maud Cowles.

Littell's Living Age for December contains an article by Goldwin Smith on George the Third which originally appeared in the *Cornhill Magazine.*

Macmillan's English Classics.—"Poems of England," by H. B. George and Arthur Sedgwick. This will rank with the best text-books of English poetry. Sixteen different authors are represented, and the time of writing extends over three centuries, from Drayton to Tennyson; but each speaks with the same patriotic fire. The authors and publishers are to be congratulated on this excellent number of the English classics. We heartily recommend it to our readers.

"Hegel's Philosophy of Right," translated by S.W. Dyde, M.A., D.Sc., Professor of Mental Philosophy, Queen's University. London: Geo. Bell & Sons; Toronto: The Copp, Clark Co. There is nothing more natural or gratifying than that one who wins distinction should seek to share it with those whom he feels have given him of their best to make him what he is. In a recent issue of the *Critic*, Bliss Carman, in a more or less humorous account of himself, mentions gratefully that Geo. R. Parkin was at one time his teacher, and that he still considers him the greatest teacher he has ever met. The inscription of the present book is to Dr. Watson, who gave to the author his "first lessons, not in Hegel only, but in philosophy." Of such ties and remembrances the best part of life is made. We take pleasure in noticing such a satisfactory translation of a great book as this of Prof. Dyde's.

In the December number of the *Atlantic* will be found an able review of "Sir George Tressady." Opinion is shifting slowly concerning the latest of Mrs. Ward's books. "The American Voice" is the subject of one of the contributors to the club. Whoever the writer is, he kindly finds the Canadian voice sweeter, but in spite of that the Canadian voice needs more care than we give it.

There is a terrible cat story in the December *Bookman* from the French, which would suit anyone in want of a nightmare after Christmas.

THE CANADA

EDUCATIONAL MONTHLY

AND SCHOOL MAGAZINE.

FEBRUARY, 1897.

REST FROM FEAR.

By the Rev. Hugh Black, M.A.

"The Lord shall give thee rest from thy fear, and from the hard bondage wherein thou wast made to serve."—Isaiah xiv. 3.

THIS section of the Book of Isaiah, the Burden of Babylon, is a prophecy of the Exile, coming with comfort and good cheer to the heart of the broken nation. The doom shifts from Jerusalem to Babylon. And for Israel, their redemption draws nigh—and, meanwhile, they are saved by hope. God's great purpose for them will again appear. It speaks of deliverance, first of all from the outward lot of oppression, and also from the inward grief and despair. This spiritual part of the deliverance is meant to begin at once. It is an anodyne from present pain. The dawning of the hope brings instant relief. They need not wait till God fulfils His promise. The very faith in that fulfilment lifts the cloud from their hearts. To believe that God will give them rest from their hard bondage, at once lightens the bondage. If the Prophet can make them against hope believe in hope, the pressure on their souls will slacken immediately. What the exiles needed supremely was deliverance from despair, rest from the fears that oppressed them; and faith in God's loving purpose would give them that at once, even in the midst of their hard bondage wherein they were made to serve. Faith is the ground of hope. "Faith is the assurance of things hoped for, the evidence of things not seen." This is the application we may bring near to our modern life from this sweet promise in the Burden of Babylon.

Life is never without its hard bondage wherein men are made to serve, the bondage of an untoward lot as in the case of exiles, or the bondage of soul in one of its many forms—sorrow, fear, doubt, habit, sin. All progress is emancipation. All advance is towards freedom. Reform is nothing if it does not mean liberty. God's work means always and everywhere the loosing of bonds and setting the captives free. This is true physically and politically, as well as spiritually. It is the former because it is the latter. Christ will yet set all prisoners free, will yet break all oppression and injustice and cruelty; but He can set them free even in their prison. He emancipates from the terrorism of the material, from the slavery of sin, and sets the soul in the glorious liberty of sons of God. The man whom Christ sets free can henceforth and forever be bondsman to none but his Master. "If the Son make you free, ye shall be free indeed."

The greatest obstacle in the way of that spiritual freedom has been fear. The bondage of fear has been the weariest slavery of the race. It has its roots no doubt in sin. Fear entered Eden when sin entered. "They heard the voice of the Lord God, and Adam and his wife hid themselves. And the Lord God called unto Adam and said, Where art thou? And he said, I heard Thy voice in the garden, and *I was afraid.*" Fear has gripped man and held him in spiritual tyranny. Men have been afraid of life and of death; afraid of to-day and to-morrow; afraid of the living and the dead; afraid of man and of God; afraid of everything and of nothing. The primitive instinct of dread, so forcibly described by Kipling, has its abode still in life.

"Through the Jungle very softly flits a shadow and a sigh—
He is Fear, O Little Hunter, he is Fear!
Very softly down the glade runs a waiting, watching shade,
And the whisper spreads and widens, far and near;
And the sweat is on thy brow, for he passes even now—
He is Fear, O Little Hunter, he is Fear!"

Society has been cemented by fear. Religion has been colored by it. The race has been hag-ridden by it. The two great forces of the world, which have built up history, our social institutions, and life itself, have been fear and love; fear, the offspring of the spirit of evil, and love, the effluence of God. These have ever striven for the mastery—and strive.

We say that the spread of education has killed fear. We point to superstitions, the dread of unknown powers, the terror of the unseen, which have been mitigated, if not destroyed, by knowledge. There is truth in this, and true knowledge is of God; for God is light, and in Him is no darkness at all. But it is not true that fear is dead, or that mere knowledge ever can give it its quietus. Knowledge can only glean in the fields after the reapers. The mind of man can only set in terms of reason what the soul of man has discovered. Superstition is killed, not by reason but by faith. A false religion is displaced not by criticism but by a true religion. And it is not true, as a matter of fact, that fear has ceased to be a bondage to men. To think so a man must be ignorant of life, must have had his eyes shut to the hunted look on human faces. To think so he must have never faced the spectres of his own mind, the troubles of his own brain. Black Care still rides behind the horseman. Fear lurks in the bottom of our hearts. There is ever a death's-head at the world's feast. We no longer tremble at mystery, and bow before idols which represent the dreaded forces of Nature. But have we solved the mystery? Has knowledge robbed life and destiny of their unknown elements? Philosophy may conquer the fear of death, but there is left still the *fear of life.* A spurious peace can be got from forgetfulness of the problems of life, by shutting the eyes, by hiding despair from oneself, or by hopeless acquiescence in the sordidness of existence. That sort of peace could always be got in that way. Life has still its appalling changes, its uncertainties. Men can still be mastered by an unspoken dread. Are there no misgivings in men's minds, no heart-sinkings about the future, no distrust of self, never an apprehension of evil, never a shiver at the possible? I speak not of the fear of death, though that must always be our portion. For the love of life is natural, and therefore the fear of death is natural. It is only when the spirit is broken, when nerve is lost, when body or mind or heart is diseased, that death can seem a gain. And if in our modern world-weariness there is a school with their morbid high-priests of literature and art, who worship at the shrine of death and speak of it affectedly as our gentle mother—even that is but another proof of heart-sickness and the fear of life. Doubt is the disease of thought, and is twin sister of fear. We may lay all the ghosts we can, and, whistling to keep our courage up, go boldly to prove that there is nothing but shadows to frighten us. But the ghosts will not be laid. The wraith of the White Lady rises at the well. Fear clings to life, elusive as the mist on the mountains.

And even when fear *for* self is beaten back from the gates, there remains for every true man fear *of* self. When we stop to think and look back on the past we can be afraid of our own base impulses and cravings. We can be afraid of our own weakness. It may be a wholesome fear, and be to us the mother of safety, as Burke called it. It may be one of the hounds of heaven to drive us from the wilderness into the fold.

And further, if self can be forgotten altogether, as it can be, there is *fear for others* in our hearts. Perfect love casts out fear, and even our imperfect human love casts out fear of the loved, but not always fear for them. There are noble forms of fear that seem almost born of love itself. Job is depicted in all his happiness and prosperity rising up early in the morning to pray and make offerings for his sons and daughters; for Job said, "It may be that my sons have sinned and cursed God in their hearts." And when the blow fell, he knew that he had been dreading something like this all his life. "The thing which I greatly feared is come upon me."

There are also fears of the future on a larger scale, fears which find voice in our books to-day about the forces at work in society, with their possible social changes, the common timidity which looks with shrinking on new and untried paths. We speak glibly of this as a transition period. We even believe that conditions more true and just may emerge, but everywhere we find men dreading the plunge, the passage through the cloud. Life is open to fear on every side. Somewhere or other it can grip us by the throat, if not at this turn of the road, at the next, possibly. Fear is the sign of evil in the world. We have all to fight it sooner or later in some form or other. Life is so often lived under a grey sky and on a sodden earth. The weight of to-morrow burdens to-day. Is there not need now as ever for the blessed promise, "The Lord shall give thee rest from thy fear"?

If the cause of our modern sickness of heart is doubt—doubt of self, of life, of God—the cure for it is faith. The owls and bats and dark night-birds that hoot in our ears, are driven from us by one stroke of the flashing sword of the rising sun. If we realize that God's love is the heart of the universe and the centre of life, fear of all kind must depart. We walk serenely in the light of that love. If we accept that love, if we apply it to our every need, if we breathe in it, live in it, where is there room for fear? Want of faith in God means want of faith in human destiny. To be without God is to be without hope; for the world becomes a riddle and life a terror. Faith in the moral order of the world, in the protecting love of the Father, saves from despondency. In God there is no room for fear and no place for care. Living in the filial relationship with God in which Christ lived, we are emancipated.

Christ's gospel is the gospel of the grace of God, good news of great joy to the sorrowful, glad tidings to the sinful and fearful. "Fear not" was a word often on His lips. He comes to-day, as then, to bring men to God. He comes bringing God with Him. He comes over life's broken waters, making a great calm. "It is I, be not afraid." A touch of His hand quietens the fevered pulse. A look of His eyes brings peace. A smile of His lips illumines the world. Christ's very presence in the world is a message of courage. Why are ye fearful, O ye of little faith? Look up to the bright light that is in the clouds. You are not unregarded. Be of good cheer. Life has a meaning. God has a purpose with you in your struggle, and patience and service. It is a purpose of love. To live in the light of that is to have rest from anxiety for self, and from fear of others. "The Lord is on my side, I will not fear. What can man do unto me?" It saves also from the fear of sin and its power. Love's redemption will snatch you from the very jaws of the dragon. Courage! Take heart of grace! "Sin shall *not* have dominion over you." Christ transmutes fear into faith. Faith grips the quiver of trembling flesh with a strong hand. The true fear of the Lord kills all other fear, even the fear of self.

Even love's fear is swallowed up by the higher love. There is no room for fear in that love with which Christ loved us. The cloud which hovers over our imperfect human love withers in the sunshine of God's perfect love. We need not fear for the world and grow craven over impending changes; for it is God's world and is the scene of His redemptive work. Nor need we fear for the Church, for the cause of truth and righteousness and peace. It is notfor us to tremble for the ark of God. Truth is inviolable. Love is invincible. God's will shall be done on earth. His kingdom shall come—oppose it who dare! Fear not, little flock, it is your Father's good pleasure to give you the kingdom. We need back again in our midst the regal days of faith. Lift up your face with its stain of tears and believe. Courage! Faith shall live —fear and all the dragon brood shall die. Take up the burden of your life again for another year of service, with comfort in your heart, and let Christ's peace rule within. Abiding in Him, He shall give thee rest from thy fear.

"He that dwelleth in the secret place of the Most High shall abide under the shadow of the Almighty. Thou shalt not be afraid for the terror by night, nor for the arrow that flieth by day, nor for the pestilence that walketh in darkness, nor for the destruction that wasteth at noonday."—*Sunday Magazine.*

Changing conditions are affecting us. It was supposed thirty years ago that the cotton of the world must come from the United States. But Egyptian cotton is far better for the finer fabrics now demanded, as it has a long fibre; 60,000 bales were used in this country last year; the Egyptians are increasing their cotton acreage. English engineers are planning to improve the irrigation and extend cotton raising; it is said an acre on the Nile will give a bale of cotton. Then, too, thirty years ago the Argentine Republic sent no wheat to Europe; neither did India. She as well as Russia has laid down railroads and opened up a vast territory just suited for wheat; to these must be now added Egypt since the English have gone there. So that the world will no longer get its main wheat supply from the United States.

ELEMENTARY EDUCATION IN QUEBEC.*

NO body of people who come together for purely selfish ends can ever rise above the mud of grovelling egoism from which such ideas are sure to germinate, and if we, individually and collectively, are here in Montreal this week, and in this hall to-night, merely to further our own interests without any thought of the public weal, the sooner this Association dissolves into its original atoms and goes down into blank oblivion, unhonored and unsung, the better will it be for the cause of public education. If, on the other hand, we, as a body, are inspired with the divine spirit of progress, forgetful of vile self, equal to our opportunities, willing to do our whole duty without fear or favor; then may our Association become a mighty influence for good; then may it indeed be a true leaven of improvement, permeating the mass of apathy which has so long rested, incubus-like, on the breast of educational public opinion in this Province. Shall we yield to atrophy; or, standing on the broad basis of humanity and human thought, shall we catch the dawning gleams of awakening sentiment in that hulking giant, public opinion, who now lies supine, but yawning and stretching so that those who are awake to the influences which are at work around us can hear his mighty muscles crack; and, extending the guiding hand, shall we place his feet straight on the road which will ever lead him onward and upward to higher and better things?

Education in every land, to be true, must be based on true principles. It, in all its parts, must belong to the people, and they must feel that it so belongs. It must be of such a kind as to suit the circumstances, the environment, the genius of the people. Its warp and woof must be spun from their finest heart fibres; it must be, in short, an embodiment of the mental activities of the people themselves.

Is this true of the educational system of this Province; is it at one with itself? As we follow it from the elementary school, through the secondary school, the college, and the university, to that body which is supposed to rule and guide its destinies, are we impressed with the conviction that they are integral parts of the same unit? Do we feel one part respond with heart throb to the heart throb of another? Are we convinced that it fulfils the demands of a true education for a whole people? As we watch that little one yonder with bright eyes and curls, following the dusty road, slate in hand, to the little red school house at the crossroads, as we think of the educational idea represented by that picture, let us place our finger on the pulse of the body to whose care that idea has been committed, and ask ourselves if that idea is represented there? Can we feel the responsive throb, or can we see, as it were, where the axe of the executioner, opportunism, with cruel stroke, has severed the life-giving artery? I leave the thought with you; it must be faced; it will not down till a satisfactory solution of the difficulty is found. No amount of sophistry will remove the obstruction.

A mighty monarch once called before him the noblest, the wisest, the best of his courtiers, and pointing

* The President's address delivered at the Montreal Convention of teachers by R. J. Hewton, M.A., Inspector of Schools.

to the far horizon where earth and sky melted into one shimmering haze, —"Go," said he, "and find for me the greatest good." Joyful they started on their quest, expecting soon to find that which they sought and receive the reward of their labors. As they journeyed, they came to a spot, a more beautiful than which, never delighted the eye of man. A mighty mountain reared his rounded head above the surrounding country. From base to summit it was clad in vivid green. As they looked in rapture, this changed to a deeper hue, and still again, as the great magician nature waved his wand, scarlet, and crimson, and gold, and russet, and all the prismatic tints snatched from heaven's own treasury, took the place of the duller shade. Anon with rustle, rustle, rustle, the gorgeous garment came floating down, and the mighty monarch was clad in a dazzling garment of diamond-studded ermine. At his feet, with head resting lovingly against his knees, they found a plant of beauty rare, and fragrance marvellously sweet; graceful leaves adorned its stem and luscious fruit pleased eye and taste. "Surely," said they, "this is that which the king desired," and they gathered of its fruit and sent their noblest to bear it to the king. But, alas, they returned sorrowing, with the command to search farther. So they encamped about the tree and ate of its fruit. It, however, was not enough for all, and out from the shelter of the mountain where the north wind blew not, and where the golden sunbeams fell, in pulsatory rays, upon the open windswept plains, shelterless and forlorn, they were forced, in quest of nourishment. O'er stony plain and black morass they travelled with down-cast looks and sorrowful hearts, for where in such a region would they find the greatest good? They sought for food, nor was their search in vain, for at their feet, with leaves prone on the ground, with blossoms exposed to frost, to hail, to whirlwind, they found a humble plant; hunger driven, they tasted of the humble fruit and found it wholesome. Forced of necessity, they paid some attention to its culture, when, behold, a marvellous thing came to pass, for under the slightest care the lowly plant extended its leaves till they covered barren plain and dank morass with pleasing verdure. Its fruit became larger, and in ever widening circles it extended till it reached the very roots of the glorious mountain sheltered tree they had mistaken for the greatest good, and this, as though it received new life from the lowly plant, took on new beauty; new leaves sprang out as if by magic; its fruit became larger and more abundant. At last, cried the courtiers, we have found that for which we came, and once more they bore the fruit of the royal plant to the king, and once again they returned. What said the king? "Search again, for though ye found it ye knew it not."

Then there arose from the outskirts of the throng one who was a toiler in the flower field, whose experience had not been utilised when the message was sent to the king. He exclaimed, "The message is plain, the fruit of the star plant is not the greatest good, because it is not sufficient or suitable for all, but this lowly plant affords nourishment for all who come, and gives life and beauty to the royal plant itself." And it was even so.

This is true of the educational system of the Province of Quebec. We have been devoting our attention almost exclusively to the lordly university, the stately college, the fine institutions in the centres of population; but the little red school house on the dusty plains sleeps under the dust of neglect. Learned dons and literary dignitaries have labored for superior education; multi-millionaires have vied with each other in founding names for themselves by building faculties for the children of the classes; but we yet await the advent of the man, the prophet, who, with the cause of elementary education woven into the fibre of his being, will, with clarion voice, wake this province from west to east, and convince those who have charge of our affairs, educational or otherwise, that the question of common education has sprung to life and must be faced. O, for the eloquence of a Demosthenes or a Cicero, the power to fire men's hearts and stir their blood, then would I make this Province, from the farthest recesses of the Laurentides to the dark waters of the Gulf, reverberate with the grand truth that the common education of its children is the primary duty of every people, that we have no right to expend lavishly of public moneys on higher education, at the expense of the common schools.

It is commonly said that on such occasions as this we ask for the unattainable. I do not do so; I ask you to face the question as to who is responsible for the indifference to education which obtains in this Province. I say to you that you are responsible, that those who are with me on this platform to-night are responsible, that we, as individual and corporate members of this Association, are responsible. We all know that rural elementary education is not represented on that body which is supposed to rule its destinies; we know that the legislative grant for elementary education is $14,000 a year less than at Confederation; we know that our teachers are underpaid; we have seen the candidate for legislative honors, with smile and bow and hand shake, seek the public sufferage; we have, perchance, worked for him; we have heard him pledge himself to secure that road, this bridge, the other railway for his county; but when have we heard the matter of education brought forward; when have we, who call ourselves educationists, asked what was to be done for education?

I am, however, thankful to say that I see the dawn of better things. Though the words of those of us who dared, in the past, to raise our voices on behalf of common schools, seemed to have fallen on deaf ears; though those for whom we spoke listened and seemed to slumber again; those to whom we spoke forgot or did not hear; those to whom we, in our inexperience, had looked, as our natural leaders, were found wedded to other interests; our words have, in the silence of public intelligence, our words have had their effect. A sign of the times was indeed visible when the first minister of this Province, but a few nights ago, spoke from a platform which bore the legends, "Elementary Education," "Better pay for our teachers." It is our duty to do all in our power to assist in carrying such objects to a happy issue. Here, from this platform, feeling the full responsibility for my words, I wish to repeat and emphasize what I said last year at Sherbrooke, when I declared that there was rank, fame and honor for the man who made education a living issue. To-night I say this and more; I say, judging from my knowledge of a considerable extent of country, that the party which takes up education and gives it the support it deserves will rule this Province for many years to come; that the man who leads such a party will be like him who found in the mud of a dark valley a jewel of inestimable value, and raised it high on a beacon, where, catching the heaven-strayed beams of light, it illuminated the dark and devious ways of the valley, and guided the toilers therein from the deep treacherous pits of ignorance and crime, on and upward to the firm ground of knowledge, and opened to their wondering view new vistas in the realms of human activities.

SOME NOTES ON POETRY FOR CHILDREN.

(Concluded from last month.)

WE would have in the Child's Anthology the Raggedy Man's account of the man in the moon, which there is no space to quote. We would also have Mr. Eugene Field's Dutch lullaby, "Wynken, Blynken, and Nod," which is well known; and William Miller's "Wee Willie Winkie," which is better known. Another but less popular Scotch poem, belonging to the same family, is "Wee Davie Daylicht," by Robert Tennant. This class of poetry, wherein a bold figure (such as Jack Frost) is employed to make the picture more real and vivid, is good for children. It stimulates the imagination, and that, in this world, is a most desirable proceeding. There is a capital poem by William Howitt beginning:—

The wind one morning sprang up from sleep,
Saying "Now for a frolic! now for a leap!"

which I have not heard since I was in words of one syllable, yet to this hour I never see a gusty day without recalling the piece, and thinking momentarily of the wind as a huge, humanized, practical-joking rebel. I don't claim to be a better citizen for this memory; but life is more interesting.

One of the larger sections of the Child's Anthology would consist of what may be called dissuasive verse: the chief producers of which are Jane and Ann Taylor, author of "Original Poems," the first deliberate effort to make a book of verse to please children first and other people afterwards. Although seventy years and more have passed since this collection of lyrics and tragedies first appeared, the book still sways the nursery. In this continued popularity we may perhaps find another proof of the distaste of children for poetry. The manner is prosaic, almost bald; the matter is, beyond words, alluring. The fascination excited by a history of human disaster is ever powerful; and the author who deals faithfully with elemental faults and passions is assured of longevity. Jane and Ann Taylor did this. They took cruelty and greed, covetousness and theft, impatience and anger, and made them the centre of human narratives; vividly real and human narratives—that is the secret of their power. Children never change; the same things that interested the infant Moses interest infants to-day; and there is still something not unattractive in the misfortunes of others. Hence is it that the "Original Poems" hold little audiences spell-bound in 1896 just as they did in 1826, and will hold them spell-bound in the thirtieth century, if mothers are wise. Their influence for virtue is another matter. They are popular, I fancy, rather for their dramatic interest than their didacticism. Sinners in real life are not so easily daunted. At any rate they would be included in the Child's Anthology, not for their dissuasive powers, but for their capacity to interest.

"False Alarms" is one of the most terrible; the story of Little Mary, who called for her mamma in alarm when there was no cause, by way of pleasantry, and laughed when her mamma came. In the end she catches fire in her bedroom, cries vainly for help, and is almost incinerated. Who (for twenty-four hours) after this, could play with fire or hoax a parent?

In "The Boys and the Apple-tree," disaster is indeed averted, but so skilfully that we experience a thrill as intense as if the catastrophe had really occurred. Tommy and Billy see apples hanging over a wall. Tommy would steal some, but Billy, the blameless Billy, says No—"To steal is a sin." They call on Bobby, to whose father, it seems, the garden belongs, and he, in the course of the afternoon, shows them a man-trap guarding the identical apples which Tommy had coveted, a weapon of peculiar horror.

Cried Tommy, "I'll mind what my good mamma says,
And take the advice of a friend;
I never will steal to the end of my days;
I've been a bad boy, but I'll mend!"

We are to suppose that he did mend. The sisters Taylor were wise not to carry their histories too far.

"Greedy Richard" has a fine aristocratic flavor:—

"I think I want some pies this morning,"
Said Dick, stretching himself and yawning;
So down he threw his slate and books,
And saunter'd to the pastry-cook's.

There, of course, he ate too much. To this day, if any one were to say to me suddenly, "Quick, tell me who is your ideal among millionaires," the figure that would jump to my mind would be Greedy Richard. I should not think of Mr. Barney Barnato until afterwards. And not only is there his wealth to admire, but look at the splendid liberty of the boy—he could fling aside his slate and books whenever he wished!

One does not realize how admirable was the work of Jane and Ann Taylor until it is compared with that of inferior writers. They had a rival in Louisa Watts, whose efforts—to be found in a volume painfully entitled "Pretty Little Poems for Pretty Little People"—attempt to cover the same ground. Her style lacks the vigor of that of her exemplars; but none the less the book attained very considerable popularity, among parents and instructors, in the forties and fifties. She seems to have considered narrative less her strength than the popularization of science, a large portion of the book being occupied by lessons, presented in the most distressing doggerel, in astronomy, mineralogy, botany, and other branches of learning. The lecturer is mamma, and the audience, consisting of Ann, Julia, Harry, and others of a strikingly considerable family, are always disproportionately grateful for the information tendered to them. Thus:—

One evening very fine and clear,
Ann and Eliza walking were,
And being very near the sea,
They viewed it each attentively.

Curious Eliza very soon
Said, "Dear mamma, pray is it known
What water is? If you can tell,
Ann and myself would like it well."

Mamma delighted to be drawn, breaks off at once, at a hand gallop:—

The element of water is
Composed of only two gases;
One part of hydrogen is there,
Four oxygen, or vital air,

and so on.

But Louisa Watts's highest achievement was the ballad entitled "The Benefit of Learning and Good Behaviour." In this poem the progress of a virtuous and industrious child from penury to wealth and position is narrated with convincing spirit. In the hope that we all may profit by her example, I will quote the lines. In reading, mark how inevitably one incident follows another:—

There was a little cottage girl,
Once forced from morn till night to whirl
The spinning-wheel, to earn the bread
With which her mother might be fed;
But though she had so much to do,
She learn'd to read, and spell and sew.

Soon as her poor old mother died,
Her wants were comfortably supplied
By a good clergyman—and she
Taught all his little family;
But soon a dreadful war began
And many people in the town
Were kill'd, and had their houses too
Burnt, then what could poor Catherine do?
To hide, she in an oven got,
But soon the soldiers found her out
And would have killed her very soon,
But as she screamed, her voice was known
By a young gallant officer,
Who took her home and married her;
But he was forced to go away
To battle, and was killed that day.
Poor Cath'rine then became a slave
To a rich man, who one day gave
An entertainment to the king,
Whom Cath'rine served, and a sad thing
He thought it, she a slave should be,
With so much grace and modesty,
He heard with wonder and delight,
Poor Catherine her tale recite;
But more delighted was to find
She had a cultivated mind;
And very soon was changed the scene,
For Catherine became a queen.

The compiler of the Child's Anthology would, after examining, however thoroughly, all previous collections of poetry, have completed but a small portion of his task. For then would come the search for these playful verses which so many men, not professionally writers for children, have thrown off with the aim of pleasing little friends. Just as "The Giant's Shoes," written by Professor Clifford for the entertainment of his children, is one of the best nonsense stories in the language, so are some of these rhymes without parallel. Sir George Trevelyan tells us that Macaulay, posing as The Judicious Poet, a myth in which his young readers more than half believed, was much given to this kind of composition. "Some of his pieces of verse," writes Macaulay's biographer, "are almost perfect specimens of the nursery lyric. From five to ten stanzas in length, and with each word carefully formed in capitals—most comforting to the eyes of a student who is not very sure of his small letters—they are real children's poems, and they profess to be nothing more." I have not made any extensive search in other biographies for kindred verses—that is a labor for the anthologist—but as a foretaste of the quality of the material now waiting to be unearthed and collected together for the contentment of the nursery, I will quote the following lyric, the authorship of which I have tried in vain to trace:—

There was a little girl, she wore a little hood.
And a curl down the middle of her forehead,
When she was good, she was very, very good,
But when she was bad, she was horrid.

One day she went up-stairs, while her parents unawares,
In the kitchen down below were occupied with meals,
And she stood upon her head, on her little truckle-bed,
And she then began hurraying with her heels.

Her mother heard the noise, and thought it was the boys,
A-playing at a combat in the attic,
But when she climbed the stair and saw Jemima there,
She took and she did whip her most emphatic!

Authorities differ as to the opening of the poem:—

There was a little girl who had a little curl
Right down the middle of her forehead,

is a common and preferable reading; and more people than not believe that when the word "horrid" is reached the poem is over. Few know that Jemima was the rebel's name. Few but are astonished to learn of the versatility of her heels. That the above quotation of the whole piece is correct may be accepted as gospel, for the sufficient reason that the *Spectator* says so. In such matters (as in records of feline vagaries) the *Spectator* is to be followed blindly. Technically, the poem is masterly. For force and vividness the phrase

" occupied with meals " stands alone in poetry for children.

Perhaps, then, some one will compile for us these Anthologies. That for the child should, I think, come first, because he has been defrauded too long ; because, for too long, he has been offered little but doggerel on the one hand, and fine, but to him incomprehensible, poetry on the other. Such a collection might be satisfying enough to discourage parents and guardians in the purchase of other and less worthy new children's books, and so, in turn, deter publishers from adding to the congested yearly output of this kind of literature. For there is no doubt that the children of to-day are too wantonly supplied with reading. Our grandmothers and grandfathers, whose nursery shelves held a poor dozen books, but who knew that dozen well and remembered them through life, were more fortunate than their descendants, who are bewildered by the quantity of matter prepared for them by glib writers, and who, after reading everything, find little or nothing worthy of recollection. The need for the Grown-up's Anthology is not so pressing. The Grown-up's can harvest it for themselves. Indeed, it probably is the duty of every lover of poetry to be his own Palgrave.—*Fortnightly Review.*

E. V. LUCAS.

THE BIBLE.

ONE of the best known of modern veteran journalists has given it as his opinion that there is no book that it is so important for a journalist to study as the Bible. This is perhaps a somewhat utilitarian way of regarding the Scriptures. Mr. Dana simply meant probably that the young newspaper man should study the Bible for style, for terse English, for simple and forcible expression ; just as he might have recommended Defoe, or Shakespeare, or the Pilgrim's Progress. There is no doubt much to be said about the Bible from this point of view. It is a fact that many of our best writers have come of families in which the Bible was a household book, and its words and phrases on the lips of father and mother. The children of such households are furnished, from the time they begin to understand the meaning of words, with a vocabulary at once terse, direct, and full of meaning. He who would write for, or talk to, the people finds Anglo-Saxon a fitting medium for his thoughts, and the Bible is a grand Anglo Saxon library. But to many people the wording of the Bible is dear for far other reasons. They do not look at it merely as a mine of pure English. Its sentences have become surrounded with associations and meanings such as gather round the words of no other book. Wilkie Collins, in his famous novel "The Moonstone," gives us a queer old character whose favorite book is " Robinson Crusoe." He knows the volume from beginning to end, and in whatever circumstances he happens to be placed some happy sentence or situation, either of Crusoe or his man Friday, comes to his mind. That is but a whimsical invention. But there are thousands of people in real life to whom the Bible is a daily guide and inspirer. Its noble words help them to fight the battle of life, comfort them in sorrow, brim to their lips in joy. The same thoughts put in other words would not be so satisfactory to them as are the antique sentences which for generations have more or less moulded English-speaking people. It was for this reason that when the Revised Version was planned there was much unuttered as well as uttered distaste for it. The minds of men and women approved, but there was, and still is a clinging to the old "Authorized Version appointed to be read in churches." The inborn conservatism of people is nowhere more apparent than in their dislike of any intermeddling with the Scriptures.

There is still room, however, for intelligent and helpful work in the elucidation of the Bible. To be acquainted with some parts of the Scripture, and to have certain well-known texts and passages ingrained in the mind cannot be regarded as the comprehensive knowledge of the Bible which its greatness deserves. The Bible, as literature, is not so widely studied by the people as it might be. There is time for reading multitudinous novels and magazines, but comparatively few people read the Bible at all thoroughly. Yet there can be no doubt that no course of reading could be more interesting and improving. It is on this account that most attempts to bring the Bible before the modern reader in any fresh and striking way are valuable. Prominent among such attempts must be reckoned the translation of the Bible which is shortly to come from the press of the Johns Hopkins University of Baltimore. It is being edited by Prof. Paul Haupt, a young German scholar, who is not only a competent Orientalist, but deeply interested in the Bible from various points of view. He has gathered to his assistance an array of scholarship such as has seldom been employed in the production of any volume, and the result of their labours must naturally be looked for with eager attention.

The feeling that the same sort of criticism that is applied to other books must be applied to the text of the Bible is one that can no longer be treated as if it were irreverent or unholy. The meaning of the Scriptures can only be found by continual comparison and inference. Human language admits of various interpretations, and every word and every sentence must be modified and explained according to the subject which is discussed; according to the purposes, feelings, circumstances, and principles of the writer; and according to the genius and idioms of the language which he uses. These things must be considered in any intelligent appreciation of the Scriptures, and it is on a basis such as is here indicated that the new translation of the Bible has been made. The attempt has been made to secure a perfect text. In addition to this, what may be called mechanical means have been taken advantage of in its production. The text will be printed on different coloured backgrounds. Original passages, in which criticism can find nothing to alter, will be printed on white. Interpellations, notes, and various changes that are believed to have been made subsequently will be printed on backgrounds of different colours. From this method the book will derive its name of "The Polychrome Bible." It sounds rather fanciful, and American, and modern, but for all that the method may prove to be a useful one. British, American, and German scholars have combined their efforts in the production of the volume, which will be a very complete compendium on Biblical literature. The work has been described as somewhat revolutionary, but there can be no doubt that it will lead to an interest in the Bible as a book such as could hardly be awakened by any other means.—*Mail and Empire, Toronto.*

You have too much respect upon the world;
They lose it that do buy it with much care.

Merchant of Venice, i. 1.

THE THEOLOGICAL LIFE OF A CALIFORNIA CHILD.

BY PROF. EARL BARNES, OF LELAND STANFORD JUNIOR UNIVERSITY, CALIFORNIA

THIS study is not intended in any sense as an inquiry into the child's religious life and feeling. It is intended simply to show the theological atmosphere in which California children live, and their mental attitude toward their theology at different ages.

The materials on which the study is based are :

I. One thousand and ninety-one compositions written by children from six to twenty years old in the various schools of California, on the subjects of heaven and hell. They were simply given the subjects and asked to write compositions in the presence of their teachers without suggestion or comment.

II. Sixteen reminiscences prepared by adults, in which they tried simply to recall and state their early beliefs.

III. Twenty-seven studies on young children made by mothers and teachers through conversations, working along the lines of this syllabus :

God—Where is He? What does He do? Why can not we see Him?

Death—Why do people die? Where do they go?

Heaven—Where is it? Who goes there? What do people do there? What will children have there?

Hell—What must a person do to go there? What is it like?

Angels—What do they do?

Ghosts—Why are people afraid of them?

Witches—What can they do?

Prayer—Why do we pray? What do we pray for? Why do we not always get what we pray for?

Religious ceremonies—Why do we celebrate Christmas? Why do we go to church?

Every variety of faith was represented in the papers — Catholics, Methodists, Presbyterians, Universalists, Christian Scientists, Mormons, Baptists, Adventists, and Spiritualists. With only two or three exceptions the children treated the questions seriously, and the papers bear internal evidence of honest effort to express the truth.

The data were collated in the following groups :

God, His appearance and activities.

The devil, his appearance and activities.

Heaven, its location, its inhabitants, and their appearance and activities.

Hell, its location, its inhabitants, and their appearance and activities.

Indications of a critical attitude; acts which take people to heaven; acts which keep them out of heaven.

Since the children were not answering any set questions, we cannot state what proportion accepted any partienlar idea, but only how many of the children who mentioned an idea accepted or rejected it.

In studying the data an attempt was first made to bring together the theological conceptions expressed in the compositions, and then to determine the attitude of the children toward these conceptions.

The central figure in the theology is naturally God. The pictures drawn of Him are often misty and indistinct, but more than half the papers represent Him as a great and good man. He is so large that "He could stand with His feet on the ground and touch the clouds with His arms upraised." "He is a man that has six hands and feet and eyes"; or, "He is a huge being with numerous limbs spread out all over the sky."

He is generally an old man with a long white beard and flowing white garments; often He is represented as having wings, and a crown on His head.

He is most often described as good and kind; the stern quality is seldom apparent, but the whole figure is shadowy, unreal, and indistinct.

A considerable number of children speak of Him as being able to do anything, as being everywhere, and as knowing everything. Omnipresence seems hard for the children to conceive, and it probably accounts for His being represented with several heads and members.

Omniscience is easier: "God can see everything you do and hear everything you say, even if you are inside of a house." "I have thought and been told that He can see through anything; it makes no difference if it is iron, steel, glass, wood, or anything." Many of the children feel that God is watching them, and some say "He writes it all down."

Omnipotence is mentioned by many children, but there are few concrete instances given. One girl of twelve says that "God could have an earthquake at any time." His activities are seldom described; less than five per cent. of the children speak of Him as ruling the universe, making things grow or caring for our material needs. One boy of ten says in perfect earnestness that "God isrcnesgsa the world."

Christ is seldom mentioned, and his relation to the Father is rarely brought out; where it is, in one-fourth of the cases the relation is reversed and God is spoken of as the Son of Christ. The Trinity is mentioned by only two children. Christ is mentioned as our Redeemer by some twenty-five children.

Heaven is generally, even with children up to the age of twelve and beyond, simply an improved earth. More than 500 children locate it "in the sky," "in the clouds," or "up." The next most common location is "where the good go," or "where God is," while a few say it is "in the earth," "all about us," "on some star," or "in the east," and "no one in a balloon could reach it, it is so far away." More arguments are produced to prove the location of heaven than to prove any other one point. Christ, they say, ascended; Elijah went up; and several close the argument for locating it in the sky by saying: "Besides, where else could it be?"

Among those who are in heaven, 482 mention angels; 367, God; 412, the redeemed; and 64, Christ. A few mention dead relatives, the saints, Santa Claus, and unborn babies.

(*To be continued.*)

THE HERBARTIAN "STEPS OF INSTRUCTION."

THE subject matter of each branch is supposed to be divided into suitable lesson-units. In arithmetic, such a lesson-unit might be "The division of a Fraction by an Integer;" in geography, "The Basin of an River;" in the United States History, "The Battle of Gettysburg." In teaching the lesson, the teacher will, according to the theory of formal steps, observe and pass through the following stages successfully:

1. Preparation, that is, recalling the previous lesson and other knowledge familiar to the child as aids to appreciation, indicating also what is the aim of the present lesson.

2. Presentation, the gathering of all

the facts on the lesson topic in hand. The method of presenting the facts will, of course, vary with the nature of the lesson.

3. Comparison, viz., of facts with facts to discover their meaning. (A fine field for the cultivation of a most useful mental power, too often neglected.)

4. Generalization, that is, the pupil's reaching, as the fruit of his own investigation, those conclusions commonly called principles, definitions, laws, rules, formulas, etc.

5. Application, that is the bringing back of the laws and principles already learned and applying them to new particular cases in science, business, and social, political, moral or religious life. This completes the cycle. The pupil starts from individual facts or events, and returns again to them, but this time with power to interpret them. Higher than this no knowledge rises; greater power none can possess. Herbart's system is by no means mechanical, although thoroughly systematized and formulated. On the contrary it brings into the elementary school the charm of reality and invests each subject with greater interest. It promotes correct thinking habits, gives clear apprehension of knowledge, economizes thought and effort and furnishes to the pupil the broadest and best basis for future acquisitions. Herbart and his followers have given to Germany a body of over eight thousand enthusiastic teachers, who follow progressive and scientific methods in pedagogy. It is not given to one man to grasp all of truth, or to perfect any system of education, but may it not prove that Herbart, more than any other, has solved the problem of elementary education?—*Selected.*

THE SPELLING QUESTION.

BY EDWARD R. SHAW, SCHOOL OF PEDAGOGY, UNIV. OF NEW YORK.

DURING the past three years four separate investigations upon the spelling problem have been made in the School of Pedagogy. Two of these investigations were made by myself and the other two were carried forward under my immediate direction. The object of these investigations was to see whether some new knowledge might not be gained that would render more specific guidance in the teaching of spelling. Other investigators have been working on this problem but no reports of those investigations have come under the writer's notice, except that of Miss Adelaide Wyckoff, on Constitutional Bad Spellers, in the *Pedagogical Seminary* for December, 1893, and that of Supt. H. E. Kratz, published in the *Iowa Normal Monthly*, and also in *The School Journal* for May 16, 1896. Miss Wyckoff made tests upon an extremely small number of spellers, but her study is especially valuable in its suggestiveness as to lines of investigation.

Spelling is a very arbitrary matter, and yields to but slight extent to the logical and causal helps which are employed in teaching other subjects. Motor elements are important elements in association, and with so arbitrary a subject as English spelling every aid in strengthening the association should be employed. From the experiments made and the verification of the conclusions in actual school application, I am convinced that the motor apparatus used in speech should be employed to a large extent in teaching spelling. All preparation of words to be written should be oral preparation, and very careful preparation at that, particular- in the second, third, fourth and fifth school years. Writing should be the final test, but only after careful preparation orally. And in that preparation the letters should be grouped into syllables and the syllables pronounced according to the method of a generation ago. The poor results now so common in spelling would thereby be greatly bettered. In the end, time would be gained, and the pupil rendered better able to help himself. The method of leading the pupil to grasp the word as a whole through the eye has made confused spellers of large numbers of children. With some, however, it has produced excellent results.

The tests show that in the employment of this method many children seize the first and the last letters of the word, but leave out some of the middle letters or mix them The naming of the three, four, or five letters, as the case may be, that constitute a syllable, and then attaching a name to these grouped letters, thus binding them into a small unity, aids the pupil to a remarkable degree. And the putting of these small unities together into the larger word unity, gives the pupil a synthetic power to this end and makes his progress more rapid and easy on the long road he must traverse in learning to spell. "Shall we turn the hands back on the pedagogical clock?" it will be asked. Yes, if the hands have got ahead and have been keeping false time.

For the last two decades or more this method has been almost wholly repudiated as an aid in learning to spell. The false notion that the eye is the avenue to which to appeal in teaching spelling began to obtain at that time a very firm hold upon the minds of teachers. Institute lecturers made strong efforts to inculcate this idea and their efforts met with large success. As much greater power was imputed to the eye in this regard, than it actually has, the time devoted to learning to spell naturally became shortened, and the spelling lesson passed from the place of prominence in the program of work to a place of subordinate importance, and quite generally the spelling lesson was merely the writing of words selected from the reading lessons, with repeated drill in writing upon words incorrectly spelled.

The larger knowledge which has resulted from the great development of psychological study of recent years leads us to see that the teachers of a generation ago were not so wholly wrong after all in their teaching of spelling. They were right as far as they went, but they did not go far enough. Those who repudiated the old method and made the appeal almost wholly to the eye, were right in holding that for most pupils the eye is a stronger sense avenue of appeal than the ear when only these two are considered. But the motor speech apparatus was not regarded as a factor in the matter. It is true that in testing any hundred pupils according to the methods which are supposed to determine whether they are eye-minded or ear-minded, we shall find a large percentage of the hundred eye-minded, and only a small percentage markedly ear-minded. But it will also be found that a very large percentage will give good returns to the tests for determining eye mindedness and also to the tests for determining ear-mindedness, with the returns usually in favor of the test for eye-mindedness. In every grade of pupils, it must be remembered, such differences will be found. The method in teaching spelling should therefore be broad enough to appeal fully to these differing aptitudes in different pupils and also to those pupils in which these aptitudes are combined. The method already suggested is broad enough to make this varied appeal. —*School Journal.*

RELIGIOUS INSTRUCTION.

THE question of the religious education of the people has been very much under discussion for five or six years, but in a form to cause Protestants rather to slight than to dwell on its importance. Determined that the system of general education, none too effective at best, should not be broken into hopeless fragments by religious misunderstandings, they are inclined either to banish religious instruction from the schools or to accept a very imperfect apology for it. In places like Montreal, where there are two complete systems of schools, it is possible in each to give more or less of what may be called religious teaching. The Roman Catholics teach doctrine and ecclesiastical duty, while the Protestants use the Bible as a classic, and communicate without comment a fair general knowledge of its contents. In many places there is not even this approach to religious teaching in the schools. "Why cannot children be taught religion in Sunday School?" says the advocate of the state secular school, "or at home, which is the right place for it. It is utterly wrong to absolve the parent from responsibility for his child's religious training." Granting that this was done, it would not solve the school problem. It is not desirable that children should learn to look upon religion as a thing that may be put on and off, that ought to be suppressed in the regular occupations of the day and in the institutions by which he is formed. Moreover, the excusively separatist teaching of religion will leave narrow and sometimes conceited ideas on a child's mind, as though his own people were the only ones who were devout or who were accepted by God.

Taking the facts as they are, however, the Sunday School has become practically the only means of religious instruction for a very large proportion of children. The Sunday school has its origin in England as a means of teaching neglected children, who otherwise passed the day in idleness and vice. In America it was adopted as a means of organizing the religious teaching of the children of the church, which was being eliminated from the courses of the day schools. It was never meant to supersede family training where such existed; but it did very largely. It was certainly not meant to supersede church attendance, but this also it did to a great extent, and so the children grew up with a habit of not going to church. which was afterwards hard to eradicate. Practically, the Sunday school is looked to by the community, if not for the only teaching of ethics or of bible facts the children get, at least for all the teaching of religious doctrine, for all the knowledge of salvation, and for all the incitement to holiness the children are to get. They may, of course, get religious knowledge and impressions from other sources, but this is practically the only means made and provided for them, as the day school is for their secular instruction. It is a curious comment on the faith of our age when thirty hours of well-braced and alert attention is given in the week to worldly instruction, under teachers trained to teach and with authority to rule, and an hour and a quarter in a sort of amateur, go-as-you please way, to all the supreme interests for which the Sunday school has been practically made responsible.

This may seem to be putting a

slight on the earnest people who in many cases devote themselves most conscientiously throughout the week to preparation for making the half-hour of teaching in Sunday school effective. Yet this class will be the first to admit and deplore the fact that there is not in the scholar the same sense of responsibility and duty to the Sunday school as there is in the same scholar to the day school. Children look upon their Sunday school as a place where they are to be coaxed and where they may yield to coaxing or not, as may best please them. Methods taken to win the children's attention and approval often tend to weaken their sense of duty towards the matter in hand; and with many teachers it is a fight to get as much as five minutes' attention from their scholars. While no one can overvalue the importance of substituting in all education attraction for driving and appetite towards the lessons for dislike of them, on the other hand it would seem as though more imperative methods than those which for the most part exist would have to be adopted if even the small fragment of time now accorded to the development of the spiritual nature of the child is going to bear the fruit it is capable of doing. The impression we would leave is that the religious education of children is in the case of most children hardly provided for at all.—*Selected.*

LITTLE THINGS.

THERE are few men and women who do not take pleasure in giving information or making themselves useful to strangers. There is one little reward they expect, and one only, and that is a nicely spoken "thank you." The reward is not a very costly one to the giver, but there are times when the pleasant, grateful smile, and the simple words expressing appreciation for the trouble taken in their behalf, not only produce at the time most pleasurable sensations, but the smile and the sweet spoken words linger in memory, and again and again come back. Dull moments are brightened by the remembrance, and times of suffering and anxiety have been softened by the reappearance before the mind of a fair young face, or a stately lady, or a lady-like poor woman, or a man courteous and well behaved. The little scene and the trifling incident returns as in a dream; it becomes a cherished recollection. Still some people deny us this satisfaction, they do not say "thank you." Several little occurrences lately have started us thinking upon this subject, and we have been trying to fix a reason for what has appeared to be inexplicable conduct. A gentlemen, well dressed and well able to enjoy art and beauty, accosted us the other day as he stood before a large public building, and asked if the public were permitted to enter. We answered, "oh yes!" and then added, "if you will come with us we will show you what there is to be seen." Now we spent some time in this effort to oblige him, but when we parted he did not say "thank you." We think we deserved it. A lady the other day, a stranger in the city, was enquiring of a man for the house of some friend. She evidently had made a mistake as to the number. We were appealed to. Though very busy, we tried to help her, and at last suggested that she should come with us and consult a directory. She walked a short distance with us and then abruptly left us and never said "thank you." A boy riding in a cart shouted out to us as he passed by,

"Say, is that——street over there?" pointing exactly in the opposite direction from where it was. He knew nothing about it, but it was a rough way of obtaining desired information. We put the boy right, but he did not say "thank you." Now, what was the matter with these people? We are sure they did not mean to be rude or uncivil. We think it was simply because they did not see how to perform this little act of politeness, and that very likely, while in their hearts they were deeply sensible of a kindness done, they were too shy to express it. They did not see the way to make a graceful acknowledgement, and so clumsily shirked it altogether. Such people deserve our kindest consideration. It is a thing to be thankful for that the Church comes to our aid in this matter of politeness. Every Church child is taught to say, "My duty towards my neighbor is to love him as myself, and to do unto all men as I would they should do unto me; to love, honor, and succor my father and mother; to honor and obey the Queen, and all that are put in authority under her; to submit myself to all my teachers, spiritual pastors and masters; to order myself lowly and reverently to all my betters." Love lies at the root of politeness, and though some people may not like the language of the catechism, it is the teaching of the Church and her Scriptures. It is taught by the example and teaching of our Lord, and in the writings of St. Paul, who besides being a great apostle, was a refined and courteous gentleman. He gives us over and over again precepts concerning courtesy and politeness to others We are fortunate in having such instruction given us when young, and more fortunate still if we have had parents or friends who have taught us how to act up to it. These good things grow with us and become habits, and bring any amount of happiness and prosperity with them.—*Canadian Churchman.*

TECHNICAL EDUCATION.

THOSE who are interested in the progress of technical education in connection with the school system of our province will be glad to learn that another point has been gained in the opening of classes in Domestic Science under the care and supervision of the Board of Education in the city of Hamilton. For some time the ladies of the Local Council of Women have been discussing the matter, and pressing on the members of the Board the advisability of establishing such classes, with the result that the Board at its last regular meeting decided to undertake the expenses of such classes for the present term.

The progress of these classes will be closely watched not only by those immediately connected with them but by everyone interested in the progress of technical education. Judging by the energy and ability of those in charge, there is little doubt of the success of the classes, and thus will be furnished a strong argument for the extension of this and similar work. In this connection it is to be hoped that the interests of the boys in technical education will not be overlooked.

There are some who desire to know with the sole purpose that they *may* know, and it is curiosity; and some who desire to know that they may be known, and it is base ambition; and some who desire to know that they may sell their knowledge for wealth and honor, and it is base avarice; but there are some, also, who desire to know that they may be edified, and it is prudence; and some who desire to know that they may help others, and it is charity.—*S. Bernard.*

WAGES.

Glory of warrior, glory of orator, glory of song,
  Paid with a voice flying by to be lost on an endless sea—
Glory of Virtue, to fight, to struggle, to right the wrong—
  Nay, but she aimed not at glory, no lover of glory she ;
  Give her the glory of going on, and still to be.

The wages of sin is death; if the wages of Virtue be dust,
  Would she have heart to endure for the life of the worm and the fly?
She desired no isles of the blest, no quiet seats of the just,
  To rest in a golden grove, or to bask in a summer sky :
  Give her the wages of going on, and not to die. —*Tennyson.*

EDITORIAL NOTES.

THE CANADA EDUCATIONAL MONTHLY has entered upon its career for 1897, with the bright object in view of becoming more than ever an organ for the teachers of the whole Dominion, and it is the intention of those who have charge of its affairs to make improvements in its appearance and matter, commensurate with the encouragement which it receives from those whose interests it upholds. Teachers ought to be loyal to themselves in the professional sense, just as much as are the members of any other profession; and as we have now a general association of teachers for the confederation under which we live, there is no reason why there should not be a rallying round the journal which assumes the rôle of being a mouthpiece for the general educational tone of those engaged in educational work. And while it is true that the immediate constituency of such a periodical must be teachers, there is no reason why it should not have a support, a very large support, from our colleges, school trustees and commissioners and even the general public. The parent is, or ought to be, as much a factor of school life and work as the pupil, or even as the teacher; and when the teachers have shown towards our enterprise that they mean to help it, there is reason to suppose that everyone interested in the educational progress of Canada will follow their example. Come then, we say to our readers, let us counsel together, and consider how in our strivings after a developing professional pride, legitimate in its ambitions, we may help in weaving the threads of a true Canadian nationality.

It has often been asked why so little progress has been made towards the nationalizing of the spirit of the people of Canada. The country has been consolidated now for thirty years as a politically united colony, and yet the Nova Scotian, even after so many years of alliance between his province and the sister provinces, is still as much of a Nova Scotian as a Canadian, if not more so, and an Ontarian is the same. We hear a great deal about a Canadian nationality, but see too little of it. Cape Breton is still all but a foreign country to Vancouver Island, while there may be just a grain of truth in the ravings of an editor of Prince Edward Island who used to classify all who came from the mainland to the "rosy little circuit" as foreigners. Why the assimilation process should have been so slow is an inquiry we need not press upon our politicians, for these gentlemen will at once tell us, biased by the narrow vision and phraseology of partyism, that such is not the case. The people of Canada are not one, it is true, they will inform us; but they are at least two in one, Grits and Tories; and if any one desires to have a corroboration of the statement he has only to read the history of the Manitoba School Question, or any other question that comes to be discussed in the House of Commons and the daily press. While one political party rushes at the throat of the other political party, partyism becomes the watchword, while the maturing of a true national opinion, and the furthering of a true national interest, may be left to a few, a very few, of our literary men. And to such an extent has this become a prevailing programme in our public discussions, that Canadians are even yet saying to themselves, thirty years after Confederation, "Can any good thing come out of Nazareth?" Have we a national sentiment? Have we a Canadian literature? Have we a true patriotism amongst us?

The Manitoba School Question in itself shows how far we are from the realization of this national spirit. "To be or not to be" in this instance is not to be decided, it seems, by what is best for Canada, but by what is best for a prejudice. A writer lately pointed out that the settlement of this question was not for Canada as a whole, but for the Education Department at Winnipeg. The whole question, he said, was one of administration in which there ought to be no politics. But a politician, one of the prime ministers, of our multi-prime ministered country, sat down upon the suggestion and dismissed the man who made it from office. The prime minister's trade was politics, and all were fish that came into his net, and as the Manitoba School Question had come into his net, or rather, as he expected to come into higher emoluments and honors through it, he was intent on making the most of it. And is there not in this instance something that should force all Canadians to ask themselves in ordinary parlance: What does our so-called Canadian nationality amount to? Have all our interests been hidden away in our party politics? Is there a national right or wrong in Canada, or is it only a party right or wrong? This journal knows no party politics as its own, nor ever will, as it looks forward to its widening field of usefulness in helping to consolidate a slowly consolidating national sentiment among Canadians. The educational organization of each province of the confederation was left in the hands of each province when the constitution of the country was written in black and white by the Fathers of Confederation; and, as it seems now, with our longing for a closer consolidation, there never was a greater mistake made. But the mistake was the outcome, not of halting wisdom, but of necessity. Confederation was what was wanted in 1867, *coûte que coûte*, and the politicians of the time were ready to sacrifice every interest in order to inaugurate its birthday, wreathed as it was with their own prospective honors; and it can hardly be expected that their successors would ever come to see the mistake that had been made, unless they should happen to be brought face to face with necessity, pressing around their own political aggrandizement. As has been said, that necessity now presses upon both parties. They do not know which way to turn. The Manitoba School question is the *bête noir* of Liberal and Conservative alike, and yet they are both unwilling to go back to first principles either for the cause or a remedy.

A nation without a national system of schools is no nation, nor ever can be a nation, and the sooner we Canadians come to recognize this ethical principle, the sooner will there be born among us a true national spirit. "Let me write the ballads of a people, and I will soon make a nation of them," says some one of our so called Canadian statesmen repeating from the statement of another. But the prophet has yet to come into sight who will say in our hearing "Introduce some function in our political administration that will lead to the consolidating and assimilating of our school systems and educational interests, and before long it will not be difficult to see a new force at work, weaving the threads of a permanent sentiment that will bring all the Canadas together as one Canada, working for her legitimate national aggrandizement. To discuss such a broad question as the above will require time, and yet in its enunciation, there is to be caught a glimpse of what every Canadian desires, if only the means were at hand to bring it about. It will be the policy of the CANADA EDUCATIONAL MONTHLY to keep this ultimate point constantly in view, and to work for its realization. Far be it from us to advocate any change in the constitution of the country which would tend to undermine our so-called provincial autonomy. Each province must be in charge of its own school system. All that may be urged in this connection is that the central government of our country, in whose direct keeping is our national pride, should not be kept at arm's length in regard to our schools and school systems, only to find itself in hot-water now and again when party spirit and denominational strife sets the political pot a-boiling. In other words, the time has come when the Dominion Government must have official cognizance of what is going on in the various parts of the country, and it is our intention to see that this is done, either in connection with some of the present departments, or in connection with a regularly organized Canadian Bureau of Education.

CURRENT EVENTS AND COMMENTS.

APROPOS of the agitation which Monseigneur Langevin feels bound of necessity to keep up in Canada, the following anecdote may be put on record. It is told by one who had it from the master of a Board School in England.

"The head master of a Board school told me an amusing story this week. We were sitting in the room in which he transacted the business of the school, and wherein he constantly received the parents of the children—he declines to take a child, I may say, until he has seen the parent. The room was hung with pictures and photographs, and looked uncommonly comfortable. 'Do you see that?' said the master, pointing out to me a photograph of Cardinal Newman. 'Yes.' 'Well, a parent came here the other day, and his eyes at once fell upon the Cardinal.' 'Oh!' says he, 'I'm sorry you are a Roman Catholic'—and his face fell very low, for he was going to place his child under my charge. 'A Roman Catholic!' I laughed. 'I'm not a Roman Catholic. Why, what makes you think that?' 'Well,' says he, 'that cture, of course,' scowling at it. 'But look here, sir,' said I, 'Now, who's that?' You should have seen his face—all smiles in a moment." It was John Wesley. His child is in the school now. But he was a very artful master, I'm afraid, for not only did I see portraits of Newman and Wesley, but Martineau (a Unitarian), Benson and Dean Stanley (Church of England), and many more, to suit many fancies.'

The account given in the newspapers of the Montreal teacher who, in carrying out some of the educational principles of Herbert Spencer, found himself in presence of the ridicule and indignation of the whole community, has its counterpart in a story that comes from St. John, New Brunswick. Mr. Kneeland, of the Montreal Riverside School, who has more than once shown how ambitious he is to be in the public gaze, thought to cure his boys of smoking by making them swallow a decoction of tobacco. The agony of the boys became the agony of the teacher, when he was called before the school commissioners to receive a reprimand. Mr. Kneeland's only consolation, under the circumstances, was no doubt the conscientious feeling that he was acting according to first principles, just as the New Brunswick teacher's reward was in the punishment of the man who sold the tobacco materials.

As the *Review* says: A case of school discipline came up recently in St. John which caused a ripple of excitement—some praising and others condemning the action of the principal. In a building in the city pilfering had been going on for some time, greatly to the annoyance of the teachers. Marked money was placed in one of the teachers' satchels—not exposed as a temptation but hung upon the wall. The money was found in a shop where cigarettes were sold and it was traced to the boy who had spent it. The principal immediately reported the matter to the police magistrate, who, at the request of the teacher, inflicted no severer punishment upon the boy than a reprimand, but fined the vendor of cigarettes ten dollars.

We are all agreed that quite a number of good things have come out of Nova Scotia. The first Normal School in the country was established there by the Rev. Dr. Forrester, under fearful odds, in the opposition of the politicians, and we now learn that the first Teacher's Union has lately had its birth there. The teachers of the whole Dominion will no doubt linger with interest over the details of its constitution. The object of the union shall be:

1. To elevate and unify the teaching profession in Nova Scotia.

2. To bring the claim of the profession before the public and legislature of Nova Scotia, as occasion may require.

3. To watch the educational outlook, and trend of thought in other countries, with a view to keeping the profession in Nova Scotia abreast of the times.

4. To endeavor to advance salaries by increasing the capability of the teachers, and improving the quality of the work; by educating the public to a proper appreciation of the value of skilled teaching; and by developing among the members of the profession such a feeling of *esprit de corps*, and such a high sense of professional honor, as will effectually put an end to the practice of underbidding.

5. To protect teachers, who through errors in agreements, or otherwise, are in danger of being defrauded by unscrupulous employers.

6. To diffuse among members of

the profession such a knowledge of law, in its bearing on teaching, as will enable teachers to know what is and what is not an actionable offence.

7. To advise teachers against whom legal proceedings, on charges connected with their profession, are being taken; and in case of an unjust decision, to aid in an appeal to a higher court.

8. To arouse teachers, not only to a full sense of their duties as teachers, but also to a realization of their obligations and responsibilities as citizens, in the broadest and fullest meaning of the term.

In the coming contest of a general election in the Province of Quebec, the politicians hardly know which side to look towards. They are not sure whether the story of the Dominion elections will repeat itself in the Provincial. The educational progress of that province for years back—in fact the only educational progress to be reported—has been supervised by a body and superintendent over whom the education department has had virtually no control. The rest of the system has been gradually on the decline. The elementary schools are said to be in a deplorable condition while the Catholic superior schools and colleges cannot, in any sense, be ranked as being very efficient. The Normal Schools are also requiring reorganization—English, as well as French, being at least a quarter of a century behind the times; and the inspection, notwithstanding the enthusiasm of many of the inspectors, amounts to next to nothing in its influence to force the school districts to do their best in the matter of the erection of school buildings and the supplying of the necessary apparatus and furniture. The Conservatives have sanctioned the setting aside of a subsidy of fifty thousand dollars towards school improvements, but they have kept in their own hands the distribution of this subsidy, and most of us know what that means, the building of a bridge at the double of what it ought to cost, and the bridge a rotten one in the end. Nevertheless, let us hope that the situation is only what a contemporary says it is, in these words: "An agitation is being carried on in the Province of Quebec, looking to radical changes and improvements in the Public Schools of that province. This is one of the cases in which party rivalry seems likely to be productive of good. The opposition are, we believe, making school reform one of the planks in their platform, on which they hope to win at the approaching election. On the other hand, the Government are, it is said, quite ready to introduce and carry through important reforms in the educational system. Consequently, marked improvements may be hoped for in the near future."

The news that comes to us from Prince Edward Island tells us of the death of Ex-Inspector Arbuckle, who, some years ago, became a victim to the "spoils system," which is still in vogue among the politicians there. For eight years he had been an Inspector—an Inspector who gave satisfaction to everybody, but when a change of government took place, he was not of the "faithful," and had to go. For some time he had been Vice-Principal of the Summerside High School, being held in high esteem by his pupils and associate workers.

Considerable interest has been excited in Halifax in a project for gathering into kindergartens those children who are too young for school, but too old to be allowed to go without some suitable training. It is felt that this preparation for school life will render our system more effective, and it is hoped it may diminish truancy. Mrs. Hinkle Condon, who has publicly advocated kindergartens for the children from three to five years, is urging the churches to unite their forces and take the matter in hand. If all will help there is a reasonable hope of success.—*Review.*

Speaking lately at the Battersea Polytechnic Prize Distribution, John Morley said: "There is a second point on which we all are agreed—that is, it is difficult, it is impossible to teach science, scientific methods, and skill to persons who have not undergone a preliminary training, and my point is that there is a direct connection between Technical Education and an important thing in our national system which does not exist—Secondary Education. I understand that in some Technical Schools in London and elsewhere, instead of beginning to teach the students science and what is called scientific methods and spirit, they have to be started with the three humble R's—reading, writing, and arithmetic. I hope that the Government of which Mr. Thornton is an ardent supporter will, before many weeks are over, bring before the House of Commons a scheme for Secondary Education. You, Mr. Thornton, will allow me to say without offence that I hope they won't muddle it up with a number of other things. There is a third point as to which there is no difference. Everybody sees that a higher appreciation of science and of the Technical arts and of the importance of scientific research and scientific investigation on the part of great British manufacturers is a thing of the very utmost importance. You often hear of workmen being complained of, but it is now being seen that the leaders of industry, whether workmen or employers, especially employers and heads of great manufacturing enterprises, must open their minds, which they have hitherto been too slow in doing, as to the importance of science, scientific research, and training, both for those who are the heads of those enterprises and undertakings, and those who have the actual conduct and carrying of them out." While our *statesmen* are wondering what is going to happen to the country if the tariff be, or be not remodelled, where is the statesman who wants to know what is being done in Canada in the direction Mr. Morley speaks of?

The London *Globe* gives us the following, which is well worth republishing: "Is patriotism a virtue, and, if so, ought it to be inculcated in the minds of the young? These questions are suggested by a very interesting discussion which took place at the Finchley School Board. The head-master of the East Finchley Board Schools had asked to be allowed to fly the Union Jack over the building, and Mr. Royston, a member of the School Board, moved a resolution to the effect that the requisite permission should be granted. The "flag," he said, "would help the children to realise the glorious inheritance that had been handed down to them." The resolution was seconded by a lady member of the School Board, and it might have been expected that a proposal so reasonable and so innocuous would have received a unanimous assent. But the sickly cant of cosmopolitanism has permeated, it would seem, even the wilds of East Finchley. A Mr. Kershaw opposed the motion in a speech full of fire and fury. "The Union Jack," he said, "would be out of place at a Board School, and would soon become ridiculous. Votaries of the flag are not in full sympathy with the cause of education, because as education advances the influence of the flag must wane." We are not surprised to learn that these remarks were received with ironical laughter, or that it should have been shown in clear and unmistakable fashion that whatever may be said of the Union Jack, unpatriotic nonsense of this type was "out of place at a School Board." Nevertheless, the tide of the speaker's turgid eloquence rolled serenely on. "The flag," he said, "has made the people the craven tools of those who lord it over them. It beguiles the mind with false ideas of duty. It is principally associated with barbaric traits which it is the purpose of education to efface. It is a reminder of national jealousies and the symbol of human strife. It is far removed from that ideal in which society is to be led by the little child; and it would be as much out of place at a Board School as would be the feudal system in the present age." Never, surely, was the Meteor Flag of England assailed in such terrible fashion!

The Finchley School Board, to its credit be it said, showed little inclination to accept the cosmopolitan orator's views. When, after metaphorically trampling on the Union Jack, he had subsided into his chair to dream of "the Parliament of Man, the Federation of the World," one solitary word of scornful criticism demolished the pretentious argument which he had built up with so much labor and so much expenditure of midnight oil. "Rubbish!" quoth Mr. Frederick Tinsley, one of the working-men representatives on the Board. We congratulate the Finchley School Board on the possession of Mr. Tinsley, and Mr. Tinsley on his membership of the Board, for in truth the best method of dealing with faddists of this curious species is to snub them with promptitude and decision. The East Finchley Schools are to have their Union Jack, and the flag will teach the children, as Mr. Donald Macfarlane very rightly observed, that "they owe a duty to their country as well as to ourselves." Cosmopolitanism, with its affectation and its specious sentiment, is simply selfishness writ large. The man who affects to regard the love of country as an exploded delusion has generally little love for anything except himself. He may boast, indeed, that his patriotism is merged in that wider and more comprehensive faith, the Brotherhood of Man, but, in his heart, he knows that he has given up the substance for the shadow, and wilfully abandoned an ideal, rich in great deeds and acts of self-devotion, for one which never yet inspired anything more useful than Mr. Kershaw's oratory. If *esprit de corps* is the life of an army, that larger *esprit de corps* which we call patriotism is no less the soul of national existence.

But if we hold, notwithstanding the mawkish eloquence of the Kershaws of this world, that patriotism is a thing to be encouraged, surely it follows as the night the day that we cannot begin to instil its principles too soon. First impressions are proverbially the strongest, and if a child is taught from infancy that the flag is a thing to be proud of, to cherish, and, if necessary, to die for, he will be all the better citizen for the knowledge. Having regard to the splendid part which our country has played in history, it must be admitted that far from over-doing the patriotic education of our children, we are distinctly under-doing it. Nowhere else than in Great Britain would such a victory as that of Trafalgar have had to wait ninety years for adequate celebration, and the fact is significant of much. If anyone is inclined to question the influence of early impressions, let him consider the effect which biassed and one-sided school-books have undoubtedly produced in moulding popular sentiment in the United States into antagonism to this country. That there exists in America an undercurrent of antipathy to Great Britain is indubitable, and it is equally certain that this unfortunate sentiment can be largely traced to the history primers in use in the schools, which dilate exclusively on the combats between England and the United States. If American historians could remember that Agincourt and Crecy and Poictiers were also the heritage of a large proportion of the people of the United States, possibly they would concentrate attention less exclusively upon wars which are by no means the pleasantest recollection in the history of the Anglo-Saxon race. But the mistaken sentiment which results from the abuse of patriotic education in the United States emphasizes, to our mind, the desirability of giving the rising generation patriotic education of the right kind. No one has any desire to stimulate hatred of France or Russia in the minds of our children, but it would be clear gain if, throughout the length and breadth of the country, boys and girls were taught that they were 'citizens of no mean city.'"

THE UNIVERSITY OF TORONTO.—The University of Toronto is confronted this year with a probable deficit of about $18,000, and a deputation from the trustees and the senate recently laid the case before the Government, asking for assistance. In the financial statement presented by Mr. B. E. Walker, general manager of the Bank of Commerce, some remarkable facts were brought out. It was shown that, forty-five years ago, when the number of students was about eighty-four, the annual income of the University from interest and rents averaged about $60,000. The fees were about $720, or $9 a student. In 1887, prior to federation, the income from endowment was $67,897; from fees, $13,431, about $35 a student; the number of students, 387. For the present year the estimated income from endowments is $65,313; from fees, $44,485; from occasional sources, $2,541; the number of students in arts is 1,044; in medicine, 293; in all, 1,478. It is to be noted that the medical fees are not included in the total of fees, as they do not enter into the general fund, but go entirely to the support of the medical faculty, which receives nothing from the endowments of the University.

While the income from fees has arisen in forty-five years from $720 to $44,485, the income from endowment has remained almost stationary. This means that during all that period the province has done nothing for the University, its endowments being derived from the original land grants. The only exception was the gift of $160,000 from the province to restore the portion of the building damaged by the fire of 1890. This, with the insurance money, was entirely consumed in the restoration of the building.

The deficit at present threatened is due partly to depreciation of interest and to a falling off in fees of about $2,500, owing to the hard times, but chiefly to the absorption of the capital in the provision of buildings and laboratories, necessitated by the Act of Federation. To that act the present straitened position of the University is largely due. The scheme of federation was initiated by the Government, not by the University. Moreover, that movement was carried out on the distinct understanding that it would enable the Government to deal liberally in providing for the increased expenditures necessitated by the Federation Act, and by the growth of the University. Hence a special responsibility is laid upon the Government to give the assistance so urgently needed, and to which, indeed, it is already pledged.

The progress of the province is very largely dependent upon the efficiency and completeness of the University. As Mr. Walker well said, without the University Ontario could not possibly have been where it is to-day. We would not have had as good a system of government, as good a medical system, as good doctors, as good schools and teachers, as good a banking system, or as good farmers.

No private institution can provide the laboratories and appliances necessary for the efficient teaching of science, and the efficient teaching of science is necessary for the development of the natural resources of the province.

We are glad to notice the heartiness and unanimity with which the application of the University for increased government aid is supported by the two leading journals on the opposite sides of politics. The University has the loyal support of all parties in the province, and in its well-being all take pride.—*The Evangelical Churchman.*

The Bishop of Manchester bore high testimony to the diligence and conscientiousness of elementary teachers, and endorsed Mr. Balfour's recent remarks with regard to the happy results that might be anticipated from the creation of a psychological climate of intelligence, order, and reverence. This is a point which has scarcely as yet received sufficient attention. People talk about the value of this subject of instruction and the other subject, as though education were a mere matter of curriculum, and as though its value were mainly dependent on the number of subjects that the curriculum includes. The "climate," the medium, the moral and religious atmosphere, the character of the circle of ideas, the whole environment of the child—these are more important than any single subject, or any number of subjects of instruction. We observe that in the Bishop's summary of the questions which the Conference were met to discuss, there were not one that met with a more sympathetic recognition than the reference to the question how to preserve religious instruction in the schools. Teachers know from experience that this instruction is the most important means they have for humanising their pupils, for lifting them to a higher moral plane, and for supplying adequate motive power for every department of right action. Take this instruction from them, and their work is crippled and degraded. Long may teachers take this view of the highest part of their duties! Valuable as are other parts of the machinery of elementary education for maintaining a high standard of religious instruction, they are not to be compared with the spontaneous zeal of teachers who realize for themselves the great responsibility that devolves upon them of educating their pupils for eternity as well as for time.—*Educational Guardian.*

We cannot agree with the Committee of Ten that the study of arithmetic should stop at the end of the Grammar school course. On the contrary, it should be continued through the High school. The fault we find now is that the arithmetic work required of the children below the secondary school age is too extensive; not in topics taught, but in the kind of work required to be done. Speaking broadly, the work of the lower grades should be devoted (1) to training through what is called "mental" arithmetic, and (2) to representation and reckoning upon the slate, or what is called "written work." The work of the High school should be the applying of the knowledge obtained in the lower grades to the working out of the problems of the shops. In other words, the foundation should be thoroughly laid in the primary grades. What the boy needs at 13 and 14 is a knowledge of the fundamental operations, with integers, fractions, common and especially decimal, skill, and accuracy, so far as it can be obtained, in reckoning, and such a training of the faculties as oral arithmetic will give. That is the work of this age, and is enough. The child does not get it now, simply because he is hurried into work that he very naturally cares little about; and so these processes learned remain in the mind through the examinations, and then most of them are forgotten. We would introduce the algebra into the two upper grammar grades as recommended by the committee (not doing too much, however) dividing the time with the arithmetic, and give one hour a week to the latter branch in the High schools,—the work there being as we have said, the solving of the problems of the banks and the shops.—*Exchange.*

A writer to the *Times* says:

Let me mention a few instances of doubtful spelling and yet more doubtful English.

In the Authorized Version of the Bible and in the columns of the *Times* we find "judgment," but in ordinary prayer-books and in the Revised Version "judgement" is the form. The introduction of the central e seems unnecessary. Again, some writers have a weakness for doubling letters not only at the ends of such words as "downfall," but also in the middles. "Batting" is all right, but why should a man be described as "combatting" the arguments of his opponent? "Coquetting" is all very well, as far as the word is concerned; but ought we to speak of attention being "rivetted" on a speaker?

It would be well if we could all make up our minds as to such words as "shew" and "show," "enquire" and "inquire." There seems to be a growing tendency to spell the verb one way and the noun the other, as also with "practise" and "practice," "prophesy" and "prophecy."

We must yield to necessity, and accept "bike" as British for "bicycle," and "navvy" as short for "navigator," but we need hardly give up the plural forms "dragomans" and "Mussulmans," and substitute "dragomen" and "Mussulmen." The mythical lady who treated *omnibi* as the plural of "omnibus" has been outstripped by the actual gentleman who regarded *alibi* as the plural of *alibus!* I have read—not in the *Times*—of a *strata;* and a newspaper lately informed us of an Arabic MSS.

You, sir, startled me, and perhaps others, a couple of years ago, by deliberately substituting "Tsar" for the time-honored "Czar."

Perhaps it was done "by command;" otherwise, though phonetic, it seemed needless pedantry. It reminds us, in fact, of the pedantic youth who calmly read out of the Bible, "Hoots his first-born and Boots his brother." It is curious that, whereas since Voltaire's days, the letters *oi* in certain words have given way to *ai*, we still talk of "reconnoitring" the foe; and I hope we shall never do otherwise.

Some speakers and writers tell us of an "union" and an "university;" in fact, this is getting fashionable. If we pronounced "union" like "onion" it would be right, but when the first letter is pronounced like "you" it surely needs no *n* before it.

There is a terrible word "dynamitard" which has grown up since the days of Nihilism, and has probably been imported from abroad. The final *ard* seems to connect it remotely and wrongly with petard. An Englishman would naturally say "dynamiter" if he must use the word at all.

But there is a yet more terrible word, with which I must close—viz., "pandenominational." It reminds one painfully of pandemonium, but whilst the latter is all right linguistically, the former is a cross-breed. *Pan* is all very well as part of a Greek compound. No one objects to a "panorama" or a "pantechnicon;" but then the word "pan Anglican" was created—not without protest; and "pan-Presbyterian" followed; and I suppose we may look in time for a crop of Nonconformist "pans." But why say "pandenominational" when a far better and pleasanter word has been invented—viz., "interdenominational?"

SCHOOL WORK.

EDUCATION DEPARTMENT.

ANNUAL EXAMINATIONS, 1896.

SCIENCE.

Editor.—J. B. TURNER, B.A.

FORM II

PHYSICS.

1. Take a board about 3 metres long with a groove down the centre in which a marble will roll. Elevate the board so that the marble will continne to roll downwards when once started. Suspend a weight by means of a string 993 millimetres long which will beat seconds approximately. Now, while one person counts the seconds from the pendulum, let another mark the distances passed over by the marble in the first, second, and third seconds respectively. It will be found that if the distance passed over from rest in the first second be 2 centimetres, that for the second second will be 6 centimetres, and for the third second 10 centimetres, etc., for the other seconds, the distances being proportional to the odd numbers 1, 3, 5, 7, etc.

If the space passed over in the first second be 2 cms., then the acceleration is 4 cms. per sec. and the velocity at the end of the first second 4 cms., at the end of the second second 8 cms.

To find the average velocity for any second add the initial velocity and the final together and take half the sum. The motion of the marble will be accelerated from rest, and in a straight line if no force intervene to change its motion.

2. (*a*) Energy of bodily onward motion—a moving train, a person walking.

Energy of bodily vibration—the pendulum.

Energy of molecular vibration—heat.

Energy of eletcric current—as shown in the electric motor.

2. (*b*) Energy of bodily onward motion to molecular energy or heat.

3. (*a*) Since the water remains on the glass we infer that there is a force acting between the water and the glass. This force is called adhesion

Since the drops of water take a rounded shape, we infer that there is a force acting between the molecules of the water. This force is called cohesion.

3. (*b*) *Ductility.*—Take a small tube of glass and heat it in a gas flame. After a while it can be drawn out into fine threads. Glass is, therefore, said to be ductile.

Tenacity.—Attempt to pull a rope apart by attaching one end to the wall of the room and pulling on the other. The resistance the rope offers to the separation of its parts is called tenacity.

Plasticity.—Place a stick of sealing wax near the edge of a table so that one end projects beyond the edge. Place a weight on the end to hold the stick from falling, and on the projecting end place a small weight and leave for some time. On removing the smaller weight, the stick of wax will be found permanently bent. This property of bending under a continuous force is called plasticity.

4. (*a*) Place a clean, dry sewing needle on water and it will be seen to float. The needle is held on the surface of the water by the force of surface tension.

Water dropped on a piece of plate glass takes a rounded shape at the edge, due to surface tension.

A mixture of alcohol and water can be made in which a drop of oil will float wholly immersed. While floating in this way the oil will assume a spherical form, due to surface tension.

4. (*b*) Weigh the body in air and then weigh it wholly immersed in the liquid, and the difference of the two weights represents the buoyant force of the liquid on the body.

5. (*a*) Weigh the cork in air and let the weight be x grams. Weigh a sinker in water and let its weight be y grams. Weigh the cork with the sinker attached, both wholly immersed in water, and let the weight be z grams. Then the weight of the cork alone in water would be $(y-z)$ grams. Therefore, the loss of weight of the cork in water would be $[x-(y-z)]$ grams. Therefore the specific gravity of cork would be $\dfrac{x}{x-(y-z)}$.

A piece of wood weighs 12 grams in air, a piece of lead weighing 20 grams in water is attached to it, and the two weigh in water 18 grams. Therefore, the specific gravity of wood is

$$\frac{12}{12-(18-20)}=\frac{6}{7}.$$

5. (*b*) Take two beakers, into which put water and alcohol respectively. Take also a long U-shaped tube with an opening at the bend and attachment to allow a rubber tube connection with the air pump. Stand the U-shaped tube vertical with an open end of it dipping into the different liquids. Exhaust the air from the U tube, and the water and alcohol will rise in their respective tubes. We then have equal weights but different volumes. Their specific gravities will be inversely as the heights of the columns.

6. (*a*) Wind a wire tightly around a wooden cylinder, and then heat. The wire will become quite slack, showing that it has increased in length.

Take a piece of sheet iron and place it before four fixed supports, one on each side. Apply heat to the iron and it will press the supports outwards in both directions, showing that it has expanded in surface.

Take an iron ring which will just allow an iron ball to pass through. Heat the ball and it will no longer pass through the ring, showing that it has expanded.

6. (*b*) The compound bar expands and takes a curved shape with the brass on the convex side and the iron on the concave. The experiment shows that metals expand on the application of heat, and that some expand more than others.

7. Take a Florence flask, and a cork with two holes in it, through which may be passed a small tube and a thermometer. Fill the flask with water and then put the cork in tightly and the water will stand a certain distance up in the small tube. Surround the beaker with broken pieces of ice, and after a while the water

will begin to descend in the small tube, and will continue to do so until the thermometer marks 4° C. If a lower temperature be then reached, the water will ascend in the tube. This experiment shows that water has its greatest density at 4° C.

8. (*a*) Take a beaker of water and place it over a gas flame until the water begins to boil. Remove the flame and the water will stop boiling. Now place the beaker under the receiver of an air pump and exhaust the air. The water will soon begin to boil again, showing that the removal of the air permits the water to boil at a lower temperature.

8. (*b*) Take 20 grams of shot and 20 grams of water. Let the temperature of the water be 20° C. Heat the shot in a test tube to 100° C, and then put in the water and say the resulting temperature is 22° C.

Then heat lost by shot = 20 (100 - 22) (specific heat).

And heat gained by water $= 20 \times 2 \times 1$.

Therefore, if $x =$ specific heat of shot $20 \times 78 \times x$ is equal to 40 or $x =$

$$\frac{40}{20 \times 78} = \frac{1}{39} = .025.$$

Specific heat of shot is .025.

ENGLISH DEPARTMENT.

For Entrance.

I.

Analyse the following simple sentences:

1. *There* is still in existence a part of the seminary *built during* his administration.

2. *Meanwhile several* of the prisoners, *taking* advantage of the general alarm and confusion *caused* by the explosion, had succeeded in *making* their escape from the fort.

3. *In* his dim chapel *day* by day
 The organist was *wont* to play,
 And *please* himself with fluted
 reveries.

II.

Write out in full the subordinate clauses in the following sentences, and tell the kind and relation of each:

1. The head is so peculiarly formed that the ball either passes over the brain, or lodges in the solid bones and cartilages that contain the roots of the tusks.

2. Before he wrote the sketch of Rip Van Winkle he had never visited that part of the Catskills where Rip was supposed to live.

3. Thy grasp is welcome as the hand
 Of brother in a foreign land;
 Thy summons welcome as the cry
 That told the Indian isles were
 nigh
 To the world-seeking Genoese.

III.

1. Parse the italicised words in the three sentences of I.

2. Give all the infinite forms of *wrote*, telling which are active and which are passive.

3. Tell what changes take place when a verb in a sentence is changed from the active to the passive, and give two sentences illustrating your answer.

4. Give all the separate inflections of *know*, *who*, *child*, *lazy*.

5. Form nouns from *part*, *please*, *form*, *solid*, *hand*, *foreign*.

6. Write sentences using *off* and *on* as prepositions; *up* and *down* as adverbs; *since* and *till* as conjunctions; *there* and *now* as nouns; *far* and *near* as adjectives.

7. Correct any grammatical errors in the following sentences, giving your reason in each case:

(*a*) Please, sir, can't Tom and me go when we finish this?

(*b*) She don't seem to care who she gets it from.

(*c*) He could do it easy enough if he was only in earnest.

FOR PUBLIC SCHOOL LEAVING.

And *she*, the mother of thy boys,
Though in her eye and faded cheek
Is read the grief she will not speak,
The memory of her buried joys,
And *even* she who gave *thee* birth
Will, by their pilgrim-circled hearth,
Talk of thy doom without a sigh;
For thou art Freedom's now and *Fame's*,
One of the few, the immortal names
That were not born *to die*.

1. Write out in full the subordinate clauses, and tell the kind and relation of each.

2. Parse the italicised words.

3. Select the prepositional phrases, and classify them according to their grammatical value, giving the relation of each.

4. Write out in full the subordinate clauses in the following, classify each, and give its relation:

(*a*) Not a step can we take in any direction without *perceiving* nnmistakable traces of design; and the skill we see everywhere *conspicious* is calculated, in so vast a proportion of instances, *to promote* the happiness of living creatures, and *especially* of ourselves, that we can feel no hesitation in concluding that if we knew the whole scheme of Providence every part would appear to be in harmony with a plan of absolute benevolence.

(*b*) He who ascends to mountain-tops shall find
The loftiest peaks most wrapt in clouds and snow;
He who surpasses or subdues mankind
Must look down on the hate of those *below*.
Though *high above* the sun of glory glow,
And far beneath the earth and ocean spread
Round him on icy rocks, and loudly blow
Contending tempests on his naked head,
And thus reward the toils which to these summits led.

5. Parse the italicised words in No. 4.

6. Select, classify, and give the relation of the prepositional phrases in (*a*).

7. Account for the use of *shall find* instead of *will find*, and *glow* instead of *glows*.

8. (*a*) Form adjectives from *Providence, harmony, appear, sun, ocean, tempest*.

(*b*) Form nouns from *hate, perceive, appear, calculate, ascend, conclude*.

9. Give examples to show that *when* and *that* may begin noun, adjective, and adverb clause respectively.

10. Which of the following forms is correct and why?

(*a*) Who (whom) do you suppose it could have been?

(*b*) Who (whom) did he say I was to give it to?

(*c*) One of the men that works (work) in the mill caught it.

(*d*) How long is it since you have heard (heard) from him?

(*e*) I don't believe there is (are) more than one boy in the class that has (have) seen a copy of it.

FOR PRIMARY CANDIDATES.

1. Write out in full the subordinate clauses in the following, classify each, and give its relation.

(*a*) I don't care where he goes, provided he does not trouble me any more.

(*b*) It is evident that all will depend on who the arbitrators are and whether they treat the question as one of law or of equity.

(*c*) What were you thinking of that you did not send me word the very day that you were told what they had decided to do?

2. Classify the italicised words in the following and give their relation.

(*a*) You should not drink so *much just* before dinner.

(*b*) *What* I have is scarcely *worth carrying* home.

(*c*) He happened *to have taken* somebody *else's* book that *day*.

(*d*) I feel a *little* doubtful of its *proving* a *success*.

3. Have nouns person? Give reasons for your answer.

4. Show that *his* and *their* cannot always be treated as pronominal adjectives.

5. Write sentences exemplifying an anacoluthic nominative, *as* used as a relative, *but* used as a so-called negative relative, a syntactical sense construction, a subjunctive mood used to express a wish.

6. How and why did the introduction of printing affect the spelling of English?

7. Explain clearly the origin of the term "The Queen's English."

ANSWERS TO CORRESPONDENTS.

A P. S. teacher writes: "I understand that you object to parsing *like* as a preposition or as an adverb. If not too much trouble please state your reasons."

I object to parsing *like* as a preposition because (1) to use the word seems to express *quality* or *manner*, and not merely a *relation*; (2) because *likes* and *likest* may be used in precisely the same way as *like*, and I am not prepared to admit that prepositions can be compared; (3) because in every case where I have heard it parsed as a preposition it seemed to me quite satisfactory and more natural to parse it as an adverb or an adjective. The mere fact that it is followed by an objective case, does not prove it to be a preposition, else we shall have to call *Ah* in "Ah me! what a sight that was!" a preposition. The objective may be accounted for by supplying *to* or *unto*, or more simply by treating it as a survival of the old dative, used as in Latin, after some adjectives and adverbs.

The question whether *like* should ever be parsed as a conjunction depends simply on the answer to the question "Does good English literary (not collegical) usage sanction such expressions as 'Do like I do,' 'If you had done like we did.' 'He behaved like a gentleman does.'" If it does, *like* is a conjunction; if it doesn't, it is surely wrong either to parse *like* as a conjunction, or to teach children to supply a verb after it in analysis. Speaking generally, if *like* has the force of *similar to* or *resembling* it may be parsed as an adjective; if it means *similarly to* or *in the same manner* it may be parsed as an adverb.

CLASSICAL DEPARTMENT.

PRINCIPAL STRANG, GODERICH.

QUESTIONS BASED ON CÆSAR, BOOK II, CHAPTERS 29-35.

I

1. Translate Chapter 30 into good idiomatic English.

2. Account for the tense of the verbs in the first sentence.

3. Account for the mood of *irridere, instrueretur, est, confiderent.*

4. *contemptui.* Classify this use of the dative, and give two other examples of its use.

5. *turrim.* Mention any other words of the 3rd declension that make the accusative in *im.*

6. Exemplify from the chapter five different ways of forming nouns.

II.

1. Translate Chapter 35 into good English.

2. Classify the subjunctives in the 1st sentence.

3. *daturas.* Account for the gender.

4. *inita.* Give the other participles, and the 3d pl. of each tense in the indicative active of this verb.

5. What is peculiar in regard to the case of *dies ?*

6. What is the antecedent of *quod* in the last sentence ?

III.

Translate idiomatically :

1. Sibi præstare, si in eum casum deducerentur, quamvis fortunam a populo Romano pati, quam ab his per cruciatum interfici, inter quas dominari consuessent.

2. Celeriter, ut ante Cæsar imperarat, ignibus significatione facta, ex proximis castellis eo concursum est, pugnatum que ab hostibus ita acriter est, ut a vivis fortibus in extrema spe salutis pugnari debuit.

3. Rewrite the 1st sentence in *Oratio recta.*

IV.

1. Mention, with examples, any diminutive endings you have met with in Cæsar.

2. Why may we write *proeliis nuntiato*, but not *Cæsare nuntiato ?*

3. Mention any peculiarity of the verbs *revertor* and *confido* respectively.

4 Mention any peculiarity of *moenibus, viribus, nemo.*

5. Mark the penult of *cortice, iniquo, movet, inimicos, collocat.*

6. Give the 3d sing. pres. subj. act. of *retenta, refractis, intextis, redactas, daturas, inita, poterant, consuessent.*

7. Write explanatory notes on *viniae, vigilia, supplicatio.*

8. Derivation of *vendidit, debeo, nemo, mansuetudine, cruciatum.*

9. What construction follows *sine, spolio, propinquus, prope, prae ?*

10. Exemplify as many meanings of *pro* as you can.

V.

Translate into idiomatic Latin, based on Cæsar :

1. With the unanimous consent of the soldiers we have decided to set fire to all the baggage that we can't take with us.

2. On reaching our camp the old man whom they had sent to beg for peace addressed Cæsar as follows :

3. We learned afterwards from the captives that although they had promised to give up all their arms, they had retained and concealed nearly a third part.

4. He informed me that he hoped to bring all the region lying between these two rivers under the sway of the Romans before the end of the summer.

5. We adopted this plan, in the belief that the approach to their camp from this quarter was easier.

6. On learning what had happened he ordered the gates to be broken open and the survivors to be brought forth and slain.

7. Let us sally forth and fight like brave men who know that their only hope of safety lies in their valor.

8. We learned from the letter which the messenger had brought, that the Senate had decreed a thanksgiving for eighteen days.

9. We were afraid that some of the states adjoining the seat of war would revolt on hearing of this disaster.

10. Feeling confident that this place, protected as it was by woods and marshes, could not be stormed by our men, they refused to surrender.

SCHOOL WORK.

Exercises in Decimals for Entrance Students.

1. Find the value of $17.6821_9 - .0013 + 144.2971 - 125.964321^9 + .432189 - .00011$.

2. From 101 – hundred thousandths take 683 – ten millionths, and multiply the difference by 101 – hundred millionths.

3. Find the difference between the product and the quotient of 3.125 by .64.

4. How many times can .013 be subtracted from 125.78, and what is the remainder?

5. What must 1562.5 be divided by to give 6250000 as quotient?

6. Subtract .00061765 from .001 and give the answer in words.

7. Divide 02048 by .00003125.

8 Simplify $\frac{10.101 \times .0001}{.000001}$

9. Simplify $\frac{.044478257 \div 5.48}{.036 \times 2.043}$

10. On Monday I spend .5 of my money; on Tuesday .25 of what is left; on Wednesday .125 of what is still left; what decimal part of my money is left on Wednesday night?

ANS. (1) 36 445748. (2) .0000-0000095 1117. (3) 2.8828125. (4) 9675 times and .005 over. (5) .000 25. (6) Thirty-eight thousand two hundred and thirty-five hundred millionths. (7) 655.36. (8) 1010.1 (9) 1/9. (10) .328125.

PUBLIC SCHOOL LEAVING ARITHMETIC.

BANK DISCOUNT.

1. A note for $584 drawn June 1st at 3 months is discounted by a bank on June 21st at 6 per cent. per annum; find the proceeds.

2. For what sum must a note be drawn so that when it is discounted at a bank 100 days before maturity at 10 per cent. per annum, the proceeds may be $639?

3. Find the present value of a bill for $7,051.75, drawn on March 21st at 7 months, discounted on August 12th at 2½ per cent. per annum.

4. Show that a bill broker who deducts as discount 5 per cent. of the amount of a bill due in 1 year gets $5\,{}^{5}/_{19}$ per cent. per annum for his money.

5. A note for $143 20 drawn on 13th June, and payable 4 months after date, was discounted on 27th June at 7 per cent. per annum. Find the proceeds.

ANS. (1) $576.80. (2) $657. (3) $7,016 67. (5) $140.15.

PROBLEMS INVOLVING REMAINDERS.

1. If ${}^{2}/_{3}$ of a farm is planted with potatoes, ${}^{3}/_{4}$ of the remainder with turnips, and ${}^{1}/_{2}$ of what still remains is planted with mangolds, what fraction of the field is not planted at all?

2. A person sold ${}^{3}/_{4}$ of his land to A, ${}^{4}/_{5}$ of the remainder to B, ${}^{5}/_{6}$ of what then remained to C. If there still remained ${}^{5}/_{6}$ of an acre, find the number of acres he had at first.

3. A man's income is divided as follows:—${}^{1}/_{4}$ in paying groceries, ${}^{2}/_{3}$ of the remainder in paying life insurance, and ${}^{4}/_{5}$ of what still remains is spent in taxes; what was his income, if he had $50 left?

4. ${}^{4}/_{7}$ of a farm is given to a man's oldest son; ${}^{2}/_{3}$ of the remainder to the second son, and the remainder to the third son; the second son gets 30 acres more than the third, how many acres in the farm?

5 A man having a certain sum of money, spent $2 more than ${}^{1}/_{4}$ of it, then $2 less than ${}^{3}/_{8}$ of the remainder; then $1 more than ${}^{2}/_{3}$ of what still remained. He has left at the last $2.25, how much money had he at first?

ANS. (1) $\frac{1}{24}$. (2) 100 acres. (3) $1,000 (4) 210 acres. (5) $19.20.

How would you be,
If He, which is the top of judgment, should
But judge you as you are?

Measure for Measure, ii. 2.

CONTEMPORARY LITERATURE.

The January *Cosmopolitan* presents an attractive new serial by Conan Doyle. Its name is " Uncle Bernac," and the hero to whom the uncle belongs lands upon the shore of France in darkness and mystery. There is also a timely article on " Mascagni and His New Opera," by Alma Dalma.

Scribner's Magazine in its January number begins a series of illustrations entitled " Scenes from Great Novels," thereby deserving much gratitude from those of us who keep a corner for other reading than wet print. The first is from " David Copperfield," and is by L. Reven-Hill, engraved by Florian. This number cannot be done justice to in a short notice. Such a short story as " Story of a Second Mate," nor such a re-visiting as "Thackeray's Haunts and Homes," we are not often given.

Mary E. Wilkins has " A Quilting Bee in Our Village," in the February *Ladies' Home Journal.* " The Burglar," conducted by Herbert D. Ward, is still moving Paradise in ways heard of before, but most interesting at the same time. There is an account of the famous Mrs. Rorer, which will be read with pleasure by many.

In the *Sunday School Times* for Jan. 23rd will be found an interesting paper on the " Harmony of the Old Testament," by Matthew Newkirk, D.D. Wilma Jacobs Brown writes of " Child Life in Mexico," and on the editorial page appears "The Interest of Jesus in Common Things."

The new literary departments in *Littell's Living Age* have proved most successful, especially the extracts from the books of the month.

" Danny and the Major " is the name of a charming story of child life among soldiers. It will be found in the January *St. Nicholas*, along with other stores of good things. Few serials have the color and life of John Bennett's " Master Skylark," and " June's Garden " is an admirable counterpart for girls.

" The Chronicles of Kartdale," " Our Jeams," edited by J. Murdoch Henderson, has recently been issued by William Drysdale & Co., of Montreal. It is a pleasant Scotch story which will find its way to many hearts, and is a renewed evidence of the power of the Scotch revival.

From the American Book Co., of New York, we have received " The Story of the Romans," by H. A. Guerber, a book well adapted for supplementary reading in history. Also " Immensee," by Theodor Storm, a pleasing German story, edited for school use, by F. A. Dauer. The same firm have recently published a " Handbook of Greek and Roman History," by Georges Castegnier, B.S., B.L ; Racine's " Iphigénie," edited by B. W. Woodward, of Columbia University, also an " Elementary Meteorology for High Schools and Colleges," by Frank Waldo, Ph.D. This textbook opens a new field for study for secondary schools, one which will doubtless prove beneficial in its effects.

We have received from Macmillan & Co., London, through their Toronto agents, The Copp, Clark Co., " Reynold's Hygiene for Beginners," a book which will be welcomed by all those who have used his primer, and an edition of " Steele's Essays from the Tatler," prepared for the press by L. E. Steele, of Trinity College, Dublin.

The Copp, Clark Co. have lately published "West's Elements of English Grammar," a book which has already been of assistance to many of our teachers, and which through this edition will reach the hands of many more.

From D. C. Heath & Co., of Boston, we have received "Molière's Les Femmes Savantes," edited by Alcée Fortler; "Moser and Heiden's Kopnickerstrasse," edited by Dr. Wells, and an Italian Reader, by Benjamin L. Bowen, of Ohio State University. The same firm have forwarded a fine school edition of Tennyson's "Princess," with introduction and notes by A. J. George, M.A.

"Napoléon," edited by Alcée Fortier, Ginn & Co., Boston; A French Reader consisting of extracts from various writers on Napoleon; also, the "Children's Third Reader," by Ellen M. Cyr, published by the same firm, consisting of selections from some of the best modern writers for children.

"Topics for Students of Medicine," by Alfred Daniell, F.R.S.E. Macmillan & Co., London and New York. Since 1892, when the General Medical Council of Britain made the study of physics obligatory, it has frequently been necessary for the student, in order to obtain the general knowledge of the subject required (and also in order to find adequate treatment of those parts of physics indispensable to the proper understanding of his professional work), to have recourse to advanced and difficult text-books as specially adapted for his use. Mr. Daniell, besides being lecturer and examiner in physics to the School of Medicine, and the Royal College of Physicians, Edinburgh, is a great authority on Physics, and has written a book which is at once specially adapted for students of medicine, and broad enough to give those students a good general view of the whole subject.

LORD ROBERTS' REMINISCENCES.

Forty-one Years in India. From Subaltern to Commander-in-Chief. By Field Marshal LORD ROBERTS. Cloth, 2 vols., pp. 511, 522, $12. New York: Longmans, Green & Co.

No one whose mother tongue is English and whose instincts are those of the Anglo-Saxon race can read the reminiscences of Lord Roberts of Kandahar without emotions of pride and pleasure, of wonder and of admiration; admiration for what the race has accomplished in our own times, for the deeds of gallantry, devotion to duty and unselfish heroism displayed by those whose actions are therein chronicled; wonder, that a single individual could pass through so many stirring scenes and live to tell the tale. Almost every page gives refutation to the cynic's claim that the days of chivalry are dead; that sordid aims have altogether superseded those of nobler mold, that love of mammon has blotted out all taste for what tradition sanctified as "martial glory." That the story—or history, as its literary worth and the conscientious care with which it has been prepared entitle it to be termed—is told by one who played a prominent part in nearly all the military operations touched upon adds much to its interest and value, and gives the work a charm that will render it irresistible to any one fortunate enough to take it up. The style is so free, simple, and soldier-like, and the diction so wonderfully vivid that one is forced to pay tribute to Lord Roberts' mastery of pen as well as sword, and to regret that the almost lost art of direct narrative is not more generally cultivated. He has not, however, sacrificed the dramatic in his evident desire to tell a plain and simple tale. War in all its aspects is clearly, though almost unconsciously depicted; in its hour of victory and in its hour of disaster.

HARVARD SUMMER SCHOOL.

One needs no better proof of the enterprise of American teachers and their desire to take every possible advantage of opportunities for improvement, than to look over the list of students attending the Summer School at Harvard University. There were 637 students registered there last year, and among these were professors of colleges, superintendents, and principals of high schools and academies. Some went for the purpose of learning methods, while others sought subjects with which they were not familiar. The University authorities have steadily maintained these courses for the benefit of teachers, although considerable effort has been made to have the courses more popular in their character.

That *Sturm und Drang* of the spirit, as it has been called, those ardent and special apprehensions of halftruths, in the enthusiastic, and as it were prophetic advocacy of which, a devotion to truth, in the case of the young—apprehending but one point at a time in the great circumference—most naturally embodies itself, are levelled down, surely and safely enough, afterwards, as in history so in the individual, by the weakness and mere weariness, as well as by the maturer wisdom, of our nature:—happily! if the enthusiasm which answered to but one phase of intellectual growth really blends, as it loses its decisiveness, in a larger and commoner morality, with wider though perhaps vaguer hopes. And though truth indeed, lies, as has been said, "in the whole"—in harmonisings and adjustments like this—yet those special apprehensions may still owe their full value, in this sense of "the whole," to that earlier, one-sided but ardent preoccupation with them.—*Walter Pater.*

We cannot all be masters, nor all masters
Cannot be truly followed.

Othello, i. 1.

THE CANADA EDUCATIONAL MONTHLY.

THE CANADA EDUCATIONAL MONTHLY, we beg to inform our readers, entered upon a new term of service in educational work on the first of January of this year. It is to be hoped that after the following announcements have been carefully considered by our subscribers and fellow-teachers, that their assistance will be secured on behalf of the MONTHLY in more ways than one.

The MONTHLY is by this time one of the oldest educational periodicals in Canada, and it is the intention of all connected with its management to make it of increasing interest to the teachers of Canada and others interested in the educational progress of the country as a whole. Its *corps* of contributors already includes the most prominent of our educational workers, and what with an improved classification of topics, additional help in the editorial work, and a cordial co-operation on the part of subscribers, publishers and advertisers, it may not be too much, perhaps, to expect it to become, in the near future, one of the best and most readable of our educational journals.

It is the intention of the editors to add to the reading matter two new sections at least, perhaps three. One of these will contain a *resumé* of the current events relating to educational movements in Canada and elsewhere. Arrangements have been made to have a record of such events sent by special correspondents from all parts of the Dominion in time for publication at the beginning of each month; aud it is needless to say that paragraph contributions will be gratefully received from all teachers, when events of more than local interest take place in their district.

The second section will comprise hints from and to teachers, with correspondence. In the past, our teachers have been perhaps a little too timid in making suggestions through the press, particularly suggestions founded on their own experience. Fault-finding is a very different thing from honest criticism, and to the latter no teacher should fail to subject every proposed educational change, before finding fault with it or advocating it. Making use of the MONTHLY as a medium, it is to be hoped therefore that our teachers will join with us in an open and above-board campaign against all defects, and in favor of all improvements in our school work as well as in our school systems, so that eventually through the co-ordination of educational views from all the provinces, our various school systems will tend towards the unification of our Canadian national life, and not towards its disintegration. In future any question of an educational tendency may be discussed in our correspondence section, and when a *nom de plume* is made use of, the personality of the writer will under no circumstances be revealed.

The third section, when fully organized, will refer to all matters connected with a proposed BUREAU for the purpose of finding situations for teachers or promotion in the service. Every subscriber will have the privilege of inscribing his or her name on the lists about to be opened for those who wish to have their names thus enrolled. As an experiment we hope many of our teachers will find this section of great service to them.

To the subscribers who have stood by us so loyally in the past, we present our most grateful thanks, while to our new subscribers we make promise that their tastes and wishes will always be carefully considered in the management of the paper. Indeed, we feel it is only through the co-operation of our readers that our enterprise can be fostered to its fullest fruition.

During the year, the publishers of the MONTHLY will call upon advertisers under the improved circumstances of the periodical. To our faithful contributors we trust we will be able, as soon as the revenues of our enterprise improve, to return thanks in a more tangible way than heretofore.

The CANADA EDUCATIONAL MONTHLY, our subscribers must understand, is a journal for the whole Dominion, and not for any section or province.

Communications in connection with the editorial management of the paper are, in future, to be sent from Ontario and all the provinces west of Ontario, to Arch. MacMurchy, M.A., Box 2675, Toronto; and from the province of Quebec and the provinces east of Quebec, to Messrs. William Drysdale & Co., St. James St., Montreal, who will also attend to all matters pertaining to the publishing and advertising departments for the Eastern Provinces, and Wm. Tyrrell & Co. will attend to the like business for Ontario. Publishers: Wm. Drysdale & Co., Montreal; Wm. Tyrrell & Co., Toronto; A. Hart & Co., Winnipeg; J. & A. McMillan, St. John, N.B.

THE CANADA

EDUCATIONAL MONTHLY

AND SCHOOL MAGAZINE.

MARCH, 1897.

LITERATURE STUDIES IN PUBLIC SCHOOL.

BY L. ADELAIDE CARRUTHERS.

THE cultivation of the æsthetic side of human nature is coming more and more to be a recognized essential in the education of the citizen. It has been argued, and not without some force, that if we wish to have a law-abiding, industrious, intelligent public we must first make it a reading public. Reading broadens, elevates and refines; and whatever ennobles the mind and refines the heart of man, clearly and incontrovertibly contributes to the cause of good citizenship. The man who reads brings to his work a breadth of view that lends dignity and charm to even the humblest labor, enabling the toiler to see his work in its true relation to the sum total of man's work in the world, and elevating the most trifling details to an importance worthy of the ideal whole; he brings to his contemplation of the events of the times, whether social, religious or political, a knowledge and sympathy that militates strongly against the spirit of bigotry and unwholesome prejudice which characterizes the ignorant and the one-sided; and he brings to his daily life the refinement of cultivated sensibilities, and a living interest in the past and the future that renders less vexatious and engrossing the petty cares and accidents of the present.

It is, then, of the first importance that in public schools our children should receive sufficient stimulus to the reading of what is good in the national literature, not that they may become authors or professors of rhetoric, but that they may make peaceable, useful citizens.

It affords considerable satisfaction to know that in the Province of Ontario the examination for entrance to high schools is shortly to be superseded by what is called the Public School Leaving, a change which is calculated to extend the public school course about one year. While it would be too much to expect that the 95% who now never proceed to the high school, would avail themselves of this extension of the course, yet it is to be hoped that a very large number will in this way be induced to pursue more advanced studies. In view of the fact, therefore, that entrance work is now, and P. S. Leaving work soon will be, the graduation standard for the great mass of the citizens of this province, it is with no little interest that we set out to examine the curricula of studies for the respective departments. But our special interest lies with the course in literature. The entrance curriculum for '97, includes twenty short poems, nine of which are set apart for memorizing, while of the remainder the pupil is instructed to commit to memory any of the finer passages. These, with six fragmentary prose selections, constitute the prescribed texts with which the pupil is expected to familiarize himself, and which he is to strive to intelligently comprehend. The young student is also, so we are told, expected to have some knowledge of each of the twenty-four authors whose work is here represented. For the boy or girl about to enter upon a commercial or industrial pursuit the course certainly is broad enough; whether it is thorough enough or practical enough is not quite so apparent.

There is no prose literature for P. S. Leaving; the course in poetical literature comprises one poem each from Herrick, Gray, Wordsworth, Southey, Shelley, Hood, Macaulay, Longfellow, and two poems each from Moore and Tennyson.

Besides the minute analysis of the prescribed texts the teacher always endeavors to interest the pupils in the various authors read,— in the ten for P. S. Leaving, or the twenty-four for H. S. Entrance. He incidentally refers to other poems or sketches by the same writers. Indeed in his enthusiasm he oftentimes snatches odd moments to read some of these to his class. And he strives to awaken an interest in the writers themselves by vivid biographical sketches enlivined by numerous anecdotes. It is true only the barest outline of all this is obligatory for examination; but somehow he feels that it is in the highest degree necessary if he is to foster in his pupils anything at all approaching a love of literature. But he finds that he can do very little of this supplementary work without seriously encroaching on the time of the actual work for examination. And in foregoing indulgence in these outside studies he is always sensible that he is missing the highest aim in the teaching of literature. For let us not forget that there are two aims to be kept in view in the teaching of literature in public schools: the child must be so trained that he may (1) acquire a taste for reading, and (2) learn to bend his energies to the understanding of an author. These two aims are not mutually exclusive; and if the educator seek to attain the second in such fashion that the first be lost sight of, he is ignoring the best interests of the pupil. For indeed the ultimate criterion of all literary study, in public schools at any rate, is whether the pupil is interested in reading. But it is patent to everyone that if the first aim be held steadily in view and honestly pursued, that the second shall be accomplished as a matter of course.

Does the present course tend to cultivate a taste for reading? That is the question with which we are primarily concerned. Will minute analysis of "Flow Gently, Sweet Afton" awaken a love of the poetry of Burns? Is it possible that critical study of "The Lord of Burleigh" should arouse lasting interest in Tennyson? For it is in just this arousing of an interest in special authors that the cultivation of a love of reading consists. And it is precisely this interest in special authors that the present course notoriously fails to arouse. However commendable in itself the incidental training may be, and we do not question that it is so, one cannot but think that the same training should be, and very easily might be perfectly consonant with the transcendently important aim—the awakening of an interest in reading.

It is the opinion of the present writer that if instead of fragments from a great variety of authors the course consisted of a good deal from one or two, the literature studies in public schools would have an infinitely more practical value in the life of the young student. It is in the highest degree improbable that with the attention dispersed over so wide a field as the study of twenty-four authors, as in the case of H. S. entrance, or of ten, as in the case of P. S. leaving, there can be brought about any permanent interest in literature.

When we read the lives of men who have become eminent in literature, and it is to them as we all know that the mediocre must look for guidance, we find that their chief incentive to read came to them through an interest in some one writer. And it is just this interest that the public schools should look most towards giving. We recall how Scott when a little lad stole out of bed on winter nights to read Shakespeare by the firelight in his mother's room. We remember the young Coleridge lying on his sick bed listening with eager eyes and bated breath while his brother read Homer aloud. We hear the child Macaulay shouting at the top of his fresh young voice the ballads of Sir Walter Scott. Whittier had always his Burns, Longfellow his "Sketch Book." We cannot forget what the "Faeriè Queene" was to Keats. From Spenser he went to Chaucer, from Chaucer to Milton; and so on and on, we are told, with ever-widening range, through all our sweeter and greater poets. These were geniuses, and a love of reading was probably born with them. But that they were geniuses only emphasizes the fact that the ordinary everyday child needs something more than scant bits from several authors to awaken in him an interest in literature.

The crux of the difficulty may be regarded by some to be the choice of an author, or two or three authors, most desirable to form the basis of literature studies for the young student. But, indeed it matters little in what author anyone is interested so that the interest be deep and lasting, and that the author be one of the best. It is of small consequence whether our first love in literature be Scott, or Tennyson, or Longfellow, or Parkman, or Goldsmith, the intelligent appreciation of, and interest in, any one of them brings us nearer to them all.

The present writer is strongly of opinion that the inveterate custom of having a Fourth Book and a H. S. Reader is at the root of this superficial course in literature. These Readers have been compiled from time to time to meet the wants of a certain class. They were designed undoubtedly to make in as cheap a form as possible a golden treasury of bits from the best authors which could be used at school successively by each member of the family, and at home by the older folks as books of general reading. They are really admirable works of their kind but in this age of the circulating library and of exceedingly cheap books, the causes which made their compilation a necessity have now no longer any force. The index of tendency stands towards a radical change in the aims of the study of literature in public schools, and it is highly inexpedient to disregard it.

The school should at every point of its being and action touch the two great, ever present realities—man and nature. It should in its educational work touch every pupil in behalf of physical, intellectual and moral well being. It should, for the pupil's sake, touch nature at every accessible point and exist and act, as fully and well as circumstances will allow, to keep the pupils in friendly and wholesome touch with nature.—*Education.*

CORRELATION OF STUDIES.

BY WILLIAM T. HARRIS.*

IN the report of the Committee of Fifteen on the correlation of studies it was partly assumed that the studies of the school fall naturally into five co-ordinate groups, thus permitting a choice within each group as to the arrangement of its several topics, some finding a place early in the curriculum and others later. These five co-ordinate groups were, first, mathematics and physics; second, biology, including chiefly the plant and the animal; third, literature and art, including chiefly the study of literary works of art; fourth, grammar and the technical and scientific study of language, leading to such branches as logic and psychology; fifth, history and the study of sociological, political, and social institutions. Each one of these groups, it was assumed, should be represented in the curriculum at all times by some topic suited to the age and previous training of the pupil. This would be demanded by the two kinds of correlation defined in that report as (1) "symmetrical whole of studies in the world of human learning," and (2) "the psychological symmetry, or the whole mind."

The first period of school education is education for culture and education for the purpose of gaining command of the conventionalities of intelligence. These conventionalities are such arts as reading and writing, and the use of figures, technicalities of maps, dictionaries, the art of drawing, and all of those semi-mechanical facilities which enable the child to get access to the intellectual conquests of the race. Later on in the school course, when the pupil passes out of his elementary studies, which partake more of the nature of practice than of theory, he comes in the secondary school and the college to the study of science and the technic necessary for its preservation and communication. All these things belong to the first stage of school instruction, the aim of which is culture. On the other hand, post-graduate work and the work of professional schools have not the aim of culture so much as the aim of fitting the person for a special vocation. In the post-graduate work of universities the demand is for original investigation in special fields. In the professional school the student masters the elements of a particular practice, learning its theory and its art.

It is in the first part of education—the schools for culture—that the five co-ordinate branches should be represented in a symmetrical manner. It is not to be thought that a course of university study, or that of a professional school should be symmetrical. The study of special fields of learning should come after a course of study for culture has been pursued in which the symmetrical whole of human learning and the symmetrical whole of the soul are considered. From the primary school, therefore, on through the academic course of the college, there should be symmetry, and five co-ordinate groups of studies represented at each part of the course, at least in each year, although perhaps not throughout each part of the year.

Commencing with the outlook of the child upon the world of nature, it has been found that arithmetic or mathematical study furnishes the first scientific key to the existence of bodies and their various motions. Mathematics in its pure form, as arith-

* From report of U.S. Commissioner Harris for 1893-94, issued recently.

metic, algebra, geometry, and the application of the analytical method, as well as mathematics applied to matter and force or statics and dynamics, furnishes the peculiar study that gives to us, whether as children or as men, the command of nature in this, its quantitative aspect. Mathematics furnishes the instrument, the tool of thought, which gives us power in this realm. But useful, nay essential, as this mathematical or quantitative study is for this first aspect of nature, it is limited to it, and should not be applied to the next phase of nature, which is that of organic life; for we must not study in the growth of the plant simply the mechanical action of forces, but we must subordinate everything quantitative and mathematical to the principle of life or movement according to internal purpose or design. The principle of life or biology is no substitute, on the other hand, for the mathematical or quantitative study. The forces, heat, light, electricity, magnetism, galvanism, gravitation, inorganic matter—all these things are best studied from the mathematical point of view. The superstitious savage, however, imposes upon the inorganic world the principle of biology. He sees the personal effort of spirits in winds and storms, in fire and flowing streams. He substitutes for mathematics the principle of life, and looks in the movement of inanimate things for an indwelling soul. This is the animistic standpoint of human culture—the substitution of the biologic method of looking at the world for the quantitative or mathematical view.

The second group includes whatever is organic in nature—especially studies relating to the plant and the animal—the growth of material for food and clothing, and in a large measure for means of transportation and culture. This study of the organic phase of nature forms a great portion of the branch of study known as geography in the elementary school. Geography takes up also some of the topics that belong to the mathematical or quantitative view of nature, but it takes them up into a new combination with a view to show how they are related to organic life—to creating and supplying the needs of the plant, animal and man. There is, it is true, a "concentration" in this respect that the mathematical or quantitative appears in geography as subordinated to the principle of organic life, for the quantitative—namely, inorganic matter and the forces of the solar system—appear as presuppositions of life. Life uses this as material out of which to organize its structures. The plant builds itself a structure of vegetable cells, transmuting what is inorganic into vegetable tissue; so, too, the animal builds over organic and inorganic substances, drawing from the air and water and from inorganic salts and acids, and by use of heat, light, and electricity converting vegetable tissue into animal tissue. The revelation of the life principle in plant and animal is not a mathematical one; it is not a mechanism moved by pressure from without or by attraction from within; it is not a mere displacement or an aggregation, or anything of that sort. In so far as it is organic, there is a formative principle which originates motion and modifies the inorganic materials and the mere dynamic forces of nature, giving them special form and direction, so as to build up vegetable or animal structures.

Kant defined organism as something within which every part is both means and end to all the other parts; all the other parts function in building up or developing each part, and each part in its turn is a means for the complete growth of every other part. These two phases of nature, the inorganic and the organic, exhaust the entire field. Hence a quantitative study conducted in pure and applied mathematics and biology (or the study of life in its manifestations) covers nature.

It has been asked whether drawing does not belong to a separate group in the course of study, and whether manual training is not a study co-ordinate with history and grammar. There are a number of branches of study such as drawing, manual training, physical culture, and the like, which ought to be taught in every well regulated school, but they will easily find a place within the five groups so far as their intellectual co-efficients are concerned. Drawing, for instance, may belong to art or æsthetics on one side, but practically it is partly physical training with a view to skill in the hand and eye, and partly mathematical with a view to the production of geometric form. As a physical training its rationale is to be found in physiology, and hence it belongs in this respect to the second phase of the study of nature. As relating to the production of form it belongs to geometry and trigonometry and arithmetic, or the first phase of nature, the inorganic. As relating to art or the æsthetic, it belongs to the third group of studies, within which literature is the main discipline.

But besides literature there are architecture, sculpture, painting, and music to be included in the æsthetic or art group of studies. Manual training, on the other hand, relates to the transformation of material such as wood or stone or other minerals into structures for human use, namely, for architecture and for machines. It is clear enough that the rationale of all this is to be found in mathematics, hence manual training does not furnish a new principle different from that found in the first or the second study relating to nature.

The first study relating to human nature, as contrasted with mere organic and inorganic nature, is literature. Literature, as the fifth and highest of the fine arts, reveals human nature in its intrinsic form. It may be said in general that a literary work of art, a poem, whether lyric, dramatic, or epic, or a prose work of art, such as a novel, or a drama, reveals human nature in its height and depth. It shows the growth of a feeling or sentiment first into a conviction and then into a deed; feelings, thoughts, and deeds are thus connected by a literary work of art in such a way as to explain a complete genesis of human action. Moreover, in a literary work of art there is a revelation of man as a member of social institutions.

The nucleus of the literary work of art is usually an attack of the individual upon some one of the social institutions of which he is a member, namely, a collision with the state, with civil society, or with the church. This collision furnishes an occasion for either a comic or a tragic solution. The nature of the individual and of his evolution of feeling into thoughts and deeds is shown vividly upon the background of institutions and social life. The work of art, whether music, painting, sculpture, or architecture, belongs to the same group as literature, and it is obvious that the method in which the work of art should be studied is not the method adopted as applicable to inorganic nature or to organic nature. The physiology of a plant or an animal, and the habits and modes of growth and peculiarities of action on the part of plants and animals, are best comprehended by a different method of study from that which should be employed in studying the work of art.

(To be continued.)

THE PUBLIC SCHOOL SYSTEM OF NOVA SCOTIA.

By A. H. MacKay, LL.D.

IN 1832 the province was divided into School Commissioners' Districts, averaging the territorial size of half the larger counties, the members of the various Boards acting gratuitously, and the schools being organized on the voluntary system. In 1835 the attendance of pupils was 15,000. About 1850, the present Sir John William Dawson was appointed the first Superintendent of Education for the province, and when he accepted the Principalship of McGill University in 1855, the Provincial Normal School was opened under the charge of the Rev. Alexander Forrester, D.D., who was at the same time Superintendent of Education. In 1863 the school attendance was 31,000.

The free school system was introduced into the legislature and passed in 1864, under the leadership of the present Sir Charles Tupper, the late Sir Adams G. Archibald being leader of the Opposition, which also supported the measure. While the Rev. Dr. Forrester remained principal of the Normal School, one of his staff, the present Dr. Theodore Rand, of McMaster University, became the Superintendent to administer the new order of things. In 1869 he was succeeded by the Rev. A. S. Hunt, M.A., who, on his death, in 1877, was succeeded by David M. Allison, LL.D., of Mount Allison University, who was in turn succeeded by the present incumbent in 1891.

The Council of Public Instruction is the head of the educational system, is endowed with extensive powers, and is constituted of the members of the Executive of the Provincial Government, with the Superintendent of Education as secretary.

The Superintendent has practically the same functions to discharge as a Minister of Education, with the exception of what is implied in his being responsible to the Government rather than to the Parliament and an elective constituency.

Ten inspectors are under his immediate direction, in charge of the inspection of schools, teachers, returns and educational matters generally within the ten inspectorates into which the province is divided. The inspector is also secretary of the Boards of District School Commissioners, referred to as created originally in 1832, which may be within his jurisdiction. The functions of these Boards now are little more than the modification of the boundaries of the School Sections, which are the ultimate territorial subdivisions of the province, averaging an area of from three to four miles in diameter, and the creation of new school sections, subject to the ratification of the Council of Public Instruction. The school section, of which there are now about 1,900, is really a small corporation or self-governing community for school purposes, is governed by a board of three school trustees (except in the case of incorporated towns and cities, where a larger board of "commissioners" is appointed, partly by the town councils and partly by the Governor-in-Council), of which one is elected by the ratepayers of the section present at the annual meeting, which is held shortly before the beginning of each school year, normally on the last Monday in June, and is the annual parliament of the section. The board of trustees here present their estimates for the support of the school for the ensuing year, and after discussion, sometimes vehement, and involved enough for a county or provincial legislative body, the amount to be assessed on the section next year is voted.

The free school course of study is of a normal length of twelve years, eight of which are covered in the first eight "grades," called "common" school grades, and four in the ninth, tenth, eleventh and twelfth grades, called the "high" school grades. As the twelfth year work is of university grade, students from the high schools generally enter the universities from the eleventh grade, except in a few non-university towns where there is a strong staff of high school teachers.

A county academy is the high school in each county which, in view of its engagement to provide for and admit free all qualified students from the county, receives a special grant called the academic grant, and is either $500, $1,000, $1,500 or $1,720 per annum, according to its equipment and work done.

In 1893, the normal term of a teacher's engagement in a section was changed from six months to one year, the Provincial Normal School, with which the Provincial School of Agriculture is affiliated, was made a purely training or professional school, including with its course of practice in teaching, manual training in wood work, physical, chemical and biological experimentation, drawing, vocal music, elocution, with a review and amplification of previous high school course, which the candidates must have passed before admission. In the same year the high school system was organized into the form of a provincial university, certificates known respectively as those of grade D, C, B, and A (classical) or A (scientific), being granted by a Provincial Board of Examiners on the courses respectively of the ninth, tenth, eleventh and twelfth years. A peculiarity of these certificates is their containing on the margin the value of each examination paper, so that they can be used in lieu of the entrance examinations of all colleges or other institutions, even those having the most diverse standards, providing the certificate in point shows the percentage mark on each particular subject required by the institution in point. Thus has been solved the problem of the affiliation of the public school system with all the different colleges and organizations in the province requiring a scholarship test for admission.

THE RELIGIOUS DIFFICULTY.

While the course of study makes instruction in "moral and patriotic duties" and "hygiene and temperance" imperative on every teacher, and while the "Compulsory Attendance" clauses of the law require the attendance of pupils from seven to twelve years of age in the rural sections adopting them, and from six to thirteen years of age in the incorporated towns adopting them, there has never been any serious difficulty with respect to religious instruction. Although not referred to in the Course of Study, a regulation of the Council of Public Instruction assumes that "devotional exercises" may be conducted in any school so long as no parent or guardian objects thereto in writing. If the objection be made, the exercises may be so modified as to give no offence within regular school hours. But if no such modification can be made, the exercises may be held immediately before the opening of the secular work of the school, or after its close. The trustees, who may well be assumed to understand the local conditions of their section, have therefore, under the law, very large powers for regulating such exercises where the people wish them limited, first by the provision that no one shall be required to be present at devotional exercises disapproved of, and secondly by the condition that it shall not intrench injuriously on the regular and imperative work of the school.

This explains how the only two Roman Catholic colleges in the province, St. Francis Xavier (English) and Ste. Anne (French), and many of the convents are affiliated with the public school system. In fact, no corresponding institutions of any other of the religious denominations are thus affiliated, although the law leaves it as open to the one as to the other. When mutually agreeable, the trustees of school sections can rent the school rooms of such institutions, appoint the teachers nominated by them, if they hold provincial licenses, and otherwise control the school in strict accordance with the letter of the law. Such schools having regularly licensed teachers, the same school books, the same registers to be kept and the same returns to be made out and sworn to, the same inspectors to visit and report, etc., and are paid the same public grants as any other public schools doing the same work. When it has not interfered with proper grading, trustees have been allowed to have separate schools for the boys and the girls, although co-education is the rule, with few exceptions, not only in rural sections, but in the County Academies and the other high schools.

In the city of Halifax, the Roman Catholic members of the Board of School Commissioners have been accustomed to nominate all teachers to the schools which were originally the property of the Roman Catholic Corporation, although the appointments are always made by the full Board. The majority of the children attending the most of these schools are said to be Roman Catholic (as there is no place for denominational statistics in any of the Nova Scotian returns), but there is no public inconvenience caused by insistence on denominational dividing lines in any of the schools. All the schools are public schools in the fullest sense, and the Education Department has no official knowledge and requires none of any arrangements which the trustees or the Board of School Commissioners may find convenient, so long as the requirements of the law are carried out.

In a few small towns, since the year 1864, children have been withdrawn from the public schools to form convent schools. In most of these cases at date, the parties causing the schism have acted with such tact and good feeling in the community as eventually to have elected to the Municipal Councils or School Boards those who were ready to rent the "separate" school rooms, appoint the "nominated" teachers (regularly licensed ones, of course), and assume general control over them as a part of the public schools of the section. The fact that such schools must win recognition from the public school trustees of the section in which they originate, is the highest possible premium on their peaceful and harmonious evolution where they must spring up. For what the the public school trustees can do in such cases they can also undo, or leave undone. But when the law is fully complied with in respect to any school, the fact that it also fulfils other functions useful to at least a portion of the community does not disqualify it from participation in the public grants otherwise legally qualified for.

Although the Roman Catholic denomination is the only one to develop affiliation of this kind with the public schools. it must be remembered that the law makes no concession in favor of one denomination more than another. What this denomination has been doing may be done in the same manner by any other denomination, philosophical coterie, or business corporation, if it can only similarly convince and impress the local school authorities. But the schools must be public schools in every respect defined by the law. Neither the statutes nor the regulations of the Council of Public Instruction contain a single reference to any religious denomination, but they both require the teacher "to inculcate by precept and example, respect for religion and the principles of Christian morality." And in this respect it is the general impression that the teachers of the public schools for Nova Scotia will compare favorably even with the clergy as a whole.—*Presbyterian College Journal.*

CIVIC TRAINING IN PRIMARY SCHOOLS.

BY DR. WILLIAM C. JACOBS, PRINCIPAL HOFFMAN SCHOOL, PHILADELPHIA.

IN a former article we endeavored to show that civic training is the starting point of scientific instruction in history. In this article we will briefly consider what phases of civic training are adapted to pupils in the first two or three years of school life.

As has been already emphasized, the only civics that is practical for children is a doing civics; the child learns little from hearing precept and blank instruction; he learns much more from seeing the actions of others, but the great part of his practical knowledge he has obtained by doing. It is from this natural order and method of mental growth that we must derive the governing principles of civic instruction in primary schools.

CIVICS IS A BRANCH OF ETHICS.

Before attempting to give a detailed account of a course of primary lessons in civics, we would call to mind the fact that civic training is one of the great branches of moral training, and rests upon the fundamental principles of morals in general. No one will ever faithfully perform the duties of citizenship who does not have a proper respect for the cardinal virtues of morality. Primary civics, then, may be regarded as a branch of primary ethics. "A family," said Wm. Paley, "contains the rudiments of an empire," and the same is true of the school. The school, as well as the home, must become the nursery of those traits of character that will gradually expand into the moral impulses that ever direct the law-abiding citizen. It is here, then, in the rich soil of youthful activity, that the conscientious teacher must plant the seeds of noble manhood and womanhood—seeds that will germinate, and blossom into the graces of politeness, the kindness of heart, the sense of fellowship, the earnest loyalty to duty, that ever mark the character of true citizenship.

It may be argued that in recognition of the general principles of morality alone, the true teacher will develop this side of the child's character. For instance, shall we not, as teachers, exact obedience of our pupils from other than civic reasons? But when we consider that there can be no civil freedom except in subjection to the law, that obedience to authority is the only soil that can grow the liberties and rights of citizenship, and that the child who forms the habit of cheerful obedience to the authorities in the miniature governments of the family and the school has learned one of the most essential of civic principles, shall we not feel a stronger and more enduring desire to graft upon the characters of our pupils the habit of cheerful subjection to authority?

MANY OPPORTUNITIES FOR CIVIC TRAINING.

The means for building up a definite civic character are many. The mental equipment with which the child enters school is of valuable assistance. For instance, he comes to school imbued with a love for his home and his parents. This love will soon reach out and include his teacher; and under her tactful guidance will, ere long, embrace his companions both in and out of school. He is thus laying the foundation of an earnest, sincere human sympathy that will, with advancing years, gradually broaden until it includes within its scope the people of his country if not the entire human race. Thus, love for country is but a more advanced growth of the love for home, and benevolence is but the ripened fruit of childish sympathy with playmates and companions.

Then again, the reading and language lessons will furnish excellent opportunities for awakening in the youthful heart the proper sentiments; the power of music may with great effectiveness be used to bring forth almost any desired feeling or impulse. The various conditions of every school offer many suitable channels for civic practice. Thus, in removing the banana and orange skins from the pavement or schoolyard, the child is developing the germs of mutual protection and civic sympathy; in voluntarily picking up the piece of paper thrown on the floor of his school-room by some thoughtless pupil, he is exercising the faculties of order and neatness and system, all of which have most important civic significance.

Further, we can have special lessons for the awakening of civic sentiments. We might start with the school-house or some prominent building in the vicinity and hold conversations with the pupils about such points as:

Who built it.
Why it was built.
The uses of the building.
Where the money was obtained.
Why the donors gave the money.
What we think of the donors.
What we would like to do for others.
What we all can do now.
What we will do at once.

This last statement is the only true end of every lesson designed to inspire civic sentiment. It is thought and feeling passing over into the only conclusion of value—action.

PATRIOTIC TEACHERS NEEDED.

Did space permit, other and more detailed suggestions might be given. But the teacher who feels that the preparation of youth for citizenship is an imperative duty, will have little difficulty in finding a way to discharge that duty. What we are more in need of is an awakening of teachers to the grave civic responsibilities resting upon them. When teachers, as a body, come to a full appreciation of the fact that our entire public school system is a civic institution, and depends upon the government not only for its support but for its very existence, and that just as the observance of the laws of health is necessary to the bodily well-being of the child, so civics, which is the physiology of the government, must have its principles wrought into the youthful character if we would preserve the health of our civil institutions. When the teaching profession, we repeat, rises to a full appreciation of the duty of the school to the State, and to a clear recognition of the fact that "what we do to the child to-day we have done to the nation to-morrow," it will have dignified and elevated itself, and will, we predict, receive such a recognition from the government as the world has not seen since the golden age of Grecian affluence and learning.

THE CAMBRIDGE SCHOOL FOR GIRLS.

IF the best three American schools for girls were to be mentioned, the Cambridge School would be among them, if, indeed, it did not hold the first position. The school is now in its eleventh year. Its success has been marked from the beginning. Many accounts of it have been written; but most of them, though they gave us delightful impressions of Cambridge with its ideal surroundings and opportunities for girls, of the conception of the plan by Mr. Gilman, and of its progress from the beginning, shed comparatively little light upon the real working of the school. We knew that there is a building for the classes, in which the school work is done; that it is equipped with laboratories; that its walls are colored in those neutral tints that rest the eyes; that it is evenly warmed, and that it is flooded with sunlight; but the spirit of the institution seems to evade us; though at first we thought that we knew a great deal about it.

If we begin at the beginning, we find Mr. Gilman, who has long been interested in the collegiate education of women, planning for the instruction of his own younger daughters. He and his wife wanted a place in which the gentle sway of love should be manifest, and in which the studies should be fitted to the peculiar wants of every individual girl. Seeking some plan that would thus meet their wishes for their own daughters, they found one which has proved to be adapted to the wants of all girls who seek careful and sympathetic training, and of parents who esteem character and good breeding, joined with general cultivation, supreme above the most thorough drilling of the mind, when divested of those admirable traits.

It is scarcely possible to put on paper a description of the real working of a school, for it is not like an inanimate machine which remains unmoved while we inspect its parts. A school is a living, moving entity, almost a personality, for it gains a character as an individual does, and though that character is made by the pupils and teachers who are its component parts, it does not readily change as the parts change. The heart gives its character to the individual, and there must be something which does the same for a school. We, therefore, enquire for the spirit that breathes through this particular school and makes it what it is.

There are two or three principles underlying all the work. In the first place, the school is not a mere factory, in which girls are mechanically placed, and polished and finished as one would polish a precious stone or finish an engine, beautiful and interesting as are the jewel and the machine. It is a place where mind is working on mind; where everything is done for the benefit of the *pupil*; where the teachers are continually asking themselves, "What will be the effect of this, or of that, upon the *pupil?*" They might say, on the other hand, "Here is the course of study of the school; it is skilfully arranged to meet the necessities of the average girl; it will fit her for college, or for the ordinary life of the woman; it will prepare her for society; it is ingeniously arranged in classes, so that any average girl, entering in the usual manner and passing through it grade by grade, will emerge 'finished;'" but that is by no means what these teachers say to themselves or to others.

The perennial question with them is, "What is best for this particular girl who happens to be under discussion?" If she be the "average" girl, she may fit into a graded course; but many girls cannot be classified thus. They come from a great variety of circumstances; this one has been taught by tutors and has never before been in school; this next has been all her little life passing through grades, and is even in her preparation; this one has lived in Germany, and is far advanced in the language of that country; another is an invalid and must take but little work; here is one who must go to Wellesley College, or Vassar, or Smith, or Radcliffe, and she must be fitted for their respective examinations. The teachers in the Cambridge School look upon this gathering of girls, study it, and arrange a course for each one. They fit the course to the girl, instead of making her fit herself to any course, however good.

This is difficult, it may be said. Doubtless it is, and it requires a numerous force of teachers. Classes cannot be large; but it is best for the pupils that they be not large. In fact the classes last year averaged less than seven, including all the lecture courses. With small classes, short "periods" are possible, and the frequent changes from room to room give opportunity for change of air and relieve pupils from the strain of long sessions. It is evident, too, that in a class of six a pupil gets more of the teacher's attention than she does in a class of twenty.

Another feature is found in the fact that it is expected of the teachers that they shall do all the teaching that any girl may need, and that as much as possible of the pupil's study shall be accomplished during the comparatively short school session. In order to provide for this, a large part of the girl's program is left open, and each teacher is allowed free hours also. In addition to this, every teacher has certain afternoon hours, during which she is to be found in the school-room, ready to meet her pupils for the purpose of explaining difficulties; and she takes advantage of the time to meet parents, in order to learn from them facts about the pupils that can be learned in no other way. Still further, the school has a "secretary," a skilled teacher of long experience with girls, who, however, teaches in no subject, but gives her entire attention to the work of smoothing out the pupil's difficulties and of saving the time of the teachers. The manual of the school tells us that every subject has inherent difficulties enough for discipline. The director, Mr. Gilman, is always found in the building, easy of approach by pupils, parents and teachers, and, as is plainly evident, counts no detail of the work too small for his notice and interest.

Still another feature is found in the statement that the school has no written rules, beyond that one written in the heart,—the Golden Rule,—"Do unto others as ye would that they should do to you." Neither are there marks for deportment: In the Study Hall, for the older girls, there is perfect freedom, limited only when it might interfere with the general object for which the pupils fully understand that they have been brought together. It is evident that this is not one of those oppressive establishments called by President Hall, of Clark University, the "Keep still" school! The motto of the school, chosen by the girls, is in line with this spirit. It bespeaks acquaintance with Chaucer and with the motto of Harvard college. It reads, "*Truthe and gentil dedes,*" and shows that while the girls seek truth in all their work as well as in their lives, they practise those deeds which mark the highest type of gentlewoman. It has often been questioned by visitors and by incoming teachers whether such methods are practicable; but experience has always shown them that they are not only practicable but conducive of the highest self-control, leading those who are guided by them to practise right, not by compulsion, but by choice. It is certainly the way in which Providence deals with men.

The last feature that needs to be mentioned is that which Mr. Gilman himself developed a few weeks ago in our columns. We refer to the separation of the school and the home, for those girls who come from a distance to enter its classes. By this plan the teachers are brought fresh to their pupils every morning, and the pupils have every advantage of home, with one added, namely, that which Mr. Gilman brought out, when he said that "while the real home is usually arranged and carried on for the benefit of a mixed household, these are established simply and solely for the benefit of the young girls who are to constitute their sacred charge." To many this is the most marked characteristic of the school.

We have left ourselves but small space in which to refer to the other traits of the Cambridge School. The impression has been given that it is pre-eminently a "college preparatory school," but this is by no means true, though it has sent a larger number of students to Radcliffe College than any other private school has. We have it directly from the head of the school that it has never worked, and that it will never work solely for college preparation; but that its highest aim is to give to every girl what she needs, along the broadest lines, and we see ourselves that its pupils remain long beyond the time at which preparation for college is finished, doing in the school advanced work, often, indeed, of college grade.

It is the exception to find such fully equipped laboratories of chemistry, physics, and zoology, in private schools for girls, nor do usually we notice so many girls actually interested in this class of work. Mr. Gilman holds science in high esteem for the very youngest pupils, and though it is here an elective study, it is taken up by them for the love of it. It serves to train their eyes and their hands, and as we look over their note-books, and see what their sharp eyes have detected in the "sand-dollar," the cricket, the cray-fish, etc., we are convinced that Mr. Gilman's theories in this respect are correct. The zest with which the smallest children take up such subjects as this shows plainly that their interest is no less than that of the oldest pupils in any school.

The teachers in a school constitute the school, and in this institution this is true in a marked degree. Their positions resemble more those of professors in a college, than of teachers in ordinary schools, for they are specialists in their different departments, and they are considered masters of their respective subjects. Under the general guidance of the principles which characterize the management of the school, they conduct their work in the way that their experience dictates. They are thus free to adopt the latest improvements in any respect, provided they are the best: and in conjunction with the "House-Mothers" in the Residences, they make the historic and literary associations of Cambridge of use to the pupils. They also let them know of the museums and the collections of the university, and of the many inspiring lectures which, by the courtesy of Harvard College, are open to them without cost. Thus they add to the instruction of the school those cultivating opportunities which come to Cambridge residents from the fact that all the lecturers of highest distiuction in Europe and America come to speak for Harvard sooner or later.

It is out of our plan to speak of the advantages of Cambridge and Boston as educational centres, though this might be made extra on which much could be said.—*The School Journal.*

TEACHING CHILDREN TO TALK.

IF I were asked how much education a woman should receive, I should answer unhesitatingly: "Enough to enable her to teach her children to speak English with reasonable purity." That she could get this in a grammar school, I will not deny; that she does get it in a college course, except in rare cases, I do deny most emphatically.

I do not refer to grammatical accuracy, as I am addressing a class of readers who habitually apply the laws of grammar to their every-day speech, do not get confused with their past tenses and participles, think one negative at a time sufficient, and use adjectives and pronouns in their proper places.

If any one will listen critically to the speech of those around him, even among the wealthy and cultivated classes, he will be surprised at the rarity of cases where "you" is pronounced properly. "Don't you" is called "Don-chuh," "will you," "will yuh," and so on. "To" is called "tuh," and "for," "fur."

All that can be done in an article of this length is to call the attention of readers to a few errors which are taught to children, to create a desire to examine the laws of pronunciation, as they are the only safe guides, and to impress upon them the necessity of teaching little ones to speak correctly.

This teaching must be done at home as well as in school. No outside training can make the ordinary child forget the language he is taught from infancy. I have heard families of grown sons and daughters, who have been fairly educated, repeating the orthoepical errors of the parents in a manner which would have been amusing if it had not been pathetic.

School training is decidedly defective in this essential. Authors indicate the proper pronunciation by means of diacritical markings from the chart up. The teacher in almost every case teaches her own peculiarities of speech. That this article may have some practical value to those who really wish to teach their children to speak correctly from imitation, the very best way, I will systematize somewhat. Merely a hint can be given under each heading, however, and those sounds referred to which are the first words of child speech.

Three things should be considered: The articulation of consonants; the enunciation of vowels; the placing of accent. Grown persons should try by some sort of vocal gymnastics to cultivate that flexibility of the organs of speech which will enable them to articulate consonant sounds. Children seem to have that flexibility naturally, and they will imitate clear-cut consonant sounds with surprising accuracy.

While in most mouths all the consonants are habitually muffled and indistinct, some are more badly treated than others. All singers and elocutionists are taught to form words in the front part of the mouth. I wish that everyone might master the subject of elocution; not that he might read "set" pieces from the platform, but that his every-day speech might be purified and made musical.

If the reader will pronounce the word "winter," giving the "n" and the "t" a distinct articulation, he will hear quite a different word from the one spoken usually. The same may be done with "dinner," heeding the "n's;" "water," making the "t" sharp, and so indefinitely.

It is in the enunciation of the vowels that the language is abused the worst. Why will educated people persist in pronouncing "can't," "half," "laugh," "past," "last," and many more words of the same kind, giving the "a" the sound of "a" in "at." It takes all the richness from the words, and though authors protest by means of their markings, teachers do not heed. The educated Englishman does not make that mistake, and I can imagine how the chatter of a crowd of American travellers must impress him.

I would begin right here with the first letter of the alphabet in an effort to fit myself to teach children to pronounce correctly. After a short practice of the correct enunciation of "a" wherever it appears, no one would ever wish to return to former errors. "Can't," "sha'n't," "half," "path," "laundry," "saunter," "laugh," and so on, have the sound of "a" in the word "ah." In "past," "last," and "pass," the "a" is not so broad.

The "o's" in "office," "dog," "hot," "coffee," and "orange," should be sounded exactly alike, somewhere between the "a" in "ah," and the "a" in "all," coming closer to the latter. Try it, practise it, and teach it to the little ones. The "u" in "rude," "truth," and in all monosyllables after "r," has the sound of "o" in "do." In "blue," "new," and other monosyllables without "r," the "u" sounds like "ĭ-oo." In "current" the "u" is short like the "u" in "tub." Teach a child to call you yo̤u, and not yüh; set him the example by your daily speech.

Much more might be said about the enunciation of vowels, but I shall have to content myself with saying a wo̤rd about the vowels in unaccented syllables. The rules go̤verning their sounds can be learned from any text-book on orthoepy or from a dictionary. I will mention a few common errors merely to call attention to the matter. In "imitate" both "i's" have the sound of "i" in "it," Usually the unaccented "i" is given the sound of "u" in "up." In "elegance" the unaccented "e" has the sound of "e" in "me;" this is also true in the word "benefit." In "beautiful" the "i" has the sound of "i" in "it," and the "u" the sound of "u" in "full." Try it and see how it sounds. A hundred examples might be given of common words which are taught to the child incorrectly.

The placing of accent is a matter of no little importance in securing correct pronunciation. Two accents are often given where there is only one, as in "idea," "primary," "secretary," and so on. The "a's" in the last two words have the sound of short "u" nearly.

Care should be taken not to make too much of an effort in the matter of articulation.

I wish every mother and teacher could study elocution just so far as it deals with pronunciation and breathing, so that children might reap the benefits. It is by teaching the little one to speak correctly that the speech of the future is to be made musical and pure.—*Public School Journal.*

A merry heart keeps on the windy side of care.

Much Ado About Nothing, ii. 1.

EDITORIAL NOTES.

UNREST FOR TEACHERS.

Why is the teaching profession, especially that part of it to be found in the High Schools, so restless at present? The uneasiness, on enquiry, will be found to be connected with the subject of examinations. Teachers say that Ontario, at some time in its past history, may have had, all told, more examinations than at the present time; but universally they maintain that the examination differed in kind. The former system of examination is described as "outside of the schools," the present system is described by one master as 'taking possession of the schools." Another master says that by the present series of examinations the Education Department takes the place of the staff in this part of the school work, and thus that the teacher is only a lifeless "pin" in the departmental machinery. Time was when it used to be said, more in joke than in earnest, that the Education Department was aiming at taking the promotion of pupils into its own hands. This last move on the examination ladder is referred to, as practically fulfilling that prophecy. All the changes made by the Department, when put together, are held to illustrate strongly the oft-quoted maxim that power and centralization are dear to the bureaucratic officials and their chief. These are the sentiments, moderately expressed, made known by teachers to THE CANADA EDUCATIONAL MONTHLY.

To say that a pupil can pass the whole course of the High School programme of studies without passing any departmental examination is granted to be true in the abstract, but in the concrete it is held to be a subterfuge advanced to enable one to dodge a responsibility. To schoolmasters examinations are a necessity in the proper performance of their responsible duties. If there is any mode, as yet undiscovered, by which they can be relieved from them, we are sure teachers will welcome such relief.

From every part of the world comes the same cry about our teachers, and in many cases it has recently been so intensified that there is every prospect of its being heard by those who can come to their rescue. The politicians of Quebec, in the present struggle for party ascendency, have had to take note of it, and from the hustings it is being made a party watchword in the form of "we must pay our teachers higher salaries." From the Australian corner of the Empire the same note has been sounded, while the professional periodicals of England, in their columns of "Wants," show how poorly the ordinary school teacher is remunerated for his services. This is what the *Australian Shoolmaster* says on the subject:

"That the whole of the teachers serving under the Education Department have had much to discourage them during the past few years must be conceded. Head masters of our large schools are in receipt of salaries far below those which formerly belonged to these positions. After years of faithful service and the drudgery of work required to obtain certificates and classification, they, in many instances, find themselves loaded with increased responsibility, but yet in the receipt of smaller incomes than they had when occupying much lower positions. The same may be said of the assistant teachers. Consequently a very large proportion of those occupied in one of the most important branches of the Public Service are toiling under a sense of hardship, and, to some extent, injustice. But of this more anon. What we wish now specially to press upon the notice of the Minister of Public Instruction is the cruel position of the first-class pupil teachers. When the schools were carried on under the former system of staffing, these teachers were supposed to be only doing subordinate work, while pursuing their studies for the teaching profession, and their salaries were fixed accordingly, whereas they now do the responsible work cast upon them through the reductions made in the assistant staff. Thus they are practically assistant teachers, though still called pupil teachers. Many of them have matriculated at the University of Melbourne, have passed all examinations demanded of them by the Department, and have been engaged in teaching for five and six years, and still their salaries are only £40 a year for females and £50 per annum for males. We have been in schools where classes of from fifty to eighty children were being taught—and well taught, too—by first-class pupil teachers without any assistance whatever, or at most, the occasional help of a child out of the sixth class. Considering the strain on the mind of a young teacher thus placed, to demand such arduous labor for the miserable pittance mentioned is "sweating" of the most aggravated character. We feel sure that the generous nature of the Minister of Education would not tolerate this state of things for a day were it not for the depleted state of the public Treasury. But the worst rut in the road of depression has been passed, and we appeal to that honorable gentleman and to the official head of the Department to speedily devise means for giving relief to this most worthy section of the State teaching staff. This could be done very readily by giving the first-class pupil teachers an increment or a result percentage payment, similar to that made to the head masters and assistant teachers. Were the whole facts of the case submitted by the Minister to Parliament, he would have little difficulty in obtaining an amendment of the Act that would meet the case of those sweated pupil teachers."

The revelations of the *Montreal Herald*, in regard to the condition of some of the schools of the Province of Quebec, have attracted the attention of the whole Dominion, and something must be done by the people of that section of Canada to remove the reproach of having a machinery so poorly equipped for the education of the coming generation. These revelations show how much worse the condition of the teacher is in Quebec than even in retrograding Melbourne. Forty or fifty pounds a year, even for teaching eighty pupils, will seem a large emolument to the schoolmarms who are working for from seven to eight dollars a month in many of the school municipalities of the Dominion, and we trust that irrespective of the seeming nonsettlement of the Manitoba School Question, no one will think of encouraging a continuance of the present state of affairs, far less a retrograde movement. We know it will be said that an increase of salary to the teacher will not make a more efficient teacher of him, but will a higher salary not encourage many to prepare themselves thoroughly for that occupation when the fiat goes forth that every teacher must be a trained teacher, with the mark of such training upon his credentials. The *Montreal Herald* has had to abide by some abuse for the open way it has conducted its task of investigation, but credit will be given to it and the other journals that have stood by it when the reformation comes. The *Public School Journal*, of Ohio, lately suggested that that State needed either an educational cyclone or a dynamite bomb to stir it in behalf of educational reform, and was subjected to a severe castigation from one of the leading newspapers for daring to say a word against the editor's native State. But the day for reprisal has come to the editor of the *School Journal*. "We were born in Ohio, educated in her schools, and taught in them for seven years. We do not like to have uncomplimentary things said about the State to which we owe so much. But there is more truth than fiction in what our former castigator now says: 'The State of Ohio is no longer a leader in education. She lags behind. This is due to politics—not party politics, but school politics — and bad management. School politics should surely be driven out of our school affairs in city and country.'" The *Montreal Herald* is having its reward in this way already, for many have joined in its exposures of educational inefficiencies in Quebec, and we have no doubt that a more emphatic reward is in store for it, when these exposures shall have led to the necessary reforms, both in the matter of providing trained teachers for all the schools of the Province as well as in the providing of better salaries and improved supervision. In Ontario even the question of increasing the salaries of our teachers is beginning to be a live subject for discussion, and we hope that in the near future, not only will the salaries be attached to the positions as a permanent emolument, but that the Department will inaugurate some process by means of which the minimum salary to be paid will be fixed by regulation.

It is amusing to notice how the forces that oppose educational reform come as much from within as without. When we talk of "school politics" in Canada, it is less easy to define the term than when the school politics across the line are spoken of. The school politics of Canada are only discernible when reform is urged upon those who have, or have had, the administration of a school system and they are called upon to investigate the error of their ways. The tenure of office has naturally made these administrators conservative in their ways of doing things, and when a quarrel based on the non-progressiveness of the system they have administered, arises, they often impulsively take the quarrel as their own, and attempt to justify a state of affairs utterly unjustifiable. Like some governments, they have been so long in power that they begin to deem outside interference as a kind of impertinence. For example, Archbishop Langevin, in a moment of ecstacy, after the late election in St. Boniface, had much to say in praise of the school system in force, when the schools of Manitoba were perhaps the most inefficient in the world. And lately, when the *Montreal Herald* was making exposure after exposure through the facts collected by its own commissioner in connection with the schools of Quebec, a former Secretary of the Department of Public Instruction was heard in one of the Teachers' Conventions, declaring that the state of affairs was not as bad as the facts made it out to be, while a former Superintendent shortly afterwards tried to emphasize the justification in a long and eloquent speech in the upper chamber of the Local

Legislature; and as if this sublimity of self-interested blindness had not yet reached the ridiculous, the most distinguished of the orators in the lower chamber has been repeating the tale of justification ever since. This is surely equal to the Irish polemic's manner of getting rid of the facts, with a vengeance. And yet school reform is in the air for all the provinces, from British Columbia to Nova Scotia; and as in Quebec so in the other provinces, the facts of the case are better than oratory or self-justifications when the moment is ripe for action.

If anything can convince our representatives at Ottawa that what was said in our issue of last month about the organization of a Canadian Bureau of Education had a large element of soundness in it, the last volume of the report of the National Commissioner of Education is sure to do so. Any one of them can receive a copy of it, we believe, by sending to Dr. Harris of Washington. It brings to us a general survey of the status of educational thought and practice in all the countries of the world where any serious attempt is made to provide for the education of the rising generation. There is no name better known in the United States than the name of him who is National Commissioner at the present; and while some of the educationists of the neighboring republic, inflated with the idea that the best of everything is only to be found in their own secluding or excluding development, and that a pedagogy can be made local, Dr. Harris, by his work and public teachings, stands as a reproof to all such. The principles of pedagogy are universal, and as these volumes come out, one after the other, they bear evidence in every page that such is the case. We are glad to see that a movement is on foot to increase the Commissioner's emoluments. *The Teacher* greets the movement with such a comment as this, which we are sure will be echoed by everyone who knows the great educationist:

The proposition, embodied in a bill now before Congress, to increase the salary of the United States Commissioner of Education from $3,000 to $5,000, appeals to all fair-minded and observant people. One great deterrent to securing the best talent for public service nowadays is the consequent merging of one's identity with the machinery of a great system. It is most unfortunate and discouraging when a public servant begins to realize that merit is not the sole factor in determining remuneration, but that in the mind of his employers he is but one of a class. We believe that this is the important reason why self-sacrifice, industry and ability in the teaching profession meet with a return less adequate than in any other line of employment. But in the case of the National Commissioner, a most superficial comparison will prove the injustice. The City Superintendent of Philadelphia receives $5,000; of New York, $7.500; of Boston, $4,200; of Chicago, $7,000; of Washington, $5,500; of Brooklyn, $6,000. We venture to assert that the government is securing from Dr. William T. Harris a degree of ability, zeal and judgment that could not be surpassed by any educator of this country. Common justice, as well as the unanimous opinion of the teaching class, demand that his salary be placed upon a par with those paid by our largest cities.

The knighthood lately conferred upon the author of "Maple Leaves" was made an event in the city of Quebec by the banquet given to Sir James Le Moine, and the honor thus bestowed upon one of their own caste, is surely one which every literary man in Canada ought to be proud of. Among the speeches delivered on that occasion there was one which it can hardly be out of place to reproduce in these columns, seeing it was delivered by one well-known to our readers and gives a fair estimate of what may safely be considered a definition of Sir James LeMoine's position among our writers, as well as a judicious estimate of the status of what we are ever calling Canadian Literature. We take the report from the *Quebec Chronicle*: Dr. Harper, on being called upon to reply to the toast of Canadian Literature, said that it was a marvel to him why he had been selected to perform such a duty, and he had no doubt that before he was done, those who had to listen to him would marvel as much as he did, For others to escape what he had to say was often enough an accredited blessing, and for himself to escape the danger of saying anything about Canadian literature especially was a lesson he had learned after the usual experience. The only explanation he could make of his selection was the long and unbroken friendship which had existed between him and the author of "Maple Leaves," the honored guest of the evening, and the high and important position which he now, Sir James LeMoine, had attained to as the father of "the men of the first campaign" in favor of an improved literature in Canada. "Sir James LeMoine is a man"—and here Dr. Harper seemed to falter in his speech, "Yes, Mr. Chairman, Sir James LeMoine is a man, and in that statement we have the whole history of his career, literary, personal and social. Our Gracious Majesty has been pleased to touch his shoulder with the imperial sword, but you all know how nature has been beforehand with her, tipping him with that brotherly kindness and sympathetic citizenship which have always marked him as one of nature's noblemen. And this it is, perhaps more than the late honoring of our guest by Royalty, that has brought us crowding round him this evening to take a stronger and firmer grip of the friendship of an honest man. And to speak thus of Sir James LeMoine is surely not to run away from the toast, but rather to speak to it in the most emphatic manner. Has he not been at the beginning of things in more senses than one, and if he is not to be called, without flattery, the Sir Walter Scott of Canada, even the Sir Walter Scott of his native Province, no one will deny that he has been a Sir Walter Scott to this old city of Quebec." Dr. Harper then referred to Canadian literature in its widest sense and showed how difficult it would be to deal with such a subject properly in an after-dinner speech. "There is an evolution," said he, "in the history of any country's literature, as there is an evolution in the history of any other movement among the humanities, and when we come to examine the stages of this evolution we find them concretely described in a marked degree in the powers of a Sir Walter Scott, as we find them exemplified in the history of our own old city. Take the instance of the development of a Rob Roy into a Roderick Dhu and you have in it an illustration of the various stages of the evolution of a literature; and take the literary developments of our own city and it is just as easy to learn from them whether there is a Canadian literature or not. Sir Walter Scott as an antiquary dug up the records of the blackmailing raider of Balquidder before he could give us as an historian the matter of fact biography of the red-headed outlaw, and as a novelist he had no doubt to think out the prose romance of Rob Roy before he had developed it into the imagery of the bold cateran of the "Lady of the

Lake." The stages in the development of a literature are, therefore, to be found in these, the industry of the antiquarian, the assimilating powers of the historian, the characterizations of the novelist and the imagery flights of the poet. And leaving Canada as a whole, as too wide a subject for the moment, does this grand old city of ours give any evidence of these various stages of the development of a literature of its own. Has she about her the proper element out of which to give birth to the antiquary, the historian, the novelist and the poet, and when Sir James LeMoine has answered you and Francis Parkman, and William Kirby and Louis Frechette you will have in their replies the answer to the query that disturbs so many people, though it does not disturb me, whether there be a Canadian literature or not. There is a fashion abroad when this subject is on the tapis, which I will not venture to imitate, the fashion of naming with aureolic eclât a list of writers of Canadian birth. With the usual illogical exclamation, "Did I not tell you so,—there *is* a Canadian literature after all." Were I to do so, I would be sure to omit some one and then the fat would be in the fire. I would rather contemplate the object lesson around us, and see if there is in the history of our own city, as a wee bit of the old world set down on the borders of the new, the elements that encourage us to hope for the very highest literary effects from those born within her borders. Why, we have had these effects already. We have had our antiquarians, our historians, our novelists, and our poets. What more do we want? We have a literature of Quebec, we have a literature of Canada, and what matters it whether it is to be called Quebec literature or Canadian literature. It is literature enswathed in the sweet rhythmic language of *La Belle France*, or the rounding periods of a wholesome English, and that is about all we need trouble ourselves with unless we would wish to see men laugh at our vanity. And let me go no further than Quebec, the city compassed about with every variety of the picturesque and the beautiful, to learn the lesson that Canada has in itself the elements to produce the highest type of the literary man.

The statement is frequently made, and by many believed to be a true statement, that the educational system of Ontario is responsible for the large number of our young men and educated young men to be found in the United States of America. The last census of the United States, 1890, claims that there were then in the States 1,000,000 Canadians, or about 20% of our population. For the accuracy of this statement we do not vouch. A graduate of Victoria University, who has been intimately associated with it and its work for the last forty years or more, and knows the history of all its graduates in Arts (they number now about 600), says that about 10% of these graduates have gone to the United States. Do the people then go in larger numbers than graduates in Arts? The same university has 1,500 graduates in Medicine; a very much larger percentage of them have gone to the neighboring country than of the graduates in Arts, probably 35% at least. These facts do not show that, as far as the graduates of Victoria University are concerned, that the tendency amongst the graduates is much stronger than among the people generally, to go to the United States. And still the impression is strong and general among our people that our system of education leads the young people from the farm to the city, and then, for want of work, they drift off to the more populous and more wealthy country. Is this impression on the part of our people well founded? The supporters of this magazine would do the country good service by turning their attention actively to this important educational question, and report the results of their enquiry by writing to THE EDUCATIONAL MONTHLY. The whole country is vitally concerned in the truth or falsehood of this statement.

PROFESSIONAL HINTS AND CORESPONDENCE.

ATTENTION.

EVERY intelligent teacher knows that any school work is utterly worthless without the attention of the pupil; and this is equally true of all grades and kinds of school, from kindergarten to universisty. But the troublesome question often is, how to secure this *sine qua non?* In truth, many teachers, without knowing it, do much to prevent attention; they are often inattentive themselves; they *fidget*, in their walk and in their ways; they *talk too much*, and their many words are too often spoken without reflection, the pupil learns not to attach much meaning or importance to what they say; they begin an exercise before they have secured attention, and they go forward with it when the attention has wandered. Probably there are very few teachers who are not sometimes at fault in some of these ways. It is a mistake to call often for attention, or to plead for it; and, with little children, the teacher should *never* ask for attention. The attention of little children is intense when they give it, but it is not under the control of the will; the skillful primary teacher will attract it in some demand it. It may sometimes be helpful to request the children to *look at you;* they can do that, and if they do it, they are more likely to attend, alway, but will make no attempt to though it is not certain that they will do so.

We will venture a few suggestions that may be found helpful in securing attention:

Make no demand, issue no order, announce no lesson, till you have thought just what you are going to say; then say it in the most straightforward way, clearly, in the fewest words possible, and *say it but once.*

Begin no exercise till you have a good degree of attention; if the attention wavers, stop the work.

Be careful to have nothing to distract attention if it can be avoided.

With little children, never call for attention; seldom do so with pupils of any age. It is better to stand quietly, self-controlled, and look the pupil squarely in the face till attention secured.

Occasionally some pleasing exercises may be introduced to cultivate the attention. For instance, let the teacher or some pupil repeat a sentence or a quotation, and see who can repeat it exactly. Let the teacher whisper a little story in the ear of a pupil, let him whisper it to his neighor, and he to the next one, and so on till the last returns it to the teacher. If the story has changed through someone's inattention, as it probably has, find out with whom the change ocurred.

Probably, it is not wise to spend much time in special exercises to cultivate the attention of pupils; but the truth is, that everything said or done in the school will cultivate a habit of attention or its opposite.

DISCIPLINE HINTS.

Employment, that is not irksome, is one of the first requisites of easy discipline. It is the idle who are troublesome, in school and in society; and the wise teacher will prevent rather than cure wrong. It is less expensive and saves wear and tear.

Order which has to be advertised, catered to, preached about, sacrificed for very much, is spurious. The genuine "Simon-pure" article is unobtrusive, natural, and has nothing of the tyrant in its sway. It makes few laws and fewer law-breakers. Beware the order which is only part of a huge "crushing" machine.

Distrust and deceit go hand in hand. The presence of one presupposes that of the other. The judicious teacher avoids both, but cultivates their opposites in herself and her pupils.

The discipline whose effect is most ennobling and most salutary, which uses the least friction in attaining the best results, is the ideal discipline for school, home, society, and nations.

You can create the sentiment which will secure perfect self-discipline in your school—but you can only create it by living up to a high ideal yourself. You will hardly expect to push a school to a higher plane than your own—though you may lift it to one much higher than it occupies, and your quiet, voiceless example will do infinitely more in this work than volumes of sermons or lectures on the subject.

Your weakness will be rendered visible by the conduct of your school, which in a large measure merely reflects you. Your strength will show in the same way.

Firmness does not mean obstinacy, any more than kindness is a synonym for weakness, although too often these are mistaken for each other. Be as ready to retreat from a false or mistaken position as you are to maintain a right one.

Threats are as unbecoming to your dignity as they are unsuited to your character and position as teacher. They are not only unnecessary, but absolutely detrimental, and are resorted to only by weak, cowardly, or powerless teachers. Punish when you must—but don't threaten.

Discipline is not "all there is of teaching"—but it is a large subject, and cannot be learned on paper. The theory that fits one case may miss the next dozen, or hundred. Study the art of easy discipline and you will see that it largely depends on your own perfect self-control.—*The New Education.*

CURRENT EVENTS AND COMMENTS.

THE eclât of progressiveness in the "New McGill" has lately been finding its way to the Arts Faculty, and it is almost enough to make some of the old benefactors and benefactresses of the institution turn in their graves, as many of the very pious folks of Montreal have been saying, to see the direction such progressiveness has taken. The energies of the McGill professors of classics have, as everybody knows, for months back been devoted to the task of preparing the *Rudens* of Plautus for the stage, and now that the whole local excitement over the completion of the task is a thing of the past, the patrons of the college are finding it hard to count the educational gains arising from the event. It would not do for us to throw cold water on educational progress in any form; and when it has been shown that there are to be discovered traces of a true educational progress in such a movement as this, we will be the first to encourage its repetition. A prominent actor published certain critical remarks on the subject, a day or two before the play was produced, but the "logic of the boys" came down upon him, and perhaps it was well for him that his engagement in the city was at an end before his critique appeared, or the boys might, in their own peculiar way, have backed up Mr. George Murray's accusation against the critic that he could not spell correctly. It is a good thing also that the Ministerial Association of Montreal did not frown upon the movement, or some of them might also have had their English attacked. As we do not desire to have either our English or our spelling defamed, we refrain from criticising the movement. That there has been collateral gain in the excellent articles which have appeared in the newspapers over the event no one can deny, and if it has done no other good than this, Canadians must greet it as a successful advertisement of what is becoming one of the most efficient faculties of the ever-developing McGill.

The movement in favor of the appointment of a Professor of Pedagogy in McGill University has nothing of a doubtful movement about it, and associated as the new professor must be with Faculty of Arts, it will do much to bring the work of that department into direct contact with the school movements of the Province of Quebec at least. The success of the Ontario School of Pedagogy, it is to be hoped, will be repeated in a province which, if all reports be true, is at present languishing for educational progress through an improved system of training for teachers. The reorganization of the McGill Normal School to meet the wants of the Quebecers is, it is said, all but an aecomplished fact, as far as the formulating of regulations go, and when this is done, what with an increased subsidy and improved inspection, there may be hope, educationally speaking, for the oldest province of Canada after all.

The retirement of Mr. John March from the superintendency of the schools of the city of St. John, New Brunswick, is a matter of much regret to all who know of the work which he has done in connection with the Board of Education there. As the *Review*, published in that city, says: "For twenty-five years no one has been so closely identified with the common schools of St. John as Mr. March, in his position both of secretary and superintendent. Of a genial disposition, ready sympathies, and possessed of rare tact and a skill for organization, he exercised an influence with teachers, parents and children that tended in a great degree to secure that harmony which is so essential in carrying out a system of free school education. He was always ready to devote himself without stint in the service in which he was engaged. It is a matter of regret that a man in the full possession of his powers, and at an age when he cannot readily turn to any other employment, should not be retained in a position in which, it has been shown, he has done so much excellent work."

It is reported that some difficulty has arisen between the professors and students of Morrin College on the score of discipline, and that several of the latter have threatened to leave at the end of the year. We trust that better counsels will prevail among the students, as the institution can hardly continue along the lines of its present prosperity if internal dissensions take hold of it, when it is in the way of leading its friends to hope for the best results under the management of the lately-appointed principal, the Rev. Dr. McRae.

It is difficult to know how some men reach their conclusions. At a late conference of headmasters of England, a discussion took place on the training of teachers, showing, as the report says, a growing opinion in favor of giving professional training to young men who propose to become assistant teachers in our public schools. It seems somewhat late in the day to be discussing such a question. We have had training colleges for elementary teachers for now over half a century, and whatever be the defects of these colleges we have never heard anyone suggest that elementary teachers would be improved by having no training. Dr. James, the highly successful head-master of Rugby, whose opinion properly carries with it great weight, is reported as having said that he did not believe in the training of teachers, and that the only instance he knew of its being tried was a failure. The public will judge for themselves whether a single instance, carried on under unspecified conditions, justifies so definite a conclusion. There is surely no one in Canada who is likely to hold with Dr. James in his opinion, high though his success as a teacher may be.

An admirably lucid and highly important volume on "Juvenile Offenders," written by Mr. Douglas Morrison, and published by Mr. Fisher Unwin, makes its appearance at what might be called, in two distinct senses, "the psychological moment." In the first place, the Education Department has just appointed a committee to report on the education of children of defective intellect. The committee are instructed to enquire into the existing systems for the education of feeble-minded and defective children, not under the charge of guardians, and not idiots or imbeciles, and to advise as to any changes, either with or without legislation, that may be desirable; to report particularly upon the best practical means for discriminating between the educable and non-educable classes of feeble-minded and defective children, and between children who may properly be taught in ordinary elementary schools by ordinary methods and those who should be taught in special schools; and to enquire and report as to the provision of suitable elementary education for epileptic children, and to advise as to any changes that may be desirable.

The Association of Headmasters of England, whose report for the past year gives evidence of much useful work, was formed in 1890, with the idea of bringing uniformity into the examinations which admit into public secondary schools, of attempting to guide secondary legislation, and of fully informing the public on all questions of secondary education. Starting with forty members, in the course of six years it has expanded to some four hundred. Originally it was recruited from the masters of schools which come immediately next to those represented at the Headmasters' Conference, and there was some apparent rivalry between the two organizations, for the conference passed a resolution that it was undesirable for headmasters to belong to both societies. In December, 1895, however, this resolution was withdrawn, and to-day more than a third of the headmasters who belong to the conference belong also to the association. There is possibly room for some such association in each of the the Canadian provinces.

Sir Joshua Fitch, late Senior Inspector of the Education Department, delivered an address at the School of

Arts and Crafts, Bedford Park, last week, in the course of which he referred to the subject of female education. We were living now, he said, in the reign of the most illustrious female sovereign who had ever sat upon the English throne. It was appropriate to remember that the reign of her Majesty had witnessed the greatest advance in female education ever made in this or any other country. At the commencement of the reign women possessed no university rights or privileges, and there were no schools for girls conducted upon liberal educational principles. These now existed and flourished everywhere, and many honorable and lucrative pursuits and professions were opened to women which were closed to them a few years ago. Many careers of public usefulness were offered for their choice, in connection with the administration of the poor law, with School Board work, with other branches of local government, and with the administration of charity. In these various public offices many women were engaged with the utmost honor to themselves and profit to the community. Nowadays there were more opportunities than ever before for utilizing and developing the special knowledge and peculiar qualities of women. To his mind this was one of the greatest features of the reign of Queen Victoria.

In Sir Philip Magnus's opinion, the London institutes give facilities not only for technical but also for literary and general education which are not obtainable on the same scale and on similar lines in any other capital in the world. How, then, does it happen, asks the *Journal of Education*' that our merchants' and bankers, clerks and our commercial travellers are inferior to those of Germany and Switzerland, if not of France? Simply because so much of our primary education is inferior, and, consequently, lads are not able to profit by the evening classes and technical instruction provided for them.

In a sermon preached to the undergraduates of Balliol College, Dr. Jowett declared the relation of the teacher to be "a personal one." He said that some persons did not understand that teaching had anything to do with sympathy.

"The gifts they look for in the teacher are knowledge of the subject, clearness in the arrangement of materials, power of illustration, accuracy, dilligence—nor can any one be a good teacher in whom these qualities are wanting. And yet much more than this is required. For the young have to be educated through the heart as well as through the head; the subtle influence of the teacher's character, his love of truth, his disinterestedness, his zeal for knowledge, should act imperceptibly upon them. . . . He who is capable of taking an interest in each of his pupils individually; who by a sympathetic power can reach what is working in their hearts or perplexing their understanding; who has such a feeling for them that he has acquired the right to say anything to them—has in him the elements of a great teacher."

Those qualities in a teacher are not ensured by the possession of a university degree or a training certificate. We are aware that Education Departments would regard Dr. Jowett's words as a counsel of perfection. Nevertheless in these days, when "doubts, disputes, distractions, fears" are almost synonyms for the term education, it is well to keep in view the ideal of the great Oxford teacher.

A British Expedition.—[Benin is a small kingdom of Guinea, western

Africa. The interior is hilly and the soil fertile. Sugar, rice, cotton and palm oil are the principal products. Benin City, a town situated on the Benin River, a mouth of the Niger River, is the capital. It has a population of about 15 000.]

A British expedition consisting of Consul-General Phillips, Major Crawford, Captain Boisragon, Captain Maling, Mr. Campbell and Mr. Locke, consular officers, Dr. Elliot, Mr. Powis and Mr. Gordon, with a number of native carriers, was attacked recently and all but two of the party massacred by subjects of the King of Benin. The expedition set out from Bonny, a port of Guinea on the western coast of Africa, on January 1st. The object of the journey was, it is claimed, to open trade relations with Benin City, a town in the interior on a mouth of the Niger River. The Expedition was unarmed and fell victims to the suspecting natives.

The British Government has decided to avenge the death of the members of this expedition. It has accordingly sent a number of British officers to Guinea, who will take charge of an armed force to compel the King of Benin to account for the massacre. The force will proceed in launches up the Niger River to Sapeli, and from that point by boat to Benin City. This march will be fraught with many dangers, as large malarial swamps lie between Benin City and the river, and the road is nothing but a narrow path through the jungle.

Go to your class with a sunny temper and a cheerful countenance. These cannot be assured if you do not retire early enough for a night's thorough rest of body and mind, after an evening devoted to some rational relaxation following your day's exhausting labor.—*Ex.*

CHAMBERLAIN ON COMMERCE—The commercial aspects of England's Colonial development were dealt with by Mr. Chamberlain in an address before the Birmingham Chamber of Commerce. His remarks are reported in a condensed way in The Christian World as follows: The present Government, he asserted, had, from the moment of accepting office, looked upon the maintenance of commerce as its most important duty. All the great offices of State were engaged in commercial affairs. The Foreign Office and the Colonial Office were chiefly engaged in finding new markets and defending old ones. The War Office and the Admirality were mainly occupied in preparing for the defence of these markets, for the protection of our commerce. In our Colonial policy, as fast as we acquired new territory we developed it, as trustees for the civilization of the commerce of the world. Other nations, on acquiring new territory, shut out all competition so that their own subjects might have a monoply of trade. We offered an open field to foreigners, and placed them on equal terms with our own people. In the last twelve months Great Britain, at a small expenditure of life and treasure, had rescued from the hands of two "great assassins" two provinces, Dongola and Ashanti, where trade had previously been imposible, seeing that no man could call his life or his property his own. In these two countries the number of victims of the bloodthirsty tyranny of native princes had been tenfold that of the people massacred by the Turk. "Yet I find that those who have been preaching a crusade for the Armenians say not one word of sympathy or approval for a policy which has, I believe, diminished the sum of human misery by a greater amount than even if we had secured the destruction of the Turkish Empire."

SCHOOL WORK.

EDUCATION DEPARTMENT.

SCIENCE.

Editor.—J. B. Turner, B.A.

SCIENCE READERS.

I.

Nature Study is gradually making its way towards recognition as a subject which will render school work more pleasant and profitable than, in many cases, it has been in the past.

To meet the ever-increasing demands, both of teachers and pupils, in this direction, numerous courses of study have been outlined by eminent educationists, and not a few books have been issued dealing with the subject. Among these latter are Murche's "Object Lessons in Elementary Science," which were shortly followed by "Science Readers," by the same author. The "Object Lessons" are for the use of the teacher, and outline a course in elementary science intended to cover the whole of the time spent by pupils in the public schools of London, England. In the use of these books it is not intended that the teacher shall take exactly the lessons laid down by the author, but that he shall be guided by them in conducting his work in the conditions in which he is placed. Wherever experiments are used they are such as to require only the simplest apparatus and very inexpensive material. In the conduct of classes in Nature Study, it is desirable that the actual objects be used, and not pictures or charts of them. One important point insisted on by the author is that wherever possible a specimen of the "Object of Study" should be placed in the hands of *each pupil.*

The "Readers" extend over the work of the same grades as the "Object Lessons," and they are intended for use after the work outlined in the Lessons has been taken up in the class.

The author, in his preface, says that "Although the subjects follow the general course of the Teacher's Oral Lessons, the order has been considerably altered, with the view of avoiding monotony in the character of the successive lessons, and of maintaining as far as possible a general level of attractiveness throughout each book."

This attractiveness has been secured by well-graded lessons, both as to subject matter and the language employed. The series begins with easy lessons on objects that are familiar to every pupil, and proceeds by easy steps to less familiar objects, and as the pupil advances the points that are brought to his attention become more important, so that the advanced pupils will not feel that they are being trifled with.

According to the present programme of studies in our public schools these books can only be used for supplementary reading, which is a part of the regular work in all our best schools.

By the use of these books in this department of school work, a great deal can be done to arouse the interest and excite the attention of the pupils, and at the same time there will be brought before the child much knowledge of common things, which will be useful in after life.

The style of these books is attractive, and the illustrations are particularly good, and it is to be hoped that they will be extensively used, especially in junior classes.

II.

The following are the solutions of two problems which were in the Senior Leaving Chemistry paper, published in the Science Column of THE MONTHLY in the January number of this year:

The cubic contents of the cylinder is $^{25}/_2 \times ^{25}/_2 \times ^{22}/_7 \times 50$ cc's, and this is equal to

$$\frac{^{25}/_2 \times ^{25}/_2 \times ^{22}/_7 \times 50}{1{,}000} \text{ litres.}$$

$$= \frac{625 \times 22 \times 50}{4 \times 7 \times 1000} \text{ litres.}$$

And this is measured at 25° C and 600^{mm} pressure.

∴ At standard temperature and pressure it will measure

$$\frac{625 \times 22 \times 50}{4 \times 7 \times 1{,}000} \times ^{273}/_{298} \times ^{600}/_{760} \text{ litres,}$$

but 11.2 litres of carbon monoxide at standard temperature and pressure weigh 14 grams. ∴ the gas in the cylinder will weigh

$$\frac{625 \times 22 \times 50 \times 273 \times 600 \times 140}{4 \times 7 \times 1\,000 \times 298 \times 760 \times 112}$$

grams = 22.19 grams. *Ans.*

The number of calories absorbed by the ice as it is raised from − 40° C to 0°C will be 200 × 40 × .5 = 4,000.

The number of calories absorbed by the ice while melting will be 200 × 79 = 15,800, since 79 is the latent heat of water.

The water formed from the ice will absorb 200 × 32.5 = 6,500, as its temperature is raised to 32.5° C.

The whole number of calories absorbed by the ice as its temperature is raised from − 40° C to 32.5° C is 4,000 + 15,800 + 6,500 = 26,300 cal.

These are absorbed from the 400 grams of water at 95° C, and the 200 grams of zinc at 100° C as their temperatures are being reduced to 32.5° C, and are equal to 400 × 62.5 + 200 × 67.5 × S.H., where S.H. is the specific heat of zinc.

We have then the following equation: 400 × 62.5 + 200 × 67.5 × S.H. = 26,300 ∴ S.H. = .096 the specific heat of zinc.

CLASSICAL DEPARTMENT.

PRINCIPAL STRANG, GODERICH.

QUESTIONS BASED ON CÆSAR, BOOK III., CHAPTERS 1-6.

I.

1. Translate chapter 3, *Quo consilio—defendere* into good idiomatic English.
2. What difference of idiom between Latin and English is illustrated by the use of *quo* in this sentence?
3. Classify the subjunctives in the passage.
4. Construction of *periculi, subsidio, quibus, parti.*
5. *salute.* What nouns in *us* of the 3d declension are feminine?

II.

1. Translate idiomatically chapter 6, *Quod jussi—recipiunt.*
2. *Sui colligendi.* Point out and, if possible, account for the peculiarity.
3. Distinguish in meaning and use *constare, consistere* and *constituere.*
4. Account for the mood of *fieret,* and the case of *numerum.*
5. *ne—quidem.* What peculiarity in the use of these words?

III.

Translate idiomatically:

(1.) Accedebat quod suos ab se liberos abstractas obsidum nomine dolebant, et Romanos non solum itinerum causa, sed etiam perpetuae possessionis culmina Alpium occupare conari, et ea loca finitima provinciæ adjungere sibi persuasum habibant.

(2.) Nostri hoc superari quod diuturnitate pugnæ. Hostes defessi proelio excedebant, alii integris viribus succedebant; quarum rerum a nostris propter paucitatem fieri nihil poterat, ac non modo defesso ex pugna excedendi, sed ne saucio quidem egus loci ubi constiterat relinquendi, ac sui recipiendi facultas dabatur.

IV.

1. Give the 3d. sing. pres. subj. act. of *consuerat, volebat, dato, positus, perfectæ, jussisset.*

2. Give the pres. inf. pass. of *facio, perficio, patefacio, completa, abstractos, permotus.*

3. Give the abl. sing. and acc. pl. of *omne id iter.*

4. Give the dat. sing. and gen. pl. of *nullus acer impetus.*

5. What prepositions when prefixed to intransitive verbs make them transitive?

6. *tantum periculi.* Give a list of other neuter adjectives similiarly followed by a genitive.

7. Compare *maxime, acrius, saepius*

8. Mark the penult of *demoror, dato, desperat, dividit.*

9. *viribus.* Give all the forms in use of this word.

10. *patiunter.* Write all the active forms of this verb.

V.

Translate into idiomatic Latin based on Cæsar:

1. I have promised to give them permission to cross the river and set fire to the village if they think it necessary.

2. Learning that the heights which overhung this road were held by a strong force of the enemy, we determined to return home by another route.

3. In addition to this, two cohorts had been withdrawn from the legion the previous day to defend the bridge.

4. Knowing that everything depended on valor, our men resisted bravely, and after about two hours' hard fighting put the enemy to flight.

5. Before the enemy could gather enough branches and stones to fill up the trench our men had recovered from their panic.

6. As no enemies hindered us or delayed our march, we reached the camp a little before noon on the third day.

7. Some of the officers thought we should join battle at once, but the majority were of opinion that it was better to wait for reinforcements.

8. We all felt sure they would return next day with a larger force and renew the fight.

9. Not thinking there was any reason to fear an attack, our men had not fortified the camp as carefully as usual.

10. Although their strength as well as their ammunition was giving out, not even the wounded would leave their posts.

ENGLISH DEPARTMENT.

PRINCIPAL STRANG, GODERICH.

FOR ENTRANCE.

I.

Analyse the following simple sentences:

1. *After* a long and *disheartening* struggle and the *expenditure* of a large amount of money, the attempt *to overcome* these difficulties was finally abandoned by the company.

2. *Picking* up the *noisier* of the two children he soon *succeeded* in diverting its attention and *making* it *forget* its griefs for a time.

3. *Never* probably in the history of the settlement had *there* been so good a prospect of an abundant harvest and a prosperous *future.*

II.

Write out the subordinate clauses in the following in full, classify each, and give its relation:

1. And *still*, as fast as he drew
   near,
'Twas wonderful *to view,*
How in a trice the turnpike men
Their gates *wide open* threw.

2. But not *performing what* he meant,
And gladly would have done,
The frighted steed he frighted more
And *made* him faster *run*.

3. And now the turnpike gates again
Flew open in short space,
The *tollmen thinking* as *before*,
That Gilpin rode a race.

III.

1. Parse the italicised words in I. and II.

2. Write the 3d sing. of each tense of the indicative passive of the verb *forget*.

3. Give all the other inflected forms of the verb from which *flew* comes.

4. Why are participles in *ing* called imperfect participles?

5. Mention two classes of dissyllabic adjectives that are compared by *er* and *est*.

6. Select all the preposition phrases in I., classify each according to its grammatical value, and give its relation.

7. Give nouns derived from *long*, *abundant*, and adjectives derived from *history*, *money*, *prospect*.

8. Write sentences using *long* as an adverb, *time* as a verb, *good* as a noun, and *future* as an adjective.

9. Write sentences showing what different kinds of attributive modifiers a subject may have.

10. Write a sentence containing a noun clause, an adjective clause and an adverbial clause.

For Public School Leaving.

1. Write out in full the subordinate clauses in the following, classify each, and give its relation.

(*a*) So Eden was a *scene* of harmless sport,
Where kindness on *his* part who ruled the whole
Begat a tranquil confidence in *all*,
And fear as yet was not, nor cause of fear.

(*b*) Nor less composure waits upon the roar
Of distant floods, or *on* the softer voice
Of neighboring fountain, and rills that slip
Through the cleft rock, and *chiming* as they fall
Upon loose pebbles, lose themthemselves at length
In matted grass *that* with a livelier green
Betrays the secret of their silent course.

(*c*) *Short* as in retrospect life's journey seems,
It seemed not always short; the rugged path,
And prospect oft so dreary and *forlorn*,
Moved many a sigh at its disheartening length—
Yet, *feeling* present evils, while the *past*
Faintly impress the mind, or *not* at *all*,
How readily we wish time spent *revoked*,
That we might try the ground again where once,
Through inexperience, as we now perceive,
We missed that happiness we might have found!

2. Parse the italicised words in (*a*), (*b*), and (*c*).

3. Select the preposition phrases in (*b*), classify each according to its grammatical value, and give its relation.

4. Write down all the participles of *begat*, and all the infinitive forms of *lose*.

5. Form nouns from *scene*, *betray*, *dreary*, adjectives from *sport*, *ground*, *rock*, and verbs from *tranquil*, *fall*, *short*.

6. Write sentences using *all* as an adverb, *less* as a noun, *secret* as an adjective, *past* as a preposition, and *cause* as a verb.

7. Name and exemplify as many kinds of adverbial clauses as you can.

8. Name, with examples, the different classes of adjectives that can't be compared.

9. Give four different examples of foreign words retaining a foreign plural ending in English.

10. Explain, with examples, what you mean by a verb of incomplete predication.

FOR PRIMARY.

"Thus formed, thus placed, intelligent, and taught,
Look where he will, the wonders God has wrought,
The wildest scorner of his Maker's laws
Finds in a sober moment time to pause,
To press the important question on his heart,
'Why formed at all, and wherefore as thou art?'
If man be what he seems, this hour a slave,
The next mere dust and ashes in the grave;
Endued with reason only to descry
His crimes and follies with an aching eye;
With passions just that he may prove, with pain,
The force he spends against their fury vain;
And if, soon after having burned, by turns,
With every lust with which frail Nature burns,
His being end where death dissolves the bond,
The tomb takes all, and all the black beyond;
Then he, of all that Nature has brought forth,
Stands self-impeached the creature of least worth,
And useless while he lives, and when he dies,
Brings into doubt the wisdom of the skies.

1. Write out in full each subordinate clause in the first six lines, classify it, and give its relation.

2. Select the infinitive phrases, classify each according to its grammatical value, and give its relation.

3. Classify the following words and give the relation of each: *taught*, *wherefore*, *what*, *next*, *endued*, *vain*, *being*.

4. Give the relation of *wonders*, and point out anything peculiar in regard to it.

5. Parse fully the word *take* in line 16.

6. Select from the passage an example each, of a predicate nominative, an adverb modifying a phrase, an adverb modifying a clause, a gerund, a noun in the adverbial adjective.

7. Is *will*, in line 2, a notional verb or a relational verb? Give your reasons for your answer.

8. Account, if you can, for the form *wrought* as a part of the verb *work*.

9. Is *teach* a verb of the old conjugation or of the new? Give your reason for your answer.

10. Give two examples each, of nouns having only a plural form, nouns having two plural forms, nouns having two wholly different meanings for one plural form, nouns retaining a foreign plural form, nouns having no plural form.

11. Write a sentence of ten words, all of native origin, and another of five words, all of foreign origin.

12. Give as many reasons as you can to account for the fact that our scientific terms are mostly of classical and especially of Greek origin.

ENTRANCE ARITHMETIC.

1. A boy's hoop is $3^1/_2$ ft. in circumference; how many turns will it make in going $^7/_8$ of a mile?

2. The front wheel of a carriage is $10^1/_2$ ft. in circumference, and the hind wheel $11^2/_3$ ft.; how many revolutions will each make in going $8^3/_4$ miles?

3. The front wheel of a carriage is $6^2/_3$ ft. in circumference, and makes 1,056 revolutions more than the hind wheel in going 20 miles. What is the circumference of the hind wheel?

4. The hind wheel of a waggon is 10 ft. in circumference, and makes 330 fewer revolutions than the front wheel in going $2^1/_2$ miles. Find the circumference of the front wheel.

5. The hind wheel of a carriage is $7^6/_7$ ft. in circumference, and the front wheel $6^3/_5$ ft.; how many feet must the carriage travel before the latter has made 20 revolutions more than the former?

6. A newsboy buys newspapers at the rate of 6 for 5 cents, and sells them at the rate of 8 for 9 cents. Find his gain per cent.

7. A tradesman marks his goods at an advance of 40 per cent. on cost, but gives a customer a reduction of 30 per cent.; what per cent. does the merchant gain or lose?

8. How much per cent. above cost must a man mark his goods in order to take off 20 per cent., and still make 30 per cent. profit?

9. A drover sold two cows at $60 each; on one he gained 20 per cent., and on the other he lost 25 per cent.; did he gain or lose, and what per cent.?

10. If $^4/_5$ of the cost price equals $^3/_4$ of the selling price, find the gain per cent.?

Answers. (1) 11,320. (2) 4,400, and 3,960 respectively. (3) $7^1/_7$ ft. (4) 8 ft. (5) 825 ft. (6) 35. (7) Loses 2 per cent. (8) $62^1/_2$ per cent. (9) $6^1/_4$ per cent. loss. (10) $6^2/_3$ per cent.

1. In what time will any sum of money double itself at 5 per cent, per annum? At 6? At 7? At 8? At 10?

2. At what rate will any sum of money double itself in 20 yrs? In 30? In 25? In 12? In 15?

3. (*a*) In what time will the interest on $300 be $60 at 5 per cent?

(*b*) In what time will the interest on $250 be $70 at 4 per cent.?

(*c*) In what time will the interest on $1,000 be $180 at 7 per cent.?

(*d*) In what time will the interest on $600 be $540 at 3 per cent?

(*e*) In what time will the interest on $150 be $72 at 6 per cent.?

(*f*) In what time will $500 amount to $620 at 4 per cent.?

(*g*) In what time will $250 amount to $310 at 6 per cent.?

(*h*) In what time will $200 amount to $245 at $4^1/_2$ per cent.?

(*i*) In what time will $350 amount to $434 at 4 per cent.?

(*j*) In what time will $1,500 amount to $1,900 at 6 per cent.?

4. (*a*) At what rate will the interest on $1,000 for 3 yrs. be $210?

(*b*) At what rate will the interest on $600 for 8 yrs. be $144?

(*c*) At what rate will the interest on $550 for 4 yrs. be $110?

(*d*) At what rate will the interest on $250 for 8 yrs. be $320?

(*e*) At what rate will the interest on $120 for 10 yrs. be $90?

(*f*) At what rate will $500 amount to $680 in 6 years?

(*g*) At what rate will $750 amount to $900 in 6 years?

(*h*) At what rate will $1,200 amount to $1,344 in 4 years?

(*i*) At what rate will $300 amount to $450 in 10 years?

(*j*) At what rate will $450 amount to $600 in 5 years?

5. (*a*) $50 is interest on what sum for 4 years at 5 per cent?

(*b*) $36 is interest on what sum for $4^1/_2$ years at 4 per cent?

(*c*) \$300 is interest on what sum for $2^1/_2$ years at 8 per cent?

(*d*) \$66 is interest on what sum for $5^1/_2$ years at 4 per cent.

(*e*) \$120 is interest on what sum for $7^1/_2$ years at 2 per cent?

(*f*) What principal will amount to \$324 in 2 years at 4 per cent?

(*g*) What principal will amount to \$266 in 6 years at $5^1/_2$ per cent?

(*h*) What principal will amount to \$780 in 4 years at 5 per cent?

(*i*) What principal will amount to \$1,120 in 6 years at $6^2/_3$ per cent?

(*j*) What principal will amount to \$179.20 in $1^1/_2$ years at 8 per cent?

Answers: No. 1. 20 years; $16^2/_3$, $14^2/_7$, $12^1/_2$, 10.

2 5 per cent, $3^1/_3$, 4, $8^1/_3$, $6^2/_3$.

3. 4 years, 7, $2^4/_7$, 3, 8, 6, 4, 5, 7, $4^4/_9$.

4. 7 per cent, 3, 5, 16, $7^1/_2$, 9, $3^1/_3$, 3, 5, $6^2/_3$.

5. \$250, \$200, \$1,500, \$300, \$800 \$300, \$200, \$650, \$800, \$160.

GEOGRAPHY FOR FOURTH CLASSES.

(*a*) Where and for what noted are:

1. Cannes, Nice, Saratoga, Tokay, Nanaimo, Oporto, Cronstadt, Leith, Civita Vecchia, Havre?

2. Johannesburg, Frankfort, Marseilles, Trieste, St. John's, Cacouna, Cracow.

(*b*) 1. Name the Capitals of the following islands: Sardina, Ceylon, Sicily, Iceland, Malta, Cuba, Corsica, Madagascar, Java, Japan.

2. Give the names of the leading cities on the following rivers: Thames, Rhine, Volga, Amazon, Mississippi, Danube, Ganges, Clyde, Seine, Rhone.

(*c*) 1. Tell where the following mountain peaks are: Elburz, Blanc, Popocatepetl, The Peak, Chimborazo, St. Gothard, Snowdon, Ararat.

2. Where are: The Iron Gate, The Golden Horn, The Maelstorm, The St. Gothard Tunnel, The Campagna, The Military Frontier, The Dollart, the Lighthouse of the Mediterranean, The Tundras, The Golden Gate?

Statesman, yet friend to truth; of soul sincere,
In action faithful, and in honor clear;
Who broke no promise, serv'd no private end,
Who gain'd no title, and who lost no friend;
Ennobled by himself, by all approv'd.
—*Pope.*

CONTEMPORARY LITERATURE.

We have received the Students' Edition of Canadian History, arranged according to Scaife's well-known Synoptical Plan; the period embraced is from 1492 to 1897. This chart is well compiled and attractively displayed with appropriate colors. In this way many of "the long results of time" may be seen at a glance. We trust it will be found helpful to all those who are engaged in studying the history of our country.

We have received from William Tyrrell & Co., King Street, "Souvenirs of the Past," by William Lewis Bâby, a book of reminiscences, dealing with the customs of the pioneers of Canada. The interest in the historical aspect of our country is steadily increasing, and the class to which a work such as this appeals is no longer a small one. Much that is interesting and amusing may be found in its pages. It is sincerely to be regretted that salmon no longer swarm in the pellucid waters of the Don and Humber.

"Matthew Arnold's Poems," selected and edited by G. C. Macaulay Macmillan & Co., London; Copp, Clark & Co., Toronto. A careful and scholarly addition to books which may be prescribed for reading by older scholars. Much useful and some new information about the setting of many of the poems is given.

"Selections from Malory's Le Morte D'Arthur," by A. T. Martin. Macmillan & Co., London; Copp, Clark & Co., Toronto. Once having caught the note of the romance of old England from Tennyson and Spenser, any student of literature would eagerly follow it in Malory. It is profit enough to be interested in the story.

"An Introduction to the Study of Chemistry," by W. H. Perkin and Bevan Lean. Macmillan & Co., London; Copp, Clark & Co., Toronto. A thoroughly modern book, in which methods of research will be found, given in a clear and interesting manner.

"English Literature," by Stopford A. Brooke. The Macmillan Co., New York; William Tyrrell & Co., Toronto. The teachers of English literature will derive encouragement and assistance from the excellence of this survey of the work accomplished in letters by English writers from 670-1832. It would be futile to reiterate comment on the unsurpassed succession of masters whose works are our inheritance. Few can equal Mr. Brooke in his conception of what they have done.

We have also received from The Macmillan Co., through the William Tyrrell Co., a text-book in the Elementary Classics Series, "Cornelius Nepos," edited by J. E. Barss.

And from the Macmillan Co., London, through Messrs. Copp, Clark, "Mensuration for Beginners," by F. H. Stevens and Minna Von Barnhelm, edited by the Rev. Chas. Meek.

In the Athenæum Press Series Ginn & Co. have recently issued a pleasing edition of Carlyle's "Sartor Resartus," edited by Archibald MacMechan, of Dalhousie College. Those who count this the most noble expression of Carlyle's belief will welcome any event which helps to bring it near to the minds of students. The notes are discriminating and just, while one whose knowledge has many limits will often find them necessary. We note with pleasure the name of a Canadian professor on the title page.

From Ginn & Co. we have also received "Ninth Book of Virgil's Æneid," edited by E. H. Cutler, and "Easy Latin for Sight Reading," edited by B. L. D'Ooge.

The University Press, Cambridge, "A Manual and Dictionary of the Flowering Plants and Ferns," vols. 1 and 2, by J. C. Willis, M.A., Director of the Royal Botanic Gardens, Ceylon. Any work issued under this publishing name cannot but be distinguished by great excellence in all that pertains to its furnishing. Students in Botany will at the same time derive pleasure from so comprehensive and thoroughly scientific exposition of this great division of their subject.

"The Story of the Chosen People," by H. A. Guerber. The American Book Co., New York. Many well-known books have been issued in this valuable series, but none possessing a more peculiar interest than the present one. The illustrations are particularly fine.

From the same company we have received "Our Little Book for Little Folks," by W. E. Crosby.

"Fragments from Fénelon Concerning Education." Bonnell, Silver

& Co., New York. Not only teachers, but any one interested in learning and teaching, will be interested and benefited by this little book.

The interest of our American neighbors in their war literature is certainly extraordinary. The *Century* publishers are more than satisfied with the sensation that is being produced by their historical serial "Campaigning with Grant." "Hugh Wynne, Free Quaker," appeals to every one, for it is a splendid story, but add to that the fact that it tells of the revolutionary war, and naturally does not glorify the British, and what more can the freeborn American desire? The March number is to be an inauguration one, with articles on life at the White House and the Capital.

McClure's Magazine with the March number will begin the publication of Stevenson's last story, "St. Ives." It is unfortunate that the enterprising publishers have, to some extent, been disappointed in their expectations as to the exclusive right of publishing in America, but no one else will be disappointed, for a more charming or stirring tale was never penned. There is no second Stevenson.

The February number of *Table Talk* opens with "The Lobster at Home," by Helen Louise Johnson, a comprehensive and valuable article which is at the same time bright and entertaining. The usual departments are given together with an article on the Quotation Menu.

Littell's Living Age is shortly to begin the publication of a serial by the eminent Russian author, Ivan Tourgenieff.

Blanche Willis Howard, a lady whose writings one only too seldom sees, has a charming short story called "Marigold-Michel" in the March *Atlantic*. There is also a short article, entitled "Mr. Cleveland as President," by Prof. Woodrow Wilson, dealing with that gentleman's future position in political history. Those who remember Percival Lowell's remarkable papers on Mars, will be glad to see that he has now turned his scientific and highly imaginative eye on Venus.

"The Secret of St. Florel" is concluded in the February number of the *Macmillan's Magazine* with a deplorable death rate. One had not realised that it would need so many removals to make the situation comfortable, it seems a little inartistic. There are a couple of interesting papers, one on Literature and Music, which apparently goes to prove that authors know little of the beauty of sound. This is unkind, for no class of the community celebrates music more than they.

Those who think lightly of the highest English Society would do well to study such an article as "Sunday with the Prince and Princess of Wales," which appears in the March number of the *Quiver*. W. J. Dawson has a short story entitled, "Rue with a Difference."

It would be hard to produce a better number of a reviewing and book news magazine than the February number of the *Book Buyer*. The frontispiece is a satisfactory portrait of Walt Whitman, and the illustrations throughout are excellent, while one finds a sincere pleasure in reading a review of four books of essays, by Agnes Repplier, and one on Margaret Ogilvy, by G. W. Cable. Gilbert Parker contributes a kindly criticism of "In the Village of Viger," by Duncan Campbell Scott.

We have received from the Copp, Clark Co. a copy of "Exercises in

Rhetoric," by J. E. Witherell, pp. 93, price 25 cts., and have pleasure in drawing attention to it. It contains the departmental examination papers for several years, followed by a considerable number of carefully selected passages, some with questions appended, others without, and a review of the leading principles of rhetoric. It will be found convenient and sufficient for class drill.

We have also to thank the same publishers for a set of "Elementary Composition Exercise Books," Nos. 1, 2, 3, for use in second, third, and fourth book classes, respectively, by S. E. Lang, B.A., Inspector of Schools (Man.).

The books, which have been prepared primarily, we presume, for use in the schools of Manitoba, undoubtedly contain a large number of useful exercises, but the arrangement is so different from what we have been accustomed in Ontario to regard as proper that we doubt if they will find much favor with our teachers.

The author, who claims to have followed a logical plan, begins in the second book classes with exercises on unity and continuity of paragraph structure; in No. 2 third book classes begin the study of the sentence, and not till pupils reach the dignity of the fourth book are they required to deal with such difficult tasks as to change the voice of verbs or to substitute words for phrases. Even these they do not reach till they have been asked to "Describe a locomotive engine," and to "Prepare a topical analysis of some novel that you have read."

However it may be that we are old fogies, and prejudiced, so our readers who are called on to teach composition had better get No. 3 of the series and judge for themselves.

Once more British sailors and soldiers have shown the stuff which they are made of, not, happily, in facing the cannon's mouth and with great loss of life, but in the more trying ordeal of shipwreck. The troopship *Warren Hastings* was wrecked off the Island of Reunion on Friday, 15th January. A despatch gives the following particulars: "The troopship ran ashore at 2.20 a.m. and the shock was severe. It was very dark and torrents of rain were falling. She had on board soldiers and crew to the number of 1,122 men, besides a number of women and children, the families of married men of the military force. When the ship struck the troops were ordered to retire from the upper deck, to which they had flocked on the first alarm, and fall in below. This they did promptly with perfect discipline, although the men were fully conscious of the danger which they were in. They were quietly mustered between decks. Owing to the fact that surf boats could not be used in landing the troops, two officers of the *Warren Hastings* were lowered from the ship's bow to the rocks, and when it was found that a landing could be effected in this way the disembarkation of the soldiers was begun at 4 a.m., Commander Holland hoping it was safe to retain the women, children, and sick on board until daylight. But the steamship was soon found to be heeling over so rapidly that everyone was ordered to the upper deck, the danger of capsizing becoming imminent. Commander Holland ordered the landing of the troops to be stopped, so that women, children, and the sick should be landed first. This was obeyed with admirable discipline. By 5 o'clock the decks had heeled over to an angle of fifty degrees to starboard and the boats were all swept away. The good swimmers were then permitted to swim ashore, carrying ropes. By these means many others were landed, and the disembarkation of all on board was completed, with the loss of only two native servants. Many acts of personal bravery are recorded. The French officials and inhabitants of the Island of Reunion gave the shipwrecked people every assistance possible." This recalls similar bravery on the part of the heroes of the *Royal George* and the *Victoria*, but fortunately in the present case only two lives were lost. Such heroic discipline in the face of extreme danger calls for the highest praise. Britons are still worthy of their name and race.—*Ev. Churchman.*

If your pupils are inattentive, wait. Ask yourself why they are inattentive. Perhaps physical conditions are not such as to insure their best mental condition. Look to the temperature and to the ventilation of your room. Be earnest and interested yourself, and they will be interested and attentive.

Do not repeat questions. Ask them in terms understood by your pupils, for they have the inalienable right to know just what your questions mean. When an answer is given, do not repeat it yourself to impress it upon the mind of the inattentive. As well might you try to illumine a cavern with an unlighted torch.

Do not speak in harsh, loud tones. Bring into the classroom your "home voice," your "society manners." Be at your best in the presence of your pupils. Your eyes will often be more effective than your voice in bringing back to the work in hand the pupil's wandering mind, and in preventing or in correcting a thoughtless movement or utterance.—*Ex*

There are three things essential to success in life—conscientiousness, concentration, continuity. In extremity it is character that saves a man. To one object the lines of life should converge. This should be the focal-point of thought and feeling. We must not scatter our powers. Continuity is not incompatible with change; it is the reverse of a fragmentary and desultory mode of life. Every true life is a unit, an organic whole. There is advantage in continuity of place as well as of purpose.—*President Smith, of Dartmouth, 1869.*

THE CANADA EDUCATIONAL MONTHLY.

THE CANADA EDUCATIONAL MONTHLY, we beg to inform our readers, entered upon a new term of service in educational work on the first of January of this year. It is to be hoped that after the following announcements have been carefully considered by our subscribers and fellow-teachers, that their assistance will be secured on behalf of the MONTHLY in more ways than one.

The MONTHLY is by this time one of the oldest educational periodicals in Canada, and it is the intention of all connected with its management to make it of increasing interest to the teachers of Canada and others interested in the educational progress of the country as a whole. Its *corps* of contributors already includes the most prominent of our educational workers, and what with an improved classification of topics, additional help in the editorial work, and a cordial co-operation on the part of subscribers, publishers and advertisers, it may not be too much, perhaps, to expect it to become, in the near future, one of the best and most readable of our educational journals.

It is the intention of the editors to add to the reading matter two new sections at least, perhaps three. One of these will contain a *resumé* of the current events relating to educational movements in Canada and elsewhere. Arrangements have been made to have a record of such events sent by special correspondents from all parts of the Dominion in time for publication at the beginning of each month; aud it is needless to say that paragraph contributions will be gratefully received from all teachers, when events of more than local interest take place in their district.

The second section will comprise hints from and to teachers, with correspondence. In the past, our teachers have been perhaps a little too timid in making suggestions through the press, particularly suggestions founded on their own experience. Fault-finding is a very different thing from honest criticism, and to the latter no teacher should fail to subject every proposed educational change, before finding fault with it or advocating it. Makinguse of the MONTHLY as a medium, it is to be hoped therefore that our teachers will join with us in an open and above-board campaign against all defects, and in favor of all improvements in our school work as well as in our school systems so that eventually through the coordination of educational views from all the provinces, our various school systems will tend towards the unification of our Canadian national life, and not towards its disintegration. In future any question of an educational tendency may be discussed in our correspondence section, and when a *nom de plume* is made use of, the personality of the writer will under no circumstances be revealed.

The third section, when fully organized, will refer to all matters connected with a proposed BUREAU for the purpose of finding situations for teachers or promotion in the service. Every subscriber will have the privilege of inscribing his or her name on the lists about to be opened for those who wish to have their names thus enrolled. As an experiment we hope many of our teachers will find this section of great service to them.

To the subscribers who have stood by us so loyally in the past, we present our most grateful thanks, while to our new subscribers we make promise that their tastes and wishes will always be carefully considered in the management of the paper. Indeed, we feel it is only through the coöperation of our readers that our enterprise can be fostered to its fullest fruition.

During the year, the publishers of the MONTHLY will call upon advertisers under the improved circumstances of the periodical. To our faithful contributors we trust we will be able, as soon as the revenues of our enterprise improve, to return thanks in a more tangible way than heretofore.

The CANADA EDUCATIONAL MONTHLY, our subscribers must understand, is a journal for the whole Dominion, and not for any section or province.

Communications in connection with the editorial management of the paper are, in future, to be sent from Ontario and all the provinces west of Ontario, to Arch. MacMurchy, M.A., Box 2675, Toronto; and from the province of Quebec and the provinces east of Quebec, to Messrs. William Drysdale & Co., St. James St., Montreal, who will also attend to all matters pertaining to the publishing and advertising departments for the Eastern Provinces, and Wm. Tyrrell & Co. will attend to the like business for Ontario. Publishers: Wm. Drysdale & Co., Montreal; Wm. Tyrrell & Co., Toronto; A. Hart & Co., Winnipeg; J. & A. McMillan, St. John, N.B.

THE CANADA
EDUCATIONAL MONTHLY
AND SCHOOL MAGAZINE.

APRIL, 1897.

A FURTHER WORD ON CANADIAN LITERATURE.

By Evelyn Durand.

IT might seem admissible, in order to obtain a hearing, to introduce this subject under some disguise, if a second consideration did not make it a question whether an amused curiosity about what can be said next on the matter has not been aroused in the public mind. We shall soon be able to compile a bibliography of what has been written about Canadian literature, more voluminous than the literature itself. And the different sentiments expressed in these writings, which I am venturing to swell, but only in the least degree, might be distributed among three classes, which shall be briefly indicated.

It would be interesting to know if all countries, ambitious like ours for a literature, have undergone in early stages such self-conscious throbs of pride and despair. They must be largely attributed to the circumstances of our being and growth; inasmuch as we did not exactly rise up out of wildness and barbarism, we are without naïveté. But that which we lack in the beginning shall become ours in the end, for self-forgetfulness springs from earnestness and abandonment from devotion.

Meanwhile the cries of the Prideful and the Despairing are equally obstructive. To the ranks of the former belong the men and women whose ideals in art are accommodated to their means of earning their daily bread. They become editors of magazines and writers on newspapers. They have long columns at their disposal, and they "puff" that they may be "puffed." They publish literary monthlies and determine to live by art; but they do not determine that others shall live likewise, and therefore they make no provision for the payment of contributors. It follows that their contributors are of that class to which writing is not a chief concern. It follows too that the editor falls into a certain position of dependence upon those who gratuitously furnish him with their work. And an unholy alliance is thus formed between them, while the public suffers or becomes indifferent.

When a magazine devoted purely to art is established among us on the same principles as the best magazines in England and the United States, a standard will then be formed and a more reliable public taste. The negative quality of such things as are now received with congratulations, will then make their reception a proper disregard and silence. And may not only those who are quite without discernment be set aside, but may there be for every industrious Gottsched an inexorable Lessing.

We are in utter need of such a standard, for there is a plethora of poor and innocent writers, who should be, not suppressed, but assigned to their rightful places. It is a hopeful thing to see many stirred to artistic expression, nay, more, without the many, the surpassing few are seldom found. And it only becomes a discouraging thing to see the pen or pencil in every hand, when some uninspired canvas is called a masterpiece, or when some jingling rhymes are spoken of as poetry.

The Despairing section of the community entrench themselves behind three arguments which they consider strong enough to render others as passive as themselves. And the first is our lack of nationality. Upon the necessity of this hardly definable quality they dwell with such insistence, that we must almost conclude that the great poets and novelists of the past, first paused to find out whether they had a nationality before setting themselves to their immortal work. We are obliged to assert that we are the sons of Englishmen, Scotchmen and Irishmen; that we are the inheritors of British laws and ideals. The soil upon which we live is, truly, separated by a sea from that upon which our forefathers dwelt, but it would require more seas than the earth possesses to make us less than British. The very language of our art which is to be, is the most wide, most free, most noble English tongue. Genius is no less the creator of nationality than nationality of genius. Luther and Lessing, Schiller and Goethe and Herder, were no more the products than the makers of German nationality; and in every country this relationship is reciprocal and mysterious. They are rash who say this or that is not the ground in which genius can spring, for even as they speak, it shoots above the surface.

The second argument of the Despairing is our lack of wealth. To this it may be answered that wealth has never been the best patron of art. For art is not a manufacture which fluctuates with supply and demand. It may be purchased by money, but never produced. Wealth may indeed be the foster-mother to encourage, but never the true mother to give birth to art. It is certain, however, that material rewards warm both the heart and the hearth of the artist, and it is to be hoped that the increasing opulence of our country will increase these rewards.

And the third argument which is considered to explain the impossibility of a literature for us, is the scattered nature of our population, together with the division of races. Both of these objections disappear before an examination of the history of art in the past. For the greatest poets have had at first the smallest audiences and the fewest readers; nor are there many countries whose inhabitants are of undivided races.

Here again it must be urged as in the matter of wealth, that the workings of art are esoteric, and as independent as the principle of life, of the laws of the scientist.

It may be thought that in removing the three chief barriers to the growth of art, some other obstacle must be found, or the thing itself discovered, for its absence must surely be explained. But this is a mistake—the appearance and disappearance of genius is unexplainable. As it is a perpetual glory, it is a perpetual mystery. It is present or absent without a law discoverable by man.

This being acknowledged, it can be asserted that art has already shown itself among us. We have already made many attempts and castings and approximations. In a few isolated instances the spark was struck, and the imperishable flame is already lit whose light will spread through the land.

If there are two classes distinguished by their attitudes to Canadian literature, as the Prideful and Despairing. there is also a third, the Believing. This is the effectual class, and to it belong alike many who themselves write, and many who do not. These are the men and women who have a simple faith in heart and spirit, which urge us now in the nineteenth century, and here in Canada, towards truth and beauty. They know that they must first seek to *live* in truth and beauty, listening " to stars and birds, babes and sages, with open heart." They feel within themselves, or perceive within others, the passing of desire from temporary to permanent forms of pleasure. They cherish this tendency in others, or in their quiet rooms bend humbly over their hard labor, rewarded already by the thrilling sweetness of their momentary glimpse of art.

They do not fear any kind of criticism, for they are aware that as much of it as errs, is harmless, and as much of it as does not err, is beneficial. And they would rather be found wanting than have anything unworthy pass uncensured.

These are the men and women who do not rush conspicuously forward for notice, who are more anxious for their work than for themselves. They are willing, indeed, to remain unknown, for they recognize the commonalty of art. Their hope is not to proclaim themselves from the pinnacle of their achievement, but to step forth at last, and mingling with the throngs on whom they have bestowed delight and benefit, look on what they have accomplished, forgetting in their thankfulness and wonder by whose imagination it was wrought, as some ancient architect may perhaps have looked upon the perfect outlines of his temple, contented that it was.

AIMS AND MANAGEMENT OF HIGH SCHOOL LITERARY SOCIETIES.*

YOUR minute book will show that Literary Societies in connection with this High School are an old institution, and my experience testifies that some of them have been very prosperous—have succeeded in doing much good, while others have dragged along an existence, and have done little or no good.

Now success or failure to make yours a flourishing, useful Society will depend altogether on your having well-defined aims of what you want to accomplish, on the spirit in which you set about accomplishing it, and the methods you pursue. Now, I take it that if a literary society is to be worthy of its name it will aim, of course, to make its members well and better acquainted with the literature of their own or of some other language, and to enlarge their acquaintance with the best writers in that language by studying their masterpieces. It will by discussing the beauty of thought and elegance of diction of these masterpieces endeavor to improve the literary acumen—the ability to decide wherein the excellence of a piece lies—and to improve the literary taste and literary expression of its members. Then, again, by means of its debates it will seek to increase the information of its members, by making them read up or glean from other sources facts and figures with which

* Substance of an Address given to the Port Hope High School Literary Society, by Dr. Purslow, Hon. President.

to support their own arguments or to refute those of their opponents. It will teach them to array these facts and this information in the most telling and convincing manner, and will give its members confidence and practice in presenting them in language calculated to please and persuade their audience. Am I not right, my young friends, in stating that these are the objects to be aimed at by a Society like that you are starting this evening? If I am right in stating that these are its aims, that this is what you desire to accomplish, then I have to tell you that it means work, it means effort, individual effort as well as collective effort. If good is to be gained, if benefit to mind and tongue is to be derived by each of you from membership in this Society, each must gain that good for himself; no one can gain it for you. This means that each member must read and study diligently the literary selection agreed upon, and bring to the critical discussion of its points some original thought or picked up information. It means that no member must shirk his duty when it becomes his turn to take part in reading, recitation or debate, and that in the latter, he will by diligent reading and research hold up his end of the argument, gain the approbation of the critic and the decision in favor of his side. Have I set the standard so high as to discourage you? I hope not. Remember that that person will never shoot high who does not aim high,—that he will never bring down the eagle if he aims no higher than at a rabbit. So with your Society. I, therefore, strongly advise you to set high your standard of what this Literary Society shall do for its members; with your best efforts you will fall far enough short of it, but if you set your standard low, you won't even reach mediocrity in the result.

But I think I hear some of you saying that to study critically a masterpiece of English literature so as to appreciate the beauty of the thought, and the fitness and elegance of the language it is clothed in, and then to be able to read or recite it so that others shall be able to appreciate both—to read and look up information so as to be able to support an argument in debate, all this means hard work, and our teachers impose enough hard work upon us in our lessons, without our imposing any more upon ourselves. This is true, but it is also true that there is a vast difference in our feelings when we do work imposed by ourselves, and when we do work imposed upon us by others. A boy will work like a horse to drag a heavy bus up a hill, whose back feels broken when his mother asks him to bring in an armful of wood or fetch up a hod of coal; and that girl could go on skating for hours, who is scarcely able to crawl when her mother wishes her to go up stairs for her thimble or pincushion. So, although I am not denying that there will be work about it, I am saying that that work will be attended with a certain degree of pleasure, because you do it voluntarily. Again, suppose it does entail work, I would have you rest assured of the fact, true of Literary Societies as of everything else, that no good was ever got out of anything unless hard work and brains were put into it. If you want the gold you must delve into the mine; if you wish the harvest you must plow the land, sow the seed and reap the grain. Remember, too, that the person who receives a good, or derives a benefit, that he hasn't worked for or paid for in some way is something of a dependent or parasite, pauper or sponge. Don't, then, be discouraged with the work that success will entail. Idleness is not rest, change of work is the best recreation, and your work for the society will be a change from your lessons. Let none of you shirk what work is necessary, and see to it that each one brings into the meetings of the society his very best work. Promise me this, my young friends, and I will prophesy that you will have one of the best Literary Societies the school has ever known.

Now, Mr. Chairman, ladies and gentlemen, so far I have been pointing out the straight high road which will lead to success. Kindly bear with me a little longer, while I indicate some byways and cross paths, down which you may wander and lose yourselves. Perhaps by talking so seriously as I have done, about the work that must be done, I have damped your ardor, have, as it were, thrown a wet blanket over the anticipations of pleasure you expected to get by being members of the society. I shall be very sorry if this is the effect of my remarks; it need not be. In your meetings, usefulness must have its place, and pleasure, too, must have its place, but I would give useful improvement the first place, and pleasure the second. If you reverse these positions, and make pleasure the all in all of your society, why then, by all means call things by their right names and change the title Literary Society into Pleasure-loving or Fun-seeking Society. I speak thus, because this is one of the bye-ways, down which some previous societies have come to grief and ended in failure, so far as mental improvement is concerned. Of course your society has no such members, but I have known boys and girls—I should say young ladies and gentlemen—join a Literary Society purely for the sake of having what they called "a good time;" and a "good time" as they understood it, was a time of unrestrained fun, noise and frolic. Should it be your misfortune to have any such members my advice would be, to weed them out, they will hinder and not help, their influence will tend to wreck the society. On the principle that "all work and no play makes Jack a dull boy," your meetings must be pleasurable, but seek to find your pleasure in the social intercourse, in the music and singing, in the wit and vivacity of the remarks; play pleasant music, sing pleasant songs—I would like to know that the boys make the house ring with the echo of the grand old college songs, songs which will come to their lips in after years in far distant lands. Have pleasure by all means, but don't let it usurp the chief place.

Your mental improvement and your advance in elocutionary and oratorical power, and in the accessories of gesture, tone of voice, etc., will depend very much on your critic. He or she must set high the standard of excellence, must hopefully encourage whatever tends to reach that standard and kindly deprecate every retrograde tendency, and your duty will be to profit all you can, week by week, by the criticisms. With a critic having the correct notions of propriety and the refined literary tastes of the one it is your good fortune to possess in your lady teacher, there is scarcely need for me to warn you of another crossroad—I refer to the temptation there is in young people to select for reading or reciting only pieces that are funny and amusing. The temptation to select such pieces lies in the fact that every reader or speaker naturally likes the approval of the audience, and that pieces of this nature always bring down the house. Let your Programme Committee keep a jealous eye upon such pieces when offered; they may now and then find that some are, to say the least, not elevating. Speaking of applause leads me to advise you to be sparing in the means of showing approbation. I have known literary meetings that noisily applauded all and everything.

This being the case, where was the inducement to read or to say a really good thing?—the poor article got as much approbation as the good. My advice is let nothing be applauded but what is of real merit.

The comfort and pleasantness of your meetings will depend very largely on your president, and on the attention and obedience you give to his rulings. He will have to see that all your meetings are conducted according to the strict rule of parliamentary procedure, and in doing so he will need to exercise a large amount of the *suaviter in modo* and the *fortiter in re*.

In conclusion, let me say that I was glad when I learned that you had formed this society; for I regard a well-managed Literary Society as a most important adjunct to High School training. There will come a time when you will forget much, very much of your Algebra, Euclid, French and Latin, yet, don't think for that reason that you learnt these subjects for nothing. The good they did you lay in the mental effort you put forth in the learning. But the self-confidence you will gain by appearing before this society in stating a point and supporting it by facts and arguments, the knowledge and experience you will gain of the manner in which public meetings should be conducted—these are benefits which will never leave you, but which will stand you in good stead many and many a time in your future lives.

SIMPLICITY IN POETRY.

[Delivered at a Grammar-School Literary and Debating Society.]

THERE is a story told of some children living in an enchanted land who used to play carelessly with what they supposed were worthless pebbles, until one day a traveller came and told them that those stones which they counted as nothing were indeed jewels of great value. Indifference arising from ignorance, or undue familiarity, is not by any means confined to material objects; in matters of taste also the truth of the proverb is seen—"Familiarity breeds contempt." How many boys and girls there must be in the schools of our land who at some time or other have had set them as a repetition lesson Cowper's well-known lines on the "Loss of the Royal George"! They probably think them absurdly easy, and fit only for children of tender years, which they will smile at as they grow older. But Mr. Palgrave says of this little poem: "For tenderness and grandeur under the form of severe simplicity these verses have few rivals. They are Greek after the manner in which a modern English poet should be Greek. Readers who admire them are on the right way to high and lasting pleasure."

Now, if we will but consider the matter, it is more probable that Mr. Palgrave is right in his opinion, and that we, who are somewhat disposed to underrate this poem, are wrong. For Mr. Palgrave, besides holding a very honorable place amongst the poets of the present generation, stands in the front rank of critics in art and literature, and whenever he speaks out on these subjects we ought to listen to him with respect. Let us then for a few moments examine this poem in detail, and see whether we can discover for ourselves "the tenderness and grandeur under the form of severe simplicity" which the critic commends. And first of all we will make a few remarks on what is meant by *simplicity* in poetry. A poem is properly said to be *simple* when the emotions it stirs, or the feelings of pleasure and pain it calls forth, are such as are common to all men alike, and which therefore all may share in. But there is another point to observe about *simplicity* in poetry, and that is the manner in which it shows itself. If we examine the best poems in any literature most conspicuous for this quality, we shall find that, when they are describing a scene or an emotion, they will do this in the most direct way possible; each word will be carefully selected that there may be no doubt as to what meaning is intended to be conveyed, and the necessary number of words for conveying the required impression will be used, and no more; there will be no superfluities, no indulging in flights of fancy which may tend to obscure the meaning, no playing with fine words for the mere sound alone; in short, the language of the poem will be adequate to the occasion.

Mr. Palgrave speaks of the severe *simplicity* of its form. How is this shown? In this way: its language and versification are adequate to the occasion. The "Royal George," at that time the finest ship in the navy, was accidentally overturned whilst undergoing repairs off the coast. A British admiral and nearly one thousand seamen were drowned. The event was justly regarded as a national calamity, and a whole nation mourned its loss. There is an awful silence in all heartfelt grief—words seem totally inadequate to express the sorrow that is surging below; or, if the burden of silence grows intolerable, it will find expression in the briefest ejaculations. The sympathy, too, which such a grief demands will be undemonstrative; many words, even though kindly uttered, will serve only to widen and aggravate the wound. If this is the case with individual sorrow, how much more when a whole nation is thrown into mourning, when not one, but many hearts are wrung with a sense of unutterable loss, the difficulty is increased of finding words that shall adequately express not only one's individual sense of desolation, but the inarticulate motions of despair that are agitating thousands of hearts! The very occasion was an unwritten poem—the employment of verse could hardly have added to its poetical character and significance, which all could feel. How, then, has the poet treated his subject? He has presented us in the most direct way by a series of simple and touching pictures the scene of the catastrophe as it presented itself to his imagination: there are no violent expressions of grief and despair; all is calm and restrained, and yet the thrilling pathos of the situation is fully brought out. The monotone of grief is admirably rendered in the short lines, at the close of every one of which the voice is almost compelled to pause with slowly dying cadence, like the muffled peal of funeral bells. It is a characteristic of sorrow that, though it may be for a time diverted from its object, it continually passes back again to the thought of its particular loss. Read Stanzas i., iv., and ix., and you will see how grief reiterates itself:

(i.) "Toll for the brave!
The brave that are no more . . ."
(iv.) "Toll for the brave!
Brave Kempenfeldt is gone . . ."
(ix.) "But Kempenfeldt is gone,
His victories are o'er . . ."

Again, Mr. Palgrave speaks of the *tenderness* of the poem. How is this shown? Chiefly, is it not, by the way in which the poet brings vividly before us the pathos of the situation, and the little human touches by which he contrasts and intensifies it? What an importance the most trifling acts and sayings assume in the retrospective memory when the author of them is dead! Thus the poet does not fail to remind us that, when the disaster occurred, the admiral's sword was laid by, and he was engaged in the simple act of writing. A gentle spirit of the most tender irony pervades the whole piece. The ship had weathered many a storm, and fought England's battles at sea. It was a *land* breeze which overturned her, and in the calm waters of one of England's roadsteads. All the bravery of the crew could not save them from their fate; nay, might it not, in a sense, have contributed to their ruin, for had not obedience to orders, which the discipline of active service produces,

> "Made the vessel heel,
> And laid her on her side"?

But the tenderness and pathos of the poem are nowhere better shown than in the last three stanzas. In the midst of grief arises the thought that the good ship is not actually lost to the service; she may be raised by mechanical means from the bottom of the sea—

> "Her timbers yet are sound,
> And she may float again."

Then, immediately, to check the current of exalted feeling, the thought of the transitoriness of human life as compared with the durability of material objects succeeds, and the poem closes, as it began, with the sounding of the funeral knell over the brave souls thus suddenly snatched away—

> "But Kempenfeldt is gone,
> His victories are o'er,
> And he and his eight hundred
> Shall plough the waves no more."

Finally, the critic speaks of the *grandeur* of the poem. Where are we to seek for this? Is it not to be found in the ardent spirit of patriotism which pervades and gives dignity to the whole? The poem is intensely national in feeling; it appeals to sentiments dear to all Englishmen—love for the sea, and for the sea as the chief bulwark of England's freedom, and the scene of her glorious exploits. It is this which intensifies the grief for the loss of Kempenfeldt—

> "His last sea-fight is fought,
> His work of glory done."

It is the thought of England's dependence upon her sailors which inspired the hope that the good ship might yet again be fit for service—

> "Weigh the vessel up,
> Once dreaded by our foes.
> . . . .
> Her timbers yet are sound,
> And she may float again,
> Full charged with England's thunder,
> And plough the distant main."

What a combination of *grandeur* and *tenderness*, too, is there in the lines in which the poet invokes his countrymen to let the fate of the brave souls who perished enter as a solemnizing thought on the occasion of festivities held to celebrate any of England's victories! Let us, he says—

> ". . mingle with our cup
> The tears that England owes."

Mr. Palgrave has another word of praise for these verses. He says: "They are Greek after the manner in which a modern English poet should be Greek." This is quite true; not, of course, in the sense that there is any conscious imitation of Greek poetry, but simply on account of their possessing those characteristics which the critic so justly praises, *i.e.*, "tenderness and grandeur under the form of severe simplicity," for in no other poetry are these two qualities exhibited in more complete perfection than in the poetry of ancient Greece. The famous passage in the "Iliad" describing the visit of the aged Priam to the tent of Achilles, to beg the body of Hector from the man that slew him, is a conspicuous example of those very qualities of genuine poetry which, as Mr. Palgrave truly says, conduce to "high and lasting pleasure." For the heart of man is the same in all ages, and speaks a universal language. Sorrow and death are with us still, parental anguish is as poignant now as it was in the time of the ancient Greeks, and the natural and spontaneous expression of it unites both the present and the past with one throb of human sympathy. After reading poems, or passages from poems, which possess this dateless character we are ready to exclaim with Wordsworth: "Thanks to the human heart by which we live."—*The Educational Times.*

CORRELATION OF STUDIES.

(Concluded from last month.)

THE work of art has a new principle, one that transcends life. It is the principle of responsible individuality and the principle of free subordination on the part of the individual to a social whole. It is in fact the exercise of original responsibility in opposition to a social whole, and the consequent retribution or other reaction that makes the content of the work of art. Further discussion is not necessary to show how absurd would be a purely mathematical treatment, or a biological treatment, of a work of art. Mathematics and biology must enter into a consideration of works of art only in a very subordinate degree. It would be equally absurd to attempt to apply the method in which a work of art should be studied to the study of an organic form or to the study of inorganic matter and forces.

The next co-ordinate branch includes grammar and language, and studies allied to it, such as logic and psychology. In the elementary school we have only grammar. Grammar treats of the structure of language; there is a mechanical side to it in orthography, and a technical side to it in etymology and syntax. But one cannot call grammar in any peculiar sense a formal study any more than he can apply the same epithet to one of the natural sciences. Natural science deals with the laws of material bodies and forces. Laws are forms of acting or of being, and yet by far the most important content of natural science is stated in the laws which it has discovered. So in the studies that relate to man the forms of human speech are very important. All grammatical studies require a twofold attitude of the mind, one toward the sign and one toward the signification; the shape of a letter or the form of a word or the peculiarity of a vocal utterance, these must be attended to, but they must be at once subordinated to the significance of the hidden thought which has become revealed by the sign or utterance.

The complexity of grammatical study is seen at once from this point of view. It is a double act of the will focusing the attention upon two different phases at once, namely, upon the natural phase and the spiritual phase, and the fusion of the two in one. Looking at this attitude of the mind, at this method of grammatical study, we see at once how different it all is from the attitude of the mind in the study of a work of art. In grammar we should not look to an evolution of a feeling into a thought or a deed; that would be entirely out of place. But we must give attention to the literal and prosaic word written or spoken, and consider it as an expression of a thought. We must note the structure of the intellect as revealed in this form. The word is a part of speech, having some one of the many functions which the word can fulfil in expressing a thought. Deeper down than grammatical structure is the logical structure, and this is a more fundamental revelation of the action of pure mind. Logic is, in fact, a part of psychology. Opening from one door toward another, we pass on our way from orthography, etymology and syntax to logic and to psychology. All the way we use the same method; we use the sign or manifestation as a means of discovering the thought and the scientific classification of the thought.

Much has been said in the report of the Committee of Fifteen on the abuse of grammar in the study of literary works of art. The method of grammar leads to wonderful insight into the nature of reason itself. It is this insight which it gives us into our methods of thinking and of uttering our thoughts that furnishes the justification for grammar as one of the leading studies in the curriculum. Its use in teaching correct speaking and writing is always secondary to this higher use, which is to make conscious in man the structure of his thinking and expression. Important as it is, however, when it is substituted for the method of studying art, it becomes an abuse. It is a poor way to study Shakespeare, Milton, Chaucer, and the Bible to grammatically parse them or analyze them, or to devote the time to their philological peculiarities, the history of the development of their language, or such matters. The proper method of studying the work of art is not a substitute for that in grammar; it does not open the windows of the mind toward the logical, philological, or psychological structure of human thought and action.

There is a fifth co-ordinate group of studies, namely, that of history. History looks to the formation of the state as the chief of human institutions. The development of states, the collisions of individuals with the state, the collisions of the states with one another—these form the topic of history. The method of historic study is different from that in grammatical study and also from that in the study of literary and other works of art. Still more different is the method of history from those employed in the two groups of studies relating to nature, namely, the mathematical and biological methods. The history of literature and science has many examples of misapplications of method. For instance, Buckle, in his History of Civilization, has endeavored to apply the biological method and to some extent that of physics, apparently thinking that the methods of natural science, which are so good in their application to organic and inorganic nature, are likewise good for application within the realm of human nature. The reader of Buckle will remember, for instance, that the superstitious character of the Spanish people is explained by him as due to the frequency of earthquakes in the Peninsula. In selecting a physical cause for explaining a spiritual effect, Mr. Buckle passed over the most obvious explanation, which is this: The people of Spain were for many centuries on the marches or boundaries of Christian civilization and over against a Moslem civilization. Wherever there is a borderland between two conflicting civilizations—a difference either political or religious—there is a sharpening of the minds of the people so far as to produce the effect of opposition and bigotry. A continual effort to hold one's religious belief uncontaminated by the influence of a neighboring people leads to narrowness and to a superstitious adherence to forms. Narrowness and bigotry in religion are the foes to science and the friends to all manner of superstitions.

Mr. Buckle's work has interested

people very much because it is an attempt to bring the methods of natural science into the study of human history. But it cannot be regarded as anything more than an example of the attempt to substitute for the true method in history a method good only in another province.

In biology the whole animal is not fully revealed in each of his members, although, as stated in Kant's defiuition, each part is alike the means and the end for all the others. The higher animals and plants show the greatest difference between parts and whole. But in history it is the opposite; the lower types exhibit the greatest difference between the social whole and the individual citizen. The progress in history is toward freedom of the individual and local self-government. In the highest organisms of the state, therefore, there is a great similarity between the individual and the national whole to which he belongs. The individual takes a more active part in governing himself. The state becomes more and more an instrument of self-government in his hands. In the lowest states the gigantic personality of the social whole is all and all, and the individual personality is null, except in case of the supreme ruler and in the few associated with him.

The method of history keeps its gaze fixed upon the development of the social whole and the progress which it makes in realizing within its citizens the freedom of the whole. This method, it is evident enough, is different frcm those in literature and grammar; different also from the biological and the mathematical methods. In history we see how the little selves or individuals unite to form the big self or the nation. The analogies to this found in biology, namely, the combination of individual cells into the entire vegetable or animal organism, are all illusive so far as furnishing a clue to the process of human history.

From the above considerations it is possible to see what is the relation of this inquiry into educational values to the questions of child study and other topics in psychology, as well as to the Herbartian principle of interest. First and foremost the teacher of the school has before him this question of the branches of learning to be selected. These must be discovered by looking at the grown man in civilization rather than at the child. The child has not yet developed his possibilities. The child first shows what he is truly and internally when he becomes a grown man. The child is the acorn. The acorn reveals what it is in the oak only after a thousand years. So man has revealed what he is, not in the cradle, but in the great world of human history and literature and science. He has written out his nature upon the blackboard of the universe.

In order to know what there is in the human will we look into Plutarch's Parallel Lives. To see what man has done in philosophy we read Plato, Aristotle, Leibnitz, and Hegel. For science we look to the Newtons and Darwins. We do not begin, therefore, with child study in our school education. But next after finding these great branches of human learning we consider the child, and how to bring him from his possibility to his reality. Then it becomes essential to study the child and his manner of evolution. We must discover which of its interests are already on the true road toward human greatness. We must likewise discover which ones conflict with the highest aims, and especially what interests there are that, although seemingly in conflict with the highest ends of man, are yet really tributary to human greatness, leading up to it by winding routes. All these are matters of child study, but they all presuppose the first knowledge, namely, the knowledge of the doings of mature humanity. There can be no step made in rational child study without keeping in view constantly these questions of the five coordinate groups of study.—*From Report of Com. of Education.*

"THE NEW WOMAN" AND THE PROBLEMS OF THE DAY.

AS there is a new everything these days, we suppose it was inevitable that there should be a "new woman"; though why a new woman more than a new man it might not be easy to explain. For our part we believe but faintly in the "new" woman; we believe in woman. We believe in progress; we believe that new times call for new measures; we believe that these are new times, and that it behooves both men and women to prepare themselves to meet the demands which the age is making on them.

What is really new in the world is knowledge. We see the practical outcome of the new knowledge in the transformation that has taken place in the arrangement under which the life of society to-day is carried on. With the new knowledge there has come a vast enlargement of human power in all directions and a vast development of human individuality. Custom, though still powerful, is no longer such a ruler of men's lives as it used to be. Men and women everywhere have been roused, we might almost say stung, into a sense of individual existence; and, looking round on their changing environment, they are asking a thousand questions to which as yet no very certain answers can be vouchsafed. Woman is awake because man is awake; the keenness of the times has roused them both; and from both we seem to hear the inquiry made by the jailer at Philippi, when startled from slumber by the trembling of the earth and the flashing of a strange light: "What must I do to be saved?" The difference between the so-called "new woman" and woman without that qualification is that the latter would wish to be saved with man, and the former apparently without him. The new variety emphasizes the fact that she is a woman, and in that capacity is going to do wonderful things; whereas woman without the "new" is content to know herself a woman and to feel that with her it rests to accomplish her equal part in all the best work of the future.

The great change, as we have said, is that there is more knowledge in the world, and that the rule of custom is to a large extent broken. Things that once had all the authority that convention and routine could give them are now open to everyone's criticism. Morality no longer rests in absolute security upon dogma. The time has come which Voltaire predicted would be the end of all things, when *the people* have taken to reasoning. Fortunately, there is no need to agree with Voltaire; but it is necessary to recognize that something is needed to give wise direction to the emancipated thought and action of our time. The dogmatic morality of the past was in the main sound; and the problem of to-day is to secure a sufficient sanction for whatever rules of conduct are necessary to the well-being of individuals and of society. That much in the way of wise counsel and true inspiration may be expected from the increased reflectiveness of women we most gladly recognize; but we do not feel disposed to call a woman who thus responds to the needs of the time a "new" woman, seeing that, for generations past, and particularly in times of emergency, women have more or less fulfilled the same rôle.

The two principal questions which to-day confront society relate to the future relations of men and women and the education of the rising generation. The allegation is freely made in many quarters that marriage is a failure; and no doubt frequently it is. None the less, however, is it the case that no scheme that has ever been proposed as a substitute for marriage merits a moment's consideration. It is easy to provide theoretically for the gratification of passion and impulse, but not so easy by any means to show how by any union less solemn and abiding than marriage the higher natures of men and women can be duly developed and their lower propensities kept in check. We do not look to any new woman for light on this question; but we do look to the best women of to-day, those who to purity and soundness of instinct add a trained capacity for independent and intelligent judgment to join with the best men in indicating the higher path which the generations of the future may tread. We may be sure of this, that the path is one not of less but of greater self-control, and that redemption from the miseries which attach, in too many cases, to marriage as it is will be found in an elevation and purification of the whole idea of marriage. Not that the idea has not been held in its highest purity by many in different ages; not that the world has ever lacked examples of ideal marriage, but that there has never been a sufficiently wide recognition of its true nature and possibilities. There is a gospel on the subject which has to be preached, and, so far as individual action can do it, enforced—the gospel that the true happiness of a man and woman united in marriage bonds consists in learning, as years go on, to love and respect one another more and more, and in aiding and stimulating one another more and more to right and noble action, each gaining strength through the other, each finding in the other the means of achieving a true individual completeness. The true gospel is that there is more in marriage than for the most part poets have sung or romancers dreamed, and that the failures of which we hear so much have been, in the main, failures to grasp the true conception of it and to make a right preparation for the duties which it involves.

Does not all this mean, it may be asked, that many are unfit, through defect of character, and others through ignorance and general inferiority of thought and sentiment, to make the best of marriage. It certainly does, and here the no less important problem of education comes in. In these days we look too much to the state to solve our problems for us. There are some problems which the state cannot solve, and one, we do not hesitate to say, is the problem of a true education. The state can levy taxes and employ agents and make regulations; but it cannot speak with the voice of father or mother; it cannot speak confidentially to the young of their deepest interests. It can enjoin rules of conduct, but it cannot guide aspiration; it cannot meet what, in a broad sense, we may speak of as spiritual needs. If the rising generation is to be adequately educated, the best men and women of the day must come together and consider how it is to be done—how the work of the state is to be supplemented by individual endeavor, so that growth in character may keep pace with growth and knowledge and intelligence. There are two main ways in which, at first sight, it seems possible this might be done, or at least more or less hopefully attempted; first, by an improvement of the home, and secondly, by the action of a higher public opinion on the schools. We quoted, some months ago, an eminent French writer of our own day as saying that it was necessary to put more "soul" in the public schools. That is precisely what they want, as all the best teachers are fully aware. But you cannot make an appropriation for "soul." It is not quoted in the catalogues of school supplies; it is not among the prescribed subjects in teachers' examinations. It is a very real if not a very tangible thing; and it is a communicable thing. There are those who have it and can impart it; indeed, those who have it can hardly fail to impart it! If there is enough of it outside the schools, it will leak in, and our hope is that the best men and the best women of the day will so join forces as to create, especially around the public schools, an atmosphere of higher sentiment that shall affect for good the working of the state machine, and greatly strengthen the hands of all who, within the schools, have set for themselves a certain standard of spiritual as distinct from merely intellectual accomplishment.

Then as to the home. Here is where we want women with new knowledge, but not—we speak with all due fear and trembling—"new" women. The "new woman" would set every one discussing rights; but the true woman with adequate knowledge would see what the best women have always seen, that the home requires a principle of unity and not a system of scientific frontiers or an elaborately arranged balance of power. Home life and home influence have, we fear, been suffering in our day through a variety of causes; but the home, like marriage, is an institution which only needs to have its possibilities developed in order to stand forth more than justified. Without entering into the question as to whether the wisest methods are being followed to-day in the education of women, it is beyond all doubt that women have gained a vast enlargement of their intellectual horizon, and that in many cases women are not only the peers but the superiors of men in the same station in life as themselves in knowledge and culture. Such knowledge and culture can nowhere be better employed than in the home, where the physical, mental and moral development of children has to be watched over. The question is, how far will it be employed in this way, and how far made a means of mere personal self-assertion? The true woman will use it for the good of others, and, if possible, will make it available for the improvement of the home; while others—the new type—will use it to make themselves conspicuous in the world, and, as they vainly fancy, add glory to the female sex.

The hope of the future lies mainly in well-ordered homes—homes in which children are trained to be just, reasonable and humane, in which they are taught to look with an inteligent eye upon the phenomena alike of Nature and of society, in which they learn lessons of industry and self-reliance, of honor, purity, and self-respect, and are guarded against the vulgar worship of wealth and worldly success. It is for the wise and noble women of our time to help to make such homes, and it is for men to see to it that they are worthy of partnership in so sacred a cause. It is no time for any silly rivalry or futile opposition between men and women, who are as necessary to one another now as at any previous age in the world's history—nay, more necessary. On the contrary, it is a time for earnest counsel and vigorous co-operation on the part of all who have the interest of the present and future generations at heart; and the less we hear of the separate and conflicting claims of men and women the better. There is ample scope to-day for the efforts of all, and if any stand idle in the vineyard it must be from lack of will, not from lack of opportunity.—*Popular Science Monthly.*

RELIGIOUS INSTRUCTION IN PUBLIC SCHOOLS.

WE have been greatly surprised at the ignorance of very many persons as to the existing regulations of the Department of Education with reference to the reading of the Bible and religious instruction in the public schools. For the information of our readers we give herewith the text of these regulations, as set forth in a bulletin of the department last month. They read as follows: The teacher of every Public and High School (unless excused because of conscientious scruples) is required to open his school with the Lord's Prayer, to be repeated by the teacher alone or preferably by the teachers and pupils in concert. At the closing of school a portion of the Scriptures shall be read, either from the Bible or the selections authorized by the Education Department, as the trustees may order. The Lord's Prayer, or the prayer authorized by the Education Department, shall follow the reading of the Scriptures. The trustees may also order the reading of the authorized selections or the Bible at the opening of the school. The Ten Commandments shall be repeated once a week. The Scriptures are to be read without comment or explanation. *The teacher shall, when directed by the trustees, require the pupils to commit to memory appropriate verses from the Scripture lessons.* The rights of parents or guardians to withdraw their children from all religious exercises should be carefully guarded by the teacher. (Reg. 99.) Any clergyman, or any person authorized by him, shall have the right to give religious instruction to the pupils of his own church, at least once a week after the closing of the school in the afternoon. Where clergymen of more denominations than one apply to give religious instruction in the same school-house, the Board of Trustees shall decide as to the days of the week on which the school-house shall be at the disposal of each of such clergyman. By Regulation 15 it is provided that Public School pupils shall assemble for study at nine o'clock in the forenoon, and shall be dismissed not later than four o'clock in the afternoon, unless otherwise directed by the trustees, but in no case shall the school day be less than five hours. Where the clergyman of any denomination applies for the privilege of giving religious instruction, the trustees may close the school at half past three in the afternoon, or even earlier, if by so doing the teaching term of five hours per day is not reduced. It is the duty of the teacher in connection with the ordinary work of the school "to inculcate by precept and example respect for religion and the principles of Christian morality and the highest regard for truth, justice, love of country, humanity, benevolence, sobriety, industry, frugality, purity, temperance, and all other virtues." (Public School Act, 1896, s. 76 (1).)

It will be observed that certain of these requirements are directly binding upon the teacher. He must open the school with the Lord's Prayer. He must read at the closing of the school from the Bible. He must have the Ten Commandments repeated once every week. He must inculcate by example as well as by precept respect for religion, and teach the principles of Christian morality. Ample scope is given here to every earnest teacher to promote effectively the moral and spiritual well-being of the pupils, to infuse a Christian spirit into the work of the school, and to set before the scholars the highest Christian ideals.

But, in addition, the trustees of each school have it in their power to order the reading of the Bible at the opening as well as at the closing of the school. They have also in their power to direct that the Scriptures be memorized by the pupils. This is a recent addition to the regulations which we have printed in italics to draw attention to it. It is a long step in the right direction, and one for which the gratitude of Christian men is due to the Minister of Education.

If our people appreciate these regulations and take advantage of them, without doubt the Minister of Education will be encouraged to proceed further, and at length to introduce a system of Biblical lessons as part of the regular curriculum of the schools. In the meantime, let Christian men and women bring their influence to bear upon the trustees and see that those regulations, which are optional, are adopted and introduced into every school in our land.

It is worse than useless for people to demand more in this direction, if they do not avail themselves of the priviliges now available. Then there are the opportunities given to ministers to visit the schools to instruct the children—how few avail themselves of these! Let us make the most of what is now granted and seek in every way to encourage interest in Bible study on the part of the teachers and the children, and we will see splendid results. If this is not done, the fault lies with the people themselves and not with the Government.—*E.C.*

Those of us who have been laboring in the cause of religious education in our public schools must rejoice at knowing that so much has been gained, even if they would wish to have something more; and it is greatly to be hoped that they will frankly accept and work the system now sanctioned in our schools, even if they hope hereafter to get something better. No doubt, the ideal system is that every church should teach its doctrines to its own children. It must be inferred that there will always be a certain chilliness in undenominational teaching, seeing that the teacher, if he has any strong religious convictions, will be under the necessity of suppressing them. On the other hand, the habit of merely reading the Bible, without the teacher being allowed to ask any questions upon it, will hardly lead to a satisfactory knowledge of the sacred writings on the part of the children. Still, it is better than nothing. It is something that the child should know that there is a Bible, and that it gives the religious history of the world in its earlier periods. It is something that the mind of the child should be informed by the sublime maxims of Christianity, that its heart should be stirred by the contemplation of the perfect life of the Son of God and His sublime devotion to God and to man. Moreover, although positive doctrine may not be taught, the moral and spiritual principles of the Gospel are to be inculcated by precept and example. In addition to all this, there is an important provision for the teaching of the children of different denominations by their own ministers, who may instruct their young people in all the doctrines of their own communion. We are quite aware of the difficulty of working this part of the system, and it may be that such instruction must be less frequent than could be desired. But it is something; and, supplemented by the work of Sunday schools, it may be worth a great deal. So far, then, from the point of view of reasonable men, we think we have got, if not all that could be desired, yet much to be thankful for, and the more so, that no denomination can be injured or offended by these arrangements. We are quite aware, and quite content with the knowledge, that in this country no religious body has a right to special privileges. There is perhaps only one point in which we could wish a slight change to be made, viz., that the religious teaching should not be outside the school hours. Of course, no child should be required to be present at the religious instruction, if his parents disapprove of the same. But in that case he should be put to some other lesson. It is a distinct inducement to keep away from the Bible lessons that those who do so should have so much time added to their hours of play. In this respect the children who are taught in the Scriptures should not be placed at a disadvantage. It would, generally speaking, be quite easy to find some other work for the children who are withdrawn.

EDITORIAL NOTES.

Educational Association of Ontario.

The above Association will meet at Easter. The expectation is that the meeting will be a large one. There is promise of good men to address the various sessions of the Convention, and the time of the year is favorable for securing a good attendance. The railways grant reduced rates on the usual conditions.

The appeal of The Canada Educational Monthly to the teachers of the Dominion has not been without its effect, and the encouragement it has received since the new year began leads those connected with its management to believe that before the year is out, there will be no university, college, collegiate institute, high school or graded school in the land that shall not be in touch with the new movement of consolidating a common brotherhood of teachers from the Atlantic to the Pacific. In the advocacy of this movement there is no selfish motive as far as The Monthly is concerned. Those who have had to do with the running of periodicals such as The Monthly, know that there is no money reward to those engaged in preparing its contents from month to month. Their only reward is the good-will and co-operation of those in whose favor they are content to labor gratuitously. There is one thing, however, which must be done, and that is, the labor of our contributors must be recognized in a tangible way if the sympathies of our most prominent writers are to be enlisted and secured. Many of our most distinguished educational writers in the country have already agreed to help The Monthly, and it is to be hoped that their efforts in our behalf will be gratefully acknowledged by our readers. We therefore ask for an increase in our subscription list, not so much perhaps for the sake of revenue as for the advancement of the new movement among Canadian teachers. Teachers sending their names to any of our publishers will have them put upon our lists immediately. These publishers who are interested in our work will give any information intending subscribers, contributors or advertisers may desire to have in regard to the standing of our periodical, which, it is to be hoped, will in time be second to none on the continent. The various educational systems of our common country have surely something to boast of, and there is no reason why these should not have an exponent in a well-supported educational periodical. Our readers, it is to be hoped, will excuse us, if this idea of representation is kept before them for a month or so at the start. It is no intention of THE CANADA EDUCATIONAL MONTHLY ever to place itself in the immodest position of speaking too much about its own affairs. But our readers must be taken into its confidence, for a time at least, in order that cooperation and well understood progress may be fairly inaugurated.

The examination idea, we are inclined to think, has run its course, and it is for our teachers to say, through our correspondence section, whether they agree with us or not. The philosophy of the thing has run to seed in the too palpable realism of the practice. As is so often the case, the means towards the end has become the end itself. No one can doubt that examinations are a necessity, but that they should ever become the most important element in our systems of education is something which no true educationist would think of maintaining. And in our animadversions against the somewhat ludicrous stress placed upon examinations, let it be understood that we have no quarrel with the central authorities who are inclined to make so much of them. It is our conviction that these authorities are conscientious in their efforts to make the most of systems of public instruction through this means. Our superintendents of education or our boards of education, who think they see in the examination a means of obtaining to the very highest pedagogic results, are no more to be assailed in this matter than are the teachers themselves in their emulation to be awarded a high professional status from the records made by those instructed by them, and who present themselves at these examinations. No good can come from laying the blame at any one's door, personally speaking. In Ontario, perhaps, of all the provinces, the intensifying of the standards has been considered a sign of educational progress; and yet no one need turn round and blame the Minister of Education personally for having given way to the general professional anxiety that favors the adoption of this as a sure sign of advancement on the part of our teachers and pupils alike. The notion is a mistaken notion, and that is all that need be said of it. A teacher is no worse a teacher this year than he was last year, because he has not succeeded in securing for his school as many passes as he did last year. There are fluctuations in the average ability of pupils as there are fluctuations in the school population. The examination cannot take cognizance of all the varying influences of school life; and it is this which those who have the directing of the examinations so frequently overlook when they desire to make the examination a hard and-fast rule of measuring success, as it is this which lies at the bottom of the unrest on the part of our teachers who feel the burden of preparing boys and girls for the examinations, an anxiety that is at times all but too grievous to be borne. In the other provinces examination and inspection go together hand in hand more than in Ontario. In the Province of Quebec, as we have discovered, the inspection has done more for the schools than the written examinations, while the system of examination there has less of the cram about it than it has in Ontario. In a word, there is more of a balance between the inspection and the written examination than in any of the other provinces, although in the superior schools the system is based more or less on "payment by results." In the Maritime Provinces the inspection of the school is not followed by a special period for written examinations. In Manitoba there is an inclination to follow in the steps of Ontario, though the efforts to make the examination everything has not been so pernicious as in Ontario; while in the North-West Territory and British Columbia things are more or less at their beginnings, with a tendency to improve the school through the enthusiasm and personality of the teacher. As a final word, this month, we may say that this is by no means our last word on this subject. The question is too important from the standpoint of parent, teacher and pupil, to allow it to remain a mere irrevocable anxiety any longer, and we are anxious to have the opinions of our teachers on the subject.

When we said last month that the Quebec Government had come to the conclusion to retain the distribution of the new subsidy in behalf of elementary education in their own hands, the facts had not all come to hand in regard to their later action after the passing of the Subsidy Bill in the Legislature. We give the report of the late meeting of the Quebec Council of Public Instruction as it is given to us in the *Montreal Witness*, and after reading it our readers will perhaps perceive for themselves what a leaping there has been from the pot into the fire. It will be now for the educationists of Quebec to discuss how the elementary schools will be improved under the latest proposal of the Council of Public Instruction. The report of the meeting is as follows:

"An important special meeting of the full Council of Public Instruction was held at the Parliament Buildings here this forenoon. As the public is no doubt aware, the council, which is composed of eleven Roman Catholic bishops, eleven Roman Catholic laymen and eleven Protestant representatives, seldom meets except for matters of common interest, but the two sections, Roman Catholic and Protestant, into which it is divided, meet regularly, each having control of its own schools. The meeting this forenoon was to determine the best method of dealing with the recent special grant by the Legislature of fifty thousand dollars for elementary schools. Most of the Roman Catholic members were present, and all the bishops except the Bishop of Sherbrooke, and among the Protestant members in attendance were the Rev. Dr. Shaw, the Rev. A. T. Love, the Lord Bishop of Quebec, Principal Peterson and Messrs. Finlay, Ames and Masten. By the terms of the Act three thousand of the fifty thousand dollars were appropriated to meet the current deficiency on the pension fund, ten thousand more to double the grant to poor municipalities, and fourteen thousand to teachers as bonuses for meritorious service, thus leaving only twenty-three thousand of the fifty thousand dollars to be really dealt with by the council. It was therefore resolved that in the case of the last two mentioned sums of ten thousand and fourteen thousand dollars, the same division should apply as in the case of the general legislative grant. As to the remaining twenty-three thousand some discussion arose as to the right of the council to apportion it. The Hon. Mr. Masson insisted that the administration of this money should be left to the free discretion of the Government. The Hon. Mr. Langelier urged that the entire fifty thousand dollars should be so left, but finally Mr. Masson's view prevailed."

The decisions of the council will, no doubt, pave the way for the fuller discussion of the manner in which the grants are distributed at the present time; and the electors will possibly now be placed in possession of the whole facts of the case by the candidates who are anxious to secure their suffrages at the coming elections. The true spirit of reform is hardly to be detected as yet in this increased subsidy, or in the proposed manner of its distribution.

The daily newspaper but seldom knows what is going on by way of educational reform in the province near by it until some gentleman of foreign parts writes something or other to the papers of his own country about an educational necessity which ought to be seen to at once. Then the local or provincial paper at once takes for granted that the necessity for moving in this direction must be pressing everywhere, and nowhere more so than in the province or parish for which it writes. For example, one of our more important dailies (it is not necessary to say that it offends more in this respect than any other of our important dailies), discovers that some American educationist has lately been saying that there is no civilized country in which so little is done to cultivate the correct use of the vernacular language as in the United States. This, of course, may be correct, and possibly the statement is of some international moment, but when the newspaper which repeats the statement goes on to say that as the conditions of Canada are very similar to those of the United States, it may be worth our while to take note of what he avers and what he suggests, we certainly must declare that Canada is not to be classified with the United States as a country which is doing little or nothing to cultivate the vernacular language spoken by her inhabitants. The Canadian newspaper that makes this statement ought to know, to say the least of it, that the province from which it draws the largest share of its subscribers has been making the most ardous efforts to improve the manner of speech of the rising generation. The French spoken in the Province of Quebec among the school children is possibly a village *patois*, but the French spoken in the French school is the French, we are told, of *La Belle France;* and the same may be said of our English schools in every part of the Dominion. In the Province of Quebec, the routine of the English schools has been more or less remodelled on the plan of getting the children to speak and write the English language correctly as a practical art, and possibly no man has done so much to bring this about as Dr. Harper, the present inspector of superior schools. In Ontario, the teacher is laboring in the same direction, as far as the routine preparation for the written examination at the end of the year permits him to employ himself in this seemingly unprofitable occupation. But let us quote what our daily contemporary says as it discusses the statement of the educationist who says that "there is no civilized country in which so little is done to cultivate the correct use of the vernacular language as in the United States." The quotation we make all the more readily as it is our intention to turn the attention of our teachers to this question in our next issue:

"*The Educational Review,*" says our daily contemporary, "has an article by Mr. E. L. Erskin, which was also read before the Teachers' Association of that city, which takes the ground that there is no civilized country in which so little is done, outside of the colleges, to cultivate the correct use of the vernacular language as in the United States. As the conditions of Canada are very similar to those of the United States, it may be worth our while to take some note of what he avers and what he suggests. He speaks of educated men caring, as a rule, little or nothing how they speak. 'Their speech is full of solecisms, their letters and notes are unpunctuated scrawls, and in their pronunciation the vowel sounds are summarily got rid of.' He tells of a dialect growing up among the new generation of the metropolis, which is supposed to go or to have gone to school—a dialect which has already a popular literature. If we wish to speak well, he says, there is nothing for it but to speak well every day, and this is what a large proportion of men wilfully do not do. Good speech has in the older lands been the traditional passport to good society, but good society in America exercises no such control, while newspaper vulgarity and so-called dialect tales vie with each other in depressing the general tone. Mr. Godkin thinks the cure is within the reach of the colleges, which should demand a much higher standard. It is, we believe, beyond the reach of colleges to communicate a good use of English unless the foundations are far better laid than they generally are before the students go there. A large proportion of our young people learn a very defective English at home, and if we wish to purify the speech of the country, the whole power of the schools should be turned to correct the evil. It may not be easy to deal with that quality which, for fault of a right word, is usually spoken of as local accent; but distinct errors, whether of grammar, pronunciation, spelling or punctuation, can be dealt with, and so can vulgar idioms and slang. The colleges have an immense power over the schools through their matriculation standards, which necessarily become the standards of the academies and high schools and, directly or indirectly, of the common schools also. Colleges must in some degree suit the standards of their entrance examinations to the existing conditions of the country, but far more does the education of the country take its tone and trend from them. Certainly, in insisting on good English or good French, as the case may be, they would have the convictions of the people with them. Neither the learned or the unlearned would in this case raise question about requiring a man to study what he had no natural taste for."

For many years back, it seems, the Protestant ratepayers of the Province of Quebec have been nurturing the idea that the Protestant Committee of the Council of Public Instruction, which has more or less an indirect supervision of the Protestant educational interests of that section of the Dominion, ought to be made more of a representative body,—not that the committee should be reorganized, for anything like reorganization would be unconstitutional,—but rather that its members should individually represent in some kind of an indirect way the sections of the province from which they hail as citizens. Such an idea is ever likely, however, to be a mere dream. The internal interests of the Protestant Committee are too fixedly focalized by this time to allow anything but conservative suggestions to prevail within the circle of its practically closed doors, and lately this has come to be more and more apparent. Under the presidency of the late Bishop Williams, the forces at the board were fairly well kept in equilibrium, but of late years an inner influence has been gathering strength within the committee, which has at last all but indicated, as our Montreal correspondent says, that if it is not allowed to have its own way in all things, it is determined "to add to its numbers," until there is nothing left of an independent spirit in the committee but the merest remnant. The committee is made up of members and advisory members, as far as we can make it out. The members of the council are appointed by the Government, while the advisory members of the Committee are elected by the committee. For a time the university men and college partizans used to have it all their own way, and whenever a vacancy occurred, the Government would appoint the nominee of "the university men," as they were called, or the university men would elect one to support the college interests. But now it seems, according to the showing of our correspondent, the policy of control has somewhat changed. The "Text-Book Committee" desire to have their innings. The members of that sub-committee have lately been bringing into the Committee, if all tales are true, anything but a savory way of doing things, and, having received a check, they are determined to elect a man who will stand by them through thick and thin, and the more ignorant he is of either the principles or practice of education all the better it will be for them, at least, all the better it will be for the influence that is seeking to consolidate itself as a one man power. The country at large will await developments with a good deal of interest.

Apropos of the above, the St. John's *News*, a paper which wields a great influence over the whole province, has uttered the following note of warning:

"Some time ago we took the liberty of referring to the functions of the Protestant Committee of the Council of Public Instruction, and though an effort was made, on the part of those who can perhaps sympathize more intimately than an outsider with what the committee does or does not do, to combat the position we took in favor of educational reform, the necessity for reform remains now as it did then, with the arguments we advanced as unassailable as ever. The eagerness for an improvement in one direction has, however, gone on increasing. The condition of our elementary schools can be no longer ignored; and now that the Government has espoused the cause we humbly desired to promote when we opened our columns for the discussion of the vexed question of education, the members of the Protestant Committee will hardly impugn our loyalty to the best interests of our province, when we again recommend that body to come into closer touch with the country districts in the matter of educational reform. The sympathies of the Protestant Committee of the Council of Public Instruction have been for the most part identified with the fostering of higher and intermediate education, and as the country districts think, the reason for such is not far to seek when the personnel of the committee is taken into consideration. The country districts may be wrong in their surmises; but rightly or wrongly, they have continued now for many years to attribute much of the neglect to which our elementary schools have been subjected to the fact that the members of the Protestant Committee, as it is at present constituted, are more intimately acquainted with, and interested in, university and city school affairs than in the wants and necessities of the country districts. This may be a mere prejudice, as some of the members of the committee are for ever saying. But why should the committee not disabuse the minds of our country constituencies, if the contention be a mere prejudice, and if it will cost them nothing to do so? Not long ago they had an opportunity of doing this, and those who wish well to the committee and its work, regretted, and still regret, that the opportunity was allowed to pass, and now many are asking if every such opportunity is to be allowed to pass? There is a vacancy at present on the committee, and that vacancy is in the gift of the committee itself. That vacancy must be filled at the next meeting, and possibly it is no business of ours to make premature enquiries about the choice of the committee, and yet not a few in the country districts are already asking if it is again to be a man laboring for the special aggrandizement of the universities and colleges. We hope not, if the Protestant Committee would save itself from the prejudices that have been undermining its influence for so long. Is the appointment to be a Normal School man? Again we hope not, considering how that institution is already over represented. Is the appointment again to go to Montreal, when so many of the members already hail from that city? Every friend of educational reform for our country schools earnestly hopes not. Who then is to receive the appointment? That is the question which the committee have to decide. It would no doubt be looked upon as an impertinence on our part to suggest even one name. We have been already accused of venturing too far in our animadversions, when the Protestant Committee and its doings have come up for discussion. And yet this, we do say, with the sincerity of an honest well-wisher, that if the Protestant Committee does not now endeavor to show that it is anxious to be a representative body of the various sections of the province, through men who know the needs of the country districts, then we are prepared to join with the country districts in their legitimate demands to have proper representation in the conducting of our educational affairs, irrespective of what may happen to the Protestant Committee in the near or remote future."

CURRENT EVENTS AND COMMENTS.

THE erection of a new High School building for St. John, N.B., is a step in the right direction for the people of that important centre of Canada. As an outcome of the return of Dr. Brydes, of the New Brunswick University, to St. John as head-master of the Grammar School for boys, it points, no doubt, to the time when the commercial capital of New Brunswick shall be as proud of its High School for boys and girls as is Halifax or Montreal. The Grammar School of St. John has had a record with which the names of many of the distinguished men of the province has been associated. The names of Dr. Patterson and Dr. Coster are still green in the memories of many who know of them and their work as head-masters of that institution, and it must be cheering to them to think that the near future is about to bring back the eclat of former days to the institution through the energies of one of the best teachers the Province of New Brunswick has produced.

We are sorry to see that the Governors of McGill University, a body which many were beginning to think had eliminated the word "difficulty" from their vocabulary, are raising a seeming difficulty in the way of improving the status of the McGill Normal School as an institution whose function is to supply trained teachers for the Protestant schools of the province which so liberally supports it. Notwithstanding the ruling of the Governors in regard to the capabilities of that institution to overcome the work for which it was originally established, and which it has virtually failed in accomplishing up to the present time, there are many who are of the opinion that with its present staff, and with its present accommodation, it is capable of being so reorganized on the model of the Ontario Training Schools and of the Normal Schools of the other provinces as to succeed in doing all the work that may be demanded of it. If the Governors of McGill University persevere in their raising of difficulties, such petty difficulties as the providing of boarding accommodation in the great city of Montreal for a hundred more people and the providing of class-room accommodation, it will not be out of place for the Government to appoint a commission to see how the large revenues annually voted to the institution are disbursed, and how the appliances are utilized at the present time.

This is what the Governors of McGill University have been saying on the matter: "By a recent resolution, the Protestant Committee of the Council of Public Instruction has provided that, with a few exceptions specially reserved to the action of the committee itself, diplomas to Protestant teachers shall henceforth be issued only after a course of training of at least four months' duration, received in the Normal School. In all probability, the result will be a much increased attendance at that institution during the last four months of the annual session. In consequence, three difficulties of grave import arise: first, the class-room accommodation of the building is scarcely adequate to the reception of perhaps one hundred additional pupils; secondly, the teaching staff is numerically too weak to meet the increase of labor involved, while there are no means at the disposal of the Normal School Committee for providing help; and, thirdly, suitable lodgings for a large number of women students, who will remain in the city for four months only, are not available at a moderate price. It is not too much to say that the situation constitutes an impending crisis in Protestant popular education in the province."

The Montreal School Commissioners have abolished what are called for a better name "Subject Prizes" in their schools. For some time past it has been felt that too much money was being spent upon prize books. The amount was usually about $1,400. Silver and bronze medals are in future to be given for general proficiency, punctuality and attention to study, in the order of merit. Not only was the money consideration involved in this matter of subject prizes, but many felt that the pupils were being unduly stimulated by them to excel in one special subject, to the neglect of others, which, in their totality, comprehended a good education.

They are coming to it in the Maritime Provinces, though coming to it slowly. In the last report of Dr. Inch the following appears, and the teachers down by the sea may not know how soon the examination will lie on their minds as an incubus. "A uniform system of grading into the High Schools is very desirable," says the superintendent. "Entrance to these schools should be barred to pupils unprepared or unable to take up the work of the course. The present arrangement, which leaves the work of grading into the High Schools entirely under the control of local officials, fails to secure either uniformity or efficiency, inasmuch as different standards obtain in different places, and it often occurs that expediency rather than scholastic qualification determines admission. The consequence is, that the proper work of the school is hindered, and a considerable part of the first year has to be devoted to the lower grade drilling of the unprepared, to the serious detriment and discouragement of the well-prepared pupils. The whole course of study is thus thrown into confusion, and the teacher pursues his work under disheartening influences. The only remedy that seems practicable, is the holding of a uniform High School entrance examination in connection with the July departmental examinations. It would follow that only those capable of passing such an examination could be admitted to the higher course; and those who failed would have to be provided for, either by requiring them to repeat the work of the eighth grade, or by special arrangements, as circumstances would seem to require. Some difficulty would result for a year or two by the congestion of the lower grade, or the necessity of making special provision for those refused admittance to the higher grade; but in a short time these difficulties would disappear; and the energies of the High School teachers—then expended on proper High School work only—would produce much better results than are possible under present conditions. The increased appropriations for High School work add weighty reasons to those given above why entrance to the High Schools should be guarded by the Board of Education. The additional grants are intended for the accomplishment of a specific work, and it is incumbent upon the board to take every precaution that High School grants shall not be expended upon lower grade work; and that greater claims shall not be entertained on behalf of any school than the actual number of properly prepared pupils may warrant. I propose to submit, at an early day, for the consideration of the Board of Education a scheme of Entrance Examinations, which will aim to accomplish all that is desirable in the directions indicated, without at the same time creating local difficulties or unduly interfering with local management."

The parent who had measles in his house and never "let on" but sent others of his children to school all the same, has been discovered and fined, and this is how the superintendent of schools in Montreal advises his board of the fact: "Mr. Arthy reported to the School Commissioners that the person who had sent his children to school, while members of the family were suffering from measles at home, had been fined by the Recorder, he himself conducting the case on behalf of the Commissioners. He hoped that publicity would be given to this, as it might deter other persons from following the example in this case. It is quite against the law—both school law and municipal law—for any child to be sent to school while any other member of the family is suffering from a contagious disease."

The Board of Governors of McGill in the early part of their last report, make the following allusion to the death of one of themselves in terms that will meet with the sympathy of Canadians generally. Perhaps no name was better known in Canada than the name of Sir Joseph Hickson, the late manager of the Grand Trunk Railway: "Though the sad event," says the report, "did not occur till a few days after the close of the year, reference must be made at the outset to the loss which the University has sustained through the death of Sir Joseph Hickson, who for twenty years had rendered loyal service as a member of the Board of Governors. At a recent meeting of the board the following resolution was adopted: That the board desires to express its deep sense of the loss sustained by McGill University, and by the members of the Board of Governors individually, in the removal by death of their late esteemed friend and colleague, Sir Joseph Hickson. Sir Joseph was always a leading friend of education in Montreal, and had served as a member of the Board of Governors since 1876. More especially in later years, since his retirement from the great work of his life—in connection with which he will always be remembered in the history of the Dominion—he displayed a warm interest in the work of the board, and freely placed his time at its disposal; while his eminent business capacity rendered his services of the utmost value to the University in connection with its recent rapid extension."

The *Manitoba School Question* is getting deeper and deeper into the mire of polemics and politics, so that to mention the matter in a periodical such as ours would hardly escape serious animadversion from some of our readers. Meantime the schools of Manitoba are going on the even tenor of their way, and that is about all our teachers care to know. Under the able supervision of Superintendent McIntyre, the schools of the city of Winnipeg have been brought into a condition of thorough organization. The politicians are on the *qui vive* over the arrival of the newly-appointed ablegate from Rome. Whatever heart's ease he may bring to this party or to that party, he will hardly introduce any new methods of imparting instruction among us, and our schoolmasters will therefore greet his arrival with more equanimity perhaps than they will the last reports issued by the various educational departments throughout the country.

It is a remarkable and significant fact that the last four Archbishops of Canterbury—Longley, Tait, Benson, Temple—should all have been schoolmasters. And the significance is twofold. It shows that the headships of our great public schools are posts that divert from their proper work the very flower of the clerical profession, and it shows also that the surer way to the episcopal throne is not by the pulpit, but by the desk. That this admixture of professions is a survival from a primitive age, when prophet, priest and king were undifferentiated, few will dispute. Whether the practical gain so outweighs the loss as to reconcile us to the anomaly is still an open question. Had the same principle been extended to the other professions, Lord Selborne, Sir Andrew Clark, and General Gordon would all have made admirable archbishops. So says the *Educational Journal*, of England.

A year ago the public schools of Boston employed a number of physicians at a small annual salary. Their duties were to visit schools each morning, and examine the children who gave any evidence of physical disturbances; 14,666 children were examined. Over 9,000 of these were found sick, 1,800 out of them ill enough to be sent home; 437 cases of infectious diseases were discovered, including 70 cases of diphtheria, 110 of scarlet fever, and a great many of measles. Children suffering from impaired hearing and sight were found. This physical condition was not suspected by either parents or teachers.

It seems that there is danger of a disruption in the National Union of Elementary Teachers in England. That body, as our readers are aware, is made up of the vast majority of the elementary teachers of England—both board school and voluntary teachers. The latter have taken offence at the hostile attitude assumed by the Union towards the late Education Bill. That bill was calculated to improve the prospects of the voluntary teachers at the expense of the board teachers, and for this reason, as well as for others, the latter, who form the majority of the Union, opposed the bill to the utmost.

In a letter addressed to the headmaster of Clayesmore school, Enfield, Dr. Conan Doyle, referring to the recent holiday camp tour of the school, writes as follows: "The struggle for existence applies to nations and to races as well as to individuals, and if Young England is to hold its own, it must be by preserving the qualities which made our fathers great. I confess that I fear that we are becoming soft with the increasing comforts of civilization. We seem to shun pain more, and we are not ashamed to show it when we feel it. I hate to see a young fellow wringing his hand because he has got a crack on the knuckles at cricket, or hopping about because he is hacked at football. It ought to be, and used to be, part of a gentleman's traditions not to show pain—and the same applies to discomfort of every sort. To teach our youngsters to adapt themselves to whatever may come, and to lead a natural open-air life is to teach something even more valuable than dead languages."

One cannot be surprised if Irishmen here and there are grumbling over the money which is annually paid out of the taxation of the country for the maintenance of the Queen's College, Cork. The Belfast Queen's College seems to be in a thoroughly healthy condition, and so is the Cork College in its medical department. But for some reason or other the Arts Faculty presents a contrast to the Medical Faculty. Its lecturers are paid at the rate of £2,728 for the year, and they lectured in 1895 to thirty-six students—an average of £80 a student. Twenty-seven scholarships and one exhibition were distributed amongst the thirty-six; and, of the twenty-eight recipients of State aid, only four secured their exhibitions at the open examination of the Royal University. So far as these figures warrant us in drawing a conclusion, the nation does not appear to be getting value for its money at Cork.

CORRESPONDENCE.

To the Editor of THE CANADA EDUCATIONAL MONTHLY:—

I am sure you will not consider me vain when I inform you that my last letter to you created not a little stir amongst us educational men, not to speak of the disturbance it caused among the *coterie* who would rule the educational affairs of our city, beyond the advice of anybody else. While the gossip continued, I was not a little afraid that my personality would be discovered, and when I found that nearly all my colleagues, good honest men that they are, had come under suspicion and that I had escaped, I felt still more uncomfortable; and when I further heard that "the powers that be" had actually located a whole group of us "in their mind's eye" for "things not good but unmentionable" whenever the opportunity occurred, I all but made up my mind that I would write you no more letters that would thus be likely to involve myself and others. The anonymous letter has many objectional features about it which an honest straightforward man shrinks from. But what are we teachers to do? Are we to put up with our burdens and let things drift, until they become insupportable? If we write and subscribe our own names to our letters, what heed is there given to what we have to say by men who are more concerned about who writes a thing than what one writes? Then there is the reprisal to consider. A man may have convictions, but every man is not made of the stuff out of which martyrs are made: a wife and a small family has kept many a "village Hampden" among us from taking the field against abuses, while many a Milton of the second or third degree has too often perhaps decided to remain "mute and inglorious" to save himself from dismissal from office. So there is nothing for us teachers than the anonymous statement of our grievances, if we would come to one another's rescue; and I for one, Mr. Editor, am glad that you have give us the assurance that our anonymity will be safe in your hands. In a word, I am now quite willing, with your assurance in my hands, to let the "little tyrants" pother round my personality for a time, until they come to forget me and mind what I have to say on educational topics.

I need hardly tell you, sir, that perhaps the most interesting topic of conversation in educational circles in this part of Canada is not the lately produced Latin Play, nor the coming elections, nor even the re-organization of the McGill Normal School, but is rather the fate that awaits the Text-Book Committee of the Protestant Committee of the Council of Public Instruction. What is the said Protestant Committee going to do with the members of their own body who have been accused of betraying a public trust? What line of action are the members of the said text-book committee likely to take, not to exonerate themselves, for that they cannot very well do after the confessions they have made, but to deliver themselves from their dilemma between the Protestant Committee and the public, to call it by a very mild name?

Perhaps you do not know, Mr. Editor, that there is at present a vacancy on the Protestant Committee which will no doubt be filled at the next meeting of the committee. The committee consists of two sets of members, some appointed by the government, and others by the committee themselves. The present vacancy is one that has to be filled by the members themselves, and the members of the Text-Book Committee are bound, it would appear, to secure the election for one of their own kind. And why should they not be successful? What has there been in their conduct that the Protestant Committee should not approve of? What has there been in their conduct which any body of honorable men acting for the public cannot afford to overlook?

To explain, the said Text-Book Committee have not been acting very judiciously of late. They have been serving their own purposes, I am afraid. One of them has been revising text-books for remuneration, while another has been recommending the authorization of certain text-books of which he himself was said to be the compiler. Of course such a way of doing things could not be hidden for long. The *denouement* had to come. The plates of the new series of Readers were found to have been stolen from an American firm. The would-be compiler declared that he had had nothing to do with the theft and had never received any recompense for the compiling of the books, while the other gentleman made a confession that he had certainly received money from certain publishers, but that the amounts had been very small and had been received for actual work done. The Protestant Committee, of course, have had to protect its good name from such conduct as this, on the part of those who were acting in trust for them. The action they took was naturally displeasing to the Text-Book Committee, and now to obviate further punishment from the hands of those who have dealt with the misdemeanants too leniently perhaps, the latter and their helpmates on the Protestant Committee have decided, so it is said, to do everything in their power to strengthen their own hands at the Educational Board by electing a man who shall support the Text-Book Committee through good repute and through bad. The right kind of a man to suit their purposes, I am told, has been found; and now from the McGill Normal School to the Montreal High School there is a rallying of forces to fill the vacancy on the committee, not with a representative man—that would hardly suit at this time—but with a member who shall support the text-book in their misdeeds through thick and thin—one who shall stand by them as they continue to mangle the list of text-books, to the perplexity of us poor teachers,—one who shall possibly wink at their further making a little grist by revising or compiling, or at their venting their spleen on some unfortunate publisher who may not be inclined to carry out all their suggestions. I find that this letter of mine has grown too long, and hence I will have to delay till my next, the saying of further on this subject. I may, however, tell you that the man the clique has pitched upon as their candidate is a lawyer, and now their cry is that no more university men are wanted on the Protestant Committee, no more clergymen, no more teachers, only lawyers, only a lawyer, only a certain lawyer, who by his vote shall screen those who have brought indignity on the Protestant Committee, no matter whether the whole of the northern section of the Province of Quebec be without representation, or the said committee be stultified by a loss of public confidence.

Yours faithfully,

MONTREAL TEACHER.

To the Editor of The News:

SIR,—Very many are watching with keenest interest the trend of educational matters in the Province of Quebec. The comparative listlessness on the part of the Protestant community may be misinterpreted. Your advocacy of the "common schools" might have been expected to lead to enthusiasm in its support. The quietness in lieu thereof simply evidences the gathering of forces. Canada and the Province of Quebec pay largely for educational facilities. These have been generously afforded, and sufficiently long to apply the prize of results. A superficial glance at the personnel of faculties proves that educationally Canada does not exist. Her teaching staffs are not of the soil. The prize winners and medallists vanish into obscurity. The chairs of our universities are not open to them. The blowing of trumpets as successive batches of decorated students pass from our halls of learning, are demonstrated to be blowing falsities, otherwise merit could not be denied its reward, even though to prophets in the land of their birth. The late appointment of a bursar to McGill University is a signal exemplification of a pernicious ostracism of the sons of the land. The gentleman selected doubtless is eminently qualified and may be honestly and warmly congratulated, but where are the hundreds of McGill men who fail to secure from Alma Mater even the lowest place? This, however, *en passant*, on the value and success of university education in the Province of Quebec. When we come to the common schools, there is still less to satisfy. Plainly, educational matters are in the hands of a *coterie*, which is not representative of the will and wishes of the people. In presence of distinct and ever advancing encroachments on the privileges of the latter, the servility of the large body of teachers under the regime of an oligarchy deriving authority extraneous to the teaching body itself, carries with it masked reproach and discredit of their certificates and credentials. Is teaching indeed a profession? and an honorable and creditable one at that? If so, where do we discover the first principle of this in their boards of control? The bar, the college of physicians and surgeons, the board of notaries, pharmaceutists, dentists and what not, provide for autonomy and self-government. Are the actual educationists of the country incapable or unworthy? To judge from condition and from facts, none other than an affirmative verdict can be rendered. Is such a verdict worthy of review and appeal? We think so. But if there be either the capacity or spirit of a profession it must needs find an expression at such an arbitrary proposition as the centralization of all educational sanctions in the Normal School of Montreal. Decentralization has been the demand on the part of the judiciary and all the liberal professions, and this claim has been conceded and works for the acknowledged benefit of these several callings. Presumption proceeded fár, when a few officials, nominees not of the body of teachers but the figureheads and actual representatives of interests quite divergent from the great mass of teachers bearing the burden and heat of the day, arrogated to themselves the unrestricted control, irresponsibly exercised as far as the teachers are concerned, of the annual examinations. Our heads of the educational department may be men of unapproachable culture, but their pretension is only reasonably defensible, when they can affirm "our mandate is from the whole body of teachers." Until this first principle be recognized our teachers cannot respect their own position nor expect the respect of others. Emancipation of the teaching body is the demand of the hour. Self-control and self-government are its common right. The best material of the past has sprung from the struggling units who overcome most unpropitious environments and some of our most illustrious statesmen made their first advance as teachers in the common schools.

The present Governor of the great State of New York started his illustrious career as a poor country lad, whose first prize was a district school. A hard and fast rule requiring teachers, without exception, to spend a period in the Normal School, is to close the door in the face of the most promising factor of the intellectual kingdom of our land. Make the standard of diplomas as high as you please, but do not substitute mere drill or arbitrary moulding for those more virile and native powers which, if permitted, will ofttimes rise superior to all normal advantages. If a uniform standard be maintained it is a species of ignoble cowardice to decline a race with less privileged elements. Uniformity based upon privilege or mere imitation is an extinguisher of genius and an index of palsy. Discussing the absence of any "uniform system of teaching or training" as declared by a state commission, a leading writer argues that this want of uniformity is one of the excellencies which makes common, normal, academy, schools more efficient.

EQUALITY.

Missisquoi, Feb. 26th, 1897.

POLITICS AND EDUCATION.

SIR,—Politics spoil everything in this country. We have high judicial authority for the statement; for the remark was made a few months ago by a judge of the Supreme Court sitting upon the Bench in Ottawa, and he spoke the truth. The boatman finds out the snag when he runs against it, and I have lately realized the force of this remark in connection with a discussion upon our Educational System which is now being carried on in *The Globe*. It is charged by the tax-payer that indiscriminate free higher education is largely, if not entirely, responsible for the overcrowding of certain lines of occupation, and for the exodus of the cream of our young men to the United States. The charges are admitted. But the editor of *The Globe* says that education is paramount. The educationist is not concerned with these interesting phenomena. He must not be checked by the contemplation of results. The tax-payer replies that he is not concerned with the education of American citizens, or in filling our cities and towns with a lot of young men of mediocre ability, who cannot find employment, or if they do make a living, help to drive the good man out of the country by increasing the competition when he is fighting for a start. He proposes as a solution of the difficulty that, by a system of scholarships, free higher education should be given only to those who show that they have the ability to make an honorable living by means of the education which they receive; and that all others should pay their own way in the higher branches. For it is generally recognized now that education is used directly as a means of livelihood. It is nothing short of cruelty to give a thousand dollar education to a ten cent boy; the interests of the State and the pupil alike demand discrimination by the State, for, generally speaking, both boys and parents are ignorant of the world of competition, and parents are too liable to overestimate the ability of their offspring.

Everybody will admit that the question is one of very great importance to Canadians, especially in this Province; and, because it is a very difficult and delicate question, it is absolutely necessary that it should be freely discussed upon its merits without fear of interruption by considerations which are not pertinent. And we want the advice of the best men in the country. But it seems that this is impossible so long as education is subservient to politics. Professor Goldwin Smith can talk, for he is not looking out for votes. A short time ago, before a farmers' meeting in Toronto, he indorsed the Scholarship suggestion and declared that the Government had no right to take the people's money for fancy education. On the other hand, I have been told by two prominent members of the Provincial Legislature that they hold the views which I have placed in the tax-payer's mouth, but political considerations tie their tongues. One is a member of the Government; he won't speak out for fear of embarrassing his minister. The other is a member of the Opposition, and he is afraid that his opponents may twist his words, and tell the people upon the platform that he wants to keep them down. So we see that politics hamper free discussion, and we naturally ask ourselves why is education mixed up with politics at all? Every consideration would seem to point against it. There is no man in Canada who has greater power for good or for evil than the head of our educational system. The man that we want is a man of rare combinations. A general, a scholar, a gentleman, and a man who can feel the wants of the people. We don't want the pick of a few politicians, but the pick of the whole Dominion. If he is not suited to the office, we don't want to keep him till his party is turned out of power; on the other hand, if we have once been so fortunate as to secure the man that we need, we don't want to make a change with every change of Government.

Again, if politics and education are wedded together, is there not a manifest and natural danger that the educational system may be utilized as a part of a political machine? And surely, this would be a national misfortune! In support of the present arrangement, it has been argued that it is necessary that an opportunity should be afforded to the responsible head to answer any attack that may be made upon him in the House. Is this impossible without casting the blight of politics upon our system? What is there to prevent us from having education "as it is in England," have it managed by a commission, with a non political head? One member of the commission might be chosen from the members of Parliament, and in the House he could act as the mouth-piece of the whole.

ERNEST HEATON.

Goderich, February 27th.

SCHOOL WORK.

PUBLIC SCHOOL LEAVING ARITHMETIC.

1. Find the alteration in income occasioned by shifting $1,500 stock in the 5 per cents at 120 to the 4 per cents at 96. Answer. No change.

2. Extract to three places of decimals the square root of 2.5. Answer 1.581.

3. Extract the square root of

a. .00000 3330625. Answer .001825.

b. $00027\dot{7}$. Ans. $.01\dot{6}$.

c. $28.\dot{4}$. Ans. $5.\dot{3}$

d. $.0013\dot{4}$. Ans. $.03\dot{6}$.

4. A ladder 26 ft. long stands upright against a wall. Find how far the bottom of the ladder must be pulled out to lower the top 2 ft. Ans. 10 ft.

5. What is the surface of a board 16 inches wide at one end, 23 inches wide at the other, and 21 ft. long. Ans. $34\frac{1}{8}$ sq. ft.

6. Find the area of a circle whose radius is 2 ft. 4 in. Ans. 17 sq. ft. 16 sq. in.

7. The hypothenuse of a right-angled triangle is 101 inches, the base is 99 inches; find the perpendicular. Ans. 20 inches.

8. The base of a right-angled triangle is 24 inches, and the area is 84 inches; find the perimeter. Ans. 56 inches.

9. The sides of a rectangle are in the ratio of 4 to 5, and the area is 11 sq. ft. 36 sq. inches. Find the sides. Ans. 3 ft. and 3 ft. 9 in.

10. Instead of using a yard measure, a dry goods merchant uses a measure 36.25 inches long. Find his loss per cent. from this source. Ans. $^{20}/_{29}$ per cent.

11. The perimeters of a square and a rectangle are each 80 inches. Find the difference in their areas, if

the sides of the rectangle are in the ratio of 1 to 3. Ans. 100 sq inches.

12. A rectangular field containing 15 acres is 10 chains wide, how long is it? Ans. 15 chains.

13. A side of a square field is 60 rods. Find a side of a square field twice as large as it. Ans. 84.85 rods.

14. What is the superficial area of the outside of a box whose dimensions are 8 ft., $7\frac{1}{2}$ ft. and 6 ft. respectively? Ans. 306 sq. ft.

15. The length of a log of uniform dimensions is 10 ft. and its radius is 1 ft. 9 in. Find (1) its surface; (2) its solid content. Ans. (1) 110 sq. ft.; (2) $96\frac{1}{4}$ cu. ft.

16. The area of a chess board having 6 squares along each side is 108 square inches. Find to six places of decimals the length of a side of one of these squares. Ans. 1.732050.

17. A ladder 25 ft. long, stands upright against a wall; find how far the bottom must be pulled out from the wall so as to lower the top one foot. Ans. 7 ft.

18. Which requires the more fence, a circular field 14 rods in diameter, or a square one whose side is 13 rods? Ans. The square field.

19. Find the area of a circular path, the outer circumference of which is 88 yards, and the inner 66 yards. Ans. $269\frac{1}{2}$ sq. yards.

20. A ladder 50 ft. long, placed with its foot 14 ft. from a wall, reaches within 1 ft. of the top; how near the wall must the foot of the ladder be brought that it may reach the top? Ans. $\sqrt{99}$ or 9.949873 ft.

Entrance Work.

1. Bought 7 lbs. tea and 5 lbs. coffee for $5.25, the tea costing 15 cts. a lb. more than the coffee; find the cost of a pound of each. Ans. Tea, 50 cts.; coffee, 35cts.

2. 10 geese and 8 turkeys cost $12.40, the geese costing 20 cts. each less than the turkeys; find the cost of a turkey and of a goose. Ans. Turkey, 80 cts; goose, 60 cts.

3. Eleven horses and sixteen cows cost $1,140, and a horse cost $30 more than a cow; find the cost of a horse and of a cow. Ans. Horse, $60; cow, $30.

4. A man's annual income is $2,500; find how much he may spend per day so that after paying a tax of 2 cents $2\frac{1}{2}$ mills on the dollar he may save $983.75. Ans. $4.

5. A workman was employed for 30 days on condition that for every day he worked he should receive $1, and for every day he was idle he should forfeit 50 cents. At the end of the time he received $27.50; find the number of days he worked. Ans. $28\frac{1}{3}$.

6. A and B can do a piece of work in 4 days, B and C in 6 days, C alone in 10 days. How long would it take A and C together to do it? Ans. $3^4/_{17}$ days.

7. If 4 men or 6 boys can do a work in 12 days, in what time would 8 men and 2 boys do the work? Ans. $5^1/_7$ days.

8. If 7 men or 9 women do a work in 60 days, in what time will 14 men and 2 women do the same work? Ans. 27 days.

9. If 2 men or 3 boys can remove the stones from a field in $5\frac{3}{4}$ hours, in what time can 5 men and 4 boys do the same work? Ans. $1\frac{1}{2}$ hours.

10. 3 men or 5 boys can do a piece of work in $2\frac{1}{6}$ hours, in what time would 7 men and 10 boys do the same work. Ans. $\frac{1}{2}$ hour.

It is not knowledge anywhere that is the end and purpose of man's labor or of God's government. It is life. It is the full activity of powers. Knowledge is a means to that.

Rich gifts wax poor when givers prove unkind.

—*Hamlet*, iii. 1.

ALGEBRA.

FORM II.—1896.

Editor—PROF. DUPUIS.

2. (*a*) Show that $x^4+y^4+z^4-2x^2y^2-2y^2z^2-2z^2x^2$ is divisible by each of the four expressions $x \pm y \pm z$.

This is unfortunately worded, since $x \pm y \pm z$ is only one expression, although denoting four distinct quantities; namely, $x+y+z$, $x+y-z$, $x-y+z$ and $x-y-z$.

This may be shown in a number of ways: *i. e.*, by substitution; by actual division, etc. But probably it is most easily shown by multiplication. For if the statement be true,

$$(x+y+z)\,(x-\overline{y+z})\,(x-\overline{y-z})\,(x+\overline{y-z})$$

must be a factor of the given expression; *i. e.*,

$$(x^2-\overline{y+z}^2)\,(x^2-\overline{y-z}^2)=x^4-x^2[\overline{y+z}^2+\overline{y-z}^2]+(y^2-z^2)^2$$
$$=x^4+y^4+z^4-2y^2z^2-2z^2x^2-2x^2y^2$$

must be a factor of the given expression, ∴ etc.

3. Add together the following fractions, and express the result in its simplest form.

$$\frac{1}{x(x-y)(x-z)}+\frac{1}{y(y-z)(y-x)}+\frac{1}{z(z-x)(z-y)}$$

The common denominator is $xyz(x-y)(y-z)(z-x)$. And the numerators become, paying attention to sign,

$$zy(z-y),\ xz(x-z),\ yx(y-x)$$

and their sum is $(x-y)(y-z)(z-x)$.

∴ The sum of the fractions is $\frac{1}{xyz}$

4. Simplify $\dfrac{\dfrac{1}{x^4+x^2y^2+y^4}}{\dfrac{x+y}{x^3+y^3}}\times\dfrac{x^3-y^3}{x-y}$.

$$x^4+x^2y^2+y^4=\frac{x^6-y^6}{x^2-y^2}$$

∴ The expression becomes $\frac{x^2-y^2}{x^6-y^6}\cdot\frac{x^3+y^3}{x+y}\cdot\frac{x^3-y^3}{x-y}=1.$

6. A, B and C together subscribe \$100. If A had subscribed one-tenth less than he did and B one-tenth more than he did, C must have increased his subscription by \$2 to make up the amount; but if A's subscription had been one-eighth more than it was, and B's one-eighth less, C's would have been \$17 50. Find what each subscribed.

There is an advantage in this kind of question to use *a b c* for the subscriptions of *A B* and *C* respectively; and students should be practiced in employing any letter as a variable or unknown, even in the same question, when literal.

The statements expressed in the language of algebra are

1. $a+b+c=100$
2. $\frac{9}{10}a+\frac{11}{10}b+c+2=100$
3. $\frac{9}{8}a+\frac{7}{8}b+17\frac{1}{2}=100$

These are equivalent to

1. $10a + 10b + 10c = 1,000$
2. $9a + 9b + 10c = 980$
3. $9a + 7b = 660$

The elimination of y and z is then easy enough, giving $a = 50$. Thence from 3, $b = 30$, and from 1, $c = 20$

7. (a) If $a/_b = c/_d$, prove that $\dfrac{ac+bd}{ad+bc} = \dfrac{a^2+b^2}{2ab}$

There are two prominent ways of doing this. The first consists in building upon the second equation from the first by legitimate rules of operation.

Thus, evidently, $\dfrac{ac}{bd} = \dfrac{a^2}{b^2}$, and $\therefore \dfrac{ac+bd}{bd} = \dfrac{a^2+b^2}{b^2}$

Also, $ad = bc$, $\therefore ad + bc = 2ad$. $\therefore \dfrac{ad+bc}{bd} = \dfrac{2a}{b}$

And dividing the first equation by the second, $\dfrac{ac+bd}{ad+bc} = \dfrac{a^2+b^2}{2ab}$

The second method consists in proving that the second equation is an identity, by means of the relations expressed in the first.

Thus, $a/_b = c/_d = m$, say. Then $a = bm$, $c = dm$, and by substituting these values for a and c in the second equation it becomes an identity.

(b) If a, b, c are unequal, and of the fractions

$$\frac{(a+b)(c+d)}{ab+cd},\ \frac{(a+c)(b+d)}{ac+bd},\ \frac{(a+d)(b+c)}{ad+bc},$$

any two are equal, show that each is equal to -1.

This is rather difficult for the paper in which it appears, and the "any two" makes it to some extent ambiguous. It means that only two are to be equated, and the value of the third is to be drawn from the results of this equation. Suppose the first two to be equal; then,

$$\frac{(a+b)(c+d)}{ab+cd} = \frac{(a+c)(b+d)}{ac+bd}$$

and making use of the principle that if $a/_b = c/_d$ each fraction $= \dfrac{a-c}{b-d}$, we have

$$\frac{(a+b)(c+d)}{ab+cd} = \frac{(a+b)(c+d)-(a+c)(b+d)}{ab+cd-ac-bd} = \frac{(a-d)(c-b)}{(a-d)(b-c)} = -1$$

Then $(a+b)(c+d) = -ab-cd = ac+ad+bc+bd$

$\therefore$ Rearranging,

$$ac+ab+bd+cd = -(ad+bc)$$

or, $\dfrac{(a+d)(b+c)}{ad+bc} = -1$, the value of the third fraction.

Symmetry shows us that we would have arrived at a similar result if we had equated other two of the fractions.

10. If $x+y+z=0$, prove that

$$\frac{x(y^3-z^3)}{y-z} + \frac{y(z^3-x^3)}{z-x} + \frac{z(x^3-y^3)}{x-y} = 0$$

The second expression immediately reduces, by division, to

$$xy^2 + x^2y + yz^2 + y^2z + zx^2 + z^2x + 3xyz,$$

or, $xy(x+y) + yz(y+z) + zx(z+x) + 3xyz$.

But from the first relation $x+y = -z$, $y+z = -x$, etc., which gives $-xyz - xyz - xyz + 3xyz$; which is identically zero.

GUMPTION PAPERS.

The value of periodical school examinations in the common facts of everyday life is recognized in not a few of our public and private schools. It may interest some of our readers if we reproduce the following "Observation and General Information Paper," set in December at a large private school in England :—

1. Mention a very important fact relating to the Queen, which attracted universal attention in September, 1896.

2. Give the names of the Prime Minister, Lord Chief Justice of England, Leader of the House of Commons, the M.P.'s for Clapham and Battersea, the present and next President of the United States, past and present Archbishops of Canterbury and Bishops of London, the President of the Royal Academy, and two former Presidents.

3. Name the authors of "The Pilgrim's Progress," "Paradise Lost," "Bleak House," "Utopia," "She," "The Earthly Paradise," "Sartor Resartus," "A Tale of Two Cities."

4. In connection with South Africa, give (*a*) the name of the President of the Transvaal ; (*b*) the names of three of the leaders of the recent raid into that country ; (*c*) the name of the English Colonial Secretary. (*d*) Where are the leaders of the raid at the present time ?

5. What are motor cars? Describe the conditions under which they were placed as to their progress on public roads before and after November 14, 1896.

6. In connection with Nelson, give (*a*) the date of the Battle of Trafalgar; (*b*) the exact words of his celebrated signal ; (*c*) by means of slight rough sketches, illustrate the great difference in appearance between the "Victory," Nelson's flag-ship, and a modern battleship ; (*d*) sketch the Nelson Column on October 21, 1896; (*e*) where is Nelson buried ?

7. What planet is now a brilliant object in the S.E. sky at 8 p.m. ? Make sketches of the Great Bear and Orion. During what months are meteors most common ? Compare the weather of October and November of this year.

8. In connection with cricket, give (*a*) the Champion County for 1896 ; (*b*) the name of the Australian Captain ; (*c*) the name of the batsman who made the greatest number of runs last season ; (*d*) the winner of the 'Varsity Match ; (*e*) fill in the names to the following initials of celebrated cricketers :—W. G. ——, K. S. ——, J. T. ——, W. W. ——, K. J. ——, S. M. J. ——.

9. Show by a sketch how the field is placed for Association Football, with names of the various positions ; also, by a sketch, the difference between the Association and Rugby goal posts.

10. At what times (approximately) does the sun rise and set on Midsummer Day and Christmas Day ? What are the dates of Lady Day and Michaelmas Day ?

11. Sketch, side by side, a leaf of an oak tree and one of a Spanish chestnut.

12. Illustrate, by a rough sketch map, the following details in your town :—Churches : the Parish, the Congregational, Catholic, Wesleyan. Streets : High Street, Pavement, Old Town, Cedars Road, Elms Road, Nightingale Lane. The Ponds on the Common.—*Exchange.*

Our doubts are traitors,
And make us lose the good we oft might win,
By fearing to attempt.

Measure for Measure, i. 4.

CONTEMPORARY LITERATURE.

E. L. Kellogg & Co., of New York, have recently issued three small books specially adapted for the needs of teachers in primary classes. The first is entitled "The Geography Class," and is by M. J. Dean. It follows the approved method of combining history with geography in this early stage, and outlines lessons of interest and merit, first on continents and their various counties, and then on more general geographical ideas. The second is "How to Teach Botany," by A. M. Kellogg. Tue number of scientific terms used is limited, and stress is laid on a method which will develop powers of observation rather than give a merely book knowledge of Botany. The third is devoted to what is called "Busy Work," that is simple and interesting exercises which may be given the children while they remain in their seats. These ingenious devices will be found extremely useful in school work.

"Pope's Essay on Criticism," edited by John Churton Collins. Macmillan & Co., London; Copp, Clark Co., Toronto. The notes of this edition will be found full and accurate, advantage has been taken of the many previous editions of Pope, but the present editor has wisely made his explanations fairly concise.

"Geography of Africa," by Edward Heawood. Macmillan & Co., London; The Copp, Clark Co., Toronto. Following the general plan laid down in this series, the author proceeds from a general view of the continent of Africa to a consideration of its more particular features. Especially valuable chapters will be found on "Races of Man in Africa on Exploration and Political Relations." Not only the ordinary school student, but the general reader, will find in this book information somewhat hard to procure, and yet necessary to the understanding of the political movements of the present day.

"Review of Historical Publications Relating to Canada," edited by George M. Wrong. William Briggs, Toronto. The present volume is the first of a series of "University of Toronto Studies in History," and it has been met with the favorable reception which it deserves. Beginning at page 5 will be found a notice of recent "Canadian Bibliography," written by James Bain, Jr., one who is eminently fitted to speak of such work. In this department, as well as elsewhere in the book, much will be found which is new even to many Canadians, who are interested in whatever work is undertaken in Canada. With the minor notices will be found a brief review of Gilbert Parker's "Seats of the Mighty," which may be characterised as a little severe, not so much in what it says as in what it leaves unsaid.

Two important additions have recently been made to the International Education Series, published by D. Appleton & Co, of New York. "School Management and School Methods," by Joseph Baldwin, in which the author, in a scientifically practical manner, treats of the best school environment and how to obtain it. The second volume is on "Froebel's Educational Hours," and is by James L. Hughes. This gentleman's wide practical knowledge and enthusiasm have made him a worthy exponent of the founder of a great part of modern education. The book will be found clear and interesting, but surely the author would wish to alter his closing words: "The Gospel ideal in practice is already the greatest controlling and uplifting force in the world."

"The Story of the Birds," by James N. Baskett. D. Appleton & Co., New York. Anything which helps to make us see when we look is from a benefactor. This lively and companionable book is apparently intended more particularly for boys whose circumstances have made rich in many spoils. The spirit of the book may be divined from such headings as "What mean the marking and shapes of Birds' Eyes?" (it sounds a little like guessing), and "How Some Grown-up Birds Get a Living."

"Topical Studies in Canadian History," by Nellie Spence. Chas. J. Musson, Toronto. The book consists of careful and accurate outlines of lessons in Canadian History, evidently the outcome of diligent work in classes. The author proceeds from well-known recent events to those of an earlier period.

Sometime ago, in a letter defending himself from newspaper attacks, Richard Harding Davis stated that he was proud to consider himself a reporter still. An ideal reporter he can make good claims to be, if he gives the world many more accounts such as the crowning of the Great King of sad Russia, or the Banderium of Hungary, which may be found in the March number of *Scribner's Magazine*. But it is not a reporter who writes "Soldiers of Fortune," now appearing in the same magazine—a most a greeable story, with a fairy prince, but more than one princess. Poor things, they will be sadly in each other's way. Elizabeth Robins Pennell contributes a lightly written and appreciative study of J. McNeill Whistler, the Master of the Lithograph. "The Story of a Play" is the beginning of a new serial by W. D. Howells, evidently to be of the difficulties of a young pair of Americans. "The Art of Travel," the first of a series, will appeal to all well-regulated minds.

There is a chapter taken from C. G. D. Roberts' new story in the *Littell's Living Age* for March 13th. No small praise has been given to this proof of Canadian letters.

Conan Doyle must have enjoyed the magazines of '96: he admires Napoleon. His admiration is made evident in his short serial which has appeared in the *Cosmopolitan*, and which is concluded in the March number. Zangwill, who last year was to be found at home in the *Pall Mall*, now speaks of Art and Letters here. It is also announced that Mr. Julian Hawthorne has been sent as the representative of this magazine to India, where someone is needed to bring back the story.

Rudyard Kipling told some truths about the American Boy and "saved him at the last" in "Captains Courageons." In some such plain way an American girl is being dealt with in "Miss Nina Barrow," which is at present appearing in the children's faithful friend and lover, *St. Nicholas*. It is written by Francis Courtenay Baylor. There is a most refreshing and delightful paper on "Animal Tracks in the Snow," which should help to open eyes, old and young, to the visible but neglected world. And so Laurence Hutton once hear Thackeray speak—happy Laurence.

The complete novel in the March *Lippincott* is by Julia Magruder, and is called "Dead Selves," which, in this case, appear to make substantial stepping-stones almost any distance up. "Sue's Weddin'" is a most diminutive story of a phenomenal gossip. "The Contributors his own Editor" is a sensible and kindly article which ought to do good to a head-strong race.

To the *Youth's Companion* of March 18th Justin McCarthy contributes "Personal Recollections of Great Americans." Among those of whom he has something interesting to say, are Sheridan, Logan, Grant and Sherman. The usual stirring tales of adventure will be found in abundance, as well as the little ones that have laughed away many a weary thought, never better chosen than in the *Companion.*

"The Queen in the Babylonian Hades and her Consort" is from the pen of Prof. Peter Jensen, and appears in the *Sunday School Times* for March 20th. The various writers in the *Times* are being made at presents the subjects of short biographical sketches, which will doubtless give pleasure to many readers to have come to look to them for help and guidance. A short account of Prof. A. R. Wells is given in this issue.

In the report of the school trustees of the city of St. John to the Superintendent of Education for New Brunswick, the following paragraph, which every board should read and inwardly digest, has been given a place:

"It was discovered during the year that a paper purporting to be a school debenture for $2,000 was held by a bank in the city. An investigation was made by a committee of the board, and the utmost endeavors were made to trace by whom and under what circumstances the fraud had been committed. An information was laid against a party, towards whom suspicion seemed to point, and a preliminary examination was held before the police magistrate resulting in the commitment of the accused for trial, but the grand jury did not find a bill. In the meantime the board has taken all necessary steps for the public protection, and will, as occasion may require, do whatever may be necessary to guard the interests of the citizens of St. John in respect to the matter."

THE CANADA EDUCATIONAL MONTHLY.

THE CANADA EDUCATIONAL MONTHLY, we beg to inform our readers, entered upon a new term of service in educational work on the first of January of this year. It is to be hoped that after the following announcements have been carefully considered by our subscribers and fellow-teachers, that their assistance will be secured on behalf of the MONTHLY in more ways than one.

The MONTHLY is by this time one of the oldest educational periodicals in Canada, and it is the intention of all connected with its management to make it of increasing interest to the teachers of Canada and others interested in the educational progress of the country as a whole. Its *corps* of contributors already includes the most prominent of our educational workers, and what with an improved classification of topics, additional help in the editorial work, and a cordial co-operation on the part of subscribers, publishers and advertisers, it may not be too much, perhaps, to expect it to become, in the near future, one of the best and most readable of our educational journals.

It is the intention of the editors to add to the reading matter two new sections at least, perhaps three. One of these will contain a *resumé* of the current events relating to educational movements in Canada and elsewhere. Arrangements have been made to have a record of such events sent by special correspondents from all parts of the Dominion in time for publication at the beginning of each month; aud it is needless to say that paragraph contributions will be gratefully received from all teachers, when events of more than local interest take place in their district.

The second section will comprise hints from and to teachers, with correspondence. In the past, our teachers have been perhaps a little too timid in making suggestions through the press, particularly suggestions founded on their own experience. Fault-finding is a very different thing from honest criticism, and to the latter no teacher should fail to subject every proposed educational change, before finding fault with it or advocating it. Making use of the MONTHLY as a medium, it is to be hoped therefore that our teachers will join with us in an open and above-board campaign against all defects, and in favor of all improvements in our school work as well as in our school systems so that eventually through the co-ordination of educational views from all the provinces, our various school systems will tend towards the unification of our Canadian national life, and not towards its disintegration. In future any question of an educational tendency may be discussed in our correspondence section, and when a *nom de plume* is made use of, the personality of the writer will under no circumstances be revealed.

The third section, when fully organized, will refer to all matters connected with a proposed BUREAU for the purpose of finding situations for teachers or promotion in the service. Every subscriber will have the privilege of inscribing his or her name on the lists about to be opened for those who wish to have their names thus enrolled. As an experiment we hope many of our teachers will find this section of great service to them.

To the subscribers who have stood by us so loyally in the past, we present our most grateful thanks, while to our new subscribers we make promise that their tastes and wishes will always be carefully considered in the management of the paper. Indeed, we feel it is only through the co-operation of our readers that our enterprise can be fostered to its fullest fruition.

During the year, the publishers of the MONTHLY will call upon advertisers under the improved circumstances of the periodical. To our faithful contributors we trust we will be able, as soon as the revenues of our enterprise improve, to return thanks in a more tangible way than heretofore.

The CANADA EDUCATIONAL MONTHLY, our subscribers must understand, is a journal for the whole Dominion, and not for any section or province.

Communications in connection with the editorial management of the paper are, in future, to be sent from Ontario and all the provinces west of Ontario, to Arch. MacMurchy, M.A., Box 2675, Toronto; and from the province of Quebec and the provinces east of Quebec, to Messrs. William Drysdale & Co., St. James St., Montreal, who will also attend to all matters pertaining to the publishing and advertising departments for the Eastern Provinces, and Wm. Tyrrell & Co. will attend to the like business for Ontario. Publishers: Wm. Drysdale & Co., Montreal; Wm. Tyrrell & Co., Toronto; A. Hart & Co., Winnipeg; J. & A. McMillan, St. John, N.B.

THE CANADA
EDUCATIONAL MONTHLY
AND SCHOOL MAGAZINE.

MAY, 1897.

MORAL TRAINING IN PUBLIC SCHOOLS.*

BY DAVID FOTHERINGHAM, B.A., I.P.S.

HAVING come into close intimacy with our schools for nearly forty years, both as teacher and inspector, I have been impressed with the vital importance of this question of morals in our schools; and while I firmly believe that our Ontario teachers, as a body, can hardly be surpassed in intelligence, rectitude and morality, I am also convinced that the character building that goes on in many schools is at the mercy of much untoward influence.

We have constant change of teachers. Few remain long in the profession, and fewer long in one school. We have a yearly increasing influx of young, inexperienced teachers whose own characters have hardly reached maturity, who have little true knowledge of human nature in its threefold being, and who must acquire the indispensable power of experience by experimenting on that most delicate of all structures, the human soul. There is a large number of children who receive little care in their homes as to moral development, and whose ideas, often expressed to myself, are that material possessions and having a good time are the chief aims of life.

Whilst there is improvement in the character and the care of their surroundings, our school children are, as a rule, sent to buildings and grounds that have little about them to educate taste and develop thoughtful care in manners and morals. Is it too much to say that in many rural districts the character of out-door accommodation often lowers delicacy of feeling and is such sometimes as to be positively degrading? Is it not also true that, during the absence of the teacher at noon or during his attention to routine work at recess, a few rough children will seriously mar the social tone of the school community, and neither the teacher nor the parent knows that the bloom of true delicacy of feeling and intercourse is being brushed from the youthful mind, never to be fully restored? Is it not true that, in the arrangements for seating and recitation, temptation to copy or otherwise pass off the work of others for one's own, too often occurs? and the inexperienced or over-worked teacher fails to realize that indifference to delicate shades of honor and honesty is fixing itself in the conscience of the child, never to be wholly lost in after life. Questionings like these and isolated cases, few, indeed, I am glad to say, of positive wickedness, have led me earnestly and often to enquire what could be done to lift still higher the tone of school life, good, comparatively speaking, now, so as to secure

*Paper read at O. E. A., April '97.

for every child immunity from deteriorating influence during its most sensitive and impressionable age.

"The question of religious training is one of supreme importance and interest."—B. A. Hinsdale.

No subject connected with education bulks so largely in the mind of our most earnest thinkers as that of the moral training of the young. Utilitarians do not trouble themselves, it may be, on this question, but in the estimation of all who desire that our country shall become emphatically the home of the free, enlightened, contented, progressive, patriotic people, no one subject is half so important.

In this Province we claim one of the best educational systems to be found anywhere; but its wisest provisions deal with intellectual training. Those for physical training on scientifie principles cannot be called effective; while for moral training the arrangements may be arraigned as either impracticable or out of touch with public opinion.

They are as follows:—"Every Public or High School shall be opened with the Lord's Prayer and closed with the reading of the Scripture and the Lord's Prayer, or the prayer authorized by the Department of Education. The Scripture shall be read daily and systematically, without comment or explanation; the portions used may be taken from the book of selections adopted by the Department for that purpose or from the Bible as the trustees by resolution may direct. Trustees may also order the reading of the Bible or the authorized Scripture selections by both pupils and teachers at the opening and closing of school, and the repeating of the Ten Commandments at least once a week." Following these provisions we find conscience clauses so that a teacher objecting to leading in these exercises shall be excused; and the children of parents who object to their presence while these exercises are in progress may be excused and allowed to withdraw or remain in another room.

Another clause makes provision for religious instruction by the clergy of any denomination, or their authorized representative, after school hours, to the pupils of their own church, in each school-house, at least once a week. This clause forbids the ex hi bition of emblems of a denominational character during school hours in any school.

I would submit that the reading of Scripture without note or comment, and the Lord's Prayer or the prayer authorized by the Department is not religious and moral instruction. Neither, in the ordinary sense, can the memorizing of the Ten Commandments be called instruction, although, reverently conducted, these exercises are conducive to moral results.

The only provision then for religious instruction in our school law and regulations is to be found in the clause permitting clergymen to undertake this duty at the close of the school day with the children of their own church.

It is nearly forty years since by teaching or inspection I was brought into direct contact with our public schools, and I have yet to find the first school in which religious or moral instruction is regularly or even irregularly given under the authorized regulations. It may be other inspectors can report differently. If so, I have yet to hear of one who is able to do so.

The truth seems to be that systematic and thorough instruction is impracticable at the time and in the way provided for.

Another undeniable and notorious truth is that this subject bristles with difficulties of a very perplexing character. I do not need to call attention to the existence of many denominations and many nationalities in our midst; and I hardly need to say that unless the spirit of broad-minded patriotism shall subordinate the desire for party advantage to the far higher advantage of securing non-sectarian but efficient ethical education for all our young people, we shall find the greatest difficulties in inducing our legislature to give us what we need.

That moral education is essential to good citizenship, is now a maxim of all civilized governments. Not only so; it is recognezed as far more important than intellectual training in its power to make for the safety and prosperity of the State.

In England, in Germany, in France, Italy, the United States and Canada, so important is moral instruction held to be that religious exercises are ordered at the opening or the closing of schools or both. In the first two named countries graded curricula are prepared under government supervision for regular daily instruction and periodical examinations in morals. At the same time sectarian tenets are carefully excluded and conscience clauses rigidly adhered to.

That religious instruction is of prime importance, is evident from the attitude of the German government. Hinsdale tells us that "in no states in the world is more attention paid to the religious instruction of children than in the German states; and in no other Protestant states is so much emphasis laid on the subject in public schools as in those of North Germany."

(*To be continued.*)

SCOPE OF SCIENCE.

By Alex. H. D. Ross, M.A. Tilsonburg.

AMONG men there has ever prevailed a vague notion that scientific knowledge differs in nature from ordinary knowledge, but a little reflection shows that much of our common knowledge is, as far as it goes, rigorously precise. Science does not increase this precision, cannot transcend it. What then does it do? It reduces other knowledge to the same degree of precision. That certainty which direct perception gives us respecting co-existences and sequences of the simplest kind, science gives us respecting co-existences and sequences complex in their dependencies or inaccessible to immediate observation. From this point of view, science may be regarded as an extension of the perceptions by means of reasoning. In the widest sense of the term, it includes:

<table>
<tr><td rowspan="3">1. Science proper, embracing an exact knowledge of</td><td>FACTS</td><td>Historical or Empirical Science.</td></tr>
<tr><td colspan="2">LAWS, obtained by correlating facts.</td></tr>
<tr><td>PROXIMATE CAUSES.</td><td>Rational Science.</td></tr>
</table>

2. Philosophy, or the knowledge of general principles—elements, powers or causes and laws—as explaining facts and existences.

In the narrow sense of the term, science includes an exact knowledge of facts and of laws; and if we accept the usual definition of a science, (viz: "Any department of knowledge in which the results of investigation have been worked out and systematized,") we may classify the sciences as

- *Mathematical*—treating of quantity.
- *Physical*—treating of matter and its properties.
- *Biological*—treating of the phenomena of life.
- *Anthropological*—treating of the life of man.
- *Theological*—treating of the Deity.

In this essay I purpose confining my remarks more particularly to those sciences which treat of matter and its properties, in other words to what is popularly known as Natural Science.

In the progress of human knowledge, a science in its earliest and simplest form, is usually a mere collection of observed facts, as for example the Egyptian's knowledge of the movements of the heavenly bodies. The next step is to correlate or generalize these facts, forming a system like that of Ptolemy or Copernicus; the next, to formulate these generalizations as laws, as Kepler did, and the last, to proceed to some principle or force accounting for these laws (usually by the aid of mathematical analysis) as was done by Newton in his theory of universal gravitation. Thus it is usual to regard Natural History as dealing merely with the description and classification of phenomena, whereas Natural Philosophy seeks accurate quantitative knowledge of the relations between causes and effects. Many subjects of study must first pass through the natural history stage before they attain the natural philosophy stage; the phenomena being observed and compared for many years before the quantitative laws which govern them are disclosed.

The *Physical Sciences* treat of dead matter, of energy apart from vitality, and include

Astronomy, Physics, Chemistry, and the Physical portions of	Geography, Geology, Meteorology, Mineralogy.

Considered as *Sciences of Energy*, they may be classified as the sciences of

Mass-Energy	Astronomy, Mechanics,
Molecular Energy	Kinetic theory of gas Heat, Electricity,
Atomic Energy	—Chemistry,
Ethereal Radiant Energy	Light, Heat, Electromagnetism.

Physical science deals with the whole of nature's wide domain and views it as a scene of restless activity. Some of the subjects with which it has to deal have been indicated already; but like the banyan tree many of its branches have taken root and developed trunks rivalling the parent stem to such an extent that they may be conveniently separated from it, as e.g. *Astronomy*, *Chemistry*, *Biology*.

Astronomy investigates the motions, magnitudes, and distances of the heavenly bodies; as well as the laws by which their movements are directed and the ends they are intended to subserve in the "fabric of the universe." In all ages, astronomy has engaged the attention of the poet, the philosopher, and the divine, and it furnishes the most extensive example of the connection of the physical sciences. In it are combined the sciences of number and quantity, of rest and motion. In it we perceive the operation of a force which is mixed up with everything that exists in the heavens or on the earth; pervades every atom; controls the motions of animate and inanimate beings, and is as sensible in the descent of a rain drop as in the motion of the earth around the sun.

Physics, or *Natural Philosophy*, investigates and measures the conditions and properties of matter as discovered by direct observation and experiment, and deduces the laws connecting those conditions and properties. It has to deal with

Mechanics, including the
- *Dynamics of*
  - Solids-*Kinetics*,
  - Liquids - *Hydraulics*,
  - Gases-*Pneumatics*,
- *Statics of*
  - Solids,
  - Liquids, (*Hydro*
  - Gases, (*statics*.

Phenomena of
- Heat,
- Light,
- Sound,
- Electricity,
- Magnetism.

Properties of
- Impenetrability,
- Weight,
- Hardness,
- Color,
- Solubility,
- etc., etc.

Dynamics treats of the effects of force in producing motion, and of the laws of the motion thus produced. It investigates the laws which govern matter and force. Matter is the vehicle by means of which we become acquainted with the immaterial essence which we in our ignorance call force, and until we know what matter is we cannot hope to know anything about the absolute nature of force. The principal forces known to us are those of adhesion, cohesion, gravitation, heat, light, electricity, magnetism, chemism, vital force, each a peculiar phase or manifestation of the Universal Force or power pervading all space.

The *Dynamics of Solids* includes an investigation of the general properties of matter, such as solidity, extension, divisibility, motion, attraction, repulsion, gravitation, central forces; and at the surface of our globe the phenomena of falling bodies, the motions of projectiles, the vibration of pendulums, the theory of machines and the principles on which their energy depends; the properties of the lever, wheel and axle, pulley, inclined plane, wedge, and screw, and the effects resulting from their various combinations. That branch of dynamics which treats of change of momentum is known as *Kinetics*, grandest problem in Kinetics. *Hy-* and Physical Astronomy furnishes the *draulics* deals with the motion of fluids, and their driving power. Upon its principles depend the construction of fire engines, force pumps, lifting pumps, waterwheels, steam engines, etc. *Pneumatics* deals with gases and their effects on solid and liquid bodies.

Stactics treats of the relations that must subsist among forces in order that they may produce equilibrium. It is the science of bodies at rest. *Hydrostatics* treats of the equilibrium and pressure of fluids. As the term fluid includes both liquids and gases, it is evident that the actions of siphons, fountains, hydrostatic presses, barometers, "pneumatic" tubes, the determination of the specific gravities of solids and liquids, etc., etc., depend upon hydrostatic principles.

Heat deals with the expansion of solids, liquids and gases; the laws of fusion and boiling for solids and liquids; the vaporization of liquids and solids; the liquification and solidification of gases and liquids; conduction, radiation, diathermancy, latent and specific heat; the mechanical equivalent of heat; and a whole host of other problems. The construction of thermometers, calorimeters, and hygrometers presupposes a knowledge of the laws of heat. Its principles underlie the construction of economical gas and steam engines, the heating of buildings; they explain the production of winds and ocean currents, and account for the formation of dew, fog, rain, snow, sleet and hail.

Optics, the *Science of Light*, pertains to everything connected with light itself and our conception of it. It treats of vision, light and color, as well as the various phenomena of visible objects produced by the rays of light reflected from mirrors or transmitted through lenses. Single, compound, and lacernal prisms; reflecting and refracting telescopes, solar microscopes, micrometers, spectacles, opera glasses, cameras, magic lanterns, kaleidoscopes, and other optical instruments owe their origin to the application of the principles of optics. By the use of these instruments the natural powers of human vision have been wonderfully increased, and our prospects into the work of the Creator extended far beyond what former ages could have conceived.

Acoustics, the *Science of Sound*, treats of the nature, phenomena, and laws of sound, and deals with the theory of music, concord and harmony.

Electricity deals with the origin of the current in battery cells or in dynamos, and is closely related to Magnetism. In fact, Ampere supposes the magnetism of a body to be due to electric currents circulating around the small particles of which it is composed. Telegraphing over land or under sea, telephoning, electrotyping, electroplating, electric lighting, and electric traction are only a few of the many useful applications of electricity.

Chemistry investigates the simple forms of matter, the modes or processes by which they are combined or separated, the laws by which they act, and the properties of the compounds they form. Without a knowledge of chemistry it is quite impossible to form any conception of many of the most important phenomena of the universe; and there is scarcely any process in the arts or manufactures over some part of which chemistry does not preside. The economic reduction of iron, copper, tin, zinc, lead, nickel, and silver from their ores are in a great measure questions of chemistry. Gas-making, sugar refining, and soap-boiling are operations all partly chemical, as are also the processes by which are produced glass and porcelain. Imagine, if you can, the state of civilization if all the iron, lead, soap, gas, glass and porcelain in existence were to suddenly vanish, and you will have some idea of the importance of chemistry, and how much it contributes to human welfare and to human comfort.

Biology, the *Science of Life*, includes Botany and Zoology. It treats of the origin and nature, the continuance and progress of life, and pre-supposes some knowledge of the natural history, structure, physiology and distribution of both plants and animals. Every observant person is something of a naturalist; fewer are botanists or zoologists; and still fewer are biologists. Biology is the philosophical aspect of both botany and zoology, and the study of the advanced student rather than the beginner.

In conclusion—the tendency of modern physical science is toward more complete generalization; its goal being the discovery of a principle that shall connect all physical phenomena. Its divisions and subdivisions do not remain separate, but now and again reunite in direct and indirect ways. They mosculate; they generally send off and receive connecting growths; and the intercommunion has been ever becoming more frequent, more intricate, more widely ramified. In marvellous contrast to the fragmentary and disjunctive science of 80 years ago, modern science presents the spectacle of a simple, unified and comprehensible cosmos, consisting everywhere of the same prime elements, drawn together by the same great forces, animated everywhere by the same constant and indestructible energies, evolving everywhere along the same lines in accordance with the selfsame underlying principles. Ours has been an age of firm grasp and of wide vision.

Isolated facts have been fitted and dovetailed into their proper niche in the vast mosaic. Cosmos has taken the place of chaos. In the words of Sir David Brewster, "Modern science may be regarded as one vast miracle, whether we view it in relation to the Almighty Being, by whom its objects and its laws were formed, or to the feeble intellect of man, by which its depths have been sounded, and its mysteries explored."

NATURE STUDY IN PUBLIC SCHOOLS.*

BY NORMAN MACMURCHY, B.A., ELORA.

I FEEL rather out of place in appearing before you at this time, for I am sure many members of our Science Association could present the subject which we are to consider more clearly and fully than I am capable of doing. Those of you who heard a short paper I read last year before the Natural Science Section on this subject will pardon repetition, for what I have to say to you to-day will necessarily be to some extent in the same line.

I am very glad Mr. J. L. Hughes is to speak to us. A year ago. when listening to his address "On the Influence of Kindergarten Spirit on Higher Education," I felt that I would have liked to have said what he said so well, at an earlier hour that day, when I had been speaking to our own Section on Nature Study.

This seems an opportune time to discuss Nature Study in our Public schools, particularly from the point of view of its educational value. It is a matter which is occupying the minds of teachers. At one of the meetings of the Training Department of this Association the report of an important committee,composed of the leading educationalists of the Province will be given—

1st. "On the educational value of subjects."

(a) Value for discipline.
(b) Value for culture.
(c) Value for use.

2nd. "What subjects should be taught in our public schools."

Again, in the United States the importance of the study of nature in elementary schools was pointed out and urged by the reports of the committees of ten and fifteen to the National Teachers' Association a few years ago. In those schools where Nature Studies have been introduced the results point to their educational value. In addition we seem to have come to a period in our educational progress when changes are about to be made, not alone in the subjects taught, but also, possibly, in the methods of instruction.

Before making changes we should weigh well those proposed. To do so we should inform ourselves of the relative values of subjects. At present we will more particularly confine ourselves to pointing out the value of Elementary Science or Nature Study.

We, the science masters of our high schools, hope to arrive at the same end as the Kindergarteners, viz: "the self-activity of the child." We wish to enable the child to educate himself by giving him something to do in accord with his mental development, and so to cultivate his senses that he may acquire the power to make accurate observations, a process which must always precede accurate thinking. We have been led to this view from dealing with pupils coming from our public schools, who

*Paper read at O. E. A. April, '97.

are, as a rule, unable to make observations from which conclusions may be drawn. We feel that if our pupils are taught to observe accurately they are in a great measure educated, for then this first and very necessary part of education is complete. The conclusion therefore drawn from viewing the product of the public schools is that perception is almost wholly neglected and that the other faculties are in consequence undeveloped.

If we consider the kindergarten we find that the child is there active and not passive; his activity is a self-activity and his expression is self-expression. His senses are being employed with a definite end in view for him and thus they are being cultivated. The power gained for the child is a power to use power. This is the reason, or at least one of the main reasons, why we in our high schools have our pupils perform their own experiments in chemistry and physics and do not perform them ourselves.

That can only become a part of the child's knowledge which he has obtained by a free action of his perceptive faculties and thus made his own.

To do this the senses must be trained; and if this is necessary in primary education, is it not equally if not more, required in all other departments of education, public school, high school and college?

This idea of self-development is to a great extent lost sight of in our public and high schools. In the latter, however, we are forced to consider it whether we wish to do so or not. For the training of perception is the first requisite of all good results in science teaching, and may I not add in all teaching? For no true and good results can be arrived at without clear and accurate perception, and the chief object of education—to enable the child to compare and analyse, that is, to think—cannot be otherwise obtained.

We believe that it is too late to begin to teach Elementary Science or Nature Study when pupils reach the high schools. It should be a continuation of the method employed by the child in teaching himself when he first gains knowledge, i.e., by experience or experiment. This plan should be continued through all stages of education, not used as now in our kindergartens and then departed from to a great extent. Elementary Science should be begun in the lowest forms of the public school, and other lessons should be so related thereto that the pupil should learn them in connection with his Study of Nature, not as separate and distinct subjects. Subjects need not be divided as they now are in our school curriculum, but they should be made inseparable parts of one lesson. In this way we claim that Nature Study could easily be made the basis of composition, spelling, writing, drawing, etc.

Whatever views have been held in the past with regard to the value of subjects we may to a great extent leave alone. Let us consider them as we find them to-day. What subject or subjects will best prepare youth for the struggle of life after leaving school is the living question with us; let us consider it for a short time.

We believe that we have at the present time a better knowledge of the mental activities than could be obtained at any time in the past. As a result of this knowledge the old idea that the mind is made up of separate parts is being discarded, the modern view being that the mind is a unit and should be developed as such. The material of instruction should be chosen with a view to train the whole mind, perception, memory, imagination, judgment, and reason, and together with these intellectual faculties the impulses and will should also be trained.

Perception cannot be separated from memory and reason along the line of perception. Perception being developed in any direction, the other faculties of memory, imagination, and reason will also be developed. A man's system of thought will mould his character, e g., doctor, minister, merchant, etc.

The faculties therefore cannot be separated but are phases of one process, and the intellect is inseparable from the emotions and will.

If this view of mental science is correct, the old doctrine that the work of the mind in any direction develops power that may be used equally well in all directions, is wrong. To put the case broadly, no person will maintain that the study of physics will prepare a person for the practice of law as well as if he had read jurisprudence.

And what a person studies largely determines what knowledge he can obtain in the future. He who devotes himself to the study of physics is enabled to interpret and appreciate a further knowledge of that science, but he will not be equally competent to interpret medical, legal and theological facts. What a man knows always determines what he wants to know and what will interest him. Therefore study in any particular line will limit our faculties to development in that direction. If this is so, surely no subject should be studied merely for the discipline alone it may be supposed to give, particularly if other subjects can be found that will give the necessary discipline and knowledge as well.

This is another reason for the introduction of Nature Study in our schools. The old idea of formal discipline by certain subjects is losing ground, and those subjects which will have a direct value in giving the pupil knowledge that will be of service to him in after life will in the future receive more prominence. By these, habits of attention, reflection, and industry may be formed equally as well as by formal subjects set for these purposes.

If we take it that our aim should be to have our pupils understand their surroundings so that they may adapt themselves to circumstances and utilize them for their own welfare, then they should study Nature, for it surrounds them, Nature Study should be prominent in our schools. Our pupils should be led to observe accurately and to interpret the facts of Nature so that they may become familiar with methods required in after life. These they must use whether they wish to do so or not.

The aim of education nowadays is to acquire a knowledge of symbols through the things which they represent, not to learn first the symbols and then gain the knowledge which these symbols represent. The subjects which enable us to express our knowledge, as grammar, composition, arithmetic, reading, writing, and drawing, should not be taught distinct from the knowledge or real subjects such as literature, nature studies, geography, and history, but as part of them. A symbol is learned with great difficulty, and will be of little use to the learner unless it be connected with the thought it represents. But if, on the other hand, the thought is first aroused in the mind, the task of acquiring the symbol is easy compared with what it would have been had not the pupil been seized of the thought beforehand—e.g., botanical terms—to master which would be well-nigh impossible it seems to me, were we not to first fix in the mind the thought which they are to represent. When the fact is presented to the pupil first the acquiring of the symbol needs but a slight effort.

We must endeavor to have thought suggested by symbols without effort on the part of the pupil. The symbols themselves, or the power to use these symbols, which only express thought, should not be brought into prominence. To accomplish this we must repeatedly keep the thought connected with the symbol which represents it.

If this be followed out we should not study language, grammar, reading, writing and drawing except as the expression of the thoughts gained in nature study, geography, history, etc. Let us teach the former subjects through the expression of thoughts gained from the latter or knowledge subjects. Much drill may be necessary, but we should use the real subjects, nature study, geography, etc., to obtain that drill. These subjects will give grammar, writing, drawing, etc., a value which they cannot have when taught by themselves.

From learning by doing, activities become habitual, and these are the ones that determine character. It is these impressions which have become indelible by action and expression which always affect us. It is not what we hear so much as what we say and do that affects our character and makes us better or worse.

What a pupil knows when he leaves school is but little, and unless we train him to make use of that little as he would make use of his wider after experience, this school training of his will be a failure. We must teach that which is to be of after value to the child as well as that which is to discipline. Let us teach our pupils to write and speak correctly, not by teaching these subjects by themselves but as the expression of their thoughts.

To leave science out of the public schools is to invert the natural order and process of youthful development which the child has commenced long before entering school. The interest he has in obtaining knowledge, from early consciousness, is maintained by the interest inherent in the subject itself. What the child most wants is to do something that interests him, not something that is of interest to the teacher. In this way we make knowledge real by making it a part of our pupils' existence.

Nature Study is perhaps not so much the matter as the method. We must permit our pupils to make their own observations and thereby to train perception, and so enable them to analize and compare what is before them, that is to think.

If they are to obtain facts of nature from text-books I would by no means favor such study.

It is the process that is most valuable, not so much the knowledge acquired in itself. If the facts of nature are learned from text-books, the chief end desired—the development of the child—is not gained by such study.

We believe that for discipline, for culture, and for use, Nature Study is the most important we can have in our schools, it being made the basis of obtaining knowledge and of teaching those subjects by which we express our thoughts.

"There is a pleasure in the pathless woods,
There is a rapture in the lonely shore,
There is a society where none intrudes,
By the deep sea, and music in its roar;
I love not man the less, but nature more,
From these our interviews, in which I steal
From all I may be, or have been before,
To mingle with the universe, and feel
What I can ne'er express, yet cannot all conceal."

—*Byron.*

THE REFORMATION SCHOOLS.*

"NEVER was a great reputation more easily gained and less deserved than that of King Edward VI. as a founder of schools." Thus Mr. Leach announces a complete reversal of a traditional opinion. It must be admitted that he supports his views in great detail, upon a first-hand examination of original documents and an independent and incisive criticism. He wisely puts before his readers the means of following his argument and judging for themselves as to its sufficiency. About two-thirds of this volume is devoted to a reprint of pertinent documents—the Commission of Inquiry, the Commission for Continuance of Schools, etc., and extracts from a very large number of Certificates and Warrants under the Chantries' Acts, 37 Henry VIII. c. 14, and 1 Edward VI. c. 4. The preliminary matter, occupying about one-third of the book, deals with the significance of the facts, under about a score of heads. Mr. Leach does not, of course, profess that his investigation is complete, in the absence of much necessary material. But, so far as the available materials go, he comes to decided conclusions. He definitively dethrones King Edward VI. from his pride of place as the founder of our national system of education, even by proxy. The only foundation with which Edward VI. is even reported to have any personal connection is Christ's Hospital, and that institution was founded, not as a grammar school, but as a foundling hospital, and Edward gave it little but his name. And as for his ruling councillors, they, says Mr. Leach, "can at least claim the distinction of having had a unique opportunity of reorganizing the whole educational system of a nation from top to bottom, without cost to the nation, and of having thrown it away."

Henry VIII. cannot be charged with any intention to damage education. But he was in straits for money. Other people, it was found, were devouring the chantries without license; why, then, in the intolerable drain of the wars, should not the king rather put the plunder in his own sack? That is the substance of the argument of the first part of the Chantries' Act, 37 Henry VIII. c. 4. The second part deals with unsuppressed institutions. It does not give the colleges and chantries to the king out and out at once, as the first part does; it only empowers him to issue commissions, and take what he pleases. Only such chantries, hospitals, brotherhoods and guilds as were liable to first-fruits might be dissolved, but all colleges might be destroyed, whether they paid first-fruits or not—and so the colleges in the Universities, and Winchester and Eton, which only ten years before had been expressly treated as non-ecclesiastical, "were deliberately swept into the net." It may be that the purpose was to sweep away the "superstitious uses," and thereafter to refound the colleges. Anyhow, the Act passed in 1545 or 1546; Henry apparently took a turn of reaction, and died in January, 1547; and the power to seize the chantries died with him unexecuted.

A new Act was therefore necessary. The advisers of Edward VI. based their action, not on lack of money, but on religous opposition to the objects of chantries. Much might be advanced in justification of that view. The Act of Edward apparently intended that the same Commissioners should first inquire into and then

* "English Schools at the Reformation, 1546-8." By Arthur F. Leach, M.A., F.S.A.. (Constable & Co.)

continue the schools, giving them either their former lands or other lands in order to form an adequate endowment. But this intention was not carried out. Two separate Commissioners of Continuance were appointed, Sir Walter Mildmay and Robert Kelway (a lawyer whose name is still known in the courts as the compiler of a series of law reports). Their commission was pretty comprehensive, and the schools were "made quite a subordinate part of the business they had to do." The fatal part of their commisson, as stated by Mr. Leach, was this:—

"And forasmuch as present order and direction cannot be had and taken for and concerning the said grammar schools and preachers, and for the continuance and alteration of the same," and all the rest of it: "our pleasure is that so much money as heretofore hath been yearly employed towards the maintenance of any such schools, preachings, schoolmasters," etc., "shall be paid from Easter last to the sustentation of the same in such manner as the same has been used to be paid, until such time as other order and direction shall be taken therein, in manner afore rehearsed." And so they were directed to issue their warrants accordingly, on the strength of the certificate of any of the said auditors or particular surveyors, or any of their deputies. It therefore came down to this, that the question of schools was really settled by the clerk of a person who occupied the same sort of position as a local agent of the Woods and Forests now. He took out of the certificates what schools were kept and were to be kept, and Mildmay and Kelway signed the warrants, which the deputy of a deputy of a deputy drew up. . . In such a fiasco ended the great promises of Henry to his Parliament, and the expressed will of the Parliament of Edward VI., for the reform of the chantries and the advancement of learning. For most of the schools the "other order" never came.

The value of the "so much money as heretofore hath been yearly employed towards the maintenance of any such schools," etc., steadily fell; and the painful illustrations cited by Mr. Leach may be commended to the study of those who laud Edward VI., and who approve of piecemeal interference with a comprehensive existing system.

Mr. Leach gives an interesting sketch of the various classes of schools of the time—schools connected with cathedral churches, with monasteries, with collegiate churches or colleges, with hospitals, with guilds, with chantries, as well as independent schools, unconnected with and in no way dependent upon other such institutions. He speaks of the re-foundation of certain schools in consequence of the dissatisfaction prevalent on the outcome of the Acts. "By their wealth and by their good works," he points out, "we can measure the loss sustained by their contemporaries and compeers, which were restricted to a fixed sum, adequate in some cases at the time, but long since shrunk into a miserable pittance." He shows that many of our existing schools go back not simply to Edward VI., but to a remote antiquity. "Grammar schools, instead of being comparatively modern post-Reformation inventions, are among our most ancient institutions, some of them far older than the Lord Mayor of London or the House of Commons." The records he reprints, which are by no means complete, show close on two hundred grammar schools in England before the reign of Edward VI., "which were, for the most part, abolished or crippled under him." He thinks three hundred is "a moderate estimate of the number in the year 1535." "Most of them were swept away either under Henry or his son; or if not swept away, plundered and damaged." Much interest will be found in the treatment of the statistics, from the documents now published, as to the number and character of the schools, and the educational payments. Taking the bare stipends, "the average pay of a schoolmaster works out at £6. 9s. 6d. a year." "In the Edward VI. re-foundations, £20 a year seems to have been the standard aimed at, which, with outgoings for repairs, allowance for an usher, and the like, would give about £12 a year to the headmaster. That is about the sum the larger schools, though not the largest, paid before the Reformation." "The school and University exhibitions absolutely disappeared. Most of the latter were perversions, excellent perversions, of the original foundation." As to the numbers in attendance, Mr. Leach has some very striking remarks. "The proportion of the population which had opportunity of access to grammar schools, and, as we can see, used their opportunities, *was very much larger then than now*." The italics are ours. There is very little direct information in the records as to what the boys learnt. But Mr. Leach pieces together a good deal of suggestive matter. As to Latin, he concludes that "for all practical knowledge of the language, for readiness in reading, in writing, and still more in speaking, Latin, the young Beckets, or Mertons, or Wolseys, might be safely pitted against their modern successors." At Ipswich school, he shows from Wolsey's statutes, the boys "were also to learn *précis*-writing and to write essays." The whole programme at Ipswich he declares to be "a much more liberal *menu* than that provided by Colet, ten years or so before, for St. Paul's School." As to the classes in attendance, "it was the middle classes, whether country or town, the younger sons of the nobility and farmers, the lesser landholders, the prosperous tradesman, who created a demand for education, and furnished the occupants of the grammar schools." Apparently we have not made appreciable extensions yet in England, although the laboring classes are no longer serfs, and although Parliament does not now petition the Crown against their being allowed to go to the Universities or schools. Let our Minister of Education give an occasional glance at what is doing in Scotland or Germany. Meantime, it will be seen that Mr. Leach has produced a work of substantial original research, of extreme interest in varied directions, and of much historical importance and practical suggestion.—*Educational Times.*

THE SNOBBERY OF EDUCATION.

The College Girl who Affects an Air of Superiority.

EDITORIALLY, in the April *Ladies' Home Journal*, Edward W. Bok expresses himself vigorously in depreciation of the tendency to introduce a dangerous element of snobbery into education. He notes the pervading "I know so much" air that is encountered on all sides, and the feeling that a line is being drawn on a so-called educational basis. Mr. Bok contends that "an educational process which sharpens and polishes only a girl's intellect, and either deadens or neglects her heart or soul, is a sorry imitation of what an education really stands for and is. . . The practice followed by some girls who have been at college of holding their heads above those who have not is a foolish proceeding, and smacks of the most repulsive kind of snobbery. It is never safe for us to assume that we know more than the people around us, whether we are college trained or not. The longer we live in this world the more we become convinced how little we know. The people most humble in their opinions are generally the best educated. It is an art which only a few of us learn: to be reticent of our own opinion when every one around us is expressing his. Yet this is one of the attributes of the well educated. Silence often speaks louder than speech. But the girl fresh from her books and college does not always perceive this. She is apt to assume, for example, that people are uneducated if now and then they speak ungrammatically. But she does not know that the most vital truths ever spoken or written, the truths which have done mankind the greatest good, have not always been those which would have borne grammatical dissection. Their good lay in what was said, rather than in the way in which the sentences were constructed. It is when we are young that we believe that all that is worth knowing is printed in books. When we are older we find that the deepest truths are never written. It is well enough for a girl to hold up for herself a standard in grammar or anything else. But she is unwise when she believes that her standard is the one by which she may judge and measure others. She has no right to do so in the first place. And in the second, she is far more apt to be wrong in her deductions than she is to be correct."

THE GROWTH OF CRIME.

SOCIOLOGISTS in America have been notifying the world for several years that crime is steadily increasing. A good many persons have heard the statement, and have merely considered it as they consider weather predictions—as not affecting their business, and, therefore, not to be worried over. Practically, the prisons are better tenanted, the courts are busier, safe-deposit vaults are increasing, more policemen are employed, and windows and doors are heavily barred at night in city and hamlet.

The yearly report of the magistrates in this city confirms the estimates of sociologists; crime is increasing more rapidly than the population. For example, the population in this city has increased 33 per cent., and crime 50 per cent. And the increase is remarkably in the case of serious crimes; that is, there are far more felonies committed than formerly. In 1886 the felonies were 4,000; in '96, 7,000.

Another feature is that a large proportion of crimes is committed by young persons; youths are now guilty of robbery and burglary. Again, there is an increase of women guilty of felonies, sixteen being tried for burglary. Along with crime, suicide always keeps pace. In a community where there is little or no crime there are few or no suicides. In this city, in 1886, eight women and 106 men were charged with homicide; in 1896, ten women and 168 men.

It is noticeable that all these criminals had more or less of the education our public schools supply so freely. It cannot be inferred that the possession of this ability to read and write made them criminals. If the compulsory law is put in force, the criminal cannot but be more or less educated. If we must have criminals, educated criminals are to be preferred to ignorant ones. We doubt whether there is any solid connection between 3R education and crime; as we have just said, if the compulsory law is put in force, in a few years all criminals will have a 3R education. If the law commands all men to wear cutaway coats, then all criminals will wear cutaways.

That the public schools should be active in preventing our youth from becoming criminals is a proposition all will admit; that they are not doing what might be done, all will admit likewise. The consideration of this subject might well employ the National Association this year for its entire session in all its departments. Attention has been called to the absence of the ethical in the aim of the public school. The Catholics, especially, point this out; they have prophesied the present results. It would be interesting and valuable to have statistics concerning the schools criminals of all kinds have attended; whether public, parochial, or private, and the amount of education. We lack, too, a history of criminals. The state ought to get a minute account from every criminal (not to be published with name and incidents, of course), as to ascertain with some precision the cause of crime, at the outset.

The great defect in our American educational process is the trusting to good fortune for the development of the ethical; the teacher does not hold himself responsible for the training of his pupils to do right. This is not stated too broadly. The effect is to have good order, of course; but if the reason is asked why good order is sought, it will be replied that progress in studies cannot otherwise be made. What is the supreme object of the school? We must admit it is of an ethical nature. But if the superintendents of New York, Brooklyn, and Chicago, and even Boston, be asked if, in their examination of the schools, they make this supreme, they will certainly say no; they make useful knowledge, mental discipline, supreme. They want the pupils to do right, of course; they demand that the teachers set a good example; but both superintendents and teachers aim at the 3R's and leave the ethical to the parents, to the Sunday-school, the church, and good fortune in general.

With the statistics given in a preceding paragraph before us it is well worth inquiring whether American educators are ready this year to take up the consideration of this pressingly important matter; a matter of more over-shadowing interest than any other. It is probable that Supts. Jasper, Brooks, Lane, if asked as to the possibility of making the ethical the first aim in the schools in their cities, they would say that it was impossible to have religion taught. But does this meet the case? We think not.

In American schools the means relied on are wholly the personal influence of the teacher, together with his example. And, yet, vast numbers every year are licensed to teach, and no examination is made to see whether they have employed personal influence to start their pupils on ethical tracks.

But there is another great failing. We have said the American teacher relies on personal influence and example to attain ethical results, and this has been true until within the past few years. It has finally been perceived, by a study of pedagogy, that the instruction given in the schools is a powerful means of producing ethical results. So long as it was bare 3R instruction there was no tendency given to the mind; it did not act at all as a stimulus in any direction whatever. It has been perceived that the knowledge must arouse feelings, desires, and end in resolutions. All human beings come under the control of convictions, which take the form of maxims or dogma. These convictions arise from ideas which have aroused feeling. Now ideas can be aroused by the teacher; if a real teacher, he can and will cause interest; thoughts that interest will be retained, reviewed, pondered upon, and produce resolutions and determination to act.

This fundamental principle has not been kept in view. The teacher has aroused an interest that the pupil should know more; that is one thing; but that is wrong. The teacher arouses an interest, so that a love for the subject matter itself appears; that is another thing. Pupils of six, seven and eight years of age have been seen who have been drilled to add columns of figures with surprising quickness. What was the motive?

The instruction given is then a most important factor in attaining ethical results. Herbart says, "out of the thoughts arise feelings, and out of them, principles and modes of conduct." The pupil must have thoughts that interest him; interest is, therefore, the immediate purpose of instruction. It has been with us, however, of little account, except to make acquirements.

The growth in crime has not come from a want of personal sympathy; every teacher wants his pupils to turn out well. But may the teacher rightly expect to have an ethical foundation by this personal sympathy? Must there not be determinations? How are determinations reached? These are fundamental questions, and well worth pondering upon.—*School Journal, N.Y.*

Heaven will not be pure stagnation, not idleness, not any more luxurious dreaming over the spiritual repose that has been and safely and forever won; but active, tireless, earnest work.

—*Phillips Brooks.*

THE OUTSIDE INFLUENCE.

THE teacher enters his school-room to find a company of boys and girls apparently ready to be molded to his will. They appear to be ready to be influenced to choose right courses of conduct; they appear to have been influenced to act according to settled principles. He dismisses them at night often in the full belief that he has accomplished something that very day that will make them proof against temptation, active in ethical ways, and only needing more of his teaching to bring them to a full manhood of earnest endeavor.

But he has an outside influence to contend with that is mightier than he. The water between New York and Brooklyn seems peaceful and harmless, but the ferry-boat that launches into it feels a mighty current that grasps it as with giant arms; and though it combats the water's force with intense effort it is often swayed far out of its intended course. And so the pupil who leaves the class-room for the street or the home encounters influences that set at naught the teachings of the day.

In the early days of this country the pupil found in the home or the street the same urgent pressure towards a virtuous life that he experienced in a school-room; but a momentous change has taken place, and the teacher now feels very doubtful as to his influence over the lives of his pupils. A gradual deterioration in public morals has been going on for a quarter of a century; though all that time the expenditure for public schools has increased, fine buildings have been erected, and a more philosophical course of procedure is pursued; yet from various causes the pupil is met on the outside of the school-room by adverse influences that nullify what has been done for him within its walls.

At the meeting of the National Educational Association, at Buffalo, last summer, it was noticeable that little knots of men and women would be found in parlors of hotels, and the topic of conversation would not be what had been said in an address but the disorganized and unbalanced public sentiment. One lady told of hearing several of her young women pupils debating whether it were not better to commit suicide than constantly to be made to do disagreeable things. A gentleman who had been long in the field declared that the antagonism to the influence of the schoolroom often kept him from sleeping at night.

The papers of this city lately contained an account of a girl fifteen years of age who, not allowed to go back to her boarding school but instead kept at home to work, undertook to commit suicide. The Indiana papers contained an account of an eleven-year-old girl of Anderson, who, upon being rebuked for truancy, bought a box of rat-poison and swallowed it.

There have been thoughtless people who charge this attitude of youth towards morality upon the schools; but these girls got their notions of suicide from newspapers or from their companions. It is the universal testimony of those who have looked into the work of the school-room of the past twenty-five years that it is far higher in character, that it reaches deeper, or is calculated to reach deeper, into the life of the pupil than ever before. The fault assuredly is not with the teachers. This period might be called the normal school period, so rapidly has this class of school been developed; so that the kind of teaching is of a more professional character; and this again proves that the influences inside of the school-room have increased in power and adaptation.

The outside influence has come at last to be an opposing factor of threatening magnitude. There are few groups of teachers in the cities that do not refer to it; they speak of it as something in the air. Boards of education refer to it. The interest in schools they see is unabated, but they see an unwillingness in the older classes to yield to the restraints that must be imposed. The college faculties are not wholly agreed on declaring there is a disorganized public sentiment; they admit that the football game has introduced experiences that are decidedly opposed to the welfare of the students.

This is not the place to discuss the causes of the demoralization. We must recognize the existence of what will be a fatal disease if not checked and apply all energies to get on a healthful basis. The teacher ought to be a religious man and to do all he can to promote religion among the community. The community, it will be plainly seen from what is said, needs his influence; he must do more than his work in the school-room. As the Christian ministers have felt it necessary to form Endeavor and Epworth societies, so the teacher must go out into his community, form associations, and construct rightly and solidly this disorganized public sentiment.—*School Journal.*

No man can be really safe, really secure that the world shall not harm him, unless there is going out from him a living and life giving influence to other men. And no man is really helping other men unless there is true life in his own soul.

—*Phillips Brooks.*

It's wiser being good than bad;
  It's safer being meek than fierce;
It's fitter being sane than mad,
  My own hope is, a sun will pierce
The thickest cloud earth ever stretched;
  That, after Last, returns the First,
Though a wide compass round be fetched;
  That what began best, can't end worst,
  Nor what God blessed once, prove accurst.
—ROBERT BROWNING.

EDITORIAL NOTES.

WILLIAM Drysdale & Co., publishers etc., Montreal, have arranged for an excellent picture, chromo-litho., of Her Majesty the Queen, nicely colored, which they expect to furnish to schools, framed, at $1.50. The supply is limited. Orders will be filled in the order in which they are received. Application to be made direct to Messrs. Wm. Drysdale & Co., Montreal.

As we informed our readers last month, every effort is being put forth to extend the usefulness of our journal among subscribers, contributors, and advertisers, and the spirit of co-operation that has already been exhibited in favor of our enterprise encourages us to make a direct request to our present subscribers, which will only cost them the price of a postal card to comply with. We want each of our present subscribers to send in to our central publishers, William Drysdale & Co., Montreal, three or more names of possible subscribers with their addresses and the address of the reader who sends them. This is no empty request, having for its sole object an increase in the number of subscribers, but is made with the object of arriving at a mutual benefit. To all who send us the names of three or more possible subscribers, we will give special terms of subscription, and we will likewise enroll them as participators in the benefits of our Mutual Benefit Bureau for promotion in the service of teaching. All subscribers who send immediately to William Drysdale & Co., their subscription of One Dollar will also have their names entered upon the lists of our Mutual Benefit Bureau. Of course, very many of our subscribers will have no wish to be enrolled on these lists, their positions being permanent; but to the young teachers who are anxious to rise to the more responsible positions in the profession, the organization of our Mutual Benefit Bureau will no doubt be recognized as a means to assist them in their laudable ambitions. See advertisement elsewhere.

From latest reports from Montreal it is learned that the usual anxiety has been witnessed in certain quarters as to the personality of "A Montreal Teacher." Our correspondent hinted that such would be the case when he sent in his last communication, and spoke of the men "who are more concerned about who writes a thing that what one writes." The critic who troubles himself in this way is a man of a very weak turn of mind, who usually rounds off his criticisms with "I'm sure he didn't write it himself anyway," or "any one can see that the fellow cannot write decent English," or some nonsense of a kindred character. But our correspondents may rest assured that the reader, who has no self-folly to fear in connection with a discussion, looks more carefully at the facts than the manner of putting them. And of another thing our correspondents may also rest assured, namely, if it be in the public interest that they write to the CANADA EDUCATIONAL MONTHLY under a *nom de plume*, no person connected with the issue of that journal need be asked to reveal the personality of such writers. An attempt has already been made to find out who "A Montreal Teacher" is, but the attempt has been altogether unsuccessful, and so we will no doubt hear further from that gentleman in future issues and from numbers of other correspondents when they learn that their personality be held inviolate as far as the management of this paper is concerned. The anonymous correspondent is often a necessity when a reform is urgent, and the "powers that be" are vindictive.

Those who have read the Hon. G. W. Ross' speech delivered in the Ontario Legislative Assembly on the 4th of March last, and who missed hearing it *viva voce*, must feel that they missed a treat, while those who heard it will hardly fail to read it. The government have done well in having it printed, if it really be at the expense of the government that it has been published. When it is said that the Minister of Education and the CANADA EDUCATIONAL MONTHLY are at one in the matter of the examination idea, there is no great exaggeration in the estimate of our relative positions, though further explanations may be necessary to make the most of the estimate. But should it be said that every Ontarian is not gratified with the report of progress which the Minister of Education has been able to make in regard to the later educational progress in Ontario, then it may also be said that there are some Ontarians very difficult to satisfy. Naturally enough, there is an aggressive tone about many of the Minister's sentences which we must lay at the door of the politician; but there is also a wholesomely honest tone about every statement he made, which brings the more interesting portions of his able speech at once within the region of fact to those who take no side in politics. The misfortune of the Minister is perhaps that there are too many politicians in the Province over which he educationally presides.

The lesson of loyalty is one that is being learned by the pupils in all the schools of the Dominion, though we still are told pupils near the border-line who are able to give glibly enough the name of the President of the United States but stammer reluctantly over the name of the Governor of their own Province. The approaching Diamond Jubilee of Queen Victoria is, we are glad to learn, not to be a mere *feu de joie*; and we trust that as the plans of the various celebration committees become matured, there will be something of a permanent character arranged for as a legacy in each community. The streak of common sense in the cry of one of our Lord's disciples, "Could not this have been sold and given to the poor?" would possibly have been less decried but for the after circumstances of the betrayal. One of our correspondents has written on this subject of loyalty and the flag, and we trust that his influence in the remote district where he teaches will be followed by every country teacher at this Jubilee season, when it is perhaps well for the youngest and even the oldest of us to be told that our Province is the greatest of the Provinces, that the Dominion itself is the largest and most progressive of Britain's colonies, and that Britain is the greatest nation in the world, even if the figures of exaggeration employed have afterwards to be modified a little, when the Jubilee season is over. Nor is the query of the betrayer likely to be repeated very often as the celebration festivities proceed, even should the Federal authorities spend two hundred thousand dollars on the Canadian army that is to be sent across the ocean, or give the premier *carte blanche* during his mission to the old country; for is he not to be sent there to emphasize our loyalty towards Britain and Britain's Queen, and are they not to accompany him to give *éclat* to his mission?

The Hon. Sydney Fisher, Minister of Agriculture, in emulating the excellent example set by the Protestant Committee of the Council of Public Instruction of Quebec, who have taken practical steps to improve the school grounds, lately advocated the planting of kitchen gardens near every school-house in the country, though he failed to say for whose benefit they were to be planted or who were to tend them during the long summer holidays. A good deal of the "earnestness" in favor of introducing agriculture as an element on the school course of study, is founded upon a like uncertanty in regard to the "professional properties." In this connection we cannot forbear from making a quotation from the much-talked-of speech of the Minister of Education for Ontario: "But it is said that the Course of Study should have an Agricultural trend, and it is the want of this that works so much mischief. In reply, allow me to say that the farmers of Ontario above all things want their children to have as good an education as the children of any other class of the community. A knowledge of the three R's, with such related subjects as constitute any well accredited school curriculum, is the foundation of all education, without which neither Agriculture nor any other specialty can be effectively taught. As a matter of fact, therefore, during the limited school course, if these subjects are well taught, all is done that most teachers can do with a proper regard to efficiency. To attempt less would be to weaken the educational value of our Course of Study. To attempt more is not without danger to the success of all. In order, however, to give elasticity to our Course of Study, provisions were made in the Regulations of 1891 that Agriculture should be taught in any Rural School when so directed by the trustees, and although five years have elapsed since that Regulation was approved, so far as I know, not a single Rural School has availed itself of the privilege thus afforded. For over ten years High School trustees had the privilege of ordering that Agricultural Chemistry should be taught in the High Schools, and so far as I know, not a single Board of High School Trustees has directed instruction to be given on that subject. If these two circumstances are indications of public opinion with regard to the study of Agriculture, then there is but little demand for its introduction either into Public or High Schools."

Apropos of the above view of a question, this month's *Journal of Education* in referring to Prof. Lloyd's pamphlet on "Technical Education," comes to us with the following: "To the farmer education means—though, doubtless, he would not so express himself—training of the memory by the study of books. He has not found his old school days any practical help to him in farming. But if he can be convinced that education means—as it assuredly ought to do—the training and development of all faculties, then he will cease to scoff or hold aloof. He will not be convinced by "donnish" graduates, who have no experience of their subject beyond their books, and no sympathy with their audience. There is need of thoroughly capable lecturers, who know how to combine theoretical knowledge with practical skill, and who realize that each is the complement of the other, and that each without the other is doomed to failure. The mere student fails to convince."

It is more than likely that the preparations for the Queen's Jubilee celebration will throw into the shade the Arbor Day programme; yet in view of its approval, we quote the following advice from a practical teacher: "Upon the teacher, however, will rest the burden of the work of improving our school grounds. The teacher should arouse interest in the pupils in behalf of this movement. The benefits and pleasures derived from shelter in winter and shade in summer, together with the satisfaction which will come from having in their district a school-house and school grounds which bear evidence that the people believe in education in the broadest sense, should be impressed. As for the kind of trees to plant, it may be said that no one kind should be used exclusively. There should be a variety if possible. School grounds which have evergreens on the rear and sides of the yard and elm on the front present a very attractive appearance. The evergreen is a hardy tree if well planted and guarded the first few years. The elm will grow in most of the Provinces and is almost sure to live if well planted. Care should be taken in the arrangement of the trees about the yard. Nor should the ornamentation be confined to trees. Flowering shrubs such as the lilac would add greatly to the beauty of the grounds. A corner of the yard could be reserved for a flower bed. Through any public spirited citizen of the district, teachers could secure packages of choice flower seed free. This flower culture would afford excellent material for language and observation lessons. Why should not the school be the garden spot of the whole district while school is in session? And why should it not present an attractive appearance at other times as well? If there is any one period in life that should fill the soul with delight it is the period of school days. Yet thousands of children while away the hours in and about school-houses open to the blasts of winter and the withering sun in summer. It is a blight on child life and should not longer be endured. The effects of beautiful and improved grounds will be far reaching. The pupils will learn the lesson of order and system. There will be a reaction upon the home life. More interest will be taken in trees and flowers at home. And how many rural homes need culture of this sort. 'To him who in the love of Nature holds communion with her *visible* forms she speaks a *various* language.' I wonder what kind of language Nature speaks when the 'forms' are not 'visible'! The language of monotony and melancholy, most generally. Let there be an awakening along the line until the treeless school lots are 'made to bud and blossom as the rose.'"

Labor shall refresh itself with
hope.

Hope V., ii. 2

CURRENT EVENTS AND COMMENTS.

THE settlement of the Manitoba School Question is again near at hand, though the announcement has been made in a somewhat indirect manner—so indirect indeed that many people are slow to believe that the much-desired for result of peace and co-operation has been reached at last. The whole question, it is to be hoped, will now resolve itself into a matter of good or bad administration, and, as in the case of Nova Scotia and the other Maritime Provinces, the parties who thought themselves at first aggrieved because they could not get what they wanted, will be more than gratified in time to come to find that they have more than they could have got in 1896, had they then obtained from the Federal Government all that they craved for. There will be no Separate Schools in Manitoba, as there perhaps ought never to have been in Ontario; but there will be good Public Schools with which every Protestant and Roman Catholic in the province will be satisfied.

In connection with the spring-hatching of medical men in our colleges, a correspondent to one of the papers has the following: "McGill sent forth the other day seventy-five fine young fellows armed with the degree of M.D. and C.M. She does this every year. There are probably, in all our medical schools, about three hundred doctors turned out every year in this country. Only a small proportion of the whole can hope to make a living in Canada. The ranks of the medical profession are overcrowded. We furnish the best education at a cheap rate; we turn out clever young fellows, trained in the latest scientific methods of healing, and, having done so, we lose them. The majority of them go to the United States, where Canadian physicians, and particularly McGill men, are warmly welcomed for the reason that doctors are made there by a patent process which guarantees rapidity at the expense of efficiency.

"This serious evil remains to be remedied—different licenses are required for different portions of the British Empire. We have not even attained to interprovincial reciprocity, although the examinations required in any province outside Quebec are mere formalities; but there must be fresh studies, there must be additional examinations in Great Britain itself before a Canadian physician can practise there. This should be remedied as speedily as possible. It is a blot upon a liberal profession. Sir Donald Smith said he would work hand in hand with the college authorities to bring about the uniform law which would apply to all British subjects in any portion of the broad dominion of Her Majesty the Queen. Let there be united effort to attain this end."

In the recent School Board elections in Great Britain the proceedings, it is reported, have been characterized in most places by a marked apathy. In Edinburgh there has been very free criticism of the finance of the last Board, and in Aberdeen the Westfield school case (to which reference has been made here) has caused considerable heat; and in various quarters there have been ineffectual protests against the running of church candidates; but, on the whole, the election campaigns have been conducted with decorum and dulness. The Health Committee of Glasgow corporation would like the School Board to equip the playgrounds with gymnasia, and otherwise make them more serviceable as areas for recreation for the children of the city.

Lord Balfour, of Burleigh, did not speak soft words to the deputation that waited on him in behalf of Gaelic. He takes the common-sense view that the Highland children should not be encouraged to cling to Gaelic at the expense of English, since that means shutting them out from a wider area of employment than their native glens can offer.

At the last regular monthly meeting of the Protestant Board of School Commissioners, this morning, a memorial was presented from the Christian Endeavor Union of the city, asking for permission to introduce into the schools a set of temperance pledge blanks which the pupils might take home and sign if their parents were willing that they should do so. Two or three members of the Board strongly objected to the proposal, with the result that the matter was referred back to the committee for reconsideration. The Board as a whole was unanimous with regard to the desirability of inculcating principles of temperance and morality into the minds of the pupils, but the members were divided as to the advisability of accomplishing such by means of pledges.

The number of conventions which a teacher takes an interest in during the year always includes the provincial convention, and the great national convention held in the United States. Our own national convention of teachers does not seem to have the necessary life about it, and some means will have to be adopted to make it more of an active, assimilating power in the land, if it is to receive the attention from our teachers it deserves. There is to be a convention of teachers in Montreal this summer, but we have not been taken into the confidence of its promoters, nor do we know why those, who were once so active in the organization of our Dominion Association but are now not even lukewarm towards its perpetuation, have come to invite this association to Canada. Attention begins to be turned toward the annual meeting of the National Educational Association, Milwaukee. Literature on it begins to circulate. A list of side-trips has just been issued showing of how much that is interesting Milwaukee is the centre. The officers of the association are apprehensive lest the recent dissolution of the Railroad Traffic Association may spoil the arrangements as to rates which had just been consummated when the decision of the Supreme Court was announced. But the indications are that new combinations, or organizations, or understandings, will soon be arranged between the roads which will practically be an equivalent in many ways for the dissolved organizations. It is to be hoped that the N.E.A. officers will yet succeed in eliminating the 50 cents from the rate now fixed, which the railroad associations demanded to pay the expenses of a joint agent at Milwaukee to take care of the tickets. How the local executive committee is going to succeed in its work it is too early to judge. We have been informed from New York that Dr. J. M. Harper, of Quebec, has been reappointed as one of the managers for Canada, a position which he held last year. The bulletins for the year have not yet been issued.

The convention of the Provincial Association of Ontario has been held this year, as last, during the Easter recess, and elsewhere the reader will find a synopsis of its proceedings. The conventions of the Provincial Associations of Nova Scotia, New

Brunswick and Prince Edward are held during the midsummer recess, of which due notice will be given. The convention of the Protestant teachers of Quebec will take place during the latter part of October, and it is said that the executive are already busy preparing the programme, with the object in view of making it a representative gathering. The annual meeting of the Dominion Association of Teachers is to be held in 1898, with the meeting place of Halifax, Nova Scotia. Dr. Mackay, Superintendent of Schools of that province, is the president.

The news from the universities and colleges includes an announcement that Bishop's College, of Lennoxville, intends to seek affiliation with Oxford and Cambridge, though it is said that they are unwilling to have a common matriculation with the other colleges of the Province of Quebec. The three colleges in the Province of Quebec that take the matriculation papers prepared by the McGill authorities are Morin College, Quebec; St. Francis' College, Richmond, and The Wesleyan College, Stanstead. McGill University is thus the strongest of the educational institutions of the province, though the university of Bishop's College is perhaps the most ambitious. The latter institution has had a very successful year if one is to judge from the numbers in attendance.

The withdrawal of the Rev. Dr. Barbour from the principalship of the Montreal Congregational College is a serious loss to that institution, and is thus spoken of by a student at the late convocation:

"But here let me reverently pause. Why should I speak further? Is it not true that this year the valedictory is not to be spoken by the student, but by the master? Yes, the real farewell this night must come from the lips of him who for the last ten years has been at once the head and heart of this college. In his presence I would feign be humbly silent. But should I not speak, my fellow-graduates would cry out and demand that somebody should try to express, even though feebly, those sentiments which we all so deeply feel. Throughout our Canadian churches this night, among all those who are interested in the college, there is a feeling of sincere regret. But no one can grieve as we grieve, for no one has lived so near to him. It is for us that he has lived and learned and labored. To-night we cannot express our feelings. We stand near him even as little children gathering around the bedside of a beloved mother soon to leave them. They do not know what a loss they are about to suffer. They cannot understand now, but in the days of sorrow and loneliness that are to come they will feel a great emptiness in their lives and an aching void in their bereft hearts. And yet must we be hopeful. We would not hinder his rest. Long and faithfully has he toiled for the benefit of others. If we were to say to him—'No, you must not leave us, we cannot spare you, you must toil on for us, there is no rest'—if, addressing him thus, we endeavored to rob him of his rest, verily, I believe there would come a mighty voice of protest from Yale and Andover and Oberlin—'Hold! Hold! Enough! Enough! Let that veteran lay aside his armor; let that venerable student put down his pen; let that honored servant of God enter into his rest.'"

At the late convocation of the Presbyterian College of Montreal, the Rev. Dr. McVicar, as a last word of advice to the graduating class of that institution, made use of the following language, which would almost be appropriate if it were addressed to our teachers: "Finally, your ministerial success will be greatly helped or marred by the life you live among the people. There is mighty potency in personal character and conduct. It tells for good or evil upon the godly and the ungodly. Both classes will look for harmony between your doctrine and your conduct, and the lack of it will be most detrimental. What I mean is this: You will preach regeneration. Then convince your people by holy living that you speak from experience, that you testify what you know from your own hearts, and not merely what you have learned as a theological dogma. You will preach faith as the root of all our Christian virtues. See, then, that you show your own faith by your works—a faith that worketh by love and purifieth the heart. 'By their fruits ye shall know them,' said the Saviour. You will preach self-denial and self-control. Then beware lest by self-indulgence in any form, or by the exhibition of ungovernable temper, you neutralize your own sermons. Remember that the very presence of the man of God in the parish should be a sermon and a benediction."

The report of the Superintendent of Education in Prince Edward Island must be gratifying reading to the dwellers by the sea, for it says, among other enconiums, that the "general results of educational work during the past year have been satisfactory. The attendance was larger and much more regular. The character of the instruction was better. In comparison with former years, a larger number of schools were in operation; a greater number of teachers with higher qualifications were employed. There was a marked and very general increase in the number of pupils receiving instruction in the several subjects on the School Course, and an increased attendance at the Provincial College and Normal School. There was a larger outlay by the people for school purposes, and an increased demand for good and experienced teachers. All these attest more loudly than words, the high estimate put upon our Public Schools and the work they are doing, by the people of the province."

Dr. W. H. Drummond had an important word to say to the members of his classes when the Dental College of Montreal was having its "closing exercises." "In your intercourse," said he, "with brother physicians, be careful to observe, and carry out faithfully, every detail of professional etiquette. Remember that even physicians are not infallible; that they have their failures as well as their triumphs, and, whenever you may succeed where others have failed, be modest, and do not boast of your success for you never know when your own turn may come to be corrected in diagnosis by another. And bear in mind that 'whatsoever a man shall sow that shall he also reap.' In a word, be gentlemen, and then you will always be ethical."

Dr. Yule Mackay, Professor of Anatomy in Dundee University College, has been selected for the post of Principal in the College, in succession to Principal Peterson, who was appointed Principal of McGill College, Montreal, some eighteen months ago. The post was left vacant owing to the litigation between Dundee and St. Andrew's, and has now been filled, the Privy Council having declared the union between the two institutions to be valid.

At the Baptist Ministers' Conference, John D. Rockefeller's proposed gift of $250,000 to the Baptist ministry was the subject which consumed the greater portion of the morning. Mr. Rockefeller will make the donation for the purpose of liquidating the large indebtedness of the Foreign and Home Missionary Societies, with the provision that the Baptist ministry raise $236,000, the amount he requires raised to meet his proposition. This amount will be gathered among the Baptists in the various cities of the United States. Chicago's apportionment is $10,000, $1,000 of which was pledged at the conference by the ministers. The latter will request their congregations to contribute the remainder.

In the report lately made by the Hon. Col. James Baker, Minister of Education for British Columbia, the following is said in behalf of the high schools of that province: "The many benefits conferred by our four high schools are fully proved by the work accomplished since the establishment of each, and by the high esteem in which each is held. These schools not only afford to all children who pass the standard required for admission the opportunity of obtaining a knowledge of the advanced subjects of study essential to a higher education, but they elevate the character of the lower grades and perfect and diffuse all the most valuable points of our school system. The scholarship demanded for entrance to a high school is certainly equal to, if not higher, than that required in the other provinces. The necessity of this arises from the fact that with us these schools form the apex of our system, while in the other provinces, in addition to high schools, we find collegiate institutes, normal schools, colleges and universities. Our high schools have, therefore, to afford to our children, as far as possible, all the benefits accruing from these other higher institutions of learning—the university excepted."

As we said last month, the principle of payment by results was about to be put in practice, and Dr. Inch's last announcement shows that we were not far wrong. The following regulation bears witness to the fact: "In order to be entitled to Grammar School Provincial grant, after the close of the present school year, grammar schools in towns must have enrolled not less than fifteen pupils who shall have passed the High School Entrance Examinations, and grammar schools in villages must have enrolled not less than ten pupils who shall have passed the High School Entrance Examinations. In order to be entitled to Superior School Provincial grant, after the close of the present term, schools must have at least two graded departments, and must have enrolled not less than ten competent pupils above grade VII."

The Educational Association.—We are glad to see the Ontario Educational Association holding its annual meeting again in Toronto, and showing signs of increased vigor in its handling of school affairs. Of these signs the most striking and gratifying is the freedom with which its members criticize the course of the department on various points. Anyone who follows the proceedings will detect a new temper in the teaching profession. The programme marks a departure, as the following items of it indicate: "Effects of High School Regulations on the Qualification of Public School Teachers," "Public School Leaving Examinations," "The Educational Council," "Overcrowding of Subjects," "Obstacles to Public School Education from the Nature and Range of Subjects," "School Law Changes," "The New Regulations," "What Can be Done by Means of Our School System to Advance Agriculture?" In the Public and High School Trustees' Section the following are some of the subjects to be discussed: "The System of Departmental Examinations," "Too Many Examinations, Costing Too Much in Fees," "Formation of the Educational Council," "Literary Qualifications for High School Trustees." These topics, all but the last of them, arise out of our educational administration. The names of them on the programme are for the most part labels of grievances and blunders from which our school system is suffering. That they are serious evils is recognized even by the apologists of the department. A few weeks ago the Toronto *Globe* drew a gloomy picture of the state to which the profession is being brought by the tidal wave of third-class teachers that strikes it every year, displacing or swamping the men of experience and ability. Our contemporary showed that this was a bad thing for education, and suggested as a means of escape from it more fees—tuition fees at the normal schools and college. But the teachers who are injuring the profession and education do not go to the provincial training schools, at least not before they have done the mischief. To remedy the evil of which they are the cause it will be necessary to remove the cause of which they are the effect. The examination system is the head and front of the educationists' grievance. To it everything else has been shaped—the teaching, the curriculum, the regulations, the recent changes in the law. It is the cause of the overloading of the course of study, the cramming of pupils, the overcrowding of the teaching profession, the decline of that profession, the poorer results in our public schools, the general dissatisfaction with the system, and the desire for a change. The latest aggravation of the evils is the October batch of regulations for high schools. How these operate to increase the output of third-class teachers and the train of disturbances which follow was well shown in the paper read by Mr. Strang. They are very fully discussed, also, in the latter part of the excellent paper read by Mr. Wetherell. He pronounces them objectionable from many points of view. They prescribe 22 to 24 different subjects, on all of which the third-class candidate must write. The candidate can scarcely be expected to be well grounded in any of them. If he takes all these subjects in one year he will have to undergo two examinations in seven of them. Thus the examinations have been increased, and have been made most burdensome on the youngest pupils of the high schools. As Mr. Wetherell says, "the number of examinations has been nominally diminished by one, while the number of examination papers for each poor primary candidate has been actually multiplied by two." The effects the arrangement is certain to produce are shown by Mr. Wetherell to be numerous and serious, among them being this one—a great diminution of first and second-class teachers, owing to the increased manufacture of third-class teachers. From the reception Mr. Wetherell's paper met, and the outspoken condemnation of many who took part in the discussion, it may be safely taken as a temperate expression of the sense of the high school teachers. It is a healthy sign, however, that the teachers are asserting their independence.

This meeting of the association was the best attended meeting in the history of the association, over 500 delegates from every part of the province having taken part in its deliberations. The importance of such a large representation cannot be overestimated. It means that in every school district in Ontario at least one teacher will resume his or her duties —next week—with a deeper knowledge than ever of the responsibilities of the profession. It means also that the earnest teachers who have just started their life's work will apply to their work practices which clear-headed men and women, of great experience, have found to be of incalculable benefit in the training of the young. Although the papers read, and discussions held, covered a wide range of subjects, all had one end in view—the advancement of education. A noticeable feature was the attention paid to the pupils. In years gone by the tendency was to study and legislate for the teacher. To-day the pupils are receiving an amount of consideration which teachers and parents alike of by-gone generations would have characterized as ridiculous, but which is now recognized as being absolutely essential. One section of the association devoted its time to the subject "Child Study," and in every other section this, the most important of questions, was dealt with. Glancing over some of the papers that were read, it is easily seen what a prominent place this subject holds. "School-room Fatigue; Its Prevention and Remedy," "Manual Training," "Moral Training," "Is Our Educational System the Best Fitted to Prepare Young Men and Women for the Practical Duties of Life?" "The Practical Results of Child Study," "Practical Games" (in kindergartens), "The Public School Course as a Preparation for the Duties and Responsibilities of Life," these were the titles of papers read and considered by thoughtful men and women on whom Ontario places the larger share of the responsibility for the proper training of its future citizens. In the address of the retiring president, Mr. John Dearness, of London, lengthy reference was also made to the sanitation, light, and temperature of our schools, and here it was shown that Ontario has much to learn. On the whole it appears that while in many respects Ontario's school system is equal to that of any other in the world, it is wofully lacking in many respects. Reforms that long ago should have been put into operation are knocking imperatively at the doors, and to quote the effect of the language used in many of the papers, "it is time the doors were opened wide."

Referring particularly to the delegates, it is worthy of note that they were unusually outspoken in regard to their views on many matters. Without any desire to reflect on past meetings in this respect, it may be said that in the one just closed there was an entire absence of a cut-and-dried mode of procedure. While, of course, obeying the rules laid down in the constitution and by-laws, the delegates gave expression to their views in a fearless manner, believing that only in this way could they convey to the public a fair impression of the disadvantages under which the system labors. For they know that unless the public thoroughly understand these questions not only will the dawn of reform be retarded, but the difficulties of the profession—too often increased, though not wilfully, by parents and guardians—will become unendurable. One question which, in so far as it affects the teacher, was perhaps transcendent, was that of the new regulations. The manner in which this was dealt with proved that the delegates possessed a goodly amount of tact. The regulations were discussed calmly, and no heated language was used. A few of the delegates, perhaps, comforted themselves with the reflection that, as in the past, they would try and conform, but the majority were emphatically of the opinion that the regulations could not be put into operation satisfactorily. Many of the majority went further, stating that they would inevitably lead to serious mischief.

The above report we have condensed from the report of the *Mail and Empire.* Anyone who attended the association meeting of April, 1897, and went from one room to another, taking part occasionally in the discussions, as we did, will, we venture to think, say that the above report is a fair one. If anything it rather under than over estimates the intensity of the feeling *re* examinations in our schools. The opinion is very common and pronounced, that, if secondary education in Ontario is to be an education worthy of the name, and aid, as it should, to develop the life of the country, there must be a radical change.

HIGH SCHOOL ENTRANCE.

The report of a committee on high school entrance examinations was presented by Mr. Chancellor Burwash, Victoria University. It recommended the division of the high schools into two distinct classes, the one literary and classical, preparing for university and higher professional courses; the other English and scientific, preparing for agricultural and other industrial pursuits.

2. That the entrance to the first division should be such as to enable pupils to enter not later than 12 years of age, so that they may advantageously begin their language studies; while the entrance to the second division might be placed at a more advanced stage of the public school programme, and thus tend to raise the character of the public schools.

3. That in the selection of examiners for entrance to the schools of the first division representatives of high schools of this class, or of the universities, should have a controlling place. For entrance to those of the first division representatives of the public schools, and of the second division of the high schools, should have prominence.

THE ANNUAL MEETING OF THE NATURAL SCIENCE ASSOCIATION.

SCIENCE EDITOR, J. B. TURNER, B.A.

The meeting of this Association, which closed on the afternoon of Thursday, April 22nd, was a most successful one. The attendance was large, the subjects discussed varied and interesting, and the enthusiasm of the members all that could be desired. All the papers that were on the programme were presented. The president's address was a comparison of the state of science teaching in different countries, and showed that while we have made good progress in this respect there is yet much remaining to be done. Abstracts of all the papers will appear in the Proceedings of the General Association and will amply repay a careful perusal by all interested in educational work. The address by the Honorary President, Mr. E. C. Jeffrey, B.A., was a carefully worked out treatment of evolution in plant life. The address was illustrated with photomicrographs and showed conclusively that there is an evolution in plant life quite as pronounced as that which has been shown to exist in animal life. The conference of the section with the public school section on Nature Study in the public schools was particularly opportune at this time of the year, when the material necessary for carrying on this work is so abundant.

NATURE STUDY.

The first essential to successful work in Nature Study is to bring the student into contact with the actual objects. It is not sufficient that the teacher have a specimen to show to the class, but every member of the class should have a specimen of his own. No one, even after long experience, can observe all the peculiarities of any object when he is at a considerable distance from it, hence the necessity for providing each pupil with a specimen of his own. Unless this point is observed no successful work in Nature Study can be done. The great obstacle in the way of undertaking this work in our schools is the want of time. Already the programme is so crowded that, it is claimed, the best work cannot be done. It is not proposed by anyone that Nature Study be introduced as a separate study, much less one for examination, but rather as aid in lightening work that is now found so onerous. One of its most obvious advantages is that it affords relief from the extreme pressure due to steady application to the usual routine of school work. It interests the children by furnishing an outlet to their restless activities, the desire of a child to be *doing* something. It aids the teacher in the ordinary work of the school. In illustration of this statement its use in the teaching of composition may be mentioned. The greatest obstacle to be overcome by pupils in the study of composition is apparently a lack of words with which to express themselves. The difficulty lies deeper than that, however, and is, as a matter of fact, a want of thoughts and ideas; once these are provided the supply of words adequate to the expression of them will soon be found. Nature Study will furnish abundant material for supplying the ideas which are to find expression in the composition. Its advantage as an aid to the teaching of geography needs only to be mentioned to be at once appreciated, and its applications to the teaching of other subjects will readily suggest themselves to the thoughtful teacher. The season of the year is at hand when material is most abundant and the interest of the child in nature the greatest. Let every teacher take advantage of this happy conjuncture of circumstances, and the results will doubtless be a great surprise to those who have never undertaken such work.

EDUCATION IN ONTARIO.

From the annual report of the Minister of Education we learn: The total number of pupils registered in the common schools of the Province, up to the 31st December, was 484,551, and the average attendance was 271,549. Of these 482,616 were between the ages of 5 and 21; 1,545 were under 5 years, and 390 were over 21. The number of kindergartens was increased to 95, with 201 teachers and an attendance of 5,901 pupils, under six years of age. The number of night schools was 31, with 56 teachers and 2,130 pupils. The number of public school teachers was 8,913, including 2,843 male and 6,070 female teachers. The highest salary paid is $1,500; the average salary of male teachers is $408, and of female teachers, $298. The total receipts of the public schools were $4,868,315, of which $3,332,995 came from municipal taxation; $298,419, legislative grant, and $1,236,901, clergy reserve fund and other special sources. The number of pupils in attendance at the 334 Roman Catholic separate schools was 39,773. The number of teachers was 755, the total receipts $331,561, and the total expenditures $296,655. The Protestant separate schools in L'Orignal and other French districts number 10, are attended by 492 pupils, and cost $6,183 for maintenance. The number of collegiate institutes and high schools is 129, employing 570 teachers, having 24,662 pupils in attendance. The total receipts were $746,727, of which $114,862 was contributed in pupils' fees. The total expenditure was $720,583, of which $526,274 was paid teachers. At the entrance examinations for 1896, the candidates examined numbered 16,696, of whom 10,240 passed.

CORRESPONDENCE.

On the Teaching of Morality in Schools.

To the Editor of The Journal of Education :

Sir,—As your correspondent "A Veteran Teacher" touches on that most important of all subjects, the teaching of morality in our upper or so-called public schools, may I ask for space to say a few words? These schools train our statesmen, lawgivers, members of Parliament, civil servants, etc., and, in fact, all who make our country what she is. Why is it that every right-minded mother who sends her young boys to these schools does so in fear and trembling, well knowing that the chances are that they will come back less pure and innocent than when they left home? Surely it is a blot upon our boasted civilization that this should be the case, and I cannot help thinking that if parents were to ask the following questions before sending their children to school it might be different: How are the men chosen who are put in authority over the boys? Are they the men of the highest moral character and intellectual abilities, or are they chosen because they can run the fastest, play the best games, and pledge themselves to teach certain antiquated doctrines, whether they believe them or not? How is religion taught in these schools? Why, *real* religion is not taught at all! Long chapters out of the Old Testament have to be learnt by heart. Chapters out of the same book are read to them, in which certain sins are spoken of as the natural conditions of life! What wonder, then, that there is need of a White Cross Society to help to cleanse our streets of a foul pollution? The public has kept silence too long, and ignored stern facts which stare them in the face. Surely, as evolution teaches that like produces like, it is all-important that the young should be trained in their moral as in their physical natures, that they may transmit high and noble feelings to their posterity. All social reforms work from the higher to the lower classes of society, so that the responsibility of the former is double. By all means let games and sports of all kinds be encouraged—they are a safeguard; but do not let the men of schools and colleges be brought up to think they are of supreme importance! There is a confusion in the minds of men as to the meaning of the words religion and morality. They see as in a glass dimly, and so long as denominationalism represents the former and the Old Testament the latter, in the teaching of the young, there is not likely to be more light.

I am, yours faithfully,
Veritas.

History Teaching.

To the Editor of The Canada Educational Monthly:

Sir,—I think the enclosed is excellent advice to the teacher of history, and will come to many of our teachers as a revelation. In our schools we force our pupils to memorize facts, but too often forget to draw the lesson these facts are competent to formulate. As the paper from which I quote says: "Most of the subjects in our school's curriculum are valuable chiefly for their disciplinary importance, and are sometimes wrongly called not practical because the information they afford is very small. History, however, is to a very important extent an information study, and the information it affords has both a special and a general value. In its special value it is a preparatory study for other studies, as arithmetic is for algebra. To the student of law it is as important as physiology is to the medical student. To the journalist it is not much less essential. Its general value is for the average citizen, by whom its information is needed, that he may interpret literature, that he may read the daily papers, even, with understanding. How often Demosthenes, Alexander, Hannibal, Cicero, and the long line of great men of long ago appear before us on the printed page to illuminate the present by an appropriate reference to the past. Poetry and prose alike abound in these references.

"The problems of history are in kind just the problems of everyday life with all their complexity and intricacy. Why did the Roman republic lose its vigor? Was Pericles justified in spending upon Athens the moneys of the Delian confederacy? Was Washington right or wrong in his refusal to give to France that aid against England which France had so recently given to the United States? Was Champlain right or wrong when he took up arms against the enemies of his friends the Hurons? These are questions which contain all the elements of the problems which will so often confront every one of us, and repeated enquiry into such as these tends to develop the judgment. History deals with men and women, with motives of human action, with natural forces that influence life now as they always have. No other studies tend so much to give training in estimating men, their characters, their powers, their probable courses of action, as does the study of history in the knowledge of mankind, and the acquaintance with men's motives which it may be made to give. This is what Cicero meant when he said, 'History is the witness of times, the light of truth, the mistress of life.' And how few of life's problems do not have to do with men and women?"

Yours
Sincerely,
SELECTER.

OUR SCHOOLS AND THE DIAMOND JUBILEE.

To the Editor of THE CANADA EDUCATIONAL MONTHLY:

SIR,—A people is unworthy the name of a nation unless there is a strong national spirit, and a citizen usurps his citizenship unless he be a patriot. Patriotism is not always hereditary, for were it so there would be less of mobocracy to mar the pages of history.

Federated Canada is a young country, and as such is somewhat defective in national sentiment. A Nova Scotian is too much a foreigner in British Columbia and *vice versa.*

Each Province has a thoroughly provincial sentiment, but the complete and harmonious unification of these for all Canada has yet to be accomplished. It has begun to grow, but as yet it is insufficiently mature.

Not for a moment would we infer the disloyalty of Canada or of any integral portion thereof, for the generosity of our people lately evinced toward their fellows in India would immediately prove the inference without foundation.

The aim of all our statesmen should be to effect the speedy establishment of a national sentiment more thoroughly national than anything at present existing; and Canada has never had an opportunity whereby she could create and foster the growth of such a spirit more favorably than the one to be presented to her in June—the Diamond Jubilee.

This event should arouse in the minds of the inert the significance of their opportunities, and the flagrancy of the crime of inactivity. It should engender such an overwhelming flood of loyalty as to drown for ever all poltroonery and indifference. It should kill the annexationist, and should weld into one the political parties of this vast colony toward the speedy advancement of that high and loyal ideal—the advancement of the Empire.

Nothing is more praiseworthy and noble in any character than true patriotism, but for the perpetuation of this cardinal virtue we must trust in and look to the younger element, the rising generation, the children of our country. Hence,should this celebration appeal most strongly to every child throughout the length and breadth of Canada—of what nationality soever. To them it should be an object lesson in patriotism.

We should so emphatically impress upon the mind of every child a truthful and fully realized conception of the present greatness and glorious victories of the empire in which he dwells, as to mature within him a thoroughly vigorous patriotic spirit, an exultant joy in present triumphs, and a never-dying love for the Union Jack.

There are probably hundreds of Canadian children who have never seen the British Flag, and the "jubilee" should be a means of exhibiting it from corner to corner of the Dominion.

Loyalty to one's country and the flag can be taught to a great extent at home, but the most prolific germ has its beginning in the little "red schoolhouse," where the teacher recounts to the many eager listeners interesting stories of history, and where are learned—sometimes—the national songs.

Every one of these institutions which appear so unimportant—but which, when properly superintended, are the base and foundation of every nation—should not only possess but should fly the Union Jack as well as our own Dominion ensign, which, we are sorry to remark, is foreign in appearance to many Canadians—and thus will the children become acquainted with its appearance, learn its significance, and of what it is a symbol, make its glory their glory, and as a consequence would love, revere and if necessity demanded would give their lives for that empire of which Canada is a gem, and whose flag and noble institutions they have learned to love.

What a glorious and memorable event it would be to see every school from the Atlantic to the Pacific celebrate Queen Victoria's Diamond Jubilee by at least hoisting the Union Jack and heartily singing "God Save the Queen!" And when the flag is once up do not take it down, but let it float with every breeze, and thus our children will learn to ever respect and guard it.

FREDERICK VAUGHAN.

Montreal, April, 1897.

Do not draw back from any way because you never have passed there before.

The truth, the task, the joy, the suffering on whose border you are standing, O my friend, to-day, go into it without a fear, only go into it with God, the God who has been always with you.

—*Phillips Brooks.*

SCHOOL WORK.

PUBLIC SCHOOL LEAVING ARITHMETIC.

BY P. S. HEAD MASTER.

1. A man invests the present worth of $2,662.40, due 8 months hence at 6 per cent. per annum, in bank stock at 95½ (brokerage ½) paying 4½ per cent. yearly dividends. Find the yearly income.

ANS $120.

2. I sell out $6,000 stock in the 6 per cent at 108, and invest the proceeds in 4½ per cent. stock at 72. Do I change my income, and how much?

ANS. Increase it $45.

3. I invest $10,175 in Bank of Montreal stock at 203, brokerage ½, paying 8 per cent. yearly dividends, and $4,950 in Bank of Toronto stock at 197½, brokerage ½, paying 7½ per cent. yearly dividends. Find my total income.

ANS. $587 50.

4. A and B invest capital in the proportion of 5 to 9. At the end of 5 months A withdraws 25 per cent. of his capital, and at the end of 6 months B withdraws 33⅓ per cent. of his. If their profits for the year are $3,051, divide it fairly between them.

ANS. A, $1,107; B, $1,944.

5. $159 due in nine months, when money is worth 8 per cent. per annum, is invested in Ontario Bank stock at 85, paying 4 per cent. per annum. Find the yearly income.

ANS. 7 1-17.

6. A man derives an income of $350 from an investment in the 3½ per cent. stock at 88; how much stock does he own, and how much is it worth?

ANS. $10,000 stock; value $8,800.

7. Find the change in income made by transferring

(1) $5,000 from the 4 per cents. at 84 to the 3½ per cents. at 70.

ANS. $10 gain.

(2) $12,750 from the 5 per cents. at 80 to the 5⅔ per cents. at 85.

ANS. $42.50 gain.

(3) $4,275 from the 4 per cents. at 80 to the 5½ per cents. at 99.

ANS. $19 gain.

(4) $2,500 from the 5 1-5 per cents. at 114⅛ to the 5 per cents. at 94⅞; brokerage ⅛ each way.

ANS. $20 gain.

(5) $3,600 from the 4 per cents. at 85 to the 5 per cents. at 102.

ANS. $6 gain.

8. A man has left to him $2,500. He invests one-fourth of it in the 6 per cents. at 112½, one-third of it in the 4½ per cents. at 80, and the remainder in the 3 per cents. at 75. Find his income.

ANS. $121.87½.

9. I invest $27,225 in the 3 per cents. at 90⅝, and when they have risen to 91⅛ I sell out and invest in the 3½ per cents. at 97⅜. What is the change in my income (brokerage ⅛)?

ANS. $80 increase.

10. I invest $25,500 in the 4 per cents. at 85, and when they have risen to 90 sell out and invest the proceeds in the 4½ per. cents. at 108; find the change in my income.

ANS. $75 loss.

ENTRANCE ARITHMETIC.

1. Forty pounds of tea and sixty pounds of coffee cost $43; a pound of coffee costing twenty cents less than

a pound of tea; find the price of a pound of each.

ANS. Tea, 55 cents; coffee, 35 cents.

2. A farmer sold 3,240 pounds of wheat and 952 pounds of oats for $54 40; the wheat is worth 40 cents a bushel more than the oats; find the value of each per bushel.

ANS. Wheat, 80 cents; oats, 40 cents.

3. A man buys land at $64.50 an acre. If he sells ¼ of it to A at $65 an acre, 1-5 of the remainder to B a, $48 for ¾ of an acre, and the remainder which is 108 acres to C at the rate of $36 for 4-7 of an acre, find his gain or loss.

ANS. Loss $153.

4. A man buys land at $80 an acre. If he sells ¼ of it to A at $60 an acre, ¼ of the remainder to B at $25 for 1-5 of an acre, and the rest to C, which is 144 acres at $50 for 2 5 of an acre, what is his gain or loss?

ANS. Loss $7,360.

5. If 4 men or 5 boys can do ¾ of a piece of work in 24 days, in what time can 3 men and 15 boys do the rest?

ANS. 2 2-15 days.

6. 7 men or 9 boys can do a piece of work in 21⅔ hours, in what time would 9 men and 7 boys do the remainder?

ANS. 10½ hours.

7. A train running 40 miles an hour takes 18 seconds to cross a bridge 64 yards long; what is the length of the train?

ANS. 256 yards.

8. If a train running at the rate of 30 miles an hour crosses a bridge 150 yards long in 24 seconds, find the length of the train?

ANS. 202 yards.

9. A train 20 rods long overtakes a man walking at the rate of 4 miles an hour and passes him in 10 seconds, how many miles an hour is the train running?

ANS. 26½ miles.

10. A train 220 yards long overtakes a man walking at the rate of 3 miles an hour and passes him in 15 seconds, find the number of miles per hour the train is running.

ANS. 33 miles.

11. Twelve months' wages are $380 and a watch, at the same rate 10 months' wages are $310 and a watch, find the value of the watch.

ANS. $40.

12. A servant agrees to work a year for $128 and a suit of clothes, but leaving at the end of nine months he gets $92 and the suit; what was the value of the suit?

ANS. $16.

13. A grocer mixes two kinds of tea, worth respectively 45 and 55 cts., per lb., in the proportion of 3 lbs. of the cheaper to 2 lbs. of the dearer, and sells the mixture at 56 cts. a lb.; find his gain per cent.

ANS. 14 2 7 per cent.

14. 5 gallons of wine worth $3.20 a gallon are mixed with 3 gallons at $4.80 a gallon, and the mixture is sold at $4.75 a gallon; find the gain per cent.

ANS. 25 per cent.

15. A plate of copper 2 ft. 3 in. long, 8 in. wide and ⅔ of an in. thick, is rolled into a sheet 2 ft. 8 in. long, and 6 in. wide; find its thickness.

ANS. ¾ inch.

16. A cube of gold, 2 inches to the side, is rolled into a sheet 3 ft. 4 in. long and 3 in. wide; how thick is it?

ANS. 1-15 inch.

17. Trees are planted 10 ft. apart around the sides of a rectangular field

80 rods long, containing 10 acres; find the number of trees.

ANS. 330.

18. A rectangular garden containing 24 square rods is 99 ft. long; how often can a boy measure the distance around it with a six foot pole?

ANS. 55 times.

19. I buy 60 gallons of syrup at $1.25 a gallon, pay $1.50 for carriage and $4.50 for duties; if ten per cent. of it be lost by leakage, at what price per gallon must the remainder be sold to gain by the whole tranaction $9?

ANS. $1.66⅔.

20. Bought 200 gallons of wine at $3.00 per gallon; paid for carriage $20.60, for duties $9.40. If ten per cent of the wine be lost by leakage, at what price per gallon must the remainder be sold to gain by the whole transportation $18?

ANS. $3.60.

21. A tree 91 ft. in length broke in falling into two parts, such that 5·12 of the longer piece was equal to ⅔ of the shorter; find the length of each piece.

ANS. Longer, 56; shorter, 35.

22. Three-quarters of John's money is double that of James's, and the two together have $55.44; how much has each?

ANS. James, $15.12; John, $40.32.

23. Find the cost of the lumber at $16 00 per M. that will be needed for a sidewalk three-quarters of a mile long, 4 feet wide and 2 inches thick.

ANS. $506.88.

24. What will the lumber cost at $18 per M. that will be required to build a sidewalk a quarter of a mile and 6 feet wide, the plank being 2½ inches thick?

ANS $356.40.

25. Find the L.C.M. of 45 cents, 60 cents, $2, $5, $9, $8.40, $12, $14, $21, and $28.

ANS. $12.60.

FOR ENTRANCE.

ANALYSIS OF SIMPLE SENTENCES.

BY P. S. HEAD MASTER.

A.

1. The noble mansions of the rich and the lowly cottages of the poor added their respective features to the landscape.

2. In another moment the livid lips and sunken eye of the clay-cold corpse recall our thoughts to earth, and to ourselves again.

3. Amid the solemn stillness of the chambers of death, imagination hears heavenly hymns chanted by the spirits of just men made perfect.

4. The beautiful river and the busy town of Marquette perpetuate the honored memory of the discoverer of the Great West.

5. The lives of these early Canadian Jesuits clearly indicate the earnestness of their faith and the intensity of their zeal.

6. By her writings and by her own personal example, Hannah More drew the sympathy of England to the poverty and crime of the agricultural laborer.

7. The cautious, old gentleman knit his brows tenfold more closely after this explanation, being sorely puzzled by the reason given.

8. Mr. Carlyle visited the leading battlefields of the Seven Years' War, while collecting material for the concluding volumes of his history.

9. The Latter-Day pamphlets assailed, with most galling invective and contemptuous ridicule, the leading politicians and institutions of the country.

10. He tells with great pathos the domestic tragedy of poor old Farmer George, third of the name; closing the sorrowful story with a possage in his own peculiar vein, full of mournful beauty and deep feeling.

B.

---

1 Sullen and silent, and like couchant lions,
Their cannon through the night,
Holding their breath, had watched in grim defiance
The sea-coast opposite.

2 Him shall no sunshine from the fields of azure,
No drum-beat from the wall,
No morning-gun from the black fort's embrasure
Awaken with their call.

3 High o'er the sea-surge and the sands,
Like a great galleon wrecked and cast
Ashore by storms, thy castle stands,
A mouldering landmark of the Past.

4 Bear through sorrow, wrong and ruth
In thy heart the dew of youth,
On thy lips the smile of truth.

5 Then, with nostrils wide distended,
Breaking from his iron chain,
And unfolding far his pinions
To those stars he soared again.

6 Steadfast, serene, immovable, the same,
Year after year, through all the silent night,
Burns on for evermore that quenchless flame,
Shines on that unextinguishable light!

7 The sea-bird wheeling round it, with the din
Of wings and winds and solitary cries,
Blinded and maddened by the light within,
Dashes himself against the glare, and dies.

8 From each projecting cape
And perilous reef along the ocean's verge,
Starts into life a dim, gigantic shape,
Holding its lantern o'er the restless surge.

9 Encamped beside Life's rushing stream,
In Fancy's misty light,
Gigantic shapes and shadows gleam
Portentous through the night.

10 Stripped of his proud and martial dress,
Uncurbed, unreined and riderless,
With darting eye, and nostril spread,
And heavy and impatient tread,
He came.

CONTEMPORARY LITERATURE.

In the interesting department, Men and Letters, of the *Atlantic Monthly* for April, Mary Hartwell Catherwood has a charming short writing on "The Book That Is Not Written." In her case it is the book of a mother. For felicity of language and tenderness of thought it would be hard to surpass in its own line this little fragment. "The Story of an Untold Love," which seems to bind its narrator in a net of inactivity, is continued. Amongst other literary and critical articles may be mentioned one on "Mark Twain as an Interpreter of American Character."

Again, in the April *Century* Mary Hartwell Catherwood has attained a singular success with her story of

"Jeanne D'Arc." There is a sympathy in sentiment and a moderation in expression that wins for this study of the maid's character an involuntary approval. Here is no pinchbeck glitter, but a refreshing nearness to the life of the soil. "Hugh Wynne, Quaker," is a novel of the Revolution, of which, at last, Americans may well be proud. In the poetry must be mentioned "Easter Flowers," by Clarence Urmy, and by itself for those who are interested in the great novelist, "Thackeray, in Weimar," with illustrations taken from unpublished drawings of his own.

"Our Gentlemanly Failures," an article on men trained by sports and in no other particular way, is reproduced from the *Fortnightly Review* in the "Littell's Living Age" for April 17th.

In the *Ladies' Home Journal* for April is published a hymn entitled "The Beautiful Hills," by Ira D. Sankey, with words by J. H. Yates. C. W. Gibson's illustration of "People of Dickens," in this number, is "Tom Pinch and his Sister." It is always a pleasure to look at Gibson's drawing, but these are not our old friends. "The Burglar Who Moved Paradise" still continues to amuse.

The April *Review of Reviews* contains a valuable article by President Thwing, of the Western Reserve University, at Cleveland, on "How to Choose a College." The question of cost is fully gone into. In "Cleaning Streets by Contract," by George E. Hooker, we learn that New York and Toronto are the two cleanest cities on the continent.

In the May *Quiver* is a complete story by David Lyall, the latest of Dr. Robertson Nichol's literary discoveries, although one takes a risk in saying "latest," they succeed each other so rapidly. There is also an account of the ragged schools, and letters for the children, by Canon Shore.

"The Practical Mental Arithmetic," illustrating contractions in multipliction and abbreviated methods of calculation, by C. E. Lund, D.L.S. J. & A. McMillan, St. John, N. B. A useful text-book for teachers, giving assistance in class work and containing a number of examples for exercise.

We have also received from Messrs. Moffat & Paige "Brush Drawing," by J. Vaughan, Art Master and Organizing Teacher, of Manual Training School Board for London.

"Vittorino Da Feltre, and other Humanist Educators," by Wm. H. Woodward. At the University Press, Cambridge. The author tells us that this volume is intended as an introduction to the study of the education of the first period of Renaissance. To achieve this purpose, the book is divided into three sections; the first of which treats in a highly interesting manner of the life of the Humanist Vittorino Da Feltre, termed "The First Modern School Master"; the second is composed of translations of four treatises on education produced during his period, and containing principles and deductions which are often considered peculiarly of to-day; the third and last is devoted to a general review of education as conceived by humanist scholars. The work is characterized by the thorough scholarship and penetrating conception of life and thought in which alone a student can find satisfaction.

"Chapters on the Aims and Practice of Teaching," edited by Frederic Spencer. At the University Press, Cambridge. These chapters are written by well-known educators of England and Wales, and treat of the importance of teaching and the methods that may be employed in teaching such subjects as Greek, Latin, French, German, English, History, Geography, Algebra, Geometry, Physical Science, Chemistry, Botany and Physiology. They deal with questions vitally important to Canadian teachers, and in so dealing do not lose sight of the fact that "the true worth of instruction—that is to say its vitalizing influence on the scholar's mind—depends less than is commonly supposed upon the particular subject through which the mind is approached, and more upon the stimulative method by which the mind is roused."

An "Experiment in Education," by Mary R. Alling-Aber. Harper & Bros., New York. This is an account of an endeavor to reach a more satisfactory arrangement of studies in our schools—a subject which is arousing great interest in the minds of those concerned with education just now. In the present instance the author considers herself justified in teaching children to read and write in connection with the study of the natural and physical sciences, mathematics, literature and history.

There has also been received from Messrs. Harper & Bros. an edition of Dr. William Smith's "Smaller History of Greece," revised, enlarged and in part re-written by E. L. Brownson, instructor in Greek in Yale University.

"Theory of Physics," by Joseph S. Ames, Ph. D. Harper & Bros., New York. This is an extended and advanced text-book which aims at giving a concise statement of the experimental facts on which the science of physics is based, and to present with these statements the accepted theories which explain them. An endeavor has been made to emphasize the theory of the experiments in terms of more fundamental principles—from this has been taken the name, Theory of Physics.

"Experimental Physics," by W. A. Stone. Ginn & Co., Boston. Not so elaborate a text-book as the one mentioned above, but specially intended for use in the laboratory, giving details of instruction, etc.

THE CANADA EDUCATIONAL MONTHLY.

THE CANADA EDUCATIONAL MONTHLY, we beg to inform our readers, entered upon a new term of service in educational work on the first of January of this year. It is to be hoped that after the following announcements have been carefully considered by our subscribers and fellow-teachers, that their assistance will be secured on behalf of the MONTHLY in more ways than one.

The MONTHLY is by this time one of the oldest educational periodicals in Canada, and it is the intention of all connected with its management to make it of increasing interest to the teachers of Canada and others interested in the educational progress of the country as a whole. Its *corps* of contributors already includes the most prominent of our educational workers, and what with an improved classification of topics, additional help in the editorial work, and a cordail co-operation on the part of subscribers, publishers and advertisers, it may not be too much, perhaps, to expect it to become, in the near future, one of the best and most readable of our educational journals.

It is the intention of the editors to add to the reading matter two new sections at least, perhaps three. One of these will contain a *resume* of the current events relating to educational movements in Canada and elsewhere. Arrangements have been made to have a record of such events sent by special correspondents from all parts of the Dominion in time for publication at the beginning of each month; and it is needless to say that paragraph contributions will be gratefully received from all teachers, when events of more than local interest take place in their district.

The second section will comprise hints from and to teachers, with correspondence. In the past, our teachers have been perhaps a little too timid in making suggestions through the press, particularly suggestions founded on their own experience. Fault-finding is a very different thing from honest criticism, and to the latter no teacher should fail to subject every proposed educational change, before finding fault with it or advocating it. Making use of the MONTHLY as a medium, it is to be hoped therefore that our teachers will join with us in an open and above-board campaign against all defects, and in favor of all improvements in our school work as well as in our school systems, so that eventually through the co-ordination of educational views from all the provinces, our various school systems will tend towards the unification of our Canadian national life, and not towards its disintegration. In future any question of an educational tendency may be discussed in our correspondence section, and when a *nom de plume* is made use of, the personality of the writer will under no circumstances be revealed.

The third section, when fully organized, will refer to all matters connected with a proposed BUREAU for the purpose of finding situations for teachers or promotion in the service. Every subscriber will have the privilege of inscribing his or her name on the lists about to be opened for those who wish to have their names thus enrolled. As an experiment we hope many of our teachers will find this section of great service to them.

To the subscribers who have stood by us so loyally in the past, we present our most grateful thanks, while to our new subscribers we make promise that their tastes and wishes will always be carefully considered in the management of the paper. Indeed, we feel it is only through the co-operation of our readers that our enterprise can be fostered to its fullest fruition.

During the year, the publishers of the MONTHLY will call upon advertisers under the improved circumstances of the periodical. To our faithful contributors we trust we will be able, as soon as the revenues of our enterprise improve, to return thanks in a more tangible way than heretofore.

The CANADA EDUCATIONAL MONTHLY, our subscribers must understand, is a journal for the whole Dominion, and not for any section or province.

Communications in connection with the editorial management of the paper are, in future, to be sent from Ontario and all the provinces west of Ontario, to Arch. MacMurchy, M.A., Box 2675, Toronto; and from the province of Quebec and the provinces east of Quebec, to Messrs. William Drysdale & Co., St. James St., Montreal, who will also attend to all matters pertaining to the publishing and advertising departments for the Eastern Provinces, and Wm. Tyrrell & Co., will attend to the like business for Ontario. Publishers: Wm. Drysdale & Co., Montreal; Wm. Tyrrell & Co., Toronto; A. Hart & Co., Winnipeg; J. & A. McMillan, St. John, N.B.

THE CANADA

EDUCATIONAL MONTHLY

AND SCHOOL MAGAZINE.

JUNE-JULY, 1897.

THE EFFECT OF HIGH SCHOOL REGULATIONS ON TEACHERS.*

By H. I. Strang, B.A., Prin. Col. Inst., Goderich.

ALTHOUGH the task assigned me is not one that I sought or that I consider myself specially fitted for, yet for some reasons I am glad to have the privilege of appearing before this joint meeting as in some measure the representative of the High School masters of the Province. As one of the older members of the Provincial Association I have felt of late years a growing regret that in this age of specialization we are getting so divided up into departments and sections, so absorbed in our own special work, and so bent on magnifying its importance and asserting its claims, that we are in danger of forgetting that we are all co-workers in a common cause, and that if we wish to exert our proper influence on the educational policy and system of the Province we can do so only by united aims and united action. That of late years we have too often been pulling in contrary directions instead of together will easily be seen by anyone who reads and compares the resolutions passed and the requests made by the various sections and departments; and that we do not wield the influence we should, and doubtless might if we were only heartily united, is abundantly evident from the refusal of the Minister of Education to give us the representation in the Educational Council to which we are justly entitled, and which, we had been led to expect, was at last to be given us.

Feeling thus, it has been to me a cause of special regret to observe that for some time past there has been a manifest disposition in certain quarters to foster antagonism between the Public Schools and the High Schools by raising the cry that the latter are degrading the former by robbing them of pupils and funds that rightfully belong to them. Now, in so far as this is alleged to result from the operation of the school law and regulations it is not my intention to deal with the matter. I wish, however, speaking for myself and my fellow principals, to deny that there is any hostility on our part to the Public Schools, or any disposition to underrate their work and importance. Why should there be? Many of us were for a time public school teachers, and the great majority of the schools to-day are in the hands of our ex-pupils, with whom we are as a rule on the best of terms, and whose success in their work is a matter of interest and pride to us. We know, too, that the more efficient the

* Paper read at O. E. A., April, '97.

public schools are the better prepared will be the pupils that we receive from them, and, consequently, the easier, pleasanter and more satisfactory will be our task in dealing with them afterwards.

In former days, when the amount of the High School grant depended largely on the average attendance, there was no doubt a temptation to relax the stringency of the entrance examination in order to swell the number of admitted candidates, but that day has long gone by, never to return; and under the regulations as they stand to-day and have stood for years average attendance is of practically no consequence in determining the government grant, and quality is of much more importance than numbers in admitting pupils to our schools. Moreover, we know that every pupil whom we admit before he is properly qualified imposes just so much additional work on the teachers to bring him up to the level of the class, and increases the risk of a low grading of the work by the High School Inspector at his next visit. I fail to see, then, how or why we have any interest in admitting pupils before they are properly prepared to pass the prescribed standards.

As to the other charge, that the High Schools and Collegiate Institutes representing, it is said, but 5 per cent. of the school population of the Province, receive the lion's share of the grant, and that the Public Schools, representing the other 95 per cent., are, in consequence, impoverished and rendered less efficient, I leave it to the Minister of Education to answer, as he has in fact so ably done in his speech of March 4th before the Legislature. Of course we take all we can get for our schools, and we may even have had the presumption to ask for more, but we have never asked that our grant should be increased at the expense of the Public Schools; and that our requests have fallen on rather deaf ears is surely evident from the fact that while the number in attendance at our schools and the local expenditure for their maintenance increased by leaps and bounds, the grant per head declined from $6.81 in 1882 to $4.05 in 1896.

It is, therefore, not merely with no hostility to Public School teachers, but with the fullest sympathy with them in their work, their difficulties, and their discouragements that I have considered the question before us. In dealing with it I have assumed that it is a settled principle now of an educational policy that the non-professional training of Public School teachers shall continue to be obtained mainly in the High Schools and Collegiate Institutes, and that the two classes of schools will continue, therefore, to exercise a powerful influence on each other. The wiser the course prescribed for the High Schools and the more efficient the teaching in them the better prepared the Public School teachers will be for their work; and, in turn, the better qualified the latter are for their duties, and the more efficiently they discharge them, the better able shall we be to do good work in our schools.

Before dealing directly with the effects of some of the present regulations allow me for a little to take a wider range, and to point out what I consider to be some serious mistakes that have been made in the past by our educational authorities, mistakes which, in my opinion, go far to account for three unfortunate, but I fear unquestionable, facts; viz.:

(1) That there is less stability in the ranks of the Public School teachers to-day than there was a quarter of a century ago; i.e., that there are fewer teachers in them or preparing to enter them who are likely to remain in the profession and to make teaching a life work.

(2) That the trend of salaries, at least outside of the cities and the larger towns, has been for the last few years distinctly downward.

(3) That notwithstanding the raising of the legal age for certificates the average age of our Public School teachers has lowered, and that our schools are getting more and more into the hands of comparative boys and girls, cleverer, quicker and better furnished intellectually, perhaps, than their predecessors of a generation ago, but lacking the steadiness and weight that only age and experience can give.

What, then, were the mistakes to which I refer?

(1) It was surely a mistake to make third class certificates provincial. If there was any valid reason for the step I do not remember ever hearing it advanced by any one. They ought, in my opinion, to have been confined to the counties where they were issued, unless perhaps when it was clear that the choice lay between endorsing a third class certificate from another county and granting a permit to some one belonging to the county. Moreover, County Boards of Examiners should always have had full power, if they judged it advisable, to raise the minimum qualifications for passing the professional examination, on giving a year's notice of their intention to do so.

(2) It was a mistake to make no difference between the experienced first or second class teacher and the untried holder of a third class certificate in regard to their legal right to accept the charge of any Public School (except Model School) without regard to its circumstances or needs. Now I am quite aware that it is possible to find *third-rate* teachers with first or second class certificates, and *first-rate* teachers with only third class certificates. I know, too, that some young and untried teachers have proved eminently successful from the first, and therefore I am not going to argue that every third class teacher should be forced to begin and serve a year as an assistant. All I claim is as it was found by experience that it was not wise to allow college graduates, even after a term at a Training Institute or a year at the School of Pedagogy, to take charge of High Schools till they had served a successful apprenticeship as assistants, it is not too much to ask that some check should be placed on the power and right of Public School trustees to appoint an untried third class teacher, holding it may be only a primary non-professional certificate, to the charge of a school which in the judgment of the Public School Inspector for the district requires the services of an experienced teacher with at least a junior leaving certificate. May I not safely appeal to the experience of the Public School Inspectors present, if they have not known of cases where a school has been practically disorganized, and six months, if not a year, virtually lost to the majority of the pupils, simply because a Board of Trustees, in order to save $50 or $100, or it may be more, or to find a place for somebody's son or daughter, filled the place of an experienced and successful second class teacher by the appointment of a raw, untried and poorly qualified third class teacher. What the check should be I do not stop to discuss or decide. I merely claim that there should be some restrictions, and that it ought not to be a very difficult task to devise suitable ones. Certainly if the Public School Inspectors are the right men in the right places, they ought to have something to say in this matter.

(3) May I not add that when the Education Department saw, as it could hardly help seeing, that things were tending towards the results I have mentioned, that with the machinery,

if I may so speak, provided by it for turning out teachers, the supply was fast exceeding the demand, it was a mistake not to take decided measures to meet the difficulty, and in the interests of the schools to prevent the older and more experienced teachers from being displaced by the increasing influx of third class teachers from the Model Schools. Surely it must have been evident to all that with only a a trifle over 8,100 positions to fill, and the Model Schools, Normal Schools, and School of Pedagogy sending out 2,100 freshly stamped Public School teachers each year (of whom over 1,500 are from the Model Schools), and with human nature constituted as it is, Gresham's law that "Bad money drives out good" is not more certain in its operation in the financial world than that a similar result would follow in the educational world, and that the tendency would be for the cheaper low-grade teachers to displace the dearer high-grade ones.

Fortunately all these mistakes, if such they were, as I honestly believe, can easily be rectified within a comparatively short period, and that, too, without injustice to any one. All that is required is courage and firmness to deal with the question. If the Department would promptly decide and forthwith announce that after 1897,

(1) Any new third class certificates granted would be valid only in the counties in which they were issued.

(2) The Department would exercise the right to say, on the representation of Public School Inspectors, that untried third class teachers should not be at liberty to take charge of certain schools which in the judgment of the Inspectors required teachers of experience.

(3) County Boards might, on giving a year's notice, decide that no one should be admitted to the Model Schools in their counties under the age of 19 (or 20), or with a lower non-professional standing than a junior leaving certificate.

I do not see that any injustice would be done to any one, and I firmly believe that within three years we should see a marked improvement in the state of affairs.

So far I have been speaking of the effect of the regulations in the past, and with special reference to the overwhelming supply of third class teachers. I come now to speak of recent changes in the regulations, and I shall devote my attention mainly to the following points:

(1) The requiring of at least two languages for a junior leaving certificate.

(2) The dropping of grammar and arithmetic and of the 50 per cent. on the total from the junior leaving requirements.

(3) The New Form I. Examination for High Schools and Collegiate Institutes.

And I shall endeavor to show that unfortunately the tendency of these changes will be to increase still further the number of third class teachers and to decrease the proportion of seconds and firsts.

Now I am free to say that I was not an advocate of any of these changes, and that in fact I did all I could to prevent some of them from being adopted. Although not fully convinced that it would be wise to insist on even one language being made compulsory, yet believing, as a classical teacher of many years' experience, that Latin, when properly taught, is an excellent means of training and culture and that not only would a course in it be of advantage to a teacher if ever he wished to enter a profession or a university course, but what is of more importance, that it could not fail to give him a better knowledge and a more accurate command of his own language. I was willing to see the experiment tried of making Latin compulsory for junior leaving certificates. I have seen no reason, however, to change my belief that the putting on of a second language was, to say the least, unnecessary and unwise.

The grounds on which the language requirement was defended at the time the change was made were, I believe, substantially as follows:

(1) It was desirable as far as possible in the interest of simplicity and uniformity to assimilate the matriculation examination and the teachers' examinations.

(2) It was in the interest of the teachers themselves to do so, because (a) a teacher having passed the junior leaving examination would then be able at any time to enter a profession or a college course, and that many would thus be encouraged to seek a higher rank in the profession, either as first class teachers or as High School masters; (b) the languages furnished a superior culture.

I may add that the dropping of arithmetic, grammar and rhetoric, and British and Canadian History from the junior leaving examination was a direct result of the action of the University Senate in making three languages compulsory for matriculation, and of the decision of the Department requiring two for junior leaving. Owing to the numerous options resulting from these decisions it became practically impossible to provide time for all the subjects, and when the question arose which should be dropped the lot fell after much discussion on these three.

Now I am not going to deny that there is some force in the arguments which I have mentioned. Looking back to the time when each University, the Law Society, the Medical Council and the Education Department had its own examinations, and remembering that these examinations differed more or less in the times that they were held, the work required, and the percentages to be obtained, I should be ungrateful indeed if I did not frankly acknowledge our indebtedness to the Education Department for the relief it has given us by securing the adoption of a uniform examination for the various bodies I have mentioned. It cannot justly be affirmed, however, that it is essential to this assimilating and unifying process that the junior leaving examination should coincide in every respect with that for University matriculation. Indeed, the Department has itself conceded this, for while three languages are required for matriculation only two are compulsory for junior leaving.

As a High School Master I do not see that it would cause any special difficulty if the junior leaving candidates were relieved of the second language, and, having thus more time to devote to the other subjects, were required in return to obtain a higher percentage than the mere matriculant. Under the present regulations a candidate who has passed Form I. or the Public School leaving examination may obtain a junior leaving certificate with only one-third of the marks in each subject. Now it is hardly necessary to point out that the ordinary pass matriculant, who is either going to enter on professional study or to continue his University course for four years, is in a very different position from that of a junior leaving candidate, who, after a brief term at a Model School, is going forth to teach the very subjects in which he passed, it may be, by a bare one-third. Apart from the fact that, as a rule, students at the stage of the primary examinations are not mature enough to get a sufficient grasp of grammar and arithmetic, will anyone say that the ability to obtain one third of the value of a grammar or an arithmetic paper, a third made up too often of "a little here, a little there, but nothing well done," is a sufficient guarantee of a candidate's fitness to teach the subject satisfactorily?

Again, take the subject of Euclid. Is it not a fact that under the present regulations our mathematical masters are finding it very difficult to get many of the candidates to work deductions. The latter know that only one-third is required to pass; they have been told that at least half of the paper is sure to be book work and, accordingly, believing that they can make a pass on that half they do not see why they should be worried with these horrid deductions.

One of the strongest arguments in favor of retaining the 50 per cent. of the total requirement is that it enabled a teacher to bring pressure to bear on indolent or careless pupils, for while under the present regulations a candidate may be weak in every subject, provided only he can make a third of its value, with the 50 per cent. on the total requirement there was a reasonable assurance that weakness in one or more subjects would in some measure be compensated by excellence in others. I think, therefore, that in the case of junior leaving candidates either the 50 per cent. on the total should still be required, or that the minimum for passing in each subject should be raised to 40 per cent.

As to its being in the interest of teachers themselves to have the junior leaving coincide with matriculation, it will no doubt be a convenience to individual teachers, and it may perhaps induce some who would not otherwise do so to go on for first class or High School Master's certificates. I cannot think, however, that it will be an advantage to the teaching profession or to the country, since, if I mistake not, the change will have a direct tendency to increase the number of those who will use the profession merely as a stepping stone to something else, and who for that purpose will content themselves with primary certificates. For instance, a young man who has passed Form I. examination will stay at school until he has passed the matriculation examination. Then, needing funds, and finding that his matriculation gives him junior leaving standing, and that a term at a Model School will put him in possession of a third class certificate, he will try the experiment, and with the whole Province to roam over in search of a school, he will teach his three years, drop out of the ranks and be heard of no more as a teacher. Thus the number of temporary teachers will be swelled.

As to the culture argument, it would ill become me as a language teacher to depreciate the value of language study as a means of culture. I go further and say that when properly taught and studied for a sufficient length of time the languages afford a most valuable training, and a culture which can not be obtained in any other department of school work. At the same time I must frankly admit that the culture obtained by cramming, with the aid of translations, examination papers, and approved methods of coaching enough of two or three languages to get a third of the value of the papers, is not of a particularly valuable or lasting character. To insure the best results of language teaching the work must be begun and the foundations carefully laid in Form I, and not left to be begun in Form II, or, worse still, to be hurriedly done after the student has reached Form III.

This brings me then to the last point with which I intend to deal, viz: the probable effects of the new Form I. examination on the qualification of Public School teachers; and as its probable effect on the organization and work of our schools has stirred up a very strong feeling in our ranks, I ask your special attention to what I believe is a fair statement of our feeling in regard to it.

In the first place, then, we have nothing to say against it as a Public School leaving examination, except that we believe you will find it too heavy for a single examination. If the Public School Inspectors, teachers and trustees wish to have fifth forms in their schools, and this examination as a graduating test of the work done in them, why should we object? Besides serving as an incentive to the Public School teachers and pupils, and as a test of the work done the examination will be of use to us as a measure of a candidate's fitness if he wishes to enter Form II. The number who take the examination in any school will not generally be large; the candidates will, as a rule, be the oldest, strongest and cleverest pupils of the school, and, therefore, presumably the ablest to bear the burden. Moreover, it will not be a promotion examination. The failure of a majority of the class to pass it will not affect the organizations of the school. The unsuccessful candidates will either drop out, or, if they continue at school, will remain as before in the highest class in the school.

Now with us in the High School the case is totally different. Coming as it does about half way between entrance and primary, and effecting, as it will, whole divisions of the schools, it will practically and necessarily become a promotion examination; and thus while the regulations distinctly recognize that the Principal shall have the control of the promotions the effect will be virtually to take it out of his hands. Now when you bear in mind that there are 12 subjects—11 papers and 1 oral test—that the papers will be prepared by one set of strangers and examined by another; that a percentage of one-third of each subject and one-half of the total is required and when you think of the number of failures at the present Form I. examination with its five subjects, I ask if any experienced teacher will say that such an examination is likely to prove satisfactory as a promotion examination. Think of a whole division of from 25 to 40 pupils grinding away at 11 different subjects (12 in reality, since rhetoric, though on the same paper as grammar, requires separate preparation), stimulated by their own ambition, and urged on by their teachers, each of whom will naturally be anxious that the failures, if such there must be, shall not occur in his or her department. Why, we groaned under the old primary with its 10 subjects and its weary hours devoted to drawing and book-keeping, and protested so vigorously that at length we got relief. Now the burden is to be made heavier, and to be laid on the shoulders of pupils younger and less able to bear it.

But this is not the only consideration that we have to look at. You will remember my saying that if the languages are to be taught so that the culture which it is claimed they afford may be obtained by those who study them, they must be begun early, one of them at least as soon as the pupil enters the High School, and carried on steadily throughout Form I. Now with 11 examination papers to prepare for, and the regulations strictly enjoining that a certain number of half hours a week shall be devoted to physical culture and reading, where is the time, not to speak of the strength, to be found for the languages? What Principal, even if he can devise a time table to meet the difficulty, finding himself constrained to treat Form I. examination as a promotion examination, will have the heart or the conscience to burden his hard worked young pupils with any real work in the languages? To show that I am expressing not merely my own opinion I may say that every High School Principal that has spoken or written to me in regard to the matter has expressed his belief that to impose the Public School leaving examination on the High Schools according to the present regulations will be to strike a severe blow at language teaching in these schools.

Nor is this a matter of interest to us alone. If we assume, as I do, that the present regulations dropping grammar and arithmetic after the primary, and requiring two languages for junior leaving, are to be continued in force, then it is surely reasonable, if not necessary, that pupils should be encouraged to begin language work as soon as they enter the High School and to make as much progress as possible before they reach the primary stage. Now there is no doubt I suppose that very few of those who enter Form II. with P.S.L. certificates will have taken up any language work. If, then, in addition to these, our Form I. classes are to be so burdened with preparation for this examination that the languages have to be neglected, the great majority of those who enter Form II. will be practically ignorant of the language. Will not the consequence be that those who wish to become teachers, finding that they can reasonably hope to obtain a primary certificate in one year without taking a language, but that if they wish to obtain a junior leaving certificate they will require two languages, and that to master these and to pass part one of Form II. and the other subjects of Form III. will probably take three years, will, as a rule, choose the easier course, and content themselves with a primary certificate? If they do, how many of them think you are likely to return at the end of the three years and take two years more at school to prepare for a junior leaving certificate? Is it not then all but certain that the effect of the Form I. examination as at present provided for will be to swell the number of primary certificates and to reduce that of junior and senior leaving ones?

What then do we ask or propose? Speaking for myself and those whom I have consulted in regard to the matter, I would suggest that Form I. examination be, like that of Form II., divided into two parts, part one to include the five subjects of the present Form I. examination, viz: reading, drawing, book-keeping, geography, and botany; part two to include the other seven, viz: arithmetic, algebra, euclid, history, grammar and rhetoric, composition and literature; both parts to be required (allowing them to be taken in either order and in different years) for a Public School leaving certificate, but only Part I. to be compulsory for those wishing to obtain a primary junior leaving or senior leaving certificate.

The basis of the division will be evident at a glance. Every one admits the right of the Department to insist that a candidate for any one of these three grades of certificate shall pass at least one examination under its own control in each subject prescribed for them. Now as the subjects included in Part I. are, with the exception of reading, dropped in Form II. the natural time to test the candidate's knowledge of them is when he wishes to leave Form I. The other seven, however, are all continued in Form II. The Department will, therefore, have another opportunity of testing the candidate's knowledge of them, and so can afford to let him pass into Form II. if in the Principal's judgment he is fit to go on with the work of that form. In other words if the regulations as they stand allow the student of Form II. who does not wish a primary certificate, to enter

Form III. and take up junior leaving work on passing merely part one of Form II. why should not the principle be extended, and a pupil of Form I. who does not wish for a Public School leaving certificate be similarly allowed to enter Form II. on passing part one of Form I. examination? If this were done I cannot see that injustice would be done to anyone. On the other hand our burden would be lightened so that masters and pupils would find it possible as at present to do a fair amount of language work in Form I., and many Public School teachers and pupils who could not undertake the examination if required to take all the subjects at once would be encouraged to try one of the Parts.

Moreover, with the division I have suggested, the examination of the papers of part two might be left, as heretofore, in the hands of the local boards, and the Inspectors could, after receiving the results of part one examination from the Department, issue as at present Public School leaving certificates to those who were entitled to them.

And, now trusting you may find something worth considering in what I have said, I leave the subject with you.

CANADIAN UNITY AND A NATIONAL BUREAU OF EDUCATION.

By Dr. J. M. Harper, Quebec.

THE temerity that would venture to criticise the constitution of our Canadian Confederacy in this the year of grace, 1897—in "the year of grace" as the Liberal party may well call it, with the federal as well as the provincial oversight of the country in its hands—is a temerity that is hardly safe to keep company with, in the glare of our present loyalty rejoicings. And yet it has to be said, as I have had occasion to say before, when advocating the organization of a Dominion Bureau of Education at the Toronto Conference of the Dominion Association of Teachers, that the British North America Act was evidently not a complete embodiment of all the unifying forces that tend to make a nation out of diverse elements. And if any of these unifying forces more than another came in for semi-elimination at the hands of the fathers of Confederation, it was none other than that of education; for the question of providing a common school education for every Canadian boy or girl, was simply relegated to the provinces themselves by the politicians of 1867, from the fact that they feared the shipwreck of the whole scheme of confederation should they dare to bargain for the common school being made a national institution. And what has been the effect of this elimination? Those who have followed the history of the New Brunswick School Question, and the Manitoba School Question, know now how the legacy of omission of 1867 became ours in 1872 and 1896. The common school has not become a national institution, but it has none the less disturbed the Dominion from one end to the other as much as it would have done had the strife been conducted on a broader basis.

And now in view of the verdict of the confederation that the common school must ever remain a provincial institution—for no one would think of having it organized otherwise now—it is pertinent enough for us to look at the effects produced by the decision of 1867, before emphasizing what may come to be a remedy in the organization of a Dominion Bureau of Education such as that which is to be found in the capital of our neighbors on the other side of the line.

When speaking of the purposes to be fulfilled by the Dominion Association of Teachers, the formation of which I was the first to advocate, I tried to point out in the concrete the constitutional elimination that had led to the keeping of the seven sister provinces so far apart, notwithstanding the loudness of our singing about a Canadian nationality and loyalty, born or about to be born, that will dominate all other political tendencies from Vancouver to Halifax. And in order that I may emphasize the later phases which this question has assumed, I may be excused from placing before the readers of the CANADA EDUCATIONAL MONTHLY some of my words on that occasion :

A great work, as I said, has been marked out for this Dominion Association of ours to accomplish, the maturing of a professional sympathy, the development of a common pedagogic that is expected to end in something even more tangible than a common pedagogic. Nor is this "something more tangible" far to seek, in view of what has been called the seeming failure of the political forces of 1867 to mature our provincial sympathies into the true national plebiscite we are ever longing for. For if it be proper to ask why the Nova Scotian trader is as much of a Nova Scotian as he was previous to Confederation, may we not also ask why a teacher cf the Canadian Maritime Provinces, east or west, has as weak a professional claim in the province of the interior of Canada as a Russian would have in Prussia or an Irishman in France. Yes, we may surely pause at the threshold of our search for pedagogic fallacies, to put the question in all seriousness, as I put it at our last meeting of this Association. "Why am I not directly eligible to take charge of a school in Ontario?" asks the certificated Normal School trained teacher of New Brunswick, and the answer comes from perhaps our Ontario brethren, "For the same reason that *we* are not directly eligible for appointment in New Brunswick, Nova Scotia, Prince Edward Island, or Quebec." But why should this be so? Is it professional prejudice or pedagogic pride that bars the way to reciprocity?

It is reassuring to learn that this Association, seeking a practical outlet for its counsels, has already taken steps to bring about an assimilation of our interests in this respect. What the final issue may be of such a movement, judiciously continued, is perhaps by some not easy to foresee. But what it ought to realize for our Dominion, tending seemingly nationwards, is a theme the most of us would not be loth to enter upon. The burdens laid upon our schools and schoolmasters are perhaps already grievous enough to be borne, and it is often urged against the many educational reformers of the present time, that the exceptions they, in their turn, urge against our system of public instruction and courses of study, seem to focus on some additional subject or pet routine they are anxious to have introduced. But the reforms that would arise were the experienced teachers of one province, to have ready acceptance in any of the provinces, would reduce the burdens of the school if there is anything beneficial in the process of assimilation. The faddist from New Brunswick would have the conceit taken out of his fads when he came to Ontario ; while the Ontario man when he came to Quebec, would have to take his hands out of his pockets out of sheer respect if not from industry. In fact there would be little or no room for the faddist whose only faith in the novelty he crows and croons over is in the declaration that it has been introduced elsewhere.

The pedagogic necessities would have to be respected as paramount in every discussion over school reform. The true function of the school would less frequently be lost sight of in the craving for change. Assimilation would lead to consolidation, and consolidation would help the national tendencies of our populations. In a word, the schools and the schoolmasters of our Dominion, without the prospect of having imposed on them additional burdens, would become agencies in developing that community of thought and national feeling which has the minimum of a provincial *penchant* about it. And if the republic of the St. Lawrence is something which a remote posterity only may see, may it not be for some of us to hail the organization of a Dominion Bureau of Education which, while it disturbs no provincial constitutional rights, may foster the pedagogic principles on which every system of public instruction ought to rest.

And it is very pleasant to me to notice that the note struck at the conference of the Dominion Association of Teachers in 1895 is likely to develop itself into a definite demand for the organization of a Bureau of Education. No more opportune time could be seized than the present to advocate the formation of such a department at Ottawa. The Hon. Mr. Laurier has come to power, with the words on his lips that the consolidation of a people and their progress can only be secured by a purity and unity of national action. And how, may we ask, can this purity and unity of national action be better secured than by the common school and the co-ordination of its interests, as well as the assimilation of the social and good citizenship forces it has for its highest function to propagate. I shall endeavor in a subsequent article to point out the further necessities that press upon our common country to make the most of our position, while loyally maturing a sound national spirit among all Canadians irrespective of the provincial tendency to isolate and prejudice, and how this can best be assisted towards fulfilment in a practical manner by a Dominion Bureau of Education.

The lack of co-operation on the part of the elements that enter into the practical conduct of our schools is the usual way of enumerating the main difficulties in this connection. Could we get our educationists and our non-educationists to adopt some practical focus-point of school work, such co-ordination would lead to the necessary co-operation and all would be well. A second Herbart would have to come to the rescue and assimilate the ideas of the utilitarian and the theorist. It has come to be a habit on the part of many of our publicists to lay social irregularities at the door of the school, a practice which would certainly all but disappear were the proper function of the school to be kept in view, when any reform is advocated or any innovation proposed. This function in my opinion is to be found in a principle which I have enunciated again and again, and which I am prepared to repeat everywhere, namely: It is not that which goeth into the mind of the child that educates, but the manner of its coming out. And when we think of this as a practical pedagogue we find it in the simple statement—if we would think correctly we must learn to speak correctly and write correctly—a point which can only be reached by a daily practice in the making of sound English sentences.

J. M. Harper.

EDUCATION, HISTORY AND IDEALS.

EDUCATIONAL ESSAY.

BY SAMUEL MOORE, B.A., TEACHING STAFF, B.C., CAN.

THE word education is of Latin origin, and means the drawing out or developing the prominent faculties of the mind by various activities. The term education is slightly different from instruction, which means the systematizing the elements of knowledge.

When we study the history of civilization we notice that many systems of education have been in use, notably three: National, Theocratical and Humanitarian.

The national system of education is the most primitive, and had the family as the organic starting point, out of which the nation grew. For example we have the systems of education in China, Persia and Greece.

The Chinese system was passive and non-progressive in methods and character, while the Persian was active and progressive.

The system in Greece aimed at individual education. The objects of this system were in many respects praiseworthy, and each individual was taught to set a value on his own personality, resembling the teachings of the Puritans in modern history.

In the theocratic system, as represented by the ancient Jews, education is at first patriarchal, because the family is the link that connects the individual with the chosen nation.

The humanitarian system of education arose in the Roman Empire and was founded on the Christian idea. The Christian ideal in education embraced the brotherhood of man and the sisterhood of woman. In this new ideal Art, Science, politics, morality and industry are included and harmonized.

In the history of Christian civilization we notice that the goal of progress is reached by the community through the education of the individual.

The chief aim of the humanitarian system in education is to fit and train young people for civil life, so that they may perform their duties intelligently and observe the moral obligations of society. The above conception represents the aims of the Public School system in the several Provinces of Canada, and also in the States of the neighboring Republic.

The best authorities on educational work show that education is both a science and an art, and that it is divided into three parts, viz, Physical, Intellectual and Moral. Education as a subject is a mixed science, as it is correlated to many other sciences, as Ethics, Psychology, Physiology, etc.

In the modern programme of studies for the teacher Psychology, or the science of the human mind, is preeminently important. The special and general senses which convey perceptions and sensations to the mind require adequate training so that they perform efficiently the primary function of intellect and be responsively active to the will. Again, as physical culture is receiving some attention at present, it is necessary for the teacher to be familiar with the subject of Hygiene and the kindred subject Physiology.

The subject of physical education received special consideration from the Greeks and Romans in ancient times, as these peoples included gymnastics and calisthenics in their regular school course.

It was by such systematic drill in physical exercises that the statesmen, orators, philosophers and poets of Greece and Rome gained strength of mind and muscle. The old Latin author stated the pedagogic truth in a nut-shell, "Mens sena in corpore sano," or A sound mind in a sound body. It is essential that the physical organs and muscles be trained so that they be responsively active to the will. Nowadays many are beginning to recognize that while intellectual studies and physical exercises are being vigorously prosecuted in the modern school system the moral training is not receiving the attention which it should. From the fact that questions of right and wrong are more frequently discussed in our social and business relations than the weather, it becomes evident from history and experience that the subject of good morals ought to be systematically taught in all educational work. No less an authority than Dr. Eliott, President of Harvard College, points out that Logic and Ethics should find a place on the programme of studies in the Public School; that is, right thinking and right acting are primary social requirements of the new education.

The educational maxim "learn to do by knowing" is as true in ethics as pedagogy. In addition to the regular mental and physical drills there ought to be a moral drill in the ethics of Christian morality.

We send missionaries to heathen lands to teach the principles of Christianity and too often leave the youth of professing Christian parents without systematic instruction in the minor morals and major virtues, to the influence of heredity alone, to relapse or decay in morals.

Sir Isaac Newton, in his "Principia," lex iii, proves that in the physical world "action and re-action are equal and opposite," and from the reasonings of some moralists and the teachings of history we conclude that a similar law is true of the moral world. *Vide* History of the French Revolution in Paris—1789-95

Education as a science and an art is at present in a transitional period; in fact Pedagogy in modern times, like the chameleon, assumes a variety of phases. At times we are bewildered by the innovations of the Herbartian kind, yet while we cannot swear to the "ipse dixit" of every particular innovator in educational work, we can, like the eclectic philosopher, Horace of old, accept what is good and true.

It often seems desirable to form a combination method which would establish a closer relationship between the old and modern methods of imparting instruction. The question is a practical one in the closing years of the nineteenth century.

The true aim of education is of primary importance to the teacher and the scholar. It is very important that we attain the correct ideal which is culture and practical power. We should aim to combine literary culture with a considerable amount of executive or practical ability. The Public School is in many respects a benevolent institution, it is by no means a "close corporation" but rather a republic of learning and sociability.

Here the children of rich and poor are alike offered free the beauties of Literature and the discoveries of Science.

Do not draw back from any way because you never have passed there before. The truth, the task, the joy, the suffering on whose border you are standing, O my friend, to-day, go into it without a fear, only go into it with God, the God who has been always with you.

—*Phillips Brooks.*

QUEEN'S ENGLISH.

IN the current number of the "Review of Reviews" a subject of the highest importance is raised—that of the conservation, in its present form and purity, of the "Queen's English." It is pointed out with great force that this year of the Jubilee must be considered a crucial one as regards the permanence and diffusion of the English language. There is nothing more remarkable in modern record than the prevalence of our mother tongue over the earth during the auspicious reign of her Majesty. Some of the leading facts are thus given. At the beginning of the century there were not more than twenty millions of people in the whole world who spoke English. In 1801, one hundred and sixty million people spoke seven European languages—English, French, German, Russian, Spanish, Portuguese and Italian. The population using these seven languages has now grown to four hundred millions, and of these one hundred and thirty-five millions speak English. At the beginning of the century English speakers were less than thirteen per cent., of the total. They are now over thirty per cent., and outnumber those speaking any other European language. By the end of the century it is probable the English speakers of the world—that is to say, the persons who habitually use English as the vehicle for expressing their thoughts and ideas—will be one hundred and fifty millions, or more than seven times as many as used that instrument of conversation one hundred years before. This immense preponderance of English speakers tends naturally to increase enormously the diffusion of a language. It is more and more coming into use as the "lingua franca" of the world. Nowadays it is possible to touch at every seaport on the planet, and to transact business without speaking a word of any language but that of Shakespeare. This is very notable, and very momentous; and while so marvellous an expansion of Shakespeare's tongue is manifesting itself over land and sea elsewhere, the silent conquest of all India by English speech is slowly progressing, as, of yore, that of Rome progressed in Italy, Spain, France, and Britain. English is year by year becoming the "free language" of the East, uniting all portions of the Indian Continent, and gradually establishing itself as the universally current speech of Oriental commerce and intercourse. Even in Africa the Germans, French and Portuguese have practically abandoned their struggle against the dominant use of English. "Whether it be Pigeon English," writes our contemporary, "as in some parts of the far East, or the curious compound that is spoken in tropical Africa, everywhere the Queen's English, however mutilated and defaced, is the recognized currency." Grimm, the renowned philologist, among many others, foresaw this result of the ubiquity of British enterprise and commerce, and did not even as a linguist regret it. He wrote: "The English tongue, which by no mere accident has produced and upborne the greatest and most predominant poet of modern times, may be with all right called a world-wide language, and, like the English people, seems destined to prevail with a sway more extensive even than at present over all regions of the globe; for in wealth, good sense, closeness of structure, no other language now spoken deserves to be compared with it." This is a significant tribute to come from a

German grammarian, and, properly considered, constitutes perhaps the noblest and fullest homage which could be paid to the great position of England among the nations now, in this eventful and unparalleled year, when, amid a world reeling with revolutions and transformation, the power and authority, the peace and prosperity of the Queen's people go on augmenting, irresistible, unquestioned, towards some vast future destiny, which cannot be frustrated or diminished except by the failure of British patriotism and British spirit.

The writer we have quoted, however, very usefully and wisely asks whether something ought not to be done this Jubilee Year to preserve unimpaired and immortal the "Queen's English." Latin—the imperial language of the Masters of the then known world—stood once precisely in the position of the English of to-day, but every student knows how it became corrupted in mingling with different races and uses, so that the mother tongue was at last "dead," and Spaniards, Portuguese, Frenchmen, Italians, Roumanians, and others now talk a broken and altered Latin without mutual comprehension. This in some measure springs from local carelessness on the part of people who have no idea of the nobleness of pure speech, and who speak in the way of which we are given the subjoined example. "One may enter a good London restaurant and hear the average well-dressed person discourse as follows: 'Beesliot (a beastly hot day). Ah, st'awb'iza k'eem (ah, strawberries and cream). Ven nice, eysh think (very nice, I should think). Shleyg vew sam? (shall I give you some?) St'awbiz vef fine thish yah (strawberries very fine this year). Ha suthinta drink withem? (have something to drink with them?) Pawt? She'y? (port? sherry?). Sowdernmilk? (soda and milk?).'" Against slipshod conversation like this no lover of pure language can contend. But it does not do so much harm as the ignorance of those who daily admit into written English such solecisms as "scientist," and "reliable," and the Americanisms which reek of the bar and the mine, and which actually pride themselves upon being without classical or grammatical authority. Great cities are great sinners in respect of debasing and defacing a national language. One can see in Clautus and Terence how the Romans clipped and mutilated the magnificent vocabulary of Scipio and Cicero, and East London has done her worst to efface the vigorous aspirate, to alter the "a" into "i" in such words as "day" and "lady," and to introduce slang expressions which are occasionally picturesque, but seldom deserving of perpetuation. There is so much of this vulgar corruption of the mother tongue going on in America, in Australia, and among the literary men who have not enjoyed the corrective benefit of a classical training, that it may quite easily become the phenomenon of a hundred years hence that English-speaking races will not easily understand each other. It is feared that this change is already commencing, that the language of Shakespeare and Tennyson will soon become a literary language, like the ecclesiastical diction of the modern Papal Bulls, in the midst of the various and different Latin tongues spoken around. We shall some day, we are warned, be as little able to understand an American or an Australian in London as the unlettered Spaniard is able to read Virgil, or the uneducated Parisian to appreciate the grace and taste of Horace.

It is proposed by the ingenious propounder of these linguistic anxieties that all sorts of precautions shall be adopted to make this year of

Jubilee a season of defence and preservation for the "Queen's English." He would invoke a council of philologists, editors, and literary men ; he would establish a league of authors and speakers to maintain the purity of the mother tongue ; he even talks of an "Academy for the English-speaking" world on the model, doubtless, of the "Della Crusca," or the French Institute. For our own part, we are of opinion that no such artificial preventives can effect much. A language, however imperial and world-wide—nay, the more certainly in proportion as it is dominant and widespread—must submit to the law of use, in becoming time worn, obliterated, defaced, and abbreviated. It is the fate of all human speech, as much as of coinage, that ignorant and rude hands shall wear away the original sharp and beautiful "image and superscription," clip the bright initial silver of the vocables, and sweat away the good gold of the new-created words. What preserves the purity of a speech must ever be its literary monuments, and next to that the conscientiousness of authors, imitating and reverencing these. No Academy, no Institute can save in its simple original perfection the language which has to furnish daily currency for the world. It must and will lose its clear edges, its etymological milling, its pristine inscriptions, and suffer the consequences of belonging to the uneducated, and being at their service. But we do most heartily agree with the spirit of this appeal in trusting that men of letters will recognize their responsibility towards such a bequest as the speech of Shakespeare and of Milton, and not wantonly infect, or allow to be infected, the chastity and nobility of their mother tongue, with such vile vulgarisms and such unauthorized innovations as day by day at the present time pass muster with the hasty public for literature and correct English writing.

It is not so with Him that all things knows,
As 'tis with us that square our guess by shows;
But most it is presumption in us when
The help of Heaven we count the act of men.

—*All's Well that Ends Well*, ii. 1.

A SCHOOL OF PRACTICAL AGRICULTURE.

THE following report upon a school of a type not very familiar to us in England is of considerable interest at the present time, as it shows the possibility of a practical solution of certain difficulties which have in some quarters at least been held to be virtually insuperable. It is the Dauntsey School at West Lavington in Wiltshire.

An Inspector of the Educational Department of the Board of Trade states : "I found the present pupils an intelligent set of lads, taking an interest in their work, both practical and scientific. As regards the latter, mention may be made of the collections of grasses which many of them made last summer, doing credit both to the teaching they had evidently had on this useful subject, and also to their own power of observation. So far, too, as the class of teaching pursued is concerned, the work seems to be of a thorough character, the practical application of what is taught being as much as possible shown. Although there is always a danger of erecting a superstructure of 'applications' without having laid a sound foundation of elementary knowledge, I do not think in the present instance this is at all likely to be the case. On the contrary, I think the pupils turned out from this school, as at present conducted, should possess a sound knowledge of the various subjects brought before them, and that those of them who are anxious for further instruction would then be qualified to go on to a place of still higher education, and when there, be capable at once of taking full advantage of the facilities for advanced education which such an institution would possess. In the foregoing remarks reference has been made to the indoor work of the school. However important that work may be one is pleased to find that in an institution of this nature it is entirely subsidiary to the outdoor work. According to the weather, the lads are taken out on the land, and there they take part in every operation, for which machinery and horses are hired when required. The actual work is necessarily more of the nature of the spade than of ordinary cultivation, yet the principles are the same, and the lads get an insight into the growth of a great variety of crops. . . . Since the school was opened in May, 1895, there have been fifty-eight pupils, of whom six have since left. Of the remaining fifty-two there are thirty-two boarders and twenty day boys. A proposal is stated to have been made to convert this place into an 'Organized Science school.' I would submit that such a course would, as affecting the agricultural work, be fatal to the best interests of the school, should it tend to stereotype the scientific teaching and subordinate the practical to it. At present, as far as can be seen, the same amount of scientific work is on the average done as would be required if the place were actually an Organized Science school, but it is done freely, as the practical work permits, and not of weekly necessity. Grants are not sought after, outside examinations with all their attendant disadvantages are not made use of, 'text-book' teaching is not indulged in, but the work seems really that of education, and not the mere 'getting up' of a number of subjects, and as such it should be allowed to continue. It may be, perhaps, worth consideration whether instruction in minor industries of the farm should be well developed. The boys are just at an age when they might take an intelligent interest in poultry-keeping. Bee-keeping also might engage attention, but except in a general way I think instruction in dairy work should be left for a later period.

———

I should say that the most grievous fault in our entire American system of education from university to kindergarten, in class-room and in teachers' meetings of all kinds, is the everlasting failure to distinguish between commonplace teachers, students, text books and speakers and those really superior. When a university has a president, or a city a superintendent, or a session of the N. E. A. a chairman who sees the difference between a $5,000 man, a $500 man, between a good and a so-so fellow or professor and permits natural selection to do its work—there is progress.

G. Stanley Hall.

———

The pride of all conservative forces in local and individual phases of administration, and the reasonable prejudice of the progressive men against all existing conditions and work, shows there is some good in the work and workers, in the methods and devices of every community. The best teaching is as good as the best preaching, or as the best practices of law or medicine, but the possibilities of reform are greater than in any other line because teachers deal with developing life; but pride and prejudice are most tyrannical.

E. A. Winship.

EDITORIAL NOTES.

THE REV. DR. RYERSON, D.D., LL.D.

THE late distinguished founder of the Public School system of Ontario was a thorough Canadian, having been born on the 24th March, 1803, in the township of Charlotteville, near the village of Vittoria, in the then London district now the county of Norfolk. His father was Col. Ryerson, a U. E. Loyalist, and a member of the Church of England. Of gentle birth, he had to maintain himself by manual labor, doing ordinary farm labor for some years, until he left to pursue his studies at Hamilton, under John Law, Esq., of the Gore District Grammar School, While doing farm work, he rose at 3 a.m., and studied till 6, carried a book to study during the "noon spell," and reviewed his reading while walking abroad in the evenings. At Hamilton he worked with such energy that he was attacked by brain fever and nearly succumbed. After his recovery, when only 18, he became Usher in the London District Grammar School. Upon conviction, he attached himself to the Methodist Church, and this so displeased his father that Egerton had to leave home and seek his own living. In 1825 he became a duly licensed minister of the Methodist Church, serving in various circuits with much acceptance, and subsequently occupying high office in the Church of his choice. He obtained a Royal University Charter for the Upper Canada Academy at Cobourg, and was appointed its first President in 1841. In 1844 he became Superintendent of Public Instruction for his native province, and administered it with conspicuous success for thirty-two years, resigning in 1876. Dr. Ryerson occupied the remaining years of his life in literary work, and died on 19th February, 1882. During his long, useful and busy life, Dr. Ryerson's voice and pen were ever at the service of his Church and country, and as a champion of civil and religions liberty, as well as the founder of a most unique and successful system of public instruction, his name is imperishably inscribed in the annals of his native country.

THE REV. DR. RYERSON, D.D., LL D.

The Minister of Education has issued the following circular for the information of pupils, parents and teachers. We ask the special attention of all schoolmasters to it. The undue importance which has been given to examinations is much to be regretted, and we hope this action of the Minister may be helpful in causing the educational work of the country to recover its equilibrium :—

"As the time for receiving applications for the annual departmental examinations is near at hand, permit me to call your attention to the following:

1. These examinations are specially designed for candidates for a teacher's certificate, or as a preliminary qualification for some other professional course of study. It is therefore desirable that those who are pursuing their studies for any other purpose should be allowed the fullest discretion with respect to these examinations.

2. Under Regulation 38 of the Education Department, the Principal of the High School has ample authority to make "such promotions from one form to another as he may deem expedient." It is not intended that High School pupils should be required to take any departmental examination in order to be entitled to promotion. Such a test, apart from the expense to the pupil, would be objectionable on many grounds which must be obvious to every teacher. Although the Education Department has no desire to interfere with the discretion of any pupil as to the examinations he should take, or to prevent any teacher from giving such advice to pupils with respect to examination as appears, in his judgment, to be for their best interests, it is to be distinctly understood that a departmental examination is not considered a necessary part of any Public or High School course of study.

3. The departmental examinations should not be taken as the chief test of the teacher's efficiency. Sometimes teachers are exposed inadvertently to the application of such a test by comparisons made with other schools before the annual school opening; at other times trustees inconsiderately make such a test the chief basis of a teacher's promotion. A more correct view of the purpose of examinations on the one hand, and of the dignity and qualifications of the true teacher on the other, would greatly assist in establishing standards of efficiency which would amply protect the good name of every well-conducted school."

SALARIES.

With regard to the salaries paid civic and Government employees in Toronto, there appears a most unjust discrimination against women teachers.

There are at present on the teaching staff of the Public Schools of Toronto 445 teachers and 54 principals: of these only 60 are men. The 421 women teachers are most wretchedly paid compared with other employees of the government or the city.

After several years devoted to academic and professional training for the duties of her high office, a woman teacher takes a position on the Toronto staff at a salary of $324 00 per year—just $3 00 more than the yearly wages of the charwoman of the Toronto P. O ($321), and exactly $26 less than the amount paid the youth who runs the errands for the office of the Inspector of Prisons, ($350).

In her fifth year of service a woman teacher receives $396—just $4 00 less than the salary of many of the young women assistants and attendants at the Public Library ($400) and $26 less than the street sweepers ($421). The laborers at the cattle market are paid at the rate of $546 per year.

The average salary of women teachers in Toronto is only $465—just $50 less than the average salary of letter carriers of the P. O. ($515), whom every one acknowledges are none too well paid; while the average salary of stenographers at the City Hall is $528.

After fourteen years of meritorious service the woman teacher receives $636—just $10 more than the attendant in the Mayor's office ($626), just $12 more than the messenger at the City Hall ($624), and just $14 less than the baker at the Central Prison ($650).

To sum up, there are 155 teachers who receive less than $400—the very lowest salary paid a clerk in the P. O. department; 343 teachers who receive less than the poorest paid clerk in the Customs department ($600); 309 teachers who receive less than a laborer at the cattle market ($546); 237 teachers who receive less than a scavenger ($477); and not one of the 421 teachers receives as much as the scavengering foreman of the street cleaning department, ($912). Not one of the women teachers receives the average salary paid subordinate clerks in the Toronto Post Office ($785.)

Do the high qualifications of a teacher count for nothing? Does it not require a higher grade of intelligence to instruct and train the youth of our country than to drive a scavenger cart or to do clerical work in an office?—A MEMBER OF STAFF.

The professional sympathies in favor of a Canadian Bureau of Education are gaining strength, as the necessities for such come to be understood; and we are not going to be surprised should the Federal Government, amid the excitement over tariff amendments, Quebec bridges, fast steamship lines, and Rocky Mountain railway approaches, be called upon to take the formation of such a Bureau into consideration at an early date. We have already pointed out the character of the work which such a bureau could safely undertake, in the matter of collecting and disseminating information regarding public scholastic institutions. But one of our contributors, Dr. Harper, of Quebec, has pointed out—in an article which we publish this month and which he promises to amplify—a fundamental function to be performed by a Bureau of Education that cannot but recommend the immediate organization of such a department. Once open the way for an interchange of teachers all over Canada through the assimilation of licenses and diplomas, and the true national feeling that must come and is coming to us as Canadians will speedily, through cosmopolitan school influences, bud and blossom, to the surprise of the remotest communities. There is a *theory* in the air about Canadian patriotism, but once set the Canadian schoolmaster free from his provincial trammels all the way from Nova Scotia to British Columbia and we will soon have the genuine article itself—the product of an assured prospect developed in every school-room in the land, through the school craft of teachers, who are neither Nova Scotians nor British Columbians, but Canadians. And with a co-ordinating force at Ottawa to bring about that community of feeling and action we are all hoping to experience soon, in a direct line through the little red school-house by the roadside, as well as through our largest institutions, even the more elderly of us may live to see our Canadian patriotism more than a mere peradventure or a piece of provincial affectation. In a word, the school-house by the roadside, in our opinion, will do more for us in this connection than a perennial hundred days' session of the House of Commons or even of the Canadian Senate.

While many of the people of Ontario are "looking backwards" to the time when the educational affairs of their Province were in the hands of a Superintendent of Education, and are some of them longing for a return to the old *regime*, the people of the Province of Quebec are taking it for granted that the organizing of a department under the Minister of Education is their only hope of progress in school affairs. There has always been a difference of opinion as to whether there should be any mixing up of politics and education as between politics and denominationalism, as between politics and anything that is not politics. And to such an extent have the politicians as well as the non-politicians amplified their arguments on either side, that some people are beginning to think that it is unwise to have anything to do with politics unless one, is on the *qui vive* for a situation. What then is *la politque*, even should the query be put in French? Is it the right or wrong examination of something tangible, or is it only the swing between the two in party strife? Is the science of government a question of ethics or only a sectional convenience? If it be the former, as it certainly is, wherein consists the informality or rather abnormality of mixing up the people's affairs with the affairs of the people? The question of Superintendent or Minister is therefore an open question, a question of provincial convenience, and there is no more, perhaps not so much, wrong doing in a Minister of Education being a politician than there is in a Superintendent of Education being a politician *sub rosa*, as he nearly always is. And in drawing the attention of our readers to this first principle, we have it in mind to justify our own references from month to month to the political tendencies of the times. *La politque vraie* is every citizen's business, every intelligent man's birthright, to see to; and as such we claim it as our business as educationists and teachers to see to the advice we have to give in the administration of educational affairs. As has been often said before, this journal knows no pronounced party politics; and perhaps it would be better for our Canadian journalism if the general tendency were in this direction. But the fact that a man who is a publicist is also a politician should in no way deter us from putting our faith in him either as an educationist, or as a minister of the gospel, or as a public school teacher, or even as an editor of an educational magazine. *Je suis l'etat* every citizen may justifiably exclaim, as long as he does not claim to be such in the spirit of the old monarch of France or the modern party politician.

The question of "open doors" in our educational councils comes to be discussed every now and again, and the recurrence nearly always arises from the indiscretion of some member of the Council forgetting himself while indulging in personalities that can hardly escape being reported indirectly afterwards to the person or persons thus covertly attacked. No more reprehensible act can be conceived than this; and when the cowardice comes to be exposed, as it always is, sooner or later, it is all but impossible to repress the demand to have the proceedings, where such conduct is tolerated, conducted openly in the hearing of the press. Many of our school boards in the cities have been obliged to open their doors, for no other reason than this; and when they are opened it soon becomes apparent that there is another side to the question, as the public comes to read in the newspapers the reports of a discussion which, for the sake of the right relationship between pupils and teachers, between supervisor and supervised, ought never to have been printed. The indiscretion of one man in giving way to the censorious bumptiousness of the *parvenu* thus becomes the punishment of many of our best teachers, as is to be borne out by the later experiences in some of our large cities. The *parvenu* has had his little bit of revenge, and what cares he who may suffer, as long as he can consider his animadversions privileged.

Then there arises a state of affairs which we will not venture to illustrate other than by the following:—

"We hear of wars and rumors of wars in the secret councils of Tyrone House. All the operations of the National Board go on in privacy, and it is only occasionally that news leaks out, or that public official information is given. It is said that, through false economy, the work of the Board has got into much confusion and arrears, and that some sweeping reforms must soon be instituted. We also hear of some arbitrary and unexplained dismissals of model-school teachers. Moreover, an investigation into the working and results of these model schools is being carried on, which is likely to result in a proof of the failure of the schools. This failure is chiefly due to the steady persecution they have met with from the Bishops, who object to them because their constitution is more mixed and secular than that of the ordinary schools, and because they are less under the direction of the Church. A good deal of the failure, however, must be attributed to defective management, especially in the mode of choosing and promoting teachers."

Tyrone House is not in Canada; but there are Tyrone Houses in Canada all the same, and in connection with their existence there is always to be found the outside demand for "open doors;" and the average newspaper would no doubt feel justified in greeting the opening of their doors much as the Harbor Commission of Montreal was complimented for conducting its proceedings in the hearing of the public.

"The decision of the Harbor Board to hereafter open its meetings to the press and the public is an act of shrewd policy and in accord with the public interest. They constitute a public body doing public business, guarding public interests and spending public money, and there is every reason why their proceedings should be open to the public eye. Then secrecy always fosters suspicion, whether it be well founded or no. When blame for some sin of commission or omission lies between two bodies, one of which deliberates in public and the other behind closed doors, the average citizen is always ready to believe that the weight of it rests upon the "star chamber" corporation. Publicity is the best defence that a public body can have when it is innocent of wrong-doing; and determined secrecy is always regarded as *prima facie* proof of something to conceal. Hence we congratulate the Harbor Board on having yielded to the public demand and opened its doors. And we congratulate the public upon being in a position to know at last how its harbor business is done."

It is needless for us to say that though the above logic may be justifiably deemed sound enough when applied to a public trust like a Harbor Board, it is too often unthinkingly applied to our educational councils when their affairs become entangled through clique usurpation or the *parvenu*'s unmannerly snarling.

And to this question of "open doors" there is another phase which is to be specially noticed when the one-man-power seeks to work out his plans "on the quiet," and comes to be suspected of ignoring public opinion even to a very slight extent. Again we do not venture to give any definite illustration of this, but the suspicion is sure to excite some such criticism as the following sooner or later, though, in the opinion of many, such criticism, no doubt, but imperfectly represents all the aspects of the case in point:—

"In the second place the chief should have the assistance and support of a council of public instruction. Experience has fully shown, elsewhere as well as in Ontario, that it is necessary to have an advisory body for the proper conduct of educational matters. The composition of that advisory body is evidently important. It should not be nominated solely either by the chief officer or by the government. In Ontario and elsewhere the direction of educational matters is too much in the hands of politicians; the Chief Officer is too often too much in evidence. Would it not be better for the interests of education if the Chief Officer were elected by the people every five or six years as is done in several States of the Union, rather than that he should be some member of a government that may be in power for only a year or for twenty or twenty-five years? In the one we have the same political tendency, broken off too suddenly or continued too long; in the other we would have either no politics at all or an opportunity for a change."

———

In connection with the meetings of the British Association for the Advancement of Science, a suggestion has been made that the various provincial governments should be called upon to defray the expenses of delegates hailing from the respective provinces. It will soon be said of us in Canada that our public spirit is to be found only in the public exchequer, even to the payment of the railway fares of delegates on their way to and from some annual convention or other. At the formation of the Dominion Association of Teachers, the various governments were called upon for subscriptions which, when received, were said to have been squandered on assistant secretaries, newspaper puffing, picture-taking, advertising, circular printing, and the genuine aggrandisement of the so-called "king makers," and, what is more, the rumor is abroad that no audited account has ever been presented of the disbursements. The Royal Society has also its five thousand dollars from the Central Government, and if the delegates to the meeting of the British Association succeed in having their way paid by the local Governments, the latter will no doubt soon be called upon to pay also the expenses of those who adorn themselves with the equivocal insigna of F.R.S.C., as they proceed on their annual mission to partake of the hospitality of the Governor-General, and to read a few papers that, as still-born productions, are buried away in an annual volume that few ever see and fewer ever read. Then there is the escapade in connection with the preparation of a Canadian History for our schools, and the sums of money spent on secretarial pilgrimages, the fêting of judges, and the bestowing of a monopoly, which have all yet to be accounted for in the blue-books of our various provincial secretaries. The cry against the member of parliament, who with all the railroad and steamboat passes he can clutch, safely stowed away in his pocket-book, demands his travelling expenses from the Government, should become the cry against all such attempts at pilfering the people's money from the public chest. If the literary and scientific investigator is not working on a higher moral plane than the ordinary bridge-contractor or political hustler, he is expected to be doing so; and in their convention ceremonies they should show an example which is above suspicion in the matter of speculation, direct or indirect. If the poor teacher has to pay her way to attend her convention, why should the literary or scientific magnate not do the same?

CURRENT EVENTS AND COMMENTS.

THE event of the year in Canada will no doubt be identified with the meetings of the British Association, which will be held on August 18th and continue until August 26th. Dr. Bailey, of the New Brunswick University, in making his announcement about the gathering includes the teachers of the Dominion in his invitation, an invitation which many will gladly accept, even if they have to pay their own way. Some of the most distinguished scientific men of Great Britain are expected to be present, as he says, as well as others from different parts of Europe and the United States, and the gathering will no doubt be the most important of its kind ever held upon this continent. In addition to the more solid work of the meeting, including practical lectures by such eminent men as Prof. Dewar, F.R S., Sir John Evans, J. Milne, F. R. S, Lord Kelvin, and Lord Lister, social intercourse and interchange of ideas will be promoted through conversaziones, garden parties and other hospitalities extended to members by the city and the citizens of Toronto, as well as by excursions freely offered to Niagara, Hamilton, the Muskoka Lakes, etc. The railway fares from any part in Canada will be one-half the ordinary figures, and tickets will be good from the first of July to the first of October, by any route desired. The fee for membership is $10.00, which entitles the holder to all the privileges of the meeting. The local executive committee have power to elect members of the Association for 1897, and it is desired that early application for such membership be made to the above mentioned committee.

The University of Manitoba from being a mere examining and degree conferring body, promises in the near future to become also a teaching institution, which it should be, and to have a local habitation. The latter is provided for in a sum of $60,000 in the Provincial estimates, which will be chargeable against the land grant of the University. At a late meeting of the University Council a suggestion was made that instead of spending a large sum in the erection of a new building the present Government House could be converted at comparatively small expense into a suitable University building. The idea was not entertained at the time, but it is quite possible that a little examination will show that such an arrangement would be advantageous both to the Government and the University. The University land grant is 150,000 acres. At present land prices, $60,000 is a heavy charge to stand against it for a building; especially as it is intended to create from the grant an endowment to keep up the current expenses of the University. If these expenses amount, at the very start, to $6,000 a year over and above the Government grant, as estimated by the Premier, all the proceeds from the lands will be needed for some years for this purpose. Any proposal therefore, towards providing a building at less expense than the amount intimated, will be a decided boon ; and the idea of adapting the present Government House to University uses is worth consideration.

The newspaper which discusses the question of a University building, refers in the following terms to the assumption of Government House as a place suitable for College purposes : The Government House as it stands at present, is an anomaly. It was built for a certain purpose ; and for some years the Legislature kept it up for the purpose for which it was designed. The Government then bebecame economical and left the Government House to take care of itself. The only immediate effect was to transfer the cost of maintaining it from the Legislature to the inmate for the time being ; but as time goes on, other effects become apparent. The building falls into a state of dilapidation and decay, and becomes a sort of white elephant, neither useful nor ornamental. Already the signs of this are becoming apparent, as it is said that it has been hardly habitable during the present winter for want of proper repair. This cannot last ; for either the building will eventually be abandoned and left unoccupied upon the hands of the Province, or the Legislature will condescend to give it some attention. This last, it may do, either by spending enough money on it to keep it to be a credit to the Province, as it was intended to be, or else get rid of it by handing it over to the University. The alternative will have to be faced sooner or later. In New Brunswick and British Columbia, the respective Legislatures did exactly what Manitoba has done, that is, declined to do anything towards keeping the provincial Government Houses. The inmates thereupon promptly retired from them and shut them up. British Columbia has since resumed the charge of keeping up its institution ; but New Brunswick would probably be glad to get a University or some other institution to take its Government House off its hands. Manitoba may as well face this problem at once. The cost of keeping up Government House creditably is no appreciable tax upon the Province, after it is once put in a proper state of repair. It would not amount to one cent per head of the population. But if this will not be done, by all means get rid of the place before it drifts into an unoccupied eye-sore.

In Boston, New York and other cities there are schools for poor children who cannot leave the city during the holiday season. The work is made as interesting as possible, and consists of exercises in manual training, needle work, gardening, cooking, gymnastics, etc. These schools enable poor children to pass the time away from the haunts of vice and to learn many practical lessons.

We do not think that this practice has so far reached any of the cities in Canada, but as a complement to the philanthropic movement of the Montreal *Star* in favor of the Fresh Air Fund, it might be well for the local school boards of Montreal and Toronto to take compassion on the *gamins* of these cities in this way, if recreations with an elevating tendency can be provided for them in some one of the cool, shady school buildings of these cities, sufficiently attractive to draw them from the deteriorating influences of the street corners and other public places.

At the last meeting of the Protestant Board of School Commissioners of Montreal, there was the semblance of a breeze on the granting of privileges to certain religious and kindred societies in the use of the various school buildings. These societies from time to time have made application to the commissioners to be allowed to prosecute certain aspects of their work in the public schools, with a view to influence the pupils. The W.C.T.U., for example, applied for the use of a room in the Aberdeen School in which to hold at least one meeting a month for the purpose of reaching the children after school hours, while the Christian Endeavor Society wanted a temperance pledge to be circulated among the pupils of the public schools. This last request led Archdeacon Evans to say that while he sympathized with the object in view, he thought the Board should take a definite stand upon this matter of external work and teaching, as otherwise they would be opening a very wide door indeed.

"Temperance and moral work of that sort is excellent," he observed, "and the place to teach it is the home, the church, the Sunday-school. We should be able to do all the work of the school ourselves by our own staff of teachers. I am quite in sympathy with the object in view; but we will place ourselves in great difficulties if we encourage outside bodies to come into our schools teaching their principle. We teach hygiene and kindred subjects in our schools by our own teachers; other subjects should be taught outside, in my opinion. Anyway, all the work of the school proper should be taught by the members of our own staff."

A committee of the same Board had been appointed on the subject of the pledge and Dr. Shaw, as convener, reported to the effect that those principals who felt disposed, might circulate the pledge amongst the children, but only with the consent of the parents, and without the exercise of any pressure whatever. The pledge itself was to the effect that the signer promised to abstain from all intoxicating liquors until he was twenty-one years of age.

"Is he at liberty after that to drink as much as he likes?" asked the chairman, smilingly.

"I will not vote for such a pledge," said Ald. McBride, "because it seems to imply that after twenty-one, one may do as one pleases."

"Oh, that is only your interpretation of it," remarked the archdeacon.

Dr. Shaw thought the matter should be settled one way or the other, but as His Worship the Mayor, who was absent, had taken a good deal of interest in the question, it was decided to do nothing for the present.

The announcements in connection with the meetings of the National Educational Association, which begin at Milwaukee this year during the first week of July, have been delayed. The usual half rates will be granted.

The October convention of the Teachers' Association of the Province of Quebec bids fair to be a successful gathering. The regular meetings will be held in the McGill Normal School while the University authorities have placed at the disposal of the executive the spacious halls of the Peter Redpath Museum for a conversazione and representative gathering. Among the speakers from the other Provinces that are expected to be present are Hon. G. W. Ross from Ontario, Hon. Attorney-General Longley from Nova Scota, the Rev. Mr. Maxwell, M.P., from British Columbia, and from the Province of Quebec itself, Principal Peterson, Dr. Robins, Dr. Harper, and other representative men. The last mentioned is the president of the Association this year.

Mr. H. H. Ewart, inspector of Mennonite schools in Manitoba, says in his last annual report, issued a few days ago: The prejudice against the English language is gradually disappearing; in some districts, of course, faster than others; while in a few schools the amount of teaching that is done in English is only nominal. I am pleased to observe not only that the people become willing to have the English taught in their schools, but that an increasing number of schools also use the English language as the medium of instruction, limiting the use of the German language to that portion of the day which has been set apart for the study of German. . . . . It is found that an hour-and-a-half per day is sufficent to teach children to speak, read and write the German language properly. I believe that after the more conservative among the Mennonites will have seen it demonstrated that learning the English language does not necessarily mean giving up the German, a great part of their reluctancy to the teaching of English to their children will be overcome.

THE number of schools in the Province of New Brunswick increased for the first term embraced by the report, 39; for the second term, 25; the number of teachers increased for the first term 38, for the second term 39 The average proportion of population at school was 1 in about 5.30; the percentage of the total population at school is 21.3; the average attendance for the full term is about 60 per cent. for the province. The number of pupils receiving instruction above Standard VIII is 1,133 for first term, and 1,138 for second term. There were only twenty-one teachers employed not holding licenses. First class teachers have increased while third class teachers have decreased. The total number of student teachers admitted to the Normal School was 246, a decrease of twenty-seven on the number admitted the previous year. The number who succeeded in obtaining licenses in the several classes was as follows: Grammar School, 13; Class I, 50; Class II, 130; Class III, 87. Eleven hundred volumes were added to the school libraries during the year. Since 1892, 150 new school buildings have been erected, and more than an equal number enlarged or repaired and re furnished, the whole at a cost more than $250,000.

The Senate of Queen's University, Kingston, has nominated Mr. F. J. Pope, M. A., for the Royal scholarship given by Her Majesty's Commissioners for the exhibition of 1851. The scholarship amounts to $750 a year, and may be had one, two or three years. It is given only to men who have shown themselves likely to make discoveries in science. Mr. Pope has already distinguished himself in chemical research. The only universities in Canada that receive these scholarships are Dalhousie, McGill, Queen's and Toronto. The last Queen's student to hold the scholarship was Mr. Walker, who has just been appointed assistant surveyor of the Geological Survey of India. Mr. Pope will probably proceed to Germany and enter upon research there.

Bishop Douglas, Aberdeen, is responsible for a mild disturbance in Aberdeen University. The Dean of Norwich had agreed to preach in the University chapel, but cancelled his engagement owing to a remonstrance by Bishop Douglas against his preaching in a Presbyterian place of worship —a piece of ecclesiastical intolerance that has given great offence. The Principal, Sir W. D. Geddes, issued a statement detailing the circumstances, and concluding:—"We deem it right to enter a protest against an assumption of authority unfortunately and unwarrantably advanced." There is a feeling that Dean Lefroy should not have submitted to the Bishop's remonstrance.

———

There is much indignation in Hartford—throughout the state, indeed—over the U. S. Senate's rejection of the $4,000 memorial appropriation to Hon. Henry Barnard. The *Hartford Courant* proposes to utilize the indignation in material fashion, and already a large amount has been subscribed. It has already amounted to $1,986.83. Dr. Barnard has sacrificed more for the cause of education than it has been the lot of most men to sacrifice, and it is eminently fitting that in his eighty-eighth year, in the possession of all his faculties and in general good health, he should receive a substantial token of respect from the friends of education.

———

The Privy Council has heard what counsel have to say for and against the decision of Aberdeen University Court, to retire Professor Johnston on a pension of £250 a year. One's impression is that the members of the Privy Council were not disposed to recall the decision of the court, but the opinion of the Privy Council has not yet been made known. In connection with the case Professor Johnston issued a book containing his petition and memorial to the Queen in Council. It also contains a preface, a table of contents, an index, and an explanatory index. This last is compiled on a plan novel enough to justify illustration:

"X.—Evident Eagerness to get me ejected from my professorship.

"Y.—"Weak and facile Yielding of sane students.

"Z.—Statements showing that this wretched case . . . ought to have been promptly *ended*," etc.

He defends the use of the words "mendacious," "mendacity," and "miscreant"—"The 'mendacity' of the aforesaid memorial and petition [of the students] is a proved fact, which no truthful person can deny, and none but a 'miscreant' could have perpetrated the bad deeds which led me to use that word." Fourteen references are given to "mendacious" and "mendacity," and six to "miscreant." Professor Johnston is a Hebrew scholar of undoubted ability, but he is obviously rather eccentric.

———

It is proposed to establish a memorial library at Harvard in honor of the late Professor Francis James Child. About $10,000 have already been subscribed for the purpose and a number of books have been donated. The collection is to be especially intended for students of English literature.

———

The question as to the number of pupils there ought to be in the ordinary department of a graded school is adjudicated upon by the Superintendent of Education in British Columbia in the following words: Taking into consideration the large number of subjects of study required to be taught in a high school, it must be apparent that the more complete is the staff of teachers, the greater the assurance of the best results; yet it may be proper in this connection to state that, as a rule, each teacher should have twenty-five or more pupils under his charge. In the report of the Honorable, the Minister of Education of Ontario for 1895, we find it stated that the average enrolment for each teacher in high schools and collegiate institutes is over forty.

———

In connection with the Jubilee Fund of Bishop's College, it is reported that a sum of $47,000 in round numbers is promised, but a further sum of something like $4,000 is necessary in order to earn the grant of

£1,000 promised by the S.P.C.K. When this is gained the total of the Jubilee Fund will exceed $50,000, and the endowment of the Principalship is to be raised to $20,000; that of the Professorship of Pastoral Theology to $25,000. Besides these the restoration of the Chapel has profited to the extent of $2,000 ; a smaller sum has been received by the Gymnasium. The Professorship of Classics has been endowed with more than $10,000. The School has received $17,000 in endowment. It was also reported that the annual statement of profit and loss for 1896 was a favorable one, a former debit balance having been obliterated and a small balance remains on the right side for the College; and that the financial result of the year ending June 30, 1897, is likely to be favorable.

The 150 medical examiners recently appointed by the board of health of New York to examine school children, in order to detect and prevent the spread of contagious diseases, have begun their work. For the present the examination is confined to the primary schools and the primary department of grammar schools. As the time for examination is limited to one hour a day, of course it is impossible to examine each child every morning. The teacher is to select those children who look sluggish or ill, and place them apart from the other pupils. The medical examiner then examines each one of these pupils, and if he finds the least symptom of illness it is sent home. The physicians will also investigate the cases of absence where parents have failed to notify teachers of the cause of absence. The examiners are required to make out written reports at stated intervals.

Mr. Charles Innes, one of the best known men in the north of Scotland, is at present on a visit to Canada. As chairman of the School Board of Inverness for fifteen years, he is *au fait* with the system that has made the schools ot Scotland famous in modern times. The schools of Inverness have reached a high state of efficency, and it is a pity that the high school or academy is still outside the operations of the School Board. Mr. Innes is a keen observer and his notes on Canada, in a series of articles entitled "From Quebec to Vancouver," are exceedingly interesting reading. It is now nearly ten years since he first visited this country, and we trust that the issue of his present visit will be an amplifying of these notes into a volume which every Scotsman in Canada will be only too glad to have in his library.

One part of the Irish National school system is neither silent nor secret, and that is the teachers, who carry on a ceaseless agitation for the redress of grievances, loudly and publicly. At present they are profoundly dissatisfied with the acceptance by the Board of the offer of the Government to give money to make the Pension Fund solvent, as compensation for the arrears of which they have been unjustly deprived. The teachers point out that from the non-payment of the arrears, they, the present teachers, have suffered, while the proposed substitute will only be a benefit to their successors many years hence.

The following interesting information concerning the pensions of teachers in the various European states, is taken from the annual report of Commissioner Harris: "All the twenty-six states that form the German Empire pay pensions, both to teachers and their widows and orphans A teachers' Union in Great Britain, in the form of a mutual aid society, pays annuities to disabled teachers. In Austria the pension schemes vary in different parts of the empire. One example will suffice: The teachers pay annually two per cent. of their salaries, and the first tenth of their first year's salary, as well as the first tenth of every increase. The remainder of the fund is supplied by the state and the communities, Sweden, Norway, and Denmark, and also most of the cantons of Switzerland have recognized the advisibility of removing worn-out teachers. In Russia the teachers in the town schools may also look forward to receiving a pension. Holland has had a state scheme for pensioning teachers since the year 1878, and teachers can claim retirement with a pension, if incapacitated, after ten years of service, or for old age at 65. In Belgium the fund is formed in this way: Two-fifths are paid by the community, two fifths by the state, one-fifth by the province, and nothing by the teacher. The pension may reach $1,000 a year. In France the salaries of teachers are paid subject to a deduction of five per cent, plus one-twelfth of the first year's salary, plus one-twelfth of each increase for the first year of such increase. This second form of deduction is productive of great evil. The pension is payable after thirty years of service, the other factor being incapacity or 60 years of age. The amount of pension depends upon the years of service. In Greece teachers contribute five per cent. on the salaries, and the state finds the remainder, in order to superannuate teachers after twenty-one years of service, regardless of age. In Portugal provisions are made for pensioning those engaged in education."

CORRESPONDENCE AND ADVICE.

To the Editor of the News:

SIR,—At last the public mind has exerted itself upon the subject of common school education to good purpose. The Government has determined upon improving the condition of district schools if money can do it. And no one doubts the wisdom of making our heritage of unsold land bear the expense of the improvement. But I have a fear, founded upon the experience of the past, that the efforts of a progressive government at Quebec will not have full effect so long as our present system of management is in force. The Council of Public Instruction, composed of ecclesiastics, professional men, and university representatives, has naturally enough diverted education towards the professions and the universities until Quebec has more professional men *pro rata* of the population, than any other portion of the world, without any exception I am told. A glance at the curriculum will show how thorough is the determination to educate young people away from the land, or from home work, and to see the goal of their educational life in a profession. That these gentlemen are without the saving grace of practicability, most of their actions prove. Consider the vacillations with regard to text books, the lack of system regarding inspections, the payments of portions of the grants according to results, where the school which needs it most gets the least encouragement, and now and most brilliant of all the declaration that to obtain the right to teach, and thereby to earn $120 or $150 a year, would-be teachers must either reside in Montreal, or be possessed of sufficient means to pay a good price for the unspeakable privilege of taking a special course at the feet of Prof. Robins in that city, this latter decision being based solely upon the plausible theory that the best elementary teachers are, and have been those trained at the Normal School, which theory is certainly not uniformly borne out by facts. (Be it understood that the relative standing of teachers of superior schools is not in question.) Need I further particularize? Has not every thinking friend of education been convinced long ago of the cumbersomeness, the purely theoretical nature of our present system? And is it not, to say the least of it, inconsistent with our institutions in general, to have a great spending department removed from the sphere of criticism or of public enquiry, excepting by perhaps an expensive commission? Let the gentlemen who will come forward next Tuesday to ask for our votes, make the abolition of the Council of Public Instruction and the substitution of a responsible minister therefor, one of the issues of the campaign, and I know that if the question is put simply and not darkened for them the voice of the voters will be decidedly for the change. The diverging interests of the two elements in our population might easily be safeguarded by the retention of the secretaryships, etc. And the gain in having the department where the public could reach it, interpellate it, and influence it, would be great. But greatest of all would be the benefit of removing this most important department from the control of the estimable gentlemen, who are purely but sadly theoretical in their management of it. After all, Mr. Editor, the future of the province depends in a great measure upon the manner in which we maintain the apparently insignificant district school, which must be my excuse for troubling you with this long epistle at this busy season.

Very truly,

W. PERCY CHAMBERS.

The Rectory, Knowlton, April 26.

To the Editor of the EDUCATIONAL MONTHLY:

DEAR SIR,—The facts which I have recorded in my previous communications to you seem to have been very unpalatable to those to whom they referred, and probably gave offence to some who ought not to have been offended. The latter may perhaps help themselves to a perusal of the enclosed newspaper paragraph which surely speaks for itself, and which just as surely will bring credit to my further utterances next month on the vexed text-book question in this province. Mark the final statement of the paragraph, Mr. Editor, and then try to tell your readers what the essential stages are, that permit of the adoption of a text-book in this province. Parents and teachers are alike anxious to know all about these "essential stages."

Yours respectfully,

A MONTREAL TEACHER.

N.B.—The paragraph reads as follows: "On Saturday night there was a special meeting of the Protestant School Commissioners, at which the question of text-books came up for discussion. The Principal of the High School recommended the augmentation of the educational series of text-books at present in use by the addition of the 'Royal Story Book Series,' and a publication entitled 'Things New and Old,' which had already been found to be of great value in the High School. Dr. Shaw had previously doubted whether the commissioners should pass upon this subject of text-books until the Protestant Committee of the Council of Public Instruction had discussed and pronounced upon the matter. Dr. Shaw, who was unable to be present, wrote a letter in this sense, but it was pointed out that these particular books had passed all the essential stages to permit of their adoption."

Montreal, June, 1897.

Exhibition of Drawings.

To the Editor of the Star :

Sir,—The attention of the public is requested to the exhibition of drawings, etc., lately held in Montreal, of the work done by the pupils of the Free Evening Classes for Architecture, Mechanical Drawing, Freehand Drawing, Modelling, Lithography, Pattern-Making, Stair Building, etc., under the auspices of the Council of Arts and Manufactures of the Province of Quebec.

These classes have been attended during the past winter by several hundred pupils, and the result was lately to be seen in the Exhibition of Industrial Art in the Monument National, St. Lawrence Street.

As already intended by the Council, the object in establishing these classes, was to reach the working man, "He who earns his bread by the sweat of his brow," and to assist him in his daily avocations by teaching him the use of lines, the knowledge of plans, construction, proportion, etc., etc., and to enable the mechanic to become something more than a "hewer of wood and a drawer of water," to give him ideas how to take hold of his work in an intelligent manner, not only for the benefit of his employer, but for his own advancement.

The result of the patience and perseverance of the pupils of the different classes was to be seen in the exhibition of drawings, drawings made by carpenters, bricklayers, stone cutters, tinsmiths, tailors, piano-makers etc., etc., in fact all trades can learn something by following these useful classes.

It is not the intention of the Council to bring these pupils into competition with the draughtsmen in the architects' and engineers' offices, but to give the mechanic, no matter in what trade, a knowledge of that trade which will not only elevate him as a mechanic, but knowledge that will make him a better and more useful mechanic, a benefit to himself and his employer. Many of the young architects and draughtsmen in Montreal to-day got their first ideas, and acquired a taste for their profession as pupils in these classes.

One of our public citizens and a member of the Council (a true philanthropist) has donated the sum of five thousand dollars towards the erection of a permanent school of technology in Montreal, where all the drawing and practical classes would be concentrated and where a library would be established for the benefit of the pupils, should the city come to the assistance of this permanent school with a like sum.

I feel confident that many of our wealthy citizens would do likewise, especially this Jubilee year of our Most Gracious Majesty Queen Victoria, a fitting tribute for so auspicious an occasion. Then our young mechanics would be enabled to perfect themselves in their own special trades, a taste for art would be fostered in the coming generation, and wages would increase as the knowledge of the wage-earner would be developed by the teachings of these valuable classes.

Henry J. Peters.

Montreal, June, 1897.

'Tis the mind that makes the body rich.
—*Taming of the Shrew*, iv. 3.

PROFESSIONAL OPINION.

AT the great annual gathering of teachers in Buffalo last year an enterprising newspaper inaugurated a movement which was not the least of the gains to the professional spirit that prevailed at that assembly of teachers from all parts of America, and we take advantage of the idea in inaugurating a new department of the CANADA EDUCATIONAL MONTHLY which we trust will be duly appreciated by its readers. In introducing its scheme the great newspaper made the following announcement:

The subjoined opinions were written by the leading educators of the country who were present at the great convention of fifteen thousand members of the National Education Association in Buffalo. They represent the widest experience in educational matters possible to bring to bear on the subject. These teachers met for the purpose of improving practical school methods, of discussing the theory of teaching, of heightening the efficiency of our educational system. "What must we do?" was the question always presenting itself. This question is answered better and more fully than it has ever been answered before in the subjoined collection of opinions. When it is remembered that the training of 16,000,000 prospective citizens and of half that number of future voters depends on the nation's schools, the importance of their welfare and the significance of what these men have written for our columns becomes apparent.

The German or French boy of sixteen is more advanced from an educational point of view than the American—more mature mentally. I think that the reason for it is that the teachers there are better trained. I am not a pedagogic expert and therefore not competent to more than suggest what may be a reason. I think it possible the fault is in our lack of a sufficient proportion of highly trained teachers. We have as good teachers as any country, but not as many of them. With us teaching is only too often looked on as a stop-gap while the man is making ready to study for a profession or the woman is unconsciously awaiting matrimony.

BRANDER MATTHEWS.

The most obvious and obstructive defect in the public schools of America to-day is the insufficiently prepared teaching—with all that that implies. Teaching as a profession is in its infancy. Public provision for training teachers is wretchedly inadequate, though increasing. Public sentiment as to the need of trained teachers is weak and halting. The State of New York has recently taken advanced ground on this question, and after Jan. 1st, 1897, no city, town or village in the State employing a superintendent of schools may use any public money for the employment of untrained teachers. The practical efficiency of this law will depend upon the administration of it by the State Superintendent. That the present incumbent, Mr. Skinner, will enforce it in spirit as in letter, I am confident. But the problem of supplying adequately equipped teachers for the rural schools remains to be met.

But the statute law must be supported by a public opinion that will not tolerate personal, sectarian or political influences, promotion, transfer and dismissal of teachers, before the school will improve permanently.

NICHOLAS MURRAY BUTLER.

The most important thing before the professional educators to-day is the broadening going on so rapidly in their conception of their duties to their profession and to the public. Too many have thought of their work as limited to schools for the young and during a short period of tuition. The true conception is that we should be responisble for higher as well as elementary education, for adults as well as for children, for educational work in the homes as well as in the schoolhouses, and during life as well as for a limited course. In a nutshell, the motto of the extended work should be "Higher education for adults at home through life."

To the great mass of boys and girls the school can barely give the tools with which to get an education after they are forced to begin their life work as bread-winners. Few are optimistic enough to hope that we can change this condition very rapidly. The great problem of to-day is, therefore, to carry on the education after the elementary steps have been taken in the free public schools. There are numerous agencies at work in this direction, reading-rooms, reference and lending libraries, museums, summer vacation and night schools, correspondence and other forms of extension teaching, reading circles and study clubs, but by far the greatest agent is good reading, and the greatest work before the schools is to send out their pupils with more practical skill in the use of books and libraries, with a stronger taste for good reading and a corresponding dislike for the weak, frivolous and sensational, and with a genuine love for the best literature.

This view is taking strong hold on all sides; in New York the regents have just appointed an expert in literature to give his whole time to the development of this needed inspirational teaching in the 640 high schools and academies of the State. At the National Educational Association in the past week the demand was officially recognized by unanimous vote in amending the constitution to provide for a distinct department devoted to libraries as a reading factor in education. The end seems at hand of an educational system which contents itself with teaching to read, and then fails to see that the best reading is provided, when undesirable reading is so cheap and plentiful as to be a constant menace to the public good. As a great thinker has said, this is exactly analogous to teaching our young children the expert use of a knife and fork and then failing to provide them with food.

MELVIL DEWEY.

The progress of public schools is retarded more by the failure of the public to keep up with the rapidly advancing educational ideals than by any other cause. There are comparatively few people who yet believe that there is a science of education, and therefore every parent believes he understands how to train children as well as the teachers or superintendent. This makes advancement along the line of the new education somewhat slow.

The greatest difficulty in the way of public school teachers in cities is the lack of opportunity to develop the individual self-activity of their pupils. This results chiefly from the fact that the pupils are graded and are therefore taught most of the time in large classes. The developments of the next decade will be along the lines of individual growth, and securing the active co-operation of parents. Education will become the central thought around which the home, the church and the business leaders will concentrate their efforts for the development of the community and the State.

JAMES L. HUGHES.

The main obstacle in the way of the more efficient management of popular education is the employment of incompetent teachers. The spoils system has found its way into the schools. Industrial enterprises, looking towards satisfactory dividends, make efficiency the sole test of fitness. But the public has yet to learn that there is a technic in teaching as there is a technic in the arts of production. When boards of education will employ only expert superintendents, clothe them with authority to nominate their assistants and remove incompetents, and will hold them responsible for results only, the methods of the successful business organizations will be the methods of the schools. Tenure, based upon fitness alone, is the cure for our chief educational ills. A professional teacher in every school is the only condition that will ever satisfy the people that their money is properly expended and that the children are coming into their birthright of education. JOHN W. COOK.

The highest progress of the public schools of the country is greatly retarded by the lack of a proper classification of the various branches of the work. In each and every school system of any magnitude there should be three heads of departments, viz.: a department of buildings, a department of finance, and a department of instruction. At the head of each department should be placed a competent man, into whose hands should be given great responsibility and full power to discharge that responsibility; then he should be held acountable for results. Over all should be a Board of Education of representative citizens, small in number, men of character and broad-minded enough to study every question from the standpoint of the child and his needs, and never from personal or local prejudices and desires. The superintendent of Schools, as the head of the Department of Instruction, should have wholly and solely to do with that department and with no other, except in an advisory sense. In a word, stated points, at which responsibility can be fixed and to which failure can be definitely traced is the great need in the educational field of to-day. A. B. BLODGETT.

SCHOOL WORK.

ARITHMETIC.

BY P. S. HEAD MASTER.

1. A sells a watch to B, gaining 1-7 of what it cost him; B sells it to C for $42, losing ¼ of what it cost him. How much did it cost A?

ANS. $49.

2. A sells a farm to B, gaining 10 per cent.; B sells it to C, losing 20 per cent.; C sells it to D, gaining 40 per cent. If D pays $3,696 for it what did it cost A?

ANS. $3,000.

3. When 19 lbs. of sugar are sold for a dollar, there is a gain of 8 per cent; what per cent. is gained if the rate is increased to 18 lbs. for the same sum?

ANS. 14 per cent.

4. By selling maple syrup at $1.25 per gallon, a merchant gains 26 per cent. What per cent does he gain if he gives only 3 quarts 1 pint for the same sum?

ANS. 44 per cent.

5. A man had $16,000 in a bank. He drew out 25 per cent. of it, then

30 per cent. of the remainder, and afterwards deposited 10 per cent. of what he had drawn out; how much had he then in the bank?

Ans. $9,160.

6. A young man has $150 in a Savings Bank. He draws out 1/3 of his savings, then 1-10 of the remainder, and afterwards deposits 3-5 of what he draws out. How much money has he now in the bank?

Ans. $126.

7. By selling oranges at the rate of $3.30 for 5 dozen, 10 per cent. of their cost was gained; find the selling price at which each orange should have been sold in order to gain 20 per cent. of cost.

Ans. 6 cts.

8. I gain 16⅔ per cent. by selling bananas at the rate of 3 doz. for 30 cents; at what price must I sell a banana to gain 40 per cent. of cost?

Ans. 1 cent.

9. If a garrison of 1,600 men have provisions for 11 months, how long will their provisions last, if it be increased by 160 men?

Ans. 10 months.

10. A garrison of 1,200 men, provisioned for 50 days, was reinforced at the end of 20 days and the provisions were exhausted at the end of 10 days from that time; of how many men did the reinforcement consist?

Ans. 2,400.

11. A garrison of 1,800 men has provisions for 25 days, it is reinforced at the end of 15 days and the provisions are exhausted at the end of 9 days from that time; of how many men does the reinforcement consist?

Ans. 200.

12. A tax collector gets 2 per cent. of all the money he collects; how much money must he collect in order to have $1,960 left for a bridge after retaining his own salary?

Ans. $2,000.

13. After paying a tax of 4 cents on the dollar out of his income, a gentleman has $768 left. What was his gross income?

Ans. $800.

14. A garrison of 6,000 men has provisions for 30 days, after 12 days 600 men are killed; how long can the garrison now hold out at the same rate?

Ans. 20 days.

15. A garrison of 1,000 men has provisions for 100 days, and after 60 days is reinforced by 250 men; how long will the provisions now last at the same rate?

Ans 32 days.

16. A dealer in cattle gave $5,600 for a certain number, and sold a part of them for $4,200 at $28 each, and by so doing lost $4 per head. For how much a head must he sell the remainder to gain $100 on the whole?

Ans. $60.

17. A dealer in cattle gave $3,240 for a certain number, and sold a part of them for $2 800, at $20 each, and by so doing gained $2 per head. For how much a head must he sell the remainder to gain $80 on the whole?

Ans. $13.

18. A drover bought a number of cattle for $8,775, and sold a certain number of them at $52 a head for the total sum of $7,020, gaining $945. For how much per head must he sell the remainder so as to gain $300 more?

Ans. $50.

19. A speculator gave $7,743 for horses and sold a certain number of

them for $4,536, at $81 each, losing thereby $6 each; for how much each must he sell the remainder so as to gain $27 on the whole?

ANS. $98.

20 Add together .6 per cent. of $70; .5 per cent of $10; .7½ per cent. of $60; .03¾ per cent. of $10,000.

ANS. 42 cts. + 5 cts + 45 cts. + $3.75 or $4 67.

21. Add together .02½ per cent. of $60; .00⅓ per cent. of $900; .00¼ per cent. of $1,760; .¼ per cent. of $25 600; 25 per cent. of $25,600; 1⅔ per cent. of $840.

ANS 1½ cts. + 3 cts. + 4 2-5 cts + $64 + $6,400 + $14.00 or $6,478.08 9-10.

22. Multiply 625 hundred millionths by 128; add the result to the difference between 999 ten-thousandths and 676 millionths.

ANS. .0008 + .099224 = .100024.

23. To the sum of seventeen and four-thousandths, two hundred and thirty-one millionths, sixteen and twenty-nine hundred thousandths; add the difference between 1,001 ten-millionths and 675 thousandths.

ANS. 33.004521 + .6,748,999 or 33.6794209.

24. (1) How many lots of ½ an acre each can be made out of a piece of village property 40 chains square?

ANS. 320.

(2) If the lots contain 4-5 of an acre, and the property is 60 chains square?

ANS. 450.

25. Brown's farm is ½ a mile square; Smith's contains ½ a square mile; Jones' is ¾ of the size of the other two together. How many acres in the three farms together?

ANS. 840.

CONTEMPORARY LITERATURE.

COLLEGE undergraduates in Harvard and Princeton must be gathering an atmosphere of historical romance about themselves from the successive numbers of *Scribner's Magazine*. But it is extremely pleasant and apparently artistic like the newest photograph. In the June number Princeton is celebrated, and the edition should have disappeared in consequence long ere this. What remains to be said now that the Soldiers of Fortune have filibustered and loved their way into paradise? Only that Mr. Gibson's extremely handsome and spell-bound people leaning against the rail of an ocean steamer remind one irresistibly of Mr. Kipling's "Three Decker" and the happy old art of sweet fiction. But there is still Howells' "Story of a Play," and Octave Thanet's "Non-combatant," neither of which should be passed over, and "The Open Boat," by Stephen Crane. Of this one hesitates to say much. The sea has spoken to so many who can never forget. The story of the great deep will convince where his vision of war was almost resented.

In the June *Cosmopolitan* people who have read Fitzgerald's translation of "Omar Khayyam" are asked to believe that Mr. Le Gallienne has done rather better. His translation will appear in the July number. Will he perhaps mention lawns and laces, and the stimulating effect of such imaginings? "The War of the Worlds" is continued. There seems to be very little chance of a hopeful conclusion, but Mr. Wells should really think of it lest some of the defenceless earth-dwellers get too frightened and escape not courageously but effectively. "The House of Life," by Mary Stewart Cutting, is an entertaining short story. One of the most interesting articles in the issue is the "Secret History of the Garfield-Conkling Tragedy," by T. B. Connery. It is as pathetic as only life can be; the story recorded looks at this distance so futile, the ends sought for so aside from the proper intent of government.

In the June *St. Nicholas* is a charming account of a birthday shared by Tennyson in the Isle of Wight; it is called "A Great Poet and a Little Girl." John Bennett's "Master Skylark" is surely a success among little people, the old time has been made so vivid that one reading feels almost as if he had been at a fair and had seen everything. Miss Nina Barrow continues her perilous career.

Macmillan's Magazine for May contains the opening chapters of two serial stories, "The House by the Howff," by W. L. Watson, and "A Chapter of Accidents," by Mrs. Fraser. Both stories bid fair to be extremely interesting, with most diverse local color and entanglement of fortune. In the same number also appears an amusing short story, "Nell," but Nell was a dog. There are several historical papers and an article on "Sunday Observance."

Edgar Allan Poe, unfortunate when he was here, and extremely unfortunate since his departure, is the fourth in the series of "American Bookmen," at present appearing in the *Bookman.* He seems to have been very unsatisfactory, but a great many of us are that still. William C. Wilkinson contributes rather an upsetting analysis of a little thing that Keats wrote on a Grecian Urn, in which he proceeds to do in the clear light of day what Browning's painter hesitated to do even in the twilight—he rubs out the lines and puts them in again as he sees correctly. Andrea's judgment may have been better too, and he added something sadly about his soul, a phase of the question which the present critic omits. But then, after all, he does say that it has given him pleasure.

A Canadian poet, who is not so often celebrated as some others of her country, and for no apparent reason, has a poem in the last issue of *Littell's Living Age.* The verses are called "At St. Bartholemi," and the poet is Mrs. Harrison.

Sir Philip Magnus and his brother Commissioners, in their report on the progress of technical education in Germany, point out the following differences between Germany and England. In Germany both the Government and the teacher seem to have a keener appreciation of the value of scientific training as a basis of commercial success. Secondary education is more easily accessible in Germany than in England. "The instruction is more disciplinary, and exercises a deep influence in the formation of habits and in the training of character. The teaching of modern languages is insisted upon to a far greater extent than in any of our own schools, with results of the greatest possible benefit to the German Clerk and Commercial Agent; the absence of frequent and conflicting external examinations gives more time for careful study. The fees are much lower than in schools of corresponding grade in this country."

Col. Parker sends the following quotation from a lecture of State Supt. Henry Sabin, of Iowa, which, he writes, should be read by every educator in the land: "I believe that to hold up before the pupil a high percentage in examination or recitation as a criterion of success is vicious in the extreme; that such a course gives him wrong ideas of the worth of knowledge, and induces him to study through unworthy motives; that the entire marking system is a relic of past ages and unworthy an enlightened civilization; that our children should be taught that learning is valued for learning's sake alone, and that the intrinsic worth of knowledge cannot be measured by figures; that the memory of words can be estimated and tabulated, but not the power of thought, which is the outcome of knowledge properly assimilated."

Praising what is lost makes the remembrance dear.

—*All's Well that Ends Well, v. 3.*

I am directed by the Minister of Education to say that Gage's Vertical Series of Copy Books are not authorized and that their use in the Public Schools will not be allowed by the Education Department. The only authorized Copy Books are the Public School Writing Course, Vertical System, published by the Canada Publishing Company, and the Public School Writing Course, issued by the Hunter Rose Company.

JOHN MILLAR,
Deputy Minister.

Education Department, Ont.,
Toronto, 18th May, 1897.

Let never day nor night unhallowed pass,
But still remember what the Lord hath done.

—2 *Henry VI.*, ii. 1.

THE CANADA EDUCATIONAL MONTHLY.

THE CANADA EDUCATIONAL MONTHLY, we beg to inform our readers, entered upon a new term of service in educational work on the first of January of this year. It is to be hoped that after the following announcements have been carefully considered by our subscribers and fellow-teachers, that their assistance will be secured on behalf of the MONTHLY in more ways than one.

The MONTHLY is by this time one of the oldest educational periodicals in Canada, and it is the intention of all connected with its management to make it of increasing interest to the teachers of Canada and others interested in the educational progress of the country as a whole. Its *corps* of contributors already includes the most prominent of our educational workers, and what with an improved classification of topics, additional help in the editorial work, and a cordial co-operation on the part of subscribers, publishers and advertisers, it may not be too much, perhaps, to expect it to become, in the near future, one of the best and most readable of our educational journals.

It is the intention of the editors to add to the reading matter two new sections at least, perhaps three. One of these will contain a *resume* of the current events relating to educational movements in Canada and elsewhere. Arrangements have been made to have a record of such events sent by special correspondents from all parts of the Dominion in time for publication at the beginning of each month; and it is needless to say that paragraph contributions will be gratefully received from all teachers, when events of more than local interest take place in their district.

The second section will comprise hints from and to teachers, with correspondence. In the past, our teachers have been perhaps a little too timid in making suggestions through the press, particularly suggestions founded on their own experience. Fault-finding is a very different thing from honest criticism, and to the latter no teacher should fail to subject every proposed educational change, before finding fault with it or advocating it. Making use of the MONTHLY as a medium, it is to be hoped therefore that our teachers will join with us in an open and above-board campaign against all defects, and in favor of all improvements in our school work as well as in our school systems, so that eventually through the co-ordination of educational views from all the provinces, our various school systems will tend towards the unification of our Canadian national life, and not towards its disintegration. In future any question of an educational tendency may be discussed in our correspondence section, and when a *nom de plume* is made use of, the personality of the writer will under no circumstances be revealed.

The third section, when fully organized, will refer to all matters connected with a proposed BUREAU for the purpose of finding situations for teachers or promotion in the service. every subscriber will have the privilege of inscribing his or her name on the lists about to be opened for those who wish to have their names thus enrolled. As an experiment we hope many of our teachers will find this section of great service to them.

To the subscribers who have stood by us so loyally in the past, we present our most grateful thanks, while to our new subscribers we make promise that their tastes and wishes will always be carefully considered in the management of the paper. Indeed, we feel it is only through the co-operation of our readers that our enterprise can be fostered to its fullest fruition.

During the year, the publishers of the MONTHLY will call upon advertisers under the improved circumstances of the periodical. To our faithful contributors we trust we will be able as soon as the revenues of our enterprise improve, to return thanks in a more tangible way than heretofore.

The CANADA EDUCATIONAL MONTHLY, our subscribers must understand, is a journal for the whole Dominion, and not for any section or province.

Communications in connection with the editorial management of the paper are, in future, to be sent from Ontario and all the provinces west of Ontario, to Arch. MacMurchy, M.A, Box 2675, Toronto; and from the Province of Quebec and the provinces east of Quebec, to Messrs. William Drysdale & Co., St. James St., Montreal, who will also attend to all matters pertaining to the publishing and advertising departments for the Eastern Provinces, and Wm. Tyrrell & Co., will attend to the like business for Ontario. Publishers: Wm. Drysdale & Co, Montreal; Wm. Tyrrell & Co, Toronto; A. Hart & Co., Winnipeg; J. & A. McMillan, St. John, N.B.

THE CANADA

EDUCATIONAL MONTHLY.

AUGUST-SEPTEMBER, 1897.

THE CLAIMS OF INDIVIDUALITY IN EDUCATION.

By R. Wormell, D. Sc., M.A.

JUST ten years ago, in the Jubilee year, 1887, I read a lecture here on "Fifty Years of Educational Progress." After the retrospect I indulged in a forecast, and spoke of some dangers that seemed to be looming in the future. I affirmed that we need not fear that the desire for education, which had been fairly aroused, would subside; but that there was danger in the tendency to require all men to pass through the same mould and the same gauge. It seemed that Procrustes was bound to have his victims, the dunces on the one hand being stretched beyond their powers, and the geniuses on the other hand stunted to an average capacity.

I drew attention to this danger in the changed condition of education by describing an analogous change in the philosophy of science. When it was believed that the supply of energy in the universe was being gradually exhausted, men often pictured the end of all things as coming from that ultimate exhaustion. The discovery that energy is transmutable but indestructible was accompanied by the discovery that energy is available for the service of man only in its transformations. If, for instance, all the parts of an enclosed and impervious region had the same temperature, no work could be done between the parts, however high the temperature might be. To get work from heat, we must have bodies of different temperatures. If all the bodies in the universe had the same temperature, there would be neither life nor motion. Similarly, if all men had the same knowledge and skill and exactly similar tastes and temperaments there could be no interchange of ideas, however highly educated each man might be. The theory of the dissipation of energy and the theory of the extinction of individual differences by a Procrustean education are therefore similar and similarly situated, and either of these is sufficent to enable us to see the last man in the dim distance. Hence I pointed out that we ought to resist attempts to produce a dull and dead uniformity by means of education, as we would resist an attack on the life of society itself. Amongst the forms of liberty to be secured the liberty of capacity is not the least important. That combination of laws which we call Nature is allowed at present to assist us by presenting an endless variety as regards natural capacities. To quote from the "Stones of Venice": "One man is made of agate, another of oak, one of slate, another of clay. The education of the first is polishing; of the second, seasoning; of the third, rending; of the fourth, moulding. It is no use to season the agate; it is vain to try to polish slate; but both are fitted by the qualities they possess for the service in which they are honored."

It requires but very little reflection to show that one factor of the prosperity of a country must depend on the extent to which individual differences and individual talents, tastes and powers are developed and utilized. If all were made alike there would be but one excellence, and many would certainly be condemned to uncongenial occupations. As it is there are many excellences. Few there are who could not excel in something, and when each is able to secure that occupation in which he succeeds best, the state reaps the largest harvest from the energies of the people.

So much for theory. Evidently theory declares that there is danger in universality. What does experiment say? The *Rassegna Nazionale* recently—that is to say, a month ago —had a very remarkable account of the working of the Italian school system, written by Signor Ajroli, a man of position and authority. He tells us that no country revels so enthusiastically in pedagogy and in educational discussion of all kinds, and none is so inefficient in practice, as Italy. "Real education," he says, "is still at a very low level there, and, as a rule, elementary scholars read badly and write worse, while their brains are muddled with smatterings of science. The Government, in its craze for centralization, has attempted to enforce a single educational programme on the whole country, without any regard for local customs, needs or interests, while the educational experts insist upon time-tables, etc., being altered with bewildering rapidity, in accordance with the latest educational craze." "Certainly eleementary education, 'free, compulsory, uniform and secular,' is not a success in Italy." And I may add it never has been a success anywhere. It may now be asserted, with little fear of contradiction, that wherever Procrustean methods have been tried they have failed to increase the prosperity of the country trying them, and therefore I cannot now say that what seemed to be a rock ahead ten years ago is still a real danger.

Nevertheless, as a principle of method in schools, the need for taking full account of individual idiosyncrasies, and of varying the general treatment as individual conditions demand, is well worth our consideration.

The main purposes of these monthly meetings, I take it, are two—encouragement and instruction. First, that we teachers may encourage each other by taking stock together of the results and difficulties, the plans and prospects of our work; and, secondly, that the experience which has fallen to the lot of a few may be made available for many. With this view I have accepted the secretary's invitation for to-night. Now we have made some progress in ten years towards a full recognition of the fact that individuality has a claim on our attention. What is the movement for technical education but a consequence of this?

The late Professor Huxley thus described the main objects of the movement:—

"A small percentage of the population is born with a most excellent quality, a desire of excellence, or with special aptitudes of some sort or another. . . Now the most important object of all education schemes is to catch these exceptional people, and turn them to account for the good of society. No man can say where they will crop up; like their opposites, the fools and knaves, they appear sometimes in the palace and sometimes in the hovel ; but the great thing to be aimed at is to keep these glorious sports of Nature from being either corrupted by luxury or starved by poverty, and to put them into the position in which they can do the work for which they are specially fitted. . . . therefore, as the sum and crown of what is to be done for technical education," says Professor Huxley, "I look to the provision of a machinery for winnowing out the capacities and giving them scope."

Let us look more closely into Huxley's notion that genius should be detected. The question has often been asked, "What forces have acted most powerfully on unfolding genius?" Not a few philosophers have tried to find out how much or how little the recognized apparatus of education has effected in the case of the preternaturally gifted.

Some have traced the influence of the parents, father or mother, others that of the schools. Long lists have been drawn up of eminent men who have distinguished themselves early by their capacity for learning.

Lists of public-school men have been arranged to justify the public-school system and to glorify the schools. Thus one writer, speaking of Harrow, boasts that this school "produced in one half century, among its five Prime Ministers, a Palmerston, a Peel, a Spencer Perceval, and an Aberdeen; and among its statesmen a Dalhousie and a Sydney Herbert ; and among its soldiers and sailors a Rodney and a Codrington ; and among its poets a Byron and a Proctor; and among its scholars a Parr and a Sir William Jones ; and among its divines a Trench and a Manning ; and among its common crowd of *alumni* a vast multitude of honourable and useful men." Similar exultations can be declared for other public schools.

But Sydney Smith maintained that "the most eminent men in every art and science had been educated in private schools." From the time of Sydney Smith we have had a greater and ever-increasing list of great men who have received all their early education in private schools, and it is not difficult to find support for the view that in private schools individuality is safer of discovery and careful nurture than in public schools.

But again, lists longer than any others have presented a terrible array of instances of complete failure. Those whom the schools branded as dunces and blockheads, or expelled as intractable rebels, have subsequently achieved greatness and fame.

But yet a fifth list has been prepared, of the so-called self-taught geniuses, who owe no debt of gratitude to any school system, except that which led them to thank their stars that they were subjected to none.

Shall we say then that genius is independent of educational arrangements, and need not be considered by them ? All know this would be a disastrous conclusion. The systems have often succeeded ; they have often failed ; therefore they need amending : but the right conclusion is that of Professor Sully. He sums up the question as follows : "Does it follow that because the possessor of genius is not well fitted to reap the particular benefits of our pedagogic system he is really independent of educational forces and influences altogether ? This is not an uncommon view, and it has much to support it. But such an idea is clearly an exaggeration of the fact. However keen and strong the impulse towards knowledge in a boy, his attainment of it obviously depends on the presence of humanly appointed sources. More than this, it is indisputable that the greatest of men will be the stronger for a wise intellectual and moral guidance in their early years. Would Goethe have been Goethe if, instead of his early home surroundings, with their comparative opulence, their refinement, their various striking personalities, and their carefully thought out plan of education, he had lighted, say, on the environment of a Chatterton? It is nothing less than a profound error to suppose that the plant of genius grows into fruitful maturity whether or no there are kindly influences of sun and rain to play upon it. One would rather say that in a sense that a boy or girl possessing the divine flame is more subject to the human forces of his surroundings than the ordinary child."

Hence the points I wish to maintain are that the duty of the school system, as regards the genius, is that the system shall be so elastic as to provide the training which will bring his special power to the highest state of excellence, and the duty of the schoolmaster is to detect the potential genius, that he may be brought within the proper influences. The strongest expressions on education that I know in our language have been framed to condemn want of elasticity in the curriculum. For instance, Mr. Ruskin warns us not to pour one kind of knowledge on one and all alike, like snow upon the Alps, and to be proud if here aud there a river descends from their crests into the valleys, forgetting that we have made the loaded hills themselves barren for ever.

It is not to be expected that any one school, however large, should present all the variety needed. There must be some considerable range and scope in the studies of each school, but the whole provision that is required by the country can be made only by means of a distribution of subjects and aims. Different groups, grades, or classes of schools should take up different portions of the work, each group having its one specific aim. When this arrangement is complete the claims of individuality may be met. No doubt Gray had reason to believe what he said of undetected potential merit in the lines we all learnt as children—

Full many a gem of purest ray serene
The dark unfathomed caves of ocean bear;
Full many a flower is born to blush unseen,
And waste its sweetness on the desert air.

But the merits of the gem and the flower will no longer be wasted when the search for them is made everywhere by the trained, skilled, and experienced educator.

This leads us to the personal and professional aspect of the case. For this work of selection and discovery the teacher himself must possess that faculty which a botanist or geologist uses when he recognises at a distance an unusual appearance, a natural object, a plant, for instance, not seen before—one that suggests new uses—one that requires for its healthy sustenance a particular habitat. I am inclined to think that a teacher's most essential qualification is the possession of this power. It has been my fate at times to try to help intending teachers who, in spite of all aids, have utterly failed from beginning to end. In nine of these cases out of ten the failure has arisen from inability to distinguish individual actions, individual conditions. Such men know when the whole class is listless, inattentive, disorderly, but what particular part in this condition is taken by A, B, or C, is never found out. Such a teacher may know there are some in his class who do not understand him, but whether M or N understands him he has not the slightest idea. They have been to him no individual existence. It is impossible that such should become successful teachers, for the power to see the individual in the mass and to feel and think with the individual is an essential.

Again, we have mentioned the frequent failure of the schools to meet the needs of the potential genius. What does this show? That even when, by accident or by the exercise on the part of some one of that faculty we have just described, the genius has been detected, something more is needed. He often requires very special treatment—very special care. His exceptional powers in some matters may have been produced at the cost of great defects in other matters. His furious appetite for some kinds of learning may be accompanied by a feeling that the subjects at which the boy of mediocre parts will work uncomplainingly are galling and insupportable impositions. In fact the unfolding genius often needs to be protected against himself by the exercise of both tact and care.

> Great wits are sure to madness near allied,
> And thin partitions do their bounds divide.

Geniuses and many others who are not destined to become geniuses are often over-sensitive. What are we to do with the over-sensitive? Harden them? If we had a scholar known to possess a valvular weakness of heart should we send him to compete in the long races, with a view of strengthening his weak organ? Would not a verdict of manslaughter rightly follow such a course? We may draw an analogy between this and other kinds of morbid sensitiveness.

Within the last few days the daily papers have expressed lay opinions on a case of schoolboy suicide. Such correspondence is generally more amusing than edifying, but there is one out of the many letters which seems to me to be dictated by sound sense, and hits the very " bull's-eye " of my contention. The writer asks: " How far is it possible to save a super-sensitive boy from the consequences of his own organization? What chance is there, under a public-school system, for the boy who, for whatever reason, is 'singular,' as compared with the average and convential type of British youth?" In answering these questions, the writer first acknowledges the good features of the public schools. He says: " No one but cranks will deny that, on the whole, our public-school system has been justified of its children. It has produced a manly, self-reliant race, simple, straightforward and truthful, modest and clean-minded, with a holy abhorrence of cant and rant, and an uncommonly clear—almost a petulant —perception of character. These results are due to a system which creates independence by giving responsibility, and enables men to belong to a governing race by teaching them to govern themselves and one another." The writer then shows how the influence of the headmaster may prevent this governing power from being abused and made irksome to abnormally constituted individuals. He says: " It depends absolutely and entirely upon the chief what is the character of the prefects, and therefore, that of the school at large. The prefects who come nearest to him, are quick to catch his manner, his sympathies, his influence, and become, in their way, reproductions of his personality. Everyone can see that if a dreamy, nervous melancholy boy is allowed to go from bad to worse before the eyes of his schoolfellows, some imputation must rest upon the prefects for their lack, not only of good feeling, but of common sense." This I am convinced is the righteous view. There must be an eye to discover over-sensitiveness, and there must be a resolution emanating from the head, but permeating the prefects and all in authority, to prevent all malevolent sporting with this peculiarity.

But the prospective genius is having too much of our time. Let our thoughts become more general, and especially take in those who have any given faculty in less than normal or average strength—so little strength, for instance, that it certainly can never be made remarkable. Does the fact that a particular faculty exists only in the merest germs relieve the schoolmaster of the duty of fostering and cultivating it? The special and careful nurture of a weak plant that nevertheless may be designed to fill a particular place in the general economy is the demand of individuality in such a case. Take music as an illustration. Some persons have good ears and good voices; some without training would never be able to see any difference between "God Save the Queen" and "The Old Hundredth," and never to reproduce a note of given pitch. Yet in Yorkshire I have often heard the children of a very large school almost without exception singing accurately and with expression from sight under the patient teaching and leading of Tonic-sol-fahists. It has then seemed to me that that system has set an example with regard to the development and general treatment of a weak faculty. The key of the success lies in connecting individual attention with collective exercise. The same method is sometimes found in art. I have heard persons say: "I could not draw a stroke until So-and-so took me in hand."

There is another faculty in regard to which individuality presents a two-sided claim. It exists, naturally, in different persons with very wide variations of intensity, but, in most cases, by attention to the individual conditions it may be developed. It manifests itself by reverence for good, noble and holy thoughts and for sacred thoughts and things, by a spirit of devotion and by certain qualities which bring to their possessors much calm contentment and power of endurance, and make a man or woman having them a perpetual source of happiness to others. I shall not be misunderstood if I call it the religious faculty. Seeing how much of the influence and happiness of life are dependent on its possession, I have no doubt it is the schoolmaster's duty to cultivate it in all his pupils. Probably, in most cases, he may not be required to consider the particular form its application is afterwards to take, any more than he is required to consider when he begins his labors to awake intelligence, the particular occupation or profession in which the pupil is to apply that intelligence. But *he* will have a very lame notion of his duties who tries to send out creatures in other respects intelligent but absolutely lacking reverence and devotion. But the due cultivation of this faculty requires a double attention to individualities. In the first place, the individual differences as regards the faculty are so wide that no wholesale treatment will be sufficient. In the second place, the time and circumstances must be suitable, and the treatment really called for, and not forced; so that this work cannot be wholly placed in certain fixed squares of the time-table.

A suitable occasion for the teaching may crop up in any lesson on any subject. I may mention an illustration which has for nearly forty years served me as a kind of pattern. In 1859 I was one of a class studying formal logic. No subject surely could, in its nature, be less likely to encourage the kind of lesson we are considering; yet the opportunity came. The correct forms and modes of hypothetical syllogisms had been considered, and a number of examples of fallacious reasoning had been collected from known authors. Then, at the end of the lesson, the principal's manner and tone of voice were altered, and we all knew something more serious was coming. He said there was a hypothetical syllogism drawn correctly in the last three verses of the sixty-sixth Psalm. He asked: Why did not David state the conclusion? The answer was sought in other passages of the Psalms, and then the lesson ended with a quotation from Old Thomas Fuller:—

> I find David making a syllogism in mood and figure. Two propositions he perfected:—
>
> "18. If I regard wickedness in my heart, the Lord will not hear me.
>
> 19. But verily God hath heard me, He hath attended to the voice of my prayer."
>
> Now I expected that David should have concluded thus:—"Therefore I regard not wickedness in my heart." But far otherwise he concludes:—
>
> "20. Blessed be God that hath not turned away my prayer, nor His mercy from me."
>
> Thus David hath deceived, but not wronged me. I looked that he should have clapped the crown on his own, and he puts it on God's head. I will learn this excellent logic, for I like David's better than Aristotle's syllogism, that whatsoever the premises be, I make God's glory the conclusion.

I venture to say that in that class there was not one who felt the digression was out of place, and there was no one whose feelings of reverence and devotion were not stimulated by the manner and matter of the illustration.

I have just time for reference to one other claim of individuality, namely, the special claim of women. The gifts and graces of men and women differ. There is no need to weigh them one against the other. The task would be as difficult as that of instituting a comparison between the services which great poets and great painters render to their countrymen. It is sufficient to know that the world is richer than it would if both these services were welded into one, and it is the richer when women have free scope for their special powers, and when education aims at developing the special faculties they have received, not for themselves, but for humanity—treasures of tenderness, sympathy, reverence, faith, and purity. To women great ideals are natural. They have capacities for teaching, training and elevating beyond anything we have hitherto used. Let us develop and utilize their precious endowments.

Thus you see I am advocating two kinds of elasticity, the first secured by dividing the work of education amongst schools of different types and grades, and the second by permitting the customs, methods and courses of each school to take account of individual needs and conditions. My suggestions in no way tend to disturb the unity of our great and increasingly important profession. Let us have corporate unity by all means, but corporate unity together with individual function. It is the latter that will preserve the necessary variety. It is the latter that will maintain the availability of the talents of the people, and will avert the peril of an equally diffused, and, therefore, unproductive civilization.

I have one concluding remark to make on the second point, namely, the encouragement of insight into individual temperament. I admit that the best rewards of this subtle craft will not be found in measurable results and marketable achievements. They cannot be tried by direct and present tests, but will be seen in the life of the coming age. Yet I firmly believe that he is happiest in the work of teaching who does not pine for immediate results, but will be content if he finds what he has cast upon the waters after many days.—*The Educational Times.*

Give to a gracious message
An host of tongues; but let ill tidings tell
Themselves when they be felt.

Antony and Cleopatra, ii. 5.

MORAL TRAINING IN PUBLIC SCHOOLS.*

By David Fotheringham, B.A., I.P.S.

(Continued from May)

AND that public sentiment in England is of the same opinion is evident from the evidence forwarded to the Government by a Royal Commission appointed some years ago to investigate this whole question. In answer to the question, "Do parents desire moral training?" the Commission received affirmative replies from 93 per cent. of Voluntary (School) Managers, 79 per cent. of School Boards and 98 per cent. of teachers answering. "It was manifest from the investigation that the people of England by an overwhelming majority desire religious instruction in the Elementary School."

If as thorough an investigation were held now in Ontario the conclusion could not be very different. The great body of our citizens know and realize that moral instruction is of vital importance to the well-being of the home and of the State; and would give wide and liberal scope to those who in good faith would undertake, as did the two great parties in England in 1870, to furnish a national system that would bring every child under the control of an efficient intellectual and moral training.

In Ontario, to meet the demands of one denomination chiefly, a Separate School system has been granted under careful provision for thorough instruction in the secular branches of a primary education, and with the distinct understanding that the tenets of that church may also be taught during school hours. But were this system carried to its full, legitimate issues by all denominations, the efficiency of secular education would undoubtedly be seriously impaired, if not destroyed; and a strong and growing feeling is asserting itself in favor of one and only one system of schools throughout our Province. The advocates of one system say that to unify and strengthen the brotherhood of all citizens who must work shoulder to shoulder for all that is valuable in our homes and our country in mature years, the children should be trained together. Our children, say they, cannot be brought into daily contact and mutual sympathy too soon if the conditions are what they should be. But in this case wise and ample provision must be made for their effective development in every part of their complex nature, and that in the order of awakening powers.

Why should morals be excluded or neglected? Why should the ethical nature, that asserts itself almost as early as the intellectual, be ignored or left to the haphazard teaching of a child's environment when that nature has in it far greater and graver possibilities than either of its other natures?

Many who thus speak are recognized leaders of the intelligent and religious classes. Mere secularists may trouble themselves but little with such matters; but when those who are able to take the most enlightened and patriotic view of this question keep pressing it on their own friends and on the public they would do well to take heed.

The advocates of secular (not godless) schools and those who can suggest no good working plan for common moral instruction tell us that

* Paper read at O. E. A., April, '97.

the parent and the church should give ethical training; and it is true that these are responsible in this respect and can never relegate their duty to the State. But where all educators and enlightened statesmen are agreed that morality is essential to the permanency and prosperity of the State, the State cannot forego its right to see that its subjects are so educated. Why insist upon intellectual and not on moral training? Why leave this to parents when many of them have no adequate idea of what to teach or how to teach in the line of morals?

The best authorities on the matter tell us that only 40 per cent. of our school population are enrolled in the Sunday schools of Ontario. Let us say that one half of our children are in such schools. What of the moral training of the other half? In all likelihood their parents are too indifferent to send them there; and if so these children are not likely to be sent to church service, and are practically growing up without any training of a right sort on their ethical side. Whence must our criminals be drawn in large measure? Not from the 50 per cent. who are under the training of homes, churches and Sabbath schools, but from the army of 300,000 that are outside the benign influence of these institutions.

In a similar way it is reckoned that 9,000,000 of young people in the Republic to the South of us are growing up in ignorance of the saving principles of morality.

Admit, for argument's sake, that this is a pessimistic calculation, though there is ground for believing that it is the calculation of men anxious to look on the bright side. Admit that the numbers may be fairly reduced to one-half, and still in Ontario we will find that 150,000 young people are growing up, a dangerous class.

It has been asserted again and again that it is the duty of the State to do this work of moral training, and it may fairly be asked how can this be established? It has already been shown that the most enlightened and most powerful nations of the two hemispheres practically support this theory. The common law of nations is based upon the laws of the Decalogue, and the leading principles of the Bible. This is historically and admittedly true.

In all modern civilized governments the one true and living God is recognized; and he is appealed to as the ultimate and only true source of law and order. Oaths of office are administered in His name to rulers, judges, arbitrators, jurors and witnesses. Profanity and other moral offences are visited with severe penalties. When the extreme penalty of the law is pronounced, the immortality of the soul and divine judgment are appealed to when the judge says "And may God have mercy on your soul." Days of thanksgiving or of humiliation before Him are appointed. For the army, navy, houses of correction and the like, chaplains are appointed to instruct in the principles of divine law, truth and righteousness; and the sessions of congresses, parliaments and legislatures are opened by invoking the blessing of Him by whom kings rule and princes decree justice. In short, "it is only secularists and exclusive churchmen who treat the body politic as having no immediate relation to God."

From these and similar considerations it will readily be conceded that the State recognizes a system of morals based upon the existence, the holiness, the justice and final authority of the one supreme, unchanging, eternal Ruler. It affirms more or less directly the responsibility of its citizens to His laws as the final and unalterable standard of right; that to do his will is the highest and best qualification for citizenship.

Hence the legitimate conclusion, that the Word of God is the highest authority to which to look for a knowledge of truth, righteousness, justice, love of neighbor and loyalty to rulers.

If these conclusions are fairly reached, the next question to be asked is how shall moral instruction be introduced and be made a part of school work? But before attempting an answer, it is only wise to look fairly and squarely at the difficulties that must be overcome.

First, we have the unworthy jealousies of sectarians to which broadminded and Christian men find themselves face to face whenever they argue and agitate for moral instruction in the public schools, and which charges them with hostility to the system.

Then we have too many of the secular, selfish spirit who seek only material and present success, ignoring the best interests of their children and their country. If these are left alone to advance their worldly interests they will in turn let alone our educational machinery, however imperfect. Even the intellectual education of their children will be neglected, as is clearly shown in the fact that the average attendance at our rural schools is only one day in two; and in all schools, urban and rural, only 56 out of 100.

We have also a class of high standing, educationally and morally, who object to formal moral education in the school because it savors of State-church and denominationalism. Some of these assert boldly that it is not the place of the State to teach religion. True, but to teach the fundamental principles of ethics is not to teach the religions of the churches. It surely means the teaching of the underlying principles accepted by all the churches. And if moral character is essential to the safety, permanency and progress of free institutions, then, for self-preservation, the State must insist upon the adequate moral training of the young.

Fortunately we have few, if any, Socialists or Communists amongst us and consideration of their special attitude is not really needed. Practically, they are Ishmaelites; and society should know how to deal with the enemies of law and order, of prosperity and progress.

There is further difficulty in the question of what is to be taught under the heading of morals or ethics; and of course as to how it is to be taught. Some claim that it is only to be taught incidentally, inferentially and implicitly. Others, of course, claim that there must be a syllabus and definite time for this work just as for other studies.

Then too the question is asked, who shall teach morals? The teacher or some one else? And shall time be taken out of the regular school hours for this purpose?

If these difficulties are approached as they should be in a patriotic and liberal spirit, they may all be overcome. They are no more formidable than were those to be overcome in England, where "for twenty-three years the subject (of religious instruction) had been settled upon the peaceable basis of compromise; in practice its theoretical differences and perplexities have been obviated or solved; and in point of fact the so-called 'religious difficulty' has ceased to exist." (Memorial from the National Union of Elementary teachers, 1893). The memorialists proceed to say "they venture to think that none can speak with more experience of the facts than the teachers themselves; and the teachers are aware that the instruction has been such as Christian theologians could collectively endorse. They know that the scholars have been carefully and reverently taught the essentials of the Christian faith as drawn from the Holy Scriptures."

Here we have more than mere theory. We have the "Settlement of 1870," a wise and statesmanlike compromise between the two great parliamentary parties, and we have the outgrowth of its provisions for religious instruction. We find that only 91 School Boards out of a total of 2,255 in England and Wales had failed to provide for religious exercises. "We find the London School Board elaborating a full Syllabus of Bible instruction, which is followed in all its schools and occupies from half to three quarters of an hour daily. We find "explicit directions issued to the teachers as to the carrying out of the scheme." In addition to the 450,000 children of London affected by this instruction, the influence of this scheme has been greatly extended by its adoption by 101 other boards, including several of the most important cities."

We are proud of our intimate relations with Great Britain, and proud of the inheritance we have received from her. Why should we hesitate to copy so practical and successful an example? Why should not the leaders of both parties in our legislature follow the example of British statesmen, and elaborate a workable scheme for the moral elevation of every child in Ontario? Why may we not have a commission, large and representative, to prepare, in harmony with the received principles of all denominations, an outline of truth that shall be hailed with pleasure by all right thinking people?

Having received ample scope and authority from our legislators, such a commission would acquaint itself with the special demands of Ontario as contrasted with those of England, of Germany, or any other country having a course of such instruction. It would possess itself of the curriculum of each. It might discover text-books such as that written by the Rev. J. O. Miller, of Ridley College, St. Catharines, and that published by J. A. Quay, Morganza, Pa., which is in use in mixed schools in Pittsburg and other towns in that State.

Such commission should have power to call before it educational experts and men of experience; and after the fullest investigation and deliberation, we should be provided with a scheme that should satisfy all reasonable men: and in a few years place our public school system on a par with the most liberal and advanced in moral training, as it is already in its literary course.

To discuss all the theories of educationists in reference to this subject, after pointing to a successful system, may seem unnecessary; yet it will not be out of place briefly to advert to some of these:

The broad question as to what are the limits of ethical or moral teaching in schools has never been settled. There are those, like Spencer and Adler, among modern writers, who claim and teach the humanitarian doctrine that the obligations which grow out of the relations of man to his fellowmen alone belong to morals. Alder says "ethics is a science of relations—of human interests and human ends." "Moral laws are formulas expressing relations of subordination, equality or superordination," etc. Bain and Johnnot, though admitting that the relations of man to his Maker may be considered in this connection, restrict themselves to discussing morals under the same limitations.

Spencer's dictum may be summarized in his own words, "that conduct whose total results, immediate and remote, are beneficial, is good conduct; while conduct whose total results, immediate and remote, are injurious, is bad conduct." "According to popular acceptance, right and wrong are words scarcely applicable to actions with only bodily effects; but such actions must be classified under these heads as much as any other."

This school of writers therefore excludes from the school-room the teaching of obligations to one Supreme Being and his laws as the ultimate standard of right and wrong. The law of expediency is, apparently, their ultimate standard. But, as Miller in his work on School Management, says, "Any attempt to base moral obligation solely on human authority has always resulted in the weakening of the conscience and the enfeebling of the will." "No nation has ever achieved moral excellence that did not hold the Supreme Being as the final source of obligation."

In confirmation of this position, I need only call your attention to the abject and ruinous failure of the moral systems of Confucius and Buddha, whose theories some writers of sweetness and light would have us believe should be placed alongside the Christian Code, but which have given awful confirmation to the truth of Scripture that it is the fool who says in his heart "No God."

Another class of writers on educational topics teach directly or by clear implication that moral education, to be efficient, must involve the teaching of a final and infallible standard of right and wrong to which all are responsible.

Among these may be named Currie, Abbott, Northend, Page, Rosenkranz, Fitch, Hinsdale, White, Wickersham, F. W. Parker, Fowle, Baldwin, Miller.

The dicta of this school may be expressed in a quotation from our Deputy-Minister's book: "The motives which flow from a belief in a personal God as the creator and moral ruler of the world; in the dependence of man on his Maker, and in his obligation to love and serve Him; in the immortality of the soul, and in the accountability of every intelligent person to the Supreme Being, are recognized principles of every efficient system of ethics."

Again, I agree that this is the true limit of the work to be assumed in training to citizenship in all Christian countries.

The writers of both schools are agreed that the teaching of morals is *the* subject of supreme importance for the well-being of the State. But there is a marked divergence as to the mode of teaching. Not a few of the best educators maintain that the direct inculçation of moral principles, as the principles of intellectual studies are inculcated, is a pedagogical error; and that all ethical instruction should be developed in the right teaching of secular studies and in the inculcation of order and compliance with the understood obligations of one to another, and of all to God. I quote Parker to show the theory maintained by him and others: "All teaching should be intrinsically moral, and all good books are text-books in morals. The demand for teaching morals as an isolated subject springs from the absence of moral effects in all other teaching." Again: "In developing motive we develop everything. Motive is the centre and everything comes to it." "The laws of action, or the principles of right doing, should grow out of the *doing* itself."

Others as strongly insist that not only should morals be taught indirectly in the instruction and government of the school, but also categorically, systematically, and from a comprehensive outline of common Christian belief, by the most competent instructors. Even Adler, whose system is typically altruistic and humanitarian, would have the teacher say this is right and that is wrong, but he would not have the reason given. The more rational advocates of moral teaching would follow that information with the reason, would speak, discriminateingly, of course, of the basis on which action should be tested, and would appeal to the principles of the Decalogue. This may be done without developing the self-consciousness and self-righteousness of the child; and without making such instruction distasteful.

But everything depends on the teacher: "A teacher of high moral character is the chief requisite of moral training." "The teacher leaves his everlasting imprint on every child placed under his care." (Miller.) Those who ignore the importance of indirect moral teaching make a serious blunder. Few influences are so potential in character-building as those of the teacher of noble ideas and a noble life, who has true conceptions of what life should be, and whose constant aim is the development of true character in his pupils. The whole round of studies, of movements, of duties and incidents is made to contribute to the strengthening of the motive and will power, and the exercise of self-improvement, self-control, self-denial and self-sacrifice to serve others and secure the approbation of the Divine Being whose presence is ever realized in the life of the morally strong teacher.

With teachers of such a type, it matters little whether direct moral instruction is said to be complementary to their influence or that their influence is complementary to the moral teaching. The combination is ideally satisfactory; and would satisfy the most earnest advocates of thorough ethical training in our schools.

How are we to secure such teachers? We already have many; aad it will not be difficult to have introduced into our training institutions a department for giving instructions in the duties of teachers in morals as is done in Great Britain.

What shall be our text-book? "Material for such instruction adapted to the needs of the child exists in great abundance. The Bible does not contain it all, but it contains the cream. Still it should not be taught to children indiscriminately. Highest on the roll of books stand the incomparable Gospels. The story of Jesus and His great utterances, as the Sermon on the Mount and the parables of the Prodigal Son, the Good Samaritan, the Talents and the Sower, should be fixed in every mind." Paul's Song of Love and his Ode to Immortality should not be omitted. "Some of the tales (of the Old Testament) as that of Joseph, Sermons of the prophets, passages of Job, parts of the Hebrew wisdom and many of the Psalms,are unsurpassed, if not indeed unequalled, as means for creating noble ideas and developing noble feelings. Still more, the educative value of the Scriptures is much increased by the noble language in which the thoughts are clothed. And this thought suggests again the close connection between ethical and spiritual impressions."

Having briefly presented the views of those who advocate only indirect moral teaching on the one hand and of those on the other hand who insist upon direct teaching of morals, and having directed attention to the value of the Bible as a text-book in the language of Hinsdale, it might seem fitting to close with the syllabus of the London School Board for the guidance of its teachers, which has been adopted by over one hundred other boards through England and Wales; but as my paper is already long enough, I must refer those interested to a copy to be found in Vol. of the Report of the U. S. Commissioner of Education for the years 1888-9, page 445.

I may, however, say that the work is carefully graded for seven standards, in the first of which the Ten Commandments (in substance) and the Lord's Prayer are to be learned, and simple lessons from the life of Joseph and leading facts in the life of Christ are to be told in simple language.

In all the grades memory work of choice selections is required, with recapitulation of the work done in the preceding grade, and added portions for fresh study.

EDUCATION—FROM A PUBLISHER'S STANDPOINT.*

BY GILMAN H. TUCKER, SEC. AMERICAN BOOK CO.

THE relation of schoolbook publishing to the schools, or to the broader subject of education, offers many interesting points. The development of the business of text-book publishing, say in the past hundred years, in the nations which are foremost in education, if its full history could be presented, would mark in detail the steps of progress in education itself; but this would be most emphatically true of the United States, which almost merits the distinction of being the inventor of text-books. When we compare the numbers and kinds of text-books published in our own country for the use of schools, say fifty years ago, with those that are published to-day—a comparison of hundreds with thousands—we realize what an increasingly large part books hold in our educational scheme, and what an enlarged influence and responsibility has come to the publisher. This great multiplication of books may not be an unmixed good, but that it is, on the whole, an enormous educational help, no one will be rash enough to deny; and this state of things has come about in response to the demand which you, as leaders of educational thought, have created; so that at the bottom the responsibility and the credit are yours.

The question of the use and misuse of text-books is wide and deep, and has itself been the origin of many books and endless discussion. Some cynic, I believe, has even raised the point whether the invention of the art of printing has, on the whole, been a blessing to the human race, but nevertheless text-books have remained and their use has increased. The speller was at one time banished from what was regarded as the progressive school; the mental arithmetic had a like fate; technical grammar has suffered somewhat of an eclipse; but books on even these subjects are finding their way back into favor with the leaders. The just criticism made upon the books of the old time and upon a certain class of books devoted to the older methods, was that they enslaved the schools and teachers by a dry routine, and furnished the letter which killeth, and not the spirit which maketh alive. But this is not true of the books chiefly in use in this country to-day. It may be stated as the truth, that books of this description are now used only by those who have not educated themselves up to the use of better standards and better methods; that the numbers are somewhat large,

* Delivered July, 1897, before the National Educational Association, Milwaukee, Wis.

however, is not the fault of the publisher, who simply fulfils the office of supplying the demand. The fountain does not rise above its source. But with increased numbers of books have come great improvement in methods, and especially a great improvement in the manner of using such books. Where formerly there were fifty or a hundred books forming a chain of routine which practically enslaved the schools, there are now thousands of books, but they are used by skilful teachers as the handy and efficient tools of their profession.

The question about text-books today is only one of form and method. And here there is nothing fixed or absolute ; changes in methods of teaching, fashions, fads, whims, are always in evidence and moving on, not always marking steps of real progress, possibly oftener going round in circles ; but they are an indication of life in education. Movement is life, and stagnation is death.

It does not follow that all old schoolbooks are bad, and that all new ones are good. What could be more foolish than not to hold on to so much of the world's experience as has been proved valuable up to the present time? Conservatism must be joined with radicalism if a wise balance is to be held. In the world's literature it is the old and standard, that which has really become crystallized, that comprises the chief value. Is it too much to say that there are old and standard text-books that can be very little improved upon, and that there are methods which have had the vogue of years, that cannot summarily be set aside because something else is simply new ? Books on literature, like school readers, must present virtually the same matter ; it is only their form and not their substance that can be changed. The principles of mathematics remain the same ; language, literature, history, always present the same facts ; political, social and metaphysical subjects do not vary much. The natural sciences have the same basis, and only need to keep pace with new discoveries and modern discussion. And it must also be ever remembered that the text-books which make the most efficient tools, in the hands of teachers of a high degree of ability and skill, often prove very sorry instruments in the hands of another class of teachers not so intelligent or skilful.

Books of real merit have a certain personality, and, like persons, they attract or repel. The ideal education comes from a contact of personalities, of mind with mind ; the live teaching force is always the *teacher* himself. The preeminent teacher can sometimes put the best part of himself into a book, and so the book becomes characteristic. There are really living books, attractive, popular, successful within their own circles, and yet indescribable, but containing certain elements of individuality or personality, such as distinguish the intelligent, clear-headed, magnetic teacher. They have a flavor that attracts and impresses, and which endows the subject with a living speech.

There is a shallow and dangerous popular belief, unhappily now rife in many states and communities, that a schoolbook is only so much paper, print and binding, and that anybody can produce it at short order, at its mere mechanical cost, and that the results produced by its use in schools will be just as satisfactory as the use of any book whatever. This is an emphasis of the evil of text-book routine in its worst form. State uniformity, state publication, state contracts in the interest of mere cheapness are its outcome. I have referred to the makers of schoolbooks as authors, and not editors, because the real schoolbook is a creation ; the best thought that can be put into printed pages, in the most skilful form that genuis can contrive, under the great stress of competition to produce the most excellent, is none too good to help out and supplement the teaching abilities of the average teacher, and give life and reality to the subject taught. Such books can be produced only where there is the freedom of an open and ambitious competition, and where, without fear or favor, merit shall win, and where the rewards of success are worth this intense striving. And every publisher knows to his dear cost how much oftener he fails than succeeds, even under this condition.

The part of the publisher is both to follow and to lead, to supply the want that exists and to create a new and better want. The first and obvious duty of the publisher is to supply the existing demand, and this in a way takes care of itself. The publisher's second and higher duty is constantly to watch the steps of educational progress and provide books which will, at the same time, create and fulfil a better and higher demand; and, stimulated by an ambition to lead and excel, this the progressive and live publisher is always doing. The editorial department of a well-organized publishing house keeps a close watch over educational tendencies, the development of this or that educational theory, the exemplification of this or that phase of teaching, the doings of this or that particular group of enthusiastic, growing teachers. It is easy to see what a close relation must exist between the editorial department and the teaching world to be able to form a correct judgment of the hundreds of manuscripts that are presented for inspection.

This is an age of great transition, and in no department of life's work is transition so evident as in methods of teaching. The present tendencies and transitions, wise and unwise, old and new, are sifted, put into form, and given to the educational world by such epoch-making reports as that of the Committee of Ten, the Committee of Fifteen, the Committee on Rural Schools. The editorial department must be in close touch with these reports, with the doctrines contained, with the philosophy preached, and must seek to materialize them in such a way as to make them usable in the schools.

Publishers study the educational sentiment and crystallize it into definite shape, providing text-books having a common basis; thus tending to assist in unifying the educational interests of the whole country.

Whatever interests educators, interests publishers; the same problems confront both; both should be equally alert, active and ready to take up improvements; if anything, the interest of the pubiisher is keener in these improvements than the interest of any individual. Unless the publisher plans wisely, his whole capital is jeopardized. Unless he keeps in touch with the newest and best educational thought, embraces the good and brings it to the front, and makes his house the headquarters for the best that is to be had, he loses prestige, he loses business, he loses profits, and must inevitably go to the wall in time. Hence, apart from any higher motives, the publisher is compelled by his pecuniary interests to keep to the forefront of educational progress.

The course of text-book publishing is an evolution, following closely the trend of educational discussion. Your deliberations here to day, determine the text-books of to-morrow. The publisher is a clearing house of educational ideas. A superintendent in a good place may do much by his individual effort. He preaches his doctrine, presents his views, guards with watchful care his own schools and his own teachers. The publisher gathers the personal views and personal influence of the best educators in all parts of the country and draws them together, crystallizes their thought in books, and by distributing those books throughout the country multiplies a thousand fold the influence of any individual educator.

The publisher is a conservator of educational interests. The personality of an active teacher or superintendent may tend to propagate bad methods; and wherever he goes and impresses his personality he may extend these bad methods. A publisher may publish a book containing bad methods, but under the law of the survival of the fittest, the poor book perishes and the good book survives. Hence, the publisher's net resultant effort is always toward improvement, in this respect having the advantage over any individual educator.

(*To be continued.*)

THE ETHICS OF EXPRESSION.

THE fundamental impulse which issues in language is the impulse to give expression to truth. Truth has many and varied forms. It pertains to all the different functions of life. There is a truth of the senses, of the intellect, of the feelings, of the will; and there is a corresponding language, or expression, for all of these forms of truth. Science is language; art is language; philosophy is language; literature is language; music is language; conduct is language.

The relation between truth and language, affecting as it does intelligent beings, is a *moral* one. The process by which truth is transferred into language is governed by ethical principles. When one is moved to give expression to truth, moral integrity requires (1) that the impulse be obeyed, and (2) that the expression correspond to and represent the reality.

1. Failure to give expression to truth involves moral culpability.

When truth visits the soul, stirring all its energies, and yet fails to find expression, the soul which thus allows truth to die through inanition experiences a sense of moral failure and guilt. Conviction, which is truth in individual visitation—demands utterance. "I believe and therefore have I spoken." Not to speak when one believes is to imprison the King's messenger and withhold his message. Unexpressed conviction rebukes, enervates, stultifies the soul.

On the other hand there is no joy greater than that of free and full self-expression. It is like the joy of a bird in the use of its wings, like the joy of a tree that is free to spread its roots and branches far and wide, like the joy of the wind as it sweeps unimpeded across the prairie, like the joy of the stars as they revolve in their courses.

2. Failure to give truth *correct* expression also involves moral culpability.

It is not sufficient that one publish his conviction, or embody his vision, he is under strict obligation to give truth *true expression.* He may not stumble in his message, or color his picture falsely, without moral dereliction.

Imperfect representation of truth consists (1) in excessive or extravagant expression. In art this is the fault of exaggerated idealism, the neglect of reality. In conduct it is the fault of fanaticism. In speech and literature it is the fault of over-statement.

The earnest sincere soul will be careful to limit itself to the enclosures of truth. After the vehement and lavish declarations of their affection for their father from her shallow sisters, pure, true Cordelia would simply say: "I love your majesty according to my bond, nor more nor less."

The temptation to voice more than is in the heart is very strong, and at times very plausible and deceptive. It is one of the greatest dangers of the pulpit. The consciousness that the transcendent truths with which he is dealing demand commensurate utterance leads the preacher to adopt, not infrequently, a tone and language surpassing his own experience. He endeavours to express what he thinks he ought to feel rather than what he really does feel; the result is the creation of that atmosphere of spiritual extravagance which is so repellent to the thoughtful and sincere.

Hardly less insidious is the same temptation to extravagance of expression which meets the author. In description, in argument, in theory, in appeal, he is moved by a natural disposition to overstate the case. Dean Church, in his admirable address on Bishop Butler, says of him: "We feel in every page and every word the law that writer and thinker has imposed on himself, not only to say nothing for show or effect, but to say nothing that he has not done his best to make clear to himself, nothing that goes a shade beyond what he thinks and feels; he is never tempted to sacrifice exactness to a flourish or an epigram. A qualm comes over the ordinary writer as he reads Butler, when he thinks how often heat or prejudice, or lazy fear of trouble, or the supposed necessities of a cause, or conscious incapacity for thinking out thoroughly a difficult subject, have led him to say something different from what he felt authorized to say by his own clear perceptions, and to veil his deficiencies by fine words, by slurring over or exaggerating. If only as a lesson in truth—truth in thought and expression—Butler is worth studying. He is a writer who, if there is any reason for it, always *understates* his case; and he is a writer, too, from whom we learn the power and force, in an argument, of understatement, the suggestion which it carries with it both of truthfulness and care, of strength and reserve."* The language of power is that which is "fit and fair and simple and sufficient."†

The moral obligations which attach to the use of language are not recognized and estimated at their full value. It was a severe but not an unjust application of moral law which Jesus made when He said: "By thy words shalt thou be justified, and by thy words shalt thou be condemned." Whoever assumes the office of preacher, teacher, or author puts himself under amenability to that standard of judgment. "Words, words, words" are not to be carelessly traded with, flippantly or inconsiderately employed. Moral responsibility is involved in their use.

But excessive expression is not the only fault in the way of a correct representation of truth. It is due (2) to the contrasted fault of inadequacy, insufficiency of expression. This, too, is morally reprehensible. When one takes it upon himself to express truth, whether in form or color, speech or literature, he is bound to give it a form in some sense adequate to its nature. Defective expression is as blameworthy as excessive; understatement is as wrong as over-statement. The artist in his portrayal of nature, if he fails to catch expression,

* Pascal and other sermons, p. 30.

† Robert Browning. One Word More.

or misrepresents color or proportions, is not free from moral blame. He who sets out for the stars must at least get above the house-top. The poet when he lends himself to the grateful task of reproducing the harmony that has breathed itself into his soul is under bonds to the spirit not to make poetry a jest. The orator or preacher, to whom it has been given to call the armies of righteousness to battle, may not give forth an "uncertain sound" without incurring moral guilt. It is not sufficient to perceive truth, or even to feel it. It must be conveyed. The obligation is upon the speaker to transfer the impression that the truth has made upon himself to his audience; and this requires purity and sympathy of tone, correctness of inflection, grace of action, force of presentation.

Thus there enters into the province of all the servants of truth that which we call *art*. To divorce truth and art is to put asunder those whom God has joined together. Art should not be allowed to dominate truth; but without art truth is dumb and halting.

The prominence of the ethical element in expression is indicated by the fact that the great hindrance to complete and effective expression is morbid self-consciousness, in the form either of pride or self-distrust.

> "The skin-deep sense
> Of mine own eloquence"

imparts the jarring discordant note that vitiates the work of art, weakens the message, discolors the truth. If the selfishness, the self-consciousness, but be eliminated from the speaker, the author, the artist, the musician, so that he might throw himself, with self-forgetful enthusiasm, into his work or his message, how would the world thrill with truth!

Moral obligation is ubiquitous. It pervades human activity in every form and sphere. The instant the self within seeks expression its activity comes under ethical principles which determine its character. Ethics demands and controls self-expression. Every life is under obligation to express in some way, in deed, or word, or work, the truth which has been given it.

Perfect expression of truth it is impossible to reach. Limitations exist on every side. There is something akin to pain in being unable to give expression to what is within one. To have the sea of thought and feeling thrust back by the dykes of training and habit and impotence baffles and disheartens. No one knows himself, or realizes his deficiencies, until he tries to express himself. This act reveals all his limitations and defects, physical, mental, and moral. "It is in the blossom of a plant that the plant's defects become conspicuous; it is when all a man's faculties combine for the complex and delicate office of expression that any fault which is in him will come to the surface." Yet this is no apology for remaining dumb.—*Education.*

We do not know of any detail question now pending which demands more study than, How to treat the subject of English in School. We have seen several good suggestions but not a wholly satisfactory one. There are so many different objects to be accomplished by the teaching in this subject that each person adopts a method which will best secure the object which his judgment emphasizes most. Here are some of the objects to be aimed at in the class in English in the order in which our judgment weighs them: (1.) To make the class enjoy the reading of English classics, to give the pupils a relish for such reading. (2.) To train them in the habit of sharp, thoughtful reading. (3.) To help them in English composition—a vast topic. (4.) To develop the literary sense. (5.) To expand the true critical faculty.

VALUE OF PSYCHOLOGY.*

BY JAMES GIBSON HUME, M.A., PH.D., PROFESSOR UNIVERSITY OF TORONTO.

WE may consider the importance of psychology to the teacher in (I.) the discovery of the interrelations of different lines of study; (II.) in organizing and systematizing his own mental life; (III.) in guiding the process of bringing together the subject of study and the student; that is, in helping the teacher as director, student and educator.

I. THE TEACHER AS DIRECTOR.

The teacher must know something about the interrelations of different studies. It is his work to arrange the time-table and programme of work, and frequently to teach several of the subjects. Even where he is restricted to the teaching of some specialty, he should know how his special subject is related to the others pursued by the pupils he is teaching. Does psychology occupy such a place as to make it specially valuable in seeing the interrelations of various studies? Let us examine.

When it divides studies into three great classes:

The natural sciences, the mental sciences, and the philosophical enquiries.

He claims that psychology is complementary to the natural sciences, assisting in the treatment of problems otherwise inadequately solved; that it is the foundation of the mental sciences, as dealing with the simple data and underlying principles of these, and, lastly, it is the natural preparation for and introduction to the philosophical enquiries.

That psychology is complementary to the natural sciences may be illustrated by a number of commonplace and well-known instances, as the case of the "personal equation" in astronomy, where it becomes necessary to take account of the apperception and reaction time of the observer who is using the transit instrument or serious mistakes will arise in the calculated results. Other familiar examples illustrate that the abstracted, mathematical, and physical properties of the observed phenomena do not alone fully explain the appearances, e.g., the larger apparent size of the moon when near the horizon: the apparent motion of the sun. Many simple, but striking examples may be taken from what are termed optical illusions, as when lines are drawn from a point midway between two parallel lines, cutting the parallel lines at various angles, cause the parallel lines to seem to curve outward, while lines drawn from points outside of the parallel lines to an imaginary line drawn midway between the parallel lines make the parallel lines appear to curve inward, etc. The cases of color contrasts are also simple exemplications of this psychical component, as for instance, a gray strip on a white and black background will appear whiter on the black background, darker on the white background. Or a strip of gray placed on a background of red, and the same gray placed on a background of blue will appear not as gray, but as shades of pink and yellow respectively, etc., etc. The British Scientific Association places psychology among the natural sciences in its meetings, making a sub-section of physiology. The American Scientific Association places it under the mental sciences, making it a sub-section of anthropol-

*An address delivered before the O. E. A., Toronto, Canada, April, 1897.

ogy. It belongs to both places. Only a slight examination is required to see that, for the mental sciences, psychology is just as fundamental as mathemathics is for the natural sciences. Note any recent advances in the mental sciences and you will detect it resting upon insight into and application of some psychological principle. Look at the new methods of teaching grammar, not before, but through the language to which it belongs. Look at the complete revolution in method in the manner of teaching and using rules. Once first, now last in the process. Once announced and memorized, now discovered, constructed, and applied by the pupil himself. Look at the improvement in history as in such books as Green's "Short History of the English People," going beneath the events to the life of the people, their aims and passions, and the analysis of the character and motives of the chief actors.

Look at the improvements in political economy of late years by the introduction of psychological and ethical considerations and the historical method. What may we expect in law when some of the time spent on procedure in criminal law is turned to the study of the criminal himself?

As to the value of psychology as an introduction to the philosophical enquiries an objection might be raised that all of these, philosophy, æsthetics, and theology, claiming to deal with the true and beautiful and good as ideals, are ultimately based on metaphysics, and the less we have to do with metaphysics the better. Modern philosophy, however, should not be confounded with the much misunderstood and much maligned mediæval disputations any more than modern chemistry with alchemy, modern astronomy with astrology, or modern biology and medical science with the views of Theophrastus Bombastus Paracelsus. And even the superseded past should be remembered with some gratitude and respect, as the progenitor of the present: "Honor thy father and thy mother." Those who cry out most loudly against metaphysics, past or present, are, in almost every case, the unconscious victims of the shallowest and most erroneous forms of metaphysical speculation. It is philosophical speculation carefully conducted which has done most to expose false principles and to amend crude and erroneous standpoints. If we mean by philosophy, reflection on the meaning of experience, reconsideration of the significance of the results gained in scientific investigations, then instead of saying, "No one should have anything to do with philosophy," we should rather say, "Every one should have something to do with philosophy." Every one who reflects on the meaning of life and its experiences, who desires to pass beyond the mere appearances to discover their worth and importance for life-conduct and destiny is to that extent a philosopher. It is necessary to specialize in science to gain results. But every scientist in every field has not only the privilege, but also the duty to give more than mere details connected with his specialty. He should endeavor to give hints concerning their ultimate meaning, as this is revealed to him. At any rate the teacher cannot be a mere pedant. He must be a man, as well as scholar, and he will give a respectful hearing to such investigations, and cultivate an intelligent interest in them. For this, psychology is a useful introduction and preparation.

May we not conclude that psychology stands in such a central position and in such intimate connection with every branch of enquiry that it is peculiarly fitted to assist in their coordination?

II. THE TEACHER AS STUDENT.

It is scarcely necessary to say anything about the importance of continual study to the teacher. He must keep alive his interest in what he is teaching by continually enriching his mind by new inquiries and acquisitions. Our studies should be organized. Each new discovery should be made to throw light upon everything we already know. By reflectively, actively organizing in this way, the mind gains strength and insight, keeps alive its old interests and creates new ones. Thus study is made delightful and fruitful. Thought is trained to become consecutive and successful. The teacher himself should be of this type, and he should have psychological insight to enable him to guide his pupil to attain to this standpoint.

III. THE TEACHER AS EDUCATOR.

What the teacher acquires and gains in his own self-culture is as teacher a means; the end sought by him is the training of pupils. He must stimulate and awaken interest. He desires to make the subject of study a means to transform the whole character of the subject who studies. In order to accomplish this, the teacher must keep in mind the logical order of correct presentation of the subject of study; the stage of development and powers of the pupil, and the laws and processes of his mental growth, that he may gain the result, the developed pupil. In order of presentation he must proceed from the simpler to the more complex, and the simpler is not the most abstract, but the most concrete; for he must also proceed from the known to the less known. He must arrange the presentation so that a puzzle or problem is proposed and suggested to the pupil and his curiosity aroused to endeavor to solve it. The teacher must sympathetically place himself at the pupil's standpoint, if he desires the pupil to advance to his standpoint. In order to do this, he should endeavor to recall the stages and processes whereby he as pupil proceeded when he was at the stage now occupied by his pupil. The ability to do this probably accounts for the fact that in many cases an English-speaking teacher will be more successful in teaching pupils the rudiments of a foreign language than a native. It may also account for the fact that so large a proportion of inexperienced teachers succeed as well as they do.

The most important service of psychology to the teacher is that it leads him to consciously and systematically study his pupils, and thus awakens or intensifies his interest in them. Surely if a doctor becomes interested in the discovery of new diseases and new remedies for them, a teacher should be interested in each new pupil, and in each experiment for that pupil's improvement. An individualized interest makes a teacher as careful of his pupils as a fond mother is of her children. He is on the alert to see that the physical well-being of the child is not neglected. Has the child bad habits of sitting, or standing, or walking, or breathing? He discovers the cause, and endeavors to correct, kindly, wisely, and at once. Proper physical habits conduce to health and to morality. Is the child untidy or unmannerly? The teacher leads him by example and considerate advice. The child is respected and is taught to respect himself. Is the child dull and stupid? The teacher endeavors to find out if ill-health or poor food or ill-usage at home is the cause; he encourages the child to play, and soon it will turn out that the teacher is found visiting the home and endeavoring to arouse parental solicitude, and gain parental co-operation. This teacher will not neglect lighting, heating, or ventilation; he will be careful not to unduly fatigue his pupils, and will be found supervising their plays without officious interference. He will even be found guarding the outhouses and walls from the desecration of perverted vandalism. He will be the guide, counsellor, and confidential friend of the adolescent pupils, guarding them with solicitude and watchfulness in this critical period of unstable equilibrium, when the nature is plastic and responsive to the promptings of the highest ideals, and when, on the other hand, the danger is so great of the beginnings of perverted habits and criminal tendencies arising if the pupils are neglected and allowed simply to "grow up;" like Topsy or Ruth Bonnython.

Let us now recall some examples of assistance from psychology in arrangement of time-table and presentation of the subject of study. The thoughtful teacher will distinguish between the more severely logical and mathematical studies on the one hand and the more historical, discursive, and literary on the other. For the former more concentrated attention is required, and therefore these should come in the early part of the programme. When it comes to reviewing it will turn out that the second class of studies require more repetition and reviewing. Pupils should, however, be taught to recall directly what they have previously read and studied, without using the book to assist them. The memory should be trained in self-reliance. Perhaps it is in connection with memory that most people would think of the assistance of psychology to the student.

Kant says memory may be mechanical, ingenious, or judicious. I think it must be confessed that the earliest attempts to apply psychology in assisting and directing memory training were chiefly of the "ingenious" kind, discovering curious and arbitrary connections in accordance with the law of the association of ideas through similarity, contrast, and contiguity. Many text-books seem to be constructed with the view of employing the mechanical memory. It is supposed that the briefer the summary, the easier it will be to learn and remember. The student is supposed to con over the tables and learn them by repetition.

A deeper insight will indicate more "judicious" methods. The great rule for memory is, "Take care the knowing, and the recollecting will take care of itself." Let the subject be taught and studied logically, systematically, thoroughly, and woven as widely as possible into the warp and woof of the mental interests and thoughts of the pupil. In this way the time spent on one subject is not taken from all others, but is contributing to all others. It is a popular fallacy to suppose that all the time spent on one subject is subtracted from all others. The trained and experienced teacher educates all the powers of his pupils, and utilizes every subject for this purpose. He keeps clearly before his view the results to be attained, carefully selects the most efficient means, and with solicitude and interest observes the process. He desires the full and harmonious development of all the powers and capabilities of the pupil, physical, mental, social, moral, and religious. He is aware that he is co-operating with the pupil in the formation of character. Is there anything of higher value? This thought makes the teacher reverent; it impresses him with a sense of his responsibility; it also enables him to respect his profession and see in it one of the noblest efforts of human endeavor. Although our public schools are sometimes accused of giving a merely intellectual drill, no teacher worthy of the name is limiting his efforts to this. He is bending every energy to attain discipline and training of character by means of the intellectual and disciplinary; he strives to inculcate ideals and form habits of faithfulness, honesty, uprightness, industry, truthfulness, obedience, reverence.

Mark, he is not teaching *definitions* of these. That would be a merely intellectual drill. He is molding the character into these moral habits. It is just because the public schools are so efficient that Sunday-school and home continually desire to relegate more and more to the public school.

The careful and reverent study of the child is destined to react upon home, Sunday-school and church. If child nature had been studied, should we find the text "Except ye become as little children, ye cannot enter the kingdom of God" so continually misinterpreted to mean that there should be passive admission of truth without questioning or enquiry? Is that the way the child learns or acts? Should not our religious life exhibit the same fearless confidence in asking questions, and at once put into practice the answers as the active child does? It would be a wide field to follow the pernicious effects of unpsychological methods of parents and teachers in the suppressing of questions and stifling the religious cravings of children. We have too often "offended these little ones." Sooner or later, truer psychological methods, as exemplified in the kindergarten, will permeate the whole school system and overflow into the Sunday-school, the church and the home. Let me add to the teacher interested in the study of psychology and its applications to his profession: Remember that the science of psychology, with all its intrinsic importance and immediate usefulness, is simply the portal and propedeutic to the higher reflective problems of the ultimate significance of life, and art, and moral conduct, and religious aspiration. As in your teaching you desire the intellectual to be the means to lift up the pupil to higher ground, prepare him for the reception of the highest truths. So let these lofty themes be in your own life constant topics of interest, perennial sources of new insight, continual fountains of noblest inspiration.

PEDAGOGY OF THE HAT-TAKER.

I GOT a sort of pedagogical "sermon" the other day, in a place where I least looked for one—a lesson on learning from a source that I had never before dreamed of containing anything worth mentioning.

It is written in the Book: "Lift up your eyes, and behold the fields already white for the harvest." And sometimes we think the grain isn't even sown yet! Let us go to, and lift up our eyes!

I was in a hotel, and went to dinner. As I was about to enter the dining-room, a young negro took my hat, and put it on a rack with a couple of hundred more of about the same sort, size, and description. You have all seen the same thing done scores of times. I'm not telling of the unusual. It is not the unusual that is of the greatest interest in this world.

When I came out of the dining-room, half an hour later, there stood the young negro with my hat in his hand, ready for me! He had never seen me before, nor I him. He put no mark on my hat, nor on me. He simply looked at me and at my hat when we parted company, and he was ready to unite us again when it came time for us to be reunited. That is the whole story of what he did for me. Of course, it goes without saying that what he did for me he did for each one of the three hundred men who took dinner at the hotel that day.

How did he do this? That is what I wondered about, too, and that is what I'm going to tell about, as well as I can.

When the rush of dinner was over, I went and stood beside the young negro, and began talking to him in a quiet way. I told him that I was greatly interested in what he was doing, and asked him if he could explain to me how he did it. He said he had never thought about trying to tell how he did it, and that he didn't think he could tell very much about it. However, we chatted on for a while, and gradually I got from him what follows:

"You see," he said, "in the first place, when I made up my mind to follow this business, *I knew just what I wanted to do, and I began to study on the best way to get to do it.*"

Now I would like to call your attention, my dear reader, to those italicized words, and have you pause and reflect on them for a minute or two. It seems to me they contain the very essence of the secret of learning and mastery. If we can, in any way, get our pupils to "know just what they want to do," and to studying on "how they can get to do it," we shall have solved the bulk of the educational problem for every pupil that we can get into this condition.

"I understand, then," I said, "that you couldn't always do the act, but that you had to learn it, just as other folks learn things?"

And he replied, "Oh, yes! I had to learn it, and it took me about three years to get it down fine, so that I wouldn't make any mistakes. But I've got it now. I don't want to brag, but I would be willing to bet money that I can take a thousand hats from a thousand men, as they pass by me, put the hats aside, and give them back to the men without a mistake."

"Well, can't you give me some idea of how you went to work to learn to do this?" I asked.

He scratched his head for a minute, and then said, "Well, I never told any one about it before, but, if you care to know, I can tell you just how I began, anyhow. I got some little slips of stiff white paper about as long and as wide as your finger, and I took a pencil and marked numbers on the ends of these slips, the same number on each end. Then, when a man gave me his hat, I'd tear one of these slips in two in the middle, give one-half to the man, and stick the other half in the hat-band. So you see I had checks on every hat, and when the men presented their checks all I had to do was to hunt up the hat to match, and there you were. This made a sure thing, every time, *and gave me a chance to hold down my job until I could learn what I wanted to.*"

It is marvellous what genuine wisdom there is just running to waste in this world! I commend a careful re-reading of these italicized words also.

And then he went on, "I did this, and didn't take any chances for a good while, till I got to doing it just naturally, as you might say, and then I began to branch out a little on what I was after. You see, a fellow can't make breaks, in a house like this, or he'll get fired, too quick. So I went slow, but I got there."

"The first I tried, without checks, was this way. *I began a little at a time.* I'd see, almost every day, some peculiar-looking man with a peculiar-looking hat. I'd take a good look at the combination, and put such a man's hat aside without any check. That's the way I began to do what I do now for everybody. And the more I looked at men and their hats the better it appeared I could couple 'em, so to speak ; and I kept on doing it, a little at a time, till now, just as soon as I see a man and a hat together once, it seems like they just naturally stay in my mind that way."

I asked him if he seemed to see any particular mark on each hat, but he said no, that "somehow the man and the hat just seemed to belong together, and they just stayed that way in his mind." He said, too, that he did not place the hats in any given order on the rack, or try to remember them that way. At supper-time he let me mix up the hats then on deposit—more than a hundred—and, while it took him a little longer to find them, yet, almost as though he had a sixth sense, he would pick the right hat every time!

I wonder if he had a sixth sense!

"No," he said, "everybody can't learn to do it. I've seen ever so many try it and fall down. I guess a fellow has got to be born for this sort of thing, if he ever gets perfect in it. Some can learn it pretty well, and some will blunder, even with checks; but some can learn it perfect."

He told me, later, that he had been through a high-school, but that he didn't think what he learned there did much to help him to learn his present trade. "Though," he added, "I don't go back on my schooling; it did a good thing for me; *but schooling is one thing and getting a living is another thing.*"

Pondering his words, and wondering how true they might be, I gave him my hat and went in to supper. Then it came to me that here was a good lesson in pedagogy, so I went to my room and wrote it down.—*From S. S. Times, July 24, 1897.*

THE SOLIDARITY OF TOWN AND FARM.*

IN 1870, according to Carroll D. Wright, 46.72 per cent. of all the persons engaged in gainful occupations were employed in farming. In 1890 only 36.44 per cent. were so employed. The farms lost ten per cent. in these 20 years. The same causes which produced that great movement of population to the towns are still operative. The rush to the cities continues, and will continue. Nor is this movement confined to this country. The same thing has taken place in Europe. Such cities as Berlin and Budapest have grown in recent years almost as rapidly as Chicago or Buffalo. For this tendency to leave the farm and seek his fortune in the town, it is common to lay great blame on the shoulders of the farmer's boy. Many good people have thought that if we could in some way surround the country youth with more comforts and pleasures, if we could relieve the solitude and monotony of the farm, he would stay at home and become a wiser and a better man. Various schemes to this end have been devised, and have come to naught. The fact is that, broadly speaking, men leave the farms because they are not needed there. The introduction of labor-saving machinery and rapid transportation has produced the same result in agriculture as in other kinds of manufacturing. A smaller number of men working in our fields turn out a much greater product than the greater number of laborers could possibly secure in olden times, and the products of all lands are easily carried to where they are needed. It is not

* Dr. A. C. TRUE, Director of the Office of Experiment Stations, U.S., Department of Agriculture, in the *Arena*, Boston, March.

love of the town so much as necessity to earn a livelihood off the farm which drives boys to the town and makes them competitors in the great industrial struggles at the centres of population.

The clear apprehension of the great fundamental fact that the conditions of agriculture are steadily approximating to those of our other great industries is very important at this crisis in the industrial life of the world. To be successful to-day the farmer must think and work as other business men think and work. The farmer is begining to arouse himself to the real merits of the great labor controversy, to feel that he cannot afford to be a mere buffer against which agitation may recoil, to see that at bottom his interests are one with those of the toilers in the factory and the mart. It is, I think, very desirable to lay stress upon the great common interests of town and farm at this time, because in some important ways the superficial tendencies of modern industrial development have seemed to widen the breach between city and country life. Thus far the tide of industrial success seems to have run in the direction of vast accumulations of wealth in the hands of a few men, accompanied with the rapid development of vast hives of industry where these accumulations are stored. The pomp and glory of the city are no longer a thing which belongs to the state and seems to reflect the greatness and power of the community. It is rather the material success of the individual which is impressed upon the visitor to Boston, New York or Chicago. The increase and concentration of wealth in large towns have also produced complex social habits and distinctions which make the country man feel less and less at home there. But I believe that these separating tendencies which occupy so much of the attention of the popular mind to-day are only superficial, and that down underneath them is an irresistible current of common interest and sympathy which is drawing men closer together to work for human elevation and welfare. From the farm the city largely gets the fundamentals of physical life, of manufactures and of commerce. Business men know how much depends upon the success or failure of the crops. However much the relative importance of agriculture may decline as our industrial system grows more complex, it must always remain one of our greatest industries. What folly then to propose or attempt any scheme of trade, transportation or finance based on the selfish interests of either town or farm alone! Great accumulations of wealth, wrung out by any unfair dealing with the multitude of toilers on our farms, will ruin our great cities and the civilization they represent just as surely as the treasures of plundered provinces enriched but destroyed the city of the seven hills. If the farmer borrows hard cash of his brother, and then is pursuaded to plead the homestead act, or any other poor excuse to repudiate half his debt, the city man is not the only sufferer. The farm must pay its honest debts as well as the town.

From the farm come in large measure the strength and vigor of great cities. Call the roll of great manufacturers, merchants, bankers, teachers, preachers, and officials in any large city, and you will be surprised to find how many of these leaders in metropolitan enterprises are graduates of the farm. When the new blood that flows into the city's arteries is tainted or diluted at its source, what reason have we to expect that the city's moral health or vitality will continue? History shows that it will not. To a greater extent than most men are aware of, the health of a great city depends on the quality of the products which it receives from the farm. The United States government inspects the meat as it is received at our great cities. Your purses, too, will be affected by the kind of farming done in the neighborhood of your city. In the vicinity of a certain city the farmers are too ignorant or too lazy to raise good chickens or vegetables. The market men are obliged to send long distances to get the grade of produce demanded by their customers. Can a city afford to be surrounded by an unintelligent and shiftless yeomanry? The great change which recent times have brought in the summer habits of city people is an ever increasing means of bringing into clearer light the common interests of farm and town. City boarders are beginning to see that the farmer's surroundings and mode of life may largely affect them for weal or woe. It may be truthfully said to have brought farm and town together on the matter of good roads. How all of a sudden thousands of city people have discovered that it is a matter of vital importance that good roads shall be built to aid the farmer who hauls his produce into town—and incidently to accommodate the bicyclist who rides out of town!

The attempt to purify city politics and revive civic pride and self-respect is very encouraging. But this must not be done to the neglect of the interest of the State, which, after all, is the great unit of our national life. In general, to sum up, the problem of our times is not how to send men back to the farms where they are not needed, not how to scatter population into myriads of little communities, but how to raise the level of farm life and farm product, to more thoroughly organize the great towns, to improve the means of communication between farm and town, and to harmonize the manifold elements which compose the modern state, so that each will do its appointed work in the best manner, and the interests of all the people will be conserved. There is a grand old word used in Thanksgiving proclamations in Massachuetts which, taken to heart, should bring town and farm into closest sympathy. Let us never forget that, wherever we may dwell, strong bonds unite us as members of the "commonwealth."

THE TEMPERATURE OF ARID REGIONS.

Mr. Willis L. Moore, chief of the United States weather bureau, and therefore an accepted authority on matters pertaining to climate, expressed the opinion, in a recent paper on "Some Climatic Features of the Arid Region," that the ideal climate as regards equality of temperature and absence of moisture does not exist in the United States. Such a climate, he says, is found only on the plateaus of the tropics, as, for example, at Santa Fe de Bogota, in Colombia; where the average annual temperature is about 59°. The southeastern part of the United States has the nearest approach to this ideal temperature. Even in the southwest the range of variation is too great, and the rainfall reaches from nothing to a point greater than is to be found in the Eastern or Middle States. The study of meteorological conditions is most interesting, the flavor of speculation that is about it rendering it charmingly attractive. Experts tell us that ranges of temperature depend upon the dryness of the air and the clearness of the sky. Thus, while the summer temperature of the Southwest is high, the real degree of heat as felt by animal life is not indicated by the common thermometer, but by a mercurial thermometer, the bulb of which is wet at the time of the observation. In this manner is shown the temperature of evaporation, the sensible temperature and, more nearly than can otherwise be indicated, the actual heat of the body.

The inland valleys and plains east of the Rocky mountain foothills have an average summer temperature of from 65° on the north to 80° on the Gulf coast. While the daytime heat in the arid regions seems excessive, it is not really so, owing to the extreme dryness of the atmosphere. It is, as is well known, the moist, "sticky" heat that is prostrating. Again, in these regions the radiation at night is so great that the temperature is made tolerable, and, indeed, comfortable. Estimated by the temperature of evaporation, the arid region is the coolest part of the country. The falling of temperature from the time of the greatest heat is irregular and not at all dependent upon longitude reckoned west from Greenwich. Mr. Moore cites as an example of this the fact that the temperature falls as much by 6 p.m. in Denver as it does by 8 p.m. in New York and Philadelphia. This is accounted for in the greater daily range and more rapid rate of cooling at elevated stations.—*Portland Oregonian.*

EDITORIAL NOTES.

JOHN MUNRO

(Teacher)

Departed this Life at Toronto, Aug. 7, 1897.

Requiescat in pace.

Mr. John Munro was born in Tain, Ross-shire, Scotland, August, 1852. He came to this country with his parents while he was still very young, and after taking the Public and High School courses he studied at the Normal School, Toronto, then under the Principalship of Rev. Dr. Davies, and from this institution he graduated with the highest certificate, that of First A. He also held from the Normal School an inspector's certificate, obtained at a special examination such as was then held for the purpose. He first taught near the Village of Hespeler, from which place he went to Blair, and subsequently to several schools in Waterloo County. Thereafter he went to Ottawa, where he for the past fifteen years held the position of principal of the Central School. For several years he held the Presidencies of the Teachers' Associations in Carleton County and Ottawa City, and at the last meeting of the Ontario Educational Association, which was held in this city, the teachers of Ontario evinced their opinion of him by electing him their President, the highest office in their gift. That his talents were recognized outside the teaching profession was shown by the fact that he was once proposed in Ottawa as candidate for the Local House.

There was a disposition in the Eastern part of Ontario, some seventeen or more years ago, to form another teachers' association to be independent of the one which had been organized in 1860 and which usually met in Toronto. Mr. Munro was one of the men who influenced, by word and act, the teachers in the Eastern part of the province not to form such an association. Every year found Mr. Munro in his place at the meeting of the Provincial Association, and by his presence and wisdom he contributed materially to the success and efficiency of the Annual Convention of Teachers.

He was a man of retiring disposition, simple, modest and kindly in his manner, but by those who knew him he was highly esteemed for his kindness and ability. He was one of the most ardent and enthusiastic teachers in this Province, and had travelled in Europe and on this continent for the purpose of self-improvement, that he might impart what he thereby obtained to his pupils and the teaching profession generally. He was unmarried.

The British Association for the Advancement of Science held its 67th meeting this year in Toronto, 18-25th August. This is admittedly the most important scientific meeting this year in the world. This is not the first time that the British Association has visited Canada, it met in Montreal in 1884, so that some of its members can take note of Canada's progress. But to the great majority of the members of the Association Canada is a new country. And now they have an opportunity of seeing what Canada as a country is, her wealth of natural resources, her commerce, charities and schools. Canada is glad to welcome the Association to this part of the British Empire, and hopes that its members will feel at home wherever they may choose to journey within its wide domain, for it is all theirs, British to the core.

This year the Education Department has taken special care to let the public know and understand that the fact of a candidate, passing or not passing any of the annual examinations conducted by it, has nothing whatever to do with the question of promotion in the schools. The responsibility for promotion rests entirely on the principal of the school. This is well, for the internal management of a school is what no department of a government can profitably manage.

In recognition of this obvious truth, and to make it more easily remembered by all concerned, it would be advisable to change the names of the examinations, and designate them so that there be no reference to any form m the schools. The principal must take the responsibility, therefore it is only reasonable that he should not be handicapped in any way in the performance of his duty.

One of the most interesting topics of discussion among teachers at the present moment is the appearance of the new Dominion School History, and when the character of the book has been thoroughly canvassed, there may arise a desire to know the whole history of the movement that led to its production. The opinion seems to prevail that the true school history of Canada has yet to be written, but the man who undertakes the work will hardly be as fortunate as Mr. Clements, when he comes to put it on the market, nor will he be wise to make the venture until Mr. Clement's work has been fully tested as a school text-book. The latter is now in the hands of our teachers, and from them alone is to come the verdict, that will perpetuate or condemn it, as a work in the preparation of which neither expense nor pains have been spared. One of our correspondents has raised a question in connection with its preparation, which we are sure the committee will only be too glad to answer when time has been given them to render a full account of their work.

Of the papers set for the annual July examination, the one found most fault with was the Geometry paper for the Senior Leaving, or Honor

Matriculation. Every one who knows Geometry will acknowledge that the paper in question is one well conceived and well constructed to test a candidate's knowledge of the subject. The objection to it is that what little of book-work there is on it is so disguised that the candidate might easily regard the whole of the paper as made up of deductions, *i.e.* original work, and thus become discouraged. If the plan of giving the number of the propositions were followed in this paper as in the other geometry papers, this difficulty would have been removed. The general opinion of masters is that the said paper was too difficult, in which opinion we concur. But, we add, that though it is quite true that geometry is the most difficult branch on the programme of studies, requiring, when treated as it was this summer by the examiner, a developed and active scientific imagination, yet candidates can be prepared if the Education Department will continuously set the same type of paper as was set this year. But to attain to this high requirement there must be continuity; there must be no such thing as a difficult paper one year, and an easy one the next.

Dr. Harper, one of the leading educational spirits in Quebec, has also been giving his views of the educational situation in Quebec, and we have been able to secure a report of the address of welcome he recently gave at a reception to a convention of teachers from the United States, who happened to hold their annual convention this year in Montreal. The points of reform which that gentleman has been emphasizing of late in his public addresses are three in number, and we have no doubt that, in the event of their being accomplished, Quebec will soon attain to the position in the educational world which she ought to hold, as the oldest province in our confederation of colonies. These three points are properly brought out in his address, which we will insert in our next issue, and which are as follows: (1) An improved system of training involving the re-organization of the Normal schools of the province, so that they may provide capable trained teachers for all the public schools in the country districts as well as in the towns and cities; (2) an increase in the salaries of the teachers by a change in the method of distributing the grants; and (3) an introduction of the system of superintendency as a supplement or enlargement of the inspector's influence. As is to be seen from what Mr. Marchand says, the local government is at present engaged in examining into the details of the present system, and it has become almost an open secret that the appointment of a Minister of Education is likely to be one of the outcomes of its deliberations, involving a thorough re-organization of the Department of Public Instruction, so that it may come into closer touch with the people, and be animated with a direct zeal to introduce progressive methods in every section of its administrative operations.

A breeze has been excited in the educational circles of St. John, New Brunswick, over the enforced withdrawal of Mr. George U. Hay from the management of the Girls' High School of that city. From all accounts it would appear that the affairs of the St. John Board of School Trustees are in anything but a promising condition. The withdrawal of Superintendent March, which took place some months ago, was also an enforced withdrawal, and the people of St. John are now inclined to enquire more carefully than is their wont into the ways the Trustees have of doing things, and the outer influcnees that seem to assist them so materially in coming to their decisions. There can be no doubt in any one's mind that the blending of two such important positions as the superintendency of the city schools and the principalship of the Grammar School is an unwise step to take, and if it be proved to have been only a means to an end, the end being the resignation of Mr. Hay, the matter will not in all probability die for lack of discussion. In this connection, we have to say that there is far too much of the indirect method of "squeezing out" practised by some of our school boards, and Mr. Hay's complaint of having been ignored in order that his enemies might say that he kept himself too much aloof from his employers, gives the clue to the method adopted to discredit him as a public servant, which are by no means new in the experience of other public officers.

While the attempt is being made to foster a national spirit with "Canada First" for its watchword, through the efforts of the Committee on a new School History for Canada, the rulers of the city of Quebec are running away from the historic notion, and have been seized with something like a passion against the antique on and around Cape Diamond. Of course it is said that if the modern improvements of city life necessitate the removal of walls and fortifications and other relics of the past, so much the worse for the relics of the past, and so much the better for the policy of the city corporation of the ancient capital in their attempts to improve and beautify off the face of the earth what they have never for a moment thought to contemplate as belonging to any one but themselves. Not long ago, the writer stood watching the last of St. John's Gate as it was being removed to make way for the Quebec District Railway, and when the main strength of the structure came to be laid bare, and the bystanders were overheard discussing its original cost and the ceremonial of its opening as late as 1867, it was difficult to refrain from drawing the conclusion that somebody past or present had either been foolish or extravagant. But when Sir James LeMoine comes out over his own signature, and, while entering his protest, announces to us Canadians that the city walls are likely to go next, it is even easier to suppose a projected indiscretion on the part of somebody or other. Perhaps Sir James, backed up by his friend Mr. Kirby, has only been trying to frighten us. There may be nothing in the thing but a mere surmise. But if there be, the city council may find that the discussion over the project is not likely to find its limits on the streets or in the newspapers of Quebec. The walls of Quebec do not belong to the city of Quebec, but to the country at large, perhaps to Great Britain if the disbursers of the original cost have any claims, though it is to be hoped that the question of ownership will never be raised in any antagonist spirit. We Canadians want Quebec as an object lesson to the rising generation, an object lesson on the origin and growth of the country, and we want it as a commercial outlook also. But there must be no huckstering spirit in the advocacy either for or against the removal of the antiquities of the place. We want these antiquities preserved, not because we would hinder Quebec from taking advantage of all the modern improvements of city life, but because we take a national pride in them; and the citizens of Quebec should not want to keep them, either because the city may gain in revenue from increasing sightseers, or because there would be more money gained to the city to get rid of them. There are surely some higher motives than these in Canada, when we seek to preserve what is our own, and what can never be replaced. It would be an anomaly surely for us to spend thousands of dollars in the preparation of a history of Canada which can be superseded by a better perhaps any day, and at the same time countenance the effacement of the few landmarks which are the continuing proof that we really have a history of our own.

A correspondent of ours has written stating that the widening influence of the EDUCATIONAL MONTHLY, while it may be satisfactory to the great bulk of its readers, has given offence to one or two of the teachers of Montreal, simply because it has lately been devoting so much attention to the educational affairs of the Province of Quebec. It is no intention of THE MONTHLY to offend any one wittingly. The world is too wide nowadays for a narrow policy of personal aggrandizement in public argument. And yet it is as little the intention of its editor to stay his hand in promoting the public good, merely from the unwholesome fear of giving offence to some one or other who would rather not be disturbed in his methods of doing good to himself, irrespective of the public weal. Besides, it is hardly necessary to repeat that the EDUCATIONAL MONTHLY is not a provincial periodical. It is a teacher's magazine for Canada, and there is more impertinence in the criticism which our correspondent refers to than in any consideration we may have to give to the educational affairs of any province in the union. Indeed, there is not the shadow of an impertinence in anything we have said about Quebec affairs, nor of the affairs of the other provinces. THE MONTHLY is anxious to be on the side of educational progress, as it may be witnessed anywhere in Canada or elsewhere, and as long as its editor and contributors keep within the limits of a seemly logic in presenting their views, its advoçacies and exposures are quite legitimate.

THE EDUCATIONAL QUESTION IN QUEBEC.

There is a flavor of progress in the atmosphere which surrounds the educational activities of the Province of Quebec at the present time, and the hope is being expressed everywhere that something practical will come out of the counsellings that have been going on for some time. The Hon. Mr. Marchand, Premier of the Province, is reported as expressing himself to the following effect in one of our daily journals, and we have the hope of better things from the interviewer's report, which says :—

As the subject of educational reform is one of great moment just now to the people of this province, your correspondent took the opportunity of a pleasant chat with the Premier, Mr. Marchand, this week, to broach the important question of the changes in our school system contemplated by his Government, and to try to ascertain something of their nature and extent for the public information.

"You can say," replied the affable Premier, "that we are fully determined to carry out in office the progressive policy which we advocated in Opposition and to which we pledged ourselves during the general elections. We are giving the vital question of education our most serious attention and the most careful study in all its details, and we shall make an important start next session in that necessary direction by embodying in legislation the improvements which we believe to be desirable in order to place our school system as far as possible on a footing of equality with the best in any of the other provinces and to give to our people the same facilities and advantages to fit themselves for the battle of life as are supplied elsewhere. We fully recognize the fact that, to keep pace with the progress of the age and to maintain our influence in the Canadian Confederation, it is necessary not only to extend and popularize education among all classes and elements of our population, but to give it a more practical direction, in order to better equip our youth for the parts they will have to play in the future and to make them more useful and better citizens. We believe that this can never be done merely by increasing the educational grants as proposed by our predecessors, which would involve simply a further waste of the public money. Without some important improvement in our school system in the methods of teaching, it would be altogether idle to look or hope for educational progress and improvement."

To the query whether he had any objection to satisfy public curiosity and to prepare the public mind in some measure for the changes contemplated, Mr. Marchand smiled and said :—

"I do not think that our scheme has been sufficiently elaborated yet to warrant a definite statement of its precise nature and scope before it has been fully worked out and decided upon. Of course we know in a general way what we want and what we propose to do to attain the great end in view, and I would be glad to give the press, which takes such an enlightened interest in the cause of popular education and the moral and material elevation of the masses, all the information possible for the public benefit. But, as there are some important points still unsettled, I consider that it would not be wise to make any official announcement just yet. You see our people are very sensitive on this subject of education and it is therefore necessary to exercise caution and prudence in dealing with it. You remember the Italian proverb: "Qui va piano va sano." But you must not infer from this that there is any hesitation on our part to carry out our programme, that is to say, when it has been definitely settled. Do not fear—we shall 'get there' all the same. We know what the public expect from us and have a right to receive; but we also know that there are certain apprehensions to be dissipated, and we think that it is much better to endeavor to remove these at the start and to enlist in our patriotic work all the influences that can help it, than to allow false impressions, under hasty information, to array them against our policy of judicious reform. When this has been done, as I have good reason to hope that it will be at an early day, you can rest assured that we shall not keep an interested public long in the dark as to the precise nature and scope of our educational programme."

"Then, Mr. Premier," remarked the 'Witness' representative, "you are not prepared to state just yet what shape the proposed reorganization will take, whether, for instance, the head of the department will be a minister with portfolio, a commissioner with a seat in the council, or a member of the Council of Public Instruction?"

"To this question my reply," said the Premier, "must be that I am not at liberty yet to fully disclose our plans on this head. This must suffice for the present."

The conversation then branched off into a general discussion of the changes desirable in our present school systems when Mr. Marchand said that he wished it to be perfectly understood that he was opposed altogether to what had been termed godless schools. He believed in religious and moral training going hand in hand with secular education and in allowing the religious and moral teachers of the people to exercise a legitimate influence and control in the matter. Another point which he emphasized was the determination of his Government to bring the benefits of education home to the masses of the people, to popularize it with them, so to speak, and to impress them with the paramount importance and necessity in this age to make elementary education a prime consideration of the administration and the legislature and to render it more practical in keeping with the requirements and spirit of the times in which we live. But, as he truthfully pointed out, a change of this kind could not be brought about in a moment. It would have to be gradual; otherwise the working of the whole educational system of the province would be stopped, which would be disastrous. The task of reform would have to begin with the teachers, many of whom, though competent enough in other respects, were sadly lacking in knowledge of the proper methods of teaching and school discipline. The result of this was a state of anarchy among the pupils, which was fatal to the influence of the former and the progress of the latter. The Government hoped to gradually remedy this shortcoming without any serious wrench to the operation of our primary schools by giving the teachers the benefit of a course of pedagogy by means of regular lectures on the subject to be delivered in each district by a certain number of expert educationists and by holding out to them material inducements to profit by these lectures. These inducements might take the shape of additions to the teachers' salaries or money prizes to be awarded after official examination and verification of the results at the end of each yearly or half-yearly term as the case might be. "This," said Mr. Marchand, "will cost a relatively small sum to the province, and I am sure that it will be productive of good results."

Still another point upon which the Premier was most emphatic was the necessity of providing as far as possible for a uniformity of text-books, which, he considered, was one of the first steps to be taken before education could be popularized and fully brought within the reach of the masses, the cost of new text-books for their children on every change of school being a heavy tax upon poor parents and one of the greatest obstacles to the spread of education. As for free text-books, he said the Government was not prepared to say what might be done in that direction. A great deal on this and many other heads depended upon the financial condition of the province. However, something in this respect would probably be done for the poorer municipalities.

In conclusion, Mr. Marchand added that the Government's good will to improve the educational system of the province, to ameliorate the condition of the teachers, and to lighten the burdens on the people for school purposes, if not to remove them altogether, would be only restrained by its financial ability to undertake all the expenses necessary for these excellent objects. It could be depended upon, however, to go as far as the means at its command would permit, and to even make great sacrifices, to raise the educational status of our people and to enable them to compete on equal terms with all others in the stern battle of life.

CONVENTIONS.

THE members of the Epworth League met this year in convention in Toronto, July 15. About

24,000 delegates were present. The Hon. A. S. Hardy, premier of Ontario, made an opening address in which he paid a tribute to the character and influence in public affairs of Rev. Dr. Carman, the general superintendent of the Methodist Church in Canada. Dr. Carman, in his speech welcoming the delegates to Canada, spoke in earnest defense of conservatism in religion, and advocated aggressive temperance work in a manner that called forth enthusiastic cheers.

The educative influence of such meetings must be great indeed. Our young friends from across the line have a lesson in Geography, as regards Canada, with which they are highly pleased and which they will not forget. An estimate of the Convention is given by our townsman, as follows:

Rev. Dr. Wm. Briggs, Steward Wesleyian Book-Room: The convention is very helpful in an interstate direction as well as international. It not only touches Canada, but England, and will also do good to representatives of the smaller leagues who will feel the touch of the mighty army, and will serve to cultivate higher intelligence in the young people. The particular danger of the league is that the other departments, such as the literary and the social, may dim the spiritual department. The Wesley Guild of England is wise in making the class-meeting a prominent feature of its work.

The Conference of Charities and Correction, which is composed of delegates, men and women from all states of the Union south of us held its annual convention this year in Toronto. This body deals with some of the most difficult problems of human life, the care and reformation of the weak and fallen members of society. We give the closing paragraph of the president's address, as showing what spirit animates the Conference in its hard work:

"But even if we are living in a State where all these bad things are true, what is the course for us to take? Shall we fold our hands in idle despair? I hold a cheerful optimism, which makes me believe that the best we see to-day among the best people anywhere is a prophecy of what shall be universal some day. If we see the good and the hopeful possibilities, let the very difficulty of their attainment be our greatest incentive to effort. Does the present appear a grinding, hard, unlovely time? So did the great heroic days of old to the little men among those who lived in them. The golden age has never been the present time but always in the dim past or the misty future. Let us take this age of ours, with its hard problems, its sad duties, its littleness of public men, its dearth of great leaders, its lack of faith in the things that are unseen and eternal, its over-weening confidence in the sensual and material, its subjection to the powers of wealth and greed, and make of its enormous difficulties the opportunity of heroism. Let us live our lives so well and make so deep an impression on the lives of others that even this very end of the nineteenth century shall be for us the heroic age.

"He speaks not well who doth his time deplore,
Naming it new and little and obscure,
Ignoble, and unfit for lofty deeds.
All times were modern in the time of them,
And this no more than others. Do thy part
Here in the living day, as did the great
Who made old days immortal! So shall men,
Gazing long back to this far-looming hour.
Say: 'Then the time when men were truly men:
Though wars grew less, their spirits met the test,

Of new conditions, conquering civic wrongs;
Saving the State anew by virtuous lives;
Guarding their country's honor as their own,
And their own as their country's and their sons'.
Defying leagued fraud with single truth,
Not fearing loss, and daring to be pure.
When error through the land raged like a pest.
They calmed the madness caught from mind to mind,
By wisdom drawn from old, and counsel sane;
And as the martyrs of the ancient world
Gave Death for man, so nobly gave they Life;
Those the great days, and that the heroic age."

RECESSIONAL.

God of our fathers, known of old—
Lord of our far-flung battle-line—
Beneath Whose awful Hand we hold
Dominion over palm and pine—
Lord God of Hosts, be with us yet,
Lest we forget—lest we forget!

The tumult and the shouting dies—
The captains and the kings depart;
Still stands Thine ancient sacrifice,
A humble and a contrite heart.
Lord God of Hosts, be with us yet,
Lest we forget—lest we forget!

Far-called our navies melt away—
On dune and headland sinks the fire—
Lo, all our pomp of yesterday
Is one with Nineveh and Tyre!
Judge of the Nations, spare us yet,
Lest we forget—lest we forget!

If drunk with sight of power we loose
Wild tongues that have not Thee in awe—
Such boasting as the Gentiles use
Or lesser breeds without the Law—
Lord God of Hosts, be with us yet,
Lest we forget—lest we forget!

For heathen heart that puts her trust
In reeking tube and iron shard—
All valiant dust that builds on dust,
And guarding, calls not Thee to guard—
For frantic boast and foolish word,
Thy mercy on Thy People, Lord!
Amen.

—*Rudyard Kipling, in London Times.*

SCHOOL WORK.

ANNUAL EXAMINATIONS 1897.

SCIENCE.

Editor.—J. B. TURNER, B.A.

FORM III.

CHEMISTRY.

Examiners.—J. FOWLER, M.A., A. McGILL, B.A., J. C. McLENNAN, B.A.

The following are the papers that were assigned in Chemistry for the candidates from Form III. and IV. at the recent High School examinations.

The papers as a whole leave but little to be desired either from the standpoint of teacher of the subject, or of the candidate.

The paper of Form IV. might have contained a greater range of questions with advantage; the element magnesium, for example, receiving more attention than its importance in the curriculum demands.

NOTE.—*Candidates will take* ONE ONLY *of the alternatives in question 6.*

A diagram of the apparatus required, and every detail necessary to make the experiment workable, must be given.

1. Define the following terms, as used in Chemistry, and give illustrative examples :—*Allotropism, combustion, fusion, neutralisation, reduction.*

2. Write equations explanatory of the following reactions and interpret these equations in words :—

(*a*) The effect of heat upon potassium chlorate.

(*b*) The effect of heating nitrate of potassium with sulphuric acid.

(*c*) The effect of heating together chloride of sodium, sulphuric acid and manganese dioxide.

3. Describe minutely all the effects, physical and chemical, which occur in the following cases.

(*a*) Lumps of marble (chalk or limestone) are treated with hydrochloric acid, and the gas evolved is passed into lime water, as long as absorption takes place.

(*b*) The air-holes of a Bunsen burner are alternately opened and closed.

(*c*) A glass tube, inverted over water, is half-filled with nitric oxide, the mouth closed by a glass plate and the vessel shaken. It is replaced in the pneumatic trough, and the glass plate removed. A little oxygen is now passed in, the mouth again closed and the tube shaken. It is a second time opened under water.

4. Write a short description of the compounds which hydrogen forms with sulphur, with nitrogen and with chlorine.

5. Calculate :—

(*a*) The percentage composition, by weight, of carbonate of ammonia, its formula being $(NH_4)_2CO_3$.

(*b*) The weight of chlorate of potash required to produce 22.4 litres of oxygen, measured under normal conditions,

O = 16. N = 14. C = 12. K = 39 1. Cl = 35.5.

6. (*a*) Describe an experiment to show that hydrogen, under certain conditions, removes oxygen from oxide of copper; and indicate the nature of the resulting substances.

OR

(*b*) Describe an experiment to show that finely divided iron will, under certain conditions, decompose the oxide of hydrogen; and indicate the nature of the resulting substances.

1. Explain the following chemical terms :—*Empirical formula ; molecular formula ; rational (= constitutional or graphic) formula ; nascent state ; atomic heat.*

2. Hydrogen and ammonium are frequently referred to as metals. State, in the case of each of these, the reasons for such classification.

3. Write descriptive notes on Magnesium, and Aluminium, under the following heads :—

(*a*) Occurrence.

(*b*) Preparation in the free state.

(*c*) Analytical methods for their separation and special tests for their identification.

(*d*) Position in a general classification of the elements, with reasons.

4. Explain, by equations and otherwise, what occurs under the following circumstances :—

(*a*) A mixture of fluor spar (fluoride of calcium), sand and sulphuric acid is heated and the gas evolved is passed into water.

(*b*). A bell-jar filled with air is inverted over a basin containing water colored blue with litmus. A porcelain dish floats on the water (under the jar), and in it a piece of phosphorus is burnt.

(*c*) 10 grams of iron filings and 1 gram of sulphur are strongly heated together in a test tube, and the whole product is treated with excess of dilute sulphuric acid.

Fe = 56. S = 32.

5. What volume of dilute sulphuric acid, of specific gravity 1.6, and containing 55.93 per cent. by weight of sulphuric anhydride (sulphur trioxide) will be required to convert 5.4 kilogrammes of apatite (tricalcium phosphate) into superphosphate of lime (mono-calcium phosphate)?

S = 32. O = 16. Ca = 40. P = 31.

6. Ascertain what acid and what base are present in the simple salt furnished you. Give an account of your procedure in its analysis.

CONTEMPORARY LITERATURE.

In the last number of the *Littell's Living Age* will be found Prince Kropotkin's article on "Recent Science," originally published in the *Nineteenth Century*. The article in question is reported to contain a satisfactory explanation of dreams.

Those who are interested in combatting school twelve months in the year will find this subject introduced in a paper by the Rev. E. A. Kirkpatrick in the August *American Monthly Review of Reviews*. "The Progress of the World" in the same magazine deals with Canada's relation to Britain, the new tariff, and other political problems of present day interest.

The *Century* has not given way entirely to the summer's keen appetite for stories. It insists, instead, that its readers should take vastly improving journeys down the Hudson, and through Thessaly, Alaska, Java, and Norway. But then most of us love to be taught, and won't be satisfied unless we think we know something. Particularly charming is the light pen that writes of "London at Play," on this occasion at play by the sea on Margate Sands. Elizabeth Robins Pennell and Joseph Pennell together invariably mean a holiday from everything but artistic care. The short story called "Concealed Weapons" by Margaret Sutton Briscoe, is a very good short story indeed. The uncle and the niece are both persons who carry liking away with them.

The Youth's Companion for Aug. 25th does not contain so many pages as that interesting periodical often does, but it is as full as possible of stories good enough to be in the *Youth's Companion*, and that is saying a great deal. The first is a continued story about a farmer's boy who is going to invent something, if possible the milking machine he desires, before the end of the 4th chapter. "Companions of the Voyageurs" is about our own country. We have long desired to thank the *Youth's Companion* for its friendship to Canada, not seldom warmly and judiciously displayed.

The complete novel in *Lippincott's* for September is by an English writer, Margaret L. Woods. She has called her story "Weeping Ferry," and it is sad enough, but truly and gracefully told. The publishers are already beginning to prepare us for 1900 and all we must make it our duty to know by the time of the Paris Exposition. Theodore Stanton explains what share each nation will have in the gathering.

"On Being Human" is a title which attracts readers as flowers do bees. The writer, Woodrow Wilson, could not have chosen it without an instinct for comfort; it is the kind of article one expects to find in the *Atlantic Monthly.*, "An intemperate zeal for petty things" is one of its most happy phrases. But culling phrases, one comes upon this a few pages over in a letter of Dean Swift's, the man with the general reputation for sharpness. "Pray God bless and protect you and your little fireside," which was a pretty, hearty thing for any man to say. Good stories will be found in the September *Atlantic* by Frances Courtney Baylor, Alice Brown, Elia W. Peattie and others.

The last issue of *The New York Medical Journal* (Vol. LXVI, No. 6) contains, among several noteworthy articles, an excellent one on "Wounds of the Hand," by Dr. George W. Spencer, of Philadelphia. The article is illustrated by several photographs, and is interesting, not only to the professional reader, but to others. *The New York Medical Journal* is issued every Saturday, and is one of the best medical papers in America.

From Ginn and Company we have received the fifth book of "Zenophan's Anabasis," edited by A. G. Rolfe, and "The Finch Language Primer," by A. V. Finch, introducing three hundred words to the primary class.

From Harper and Brothers, New York, "A Laboratory Course in Wood-Turning," by M. J. Golden, M. E. and Johnson's Alexander Pope, edited by Kate Stephens.

Ginn & Company and the American Book Company have both had prepared series of writing books, modifications of the vertical.

Attinger Freres, Publishers of Neuchatel have recently issued a convenient and inexpensive edition of an Introduction au Nouveau Testament by F. Godet, comprising the accounts by Matthew, Mark and Luke.

From the American Book Company, New York, we have rereceived, "Bible Readings for Schools," edited by Nathan C. Schaeffer, D.D. "Asia," in Carpenter's Geographical Readers, "The Story of Troy" by M. Clark, and "Stories from the Arabian Nights," edited by M. Clark, in the Eclectic School Readings. "Fragments of Roman Satire from Ennius to Apuleius,' selected and arranged by E. I. Merrill, and "Freytag's Die Journalisten," edited by J. Norton Johnson.

D. C. Heath & Co., Boston, have recently issued. "Drei Beleive Lustsfiele," edited by B. W. Wells. "Materials for German Composition," by J. T. Hatfield, assisted by Jesse Eversz. Baumbach's Die Nonna, with English Notes by Dr. W. Bernhardt. "La Poudre Aux Yeux," by Labiche and Martin, edited by B. W. Wells, and "First Spanish Readings," selected and edited by J. E. Mahzke.

"The Forge in the Forest," an Acadian romance by Charles G. D. Roberts. (William Briggs, Toronto.)—The scene of this novel is laid in the country which has been made familiar to us by the poets of the eastern sea-bordering provinces of Canada. In addition to the exquisite description, which one might have reason to expect, the narrative contains human interest of considerable force and great charm, and together they form the story, wholesome, sweet and stirring, of one part of the life of Jean de Mer, Seigneur de Briart. At any time of the year the book would be better to read than most of the novels of the day, but it seems to have been specially designed for the desire of summer.

THE CANADA

EDUCATIONAL MONTHLY.

OCTOBER 1897.

AN ADDRESS OF WELCOME TO THE AMERICAN INSTITUTE OF INSTRUCTION.

DR. J. M. HARPER, QUEBEC.

IN presenting greetings from the Province of Quebec to the American Institute of Instruction my task is simple enough in itself, for as far as my commission goes I have only to extend the right hand of fellowship to you, sir, and the members of this old and world-famed educational organization, and humbly resume my place, as among those who desire to receive rather than to give advice. As a citizen of what may be called the oldest province in the Dominion of Canada, as well as in my capacity of President of one of our provincial teachers' associations, I certainly wish to bid you welcome to Quebec; may your visit here be long remembered as one bringing to you the largest measure of pleasure and profit, whatever may have been your motives in selecting the city of which we provincials are so proud, as the place of your convention this year. In such conventions as this the long continued strife of the philosophies over self-interest *versus* benevolence as the fundamental lines of the humanities, seems to have found a truce in the mutual benefit idea; and who will say that the mutual benefit idea is not as safe an ethical principle as empiricism is likely to find for us in this age of self-seeking? And hence in the greeting I extend to you there must be no one-sidedness. The give and take between us must at least have a look of fair play about it. When two men meet there can be little after friendship between them without some interchange of confidences. They must know and be known of one another. And as you have granted us the privilege of taking part in your proceedings in order that we may learn of you and your work as educators and educationists, we also, in giving you hearty welcome among us, will have to render some account of ourselves and what we are doing for ourselves along the lines of educational progress; and therefore I hope you will bear with me, when I proceed to tell you, in as concise a way as possible, what we of Quebec are educationally speaking, and what our seeming destiny is as a people desiring to be ranked among our neighbors as educated people having a confidence in our future.

When we address one another in our own educational gatherings, the spirit of reform is as often the bleating of the benighted lamb as it is among yourselves, when the spirit of "the pull" with the cousin of incompetency as a candidate, and the counting of heads tries to hush its voice. We are sometimes even so far misguided as to use the negative that decries, and, when the door is safely shut against strangers, we not unfrequently belittle one another's enterprises to our heart's content. Of course we know that you never do anything of that kind on your side of the line, nor even the people of Ontario on their side of the line, as my friend the Hon. Dr. Ross may inform us. Indeed, as we are often told by those who, like the Bishop of Leicester, have no particular desire to reach a "better place," having the best of places already, we ought to feel ashamed of ourselves in being so restless, in being almost as unwise as were the people of Manitoba before events had matured themselves. But this is only when we are among ourselves. We do not admit strangers to these wicked *seances*. We would all feel very unhappy if anyone were to break in on these family pleasantries of ours. Like the Highlanders of Drumtochty we are all of the best of clay when our own minister has the making of us. Indeed, we would deem it the height of treason to speak disparagingly of ourselves before others; and therefore in full view of the respectable educational forces that are apt to plume themselves when focussing in such an assembly as this, I feel it to be my duty to put as good a face on our educational affairs as can be done within the lines of truth, and tell you what we desire and expect to be in our endeavors to be other than we are.

The people of Quebec, I may as well tell you, have a show of their own, an educational record of which we need not be ashamed, although, from what the newspapers have lately been saying about us, we are all pretty well convinced that it ought hardly to take rank as "the greatest show on earth," and I may also as well tell you that the school system of the Province of Quebec is one of the best systems in the world, in theory at least. And though in practice there may be about it too much of the peradventure perhaps in these latter days, it still has within it quickening elements that could be made to do the most for a community constituted as ours is. One of the first principles of responsible government is that the people must have what the people demand, and if there be anything amiss about our educational system, there has at least been no breaking away from this first principle. The people have been having what the people desired, perhaps I should say what the people have tolerated, and if there has been a policy of *laisser faire* fostered here and there, as the tribunes of the people have lately been proclaiming, the primary cause of such is not far to seek when the open daylight condition of some of our schools is taken into consideration. The people have been having what the people have tolerated, and we all know that every decade of these times, when the *via media* safeguards, mediocrity, does not always produce a prophet eager to sacrifice himself among the dry bones in the valley of go-as-you-please. At one time, it seemed as if self-sacrifice was to be our watchword, but when it came to be illustrated only in the poor teacher's experience with her "much less than a hundred dollars a year," it became too much of a one-sided anomaly to be perpetuated.

But this phrase "much less" has happily been changed to "not less than a hundred dollars a year," and in the change there is some measure of progress, if not the prospect of further improvement. Through the late dictum of the Council of Public

Instruction, that no teacher shall be employed in any of the public schools of the Province of Quebec at a salary less than one hundred dollars per annum, a result has been reached which, I am afraid, does not issue altogether from the will of the people. The people in most of our municipalities require further training before they see that the salary belongs to the position and not to any particular teacher. The bargaining habit is hard to cure. "How much will you take?" is still a query too often affixed to an advertisement for a teacher. I know you have no such thing on your side of the line, nor in Ontario, nor in any other part of the world—ah, I am not to be too sure of that. Well, at any rate we have it here in our province, and to such an extent too that teachers were till lately often brought together by Commissioners to bid for a vacancy as in an ordinary auction mart, while it is even yet no new thing to find a teacher offering to take less salary than his predecessor, and I need hardly say in your hearing or in our own, that until conduct of this nature on the part of Commissioners or candidates is scouted as the meanness that is worse than a crime, can we expect the teacher to assume his right position as a public servant in the community.

A great deal has been said and written among us, and among you too, by educationists and statesmen, and by other publicists of lower degree on the salary question, by way of emphasizing the fact that the teacher makes the school. But in too many instances the advocacy has run to seed in mere rhetoric. What I say is, let our teachers be true to themselves and to the dignity of their calling, and the salaries must increase even should the effect of a government donation fall short of the expectation. A subsidy of fifty thousand dollars to our elementary schools to be further increased by the government of to-day if the financial position allows it, and the fixing of a minimum salary, surely indicate how far alive we are in Quebec to the raising of the status of the teacher and the condition of the school as the proper functions of a progressive school system.

Arising from the neglect of first principles, and more particularly of the substantial fact that "the teacher makes the school," the importance of having trained teachers in every school, has been overlooked to a very large extent here as elsewhere. The value of a Normal School training has been underrated, and, I may say, is being underrated at the present moment to such an extent in our province, that when at last the step has been taken to give a training to all our teachers, the argument is advanced that the additional outlay on the Quebec teacher of the future is too much of a sacrifice to be demanded from the state or the candidate. Such a silly war cry against what is the practice in every field of skilled labor, makes one wish to re-write all that has been written in favor of Normal Schools from David Stowe's time to the time when the Cook County Normal School fell into the clutches of a Chicago School Commissioner. But I must not make any such combative attempt in a simple address of welcome. I think I hear some of you say: "We are not much better at home. The teachers of the United States are not all trained teachers." I know that, and the very fact ought to keep you humble at times, for can there be any one present in this assembly who, notwithstanding the late folly of a certain distinguished but misguided English head-master, would care to say that all teachers, Sunday-school teachers as well, need not be trained teachers, or is there any one of you who is not prepared to congratulate us of Quebec that we have reached the stage of progress, whereby it has been arranged that all our teachers must undertake a period of professional training, even should this big city of Montreal have to annex Westmount in order to provide lodgings for the increase in the attendance at our Normal Schools, or some other of our ways of doing things be made more modern?

In keeping for the moment to the text that the teacher makes the school, I may refer to another phase of progress which, with the teacher trained and his respectability assured, may lead to the best results for us. I mean the question of supervision. The three elements of reform go hand in hand, if we would make the most of the teacher. With the teacher's position in society improved by an increase of salary, his professional status secured by a period of training, and his experience properly matured and accredited through the best system of supervision, we need have no hesitation in expecting the very best results under any school system whatever of a peradventure there may be about some of its other features. Up to the present the thin end of the wedge has only so far entered the surface plane of resistance, and yet our people are coming to see, through the results secured in our graded schools, that we must have in every part of our province less of what is called here inspection and more of what you on your side of the line call superintendency. At the last conference of our inspectors it was urged that instead of two inspectoral visits during the year, there should be, lieu of one of the visits, a conference held of the teachers of a municipality or a group of municipalities under the superintendency of the inspector of the district, for the purpose of elucidating the regulations of the Department and laying down plans to secure uniformity and an improved pedagogy. Some of our people have spoken of school inspection as a failure. But inspection has been no failure. Increase the number of inspectors, competent inspectors, and intensify their functions of supervision, is what I say in the light of what you have done in the United States and of what Great Britain is at last doing, and there will soon be evidence enough given to us that the Quebec school system has in it the elements of reaching out towards the highest results.

In enunciating the above reforms, I therefore feel safe in saying that with these three fundamental progress lines fairly laid down, we are hoping for better things for our elementary schools. If they had been neglected, they have been neglected while other phases of our school system have been developing. In connection with what are called our superior schools, that have been brought in line with our university work, there has been progress in many ways. Few of our communities—villages and towns—now feel satisfied with themselves until the school environment within and without, is in a fair way of being improved. With the excellent object lesson ever before them in the equipment and organization of the large and comfortable erections of Montreal and its suburbs, there has been created an ambition in the minds of the people to have the best that is going for their children. If the central authorities are sometimes afraid of being embarrassed by suggestions that might lead to improvement, if the cry of the economy man is still heard within our borders, and the prayer of the utilitarian who heaps up the obliquities and indispositions of mankind against the school door, is still as ominous of nothing as ever;

if the would-be educationist, who has never thought of enunciating for his guidance what the legitimate function of the common school is, still carries about with him his amendments to our course of study and for the moment bemoans his position as "the voice of one crying in the wilderness," there are other signs of the times that bid us be of good cheer. In our superior schools, and in some of our elementary schools too, there is a growing catalogue of class-room appliances which some of our would-be educationists are afraid may grow too large. We have laid the nucleus of a school library in the most of our superior schools which only awaits development at the hands of the authorities. Our school-houses are being improved, and their grounds laid out, and when we want "to put on style," as the saying is, in presence of visitors such as you we never fail to point out with pride to the progress of our universities with their *clientele* of colleges and kindred institutions. Have you been through McGill? Have you been through Laval? Have you been to Quebec or Lennoxville? Have you been to any of our towns to see their local colleges? When we look for ourselves at these massive combinations of stone and lime and learning, we are apt to forget for the moment the condition of the little red school-house by the wayside, as my predecessor in office lately declared with an emphasis of eloquence not to be forgotten. But as you have not seen our little red school-house by the wayside, and perhaps are pretty well satisfied with your own, we are bold enough to put our best foot forward in your presence, and with an excusable wave of the hand point to the evidences of educational progress around you in this building, and in this great and growing metropolis of ours, and taking you up to our mountain—not an exceedingly high one—we may show you with some further excuse for our pride, the growing McGill, the spreading Sulpician, and the massive Laval, as well as the hundred and one minor institutions of learning that beautify our streets; and then when your backs are turned after coming to think well of us, we will continue to pray for the little red school-house by the wayside, knowing well that to bow down and worship these grand results of our enterprise—however far they may be taken as monuments of the benevolence of our Macdonalds, and Redpaths, and Lord Mount Royals, and Molsons—will avail us nothing as a people, should we neglect to do what is right by the least and yet the most important of our educational forges for the raising of the masses.

With these scattered hints about ourselves, and with the hope of learning a great deal more about you before you leave, I again give you hearty welcome to our province. And having opened our Pandora box just a little way, I may be excused for one last word in the general. A short time ago I was invited to one of your gatherings to make an address, but was unable to go. I sent the society holding the gathering the following message, and perhaps you may not take it amiss if I hand it over to you as a morsel of homespun advice to you in your deliberations:—"Your invitation in itself is a guarantee of the universality of the brotherhood of teachers, as instituted by the educational principles that have happily now taken hold of the world. Pestalozzi and Froebel drew aside the screen that hid away for so long the eternities of the true school work. Their names are as a watchword to all of us. But let us discriminate in our hero worship. The ordinary teacher never catches much more than a mere glimpse of these same eternities. Among the less enlightened of our teachers there is still a paganism abroad that is ever taking the sign or symbol and assuming it to be the reality, just as there is ever a proneness among others to make for change, no matter whether it involves retrogression or progress. The following word to your assembly from a Canadian, if there is room for it: The difference between the faddist and the true educationist is as wide as the gulf between the crank and the philosopher. The difference between the crank and the philosopher is, that while the former is at enmity with the world, it is the world that is at enmity with the latter. And just as striking is the contrast between the faddist and the true educationist, —the true teacher; for while the former is ever ready enough to sacrifice the true interests of his school for the sake of making a present reputation, the latter is ready too at times to jeopardize his reputation, past or present, for the sake of his school."

ON BEING HUMAN.

WOODROW WILSON.

"THE rarest sort of a book," says Mr. Bagehot, slyly, is "a book to read"; and "the knack in style is to write like a human being." It is painfully evident, upon experiment, that not many of the books which come teeming from our presses every year are meant to be read. They are meant, it may be, to be pondered; it is hoped, no doubt, they may instruct, or inform, or startle, or arouse, or reform, or provoke, or amuse us; but we read, if we have the true reader's zest and palate, not to grow more knowing, but to be less pent up and bound within a little circle—as those who take their pleasure, and not as those who laboriously seek instruction—as a means of seeing and enjoying the world of men and affairs. We wish companionship and renewal of spirit, enrichment of thought and the full adventure of the mind; and we desire fair company, and a large world in which to find them.

No one who loves the masters who may be communed with and read but must see, therefore, and resent the error of making the text of any one of them a source to draw grammar from, forcing the parts of speech to stand out stark and cold from the warm text; or a store of samples whence to draw rhetorical instances, setting up figures of speech singly and without support of any neighbor phrase, to be stared at curiously and with intent to copy or dissect! Here is grammar done without deliberation: the phrases carry their meaning simply and by a sort of limpid reflection; the thought is a living thing, not an image ingeniously contrived and wrought. Pray leave the text whole: it has no meaning piecemeal; at any rate, not that best, wholesome meaning, as of a frank and genial friend who talks, not for himself or for his phrase, but for you. It is questionable morals to dismember a living frame to seek for its obscure fountains of life!

When you say that a book was meant to be read, you mean, for one thing, of course, that it was not meant to be studied. You do not study a good story, or a haunting poem, or a battle song, or a love ballad, or any moving narrative, whether it be out of history or out of fiction,—nor any argument; even, that moves vital in the field of action. You do not have to study these things; they reveal themselves, you do not stay to see how. They remain with you, and will not be forgotten or laid by. They cling like a personal experience, and become the mind's intimates. You devour a book meant to be read, not because you would fill yourself or have an anxious care to be nourished, but because it contains such stuff as it makes the mind hungry to look upon. Neither do you read it to kill time, but to lengthen time, rather, adding to it its natural usury by living the more abundantly while it lasts, joining another's life and thought to your own.

There are a few children in every generation, as Mr. Bagehot reminds us, who think the natural thing to do with *any* book is to read it. "There is an argument from design in the subject," as he says; "if the book was not meant for that purpose, for what purpose was it meant?" These are the young eyes to which books yield up a great treasure, almost in spite of themselves, as if they had been penetrated by some swift, enlarging power of vision which only the young know. It is these youngsters to whom books give up the long ages of history, "the wonderful series going back to the times of old patriarchs with their flocks and herds"—I am quoting Mr. Bagehot again—"the keen-eyed Greek, the stately Roman, the watching Jew, the uncouth Goth, the horrid Hun, the settled picture of the unchanging East, the restless shifting of the rapid West, the rise of the cold and classical civilization, its fall, the rough impetuous Middle Ages, the vague warm picture of ourselves and home. When did we learn these? Not yesterday nor to-day, but long ago, in the first dawn of reason, in the original flow of fancy." Books will not yield to us so richly when we are older. The argument from design fails. We return to the staid authors we read long ago, and do not find in them the vital, speaking images that used to lie there upon the page. Our own fancy is gone, and the author never had any. We are driven in upon the books *meant* to be read.

These are books written by human beings, indeed, but with no general quality belonging to the kind—with a special tone and temper, rather, a spirit out of the common, touched with a light that shines clear out of some great source of light which not every man can uncover. We call this spirit human because it moves us, quickens a like life in ourselves, makes us glow with a sort of ardor of self-discovery. It touches the springs of fancy or of action within us, and makes our own life seem more quick and vital. We do not call every book that moves us human. Some seem written with knowledge of the black art, set our base passions aflame, disclose motives at which we shudder—the more because we feel their reality and power; and we know that this is of the devil, and not the fruitage of any quality that distinguishes us as men. We are distinguished as men by the qualities that mark us different from the beasts. When we call a thing human we have a spiritual ideal in mind. It may not be an ideal of that which is perfect, but it moves at least upon an upland level where the air is sweet; it holds an image of man erect and constant, going abroad with undaunted steps, looking with frank and open gaze upon all the fortunes of his day, feeling ever and again

"the joy
Of elevated thoughts; a sense sublime
Of something far more deeply interfused,
Whose dwelling is the light of setting suns,
And the round ocean and the living air,
And the blue sky, and in the mind of man:
A motion and a spirit, that impels
All thinking things."

Say what we may of the errors and

the degrading sins of our kind, we do not willingly make what is worst in us the distinguishing trait of what is human. When we declare, with Bagehot, that the author whom we love writes like a human being, we are not sneering at him; we do not say it with a leer. It is in token of admiration, rather. He makes us *like* our human kind. There is a noble passion in what he says; a wholesome humor that echoes genial comradeships; a certain reasonableness and moderation in what is thought and said; an air of the open day, in which things are seen whole and in their right colors, rather than of the close study or the academic class-room. We do not want our poetry from grammarians, nor our tales from philologists, nor our history from theorists. Their human nature is subtly transmuted into something less broad and catholic and of the general world. Neither do we want our political economy from tradesmen nor our statesmanship from mere politicians, but from those who see more and care for more than these men see or care for.

Once—it is a thought which troubles us—once it was a simple enough matter to be a human being, but now it is deeply difficult; because life was once simple, but is now complex, confused, multifarious. Haste, anxiety, preoccupation, the need to specialize and make machines of ourselves, have transformed the once simple world, and we are apprised that it will not be without effort that we shall keep the broad human traits which have so far made the earth habitable. We have seen our modern life accumulate, hot and restless, in great cities—and we cannot say that the change is not natural: we see in it, on the contrary, the fulfilment of an inevitable law of change, which is no doubt a law of growth, and not of decay. And yet we look upon the portentous thing with a great distaste, and doubt with what altered passions we shall come out of it. The huge, rushing, aggregate life of a great city—the crushing crowds in the streets, where friends seldom meet and there are few greetings; the thunderous noise of trade and industry that speaks of nothing but gain and competition, and a consuming fever that checks the natural courses of the kindly blood; no leisure anywhere, no quiet, no restful ease, no wise repose—all this shocks us. It is inhumane. It does not seem human. How much more likely does it appear that we shall find men sane and human about a country fireside, upon the streets of quiet villages, where all are neighbors, where groups of friends gather easily, and a constant sympathy makes the very air seem native! Why should not the city seem infinitely *more* human than the hamlet? Why should not human traits the more abound where human beings teem millions strong?

Because the city curtails man of his wholeness, specializes him, quickens some powers, stunts others, gives him a sharp edge and a temper like that of steel, makes him unfit for nothing so much as to sit still. Men have indeed written like human beings in the midst of great cities, but not often when they have shared the city's characteristic life, its struggle for place and for gain. There are not many places that belong to a city's life to which you can "invite your soul." Its haste, its preoccupations, its anxieties, its rushing noise as of men driven, its ringing cries, distract you. It offers no quiet for reflection; it permits no retirement to any who share its life. It is a place of little tasks, of narrowed functions, of aggregate and not of individual strength. The great machine dominates its little parts, and its Society is as much of a machine as its business.

"This tract which the river of Time
Now flows through with us, is the plain.
Gone is the calm of its earlier shore.
Border'd by cities, and hoarse
With a thousand cries is its stream.
And we on its breast, our minds
Are confused as the cries which we hear,
Changing and shot as the sights which we see.

"And we say that repose has fled
Forever the course of the river of Time,
That cities will crowd to its edge
In a blacker, incessanter line;
That the din will be more on its banks,
Denser the trade on its stream,
Flatter the plain where it flows,
Fiercer the sun overhead,
That never will those on its breast
See an ennobling sight,
Drink of the feeling of quiet again.

"But what was before us we know not,
And we know not what shall succeed.

"Haply, the river of Time—
As it grows, as the towns on its marge
Fling their wavering lights
On a wider, statelier stream—
May acquire, if not the calm
Of its early mountainous shore,
Yet a solemn peace of its own.

"And the width of the waters, the hush
Of the grey expanse where he floats,
Freshening its current and spotted with foam
As it draws to the Ocean, may strike
Peace to the soul of the man on its breast—
As the pale waste widens around him,
As the banks fade dimmer away,
As the stars come out, and the night-wind
Brings up the stream
Murmurs and scents of the infinite sea."

We cannot easily see the large measure and abiding purpose of the novel age in which we stand young and confused. The view that shall clear our minds and quicken us to act as those who know their task and its distant consummation will come with better knowledge and completer self-possession. It shall not be a night-wind, but an air that shall blow out of the widening east and with the coming of the light, that shall bring us, with the morning, "murmurs and scents of the infinite sea." Who can doubt that man has grown more and more human with each step of that slow process which has brought him knowledge, self-restraint, the arts of intercourse, and the revelations of real joy? Man has more and more lived with his fellow men, and it is society that has humanized him—the development of society into an infinitely various school of discipline and ordered skill. He has been made more human by schooling, by growing more self-possessed—less violent, less tumultuous; holding himself in hand, and moving always with a certain poise of spirit; not forever clapping his hand to the hilt of his sword, but preferring, rather, to play with a subtler skill upon the springs of action. This is our conception of the truly human man: a man in whom there is a just balance of faculties, a catholic sympathy—no brawler, no fanatic, no Pharisee; not too credulous in hope, not too desperate in purpose; warm, but not hasty; ardent and full of definite power, but not running about to be pleased and deceived by every new thing.

It is a genial image, of men we love—an image of men warm and true of heart, direct and unhesitating in courage, generous, magnanimous, faithful, steadfast, capable of a deep devotion and self-forgetfulness. But the age changes, and with it must change our ideals of human quality. Not that we would give up what we have loved: we would add what a new life demands. In a new age men must acquire a new capacity, must be men upon a new scale and with added qualities. We shall need a new Renaissance, ushered in by a new "humanistic" movement, in which we shall add to our present minute, introspective study of ourselves, our jails, our slums, our nerve-centres, our shifts to live, almost as morbid as mediæval religion, a rediscovery of the round world and of man's place in it, now that its face has changed. We study the world, but not yet with intent to school our hearts and tastes, broaden our natures, and know our fellow men as comrades rather than as phenomena; with purpose, rather, to build up bodies of critical doctrine and provide ourselves with theses. That, surely, is not the truly humanizing way in which to take the air of the world. Man is much more than a "rational being," and lives more by sympathies and impressions than by conclusions. It darkens his eyes and dries up the wells of his humanity to be forever in search of doctrine. We need wholesome, experiencing natures, I dare affirm, much more than we need sound reasoning.

Take life in the large view, and we are most reasonable when we seek that which is most wholesome and tonic for our natures as a whole; and we know, when we put aside pedantry, that the great middle object in life—the object that lies between religion on the one hand, and food and clothing on the other, establishing our average levels of achievement—the excellent golden mean, is, not to be learned, but to be human beings in all the wide and genial meaning of the term. Does the age hinder? Do its mazy interests distract us when we would plan our discipline, determine our duty, clarify our ideals? It is the more necessary that we should ask ourselves what it is that is demanded of us, if we would fit our qualities to meet the new tests. Let us remind ourselves that to be human is, for one thing, to speak and act with a certain note of genuineness, a quality mixed of spontaneity and intelligence. This is necessary for wholesome life in any age, but particularly amidst confused affairs and shifting standards. Genuineness is not mere simplicity, for that may lack vitality, and genuineness does not. We expect what we call genuine to have pith and strength of fibre. Genuineness is a quality which we sometimes mean to include when we speak of individuality. Individuality is lost the moment you submit to passing modes or fashions, the creations of an artificial society, and so is genuineness. No man is genuine who is forever trying to pattern his life after the lives of other people—unless indeed he be a genuine dolt. But individuality is by no means the same as genuineness; for individuality may be associated with the most extreme and even ridiculous eccentricity, while genuineness we conceive to be always wholesome, balanced, and touched with dignity. It is a quality that goes with good sense and self-respect. It is a sort of robust moral sanity, mixed of elements both moral and intellectual. It is found in natures too strong to be mere trimmers and conformers, too well poised and thoughtful to fling off into intemperate protest and revolt. Laughter is genuine which has in it neither the shrill, hysterical note of mere excitement nor the hard metallic twang of the cynic's sneer—which rings in the honest voice of gracious good humor, which is innocent and unsatirical. Speech is genuine which is without silliness, affectation, or pretense. That character is genuine which seems built by nature rather than by convention, which is stuff of independence and of good courage. Nothing spurious, bastard, begotten out of true wedlock of the mind; nothing adulterated and seeming to be what it is not; nothing unreal, can ever get place among the nobility of things genuine, natural, of pure stock and unmistakable lineage. It is a prerogative of every truly human being to come out from the low estate of those who are merely gregarious and of the herd, and show his innate powers cultivated and yet unspoiled—sound, unmixed, free from imitation; showing that individualization without extravagance which is genuineness.—*Atlantic Monthly.*

(*To be continued.*)

EDUCATION—FROM A PUBLISHER'S STANDPOINT.*

By Gilman H. Tucker, Sec. American Book Co

(*Concluded.*)

IN the best style of teaching, of course the text-book is always subordinate. Books are bad masters, but good servants. They are not to be used as crutches to help those who could not otherwise walk, but are to be placed in the hands of the skilful as fine-edged tools. The wise teacher may omit, may add, may modify—in a word, may adapt the text to the wants of the hour, and thus extract and use to the greatest helpfulness. While the highest type of teacher may be a living text-book, time does not suffice, and the burden is too heavy for wholly personal work.

But with ordinary or inferior teaching—and who shall say, despite all improvements, how much of this sort of teaching still prevails throughout the breadth of this country?—the good usable text-book is the chief dependence, the indispensable tool which almost wholly shapes the final teaching result.

And notwithstanding the days of talking, explaining, and lecturing, I am old-fashioned enough to believe that the real downright study of the proper book by the pupil is a most useful adjunct in any course of mental training for the young.

There is a class of text-books on such subjects as history, political economy, civics, and sociology, in which the facts and truths concerned are open to differing and partisan views. But the publisher cannot advocate the principals of a party; his true course is to give all honest and capable writers a fair hearing. He is not responsible for the views of the author; at the same time he should discourage and, within reasonable bounds, labor to prevent the propagation of injurious extremes.

In respect to United States school histories, he is in a delicate and responsible position. That thirty years after the close of our Civil War there should, in some quarters, be a revival of intense sectional feeling, giving rise to little less than a clamor for the use of such school histories as shall most markedly favor the partisan views of either one side or the other, is nothing less than a distinct national calamity.

Charles Sumner, as intense a partisan as ever fought for complete liberty, was equally earnest for a full nationality, and advocated in the United States Senate, with all the fervor of his great eloquence, that the trophies of the Civil War should not be cherished, but should be utterly destroyed. In this he was in agreement with the great and patriotic minds of all ages, from Greece and Rome down to England, Germany, and France. No more patriotic or worthy service can be performed by the publishers than to hold the balance even and to discourage the propagation of views and doctrines by extremists that tend toward disagreement and disruption, and instead to promote a broad and liber-

---

* Delivered July, 1897, before the National Educational Association, Milwaukee, Wis.

al spirit of fraternity and nationality; and to this worthy end, the leaders of educational thought in this country should rally to their support and hold up their hands.

There is another threatening, narrowing influence that may well be mentioned in this connection—the tendency in some states towards limiting and localizing the production and use of schoolbooks within their own narrow borders. This is the ambition of the local politician; but the strong tendency of such a policy cannot be other than destructive to that best education which *lives* only in the sunlight of freedom. Writers of the best text-books, like the greatest teachers, are rare; they are not to be found in every village, city, or even state. And when found, no matter where—in Kansas, in Texas, in New York, Wisconsin, or Massachusetts—no part of the country should be deprived of the fruit of their labors, and no author of merit should be content with a less field of competition than the whole country. It is by such freedom, and a fair field for all comers, and by such a market, restricted by no sectional or state line, that the scale of merit is raised to the highest attainable point and the best results achieved.

For some unaccountable reason there is a widespread misapprehension in respect to the cost of schoolbooks to the school patrons, and of the total amount expended for text-books in the different states and in the country as a whole. This false idea has taken such a strong hold on certain states and communities that under the hot breath of a certain class of politicians it has been fanned into a flame of passion, until the single aim has seemed to be to get *cheap* books, irrespective of all other considerations. The gravity of this evil necessitates its mention, and calls for the dissemination of correct information on this subject.

According to a series of investigations in different states, based upon statistics and reliable information, the conclusion has been reached that the consumption of schoolbooks in the public schools from year to year amounts, in cost to the purchaser, to a sum which would be equal to ten cents for each inhabitant, or about forty cents for each enrolled pupil. This includes high-school books and all.

According to Commissioner Harris's latest report, the total expenditure in the United States for public education for the school year 1894-1895 was $178,215,556. This, of course, does not include money expended for schoolbooks, except in the few states which at that time furnished free books. It is thus seen what a very small proportion the cost of text-books bears to the sum of other educational expenditures. It is less than three per cent. of the total.

Something can not be had for nothing, and it is for you, the makers of public opinion on educational matters, to say whether the relatively small outlay for the best text-books that wide and free competition can furnish is not about the best-paying investment for its schools which the public can make. Is it not, therefore, your duty to direct the public mind back from the mere consideration of cheapness to the higher and more vital considerations of intrinsic merit and a suitable adaptability to desired educational ends?

I have assumed throughout this paper the existence of a most active competition, in this country, in text-book making and publishing. In an experience of thirty years of active connection with this business, I have seen no period of ten years in which the competition to produce the best books—and no end of them in numbers—has been greater, or the enterprise to get them into use has been more active than in the decade just now closing. You, among the elders, are qualified to judge of the correctness of this statement. This seems a proper place for me to say also that there has never been, at any time, or in any quarter, any agreement or understanding among publishers which has in the least degree even tended to restrict any house or firm in putting such prices upon the books of its production as the demands of free competition have dictated. I say this in the interest of truth, and to clear up an existing misapprehenson, and every publisher will indorse this statement.

When you can invent a method of cornering the market of brains, you can then set up a monopoly of intellect ; and when this is done, you can establish a monopoly in schoolbook publishing, but not until then.

This topic leads directly to another cognate subject which is based upon the recognition of the existence of the competition described—the evils of the commercial side of publishing. That such evils exist it would be folly to deny, but that they have been very greatly exaggerated and too widely advertised is equally true. Questionable practices in the adoption of text-books require the consent of two parties ; the school side no less than the publishing side is involved, and it is equally for the interest of both that whatever evils do exist should be eliminated, or at least, to the greatest possible extent minimized. Let us meet the question squarely and fairly.

I beg you to recognize that schoolbook publishing, as a business, has to fit itself to the environment of to-day, which surrounds the carrying on of all other kinds of trade. It is not, in this respect, a thing apart, and cannot possibly be made so. The laws governing it have not been made by fiat or choice ; they are the laws of its development by evolution, and have to be accepted as such.

There is a widespread popular notion that schoolbooks are changed oftener than the best interests of the schools require, and that the publishers are responsible. Most states have restrictive laws, prescribing periods of adoption of from three to six years, which are in the interest of a wise conservatism. But while these laws are a useful barrier against individual cases of excessive changes, it is still true that, on an average, books remain in use two or three times as long as any of the laws prescribe, and that the life of a good book lasts from ten to twenty years. Publishers are criticised for publishing too many new books, for revising their books too often, all merely to make changes in books necessary ; they are equally criticised for continuing the publication of too many old books and forcing their continued use, and for not keeping them thoroughly revised, so blocking the way to improvements. Thus by the inconsiderate they are condemned if they do, and they are condemned if they don't ; and it is a trying position to hold the scale even. As between most extreme views, the truth lies in a middle ground.

With one almost continuous session of Congress, and the frequent and prolonged sessions of the legislatures of forty-five states, we are blessed or cursed with many laws, and with constant changes of laws. This threatens the simplicity of a republican form of government with becoming a labyrinthian complexity of laws which even judges cannot unravel and interpret. This plague of over-legislation has not omitted the schools, and especially the adoption and supply of text-books. The politician attacks this subject with a courage born of ignorance. Uniformity and cheapness are apparently the things chiefly considered, under the guise of state uniformity, by state adoption and state contract, or by state publication. All independence and individualism in text-books are killed by this Procrustean method. The needs and preferences of different communities are disregarded, the voice of teachers and local superintendents and school boards is stifled by a centralizing and paternal policy, and dangers of political jobbery are immensely augmented. If experience has taught anything, it is that those schools are best served with suitable text-books where the competition is the freest, and especially where a fair degree of local option prevails in the selection. This is a principle that ought to have the indorsement of every organized educational body in this land, as fundamentally in the interest of good schools. The adopting unit should be the township or the county, for when it gets to be greater that this the teacher whose right it is largely to determine this question, is put on one side and his influence minimized. In this way, too, local needs can be recognized and supplied, and a proper individualism maintained, as against a system which aims to take the independence and life out of a system of schools by a plan compelling all concerned to think exactly alike.

The question of text-book supply is an all-important one—how to make it adequate, prompt, and reasonably cheap. "Free books" has been the most general recent answer, but this plan is not suited to all states. Moreover, it has only been carried so far as to lend books for the pupils' use for the time being. The full possession and ownership of the books by the pupils for use and reference at all times, in the school and at home, is the further necessary step to make the free-book plan complete. When the supply is not a public one, there should be a plan for the books to reach the children's hands as directly as may be from the publishers, at the lowest competitive prices, without adding any intermediate profit, except the necessary and reasonable cost of distribution. Local option in the selection, and direct supply at the lowest publishers' prices, are the two points which meet the requirement and cover the whole ground.

Of the volume that might be written on the relation of the publisher to the schools, I have only here and there touched a few of the most obvions points. But it is easily seen that the relation is a close one, and that the work of the publisher all along the line is absolutely identified with the work of the teacher, superintendent, and school board, and that co operation and sympathy are the necessary watchwords; excellence and improvement in education profit both. We will give you our best service in an active, high-minded, business enterprise, and you will help us by approving our endeavors, and in preparing for us better and bette books. This is the freedom and union which will best subserve the public interest.

Rockall, a desolate granite rock rising only seventy feet above the sea, between Iceland and the Hebrides, is to be made an English meteorological station. It lies 250 miles from land, the nearest point to it being the little island of St. Kilda, 150 miles away, and itself nearly a hundred miles from the main group of the Hebrides. Rockall is in the path of the cyclonic disturbances on the Atlantic, and the station there would give timely warning of storms that visit the British coast.

"A land of settled government,
  A land of just and old renown,
  Where Freedom broadens slowly
      down
From precedent to precedent.

TENNYSON.

CANADA'S DEVELOPMENT.

OUR visitors are surprised and pleased to discover in Canada the evidences of industrial progress that have, up to this moment, attracted their attention. The half, however, has not been told. This larger portion of the North American continent is so extensive, its industries so numerous, its possibilities so great, that no body of men making a sudden incursion into any one part of it can be expected to appreciate and comprehend the whole. Possibly the most marked characteristic of the country is the freedom of its institutions. Here we have, under the Sovereign whom Canadians, in common with other British subjects, delight to honor, a full degree of political liberty. We rule ourselves in accordance with the British constitutional system, and we flatter ourselves that under that system we have a Government more responsive to the popular will than the Government of any land outside of the Empire to which we belong.

Has our system of self-government been conducive to the well-being of Canada and of the Empire? The answer is surely to be found in the improved conditions of the country during the past thirty years. We commenced business in a small way, a fur-trading and lumber-selling people, with scattered agricultural settlements along the river banks. The earliest efforts of the pioneers were directed to the cause of education. We see the results of the labours of that day not only in the primary schools but in the great seats of learning. Material considerations, however, affected the Canadians of the last generation. They perceived the necessity for rapid communication, and gave us the nucleus of the railway system, covering some sixteen thousand miles, which we now have. Then commenced a period of development. The settler, no longer restricted to the waterways, was able to occupy and to cultivate "the back country," and, consequently, more room was found for producers. New forces gave birth to further steps forward. We brought all the provinces under one government; we added the vast North-West and British Columbia to our area, and we connected the Atlantic and the Pacific by rail. Now Canada, though divided into provinces for the purposes of purely local administration, is one country. The circumstance which led us in the exercise of our powers of self-government to unite politically and to reach out commercially was our faith in the capabilities of the vast country which is our. It was believed that Canada was rich in minerals, rich in timber, rich in fertile areas, rich in fisheries, rich, indeed, in all that goes to make up a powerful and prosperous State. It was felt that the utilization of our resources would be a paying enterprise, not only contributing to the wealth of the country, but affording homes for British people and fields for the profitable employment of British capital. Canada has not been disappointed. A panoramic view of the Dominion to-day reveals a measure of activity that bears testimony to the wisdom of the men of all parties who labored for a united country and a progressive policy. What is being done at the present moment? Our famous business of lumbering—prosecuted in New Brunswick, where the great deals are sawn for the British market; in Quebec and Ontario, whose northern districts are rich not only in pine, but in the spruce from which paper is made; and in British Columbia, the home of the Douglas pine, the mightiest tree on earth, taller and thicker than any other giant of the forest—boasts an output of $125,000,000 in value annually, and a wages roll of $30,000,000. No less than 12,000,000 worth of our lumber goes to Britain, and last year $13,500,000 worth went to the United States. Our 60,000 fishermen, operating on the coasts of the Maritime provinces, on the Pacific, on the British Columbia rivers, and in the great lakes, report a catch $30,000,000 in value. The maritime fisheries for cod, mackerel, oysters, lobsters, and herring are unexcelled. Nowhere in the world is there such a spectacle as that presented by the salmon fisheries of British Columbia, where the king of fish, returning from his sea outing, appears in myriads in the river, is crowded by his companions up on to the banks, and can be caught by hand. The agricultural development has been marvellous, although it has experienced changes more or less serious while in process. We in the East were formerly to a large extent a wheat-growing people. Now, while cereals are produced in vast quantities, we are paying greater attention than hitherto to live stock, to fruits, and to vegetables. This applies to the entire Atlantic division of the country. Ontario to-day is a great dairy province. Her cheese is a favourite article on the English market because it is good and because it is honest. Her butter for the same reasons, is growing in public esteem, and, with cold storage transportation, is taking a foremost place. Of cheese Canada exports $15,000,000 worth, and of butter a growing quantity. Cattle are an important item. Here we export to the tune of seven or eight millions of dollars annually. A later agricultural development is the production of hams and bacons, in which we are bound to lead. The fruits of Ontario are of excellent quality. Nova Scotia certainly does well with apples from the Annapolis valley, the scene of the Acadian expulsion, which Longfellow has reduced to poetry beautiful, though scarcely historically correct. That province exports half a million barrels. But Ontario is in advance so far as quantity is concerned. Of the product of the six million apple trees of this province, two million barrels were exported last year. The less hardy fruits, those requiring milder climatic conditions, are produced in vast quantities in our Niagara district and in Western Ontario. Our half a million of peach trees, our three million of bearing grape vines, which help to swell up Ontario's 320,000 acres of orchard, are but the beginning of our fruit enterprise. Passing from the older provinces into Manitoba and the North-West, we reach the enormous wheat fields where is grown a hard grain that brings the highest price on the market. Nor is production in this wonderful region limited, as it was once supposed it would be, to wheat. A varied agriculture contributes to the rewards of toil, not the least important branch of which is the cattle industry, both on the farm and on the ranches. Here we have a territory of 900 0^0 square miles, capable of supporting millions of people. Of our mineral wealth we have known a great deal for years. Our first enterprise was with the coal measures of the Atlantic coast. The deposits there are vast and valuable, stretching far inland, aud far under the bed of the ocean. At the other end of the Dominion we have the coal of Vancouver Island; while in the Territories, at Lethbridge and in the mountains near the Crow's Nest pass, are deposits the full extent of which are matters of speculation. Iron of good quality is found in Nova Scotia, in Quebec, in Ontario, and in the West. There are but two great nickel mines in the world, and we have one of them at Sudbury, in Ontario. All the minerals of value, silver, lead, copper, asbestos, are to be found in the country, but more especially gold, which is produced far east in Nova Scotia, in Central Ontario, in the Rat Portage District, all over British Columbia, on the Saskatchewan, and, as we have lately learned, on the Yukon. Our gold discoveries challenge the attention of the world. Meanwhile, quietly and unostentatiously, we are pumping up petroleum from 10,000 wells in Lambton and Bothwell, salt on the borders of Lake Huron, and natural gas in Essex and Welland.

We have within Canada valuable forests, extensive fisheries, fertile lands, and enormous mineral deposits, in fact, everything which contributes to the material wealth of the people. Of the country, the resources of which have by our large expenditures been brought within reach of industry, we are all proud. It is a contribution to the greatness of our Empire. What it needs is more men to take advantage of its wealth, and these will surelycome as its capabilities are made known.—*The Mail and Empire.*

OUR GREAT NORTH.

NATURE entrusted to the people of Ontario a marvellous fund of wealth in the forests and minerals of the great northern part of the province. Of the extent of the deposits of valuable metals we can as yet form no estimate. The development already carried on has been sufficient merely to give glimpses of what the rocks contain. We know, however, that Ontario has in abundance nearly all the important metals of commerce. The value of mineral deposits is popularly appreciated. People need only to be told that there are so many square miles of gold-bearing rocks and so many square miles of nickel or iron deposits to understand, to a certain extent at least, the significance of the fact. This is not the case with the forests. The people of Ontario are only just beginning to appreciate what a valuable possession thousands of square miles of forests may be. Many other nations are alive to this, although some have awakened too late. Germany has so wisely conserved her heritage that she draws from her forests an annual revenue of $8,000,000. Under the system in vogue there this revenue will not only not decrease, but will increase from year to year.

Although the people of Ontario are only just becoming aroused to the magnificence of Nature's provision for national revenue, they are becoming aroused in earnest. The forests should belong to the people. They do in Germany. In France no Government forests have been sold since 1870. The Federal forest law of 1865 in Switzerland prohibits the cutting of an amount of timber in excess of the total annual increase. Russia passed a somewhat similar law in 1888. India began systematic forest management about forty years ago. Even Japan is very much ahead of us in the management of her forests. She is not content with taking only the amount of the annual increase, but is systematically planting the best forest trees that can be found in any country.

Ontario will suffer no longer the criminal sacrifice of this fund of national capital. Individuals have become wealthy by the exploitation of our forests. Acquiring cheaply vast tracts of timber lands, they have striven to amass fortunes quickly, and have ruthlessly destroyed. Ontario wants a policy of husbanding its resources, and keeping them national. Wise statesmanship at this time would keep the province wealthy forever.—*Ex.*

EDITORIAL NOTES.

"Deliver not the tasks of might
To weakness, neither hide the ray
From those, not blind, who wait for day,
Tho' sitting girt with doubtful light.

"That from Discussion's lips may fall
With Life, that, working strongly, binds—
Set in all lights by many minds,
So close the interests of all."

THE opening of the colleges of Canada, which follows a little later than the opening of the schools, is as full of interest to those who have been able to pursue their collegiate training beyond the highest grade of our High Schools; and in the activities of the reorganizing of college classes, there are many lessons to be learned even by the general public. One question, which nearly always comes up at this season, is the fitness of the professor for his work, and while so much stress is being laid upon the necessity for efficiently trained teachers in our schools, it is no matter for surprise if the enquiry be made, in connection with the appointment of professors, into the antecedent training which has led to such appointment. That a man should be fit to teach young men merely because he has scored high in his university course, is as absurd as to suppose that a good teacher needs only a high grade of a degree to fit him for conducting a school; and the discussion has point at the present moment in view of the friction that has been created among the Montreal lawyers by the appointment of Dean Walton as head of the Law Faculty of McGill University. Of late years, there has sprung up in the minds of the corporation of that institution a preference for professors who come from Britain, and notwithstanding the failure of one or two of the "imported gentlemen," the feeling in favor of importations has developed into a kind of passion, until at last it has led to the appointment of a Scottish lawyer to give lectures on Quebec law. This last straw, however, has galled the camel's back, and the Montreal lawyers, knowing the peculiarities of Quebec law, and the long years of toil that have to be spent in acquiring a knowledge of it, have published their protest against the action of the corporation. We do not know what will be the issue of that protest, except that it is a very unfortunate thing for the new professor. There is surely no one in Canada so narrow-minded as to say that no Canadian college should go in search of additions to their staff outside of Canada; but just as no one would think of going out of the country for a minister or superintendent of education, or even for a professor of education, so many will be inclined to take sides with the Montreal lawyers in making their protest againt the appointment of a Dean of the Law Faculty in McGill University, who cannot be expected, in the nature of things, to have a thorough knowledge of the subjects he may have to lecture upon, until after a period of years.

Few names were better known among the teachers of America than Dr. Sheldon's, and his death, which took place on August 26th last, will be regretted by a host of friends and acquaintances who were always glad to see his venerable face at the educational gatherings of our fellow-teachers of the United States. The *School Journal* has promised to give us a biographical sketch of him, and has already said of him—what everybody who knew him will readily endorse—"The death of Dr. Sheldon, of the Oswego Normal School, removes from the educational field one of the pioneers of advanced ideas in education. He was a disciple of Pestalozzi, and was one of the great leaders who devoted themselves to the introduction of Pestalozzian ideas and methods in this country. He organized the first training school for teachers, in 1861, where he arranged a systematic course of objective instruction, a system afterward adopted by the various normal schools of New York state. In 1862 he became principal of the Oswego Normal School. His wonderful success in the face of persistent opposition to his methods of teaching made this institution famous and attracted to it students from all parts of the country. His great power with students, in winning their confidence and arousing their enthusiasm, is due principally to his kindness of heart, his disinterested devotion to the advancement of education, and his deep and abiding interest in young people. It was 'Father Pestalozzi' to his pupils, and it will be 'Father' Sheldon to those who have been privileged to come under his influence."

One of our contemporaries says: "It is strange that the educational journals which have a large national circulation are not used more for advertising purposes. Live superintendents and principals who take an interest in the study of education are frequently asked by parents to recommend a school for their child. Besides, there are many schools that depend wholly or in part upon teachers for their patronage, such as schools of pedagogy, training schools, schools of art, conservatories of music, technical schools, etc. The standard educational journals clearly could be used to advantage by these institutions."

Such a paragraph, with some changes in its wording, we think may wisely enough be addressed to many of our readers and subscribers. THE EDUCATIONAL MONTHLY reaches every section of the Dominion, and an advertisement inserted in it about the date of opening and terms in connection with boarding schools and other scholastic institutions, will not be likely to escape those who may be of service in bringing them to further public notice. We are prepared to insert such advertisements on the most reasonable terms.

Another name that is likely to have a place in the history of education has to be numbered in our obituary list. "In the death of Mr. Mundella, England has lost one of her ablest and most disinterested supporters of elementary and technical education," and these words do not come from England but all the way from India. "His interest in these subjects," as the *Educational Review* of India says, "both while in office and out of office, has been remarkable. It was but a few weeks ago that he attended the International Technical Congress, and now all too unexpectedly comes the news of his death. Mr. Mundella's name will be permanently connected with the history of Elementary Education in England by his famous Act of 1880, which made school attendance compulsory throughout England. Mr. Foster's Act of 1870 had done much to popularize Elementary Education, but there was still by 1880 a most undesirable disproportion between the number of children in actual attendance and the total number of children of school-going age. In the same Act, Mr. Mundella introduced an educational standard as a condition of half-time employment. This standard is the necessary condition of employment of children between the ages of ten and thirteen, irrespective of attendances made. Scarcely less important were the improvements introduced into the code by Mr. Mundella in 1882. A regular course of object lessons on natural phenomena and of common life was made a condition of the receipt of a Government grant by infant schools. The kindergarten system was likewise made compulsory, with the result that more efficient infant schools than those now existing in England are scarcely to be found anywhere. Mr. Mundella was fully aware of the evils resulting from the "payment by result" system. By his "graduated" and "merit" grants he attempted to avoid the drawbacks of that system. The tone, method and equipment were to form henceforth an important element in the estimate of the Inspector, upon which estimate depended the merit grant. It is impossible to enumerate here all the reforms in Elementary Education which must ever be associated with Mr. Mundella's name."

The teachers of the Province of Quebec are beginning to look forward to their next convention, which is to be held in October next in the city of Montreal. The programme has not yet been issued, but we have been told that it will include many prominent names and many excellent papers. In view of the possible changes in the way of the working of the system in Quebec, announcements may be made that will show how the urgency to improve the educational system in the rural districts is to be met. The Chamber of Agriculture in Iberville has lately been asking that the schools be provided with competent teachers who should be paid liberally, and other French-speaking districts will no doubt be taking similar action. As we have said, the old province is bound to have her educational rights.

One of our own educationists has just passed away by the death of Inspector Smirle, of Carleton county, Ontario, which occurred in the Royal Victoria Hospital in Montreal on the 19th of September last. The *Witness*, in referring to the event, says: "After a life of earnest, faithful endeavor, Mr. Archibald Smirle, aged fifty-five, and for thirteen years school inspector of the county of Carleton, has just passed away. Mr. Smirle was of a retiring, modest, nervous temperament, although of a firm and determined will, The knowledge that his life must be brief, and death perhaps sudden, prevented him from entering further into the work on which his mind was bent, and which might otherwise have benefited more fully by his character and power—the education of the people. Restricted in his work, he made it his best, and led Carleton county into a first place in Ontario in the true education of children. Mr. Smirle leaves two daughters, who will have the sincere sympathy of many friends in Carleton and elsewhere."

The new High School for pupils o both sexes has been opened in St.

John, with Dr. H. S. Bridges as principal and a staff of eight teachers. Mr. Hay, formerly headmaster of the Girls' High School, has decided to devote his time for the present to newspaper work, while Mr. W. H. Parlee has been appointed principal of the Victoria School, vacated by Mr. Hay. This will unify the system to a large extent, and we are told that Dr. Bridges will be able to accomplish the additional duties imposed upon him without affecting the efficiency of the new institution. The new High School, as an accomplished fact at last, will no doubt be a pride to the St. John people.

The Toronto Fair.

It is frequently said that the Toronto Exhibition of one year is but a repetition of that of the previous year. It is, nevertheless, a wonderful sight and more than a redressing of what has been seen before. The Fair is the great farm festival. We have here for a few days a representation of the work of man, whether that be in the field, the machine shop, or the studio. And every year shows some improvement on the previous year. And if there were no improvement to see, the show would be well worth seeing: there are so many things appealing to the eye, ear, and intelligence of the observant and quick-witted visitor. It is a question if the people themselves are not the great feature of the show. Animate objects are more than inanimate machinery, no matter how skilfully the latter may be directed, and intelligent beings are of greater interest than dumb brutes, be the latter ever so perfect. And the people this year were a greater show than ever. There is an appearance of thrift, of hope, and of happiness never seen in past seasons. Dollar Wheat, Six-Dollar Pork, and Five-Dollar Cattle show themselves in the smiling faces at this year's exhibition. We have not space to enter into particulars, but only to say, what was acknowledged by all competent to pass judgment, that never before was there in Ontario, such a show of cattle, peaches, grains of all kind. Those who are in a position to judge, say that it is a rare thing to see anywhere such an exhibit of the industry of man as the Province of Ontario makes every year in Toronto. It is an inspiration to see it; teachers should see and tell abroad what a country Canada is.

"What is the general attitude towards Canada?" "As a rule, they simply ignore us, as they do the rest of the world. We need not wonder at this. Their own country is so great, the problems they have to face are so pressing, their own possibilities are so boundless, and such demands are made on their energy, that they really have not time to consider the affairs of what seems to them a narrow strip of land under the rule, as they believe, of 'a nine months' winter.' Ignorance of Canada is really more general in the United States than it is in Great Britain; but that should not distress us. We can be good neighbors without gossiping about each other. Each of us has work enough to do without being troubled over the short-comings of the other. If we keep our own streeets and skirts clean we shall do well. One thing is very clear to me. The majority of the English-speaking race must find its home within the boundaries of the great Republic, and it would therefore be madness for us not to do everything in our power to cultivate friendship with them and to allay irritation and acrimony. I am sorry to find a tone of irritation towards the Americans growing up in the minds of Canadians generally, such as never existed before. Of course it may be said that there are causes for this. But when a people has done the great things that they have done, at such enormous sacrifices of blood and treasure, we who have as yet done comparatively little, and who to this day are wholly dedependent on the mother country for protection whenever we trade, or travel, or preach abroad, are not warranted in sneering at them. They deserve, rather, our admiration and our sympathy. When we share Imperial responsibility we shall be less likely to say or do anything to provoke quarrels. The strong man is usually calm, whereas poor, weak creatures, unless greatly sustained by divine grace, are apt to be fussy and provoking. It is the same with newspapers as with men. A little cur snarls and barks ten times as much as a Newfoundland or a St. Bernard."

The above extract is taken from *The Westminster* of 18th Sept., and occurs in a report of an interview with the Rev. Principal Grant of Queen's College, Kingston. From the reported interview it appears that the Rev. Principal spent most of his summer vacation in New York City. The part which we wish to direct attention to at present, is the following: "One thing is very clear to me. The majority of the English-speaking race must find its home within the boundaries of the great Republic." We have noticed a statement similar to this one in reported speeches of Dr. Grant's before, but these speeches had been delivered outside of Canada. We are certain that many in Canada would be pleased to know the data on which the respected Principal of Queen's University founds his assertion about the future habitat of the English-speaking race: this is true in a special sense of the teachers in Canada.

CURRENT EVENTS AND COMMENTS.

THE serious illness of Dr. Peterson is a matter of regret to every one who knows how much he has been lately doing by way of introducing and supporting educational reforms within and without the city of Montreal. Dr. Peterson has already shown himself to be animated by an honesty and directness of purpose that needs no make-believe art to enhance it. If he is in favor of any project, be it the organizing of a new college or the selecting of a new text-book, his associates know very soon why he is in favor of either. McGill, under his influence, has now discarded the old idea which has hung round its neck for so many years like a millstone, that numbers prove success; and we trust he will soon return to Canada fully restored in health to watch the developing of the new McGill.

There is not a little of the spirit of rivalry exhibited now and again between the "board-schools" and the "boarding-schools" of Great Britain, and a good deal of interest has been excited in the English academical world by the fact that a board-school boy has just carried off the blue ribbon of the mathematical world at Cambridge University. This is Mr. W. H. Austin, who was born June 3, 1875, and has gained his senior wranglership at the age of twenty-two. He was educated first at the Jenkins-street board-school in Birmingham, then at the Camp Hill Grammar School, then at Mason College, Birmingham, and finally at Trinity College, Cambridge, where he obtained his scholarship in November, 1893, and went into residence in October, 1894, so that within considerably less than three years of the beginning of his college life he has attained its highest prize. Some enthusiasts proposed that Mr. Austin should be exhibited in the jubilee procession as a living proof of the excellence of board-school training, but the suggestion does not appear to have been adopted.

The following may be read with interest by many of our teacher-readers, though it is not likely to be immortalized among the curiosities of school literature. It was lately addressed by an extremely respectful parent (would that they were all so !) to a school board, and reads as follows :—

"Gentlemen of honor, trusting you will graciously pardon the liberties taken by me in asking a favor which is as stated. I have five children in the Crondall school my daughter being Married with a family as requested me to appeal to you she says she would like the oldest girl ada Claridge to be discharged from the school to assist her in family matters I now beg the pleasure of leaving the matter for your honorable considerations looking up unto you as my very superiors and also christian gentleman and adding that you will in return as mighty defendres of rightneous graciously grant my request I remain gentlemen of honor your Excellencies' Obedient and faithful servant."

Bathing grounds for the pupils are beginning to be looked upon as necessary attachments to our larger institutions. In Brookline, for instance, in the reports of the sub-committees of the Education Society considerable attention is given to the subject of utilizing the new bathing establishment as a part of the educational system of Brookline. The sub-committee believes that in addition to the direct hygienic mission the bathing establishment will furnish ideal conditions for a swimming school. Swimming, which is an art of educational as well as of practical value, will be taught each pupil. Facilities for swimming as an exercise will be provided for a number of months if not for the entire year. The sub-committee recommends that for a portion of the year competent instruction be provided both boys and girls, the expense to be met from the appropriation for schools.

When Mr. Du Maurier was lucky enough to pass his examination (much to his own astonishment), he wrote to his father :—

> Care mihi princeps, sum per, mirabile dictu,
> Proxima sed rasura, fuit, ni fallor, aratri.

And, as was very necessary, appended a translation, which ran, according to the *Cambridge Review* :—

> Dear Governor, 'tis no less strange than true
> That, by a lucky fluke, I'm through, I'm through,
> And yet it was, unless I'm much mistaken,
> A close shave of a plough—just saved my bacon.

Mr. R U. McPherson, chairman of the Toronto Public School Board, received some time ago from Sir Donald A. Smith a letter enclosing a letter from the Colonial Office acknowledging the address sent to the Queen by the school board on the occasion of the Diamond Jubilee. The letter from the Colonial Office is as follows :—

"Downing Street, July 24, 1897.

"Sir,—With reference to your letter of the 3rd instant, I am directed by Mr. Secretary Chamberlain to inform you that he has now laid before the Queen the address from the members of the Toronto Public School Board. Mr. Chamberlain will be glad if you will inform Mr. McPherson, chairman of the Board, that Her Majesty received the address with a gracious expression of her appreciation of the loyalty which inspired it, and that he has received Her Majesty's command to convey her cordial thanks to the members of the Board for their message of dutiful congratulations and good wishes.

"I am, Sir, your most obedient servant,

"JOHN BRAMSTEN.

"The High Commissioner of Canada."

The following is an English idea concerning Canadian affairs, and we all know what incongruity there is often to be found between the two :

"We may express here our thanks to the Hon. George Ross, Minister of Education for the Province of Ontario, for a lucid and well-ordered account of the school system of which he is the head. Probably in no part of the British Empire is the organization so complete, covering, as it does, the whole educational field, from the Kindergarten to the University. As the book will come into the hands of many of our readers, we need not communicate its contents in detail. We confine ourselves to saying that it is full of matter relevant to the great controversies of the day. Some of us, for example, believe that in England we have not merely to settle an issue between centralization and decentralization ; but that we require a careful examination of the extent to which, and the respects in which, it is proper for the State to delegate its functions to local bodies. Ontario supplies us with an instance of central control. All text-books are prescribed by the Education Department, and the teacher who uses an unauthorized book is liable to a fine of ten dollars. Yet nothing can cramp, and indeed torture a teacher more than restricting him to a book which he does not approve, or as to which he feels that, however good it may be for others, it is bad for him."

There is now no province in the Dominion of Canada where the teacher may have use of a text-book of his own selection, unless it be British Columbia. In the province of Quebec the text-book committee seems to aim at being the great *sine qua non* influence in all educational movements from the election of a member of the Protestant Committee to the classification of booksellers and publishers into two great divisions, those who should be patronized and those who should not be. And yet, notwithstanding all their indirect methods, the list of text-books they have given to the world is little short of a new "tree of the knowledge of good and evil," if we may judge from the published programme,

---

"Boys will be boys," is a true saying, and never more true than when they are at play. A city editor has been having a double game of "hy-spy" with them, and this is what he says :

"It's a gruesome place to choose for a play-ground, but boys appear to have a preference for the graveyard in New street to the public roadway, for the upkeep of which their parents pay rates. The other night as I passed they were playing hide-and-seek among the tomb-stones, and one sat in tailor fashion on the six-inch edge of a high monument, desecrating memory and outraging sentiment as he yelled out something between a war chant and a music-hall ditty. After all, when one comes to consider the matter, there is not so much to find fault with. A boy cannot be sentimental, and his rule is to discover the best place for amusement and at once proceed thither for the purpose. It is natural that he should prefer the cool grass for the hot, hard stones of the roadway, and though he disturbs the echoes in God's Acre, he does no material damage."

The meetings of the British Science Association at Toronto and the British Medical Association at Montreal have brought many distinguished men within our coasts during the summer months, and we have witnessed the academic honoring of some of them by our universities. In the festivities at Montreal the presence of Sir Donald Smith, now Lord Mount Royal, has been a tribute to the commercial development of the land, rather than to its learning and science, and there is a lesson surely to be learned when one sees Lord Mount Royal veritably copying Lord Lister as a doctor of laws. Every one in Canada who has had knowledge of Sir Donald Smith is sure to welcome him as one deservedly honored. The general feeling seems to be that one who has labored so successfully in Canada, and has expended of his means so munificently for Montreal, is well worthy having his name now so intimately associated with the hill which enabled Jacques Cartier to mark the site of the future metropolis so definitely in his descriptive notes.

The question of tax exemptions is always a very pertinent one in the city of Montreal, and as our educational institutions are all interested in the question, it may be of importance to them to note the plain speaking of one of the aldermen of that city:

"The fact is that the gentlemen of the Seminary and the ladies of the Grey Nuns hold immense tracts of land both in the west and east ends. Personally, I think it is far from just that business men and others should be made to pay taxes while these ladies and gentlemen gather large tracts of land together on which they do not pay a cent of taxation. Think of all the land these gentlemen and ladies own on Cote des Nieges hill, St. Catherine street, and in fact all over the city, and which does not yield a cent of revenue. Religious institutions, I say, should pay taxes on the property they own just as I do. If it could be said that these gentlemen of the Seminary and ladies of the Grey Nuns owned land for purely charitable purposes, I would be the last man to propose that they should be taxed; but there is not a man here who does not know that they are most actively engaged in business pursuits. Very well, then; if they are business concerns, there should be no discrimination in their favor, and they should be made to pay taxes on their possessions. I can prophecy that if we taxed all the vacant land they held (till it becomes valuable by improvements which others have to pay for) they would soon turn it into building lots, and then this city would have a chance to get some taxes from it. I am not making these remarks from any religious standpoint. I am a business man, and look upon these matters in a business light. I might add further, that many of these institutions which own so much land, are not operated by Canadians, but by persons who have come from abroad and who have grown rich here. We need money; let all property and land in the city yield a revenue."

Governor Black, in speaking lately on the subject of "The State and Education," spoke in part as follows:

"I sometimes doubt whether the obligation of the state to the scholar is as great as it used to be. In the earlier days of the Republic, the statesman, the politician and the scholar were the same. What any man possessed of education or enlightenment was devoted freely to his country. His individual attainments were his country's gain and at his country's service. It seems sometimes as though the scholar's path is narrowing as he advances. If that be true, it is not a promise, but a danger. As the world enlarges the scholar should broaden with the rest. He should grow to the size of a statesman, and not shrink to the crippled stature of a critic. I wish every scholar in the country would enter politics. If he did there would be no danger of harm to him, while the gain to his country would be lasting and substantial. There are abuses to be corrected, but nothing will correct them but work, and work can never be effective unless the efforts of many are combined. All those struggling for the same destination should be willing to reach it, even by different roads, and each should remember that losing sight of another who has proceeded by a different path is no proof that that other has turned back. Nothing should ever be based upon impulse if conviction can be attained. The same forces aided by toleration will win a thousand times, and the next thousand times governed by distrust will fail. If you are stronger than others, more can rightfully be demanded of you, and above all other things remember this, that confidence is better than distrust, better as a weapon for you, better to encourage others who bear and realize responsibility."

EDUCATIONAL REFORM IN ROME.

A.U.C. 550.

PERHAPS no educational movement has had a greater effect on the history of the world than the silent revolution which took place after the second Punic War in the teaching of Roman children. It was a change not only in the subject-matter of instruction, and in the objects immediately aimed at, but it was also and essentially the introduction of a new ideal. "Poeticæ artis honos non erat," says Cato of the ancient Romans, and this was the key-note of that method of education which moulded the masters of the world. To them the uses of leisure were unknown. "I hate men that are inactive and of a philosophic mind," says some one in a play of Pacuvius.

The methods in which the utilitarian principle was carried out are, perhaps, less obvious than the principle itself, and the nature of the facts observed is of such interest as well to repay investigation. The immediate object of the Roman parent was to make his child a likeness of himself (an object, it may be observed, thoroughly in accord with the laws of human nature). The pattern was at hand; the life-framework was ready; to mould the child's plastic nature into the form required was a comparatively simple matter, and no great thought was, apparently, spent upon it. But, at the outset, let us observe one thing—that extraordinary product of modern civilization, the boarding-school, seems never to have appeared on the educational horizon of the Romans. They did not dream —one can well believe that they could with difficulty have formed the conception—of such a thing. And, for one reason among others, because they kept clear the distinction between imparting instruction to a child and educating him for life. School for them meant reading, writing, and arithmetic; but the bringing up of a child was a very different matter; and it would be difficult to decide which would have seemed to them the most extraordinary proceeding—to hand over the solemn responsibilities of parenthood to young men who had but just completed their own education, and who had little or no experience of life; or artificially to herd together in one mass persons of the same age and sex, carefully cutting them off from the educational influences provided by nature in a world composed of men, women, and children.

In the Roman system, life was not made for children, but children for life. A place was marked out for them and they must fill it; idiosyncrasies were ignored or suppressed. They were got into line early. In domestic, social and religious affairs their lives were from the first directed in reference to their parents and kinsfolk, and they were not treated as having a standing of their own; they were τέκνα rather than παῖδες. They assisted in the family worship, being the recognized attendants of the priest-father. They dined with their parents, but in a subordinate position, at the foot of the dining-couch or on a bench by themselves, being, moreover, expected to wait on their elders. They accompanied their father when he was invited to dine with a friend; but, at both sacrifice and feast, they were present not in their own right, but as attendants on, or as subordinate to, their parents; they lived, as far as their age permitted, the life of their elders. To the Roman father, a son was rather an undeveloped man than a boy with qualities as such. The pursuits of the child were, in the main, those of the parent, the difference between them being one of degree. The son went forth in the morning with his father to plough, sow, and reap; the daughters gathered round their mother in the atrium, learning of her to spin, weave, and direct the household affairs. The model educator trained his son in "thrift, endurance, and industry;" the pattern education was a laborious ploughing and sowing of the stony Sabine soil. What the parent was, that must the child become; and this principle of conformity to a fixed type received the highest sanction from the special nature of religious worship in the home. For so great to them was parenthood, and so reverend the past, on which parenthood must always take its stand, that the divine power, in its relation to the family, was represented by the original ancestor. It is not easy to realize what an educative force must have been the worship of the Lar by the children of every Roman family; while the importance of following example rather than inward impulse was still further urged by the symbolized presence of other ancestors, whose images surrounded the atrium in which the family life was carried on, as well as by the constant renewal of the memory of the dead in funeral feasts and ceremonies, in which those who had passed away were still supposed to share. For when a Roman died, the place that had been his knew him still. He was not even then allowed to slip out of the family circle, but had his share, as of old, in its joys and griefs.

The influences by which the Roman child's nature was to be formed according to the pattern laid down, were as many as the many sides of life; for it was to life itself that his education was mainly entrusted. He learnt by practice rather than by precept. He was not, for instance, taught religious dogma, nor had "children's services" arranged for him. He took part—a necessary part—in the thing itself; his services were required by the priest at the altar, and in the worship of the Lares at home, and his religion was learnt in the performance of religious duties.

The principle of shaping education by the realities of life was also carried out in regard to such theoretical instruction as the Roman children in those early days received. Certain things were necessary in order to fulfil the duties of a citizen and of the head of a household, namely, to know the laws and to be able to read, write and count. These things therefore must be taught. Sometimes the father taught them, sometimes an educated slave, who, perhaps, had other pupils besides his master's children; sometimes they went to school, the school being probably kept by a freedman, who assembled the children, boys and girls together, in a kind of booth or arbor attached to the house. The school times and holidays, it may be observed, were arranged with a view to practical convenience, the vacation lasting for four months in the summer, and the school work continuing without interruption, except on some public holidays, such as the Saturnalia and New Year's Day, throughout the remainder of the year. In truth, the working of a child's mind did not commend itself to the Romans as a subject of study, and the idea of arranging times of work and of recreation with the view of assisting its development would indeed have been a novel one. Their business was to provide him with the tools necessary for his work in life; his mind must take care of itself.

All parents did not share the feeling of Cato's father, who objected to seeing his son under the authority of a slave, and liable to be called names or to have his ears pulled by him when he was slow in learning, and not only preferred himself to train him to ride, to swim, and to fight, but also undertook the tedious task of teaching him to read, with his own hand writing out for his use in large letters narratives from history, that the boy might be provided from the outset with information likely to be useful to him in life about the deeds of his ancestors. Not a few, indeed, of the most highly educated Romans, including both Cicero and Atticus, seem to have been taught, at least in their early years, by their fathers, and, on the other hand, schools continued to flourish from the legendary epoch down to the latest times; but the "educated slave" offered in all periods a ready and popular means of tuition, a system, it may be observed, of which the traces are discernible in far other climes and times, not having entirely died out with the generation of Charlotte Brontë.

The education which was required in the Roman slave-teacher was, however—at least, before the study of Greek was introduced—not of a high quality; though that the task was none the less laborious, for that may be gathered from scattered statements as to the means by which the infantile mind was induced to devote its unwilling energies to "learning letters, joining syllables, conning nouns, and forming sentences"; cakes and sweets being offered when the shrill little voice lisping the sounds came out with the right words—nay, flowers, trinkets, toys being pressed into the service, when, it is naïvely added, threats and the rod did not avail. One would think that a child of moderate astuteness might have scored a good many sweets and toys. Subject-matter for the reading-lessons was, at any rate in early times, somewhat scarce; portions of the writings of the poets were taken down at the teacher's dictation, afterwards to be got by heart; and the Twelve Tables of the law were a standing dish, of which, indeed, many Roman children must have had in after life the same kind of recollection that Byron had of Horace. The writing-lessons were probably more easy to enforce, the little one's hand being guided by the teacher, as it traced with the stilus letters ready cut in a wooden tablet, a further stage of advancement being to write on the waxed tablet from a copy. But the most difficult branch of elementary education, in which, indeed, we hear of specialist teachers for the elder boys, was counting; the processes of addition, subtraction, division, and multiplication being carried on, with much labor, in the concrete, with the aid of the fingers, or of the counting-board and pebbles: so that, for instance, if it were required to find the product of 17 and 9, pebbles to the number of 17 would have to be placed 9 times over on the board, and the whole number then counted; a step in advance being afterwards made by the introduction of boards with lines to denote the fives, tens, fifties, hundreds, five-hundreds, and thousands, so that 3 pebbles placed in the line of the fives would represent 15, and so on. Moreover, the cumbrous system of numerical signs must in itself have presented many difficulties to the young learner.

This instruction, narrow enough in its scope, was, however, almost universally acquired; and that it was as early as it was widely given may be gathered from such traditions as that of Romulus and Remus learning to read at Gabii—of the waylaying of Virginia as she passed through the forum to her school—of the ill-famed deed of him of Falerii—as well as of more realistic presentations of school life, such as that which incidentally occurs in the interesting picture of the peaceful and industrious town of Tusculum, in the time of Camillus, where the "workmen were each intent on his own business, the schools buzzing with the voices of learners, and the ways thronged with people, among whom women and children mingled, going hither and thither as the affairs of each one took him."

But over this simple and practical method of education a change was to pass: the utilitarian principle, which made it suffice to know the laws, to count, to read, and to write, was to be silently and completely transformed by the spirit of another nation with another ideal. In the third century B.C., the inevitable result of contact with a superior but alien civilization had begun. The ideals of Greece had dawned on the narrow horizon of the Roman educator, and imperceptibly the new influence undermined his whole system. It first took the form of a necessity for learning the Greek tongue. In families that aimed at the higher culture, a Greek tutor, generally a slave or freedman of Greek extraction, appears on the scene; he taught his pupils to read Homer and other Greek poets; soon schools were opened for instruction in Greek language and literature, to meet the increasing popular demand, and the *grammaticus*, or teacher of Greek, threw into the shade the old *litterator* or teacher of reading.

Meanwhile Roman education was rapidly, if unconsciously, shifting its goal: its hitherto undiverted course towards a practical mastery of life was checked: it had caught sight of the golden apples dropped on the race-course by a mischievous goddess: it had conceived the idea of beauty as a thing for its own sake worthy of pursuit, and the homely prize of utility seemed no longer a fit object of endeavor. With this change of thought was mingled that curious desire to be some one else, which appears from time to time in the history of mankind, creating the oddest situations. It now became necessary to adopt not only Greek ideas, but Greek names for things, Greek customs, and actually the Greek language. From earliest infancy boys must have Greek nurses, pedagogues, and teachers, nay education itself must be to a great extent carried on in Greek. The charm that lies in imitation had seized on the minds of the conquerors of the world, and as time worked out its slow revenges, the well-bred Roman was a Roman no more. But the higher education, as it developed in Rome, is not my subject. Suffice it to point out that the training by which the Romans who made Rome were formed, and that which produced the inhabitants of the imperial city, were not two parts of the same thing in different stages of development, but were two essentially and totally different things; that they answer to two principles, of which the one makes the individual pupil subservient to the general ends of education, the other places before itself as the end of education the development of the individual pupil. The former is of this earth, and aims at making the best of known conditions; the latter cannot tell whence it comes—no, nor whither it is going.—S. E. HALL.

INTELLECTUAL WASTE.

JOHN DAVIDSON, M.A., HIGH SCHOOL, STRANRAER, SCOTLAND.

THAT the increasing complexity of our educational system is contributing to smoother working is at least doubtful. That the product which the educational mill is intended to turn out is being actually realized is also doubtful. And yet, what with palatial buildings, large and well-trained staffs, school boards, county superintendents, inspectors, educational codes, *et hoc genus omne*, the superficial observer may be pardoned for thinking that a finished product—a truly educated boy or girl—ought to be forthcoming. Amongst thinking people, however, outside the charmed circle of pedagogy, there is a feeling of dissatisfaction—a more or less intelligible consciousness that all is not right with the education of our public school children.

The *Times* voices this dissatisfaction, and reflects the opinion of not an unimportant section of people, when it declares that "the average schoolboy has to forget most of what he has learned, or to relearn it in new forms and relations." This is a serious charge. We have heard it before. It is the opinion of the man in the street expressed epigrammatically. And the indictment is serious just because it is that of the man in the street. Who better than he knows what it is to live, and what is education but a training for living? But the testimony of the man in the street does not stand alone. Examine the reports of superintendents and you will find more than one wail over the profitless energy and the wasted time of our public school children. One inspector virtually says that in many cases the results of a study of history and geography are almost *nil*; another, that a former year's work in these subjects, and especially in history, disappears, whilst no training seems to have been got through the temporary acquisition. Similar though less severe complaints are made in regard to other branches of instruction. Although it would be illogical from one or two particular subjects to make any generalization in regard to each and every subject taught in school, yet such a criticism, coming from those who, on the whole, are well fitted to sympathetically appraise the value of the work in school, cannot fail to make even the most optimistic teacher pause, and ask whether, after all, the man in the street is not partly right.

In wholesale condemnation there is always an element of exaggeration. Without, therefore, going the whole way with our critic, the *Times*, every honest teacher will admit that intellectual waste is going on apace in our schools, Not that there is no progress of a kind, but that such progress is made at a considerable sacrifice. To tell truth, who knows better than the teacher of the existence of the useless grind and its resultant waste?

Does it not lie with him, then, to stay this waste? Not altogether; he is part of a system. But more, one and all of us are so intent on the false show of the examination result that neither the prayers of the central figure in the show nor of his champions are heard. Is it sufficient that that delicate instrument—a child's mind—should contribute to the senseless glorification of a school or the pacification of the almighty tax-payer? What matters it, then, should the instrument be wasted or even destroyed in the process? The end justifies the means, forsooth!

The pessimistic teacher looks upon the mental waste which he sees all around him as the inevitable result of the system under which he works. But no true teacher can be a pessimist in anything but theory. His life work demands that he should work and hope for the best even whilst oppressed with a sense of the worst. Still, intellectual pessimism is of service; it is the best antidote to the fatal optimism that is so apt to be fostered by the dazzle of the latter day examination result. It compels us to give heed to the vicious points in our method of educating, and the practical result, so far as the teacher is concerned, is an endeavor on his part to rise superior to the system that enthralls him.

Of intellectual waste, as of any other kind of waste, there are two kinds, productive and unproductive. The acquisition of former knowledge that has now disappeared from the mental consciousness has certainly proved unproductive, if the mind received no training in the acquisition. This is waste with nothing to show for it. But there is the unavoidable waste involved in the disappearance of formerly acquired knowledge whose acquisition resulted in a certain development of the mental powers. Here there is a loss and gain, the latter often far transcending the former. In a utilitarian age, when every bit of knowledge is apt to be judged from a one-sided utilitarian point of view, this latter kind of waste is often confounded with the former. It is the unproductive waste which concerns us.

The testimony of inspectors will doubtless be corroborated by that of the observant teacher, that the study of some subjects entails a greater amount of waste than that of others. Such subjects as history and geography have acquired bad prominence in this respect. Important as history is, from the point of view of future citizenship, to the average pupil of the elementary school, yet inspector and teacher alike seem to view the subject with despair. As *deus ex machina*, it is either expelled the curriculum of the elementary school, or (perhaps by way of a conscience-salve) relegated to the oft nondescript position of a reading lesson. The question is thus suggested: Are there certain subjects of school instruction of such a nature that to attempt to teach them only results in waste unproductive? Or is the waste wholly or partly the outcome of wrong method in teaching those subjects? The case of history would seem to favor the former alternative. But what does the now historical cry of the inherent difficulty of the subject amount to? It will be granted that in general any subject of study is difficult or easy, according to the way in which it is approached. A glance through the ordinary historical text-book shows the method by which the pupil is introduced to a knowledge of history. It is questionable if there is at present in the educational market a single historical manual that deviates from the orthodox plan of treating the subject "from the beginning." In general, the pupil is led through a series of facts whose sole connection is often merely chronological. He leaps from one isolated foothold of fact to another, finding neither rest nor satisfaction in any. And even in the case of those text-books that aim at giving a connected account of the life of the people in its various aspects, the same method of going forward is followed.

To the average child the study of history, as indeed that of any other subject, after this fashion, is uninteresting. His mind refuses to go forward willingly in this will-o'-the-wisp chase after effects. Even if you lead him along a line of the most perfect synthesis, his mind, unless analytically employed at each step of the synthesis, does not follow with a full interest. You have robbed him of the motive for effort—the desire to find the cause of an effect, not the effect of a cause. He is not so much concerned with what this will do as with what caused this, not so much with *how* as with *what*, not so much with *synthesis* as with *analysis*.

Never was a truer educational dictum proclaimed than the Herbartian maxim that the substitution of any other motive for effort other than interest in the subject injures the character of the child. And what is this but another way of saying that there is no real education where interest in the subject is not the motive of the mental effort? To secure this Herbartian interest the learner must be led along that analytical path which the pupil himself unconsciously points out at the birth of thought. It is, alas, too true that the little would-be analyst can be brought to submit quietly, and blindly, to the bondage of the synthetical leading string, lured on, it may be, by the poor hope that he will ultimately reach some light. Childhood is the period of faith. Yes, but a more rational faith than oft attends the child in later school life.

That psychology is not yet dead that makes much of the child memory and little of the child intelligence. It is psychology of the study, not a psychology of the class-room. It is partly owing to it, that the child of our lower standards is cursed with an *olla podrida* of meaningless facts. And yet in reality he is an embryo discoverer, unconsciously working analytically, and demanding analytical explanations of things.—*Educational News, Scotland.*

THE OLD DISTRICT SCHOOL TRIED BY FACTS.

In these days of over-teaching it might not be amiss to recall some of the virtues of the old system. The defects of the old system have been harped upon so much, that it would be quite an easy matter to persuade ourselves that it had no virtues; and that the modern improved school has no defects. One glance at national facts, however, will dissipate all this assumption. The greatest generation of Americans that has appeared so far, in the history of the country, the generation that carried the country through the civil war, and gave us that finely disciplined, magnificent volunteer army, the able generals to conduct it, and the wise statesmen to provide for it, was the product largely of the old-time public school. In the stern discipline of the old district school, where the autocratic schoolmaster was the unlimited monarch of all he surveyed, was laid the foundation of that valuable military discipline that ultimately rescued our nation from the throes of dissolution.

The old school had its defects—defects which have been remedied; but it had also its virtues, for which, in my way of thinking, the new school has furnished but scant compensation. The new school makes better scholars; but does it make better men? Those who come from the schools to-day are better equipped with the details of learning; but are they better able to think, and to do? On these questions there may be room for more than one opinion. We know what the old school did; and we may hope that the results of the new school will be even more gratifying; but we will do well to bear in remembrance the principles and methods which secured for us a manhood strength which, when tried in the severest balance in our history, was not found wanting.

The typical school of a half-century ago was the district school; as the people at the time were principally country people. Rural thought and rural manners were then the controlling forces of the nation; and country bred men were, and indeed are still, our great leaders of thought and action. Hence the district school, fifty years ago, lay very close to the national life-springs; and exercised a preponderating influence in determinating our national type. The country school then, rather than the city school of fifty years ago, was the school that gave us the men that have illumined the page of our recent history. We may, therefore, infer that the old country school, with its rude benches, its wood stove, its austere teachers, and its iron discipline, was not without its virtues. It has often been made the butt of ridicule. Does it not deserve better treatment?

Fifty years ago I shared the instruction of such a school—a school from which went forth a bishop of the church—a distinguished journalist—a skilled machinist—an officer in the army—a chaplain in the army—a noted revivalist—and several women who are doing noble work in the world; and as I look back upon my childhood days, and contrast the form of schooling with that my children are now receiving, I am not filled with unmingled regrets on my own account. My children are receiving much in school that I did not get; but I am confident they are missing, in their training, some things of great value which I received.

Prominent among the virtues of the old district school, was that of developing within the child self reliance and the mastery of his own faculties. He was not helped beforehand—not, indeed, until his own efforts had been exhausted—and then, not more than enough. Boys were given work to do, and if it were not done, the teacher, or "master," demanded the reason why; and not infrequently enforced his demand with a stinging "hickory." True, the curriculum was very narrow, but the poor boy had to plod through it alone, spurred on by the master's rod; and by the time he climbed "Parnassus' heights," he was no "ninny," as he has shown.

A second great virtue taught in the district school, was true, plain democracy. There were no higher classes; no lower classes; no cultivated children; no rude children;—all were boys and girls—"scholars." Dress received never a word or a thought. We came there to learn to read, write, and cipher; not to learn manners and fashions. Our Bennetts, Pikes, Roses and Davies were more to us than collars, cuffs and shoe-brushes. We were taught a broad honest pronunciation of the words, and an open and full presentation of our thoughts, without any fears of grammatical rules, or dictionary accents.

The third valuable thing taught in the old school was the appreciation of good English—not by a senseless, precocious analysis of works far above our heads: but by reading and committing to memory classic compositions. Our old Readers abounded in fine selections which were read and re-read, committed and recited, with never a note or word of comment whatever. We were allowed to meet the author alone, and hear his voice without let or hindrance from officious editor or teacher. The old schoolmaster knew where to stop.

I need not comment upon that careful and painful penmanship that prevailed. Our old teachers "set" our copies, and their penmanship was awe-inspiring to contemplate. On this study I always thought they were over nice, as they would rap my fingers with their rod to make me straighten them out and keep my pen pointing to my shoulder.

The old master has long since passed away; the old school house has been replaced by the modern school building with its rooms and grades, all of which are much, very much, better than the old in many respects; but in cultivating self-reliant manhood, in inculcating true democracy, in inspiring a genuine love for good English and originality of thought and freedom of expression, I know nothing in the new American educative system that more thoroughly takes the place of the old country school.

THEOPHILUS GOULD STEWART.
Fort Missoula, Mont.

—*The School Journal.*

THE TEACHER'S WORK.

THE demands of the educational system of to-day upon the energies of the teacher are tremendous. There is no other labor at the same time so exhausting, ill-paid, and unsatisfactory to the doers of it as that which is done in our schoolrooms. The work of the Ontario Public school teacher is, in fact, never done. He cannot compass it all. As prescribed for him by the programme of the Education Department, it is an impossibility. He cannot perform well the half of what there is required of him. But ill or well, the ground has to be covered—he must leave nothing out. In their respective classes boys and girls must be taken over the full sweep of the authorized course of study. There stand at the end of the term the examinations—promotions, entrance and leaving—and unless the teacher wants to lose his situation and his reputation he must make shift to pass a respectable number out of each class. To do this he must largely discard sound methods of teaching. To take the pupils thoroughly over the work required for the examination is out of the question. There is too much of it. The subjects are too numerous; in most of them the range of study is too extensive, and the questions set by the examiners are frequently beyond the understanding of the candidates. Take the scope of the work for the entrance examination in the one subject of British history. The examiner may select his questions from all periods of that history, from the time of Julius Cæsar's landing in Britain down to the Diamond Jubilee. To stand the test of such searching, ingeniously constructed questions as will be asked, a pupil should be well grounded in not only the broad facts, but also in much of the detail of the text-book. He must not only have a full and exact knowledge of the history of Great Britain, but he must know also a good deal about constitutional usage. In fact, some of the questions asked belong rather to political science than to history. It is vain for a teacher to try to put his pupils in possession of such a stock of historical knowledge as will assure them success at the examination. If he teaches faithfully, with the object of really making his class acquainted with the subject, they will all be plucked. At that rate he would not get over a third of the work required to be done. Since genuine teaching will not serve his purpose he has to resort to cramming. To force the whole subject into the brains of his pupils he must be a regular steam engine of energy. He must wear himself and his pupils out in order to get a sufficient number of the facts pumped in and impressed long enough to be of use on examination day. When the examination is over the mass of the facts passes out of the head of the average pupil so crammed like the air out of a punctured tire. So it is in regard to many of the other subjects in which the pupil is supposed to be instructed. There are too many of them, and there is too much of them. Under the Ontario system teachers and pupils have to work like slaves, and yet they accomplish but little. The main work of education—the development of the reasoning powers—has had to be neglected for want of time. The memory has been abused, and the store of matter with which it was loaded is soon thrown off. We want a more compact and practical course of study at our Public schools. —*Ex.*

SCHOOL WORK.

1. A man has $3,000 in a bank, he draws out $^3/_{10}$ of it and then $^1/_5$ of the remainder, and afterwards deposits $^1/_4$ of what he has drawn out; how much has he then left in the bank? Ans. $2,010.

2. A regiment was reduced to 480 men after engaging in two battles, in the first of which it lost 1 man in every 27 and in the second $^5/_{13}$ of the remainder. How many men were there at first? Ans. 810.

3. A man bequeathes $^1/_4$ of his property to his wife, $^5/_6$ of the remainder to his son, and $^4/_5$ of what then remained to his daughter, and the balance, $700, to a hospital; find the amount each person received. Ans., wife, $7,000; son, $7,500; daughter, $2,800.

4. A man divided a farm among three sons. To the first he gave 24 acres; to the second $^4/_9$ of the whole, and to the third $^3/_7$ of the whole. How many acres did the farm contain? Ans. 189.

5. A farmer sold $^5/_{12}$ of his grain and then $^1/_7$ of the remainder, and next $^6/_{11}$ of what then remained, and had left 20 bushels; how many bushels had he at first? Ans. 88.

6. A man divided his money among his five sons. He gave $^1/_2$ to the eldest, $^1/_4$ of what was left to the second, $^1/_6$ of what was then left to the third, $^1/_5$ of what was then left to the fourth, and the remainder, which was $160, to the fifth. How much money was divided? Ans. $640.

7. A farm is divided among three persons; the first gets 60 acres, the second $^3/_5$ of the whole, and the third $^1/_3$ as much as the other two together. How many acres did the farm contain? Ans. 400.

8. A man having $240 spends a part of it, and afterwards receives $6^1/_4$ times as much as he spent; he then had $555. How much did he spend? Ans. $60.

9. I have $100 and spend a certain part of it; afterwards I get back $3^1/_5$ times as much as I spend; I then have $298. How much do I spend? Ans. $90.

10. On $^2/_5$ of my field I planted corn; on $^1/_3$ of the remainder I sowed wheat; on $^5/_6$ of the remainder I planted potatoes; the rest, consisting

of $^1/_2$ an acre, was planted in beans. How large was my field? Ans. $7^1/_2$ acres.

11. If, when wheat sells at 80 cents per bushel, a 4 lb. loaf of bread sells at 12 cents, what should be the price of a 3 lb. loaf when wheat has advanced 40 cents a bushel? Ans. $13^1/_2$ cents.

12. A person sold A $^4/_5$ of his land, B $^1/_3$ of the remainder, C $^1/_4$ of what then remained, and received $400 for what he had left at $20 an acre; find the number of acres at first. Ans. 200.

13 Find the amount of each of the following bills:

(a) $8^1/_2$ lbs. raisins, at $6^1/_2$ cts.; $9\frac{3}{4}$ lbs. currants, at $8^1/_2$ cts., $16\frac{2}{3}$ lbs. figs, at $7^1/_2$ cts., $24^1/_4$ lbs. candies, at $5^7/_8$ cts.; $58^1/_8$ lbs. nuts, at $5^1/_2$ cts. Ans. $7 25 $^9/_{32}$.

(b) $20^5/_8$ lbs. suet, at $13\frac{3}{4}$ cts.; $16^1/_4$ lbs. bacon, at $12^1/_2$ cts.; $9^2/_5$ lbs. lard, at $8^1/_3$ cts.; $26^3/_4$ lbs. beef, at $7^1/_2$ cts.; $17^1/_2$ lbs. pork, at $11^2/_5$ cts. Ans. $9.65 $^{17}/_{96}$.

CORRESPONDENCE.

TRADUCING CANADA.

To the Editor of the Mail and Empire:

SIR,—In a recent issue of your paper you quote a long letter which appeared in Modern Society (a well-known London weekly), written by an Englishman, containing what you call "slanders that are not worth contradicting." Dickens once got into great trouble with the Americans because he spoke frankly of their failings—"traduced" them, as you would say—and showed them up with that keen power of ridicule which, as the French say, "kills." What was the result? Many of them took their medicine like men, and now the faults which he criticised are greatly minimized. A man, or a people, so silly as to resent criticism, or so conceited as to think such criticism beneath notice, is beyond redemption. There is a legal maxim that "the greater the truth, the greater the libel," and it may be from a knowledge of the truth of much of what appears in that letter in Modern Society that you denominate it a "slander."

I will take the points of that letter seriatim. (1) The writer says "the way all business is carried on requires a total reformation," and he then speaks of "the cheating and trickery that exists broadcast." Now, I will ask any business man to probe his own conscience, and say whether there is not at least some modicum of truth in this. Mispresentation is not considered reprehensible—if it is successful. Inferior stuff is too often palmed off as good, and the "bargains" about which people are so crazy are too often nothing but cheats. Will anyone but a fool think that, as we often see in the windows, "50 cents, worth $1," is the truth? If it is not the truth, what is it? It is a deception, and we know that "the essence of a lie is the intention to deceive." What did one of our judges say recently in an election trial about the want of truthfulness which appeared to prevade the witnesses; and if men lie as witnesses when on oath, what are they likely to do in private when not on oath? It is impossible to believe one quarter of the statements one hears. People apply euphemisms to such statements, but when sifted and faced frankly, they are simply lies. Is even the public business of the country carried on in a manner which is beyond reproach? Have not charges of dishonesty been made against even members of the Government—of both parties—which have never been disproved? Such charges, if made against a man occupying such a position in England, would bring him at once to the bar of public opinion; and if proved, would cause his extrusion once and for ever from the public service, and almost from public life. I said, advisedly, that there does not exist in this country the same keen sense of honor and honesty and truthfulness among our leading politicians as exists in the Old Country. As for the rank and file of politicians in this country, they are mostly busy-bodies who have thrust themselves into that position because better men will not take the trouble to do so. Independent men will not enter public life merely to become the puppets of place-hunting wire-pullers.

(2) Farming is worse than in England. Farming certainly is not as profitable as it was. In fact, farming is, in very many cases, carried on, if not at a loss, at any rate with a very small margin of profit. Go to the banks, the money lenders, and the loan societies, and you will find out that mortgages are the rule.

(3) Canadian mistresses don't know how to treat a servant, because so many have themselves risen from that post. It very often does happen that the family of the domestic may have been, and may still to a certain extent be, on something not far from the same level as that of her mistress; and as the mistress may think it necessary to assert herself, a certain amount of jarring will result. That many mistresses do treat their domestics badly is certain, but then this same class of mistresses are uncourteous even to assistants in the stores and, indeed, to all whom they think their inferiors in wealth. On the other hand, many servants are a trial even to the best mistresses. Carelessness, indifference, laziness, uppishness are frequently the characteristic of the Canadian handmaid. It is an old saying that "bad mistresses make bad servants"; and bad servants too often try the temper of the best mistress.

(4) The promiscuous mixture of boys and girls in the public schools is a bad thing. Anyone capable of using his eyes can observe how it makes the girls rough, and that it teaches them a great many things of which they would better be ignorant. As for the "system" of education, while it may be perfect on paper, it is distinctly unsatisfactory in practice. It has several drawbacks, among them being these two: It is of so superficial a nature that the mind of the pupil is not trained, but simply loaded with fact; and the teachers are very frequently unfit for the work. The writer of that letter says: "The teachers themselves speak ungrammatically." I don't make such a sweeping assertion, but I do say emphatically that "many" of the teachers do so; and they not only speak ungrammatically, but they write and compose badly. As for the so-called higher education, the result is simply the spoiling of many decent farmers, farm laborers, and mechanics, and the deluging of the already overcrowded professions, whose standards are being thus year by year lowered. As was said only a short time ago in one of your own leading articles:—

"The higher branches of the school course, instead of being bent towards practical ends, seem to the pupil to belong to another world than the work-a-day one he has been brought up in, and make him feel some contempt for the 'base mechanic arts.' One outcome of it is the drift of the young people from the country into the city, the swelling of the ranks of the professions and of the genteel employments. As a consequence, the greatest natural industry of the country suffers. Farming, instead of being taken up by the bright, better-educated, and progressive youth of the province, is left for the most part to those who have had poorer chances at school. To get the education which makes professional men of boys who should have been farmers, lands are mortgaged, and the owners of them have to struggle along under the burden of debt, while in the over-crowded professions the young fellows cannot earn enough ro repay the cost of their education."

(5) Canadian parents have no control over their children. This is the simple truth. It is not quite so bad as in the United States, but it is bad enough. There is nothing that strikes a new comer more than this, and things have come to such a pass that a man I once knew who taught his children to obey was looked upon as unkind and almost cruel.

The abuse levelled at Dickens for telling the truth to the Americans suggests that, in telling the truth to the Canadians, I had better simply sign myself, Yours, etc.,

A CANADIAN WHO HAS LIVED IN ENGLAND.

Toronto, Feb. 15th.

DEAR MR. EDITOR,—Your periodical, I am afraid, while it is being well received by our teachers generally, has offended some of the members of the text-book committee who have been saying that they know all about me and have only to hold up their little finger to get me into hot water with my employers. Now, Mr. Editor, how is it that any one knows all about me unless you have divulged the secret, and I am sure you would never think of doing such a thing. I am rather inclined to think that in trying to scare me they have only been showing how troubled they are themselves in being brought face to face with the public. They are public servants, and it was unwise of them to think of doing anything that cannot bear the light of day shed upon it. And no matter what they think, the public are now going to have it made known to them what is being done both as regards the authorizing of text-books and the framing of resolutions which have nearly always in them something to repress the personality of the teacher or the pupil. A text-book in this province is not a text-book at all unless our self-elected censor either likes the book or the person who has compiled it. The selection is never without this element of personal like or dislike, and hence it comes about that our text-book list has become a jumble of good and evil. Do you think, Mr. Editor, if you were to write a text-book, even as good a one as Euclid wrote three thousand years ago, that you would have the faintest chance of having it authorized for use in our Montreal schools, after allowing me to write to you as I have been doing. Why, sir, it would be condemned in certain quarters before it had reached the bookbinder's. Its reprobation would be an accomplished fact before either the Protestant Committee or the Montreal Board had ever set their eyes upon it. And suppose, Mr. Editor, you happened to have a book on our authorized list, what do you think would happen? Why, my dear sir, your book would be superseded in the shortest time possible, and nobody, outside of a certain circle, would know anything about the change until it had been irrevocably accomplished unless as at the last meeting of the Montreal Commissioners some simple-minded enquirer is told that all preliminary arrangements had been seen to. And what these preliminary arrangements were I will again give you a month to surmise before entering into further explanations.

Yours most respectfully,

A MONTREAL TEACHER.

CONTEMPORARY LITERATURE.

An account will be found in the September issue of the *Cosmopolitan* of the house-keeping of that magazine since it removed to its idyllic home in Irvington-on-the-Hudson. It is a genuine pleasure to learn that the experiment has been fully justified. This ought to encourage other crowded city establishments to go forth and possess the country. President Andrews contributes an article on "Modern College Education." The Cosmopolitan University will probably experience some difficulty from the circumstance that President Andrews has decided to continue his occupation of Brown University. Julien Gordon has the first part of a continued historical story in the September number; "Mrs. Clyde" is the name that she has given to it.

The Quiver publishes in its October number a most interesting account by General Booth of the Salvation Army. Any one who has exercised such a vast influence in the world cannot fail to know much that is worth telling. The name of the article is "Work in Which I am Interested," and it is illustrated by characteristic photographs of Army officers in different parts of the world. "Sayings of Our Lord," by Dean Farrar, is an account of the recent discovery in Egypt.

Every magazine has its peculiar characteristics which, if inherent, become more confirmed with time. In *Scribner's Magazine* it is becoming evident that there is a strong desire to arrive at a more sympathetic understanding with the people who have monopolized the honorable adjective "working." In the series of such endeavors that Scribner's have presented to their readers none will attract more attention nor give more satisfaction than Prof. Wyckoff's Experiment in Reality, entitled "The Workers." Along with information that is new and pleasing, he tells his audience things that they would rather not believe, but which they will decide must some day be changed if they do not of themselves pass away. "The Way of an Election," by Octave Thanet, is a story that will appeal to the same class of readers.

MacMillan's Magazine for September contains a short story by Mrs. Steel, the author of "On the Face of the Waters." The name of the story is "In the Guardianship of God," and it is characterized by the same thoughtful insight into the character of the native Indians that was so evident in the lady's successful novel. Mrs. Fraser's charming story, "A Chapter of Accidents," is brought to a satisfactory conclusion in this number. Among the articles which will be read with interest might be mentioned "Hats and Hat Worship" and "The Craze of the Colored Print."

The profits to the *Ladies' Home Journal* from General Harrison's series of articles has been so satisfactory that Mr. Bok has generously released his forthcoming book from any royalty to the original publisher of the papers. It is to be issued by Scribner's early in the autumn. *The Home Journal* itself continues to receive the support that the enterprise of its editor so richly deserves. The last issue contained a set of waltzes by a well-known composer.

Bunyan's Pilgrim's Progress, edited by John Morrison, and Goldsmith's Vicar, of Wakefield, edited by Michael MacMillan, have both recently been issued by Macmillan & Co., London, and may be had from the Copp, Clark Company of Toronto. The text of the Pilgrim's Progress has been changed into more modern English.

"The Outlines of Physics," by Edward L. Nichol. The Macmillan Company, New York. The subject is here treated so as to make it an equivalent for the mathematics required for entrance to a college course. To do this a laboratory method has been employed, with experiments as far as possible of a quantative nature.

Other books received from Macmillan & Co., London, through their Toronto agents, the Copp, Clark Co. "Algebra for Beginners," new edition, by I. Todhunter, revised by S. L. Loney.

"The Study of French," by A. F. Eugene and H. E. Duriaux.

"Lessons in Elementary Practical Physics," by C. L. Barnes.

"Virgil, Georgic IV," edited by T. E. Page, and books 5 and 6 of "Murche's Domestic Science Readers."

"The Contemporary Science Series," edited by Havelock Ellis. "Bacteria and Their Products," by German Sims Woodhead, M.D. 3s.6d. London: Walter Scott.—This book may be read with great advantage by students in natural science, medicine, and allied courses of study, but at the same time it is eminently adapted for general libraries. It is a valuable summary of the present state of knowledge on this subject, and public attention being directed more and more every day to Bacteriology, such a work will necessarily be much in demand. Two introductory chapters are followed by a most interesting third chapter on the "History of Bacteriology," which dates back more than two hundred years at least. The remaining three hundred pages of the book (exclusive of an appendix and index) deal with the general subject—a chapter or more being given to each of the better known specific diseases. The author, Dr. Woodhead, of Edinburgh, was formerly Research Scholar of the Honorable Grocers' Company, and is now Director of the Laboratories of the Royal College of Physicians and Surgeons in London.

An account of a recent address on the "Professional Education of Teachers," delivered at Oxford by the Rev. G. C. Bell, Master of Marlborough, will be found in the *Publisher's Circular* for August 14th. He emphasizes actual experiments in teaching during the course of preparation.

"A First Book in Writing English," by E. H. Lewis, Ph.D. The Macmillan Company, New York. This is a text book intended for the first two years of a secondary course, special attention being given to the difficulties of that period. The third chapter. A Review of Punctuation should be noted by teachers of composition.

From Ginn & Company, Boston: "Elements of Chemistry," by Rufus P. Williams; "A Practical Physiology," by Albert F. Blaisdell; "Outlines of the History of Classical Philology," by A. Gudeman.

THE CANADA

EDUCATIONAL MONTHLY.

NOVEMBER, 1897.

THE BUSINESS OF THE TEACHER.*

J. J. FINDLAY, M.A., PRINCIPAL OF THE TRAINING COLLEGE.

OUR exposition must commence with a definition. In order to save your time I will offer you a form of words that seem to me to cover the meaning of the term "education"; they have appeared in print before, but I may be pardoned for reproducing them here.

"The adult portion of the community, distributed in the forms of the Family, the State (local and imperial), the Church, and various miscellaneous corporations, desires to promote the welfare of the rising generation. This it seeks to do by the employment of certain deliberate modes of influence, as an addition to the inevitable influences of circumstance and environment which operate upon all human life. These specific influences are called Education, and those who exercise them (whether professionally or incidentally) are called Teachers."

You observe that this statement declares that two factors are necessary to an act of education: the giver and the recipient. You cannot conceive of education apart from an educator. True, popular speech employs the term "self-education," but popular speech should here be corrected: self-culture is an admissible term; self-education is scarcely so.

Who, then, is the educator; who is the fount, the source of educational effort? Not, surely, the teacher—he is only an agent, employed by an adult society to achieve social ends. We must get behind him, and observe how he is appointed to his task by the organized groups of adult society which we call the Family, the State, and so forth. On the first blush these distinctions may be regarded by you as pedantic, but I trust that on further consideration you will admit their necessity—as the starting point for a comprehensive treatment of educational science. It enables us to give a proper place to all those grave administrative problems relating to the control of education which it appears to be the special task of our generation to meet and to solve. The definition involves the position, now admitted by all thinking people, that education is a social duty, a matter of public concern; not, as in earlier days, a private responsibility of parents alone.

Further, you will notice the use of the terms "deliberate" and "specific." He who educates is not concerned in a vague amateur enterprise; his undertaking must be of set pur-

* Inaugural lecture, at College of Preceptors, Sept. 27th, 1897, London.

pose, with the conscious adoption of means to an end; supplementing that immense variety of other influences which promote the welfare of the young.

Finally, before leaving the definition, let us notice that it affects the status of the teacher in his attitude towards those corporations under whose authority he acts. We teachers are the servants of society, not its masters; although tradition would ascribe a domineering spirit to our profession. As private individuals we may hold many private opinions, on politics, morals, manners, religion, but as teachers employed for public ends we are bound to distinguish between matters which concern private judgment and those which affect our relations with children; and this reserve, which society claims from us, we can, in return, expect from the authorities who control our work.

I have spent some little time upon this form of definition because I wish from it to trace the three principal departments of the study of education.

Firstly, we have to determine what constitutes "the welfare of the rising generation." What are we, as teachers, to set before us as the goal for our work? In a word, what is the *Aim of Education*, the business of the teacher?

Secondly, what steps does the adult society take to achieve this end? What are the functions and mutual relations of the family, the State, and the other corporations which undertake the task? How do these stand with regard to the teacher? These inquiries, which, as I have urged above, make a special claim on our attention at the present day, may be grouped under the title *Administration of Education.* Hitherto, it has not been the custom in our training colleges or in teachers' examinations to give much attention to this branch of study, but I have found that it proves of interest to teachers. I therefore propose to assign a few lectures to it.

Thirdly, we have the large field of inquiry within which the province of educational theory is more usually confined; we contemplate the task of the teacher, when brought face to face with his pupil and his school. I have used the terms "Conduct" or "Practice" of Education to indicate this branch of study; the latter term, "Practice," is perhaps the most intelligible, but, owing to the contrasted use of the terms "Theory" and "Practice" in another sense, some confusion of thought may arise; hence I usually prefer the term "Conduct."

You will observe the order of these three divisions: first, Aim, then Administration, then Conduct. This order is not indifferent; you cannot safely arrange your ideas as to the administration of education in any community until you have resolved what are the ends that your plan is to achieve, nor can the teacher hope peacefully to enter upon his task until his status and his relations to those whom he serves have been determined.

This third department of study obviously claims the chief attention of students and teachers, and, on turning to the Lecture List, you will observe the manner in which we seek to cover the ground. First of all, we have to contemplate the child, the subject-matter around whom all our interest centres. In Courses IV. and VIII., the aid of physiology is sought in order to understand the child as a physical organism; in Courses V. and VI., the mental life of the child* is brought under review. Assisted

*It will be observed that the term "child" is technically employed to include all who are subject to the educational process.

by these subsidiary sciences, we are able to investigate the teacher's functions (Courses I., II., III., VII., VIII., XII., XIII., XIV.). In making this investigation we are confronted with one aspect of the teacher's work which enhances our difficulty both in the study of theory and in our daily business—we have to care not only for the isolated individual child, but for the community of children in a school. Theories and methods planned to suit the single pupil may prove useless when applied to the needs of a corporate society. You will find that writers on education have oft ignored these conditions—Locke, Rousseau, and even Herbart may here lead us into error. On the other hand our English tradition, of which Arnold is the chief exponent, allows great weight, perhaps to exaggeration, to the corporate influence of youthful society upon the individual.

A fully elaborated exposition of education would probably treat separately of these two aspects, dealing first of all with the unit, and then with the mass as organized in schools. For practical purposes I think it sufficient to devote one course (No. VII.) entirely to problems of organization, and in the other courses to deal with both the single child and the school as occasion arises. You will observe that in discussions on Physiology and School Hygiene (Course IV.) and on Elocution (Course XI.) this same dual treatment is rendered necessary. We cannot sacrifice the interests of the community to those of the individual, nor (in secondary schools at any rate) are we willing to consult the interests of numbers while neglecting the single child.

This study of the practice of education is confronted with another difficulty to which I must briefly refer. We cannot advance very far upon the road apart from actual dealing with children. Lecture and discussion about teaching and training in the absence of our subject-matter, the child, is, no doubt, to some extent necessary; but it is obviously incomplete, and sometimes, I fear, this procedure leads to error. I trust, therefore, that my own professed desire to correlate such lecture work with practical school experience may protect me from going very far astray in theory, and, so far as effective demonstration can be employed by a lecturer who has not actual charge of a class, we do make the attempt in all our studies to base theory upon actual experience, which can be observed and verified by the students.

Let us now revert to the first section of inquiry, to the momentous question which, as I take it, stands on the threshold of education: What is our aim? In what terms can we describe the business of the teacher? In the definition we have expressly evaded this inquiry, contenting ourselves with vaguely indicating "the welfare" of the young as the purpose of education. We have done so in order to secure separate and adequate treatment for this issue.

There are two schools of thought which appear to come into sharp conflict. On the one hand we have writers like Alexander Bain, who would limit our responsibility to the intellect of the child. The schoolmaster, they say, has no concern with ethical ideals; the pupil is sent to him for a certain definite purpose—to secure the development of mental faculty by means of lessons. Anything outside of this range is incidental and should be ignored. On the other hand you have the great masters of our craft, from Socrates and Plato down to Arnold and Herbart, urging with the utmost emphasis the opposite doctrine. They urge us to seek the end of education by enlarging our sympathy, by reaching out into those regions of conscience and character which touch the deepest springs of life. The conflict must be decided, finally, by each of us for himself. I have no choice but to place myself wholly in the ranks of those who accept the highest and fullest responsibility in discharge of the teacher's office. And I do so, not because I am out of sympathy with the desire exhibited by Bain, to treat education as a science; nay, rather, it is my very anxiety to obey the canons of scientific method which leads me to reject his leadership. For it is the first law of true science to have regard to the facts of the situation. Now what are the facts that confront us in our daily work as teachers? Surely the most superficial acquaintance with child-life shows how impossible it is for us to raise an artificial psychological limit between intellect and will, or between mental and moral influence. If you, as a teacher, propose to be responsible for memory and reason, leaving character and habit in the charge of the parents or the clergy, you are adopting a course which is not only contrary to the best traditions of our profession, but contrary to the facts of experience, and to the obligations which parents and public opinion impose upon us.

Fifteen years ago in Oxford we heard Arnold Toynbee offering a re-statement of political economy. He rejected the authority of Ricardo and declared his adhesion to the ideals of Carlyle and Ruskin. I do not think that his exposition lost value in the eyes of scientific men because he sought to base his social science upon an ethical ideal; nor need we fear the reproach (if it be a reproach) of being called unscientific, in rejecting the narrower theory of Bain and reverting to the ideals of Arnold and Herbart. We must, with them, insist that righteousness exalteth a school as well as a nation; that the first simple purpose underlying every other aim in education is the creation of character. It may be that in some quarters there are influences about us which tend to degrade our ideal, to turn the educator into a mere instructor. What else, indeed, can we expect in a period and a country where wealth and luxury abound, and where it is loudly proclaimed by public men that self-interest is the only motive worthy of our regard? If here and there we teachers find such influences to prevail about us, if we find that a high moral purpose is not expected from us by those whom we serve, we can readily distinguish what is temporary and abnormal from the abiding, the eternal facts of experience. Ours is not the only calling in which the individual finds it difficult to maintain the highest standard of aim and practice.

And yet in no profession, except of course that of the clergy, is it more necessary to admit our obligations to this standard. The medical man, or the engineer, deals in the first instance with the physical world, and he may achieve much apart from an altruistic ideal, but, in the social sciences, any attempt to ignore the fundamental law which binds us to our neighbor is fatal to progress and to truth.

This simple statement of the ethical basis of education does not, however, by itself satisfy the situation. Our view of what is possible in the teacher's calling should be checked by our knowledge of child-nature. The child is not an adult, and child-character must be treated according to its kind. In other words, while we are compelled to turn to ethics to guide us in our ultimate aim, we cannot safely rest here; we must look to psychology (or, if you prefer the term, to child-study) and seek there, by actual observation of the child, for the limitations which his imperfect development will impose upon our ethical aspirations.

We seek then, first of all, for the stimulus offered to us in the words and examples of the great teachers of the human race. In the Old and the New Testament, in Epictetus and Plato, in the writings of modern teachers like Emerson and Ruskin—in such illustrious teachers of mankind are revealed the lofty heights towards which our steps should bend; but, lest their inspiration should exalt our ambition beyond its proper sphere, we turn now to the child and study him: our kingdom, like the kingdom of heaven itself, can be entered only by those who are content to humble themselves as little children. At this lowly level we shall be safe from the two perils that beset the idealist: learning how limited are the powers of the child, we shall realize the true limits of our sphere of labor; learning something of the richness of the child's moral nature, we shall be saved from the reaction of unbelief and scepticism, which falls upon those who vaguely long after an ideal without the energy to pursue it.

Finally, restrained but encouraged by contact with the living soul of the child, we shall turn with confidence to the example of the great "practitioners" of our own calling, to those who have lived and worked among children, and we shall tread with confidence on the road where they have walked so safely.

Among these leaders of our profession, I have, for various reasons, singled out Arnold in England and Herbart in Germany as especially worthy of our study in connection with this problem of the educational aim. We cannot, however, entirely accept their guidance, for the world has not stood still during the last half century, our doctrines and practice are influenced, for good as for evil, by the development of ideas in every sphere of life, and our science will not remain true to facts if it ignores these changes. Doubtless it is a formidable task to interpret wisely the forces which are now moving men's minds, and you will not expect any full interpretation from me; I will only venture to point out one or two of the more obvious influences which tend, not to overthrow, but to readjust the older conceptions of the business of the teacher.

The first of these we owe partly to one great man, Frœbel, partly to the social movement of our times connected with the advancement of women. The child to us is a more sacred person than he was to our fathers. He has his claims and his rights, *as a child.* Hereafter he may have a great future, as we say, before him; but the present also has its claims; let him live his own child-life in a child-like fashion.

You observe that this readjustment of our aim springs from the source to which we have already alluded—a more careful study of child psychology. I am bold enough to believe that this movement will grow in force as time goes on, until it finally revolutionizes the practice of our schools. Much is being talked—more, perhaps, in America than in England—of the New Education. I do not like the phrase, for it suggests an impertinent contempt for the old education, and in many respects I still think that "the old is better." If, however, that phrase and that movement mean anything at all, they mean just this: that your child has a right to self-development, untrammelled by the ambitions and interests of the adult, and that we teachers have to protect him, not only from his own errors and follies, but from the alien claims of his elders. You wish your child to be successful? Very good, but let his successes be such as accord with his simple nature. You desire him to be wise? Yes, indeed, but this wisdom can only grow out of his own apperceiving concepts.

Look back upon the history of education in Europe, and judge whether the child has not just cause of complaint against his elders. Every advance in thought, from the Revival of Learning in the sixteenth to the discoveries of physics in the nineteenth century, has imposed new burdens upon the young, burdens many of them alien to his understanding and his sympathies. Am I too bold in asserting that the besetting sin both of parents and teachers is this unceasing effort to impose on children our interests and pursuits? As soon as some novelty attracts public attention, whether it be a voyage to the North Pole or the danger of paraffin lamps, we find some wiseacre anxious to plague our children with it in school lessons.

It may be our pride to have trained children so as to become prosperous, worthy, faithful men and women hereafter: so be it, but may we not be content so to control their life that here and now they may exist as happy, worthy, faithful boys and girls: if so, our conscience will be clear, even if their lives are cut short by death before the age of manhood is attained.

Now, if you will grant the gravity of the plea which I have here urged, I will readily admit that there is an opposite truth, of equal importance, which was also foreign to the minds of our predecessors in the 'forties. This truth is expressed clearly enough in the Technical Instruction movement. I admit this opposing truth in the interest of the child himself, for he will not always be a child, and it is the business of the teacher to aid him gradually in "putting away childish things." Here is the true plea for Technical Instruction: not merely as a new tool in the competition of trade and industry, to develop still further our material wealth, but rather as a recognition of the duty of every citizen to earn his bread in the sweat of his brow, reviving the ancient Jewish principle that every child should be taught the means of honest livelihood.

You will observe that in this matter we cannot abide by the counsels of Arnold or Herbart; fifty years ago education was only for the few; the term "school" then bore some relation to its origin in the leisurely intercourse of scholar and philosopher. Nowadays, when the struggle for existence appears to be more intense, our expression of the aim of education needs to be readjusted; we must see to it, however, that we still, under new conditions, maintain our hold upon the primary moral ideal.

If time permitted, it would be appropriate to observe how these two movements, the increase of sympathy with children and the need of equipment for life, have modified our view of the tools by which we seek to achieve our aim.* The teachers of former days worked mainly under the influence of the Renaissance, and sought in the Humanities alone for the weapon wherewith to train the child towards goodness; to impart knowledge, in their eyes, was the chief business of the teacher; the active and volitional side of human nature received scant recognition. We are surely advancing in the pre-

* There are, of course, other forms in which the aim of education may be stated, each containing an element of truth. Thus the doctrine of culture inheritance, which demands that the child shall be put into possession of his intellectual heritage, is at least as old as the Old Testament; the doctrine of harmonious development of faculty may be traced to the Greeks. But an adequate criticism of these would take us beyond the limits of this address.

sent day a step further: we are not content simply to follow Arnold and Herbart in giving a nobler aim to the studies of the child, but we desire also to bend his activities in recreation, in physical education, and in all the arts towards the same moral end. We need not, however, dwell upon this topic, for indeed it will occupy our attention at a later stage, when we come to consider the selection of material for the curriculum. I mention it here as a link of connection—showing how dependent we are, when proceeding to consider practical problems of teaching, upon our previous inquiry into this first department, the aim of education.

It appears, then, that the primitive ethical ideal needs to be interpreted anew under new social conditions. You will readily agree with me that in each age it is also imperilled by new dangers. To the most obvious and most oppressive of these I have already referred:—the forces of competition and wealth are a permanent foe to the simplicity of moral aims. I may mention briefly two other agencies which seem to me to be fraught with more subtle danger. The introduction of science teaching into our curricula has been, as we all agree, a necessary and welcome addition to our resources, but we shall surely also agree that it has sometimes been pushed to an extreme. After all, a knowledge of the natural world is not the highest or most important knowledge open to the child; nor does it lie closest to his affections and interests. First of all he is a human being, and in the pursuit of humanistic studies he has ever found the most direct food for moral nurture. (I of course include the study of the literature of the Bible as taking a supreme place in the Humanities.) It is widely admitted that the one-sided action of such organizations as the Science and Art Department has not only hindered literary culture in our secondary schools, but has imperilled the ethical idea which underlies our conception of "a sound general education."

Another danger, surely, is to be recognized in our excessive absorption just now in problems of administration. Formerly the schoolmaster was a clergyman; now he seems likely to become a politician! From what I have said in the earlier part of this address, you will see that I make this reference to administration in no spirit of contempt. On the contrary, we owe a great debt to the leaders of our profession, who in recent years have taught us the necessity of organizing our secondary education. But we know that these very leaders are the first to anticipate the danger to which I refer. No interest of party or of organization should suffice to draw us away from the principal subject to which we are pledged to devote our lives:—the one subject of education now and always is the child, and the society of children which we call our school. Only so far as we remain faithful to this interest we are justified in giving what remains of our energy to the common cause of our profession. The business of the teacher is obviously to teach and to train the young; in their society he finds that his aims and hopes for education take a higher range than is permitted to him in the turmoil of educational politics.

Here, then, is the standpoint from which we have sought to answer our inquiry as to the Aim of Education. In its fundamental ethical basis it can never change, but, since each period of society, each nation and civilization, produces new codes of conduct, novel readjustment of the moral life, new perils to that life, so the business of the teacher needs to be presented under new aspects, conformable to what I sometimes call "the ethics of the period." And just as to-day we cannot rest content with the standpoint of an earlier age, so we have to expect that the progress of our age will readjust again the terms in which the ethical idea will be expressed.

Is it, you may ask, for us, as teachers, to forecast this progress? Are we to attempt the *rôle* of reformers of humanity, pioneers of new thoughts, of new ideals? As teachers, surely not; we must be content with a more humble task. Humble, first of all, because we are engaged with children, and they do not require, as yet, the breath of a new ethic—for them, at least, the old paths will suffice; and, secondly, because of our relationship, in administration, to the society in whose service we are engaged. They look to us to fulfil the ethical obligations of our age with all possible seriousness, rather than to discover a new law of life. The educational reformer has scope enough for progress within the bounds of his school: if he will only improve the practice of education he will find that the social and ethical doctrine of his age answers sufficiently the needs of the rising generation. Let him faithfully train up his pupils to that level, and he may rest secure; they, when their wings are grown, will fly of their own impulse to heights beyond his ken!

I fear, sir, that in this attempt to indicate the function of the teacher I have sometimes adopted the tone rather of the pulpit than of the lecturer's desk; if so, my apology must be found in the nature of the topic before us. In treating of a moral problem of this nature, which affects so intimately our own daily pursuits, we are in danger either of employing overwrought language which betrays the dreamer, or of assuming a false modesty which belies our hearts. We English teachers, I think, are peculiarly liable to this honorable fault of self-depreciation; we hesitate to magnify our office, to talk of ideals, of ethical aims. But this modesty incurs, surely, a special danger of its own, for if we fail on proper occasions, to express our convictions, we may by our silence give encouragement to those who deny the moral obligation. We cannot be too modest in admitting limits to our personal qualifications for the teacher's office, but no barrier of reserve should hinder us from acknowledging the lofty aims of our calling. Let us contemplate this calling in its true proportion, taking our stand side by side with other professions which are "called" to the service of society.

Finally, one question suggested by the critical spirit of our age: Is our aim a reasonable one—that is to say, is it in any measure possible of achievement? Can we, by education, make children virtuous? Can we, by science, save souls? The sceptics of fifty years ago denounced the "humbug" of those who sought by legislation to improve the nation's morals. Can we, they sneered, make men virtuous by Act of Parliament? No! it was replied, but you can make the habit of virtue easy and natural: you can establish favorable conditions for virtue.

You cannot by preaching save souls, but you can touch emotion, arouse impulse, suggest reflection. Now these are possibilities within the teacher's range also; for he can bring all the armory of professional skill to bear upon this unique problem of the formation of character. Personal influence, environment, the selection of a curriculum, and methods of teaching can all be considered with reference to this supreme goal.—*The Educational Times.*

THE HIGH SCHOOL TEACHER OF MATHEMATICS.

PAUL H. HANUS.

THERE is an important sense in which the preparation of every teacher is beyond the reach of human influences. His preparation has begun before his birth. He is either endowed by nature with personal qualities that should forever exclude him from the ranks of the teaching profession, or he possesses such qualities, as under appropriate training, enable him to overcome the inevitable difficulties that will beset his path, and ultimately to attain varying degrees of usefulness from mediocrity to the highest skill in his art. If he is a physical or mental weakling, if he is stolid and heavy, if he is indifferent to nature, human nature and art, if he lacks enthusiasm in the pursuit of his subject and never feels the glow of conscious mastery, if he has a crabbed or irritable disposition, if he is brilliant but unsympathetic, if he lacks an interest in his pupil at least equal to his interest in his subject, if he has no tact, and is lacking in the sense of humor that often furnishes the silver lining to an otherwise black cloud of youthful idleness or seeming perversity—in a word, if he is not physically and mentally vigorous, alert and active, if he is not interestedly and healthily responsive to the varied interests of life, if he cannot cherish a feeling of good will and maintain a hopeful and encouraging attitude in spite of many discouragements and some failures, whatever he may be able to achieve in other callings, he ought never to be a teacher. I need hardly say that, in what follows, adequate natural capacity and a responsive nature are assumed, and that my discussion pertains only to the preparation of the would-be teacher who possesses these characteristics.

The preparation needed by every high-school teacher is both general and special; that is to say, it should cover the essential elements of a liberal education, and special training in that subject or group of closely related subjects which the teacher expects to teach; together with enough professional training to show him his responsibilities to his pupils as well as to his specialty, and help him to become as good a teacher as possible as soon as possible. That a high-school teacher should in general, have profited by an education at least equivalent to that afforded by a good American college, ought to be universally recognized. Since this is not the case, one must assume either indifference to or ignorance of the importance of a liberal culture for high school teachers on the part of those who employ the teachers, or are responsible for their employment. Under such circumstances, it becomes one's duty to do what he can toward influencing public opinion on this very important matter. I am aware that in this presence this endeavor is unnecessary, if not somewhat presumptuous; but I am sure that the deliberations of this club are intended not merely for the enlightenment of its members, but also to promote the dissemination of wholesome educational ideals in the larger community outside, which the members of this club serve as educational advisers and teachers, and the intelligent cooperation of which they aim to secure in every legitimate way. It seems worth while, therefore, to point out briefly the serious consequences of indifference or ignorance on the part of employers of high-school teachers as regards the general culture essential to real efficiency.

It must be borne in mind that high school pupils are no longer little children, uninformed and unsophisticated. Besides possessing a considerable store of general information, they have usually learned to read human nature tolerably well where their own interests are concerned. Superficial knowledge, and limited mental power, narrow views of life, rusticity of manner—all of them marks of meagre culture—rarely escape detection in a high school; and particularly for the brighter and socially superior pupils offer a serious obstacle to the teacher's usefulness, if they do not destroy it altogether. It is a serious disadvantage to every high school pupil, whether he is aware of it or not, perhaps even more serious if he does not know it than if he does, to have his mental horizon determined by the narrow mental horizon of his teacher; his intellectual vistas and sympathies limited or dwarfed by the inadequate intellectual insight and want of perspective on the part of his teacher; to have his notions of social refinement and cultivation unformed, or deformed, or even perverted by the uncultivated man or woman who happens to be his teacher. The high school supplies to most pupils their last chance at these stores of inspiration and guidance, and they should be the very best. Such disadvantages to the pupil do not appear, and such obstacles to the teacher's success can hardly exist when the general culture and refinement of the high school teachers are sufficient always to command the just respect and challenge the regard, if not to inspire the imitation, of the best pupils. For such an equipment those who have tried it will agree, I am sure, that, in general, four years of training in a good college are little enough.

This view is strengthened by the reflection that there is no period in a young person's life in which impressions received produce a more lasting effect, in which incipient interests, and habits of thought and conduct are more permanently influenced than during the period covered wholly or in part by secondary education—the period of adolescence. It is often said that the earliest impressions are the most lasting and the earliest training is the most important for intellectual and moral development, and for the future usefulness and happiness of the individual; but I cannot believe that in most instances this is a true statement of the case, so far, at least, as those pupils are concerned whose school career is continued into and through the high school. If good early training were always followed by equally good subsequent training, if the child's opportunities for growth in knowledge and power were continuous, if his moral training and his social environment improved with his growth from early childhood through later childhood and youth, if his earlier acquisitions were really made to serve continuously and progressively as the foundation for continuous subsequent growth, then the earlier and earliest training would be of the utmost importance; for it would be the foundation on which later development would be most economically and securely laid. But such conditions of development are rare. The cases are not common in which each stage of a child's progress is so nicely adjusted to the previous one. Such an arrangement of our courses of study and our teaching processes is as yet too commonly rather a vaguely conceived ideal. Moreover, the instability of the population, the perpetual migration of people in this country from one place to another, enormously increases the difficulty of approximating to such an ideal, even when it is consciously and conscientiously aimed at. But suppose that such an ideal were generally realized.

It would still remain true that childhood in its first dozen years or so, with its ready adaptability to changing conditions, its rapidly changing dominant interests, in a word, its instability, would be affected most strongly by its latest influences. In my opinion it is quite possible for the later school life to make good the defects of early training; or, it may undo very largely what has been well begun, on the one hand, as, on the other, it may build on an excellent earlier foundation a superior superstructure. If this be true, and I believe it is (in the absence of scientific knowledge one can only generalize from his own experience and observation), the great importance of good teaching, wise management, and the most wholesome and refining general atmosphere in the high school are apparent. In any event, it will be admitted, I think, that as the period of adolescence approaches, and especially during that period, the instability above referred to rapidly diminishes. The individual gradually emerges. The child becomes a youth. This is a critical period in the life of every human being. To assume the wise guidance of young people during this important period is the exalted function of the secondary school teacher. He is to be the inspiring, sympathetic, discriminating, and vigorous guide and leader of boys and girls just developing into manhood and womanhood. To be such a guide and leader in very truth he must have resources, both natural and acquired. The least that should be demanded of him is that he shall have taken pains to secure an equipment of knowledge that will give him broad, sane, and healthy views of life, with its duties and its privileges, and liberal intellectual sympathies; together with a conscious power in some one field that enables him to maintain, both for himself and his pupils, a high standard of achievement. Such an equipment every college graduate who has made good use of his opportunities may possess. It is not often that one who has not profited by such an education can be expected to possess it.

There are special reasons why the teacher of mathematics should have a liberal equipment of general culture in addition to special knowledge and power in his particular subject. Pure mathematics is profound and interesting; but its subject-matter, save in its elements, is so remote from the common interests of men that its devotees are in constant danger of what may be called a professional or academic isolation; and this isolation is almost sure to increase with increasing devotion to the subject. It has fewer points of contract with the ordinary affairs of life than natural science, or language, or history; to say nothing of subjects like economics and political science. In this respect mathematics differs from all other subjects. Factoring, radicals, and quadratic equations, polygons, paralleropipeds, and spherical triangles, sines, tangents and trigonometric formulæ, the theory of equations, determinants, and complex numbers, point and line co-ordinates, involutes and evolutes, derivatives, differential equations, and elliptic functions, may completely shut out from view the living panorama of nature and society in which most men live and move, and have their being, and from which the young, in particular, derive most of their incentives and conscious purposes. In my opinion it is therefore not asking too much that the high school teacher of mathematics should posses and understand the importance of the general training that enables him to appreciate extra-vocational, *i.e.*, for him extra-mathematical interests. It ought never to be possible for the teacher of mathematics, however high he may rate the importance of his own subject and its beneficial effect on the pupil, to become one who measures the capacity of all pupils solely by their ability to "do sums, and to work problems," and the goodness of any course of study chiefly by the work in mathematics it prescribes.

But after all has been said that can be said of the necessity of broad general culture for the teacher of mathematics, it is still emphatically true that his efficiency depends ultimately on his special training, on his resources in and power over his own subject; for it is through that subject that his special duty to the pupil is to be done. Either the pupil is to receive through him a peculiar insight into the marvellous system of the external world, some comprehension of the wonderful power and fertility of the human mind in one of its fields of activity, a quickening of his intellectual life through the knowledge and insight, the clearness and adequacy of exposition of mathematical truths characteristic of a scholarly enthusiastic, well-trained teacher; or he must forever remain indifferent to these interesting, and to some minds fascinating experiences, because both he and his teacher move about vaguely in a "world unrealized," where the intellectual fog never rises, and where the road traversed to-day must be retraversed with the same dim nncertainty to-morrow.

If the teacher of mathematics has little mathematical ability, and if at the same time he has not had sufficient training, he is almost sure to carry on his work with a benumbing inadequacy of comprehension and exposition which soon becomes chronic, and through which the pupils come to look on mathematics as a highly artificial subject of little real interest or practical utility; a subject in which success does not depend on common sense and patient study, but on a certain inborn ingenuity of manipulating postulates, hypotheses, and previous propositions, and in which absurdities are as valid as realities.

A certain college student of my acquaintance must have had this kind of instruction. She said she had studied algebra before coming to college, but she had become interested in the subject only when she took up equations and proved "things." Whereupon I asked her if she had ever seen the paradox by which, through a series of equations, any number may apparently be proved equal to nothing. As she had never seen it, I showed it to her, securing her assent to the several steps as I went on. When we arrived at the conclusion, $2=0$, I handed her the paper and looked up with the half apologetic, half triumphant manner of one who expects after a very brief triumph and a rather lame defence to yield the point in question. But nothing of the sort happened. She merely said "That's all right" and handed the paper back to me. "But," I said, "how can it be? Two cannot be really equal to nothing." "O," she said, "that's algebra."

The situation is not much improved, although it is quite different, if the teacher has good ability, but insufficient training. In that case he is oppressed by the consciousness of the heavy demands made on him and of his inability for a long time to respond to them as he should. The work must be done somehow, the classes cannot wait. He is thus obliged to carry on a discouraging struggle against tremendous odds. Meanwhile, his pupils are the losers, and the reputation of the subject suffers. Similar statements could, of course, be made with respect to inadequate preparation in other subjects as well as mathematics, but the immediate consequences are not so conspicuous. The definiteness and rigor of mathematical reasoning afford a constant and ruthless exposition of the teacher's shortcomings—an exposition which in other subjects is neither so glaring nor usually so disastrous. The teacher of mathematics must be a logical reasoner and ready in manipulation. If his training has left him without these powers, his other mental powers will avail him nothing. Either the pupil is right or he is wrong. Neither teacher nor pupil can escape the consequences of false reasoning or lack of skill in handling mathematical expressions. So, too, the glimpse the teacher gets of fields unexplored, which he vaguely realizes must have an influence on the interpretation of the work on which he is engaged, is a constant intimation of inadequacy, and so a source of self-accusation that heightens the acute "misery of conscious weakness" which he is sure to feel, and which is one of the most paralyzing of all the untoward influences that oppress the conscientious but meagrely equipped teacher. There is no heavier burden than the burden of accepted duties that one feels he cannot adequately perform.

There is, of course, always hope for the able teacher inadequately prepared, for he may, by dint of hard work, ultimately achieve at least a moderate efficiency, although at the expense of many pupils; but there is no hope for the ignorant teacher of poor ability unconscious of his own ignorance. In either case the want of adequate preparation before actual service begins casts its shadow over his entire professional career.

To teach mathematics well in the high school, it is, therefore, hardly necessary to argue that one must have a thorough knowledge of the subject, a knowledge that is far in advance of pre-collegiate study, *i.e.*, far in advance of a good acquaintance with the branches of mathematics usually found in the high school curriculum or such a presentation of them as is contained in the usual text-books. It is hardly necessary to argue that with an equipment limited to pre-collegiate study, the teacher of elementary mathematics is unable to comprehend the relative importance of the different phases of his subject. He may, and usually does, neglect important aspects and magnifies trifles. He treats facts and processes as ultimate ends in themselves, instead of means to ends. He never gets the comprehensive point of view from which the subject is unified and gains full significance in his own and the pupils' minds. His pupils not infrequently learn many things which subsequently must be unlearned—an expensive and exasperating experience. That he may escape this unfortunate situation, that he may from the start enter on his work well equipped for the demands that are to be made on him, I purpose now to enquire what should a good course of study, to be pursued by the high school teacher of mathematics as special preparation for his work, comprise?

Bearing in mind that this course of study should enable the teacher to appreciate the relative importance of the different phases of his subject and of their interdependence throughout, and so enable him to select with certainty and wisdom those portions of mathematics essential to the elements of a liberal education, or for future specialization in mathematics, if the pupil's interest and probable career should lead him into that field; and also that the teacher should know and be able to point out the significance of mathematics for the adequate development of power over other sciences, it is clear that the teacher's preparation must cover both pure and applied mathematics, and a general training in elementary physical science. Only through such knowledge is it possible to expect confidently that the teacher shall have an adequate, a wise, and firm grasp of essentials; and be able to impart to the pupil the scientific interest born of insight, unified knowledge, and perspective; and also a conviction of the fundamental utility of his subject in the pursuit of other sciences and in the practical affairs of life.

In view of these considerations, I suggest the following college course of study for the equipment of the high school teacher of mathematics:

Advanced algebra, about fifty lessons; theory of equations, about fifty lessons (together with determinants and complex numbers); solid geometry, about fifty lessons; trigonometry, plane and spherical, about fifty lessons; surveying, about fifty lessons; calculus, about one hundred lessons; mechanics, about one hundred lessons; history of mathematics, about fifty lessons; physics, about one hundred lessons (general, with quantitative laboratory work); astronomy, about fifty lessons; chemistry, including mineralogy, about one hundred lessons; application of the calculus to light and heat, or to electricity, about one hundred lessons; history and theory of education, about one hundred lessons; methods, about fifty lessons.

Such a course of study should give the teacher of mathematics the original awakening and impetus, and furnish the permanent sources of inspiration and guidance without which growth and high efficiency are impossible. It places the teacher at the centre of his subject, whence he can see and use its resources to the best advantage. The command it gives him over the resources, the problems, the historical development, and the practical and theoretical utility of elementary mathematics may be expected to enrich and vitalize his teaching. Under a teacher thus equipped, the pupils feel that they are dealing with a fertile and a beautiful subject, and that they have a steady, able, and sure guide to the mastery of it. The halting and labored procedure, so characteristic of one who is not master of the situation, will be wanting; the pupils will perceive a definiteness and directness of aim and procedure, a facility of handling mathematical expressions which shows them how real it all is, how important, interesting, and useful it all is, and how accessible it all is to patient study; and, to the mathematical spirits among them, how fascinating and how simple it all may become. Such a course of study will make it impossible for the teacher of elementary mathematics to regard high school algebra, geometry, and trigonometry as "higher mathematics," as I have heard some teachers call these subjects; but he will nevertheless have a just and high regard for these subjects, and will address himself to teaching them accordingly.—*The School Review.*

BOSTON SCHOOL ADMINISTRATION.

THE feeling that I should be called upon to formulate a course of study for a primary class, or a Latin school, or a manual-training school, became oppressive when I realized that I was not what is called "equipped" for such service; nor did I hanker for the opportunity to designate what text-books should be used in the schools; a task which, in fact, amounts to nothing more than choosing between text-book publishing houses. It would seem as though even a political boss or a machine legislature could be made to understand that a lot of citizens, chosen haphazard from the shop, the counting room, the bar, the pulpit, the household (for women serve, too), ought not to be required, and should not be permitted, to decide such questions for eighty thousand children—or for eighty children, for that matter. Of course it may be said that members of school committees are not obliged to perform these duties, or, at least, they may be wisely performed perfunctorily, by adopting the suggestions of the Board of Supervisors, which is supposed to be an advisory body. But, in my experience, this is just what a school committee will not do. It may, and often does, ask the supervisors to recommend a text-book, and to report upon some purely educational question, such, for example, as the so-called enrichment of the grammar course, departmental work, and the adoption of parallel courses. But it does not follow that the expert's recommendation must be accepted, or is even likely to be. I have frequently seen such advice disregarded and sometimes spurned. The Boston committee is composed of twenty-four members (elected at large and eight retiring each year), and as the Massachusetts statute requires a two-thirds vote of the full board for the adoption of any text-book, a clever text-book agent, if he cannot get his own wares adopted, may at least prevent any other book from going on the authorized list. Results that would be ludicrous, if they were not so serious, naturally follow. I recall a number of facts which, while they all belong to one case, illustrate more than one of the points I am trying to make. During my second year in office it was discovered that much dissatisfaction was being expressed by employers of juvenile "help" because of the ill-formed, cramped, and illegible handwriting of graduates of the grammar schools. It was found, also, that Chicago and several other large cities, besides many smaller ones, both East and West, had adopted the vertical style of penmanship because it had been found that even the "hand" that was not good-looking had almost invariably the merit of being "plain." Hygienic questions were brought in, too, but these were somewhat abstruse, and subsequently the doctors in the Boston committee disagreed very learnedly upon them—as the lawyer members nearly always do on all debatable questions. The Boston board appointed a committee of five to inquire into the vertical system. This work was painstakingly and intelligently done, and the sub-committee's report, which became a public document, was unquestionably a meritorious, if a somewhat ambitious production. The introduction of the system, at least experimentally in a few schools, was recommended, The recommendation was adopted, after a hard fight, by a slender majority. Before the close of the session, when three of the yeas had retired, reconsideration was secured and the report of the sub-committee was rejected. The subject was then referred to the committee on examinations, which reported—only one member dissenting—in favor of the introduction of the system. This report was rejected, and the question was then referred to the Board of Supervisors, whither it should have gone in the first place. The experts made an exhaustive inquiry, summoning witnesses and corresponding with school authorities and other people far and near. At length they reported in favor of the vertical system. But even this report was rejected, almost contemptuously, and the superintendent was then directed by vote of the board to write to the grammar-school masters, asking them if they liked the vertical style and would be willing to try it in their classes. Several replied, expressing a willingness to experiment with the system, but most of the masters, in the words of the superintendent, "begged to be excused." So that the school committee finally stood, that year, in the position of going over the heads of its expert advisers to get the judgment of their subordinates in rank, and, withal, it was itself impotent in the end. But those masters who were willing to try the vertical system did try it, not finding anything in the rules and regulations of the department to prevent them, and by the next year, and when the annual text-book raid was almost due, it was found that the reform writing had got quite a hold. Then the committee actually passed an order which authorized and encouraged the new system. But the next step, the adoption of a text-book, was more difficult. The copybook-makers waged a most desperate war, in which the members of the board soon became offensive partisans. Even the supervisors, who had recommended a book, were unmercifully assailed, and warned against exceeding their duties. They were to be seen and not heard, except when they were asked to speak. The result was the defeat of the copy books, sixteen votes not being secured, as required by statute. So that the school committee finally stood, that year, in the position of adopting a new style of writing, but refusing to furnish the necessary text-books for securing intelligent results on the part of the pupils; while the most hurtful direct consequence is that the individual child is taught the vertical hand in one grade and the sloping hand in the next, or *vice versa*, for the whole subject now rests, through the impotence of the school committee, with the individual teachers, who are influenced by personal experience or practice, by prejudice or caprice. It is, perhaps, needless to add that the school committee was swept from its moorings (the Board of Supervisors) by the dazzling efforts, the almost hypnotic influences, of the publishing houses.

I never for a moment blamed the text-book men in this or any other instance. The board simply invites these ravenous invasions, which are annually made. Nor have I believed that the raiders find it congenial to traffic upon such predatory ground. The house that did not pursue such methods would certainly sell very few books in the Boston public schools. The selling agents care very little, I think, about the opinions, good or ill, of the Board of Supervisors, for they know that the school committee also cares very little about them. Just before the yearly attack there is a portentous calm. Few debates occur in the open board. There is a great deal of buttonholing in the corridors and the committee rooms at school headquarters. The text-book lobby is in full swing. Members whisper together and text-book men whisper to both. The text-book men follow the members to their offices and sometimes visit their homes, where much argument may be "pumped" into the individual who intends to be a spokesman on the floor in debate. I have found them very agreeable companions, for we have usually discussed school management freely, and text-books very reservedly. Before I had been long on the board I discovered that a good text-book man knew more about the public schools of Boston than the average member of the Boston committee, and I learned much from them about the conditions of the schools in New York, Brooklyn, Chicago, St. Louis, Cleveland, and a few other representative cities. I really did not need to hear their book arguments, for I knew I should hear them exactly reiterated in the school committee. As a rule such debates were confined to a few members, certain of whom almost always spoke for one particular house, while other members followed the fortunes of another house. When the storm would break, at last, it always seemed as if there would never be any more sunshine in the Boston schools, and that the members of the board must be mortal enemies for life. As for the text-book men, one could imagine them trooping off with a crowd of seconds to some sylvan dell; but, quite to the contrary, I found them, early one morning in early summer last year, sitting and chatting together on the piazza of the Maplewood Hotel, watching, as they talked, the fleeting shadows of fleecy clouds as they chased up the great slopes of Mt. Washington and went into nothingness over the summit. I was glad to meet them again, for, after I had made it known that I would invariably vote to sustain the expert Board of Supervisors in text-book controversies, I missed them, and was very sorry. They had come to attend the annual meeting of the American Institute of Instruction, availing themselves of this opportunity to call the attention of teachers and educationists to their books and to secure written commendations where possible. I have found schoolmasters and even supervisors rather free in doing this sort of thing, and they, too, are not unlikely to "stand in" with one particular house through thick and thin. While I do not know that this is altogether wrong, I do know that I was embarrassed, and found my position with regard to expert advice made almost untenable, through the practice of supervisors themselves of launching text-books of their own upon the market through some favored houses, which promptly invited the school committee to put these books on the authorized list. I do not believe it possible to secure from a small, close body like this an absolutely fair, and certainly not an unquestionable, professional opinion on the value and applicability of a book produced by one of its own members. And this brings me back to the school committee itself, whose members, like the text-book men, soon see the shadows flee when the controversy is closed. I have suspected log-rolling in some instances, but probably there was nothing in this, though I very distinctly recall a remark made in a sub-committee room one afternoon by a member toward whom reform associations are particularly tender. The memorable fight over Frye's *Geography* had taken place; the book had been defeated. The member (whose sex it would perhaps be unfair to state) was indignant, and exclaimed: "If we can't have Frye's *Geography*, they shan't have Metcalf's *Grammar*." This was not said during the stress of battle, but several days after it. The books mentioned came from rival houses that have had a long struggle for supremacy in Boston, and the "we" and the "they" in that sentence of eleven words bespoke the position of the Boston School Committee on the whole text-book question.

This kind of mischief done or averted, the board soon settled down to the discussion of some other form of patronage. The teachership is still a spoil of office. It is more difficult, at the present time, for a Catholic than for a Protestant young woman to get a place, but, nevertheless, some Catholics secure appointments, for "trading" may always be done, while each side has a wholesome fear of the other assailing it in the open board. A member said one day, in my hearing: "I must have my quota of teachers in —— ——, anyhow." (The dashes represent the district in which he resides.) It turned out that he got at least a good part of what he demanded, and there was a remarkable sequel. One of the ablest masters in the service, an elderly, discreet man, said to me one day: "I don't know what I shall do with that Miss ——; she is thoroughly incompetent and a great injury to my school."

"It seems to me," I said, "you have only to make that statement to your division committee in charge."

"No, no," he replied, "it would never do. She was put in by Mr. ——, and if she were removed the A. P. A. cry would be raised, and that would do the whole school so much injury I had rather put up with a poor teacher."

This religious difficulty has a double-back-action. Sometimes the Catholic is kept out of her rights; at others the Protestant is wronged to give the Catholic a place. And there is no peace any more. Actual merit is one of the last things thought of, if it is ever thought of at all. It is true the candidate must have passed an examination, but the supply is always much greater than the demand, and written examination is necessarily inadequate as a test of fitness, because it does not bring out the quality known as teaching ability. If a poor teacher gets into the service, removal seem almost impossible, because it is the political factor which controls. The elective board has the "say." The superintendent and his supervisors are mere figureheads. Even an opinion is rarely asked of them in such matters as this. Transfers are made without their knowledge. Sub-masters are chosen, and, in due time, promoted to masterships without it being even said to them: "What do you think of this?" The board at one time ordered a preferred list of sub-masters eligible for promotion to be made by the supervising body, but the very first time there was a vacancy it was found that the man with a "pull" was not on the list, and the list was therefore ignored. Subsequently, it was found to have been ignored so much the board gravely voted it out of existence. "Pull" and expediency stand for merit now. If a master and his sub-master are incompatible, the sub-master is given the first vacant mastership for harmony's sake. Sometimes, and not infrequently, a master is transferred, regardless of the good of the service, from one side of the city to another, in order to make a vacancy in a school where an influential sub-master desires a promotion. The advice of the superintendent, if it is given, has no weight in such cases. It is not even thought of, I feel sure, when the board proceeds to the business of making the changes. The most inefficient sub-master in the service to-day may be elected master to-morrow, for while the salaried educationists may prefer what is best, the non-professional committee men will probably choose what is worst. There is often that very marked difference; personal advancement by mere choosing rather than by preferment. It has been suggested that the remedy may lie in delegating to the superintendent and supervisors the power to promote; or, at least, the board could adopt a rule by which, in effect, it would agree neither to select nor promote any instructor not recommended by the advisory officers. I do not expect to see any school committee accept with honest intent any such proposal. At all events, it would not be worth what it would cost to put it into type, so long as the supervisors and superintendent are not made secure by long tenure of office. I served but three years on the board, and yet voted for these officers twice during my short term of service. Few men thus situated are so natured that they can spontaneously assert the exact truth, without ambiguity or evasion, when they know it to be unwelcome, and likely, if fearlessly and too forcibly expounded, to render each of them *persona non grata* with the office-giving authority. If President McKinley should go to the custodian of the post-office building in New York and tell him he wished Mike Jones appointed a janitor's helper, it is not probable the custodian would waste much time looking up the "availability" of Mr. Jones for such a position. Of course, Mr. McKinley would not do this, but members of school committees find no office, however humble, unworthy of their personal attention. And it is not a stretch of imagination to foresee the school-board politician saying to the Board of Supervisors: "You are going to recommend Alf. Wiggle for the mastership of the Charles Sumner School, or I'll know the reason why!" The more refined worker on the board will hint to the supervisors that Mr. Wiggle seems to be a person who would fill the vacant place satisfactorily. In the end the office-seekers, who are invariably the most energetic, would get their candidates in, or the supervisors would get out.—*Educational Review.*

(*To be continued.*)

SLOUCH.

I WOULD like to see in every school-room of our growing country, in every business office, at the railway stations, and on street corners large placards placed with "Do not slouch" printed thereon in distinct and imposing characters. For if ever there was a tendency that needed nipping in the bud (alas! I fear the bud is fast becoming a full-blown flower), it is this discouraging national failing.

Each year when I return from my spring wanderings among the benighted and effete nations of the Old World, on whom the true American looks down from the height of his superiority, I am struck anew by the contrast between the trim, well-groomed officials I have left behind me on one side of the ocean and the happy-go-lucky slouching individuals I find on the other. As I ride up town this unpleasant impression deepens. In the "little Mother Isle" I have just left, the "bus" drivers" have quite a coaching air, with hat and coat of "knowing" form. They sport flowers in their buttonholes and salute other "bus" drivers when they meet with a twist of whip and elbow refreshingly correct, showing by their air that they take pride in their calling, and have been at some pains to turn themselves out as "smart" in appearance as their finances would allow. Here, on the contrary, the stage and cab drivers I meet seem to be under a blight, and to have lost all interest in life. They lounge on the box, their legs straggling aimlessly, one hand holding the reins, the other hanging dejectedly by the side. Yet there is little doubt that these heartbroken citizens are earning quite double what their London confreres gain. But the shadow of the national peculiarity is over them. When I get to my rooms, the elevator "boy" is reclining in the lift, and hardly raises his eyelids as he languidly manœuvres the rope. I have seen that boy now for months, but never when his cravat was not riding proudly above his collar. On occasions I have even offered him pins, which he took wearily, doubtless because it was less trouble than to refuse. But the next day the cravat again rode triumphant, mocking my efforts to keep it in its place. His hair, too, has been a cause of wonder to me. How does he manage to have it always so long and so unkempt? More than once, when expecting callers, I have bribed him to have it cut, but it seemed to grow in the night back to its poetic profusion.

In what does this noble disregard for appearances which permeates our middle class men originate? Our climate, as some suggest, or discouragement at not being all millionaires? It more likely comes from an absence with us of the military training that abroad goes so far toward licking young men into shape.

I shall never forget the surprise on the face of a French statesman to whom I once expressed my sympathy for his country, laboring under the burden of so vast a standing army. He answered: "The financial burden is doubtless great; but you have others. Witness your pension expenditures; while with us the money drawn from the people is used in such a way as to be of inestimable value to them. We take the young hobbledehoy farm-hand or mechanic, ignorant, mannerless, uncleanly as he may be, and turn him out at the end of three years with his regiment, self-respecting and well-mannered, with habits of cleanliness and obedience, having acquired a bearing and a love of order that will cling to him and serve him all his life. We do not go so far," he added, "as our English neighbors in drilling men into superb manikins of 'form' and carriage. Our authorities do not consider it necessary. But we reclaim them from the slovenliness of their native village, and make them tidy and mannerly citizens."

These remarks came to mind the other day as I watched a group of New England youths lounging on the steps of the village store, or sitting in rows on a neighboring fence, until I longed to try if even a judicious arrangement of tacks, "business-side up," on these favorite seats would infuse any energy into their movements. I came to the conclusion that my French acquaintance was about right, for the only trim-looking men I saw were either veterans of our war or youths belonging to the local militia. And nowhere can you see finer specimens of humanity than West Point turns out yearly.

But if any one doubts what kind of man slouching youths develop into, let him look when he travels at the hopeless appearance of our farmhouses throughout the land. Surely our rural population is not so much poorer than in other countries. Yet compare the dreary homes of even our well to-do farmers with the smiling, well-kept hamlets one sees in England or on the Continent.

If ours were an old and bankrupt nation, this air of discouragement and decay could not be greater. One looks in vain for some sign of American dash and enterprise in the appearance of our men and their homes. During a journey of over 4,000 miles, made last spring as the guest of a gentleman who knows our country thoroughly, we were all impressed most painfully with this abject air. Never in all those days did we see a fruit-tree trained on some sunny southern wall, a smiling flower garden, or carefully clipped hedge. Hardly even the necessary vegetables are grown. My host told me that throughout the West and South they prefer canned food. It is less trouble.

If you wish to form an idea of the extent to which slouch prevails in our country, make the experiment of trying to start a "village improvement society," and experience, as others have done, the apathy and ill-will of the inhabitants. Go about among them and try to rouse some of their local pride to your aid.

In the town near where I pass my summers, a large stone, fallen from a passing dray, lay for days in the middle of the principal street, until I paid some boys to remove it. No one cared, and the dull-eyed inhabitants would doubtless be looking at it still but for my impatience.

You would imagine they were all on the point of moving away (and they generally are if they can sell their farms), so little interest do they show in your plans. Like all people who have fallen into bad habits, they have grown to love their slatternly ways and cling to them, resenting furiously any attempt to shake them up to vigor and reform.

The farmer, however, has not a monopoly. Slouch seems ubiquitous. Our large railway and steamboat systems have tried in vain to combat it, and supplied their employees with a livery (I beg the free and independent voter's pardon—a uniform !), but it has had little effect. The inherent tendency is too strong for the corporations. The conductor will shuffle along in his spotted garments, his cap on the back of his head, and his legs anywhere, while he chews gum in defiance of the whole board of directors.

Go down to Washington after a visit to the houses of Parliament or the Chamber of Deputies, and observe the air and bearing of our Senators and Representatives. They seem to try and avoid every appearance of "smartness." Indeed, I am told, so great is the prejudice against a well-turned-out man that a candidate would seriously compromise his chances of election who appeared before his constituents in other than the accustomed shabby frock-coat, unbuttoned and floating, a pot hat unbrushed, no gloves, as much doubtful white shirt-front as possible, and a whisp of black silk for a tie ; and if he can exhibit also a chin whisker, his chances of election are materially increased.

Nothing offends the eye accustomed to our native "laisser aller" so much as a well-brushed hat and shining boots. When abroad, I can "spot" a compatriot as soon and as far as I can see one by his graceless bearing, a cross between a lounge and a shuffle. In reading or dining-room, he is the only man whose spine does not seem equal to its work, so he flops and straggles until, for the honor of your land, you long to shake him and set him squarely on his legs.

Now, no amount of reasoning can convince me that outward slovenliness is not a sign of inward and moral supineness. A neglected exterior generally means a lax moral code. A man who considers it "too much trouble" to sit erect can hardly have given much time to his tub or his toilet. Having neglected his clothes, he will neglect his manners, and between morals and manners we know the tie is intimate.

In the Orient a new reign is often inaugurated by the construction of a mosque. Vast expense is incurred to make it as splendid as possible. But, once completed, it is never touched again. Others are built by succeeding sovereigns, but neither thought nor treasure is ever expended on an old one. When it can no longer be used, it is abandoned, and gradually falls into decay. The same system seems to prevail among our private owners and corporations. Streets are paved, lamp-posts erected, store-fronts carefully adorned, but from the hour the workman puts his finishing touch upon them they are abandoned to the hand of fate. The mud may cake up knee-deep, wind and weather work their own sweet will, but it is no one's business to interfere.

One of my amusements has been of an early morning to watch Paris making its toilet. The streets are taking a bath, the lamp-posts and newspaper stands are having their feet scrubbed, the shop-fronts are being shaved and having their hair curled, cafes and restaurants are putting on clean shirts and tying their cravats smartly before their many mirrors. By the time the world is up and about, the whole city, smiling freshly from its matutinal tub, is ready to greet them gaily.

It is just this attention to detail that gives to continential cities their air of cheerfulness and thrift, and the utter lack of it that impresses foreigners so painfully on arriving at our shores.

It has been the fashion to laugh at the dude and his high collar, and the darky of a Sunday morning in his master's cast off clothes, aping style and fashion. But better the dude, better the colored dandy, better even the Bowery "tough" with his affected carriage, for they at least are reaching blindly out after something better than their surroundings, striving after an ideal, and are in just so much the superiors of the foolish souls who mock them—better even misguided efforts, than the ignoble stagnant quagmire of slouch into which we seem to be slowly descending.

AN IDLER *In Evening Post.*

MODERN COLLEGE EDUCATION.

BY GRANT ALLEN.

BEYOND a doubt, the course of learning Greek and Latin does afford one a single piece of good mental training; it is unrivalled as a method of understanding the nature of grammar—that is to say, of the analysis of language. But this knowledge itself, though valuable up to a certain point, is absurdly overrated; ignorance of grammar is treated as a social crime, while ignorance of very important and fundamental facts about life or nature is treated as venial, and in some cases even as a mark of refinement.

An intelligent system of higher education designed to meet the needs of modern life would begin by casting away all preconceptions equally, and by reconstructing its curriculum on psychological principles. (And, I may add in parenthesis, the man to reconstruct it would be Professor Lester Ward.) I am talking now, of course, of a general scheme of preliminary higher education—the sort of education which should form a basis for all professions alike (like the ordinary B.A. degree at present), and which would have to be afterwards supplemented by the special technical training of the lawyer, the doctor, the merchant, the manufacturer, the engineer and the parson. Such an education ought primarily to be an education of the faculties; and for educating the faculties, language and grammar have proved themselves to be the worst possible failures. It ought, however, at the same time to consider whether, while training the faculties, it could not also simultantaneously store the mind with useful facts. For both these purposes a general education in knowledge is the most satisfactory; and I say knowledge on purpose, instead of saying science, unduly restricted. I would include among the most important forms of knowledge a knowledge of man's history, his development, his arts and his literature. I believe that, for a groundwork, a considerable range of subjects is best; this may be supplemented later by specialization in particular directions. Let us first have adequate acquaintance with the rudiments of all knowledge; in other words, let us avoid gross ignorance of any; afterwards, let us have special skill in one or more.

As a beginning, then, I would say, negatively, no Greek, no Latin, no French, no German. Those languages, or some of them, might or might not come later in particular instances. For example, a man might get interested in Hellas (say by travel, or by examining Greek sculpture), and might reasonably take up Hellenic art and Hellenic archæology; in connection with which it would also be desirable that he should read Æschylus, Sophocles, Herodotus and Thucydides, not to mention likewise Pausanias and Pliny (I am aware that Pliny wrote in Latin). Or he might have business relations with Germany; in which case it would be desirable that he should learn German. Or he might take an interest in literature as a whole, and in the history of its development; in which case, of course, he could not afford to neglect French literature. Moreover, since languages are most easily acquired during plastic childhood, I do not deny that *if* exceptional opportunities exist for picking up modern languages (as during travel, etc.) advantage should be taken of them. I am not dogmatically opposed to the learning of languages; I have learned one or two (besides Greek and Latin) of my own accord. I only say their importance has been vastly overrated, and the relative importance of certain other subjects unaccountably underrated.

On the other hand, education ought certainly to include for everybody, men and women alike, some general acquaintance with the following subjects: Mathematics, so far as the particular intelligence will go; physics, so as to know the properties of matter; generalized chemistry; zoology; botany; astronomy; geography; geology; human history, and especially the history of the great central civilization, which includes Egypt, Assyria and Babylonia, Persia, Asia Minor, Hellas, Italy, Western Europe, America; human arts, and especially the arts of painting, sculpture and architecture in North Africa, Western Asia and Europe. If this seems a large list for the foundations of an education, it must be remembered that six or seven years would be set free for the acquisition of useful knowledge by the abolition of grammatical rote-work; and that a general idea alone of each subject is all I ask for.

For instance, in physics, it would suffice that students should be taught the fundamental laws of matter, solid, liquid, and gaseous; the principles of gravitation; the main facts about light and heat; and some notions of electrical science. In biology, it would suffice that they should be taught the general classification of animals, a little comparative anatomy and physiology, and some idea of specific distinctions. At present, quite well-informed people will speak of a porpoise or a lobster as a fish; such grotesque blunders ought to be made impossible; they ought to be considered far more damnatory evidence of ignorance and ill-breeding than "you was" or "me and him went there." A few weeks' practice will enable any intelligent young man or woman of eighteen to identify any plant in the American flora by the aid of a technical description; and the mental value of that training is immeasurably greater than the mental value of ten years' work at Greek syntax. And so forth with the other subjects. I contend that a man or woman ought to leave college with a fairly competent general idea of most arts and sciences, to be supplemented by exact knowledge of one chosen subject—say, beetles or chemistry, or the English literature of the seventeenth century, or Hittite inscriptions, or the fresh-water mollusks of the United States, or early Flemish painting, or the geology of the Ohio basin. The special subject ought always to be one chosen, out of pure predilection, by the student himself; the general subjects ought to be imposed from above by the educational authorities of the particular university. In this way you avoid complete and foolish ignorance of any one subject about which it is desirable for everybody to know something; but at the same time you give full and free play to individual diversities of taste and faculty.

A person brought up on such a curriculum ought to be fairly well equipped for the battle of modern life in everything except the technical training of the particular profession. And technical training must, of course, come afterwards—in the medical school, in the lawyer's office, in the engineering yard, in the merchant's counting-house. But I mantain that every man or woman will be better fitted for every position in life—he or she may fill—as a citizen, as a breadwinner, as a wife, as a parent—than when linguistically educated upon the existing basis. Wide knowledge of facts is essential to success in modern life; it is ignorance of facts that most often causes failure of adaptation. And any nation that ventured to adopt such an education in facts, instead of words, would forge ahead of all other nations with an accelerated rapidity that would astonish even those who introduced it.

But there is a preconception still more fatal to progress than all these preconceptions with which I have hitherto dealt—a preconception which vitiates as yet almost all thinking on the subject, even in America. It is the deep-seated prejudice in favor of the college itself—of education as essentially a thing of teaching, not of learning—of education as bookish and scholastic—another baneful legacy of the monkish training. I believe almost everybody still overestimates the importance of college as such, and underestimates the value of travel and experince. Let me put the thing graphically. Thousands of American parents, asked to thrust their hands into their pockets and pay a round sum to send their sons or daughters to Harvard or Vassar, will do so without hesitation. Thousands of English parents will do the same thing, at still greater expense, for Oxford or Girton. But ask those same parents to thrust their hands into their pockets and pull out an equal amount to send their sons and daughters traveling, deliberately, as a mode of education, in Europe, and they will draw back at once; "I don't want to waste so large a sum on a mere pleasure excursion."

Why is this? Clearly because the mediæval idea that most learning or all learning is to be derived from books still survives among us. In the middles ages travel was difficult. People lived much in the same place, and the knowledge of the times was really all book knowledge. To-day people travel freely; but the conception of travel as a great educator hardly exists at all in Europe, and is relatively little known even in America. I say "even in America," for I gladly admit that many more Americans than Europeans do really understand the high educational value of travel. But for the Englishman, travel in England itself is comparatively useless; so for the American, is travel in America. It is travel in other countries that is of prime importance—above all, in the motherlands of culture—France, Germany, Italy, Greece, Egypt. And the great est of these is Italy.

In my opinion a father who has sons and daughters of the proper age to go to college will do better by his children, and not less economically for himself, if he sends them for two years to travel in Europe than if he sends them for three years to an American or English university.

The knowledge gained at the university is unreal and bookish—

mere half knowledge; the knowledge obtained by travel is real and first hand; it teaches and impresses. And the things it has taught us live with us forever.

Let any cultivated man or woman of middle age ask himself or herself seriously: "How much of what I know that I really prize did I learn at school and college, or learn from books, and how much did I learn from things seen and visited in London, Paris, Venice, Florence, Munich, Nuremberg, Dresden, Brussels?" Will not the answer be, to the first half, next to nothing; to the second half, almost everything? Speaking for myself, I can honestly say I went away from Oxford without a single element of education worth speaking of, and without the slightest training in method or development of faculties. Everything that I have ever learned worth knowing I have taught myself since by observation and travel; and I reckon in particular my first visit to Italy as the greatest and most important date in my mental history. Oxford taught one how to write imitation Latin verses; Italy taught one who the Romans were, and why their language and literature are worthy of study. Until you have been in Rome it is silly and childish to read Roman books; only when you know Rome does Rome begin to live and speak for you

One's own experience is often the best guide one can have; therefore I shall make no apology for adding that on the first day I ever spent in Rome, I took a long drive round the town—a drive of mere orientation, suitable for a man who was weary with travelling all night; and in the course of it I saw the Forum, the Capitol, the Palatine, the island in the Tiber, the Vatican, St. Peter's, the Pantheon, the column of Trajan, and most of the other great monuments and churches. Now, I had been teaching Roman history half my life, and lecturing on the masterpieces of Roman literature; but when I returned from that drive I felt I knew and understood Rome as I had never understood it before; and I was ashamed of the fact that I had not earlier seen it. I realized that my education had been neglected. I re-read several of my classics, comprehending for the first time in my life what they were about, and reading them with pleasure, where before I had read from a sense of duty. The man who has once visited Italy finds all the world thenceforth something fuller and deeper for him.

"But you had already learned some Latin!" In fear and trembling, yes; as a hateful task, to be examined in. If I had never learned Latin till I went to Italy, and had then spelled it out word by word on the monuments, I should have learned it more thoroughly, and certainly loved it better.—*Cosmopolitan.*

EDITORIAL NOTES.

"Deliver not the tasks of might
To weakness, neither hide the ray
From those, not blind, who wait for day,
Tho' sitting girt with doubtful light.

"That from Discussion's lips may fall
With Life, that, working strongly binds—
Set in all lights by many minds,
So close the interests of all."

Vanity it would be in me and to you bootless, to repeat what has been repeated and written *ad nauseam* about the increase of pupils since 1847, in the then Grammar Schools, now our High Schools and Collegiate Institutes, also the great change which has come to our Colleges and Universities, as regards both equipment and attendance, and logically therefore the great increase in the wealth and population in Ontario, Canada; the last item being the basis on which the two former facts stand.

Not, indeed, that these things are unimportant, especially if we took time to analyse the characteristics of the population of Canada. If this were done, I believe the result would be eminently satisfactory to the Central British Empire.

The words given me, the Higher Education, High Schools, Colleges, etc, etc. gave me pause.

The Higher Education surely cannot be modes of conducting examinations, or the results of examinations, though these are much spoken about and written about, or even the number of graduates of High Schools and Colleges.

If the staffs in these seats of learning are cherishing the fond delusion that the country expects only, as the result of their labor, that the alumni of these institutions may be able to give a good account of themselves in examination halls or on public platforms, to the neglect or in defiance of the absolutely necessary education covered better by the word manners than any other single word, then they are woefully mistaken. No one whose opinion is worth having on any matter pertaining to life can depreciate these splendid gifts, but they are not Education.

The Crown is celestial; we must reject everything as a temptation to evil, which has a tendency to confine our efforts and energies to gathering straws, small sticks and dust, like unto the man in the immortal Allegory.

Within the last two weeks I met a man born in Toronto more than 54 years ago. His father had considerable property, a large share of which fell to this son. After the death of the father the son invested pretty freely, by which he lost $30,900. He risked unwisely and lost; all right, he himself said. He gave me unasked his views of our education. "The centre of our system of education is in the wrong place. When I see a lot of young men in our colleges, etc., come down Yonge Street, smoking, swaggering, hands in their pockets, and often talking loudly, I feel and say that they are in the wrong place, and think to myself who pays for these young men? What will these young men do at college, and worse still, what can they do for a living? Many of our young doctors live on 5 cent lunches. Many of these leave us and go to U. S. A. When I look over our town and see many families from the country, the parents having sold their farm and brought their children to the city, sons and daughters, to educate them, they say, then I ask again, what are these children to do? Every one cannot be a lawyer, or clerk in a store, or type-writer. It is *ruin* to these children; perhaps worse for the daughters than for the sons. But it is ruin; I tell you, sir, the centre of our education is in the wrong place."

"What would you suggest in order to improve matters?" I asked my communicative friend.

"We must have more farmers, more mechanics, more artisans, more producers of weath. We have too many non-producers."

Extract-notes of remarks made by the Editor of THE CANADA EDUCATIONAL MONTHLY, at a banquet held during Jubilee of Toronto Normal School, Nov. 2, 1897.

These, in brief, are the statements made by a man who was born in Toronto, and lived in the city continuously for over 54 years; several times went to the U. S A. as far south as Washington. I do not vouch for their correctness, but there is no doubt that he believes them to be correct, and blames our educational system for the desire of our people for professional life, and he gave me particulars which I must suppress."

Ontario is not alone in this respect. We find practically the same conditions existing in the U. S. A.

To give an opinion on what I constantly hear and see on every side, I would say that our great lack is lack of reverence, manifested in the lack of respect to age, lack of consideration for the work our forefathers were engaged in, and in which they lived healthily and happily.

The Mayor of Montreal the other evening at the Convention of the Protestant Teachers of Quebec, said that farming—the mainstay of Canada's prosperity—was now carried on as a drudgery. His Worship's hope for a better state of things was in the teachers of his province. Akin to his Worship's statement is that made by a writer in one of the leading magazines of the U. S. A. viz:—that quite recently he travelled westward in his country for 3,500 miles without seeing a kitchen garden on a farm. The farmers seem to feel that unless they can have the sofas, chairs, carpets, etc., etc., which are found in houses in our cities and towns, whether paid for or not, they are ill-treated. They seem to have lost the sense of appreciation of things suitable for the farm; the strength and beauty of chairs, clocks, tables, chests of drawers, etc., which have upon them the comeliness of having served more than one generation. The characteristic which is working so much damage to our country is lack of respect for the work in which the individual may be for the time engaged. We are all workers, and in the right spirit we should rejoice in our work.

The Higher Education can only be found in the direction indicated in the following three statements:

1. Do justly, love mercy and walk humbly with thy God.
(Written 2600 years ago.)

2. Not slothful in business, fervent in spirit, serving the Lord.
(Written 1837 years ago.)

3. Self-reverence, self-knowledge, self-control.
(Written during the present generation.)

" In the softly fading twilight
 Of a weary, weary day,
With a quiet step I entered
 Where the children were at play;
I was brooding o'er some trouble
 Which had met me unawares,
When a little voice came singing,
 'Me is creeping up the stairs.' "

" Ah it touched the tenderest heart strings,
 With a breath and force divine,
And such melodies awakened
 As no wording can define.
And I turned to see our darling,
 All forgetful of my cares,
When I saw the little creature
 Slowly creeping up the stairs."

" Step by step she bravely clambered,
 On her little hands and knees,
Keeping up a constant chatter,
 Like a Magpie in the trees.
Till at last she reached the topmost
 When o'er all her world's affairs,
She delighted stood a victor
 After creeping up the stairs."

" Fainting heart, behold an image
 Of man's brief and struggling life,

Whose best prizes must be captured
  With a noble, earnest strife;
Onward, upward, reaching ever,
  Bending to the weight of cares,
Hoping, fearing, still expecting,
  We go creeping up the stairs."

LESS SOCIETY AND MORE SLEEP.

THE tendency of boys and girls to enter society at an age when they are in nearly every respect unfitted for it is one that needs to be carefully guarded. While no sensible person desires to remove from the young a single source of real enjoyment and pleasure, the time has come in this country when all the friends of our grammar and high school pupils should unite in demanding for them, because it is absolutely necessary to their future happiness and usefulness, that they give less time to society and more time to sleep. This may seem like a very plain and abrupt statement, but it is, nevertheless, a true one. We have frequently heard the public lecturer accuse the public schools of overworking the boys and girls, and in many instances the accusation has been met with applause from fathers and mothers who ought to have known better. It is possible that, in very rare instances, pupils in our grammar and high schools are overworked, and as a result nervous prostration follows, but every time one instance of this kind can be found, at least a score may be found of similar conditions brought about by the attendance of boys and girls at parties and dances three or four nights each week when they ought to be at home in bed. Every parent or teacher who has ever given the matter any intelligent, honest consideration will admit that the application and hard work which are absolutely necessary on the part of each and every pupil who succeeds in his studies, cannot be developed in the midst of the distracting influences surrounding the person who gives up his time to the demands of modern society. It is gratifying to note that teachers and superintendents are beginning to call special attention to this very important question. In the last report of the Newark Public Schools, Supt. J. C. Hartzler refers to it as follows:

"The besetting weakness of public schools of the city and country over is the indifference of parents as to regularity of attendance. The premature entrance of our young people into society circles is doing more to dissipate interest in school work than perhaps all else. Loss of sleep and late refreshments always unfit a pupil for both the preparation and recitation of lessons. It is hoped that this brief suggestion may be graciously received by the patrons of our city schools."

At the opening of the schools this fall Supt. Hartzler again called attention to the matter through the Newark papers:

"May not the above suggestion be further emphasized at this time, the opening of the school year, by this additional suggestion, that no evenings of the school days, Friday evening, if it must be so, excepted, be wasted in premature attentions to society by our young, school-going people? Sleep, the greatest of all restoratives of nervous energy, so indispensable to the conditions of correct student life, cannot be interfered with without reflex injury.

"Foreigners tell us that we Americans live too fast, eat too viciously, struggle too hard in the scramble for wealth, and are thereby too wasteful of our nerve energy; all of which every observing and considerate person must accept as true. If there is any part of our present construction of society that needs reconstruction, it must be admitted to be in the premature entrance of our young school-going people into society circles. But this question needs no further discussion here. We believe that a fair, frank statement to the upper grammar and high school grades, suggesting the importance of regular habits of living as well as of study on the part of our students, will prove a sufficient guaranty that an improved condition of things will prevail in Newark in the future."

We congratulate Dr. Hartzler on the firm and sensible stand he has taken, and are glad to learn that he is meeting with the most hearty co-operation of the great majority of the patrons in his city. Let the good work go on. In these latter days when character—manhood and womanhood—is being emphasized, as never before, as the end and aim of education, it is well to remember that good habits are very essential elements in good character. Society of the right kind has its proper place in the world, and in that place is all important, but the foolishness and emptiness which characterize modern society in many instances are purchased at too dear a price, when health, and opportunity to get an education are sacrificed to obtain them.—*Ohio Educational Monthly.*

CURRENT EVENTS AND COMMENTS.

MANY cultured United States folk have been in Canada this summer and autumn, in connection with the meetings of the British Association and the British Medical Association at Toronto and Montreal, and they are carrying back to their homes a new idea of Canada and the Canadian people. Professor D. S. Martin, for instance, says: "The writer was much confirmed in the belief, formed on previous visits to Canada, that our people do not understand or appreciate our neighbors at the north, the greatness of their domain, their just pride in it and intense love for it; their educational, scientific and material progress, and their truly national spirit. Too often we hear Canada spoken of as a mere appendage to England, and its people as without a country of their own. Nothing is farther from the truth. The Dominion has an area somewhat greater than ours, even including Alaska; vast regions of it are just being opened to cultivation, and in a few years will be changed from a wilderness into a 'fruitful field'; its mineral resources are enormous; its institutions free and progressive; its society cultivated and elegant."

"If Canada," Professor Martin goes on to say, "has not absolute and separate independence, she has a feeling of being part, and a great part, of a world-wide empire of the English-speaking race, 'on which the sun never sets.' Her people are proud and loyal; and they have good reason to be so. They have no menace and no jealousy for us; they wish to be friends and kind neighbors, but any idea of absorption or annexation is intensely alien to their feelings, and can never be realized or even approached until immense changes have taken place and long decades have passed.

"In fact, Canada and the United States are like two brothers whose careers have been differently chosen and shaped. One has quarrelled with his father, gone away and set up for himself, and developed great energy and great success. He is proud of his independence and achievements, and cares naught for the old homestead and family traditions. The other has remained near his father, has built his home on the ancestral estate, and clings to the memories and associations of the family. He, too, is wealthy and proud, but his pride and his treasure are interwoven with the name and the fame of the paternal house. The two people are different; they are two nations, each with its own work to do and its own providential mission to fulfil in diffusing a free, intelligent, Christian civilization through the continent of North America.—*The Canadian Gazette, London, Eng.*

In these days we hear a great deal —perhaps not too much—about "awakening an interest" on the part of pupils in their studies. The value of this "interest" depends very largely upon its character and what it will do for a pupil after it is awakened. If the chief factor leading up to it is *eutertainment,* and it leaves the pupil in a state of mind which will be satisfied only by more *entertainment* of the same kind, then the less we have of it the better. In some schools which make a very good showing when on "dress parade," it will be observed that the teacher does all the *work,* and all that the boys and girls have to do is to be "interested" in the performance. On the other hand if the "interest" on the part of the pupil is of such a character as to lead him to *work* and what is still better *to love to work,* then we cannot have too much of it. It must never be forgotten that ability to do continuous hard work cheerfully and happily is the one factor in character, on account of the lack of which, so many people fail in life's work—*Ohio Educational Monthly.*

Have we any signs presenting themselves of the literal fulfilment of the prophecies respecting Israel's restoration to the Promised Land? We have. For one thing, it must be noted that its process will be a gradual one. The restoration from Babylon which had been predicted was of this nature. Let us, then, notice what history records, and observe some of the signs of the times.

It is an historical fact that a great change for the better has come upon the Jews during the past century. To a great extent they have become emancipated from "the yoke of the Gentiles." In England they were enfranchised in 1753. In France the yoke fell off a little later. In Austria, a liberating edict was proclaimed in 1783. In Prussia oppressive laws were repealed in 1787. In Russia the edict which excluded Jews from the country was revoked in 1805. Other countries in time followed these examples. The grasping Turk gave them toleration and liberty to possess land in Palestine in 1867; while in Italy the day of their humiliation terminated with the overthrow of the Pope's temporal power in 1870. In all this we see the fulfilment of the prediction that in "the latter days" the people should burst their bonds (Jer. xxx: 8). In England the restrictions which existed have been fully removed from the Jews. They now have seats in the national Legislature. A Jew has reigned as Lord Mayor of London, and another has enjoyed that high honor during this present year. Their influence in politics is rapidly extending throughout Europe, where they possess an extensive hold on the press of leading cities.

They have also entered into the educational arena with zest. They hold in various quarters high positions as instructors of the people; and as scholars, linguists, critics, and professors they rank among the highest.

Their influence in literature, education, and politics is not alone considerable, but is on the increase—so much so that a leading journal has said: "If this upward movement continues, the Israelites, a century hence, will be masters of Europe" (*Century*, April, 1882). This is not unlikely, because the "sure word of prophecy" has declared, "I will make you a name and a praise among all people of the earth" (Zeph. iii, 20). Combined with all this it is to be noticed that prophecy sets forth how the Jews should be possessed of immense wealth when on the eve of restoration. There is a vast accumulation of money now in Jewish hands, according to the official statistics of various European countries. They command some of the Bourses in Europe. The position of the Rothschilds is well known. Be it how it may, there is a noted tendency for capital to accumulate with the Jews; and herein we find a further prophetic fulfilment. Isaiah foretold that they should "eat the riches of the Gentiles," that is, increase in wealth at the expense of the latter.—*The Quiver.*

The University of Toronto has made a distinct advance by establishing a post-graduate course leading to the degree of Ph.D. No provision has as yet been made for post-graduate lectures, but the regulations laid down in the new Calendar are such that a graduate of the University on pursuing a special subject for two years after graduation, presenting a satisfactory thesis as evidence of research in that line, and passing an examination on two allied minor subjects, may receive his "Ph.D." on the fulfilment of a further requirement, the payment of the necessary fee. All candidates must be graduates in Arts of the University of Toronto, and registered in the University as graduate students. In order, however, that graduates of other Universities may enter on the course, if so desirous, provision has been made that they may register on being admitted *ad eundem gradum* in the University of Toronto. The subjects are arranged in groups, and the candidate is allowed to choose his special or major subject from any of the following departments: Biology, chemistry, physics, geology, philosophy, Oriental languages, political science, modern languages, Latin and Greek, history and mathematics. This major subject must be pursued for two years under the direction of the professor of such subject in the University, but on report of satisfactory study at another university, exemption from attendance for the first of the two years may be granted. In the minor subjects chosen an examination equivalent to that required for first-class honors in the examination for the B.A. degree must be taken, though this examination will be dispensed with if the candidate has already obtained first-class honors in these subjects at the University. The chief feature, and that for which the course was primarily established, is the requirement of a thesis on some topic embodying the result of an original investigation, conducted by the candidate himself. It is hoped that by this means original research may receive a stimulus in the University. The new course may be entered upon with the commencement of the academic year.

Most of our educational institutions have reopened for the fall term, and the attendance seems to be larger than ever. A word or two to parents may not be out of place: Try and get to know the men and women who are teaching and training your boys and girls, and let them know that they possess your confidence and sympathy. Do not listen to every complaint your boy or your girl makes. At least, if you do, see that you investigate thoroughly. Do not set at naught the discipline of the school, or ask for too many relaxations in favor of your children. Their teachers will probably know your children's characters as well, if not better, than you do yourself, and unless in very exceptional cases, this authority should be upheld at home. What children need particularly to learn in this age is obedience, which is simply putting one's self in a right relation to the world.

THE MONTREAL CONVENTION.

FROM the full reports that have appeared in the public press of Montreal, the late convention of the Teachers' Provincial Association of Quebec has been the most successful ever held in the history of that Association. The president of the assembly was Dr. J. M. Harper, who was ably assisted by the Hon. Dr. Ross, of Toronto, Hon. Judge Lynch, Principal Peterson, Rev. Principal McVicar, Rev. Principal Adams, and the more prominent of the educationists and teachers of the Province, in bringing about the success of the various sessions. It is our intention to refer to the proceedings next month, and to examine the discussions which promoted the greatest interest. The influence which has been exerted upon the teachers to make so much of the selection of officers is said to be a pernicious influence, and one that has for years been antagonistic to everything in the way of solid improvement; and now that one of the teachers has entered an open protest against that influence the whole history of the trouble will no doubt be exposed in time, and the teachers be led to breathe a purer air of independence of action in their co-operation. Dr. Harper uttered no uncertain sound in his inaugural address, and from time to time we will point out how these views are being endorsed and supported by the men who have evidently been living in the belief that it is the duty of every one, even of THE CANADA EDUCATIONAL MONTHLY, to defend or cover up every indiscretion they commit. In this connection, the report of the speeches of the Rev. E. J. Rexford and Mr. Truell, is especially instructive. If that report is correct, it would seem that Mr. Rexford's logic is of a remarkable kind. Mr. Hewton had asked if it was true that the teachers of the Province would have had another representative on the Central Council of Education, had it not been for the action of the members of that council who are supposed to be representatives of the teachers. Mr. Rexford, by way of reply, said that Mr. Truell had not defended him from certain aspersions made against him, and hence he had used his endeavors, with those associated with him on the Text-Book Committee, to bring about Mr. Truell's defeat as a candidate for the coveted place. When, however, Mr. Truell made his defence quite a different aspect appeared, so that now teachers and others can judge for themselves, and put the blame on the right person.

Another remarkable discussion during one of the sessions was a criticism *pro* and *contra* the new text-book on Canadian history. The merits of that discussion will no doubt be made more manifest when the teachers have had an opportunity of judging of the book, and it was a pity that Mr. Patterson should have seen fit to push the matter to a vote, the most ridiculous that perhaps was ever taken in the public assembly, in face of the fact that the teachers present had not even read the book, and that Mr. Patterson had to assume an apologetic tone when referring to the defects pointed out. At least this is the impression left after reading the newspaper reports of the discussion that took place on this subject.

The air, however, seems to have become quite excited, when Mr. Hewton made his charge about the unseemly conduct of certain men high in authority, who had led some of the headmasters of Montreal into the way of wrong doing, especially when he was challenged by Dr. Robins and others in very intemperate language, which no school boy would dare use towards another with impunity. We have heard that this matter is not likely to end with Mr. Hewton's protest, which we give verbatim as it appeared in the *Gazette* :

"I, Robert John Hewton, member of the Provincial Association of Protestant Teachers, a body politic and corporate of the Province of Quebec, and being duly qualified to vote for the election of officer of the said association, do hereby file the following protest in writing against any declaration of the election of officers made, or to be made by the president, or other officers whose duty it is to make such declaration, at the present convention of the Provincial Association of Protestant Teachers, and against all proceedings which have hitherto been taken by the said association in respect of such election; and in support of this protest I allege :—

"1. That, in violation of the constitution of this association, a number of ballots have been issued to members of this association prior to the date of the annual convention.

"2. That some of the said ballots were marked prior to the time provided for by the constitution, and were subsequently deposited, thereby rendering null and void all proceedings in connection with the present election.

"3. That influence has been exerted by certain members of this association upon other members of the said association, under their authority, to determine the nature of their vote.

"4. That certain head teachers of public schools have held meetings of their subordinate teachers, members of this association, previous to the date of the present convention, and presented to the said subordinate teachers a prepared and printed ticket, and indicated the manner in which the said subordinate teachers should exercise their voting privileges, in connection with the present election of officers of the Provincial Association of Protestant Teachers."

Notwithstanding some of these features of the convention just hinted at, it seems to have been brought through its work with the well known tact of the chairman to a successful closing scene, which is thus reported :

"The incoming officers were then presented by Dr. Harper, who, on retiring from the chair, said that he was pleased to see such a large number present at the closing meeting of the convention. He was proud personally to be able to say that this perhaps had been one of the most successful, if not the most successful conventions that had been held in the history of the association. It had certainly been the largest, and when they contemplated the pleasant experience they had had the evening before at McGill, he thought, notwithstanding the various little bits of fireworks that had been exhibited, that good fellowship prevailed and that good fellowship would continue. He spoke in a complimentary way of the character of the papers that had been read before the convention. They were of a practical and instructive nature, drawn from the personal experience of those who prepared them, and it seemed that every sentence in those papers came directly from the minds and hearts and souls of those who read them. He had to thank them all for the kindness exhibited towards him, as chairman. Unfortunately the chairman was obliged to assert himself sometimes. He could not always escape the necessity of exerting the authority of his position to cover up a difficulty. With perhaps one exception, he had been supported throughout in his movements, and he thanked them heartily for that support, and would bespeak the same kind consideration for the gentleman who was to take his place."

ASTRONOMICAL NOTES.

NOVEMBER.

THOMAS LINDSAY.

OBSERVERS of the heavens interested in planetary work, have not, during the past summer, been at all fortunate, there having been, so to speak, a dearth of planets in the evening skies. And for some little time yet it is in the early morning that the amateur may show his enthusiasm; lacking that, he will probably not observe at all. From August to October Jupiter was either lost in the sun's rays, or but feebly visible, and the satellites quite too faint for observation. But he presents his beautiful disc now before sunrise, reaching the meridian about 8 o'clock, and is well worthy of observation. His position on the celestial equator is among the stars of Virgo, and on the morning of Nov. 15th the planet will be in the same field of view in the telescope with Eta Virginis, a 4th mag. star. It may aid the observer to note that the four satellites will be on the west side of the planet and the star west and a little north of the more or less straight line running through the system, the whole forming a very pretty telescopic field.

For Mars we need not look at all; the little fiery planet is directly in the sun's rays and quite harmless to evoke a renewal of the discussion on the origin of his surface markings, for this year at least. In connection with this, we are reminded of the peculiar argument given by Mr. Percival Lowell in support of his views. He says the lines on Mars "look" artificial. It may not be strictly scientific, but we can all understand how he might become impressed in this way if his telescope does really give the exquisite definition credited to it.

Saturn is, like Mars, close to the sun and invisible. It is some little compensation, however, to know that when he does pass round to the position of morning star the ring will be more broadly opened out than it has been for years past. Recently published reductions of measures made by Prof. Barnard, at Lick Observatory, seem to decidedly negative the theory at one time advanced, that the rings were slowly drawing in upon the planet; the delicate micrometer thus supports mathematics in the demonstration of the stability of the Saturnian system.

Venus still shines beautifully in the morning sky, but is waning in lustre as she passes away from us in that part of her orbit concave to the earth. The crescent form of the planet is now almost lost, and the disc appears in the telescope nearly circular.

Mercury is as disappointing as the

others during November, except that he makes a third planet in close conjunction with the sun in one month.

When the planets are not favorably situated, the amateur turns to the ever beautiful moon and the countless objects of interest in the sidereal heavens. During November we have several occultations of stars by the moon, and one especially noteworthy. This is an occultation of the Pleiades group on the morning of November 10th, between 4 and 5 o'clock. In this case the brightest of the cluster, Alcyone, is right in the moon's path. The moon is then past the full, so that the bright edge occults the stars; but there will be no difficulty n seeing the latter with the ordinary two-inch telescope. These observations are always interesting, while to render them valuable it is only necessary to be accurate in noting the times of immersion and emersion. If this be done, any of the great observatories will gladly receive reports of the work. As winter comes on we welcome the ever beautiful Orion in the evening skies. The great nebula, photographed by all the skilled workers in this line, presents yet a very rich field for the artist with the pencil. An exquisite drawing of the nebula was recently shown at a meeting of the Astronomical Society, made with a hard black lead. It is by attempting such work that the amateur becomes thoroughly familiar with objects of this class.

SCHOOL WORK.

SCIENCE.

Editor—J. B. Turner, B.A.

The following are the papers in Physics, assigned at the Midsummer Examinations of 1897:—

The High School and University Examinations.

FORM III.—PHYSICS

Examiners: J. Fowler, M A. A. McGill, B.A. J.C. McLennan, B.A.

1. (*a*) Explain the terms: *magnetic field, line of force, inclination, declination.*

(*b*) Describe, with diagrams, the magnetic field produced by an electric current when the conductor is (i) a straight wire, (ii) a circular wire, (iii) a solenoid.

2. Explain the effect on the current from a battery of (*a*) the size of the plates, (*b*) the distance between the plates, (*c*) the number of cells in series, (*d*) the number of cells in multiple.

3. State the laws according to which electric currents are produced by variations in the magnetic field, and show how each law may be verified by experiment.

4. Find the *wave-lengths* in air corresponding to the notes of a major chord, the vibration-number of the fundamental note being 512, and the velocity of sound being 1,100 feet per second.

5. Explain the method of studying sound-waves in air by means of manometric flames. Show clearly how the flame-picture is produced.

6. Explain the terms *node and loop* as used in Acoustics. How would you demonstrate the existence of

nodes and loops in (*a*) a vibrating string, (*b*) a vibrating column of air?

7. Explain, with diagrams, how you would determine whether a mirror which you cannot touch, but in which you can see objects reflected, be plane, concave, or convex.

8. Make drawings to show the action of a convex lens when used (*a*) as a simple microscope, (*b*) for projection purposes.

9. What is a spectrum? What apparatus do you require, and how would you arrange it, to produce a pure spectrum from a gas flame? Make a diagram showing the path of the rays.

FORM IV.

1. (*a*) Show how to find, graphically or otherwise, the resultant of a number of forces acting at a point.

(*b*) Two forces, acting at right angles on a particle, are balanced by a third force making an angle of 120° with one of them. The greater of the two forces being 4 pds., what must be the values of the others?

2. A stone, *A*, is thrown vertically upwards from a high bridge with a velocity of 96 feet per second; find how high it will rise. After 4 seconds from the projection of *A* another stone, *B*, is let fall from the same point. How many seconds will elapse before *A* overtakes *B*?

3. Water is poured into a U tube, the limbs of which are 12 inches long, until they are half full. Oil (Sp. Gr. =0.9) is then poured into one of the limbs to a depth of 4 inches. As much alcohol (Sp Gr.=0.8) as possible is then poured on top of the oil. What length of the tube will the alcohol occupy?

4. A piece of iron (Sp. Gr.=7.2) is covered with wax (Sp. Gr.=0.96) and the whole just floats in water, the weight of the combined mass being 36 grams. Find the weight of the iron and the wax respectively.

5. Describe two methods of finding the resistance of a copper wire, explaining the principle of the measuring instrument used in each case.

6. (*a*) Describe any simple voltaic cell, explaining the formation of that which is called the *current*.

(*b*) Describe a series of experiments which show that the E. M. F. of a cell does not depend upon the dimensions of the cell but upon the materials used in its construction.

7. (*a*) Explain the acoustical phenomenon of *interference*.

(*b*) How would you exhibit this phenomenon by means of an ordinary tuning fork?

(*c*) Describe fully another method of exhibiting *interference*.

8. (*a*) Describe how the air vibrates in an open and in a closed organ pipe.

(*b*) An open organ pipe, 2 feet in length, when excited, emits the note C_1 of the diatonic scale. Find the length of a closed organ pipe which will emit the note G_1 of the same scale.

9. If the index of refraction for a ray of light passing rom air to glass is $\frac{3}{2}$ and from air to water $\frac{4}{3}$, show graphically that the index of refraction for a ray passing from *glass* to *water* is $\frac{8}{9}$.

10. A convex lens of focal length *f* is placed at a distance 4*f* in front of a concave mirror of radius *f*, and an object is placed half-way between the two. Make a diagram to show the positions of the images formed by refraction through the lens (*a*) direct-

ly and (*b*) after one reflection at the mirror. Also compare the magnitudes of these images.

NORMAL COLLEGE NOTES.

On Friday, Oct. 1st, the new Normal College, at Hamilton, was formally opened by the Hon. G. W. Ross. The opening lecture was given on the following Monday, at which nearly 200 students were in attendance.

The number of students at present is 205, comprising 115 ladies and 90 men. Of these about 80 are graduates or undergraduates, the remainder being 1st class candidates.

The large attendance this year is partly accounted for by the number of Hamilton students present, and by the fact that many of the students wish to come in under the old regulations, which do not require them to take Latin.

A Literary and Scientific Society has been formed with the following officers: Hon. Presidents, J. A. McLellan, LL.D., R. A. Thompson, B.A.; Patron, J. J. Mason, Chairman of the Collegiate Institute Board; President, C. E. Race, B.A.; 1st Vice-Pres., Miss E. R. McMichael, B.A.; Treasurer, G. F. Colling, B.A.; Corresponding Secretary, Miss J. P. Brown, B.A.

The first regular meeting was held on the 22nd inst., when addresses were given by Mr. R. Thompson and Dr. McLellan, the latter selecting as his topic "Thoughts on Literature." A vote of thanks was passed to the Hon. G. W. Ross, for providing a piano for the use of the society. Piano solos were interspersed during the proceedings.

In the first weeks of the term, no less than five receptions were tendered the students by the different churches of the city.

Athletics are booming at present. The ladies have formed an Athletic Association. Basket-ball is practised twice a week in the gymnasium behind screened windows.

The male students of the Collegiate and the College have combined to form an Athletic Association. Hon. Pres., Hon. G. W. Ross; Pres., J. T. Crawford, B.A.

A football team has been entered in the contest for the Spectator Challenge Cup. The Y.M.C.A. grounds are used for practice. Basket-ball is indulged in daily on the grounds in front of the Collegiate.

Dr. McCabe has been appointed lecturer in sanitary science hygiene.

CORRESPONDENCE.

MINISTERIAL EDUCATION.

BY WM. MORTIMER CLARK, M.A. Q.C.

Chairman of the Board of Management of Knox College.

THE beginning of a new session of Knox College under its strengthened theological faculty, has led many of the friends of the institution to consider whether some improvement might not be made in the literary culture of the students, before they enter on the special work of the seminary. It is felt that, while the raising of the standard in theology is a step in the right direction, and is gratifying to all interested in the welfare of the College, yet the benefit to be derived from the more complete equipment of the theological faculty, and the efforts of the professors to impart a more thorough training in the various departments of ministerial education, will be greatly minimized and hampered by the continued importation into the theological classes of men without sufficient previous literary training and culture. While the Canadian Church was in its infancy, and the means provided for obtaining an adequate literary education were wanting or surrounded by ecclesiastical or financial restrictions, which almost precluded students from obtaining the higher education of the period, and while more men were urgently required for home mission work than could be found, the Church was obliged to accept the services of such students as presented themselves, and to provide for them such educational advantages, through the preparatory course, as circumstances then permitted. This condition of affairs is entirely changed. Higher education is now within the reach of all, and can be obtained in our university at a cost almost nominal; and while in the past, ministers could not be found in sufficient numbers to supply the needs of the Church, now men are more numerous than charges.

Under these circumstances it becomes a grave question whether the Church is called on any longer to furnish at a large expense a gratuitous literary education to aspirants for the ministry, and to divert money given for theological education to foster and perpetuate a system which affords a primary education confessedly inadequate. The maintenance of the preparatory course in fact holds out a premium to superficiality, and opens a side door for entrance into a profession which requires in these times imperatively the highest culture. The policy of the Church in this respect is in painful contrast to that of the governing bodies of the legal and medical professions, and indeed of all educational institutions, and so much is this noticed that prominent laymen have declined to subscribe to the funds of the College while the preparatory course is continued. It is not surprising that under the present system of clerical education so many complaints are heard of the inadequacy of ministerial support. Congregations are not slow to realize that, if the education of a minister is indifferent, and has cost him little or nothing, he cannot expect a liberal remuneration for his services. In the Church of England of late years an increasing number of candidates for the ministry have obtained ordination without having previously had a university education. These men are known in England as "Literates," and the large increase of such has naturally reduced the already meagre rate of ministerial remuneration. The Presbyterian Church in England being fully alive to the defects of the past system, has been using every effort to raise the standard of the culture of students, and with a view to improvement has removed its divinity hall to Cambridge.

It has been said, in answer to suggestions previously made as to the abolition of the preparatory course, that if students were required to take a university degree it would extend the time required to be spent by them in study. This, doubtless, is the case, but it would only enlarge the period for one year longer than at present. If the student looks to the ministry for a *living* this is unquestionably a weighty argument with him; but if a young man has the high ideal before him of his sacred calling, the anxiety to equip himself for his life work will outweigh all such unworthy considerations. It has also been argued that if a university degree were demanded before students entered the theological classes at

Knox College, many would seek their education in other institutions. The loss would not only not be serious, but would be eminently advantageous to the College and the Church. The Church would be benefited by receiving a larger number of educated ministers, for it would be found that students would hesitate to deliberately seek their education at institutions where the education would be notoriously inferior to that of the students of Knox College. Congregations would specially note the fact in selecting pastors. The College would itself acquire a reputation and a standing which would attract the very best students to its halls. The college which will have the courage to insist upon the possession of a degree in Arts from every student who seeks admission to its theological course will be the one which will specially command the respect and liberality of congregations.

It has been further said that, were the College to insist on a university degree being first obtained before students are received, it would be a limitation on the operation of the Holy Spirit. This argument, which is somewhat questionable, appears to pre-suppose, to some extent at least, that the Spirit is more active in His energy among the "Literates" than among the university men. So far as human observation can permit of any judgment being formed on this subject, it has not been borne out by experience. It must be remembered also that the Church needs educated ministers, and that the Spirit does not provide or promise the needful literary training. It is certainly true that the Spirit of God works when and where He pleases, but His gracious operations, it must be remembered, are extended to multitudes who are utterly unfit for the public ministry of the Word. He certainly does not encourage superficiality in training for the ministry, or the desire on the part of students to get into the Church with the least possible quantum of education. Those who complain that the rule contemplated would preclude persons who are desirous of abandoning their business, and late in life studying for the Church, from entering the ministry, might peruse with profit the words of the Apostle Paul in I. Corinthians vii. 20, where he says: "Let every man abide in the same calling wherein he was called."—*Westminster.*

[In the above communication, Mr. Clark deals with a question affecting all branches of the Church, and it is high time for all of them to take concerted action in the matter. Perhaps the Presbyterian Church can show the way.—Ed. C. E. M.]

CONTEMPORARY LITERATURE.

The anniversary number of *The Atlantic Monthly* is truly a notable one. The opening article by James Lane Allan is on the two great principles in fiction, that is, as he characterizes them, the masculine and the feminine. No one can deny that there is much truth in what he says, but on the other hand facts can be quoted to support almost any literary theory. Kipling's "Recessional Hymn" is an instance in Mr. Allan's judgment of the union of both principles. "Caleb West," a new serial by Hopkinson Smith, opens with great promise. There is a healthiness and a vigor about his portrayal of character that will attract liking from any straightforward mind. No one who has been in Edinburgh should miss "Penelope's Progress," there conducted by Kate Douglas Wiggin.

It would be hard to say which is the more interesting, John C. Van Dyke's article on "Sir Joshua Reynolds" or Joseph Pennell's on "The Art of Charles Keene" in the October *Century*. But before one has been enabled to discriminate, another choice of interest is given us; here the judgment is exercised between Theodore Roosevelt's "Account of the New York Police Force" and "Marie-Antoinette as Dauphin," by Anna L. Bicknell. Add to these that in the same number "Hugh Wynne," and "The Days of Jeanne D'Arc" are both fitly concluded, and one may have an idea of the worth of the last issue of *The Century*.

"Miss Lillian Bell's Adventures in the Old Country" promise to be most entertaining reading. They are begun in the October number of *The Ladies' Home Journal* and are to be continued for some time. The writer is so sprightly and so keen in her attacks on the world in general that our filial anxiety is already aroused for our distinguished progenators who may possibly be misunderstood by so swift a lady, but the process of dissection is sure to be vastly amusing.

If the *Review of Reviews* has done nothing more, it certainly has contributed to the better understanding of the great general principles that underlie caricature. Here month by month one may see what the outside world thinks of some other part that we are intersted in, and a monstrous thinking it generally is. The force of caricature has always been a curious one.

The Book-Buyer for October contains an interesting and appreciative sketch of Henry McCarter, the illustrator, along with fine reproductions of some of his most successful work. He succeeds to an extraordinary degree in conveying the romantic and mystical atmosphere, more especially of the poems which he illustrates.

From the American Book Company, New York: "Third Year in French," by L. C. Syms; "Physics for Grammar Schools," by Charles L. Harrington; "The Student's Manual of Physics," by L. C. Cooley; "A Study of English Words," by Jessie Macmillan Anderson; "The American Word Book," by Calvin Patterson; "The Story of Japan," by R. Van Bergen; "Natural Elementary Geography," by Jacques W. Redway; "The Advanced Music Reader," by F. H. Ripley and T. Tapper.

We have also received from Ginn & Company "Exercises in Greek Composition," by Edwin H. Higley; eight books of "Homer's Odyssey," for the use of schools, by Bernadotte Perrin and Thomas Day Seymour; and "An Introductory Course in Quantative Chemical Analysis," by Percy Norton Evans.

"The Mineral Wealth of Canada: a Guide for Students of Economic Geology." By Arthur B. Willmott, M.A. B.,Sc. William Briggs, Toronto.

A more opportune time for the appearance of this book could not have been chosen so far as the interest of the general public is concerned. The author, who is the Natural Science Professor in McMaster University, has for some years been giving to his class in geology a short course on this subject, and the present production comprises these lectures, together with explanatory passages for the use of readers who are not acquainted with the elements of geology. The work has been founded largely on the reports of the Geological Survey of Canada, an enterprise which is not sufficiently recognized by the Canadian public.

THE CANADA

EDUCATIONAL MONTHLY.

DECEMBER, 1897.

THE BROTHERHOOD OF TEACHERS AND EDUCATIONAL REFORM.

DR. J. M. HARPER'S ADDRESS.*

WHEN we hear so much of what is being said in these days about the brotherhood of mankind in general, and the building up of a Canadian nationality in particular, one cannot but be struck with the difference there is between the effects produced by a sentiment and those produced by a principle. And in an assembly of teachers, come together as we have, to promote the interests of a common cause, it is surely pertinent enough for us to ask wherein lies this difference, or even, going a little bit further back, to ask what is a sentiment as distinguished from a principle. You know the difference between cause and effect, between the abstract and the concrete, between ethics and applied morals, between preaching and practice, between the ordinary prayer and consistency of conduct; and hence there can be no difficulty in your recognizing sentiment as a mere phase, principle as a substantial fact, the former a passive contemplation of what ought to be, the latter as an active and constructive force, moulding things towards the right of it; the sentiment enervating like an intoxicant, and producing prejudice and narrowness of mind; the principle, active, enobling, perpetuating.

And reducing the thesis of the brotherhood of mankind to the narrower basis of the brotherhood of teachers, it is never a waste of time for us to go back to first principles while investigating our relationships as a corporate body, in order that the individual member, even the least of these our brethren, may come to realize fully his or her true function as a member of our association. During the years that have passed over the head of our association, there have been peaceful slumbering times and there have been wakeful progressive times; and in these phases of our history we have had definite illustration of the difference between sentiment and principle. During the peaceful slumbering times, men have climbed into place, while arguments of the mutual admiration kind were being coined by the self-sufficiency that replies to everything by a vote, to be thrown in the way of proposals for the general educational good, and for the purpose of thwarting the best of progressive projects; while during the more disturbing times, when the true principle of brotherhood was

* Annual Convention of Provincial Teachers' Association, Montreal, Oct., 1897.

having its way and the sentiment of hero-worship was in the dumps, suggestions have been matured into activities, divergences of opinion co-ordinated, and self-aggrandizement thrown off the wheels of our annual gatherings and executive meetings like a patch of mud from the potter's rotary. And surely, my fellow-teachers, when through our own experiences we come in view of the principle of a common brotherhood, that has done, and can do, much more for the maturing of better things for our province, than the enervating sentiment which so often makes men and women the slaves of faction or the one-man-power, it would be well for all of us, from the officers-elect to the simple-minded teacher from the remote country district, whose vote has more than once been a source of anxiety to one or two of us; yes, it would be well for us to hold by the principle of brotherhood and let the sentiment in favor of hero-service go. Our brotherhood as teachers does not lie in our differences of opinion, so often made so much of by canvassing self-aggrandizement, but in the identification of a central affection, a common professional principle making for righteousness and progress, in whose co-ordinating presence all differences are minor, and (outside of the polemic that is always counting heads) are productive of little that is either good or evil.

I have been accused often enough of calling a spade a spade; and if in presence of the sentiment that, right or wrong, would always be victorious, I again become outspoken, there will remain only one thing for me to do, now as before, namely to bow my head in humility to the punishment of misrepresentation that is sure to follow, as one inured to that kind of thing. Ah, my friends, there is a would-be force in all societies as well as in our own, in all society I might say, in the political, social and religious world, that would put its foot on the neck of this simple, active principle of the true brotherhood of men. With a canvassing fallacy in the one hand and a voting paper in the other, its smile is as ominous as its frown. Warped and selfish instincts distort its every feature. "Vote for me or be dismissed, and I will take care to use my every endeavor that you be dismissed." That is the watch-word of this new diabolus that would destroy the manhood of men. With the prospect of place he would entice us with an emolument that is the price of our own soul, and with threats and slander let loose around us he would deter us from doing what is right and conscientious: "Don't stand in my way," is the shout of this new incarnation of evil. "Sell yourself or take the consequences. I am after votes, and the argument the right of it, may play whistle."

And as a justification of the more concrete part of my address, my advocacy of educational reform in three different respects, you will have to bear with me if I keep, for the sake of emphasizing, to the general for a few minutes more. The true leader is he who works for the good of the whole of society, and the honest man is he who works with him. Their duty is to round off and realize, to materialize, differences in a progression towards the highest and noblest, to co-ordinate, to harmonize, to focus towards the right. Why, of course they have to destroy, they have to remove obstacles; but they do so, differing from the pitiless polemic whose obstacles to be removed are always the men who oppose him, not their arguments. Encrust a truth in a dogma, and you have a fossil for your pains, with the essence of the truth hidden away within it, frog-like, for centuries perhaps, until the true leader and the honest man come along with the principle of brotherhood in their hand to liberate the long imprisoned. The dogma is smashed into smithereens, but the truth remains, and no man, no individual is injured. The reform has been accomplished as an impersonal good turn done to society in general, and men and women come to recognize, perhaps with some inconvenience for a time, the beneficence of its trend. They judge of the reform as an impersonal force; and the true leader and the honest man are quite satisfied with the reward that knows no outer loud-mouthed hurrah. With the true reformer, prosperity and victory are to be found in the peace and comfort and joy that comes, when the war of a sound logic, as conducted by him, has had its own way.

But how different from this is the false leader with his attendant hero-worshipper. Between the true reformer and the self-seeking polemic there is the gulf between the brotherhood of men as an active principle for good, and the stereotyped sentiment that seeketh but its own. "How will this movement affect me and my affairs?" the latter is ever saying to himself. "Evil be thou my good, and so much more the worse, for the good that is not evil," his henchmen join in chorus, and so they combine to oppose, and happily for all of us combine also to explode. Their condemnation becomes a self-condemnation, as they continue to decry what they cannot overturn, until their moral sense becomes a mere rag, tattered and torn with the violence of their passion to do a hurt to their opponents. In a word the dogma-producing personality as a guidance to men in the way of reform, is as much an enervating force as is the sentiment that warps and makes a distortion of the soul, and as truly is it so as is the true reformer in a convention such as ours a power for that improvement which benevolence is forevor weaving out of the bowels of its own compassion for humanity.

In view of these general remarks, which some may wisely or unwisely take as a self-justification for my persevering attitude in favor of educational reform, I may as well now run away from the general to the partienlar in explanation of what I think would be of benefit to us as an association of teachers, as well as what would be a benefit to our province and possibly lead to the further unification of our Canadian confederacy. If, as has been said in Montreal here, the teacher who becomes an educational reformer has taken to walking on dangerous ground, let us join as teachers of the city and country, precarious as our ground may seem to some, and by sympathy and co-operation, and an advocacy of the right, assume the consequences of such a brotherhood until there are no consequences of a serious personal kind to assume.

And first in regard to our own immediate affairs, the organization of our association, it has been suggested by one of our most zealous members that our machinery has become somewhat cumbersome and complicated. The association itself has a voice that is heard only once a year, and for the most part from only one part of the province, and when it adjourns the Executive Committee rules in its stead. I can see no true cause for alarm in this, though perhaps it would be more beneficial to all sections of the province were the convention to be held in other places than Montreal more frequently than it has been of late years. In regard to the large representation on the Executive Committee, it has been urged that the expense of bringing so many members together is a strong argument against its continuance, as it is at present constituted. With our committees carefully selected and their functions as carefully defined, and with more of the sub-committees raised to the rank of committees reporting directly to the association in Convention, the constitution of the Executive might perhaps be amended in such a way as to save the funds. But in doing so we must be careful not to lose any of our prestige, though in my opinion we would be adding to our prestige were we to select more of our committees direct in convention, so that they might on emergency take direct action. There seems to be a necessity in this connection pressing upon the Text-Book Committee, in order that it may negotiate, as the Committee on Professional Training did so efficiently last year, directly with the Protestant Committee of the Council of Public Instruction. It goes without saying that our list of text-books finds itself at the present moment in a phenomenally chaotic condition, and in order to provide against such contingencies in the future, it would be well for our teachers to have a little more of a say in the removing of a book from the list if not in its selection. "Why was Collier's History removed from the list?" asks one of our teachers to be answered by another "Yes, and can you tell me when the text-book on Physiology and Hygiene is to be changed again, and the Latin book, and the readers, or when are we to have a printed list of text-books for our guidance, that we can depend upon?" But I must not take up further time this evening on matters which are sure to be well sifted before the week is over, and when I myself may come in for a share of the good things going.

In regard to the reforms in our provincial affairs I have only to emphasize the three necessities that press upon every efficiently organized system of public instruction, and which I have already enunciated more than once. Every one of you knows how repetition is the best of emphasis. One of our reforms has been safely launched, and now the Normal School authorities propose to do for the province what the province has a perfect right to demand at their hands. The crowning of the movement will, no doubt, be witnessed in the near future by the appointment of a Professor of Education in McGill University, when the teachers of our superior and intermediate schools will share in the benefits of a sound professional training. It has been said that the provincial government intends to further this movement in some tangible way and to supplement it by the inauguration or re-oranization of Teachers' Institutes, and I am sure no teacher will be sorry to hear of the proposal, if the Hon. Mr. Marchand has any message of this kind for us.

Were I to speak of the two other reforms *in extenso*, I would only repeat what I said at the convention of the American Institute of Instruction held in this city in July last. The amelioration of the teacher's status needs no elaboration at my hands now; it has been dealt with often enough by way of a sentiment. I have heard that it has now fallen into safe hands, and from being a mere sentiment is at last likely to become an active principle in our educational life. You have no doubt heard of this also, at least I know some of you have been asking about the long-looked-for bonuses to be given for faithful service, not to speak of the pressure that is to be brought to bear upon the communities individually to add to your salaries. The details connected with this reform realized are not in my keeping, and you will have to be patient until the denouement is made. If the spirit of economy should again stand in the way, then the concentration of our school energies must be made on the Concord plan of having fewer schools stationed at central points. If the teachers in our superior schools are to consider themselves outside the influence of this reform, as some say they are, they at least can have an amelioration in the three years' engagement idea, and this they can readily institute for themselves as the law at present stands. I am a believer in the principle of *aut vita aut culpa* as it used to be in the old parish schools of Scotland, a principle that endowed the teacher with the spirit of independence, and which has possibly made him to-day the educational reformer *par excellence* of his native land. That principle we may never live to see accepted on this side of the Atlantic. The school commissioner, who buds and blossoms as a providence in his own right, developing in time as the poor teacher's fate, is too much of a personage amongst us to tolerate any such innovation. And yet the principle is happily accepted as an unwritten law in some of our cities, while the three years' engagement idea has come to be accepted by some of our country towns, leading us to think that in time the anxiety-producing annual notice will in time be more respected in the breach than in the observance. Our teachers have this matter very much in their own hands, as they have very much the keeping up of salaries in their own hands. Let them be true to themselves and to the dignity of their calling, and the salaries must be sustained and increased, and their individual status enhanced.

"What salary had you last year?" a teacher was asked lately.

"I had two hundred and fifty dollars."

"And you are a college graduate?" "Yes."

"And what salary have you this year?" "Four hundred."

"And what salary had your predecessor?" "Nine hundred."

Umph: there's professional etiquette for you, and in face of efforts made from year to year to bring that same position from being a five hundred dollar one—it never was four hundred till this year—to the thousand dollar mark. Will any of you tell me how long it will take the *aut vita aut culpa* principle to develop under such circumstances; will any of you say when the idea is likely to be matured in our province that the salary belongs to the position and not to the incumbent, under the influences illustrated by the above conversation?

The third reform, that of supervision, has also, I have been told, come in for serious consideration at the hands of those who are in a position to solve the problem satisfactorily. Inspection that brings the system into close touch with the people, and which has in it more of an active supervision than a mere inspection, is being introduced even in Great Britain, after having been successfully worked out in Prussia and the United States. The idea is abroad even among us that the people must have what the people demand, and that the people must have the check rein in their own hands as a means of keeping the head of things educational uplifted and on the *qui vive*. This is no place for the discussion of such a question, but it is none the less intimately mixed up with the question of supervisory inspection, and we may rest assured that those who have promised us reforms are as alive to its bearing on our circumstances as any of us are.

There are other matters which I would like to say something about in connection with our provincial affairs, but I must hasten to a close. My reference to the brotherhood of men, had associated with it a reference to our Canadian nationality, and though made partly in jest, I cannot let the opportunity pass without re-enunciating my suggestion in favor of establishing a central Bureau of Education at Ottawa. When one considers the interblending of educational influences that has taken place throughout the Union, since the Bureau of Education was first organized in Washington, the nearest possible approach to one country, one educational system that the United States is ever likely to see, and when one further considers how far we are from a truly national consolidation even thirty years after confederation, and how effectually the school house can be made a nursery ground for the true patriotism, it is easy enongh to put this and that together, and plead for the organization of a like institution in Canada. To advocate a national system of education for Canada is to cry for the moon, is at least to shut our eyes to the constitution and the rights and interests it protects. The establishing of a national system of education for Canada means revolution, and we are hardly prepared for a revolution that would be sure to rend us apart rather than bind us together, before we really have had time to become a nation. In the organization of a central Bureau of Education there is, however, not even the faintest tendency of a revolution about it, its functions being missionary, and its administration *ex officio.* All that would be required would be a vote for its support as a sub-department under the federal government, and liberty to work out its own destiny of usefulness, as a coordinating force in the educational affairs of the Dominion. As such a force it would neither be over nor under any provincial authority, perhaps not even advisory, yet bringing about by judicious and justifiable means, an assimilation of provincial efforts and pedagogic necessities that would bring all the teachers of Canada, and through them the rising generation, to see the provincial shade away into the federal, into the national. Nor is there need for me to go into particulars. I have done this already, and intend to return to these particulars when there is more time and better opportunity. Suffice it to say, if the Fathers of Confederation by any chance left out an element in the arrangements that were expected to lead us nationward, it is our duty to find out wherein lies the defect, and if it be found that the Nova Scotian teacher is still steeped in the provincial and the Ontario teacher the same, that there are Quebec teachers and Quebec teachers, and Manitoba teachers and New Brunswick teachers, there is in the fact some indication of the reason why our lads growing up towards manhood and our maidens towards motherhood, continue to look upon our nationality as a mere sentiment, thinking little of the active principle that makes for the true patriotism. "What constitutes a state?" our boys still recite, as the Fathers of Confederation recited when they were pleading from the hustings for federal union.

What constitutes a State?
Not high-raised battlement or labored mound,
Thick wall or moated gate;
Not cities proud with spires and turrets crowned;
Not bays and broad-armed ports,
Where, laughing at the storm, rich navies ride;
Not starred and spangled courts,
Where low-browed baseness wafts perfume to pride.
No:—men, high minded men,
With powers, as far above dull brutes endued
In forest, brake, or den,
As beasts excel cold rocks and brambles rude,—
Men who their duties know,

But know their rights, and, knowing, dare
maintain,
Prevent the long-aimed blow,
And crush the tyrant while they rend the
chain;
These constitute a State;
And sovereign law, that State's collected
will,
O'er thrones and globes elate
Sits empress, crowning good, repressing
ill.
Smit by her sacred frown,
The fiend, Dissension, like a vapor sinks;
And e'en the all-dazzling crown
Hides his faint rays, and at her bidding
shrinks.

There is the sentiment, and it is for us as teachers to help towards the universal acceptance of it, not as a mere sentiment, but as an active principle in our life as a people. As Emerson writes in another connection, "the fossil strata show us that nature began with rudimental forms," and the period of Canadian development in which we have part, has perhaps still sticking about it some portion of the shell of its chrysalis state. We call ourselves Canadians, but are we? Is our patriotism of the higher honesty? Is there a true nobility, not a make-believe, in its pæans? If the recognized difference between the sentiment and the principle of patriotism; if the Canadian school house as a nursery ground for Canadians; if the Canadian teacher's enthusiasm as an impulse to be imparted while breaking away from provincial bias; if the co-ordination of our superior and inferior educational forces, provincial or federal; if our ministers of education, our superintendents, inspectors and college professors acting in concert can do aught to set the national nerves throb from Halifax to Vancouver, can by united action clear away the chrysalis fragments from our common country, corporate and national, then is there to be seen a smashing of the fossil into smithereens and a breaking out of the truth, a new nation born to us in deed as well as in word.

THE STUDY OF NATURAL SCIENCE.

BY ALEX. H. D. ROSS, M.A., TILSONBURG.

THOSE things which are most familiar to us are apt to be regarded with least wonder and to occasion the least thought. It is only when we study with care the objects about us that we *begin* to see how wonderful they really are.

Without becoming a university student, the poorest lad or humblest girl in the world may matriculate into Nature's University, and enter upon studies far more exalted and varied than can be pursued anywhere else.

Where our interest in Nature will lead to, and where it will end, we need not care. It can never lead to the bad, nor end in anything but good, and the world may profit by it.

Some of the most valuable discoveries and inventions have sprung from apparently trifling accidents which happened amongst *thoughtful* people. For example, while watching a chandelier swinging in a cathedral at Pisa, Galileo observed that whether the arc described was long or short the time of vibration was apparently the same, tested the truth of his supposition by a series of experiments, and the outcome was the use of pendulums to mark the flight of time and measure the attractive force of our earth upon bodies near its surface. Again, while

---

Thrice is he armed that hath his quarrel just. *2 Henry VI., iii., 2.*

holding a pair of spectacles between his thumb and fore-finger, a watchmaker's apprentice was surprised at the enlarged appearance of a church-spire, and thus was discovered the power of lenses as applied to telescopes, microscopes, etc., by means of which the natural power of human vision has been wonderfully increased, and our prospect into the works of the Creator extended far beyond what former ages could have conceived.

The principle of curiosity has been implanted in our natures for wise and important purposes. When directed in the proper channel, it becomes a powerful auxiliary in the cause of religion and of intellectual improvement. To gratify this principle, and to increase its activity, our earth is adorned with a combination of beauties and sublimities stretched in endless variety over all its different regions. The hills and dales, the mountains and plains, the seas, lakes and rivers, the islands of every form and size which diversify the surface of the ocean, the bays, the gulfs and peninsulas, the forests, the groves, the deep dells and towering cliffs, the infinite variety of plants so profusely scattered over the surface of the earth, the marvellous productions of the mineral kingdom, the variegated coloring spread over the face of nature, not to mention the many thousand different species of animated beings which traverse the air, the waters, and the earth—all of these afford so many stimuli to rouse the principle of curiosity into exercise, and to direct the mind to the contemplation of the Creator.

Those who love Nature can never be dull. They may have other temptations, but they run no risk of being beguiled by *ennui*, idleness or want of oocupation. Sir Arthur Helps has well said, "What ! dull, when you do not know what gives lovliness of form to the lily, its depth of color to the violet, its fragrance to the rose ; when you do not know in what consists the venom of the adder any more than you can imitate the glad movements of the dove.

"What ! dull, when earth, and air, and water are alike mysteries to you, and when, as you stretch out your hand, you do not touch anything the properties of which you have mastered ; while all the time Nature is inviting you to talk earnestly with her, to understand her, to subdue her, and to be blessed by her. Go away, then ! *learn* something, *do* something, *understand* something, and let me hear no more of your dullness."

One man walks through the world with his eyes open, another with his eyes shut ; and upon this difference depends all the superiority of knowledge which one man acquires over another. While many a vacant, thoughtless person will travel hundreds of miles without gaining an idea worth crossing the street for, the observing eye and the inquiring mind will find matter of improvement and delight in every ramble. Therefore, let us not walk about with our eyes shut, but let us use our eyes and our intellects, our senses and our brains, and thus learn the lessons which God is continually trying to teach us. I do not mean that we are to stop there, and learn nothing more ; anything but that. There are things which neither our senses nor our brains can tell us ; and they are not only more glorious, but actually more true and more real than anything we can see or touch. But we must begin at the beginning to end at the end. We must sow the seed if we wish to gather the fruit.

It seems to be the plan of Him who made us, who created the vast universe, and who has endowed us with faculties for beholding Him by means of the material creation, that by seeing how widely we are separated from the shining worlds, whose motions and whose laws prove them to belong to the same system as our own, we should be led to think of another state of being, in which the knowledge we have gained here is to be enlarged, and where the mysteries that now surround us shall be among the most familiar of our thoughts.

It has been well said that the laws of Nature are the thoughts of God. Hence, it is truly surprising to see the apathy of most people in regard to a knowledge of Nature. Of those not scientists, who favor science in a scheme of education, the majority do so on utilitarian grounds only. What a degraded view to take of the universe of God—its study being tolerated because thereby we may be enabled to put money in our pockets. Nature is truly a revelation of the Creator, and seek where we may, we fail to find in its study anything that is not ennobling. Can as much be said of other subjects? But we plead for science, for philosophy, the study of the works of the Almighty on their *own* merits. By all who cherish them, they are known to be worthy of all the attention they receive. They more than repay the labor by the fruit. What can be more delightful than to trace the secret mechanism by which God accomplishes His designs in the visible world; to enter into the hidden spring of Nature's operations, to perceive from what simple principles and causes the most sublime and diversified phenomena are produced? Even as a relaxation there is more delight experienced in the pursuit of science than in the charms of poetry, or romance, or song; and the more dignified entertainment of the intellect is a much better refreshment of the faculties amidst the ordinary work of life. All those who love Nature, she loves in return, and will richly reward, not perhaps with the good things, as they are commonly called, but with the best things of this world; not with money and titles, horses and carriages, but with bright and happy thoughts, contentment, and peace of mind.

From Nature we have coldly stood aside,
And gone our ways with all sufficing pride;
Into her quickening soil a seed we sift,
Take the ripe fruit, nor marvel o'er the gift.

She is our own dear mother. She and we
Are one magnificent totality!
Through us earth wheels self-conscious on her track,
Our eyes are hers; they glass her glory back.

Through us she sees her charms unfolded far,
Green waving world, and glittering sea and star;
Through us she sees her still streams glide in grace,
And looks her blushing flowers in the face.

In man's aspiring soul she yearns and strives,
And through his cunning hand her art contrives;
Direct as dawn, or dew, or flower, or flame,
Out of earth's breast her vast cathedrals came.

You, I, all, is her speech—the poet's lines,
The player's touch, the dark sea-sounding pines.
Even as the wind through Asia's forests roared,
Not less from rapt Isaiah's tongue she poured
His fiery and forever living song.

All sounds are hers—the viol's ponderous pain,
The patter of the million-footed rain,
Through reed and roaring brass her breath is blown;
The organ's monster music is her own.

The man whose mind is irradiated by the substantial light of science has views and feelings and exquisite enjoyments to which all others are entire strangers. In his excursions to the woods he is able to appreciate the beneficence of nature, the beauties and harmonies of the vegetable kingdom in their interior aspect, and also to penetrate into the hidden processes which are going on in the roots, trunks and leaves of plants and flowers. He is also able to contemplate the numerous vessels through which the sap is flowing from their roots through the trunks and branches, the millions of pores through which their odors are exhaled, their fine and delicate texture, their microscopic beauties, their orders, genera and species, and their uses in the economy of nature. To the scientific enquirer, every object in the animal, mineral and vegetable kingdom presents new and interesting aspects, and unfolds beauties, harmonies, contrasts and exquisite contrivances altogether inconceivable by the ignorant and unreflecting mind.

Natural science alone gives us true conceptions of ourselves and our relations to the mysteries of existence. It seeks the relation of things to environments, and the relation of events to preceding or following events. In this way each thing or event is made to throw light on all others, and all things and events are made to throw light on each. This is what makes science so important to men. More than any other study, it strengthens our faith in the necessary connection between cause and effect. Nothing so tends to destroy superstitions and replace them by reason, and no other study instils such a deep love of truth and reverence for the Creator.

The scientific man's whole habit of life is a reverence for truth, and a patient effort to discover it; yet some imagine that the scholar is simply a drone in the busy hive of life, and even the theologian has been known to look with suspicion at the "dangerous tendency" of science. All this is uncharitable. We are all members of one body; none can afford to despise the labors of others, because all agencies are needed to build up the one great fabric of society. Whatever makes for the elevation of the race is sacred. The scientific workers of to-day are not empty idlers, but men who feel that to them is entrusted the noble duty of assisting to work out the mysteries of the universe. The truths which science has discovered may be regarded as so many rays of celestial light descending from the Great Source of Intelligence to illuminate the human mind in the knowledge of the divine character and government, and to stimulate it to still more vigorous exertions in similar investigations.

Now, as regards the relation of science to religion. It has been well said that "Science is the handmaid of Christianity, and Christianity has ever been the firm, the fast, and the fostering friend of Science." Nor is it hard to understand why this is. Science is nothing else than a rational inquiry into the arrangements and operations of the Almighty, in order to trace the perfections therein displayed.

Inasmuch as it generates a profound respect for and an implicit faith in the uniform laws which underlie all things, true science is essentially religious. Just as religion flourishes in exact proportion to the scientific depth and firmness of its basis, so true science prospers exactly in proportion as it is religious.

Professor Dana, the eminent American geologist, says, "There can be no real conflict between the two Books of the Great Author. Both are revelations made by Him to man—the *earlier* telling of God-made harmonies coming up from the deep past and rising to their height when man appeared, the *later* teaching man's relations to his Maker, and speaking of loftier harmonies in the eternal future."

Professor Tyndall regarded Natural Science as the most powerful instrument of intellectual culture, as well as the most powerful ministrant to the material wants of men; yet when asked if science has solved or is ever likely to solve the problem of the universe, was obliged to shake his head in doubt. As far as he could see, there is no quality in the human intellect which is fit to be applied to the solution of the problem. He compared the mind of man to a musical instrument with a certain range of notes, beyond which, in both directions, we have an infinitude of silence.

The phenomena of matter and force lie within our intellectual range; but behind, and above, and around all, the real mystery of this universe lies unsolved, and, so far as we are concerned, is incapable of solution. In the language of Carlyle, "To the wisest man Nature remains of quite infinite depth, of quite infinite expansion, and all experience thereof limits itself to a few computed centuries and measured square miles. The course of Nature's phases on this little fraction of a planet is partially known to us. Who knows what deeper courses these depend on? To the minnow, every cranny and pebble and quality and accident of its little native creek may be familiar; but does it understand the ocean tides and periodic currents, the trade winds, the monsoons and moon's eclipses which all regulate the condition of its little creek, and may from time to time quite overset and reverse it? Such a minnow is man; his creek this planet earth; his ocean the immeasurable all; his monsoons and periodic currents, the mysterious course of providence through Æons of Æons. Truly Nature is a volume whose author and writer is God. Man knows not the alphabet thereof, and prophets are happy that can read here a line and there a line."

No possible power of ours can penetrate the mystery of existence, and the further we go in either time or space the more completely we find ourselves surrounded by mystery. A cloud of impenetrable mystery hangs over the development, and still more over the origin of life. If we strain our eyes to pierce it, with the foregone conclusion that some solution is and must be attainable, we shall only mistake for discoveries the figments of our own imagination.

In our search into the inscrutible mysteries of existence (whether we follow the path of Materialism or Idealism), if we go but far enough, we are compelled to acknowledge the existence of a Supreme Being, who alone organizes and directs the movements of the innumerable parts of every organized being in existence.

In every part of the universe we may discern in the animate, the inanimate, and intelligent worlds most evident proofs of an agency which it is impossible rationally to attribute to any other being than the great I AM. This agency is conspicuous at all times, in all places, and in all things. It is seen in the sea, the earth, the air, the heavens. It is equally evident in the splendor and light-giving influence of the sun, in the development and growth of plants and animals from their germs, in the light and beauty of the stars, and in the motions, order, and harmony of the planets.

In conclusion—We should devote a certain amount of time to the study of one or more of the various branches of Natural Science: because such studies lend interest to life; strengthen our powers of observation; afford us the pleasure of discovering many new, interesting, and mayhap important facts for ourselves; invite us to use our reasoning powers in explanation of the phenomena revealed by experiment; cultivate independence and breadth of thought; show us how very limited our knowledge is and how necessary it is to make the most of every opportunity for self-improvement; increase our faith in the absolute justice of the laws of the universe; inculcate a high regard for truth; enable us to contemplate the system of Nature in its true light; and set forth the munificence of the Creator.

ON BEING HUMAN.

WOODROW WILSON.

BUT how? By what means is this self-liberation to be effected,—this emancipation from affectation and the bondage of being like other people? Is it open to us to choose to be genuine? I see nothing insuperable in the way, except for those who are hopelessly lacking in a sense of humor. It depends upon the range and scale of your observation whether you can strike the balance of genuineness or not. If you live in a small and petty world, you will be subject to its standards; but if you live in a large world, you will see that standards are innumerable,—some old, some new, some made by the noble-minded and made to last, some made by the weak-minded and destined to perish, some lasting from age to age, some only from day to day,—and that a choice must be made amongst them. It is then that your sense of humor will assist you. You are, you will perceive, upon a long journey, and it will seem to you ridiculous to change your life and discipline your instincts to conform to the usages of a single inn by the way. You will distinguish the essentials from the accidents, and deem the accidents something meant for your amusement. The strongest natures do not need to wait for those slow lessons of observation, to be got by conning life: their sheer vigor makes it impossible for them to conform to fashion or care for times and seasons. But the rest of us must cultivate knowledge of the world in the large, get our offing, reach a comparative point of view, before we can become with steady confidence our own masters and pilots. The art of being human begins with the practice of being genuine, and following standards of conduct which the world has tested. If your life is not various and you cannot know the best people, who set the standards of sincerity, your reading, at least, can be various, and you may look at your little circle through the best books, under the guidance of writers who have known life and loved the truth.

And then genuineness will bring serenity,—which I take to be another mark of the right development of the true human being, certainly in an age passionate and confused as this in which we live. Of course serenity does not always go with genuineness. We must say of Dr. Johnson that he was genuine, and yet we know that the stormy tyrant of the Turk's Head Tavern was not serene. Carlyle was genuine (though that is not quite the *first* adjective we should choose to describe him), but of serenity he allowed cooks and cocks and every modern and every ancient sham to deprive him. Serenity is a product, no doubt, of two very different things, namely, vision and digestion. Not the eye only, but the courses of the blood must be clear, if we would find serenity. Our word "serene" contains a picture. Its image is of the calm evening, when the stars are out and the still night comes on; when the dew is on the grass and the wind does not stir; when the day's work is over, and the evening meal, and thought falls clear in the quiet hour. It is the hour of reflection—and it is human to reflect. Who shall contrive to be human without this evening hour, which drives turmoil out, and gives the soul its seasons of self-recollection? Serenity is not a thing to beget inaction. It only checks excitement and uncalculating haste. It does not exclude ardor or the heat of battle: it keeps ardor from extravagance, prevents the battle from becoming a mere aimless mêlée. The great captains of the world have been men who were calm in the moment of crisis; who were calm, too, in the long planning which preceded crisis; who went into battle with a serenity infinitely ominous for those whom they attacked. We instinctively associate serenity with the highest types of power among men, seeing in it the poise of knowledge and calm vision, that supreme heat and mastery which is without splutter or noise of any kind. The art of power in this sort is no doubt learned in hours of reflection, by those who are not born with it. What rebuke of aimless excitement there is to be got out of a little reflection, when we have been inveighing against the corruption and decadence of our own days, if only we have provided ourselves with a little knowledge of the past wherewith to balance our thought! As bad times as these, or any we shall see, have been reformed, but not by protests. They have been made glorious instead of shameful by the men who kept their heads and struck with sure self-possession in the fight. No age will take hysterical reform. The world is very human, not a bit given to adopting virtues for the sake of those who merely bemoan its vices, and we are most effective when we are most calmly in possession of our senses.

So far is serenity from being a thing of slackness or inaction that it seems bred, rather, by an equable energy, a satisfying activity. It may be found in the midst of that alert interest in affairs which is, it may be, the distinguishing trait of developed manhood. You distinguish man from the brute by his intelligent curiosity, his play of mind beyond the narrow field of instinct, his perception of cause and effect in matters to him indifferent, his appreciation of motive and calculation of results. He is interested in the world about him, and even in the great universe of which it forms a part, not merely as a thing he would use, satisfy his wants and grow great by, but as a field to stretch his mind in, for love of journeyings and excursions in the large realm of thought. Your full-bred human being loves a run afield with his understanding. With what images does he not surround himself and store his mind! With what fondness does he con travellers' tales and credit poets' fancies! With what patience does he follow science and pore upon old records, and with what eagerness does he ask the news of the day! No great part of what he learns immediately touches his own life or the course of his own affairs: he is not pursuing a business, but satisfying as he can an insatiable mind. No doubt the highest form of this noble curiosity is that which leads us, without self-interest, to look abroad upon all the field of man's life at home and in society, seeking more excellent forms of government, more righteous ways of labor, more elevating forms of art, and which makes the greater among us statesmen, reformers, philanthropists, artists, critics, men of letters. It is certainly human to mind your neighbor's business as well as your own.

Gossips are only sociologists upon a mean and petty scale. The art of being human lifts to a better level than that of gossip; it leaves mere chatter behind, as too reminiscent of a lower stage of existence, and is compassed by those whose outlook is wide enough to serve for guidance and a choosing of ways.

Luckily we are not the first human beings. We have come into a great heritage of interesting things, collected and piled all about us by the curiosity of past generations. And so our interest is selective. Our education consists in learning intelligent choice. Our energies do not clash or compete: each is free to take his own path to knowledge. Each has that choice, which is man's alone, of the life he shall live, and finds out first or last that the art in living is not only to be genuine and one's own master, but also to learn mastery in perception and preference. Your true woodsman needs not to follow the dusty highway through the forest nor search for any path, but goes straight from glade to glade as if upon an open way, having some privy understanding with the taller trees, some compass in his senses. So there is a subtle craft in finding ways for the mind, too. Keep but your eyes alert and your ears quick, as you move among men and among books, and you shall find yourself possessed at last of a new sense, the sense of a pathfinder. Have you never marked the eyes of a man who has seen the world he has lived in: the eyes of the sea-captain, who has watched his life through the changes of the heavens; the eyes of the huntsman, nature's gossip and familiar; the eyes of the man of affairs, accustomed to command in moments of exigency? You are at once aware that they are eyes which can see. There is something in them that you do not find in other eyes, and you have read the life of the man when you have divined what it is. Let the thing serve as a figure. So ought alert interest in the world of men and thought to serve each one of us that we shall have the quick perceiving vision taking meanings at a glance, reading suggestions, as if they were expositions. You shall not otherwise get full value of your humanity. What good shall it do you else that the long generations of men which have gone before you have filled the world with great store of everything that may make you wise and your life various? Will you not take usury of the past, if it may be had for the taking? Here is the world humanity has made: will you take full citizenship in it, or will you live in it as dull, as slow to receive, as unenfranchised, as the idlers for whom civilization has no uses, or the deadened toilers, men or beasts, whose labor shuts the door on choice?

That man seems to be a little less than human who lives as if our life in the world were but just begun, thinking only of the things of sense, recking nothing of the infinite thronging and assemblage of affairs the great stage over, or of the old wisdom that has ruled the world. That is, if he have the choice. Great masses of our fellow men are shut out from choosing, by reason of absorbing toil, and it is part of the enlightenment of our age that our understandings are being opened to the workingman's need of a little leisure wherein to look about him and clear his vision of the dust of the workshop. We know that there is a drudgery which is inhuman, let it but encompass the whole life, with only heavy sleep between task and task. We know that those who are so bound can have no freedom to be men, that their very spirits are in bondage. It is part of our philanthropy—it should be part of our statesmanship—to ease the burden as we can, and enfranchise those who spend and are spent for the sustenance of the race. But what shall we say of those who are free and yet choose littleness and bondage, or of those who, though they might see the whole face of society, nevertheless choose to spend all a life's space poring upon some single vice or blemish? I would not for the world discredit any sort of philanthropy except the small and churlish sort which seeks to reform by nagging—the sort which exaggerates petty vices into great ones, and runs atilt against windmills, while everywhere colossal shams and abuses go unexposed, unrebuked. Is it because we are better at being common scolds than at being wise advisers that we prefer little reforms to big ones? Are we to allow the poor personal habits of other people to absorb and quite use up all our fine indignation? It will be a bad day for society when sentimentalists are encouraged to suggest all the measures that shall be taken for the betterment of the race. I, for one, sometimes sigh for a generation of "leading people" and of good people who shall see things steadily and see them whole; who shall show a handsome justness and a large sanity of view, an opportune tolerance for the details that happen to be awry, in order that they may spend their energy, not without self-possession, in some generous mission which shall make right principles shine upon the people's life. They would bring with them an age of large moralities, a spacious time, a day of vision.

Knowledge has come into the world in vain if it is not to emancipate those who may have it from narrowness, censoriousness, fussiness, an intemperate zeal for petty things. It would be a most pleasant, a truly humane world, would we but open our ears with a more generous welcome to the clear voices that ring in those writings upon life and affairs which mankind has chosen to keep. Not many splenetic books, not many intemperate, not many bigoted, have kept men's confidence; and the mind that is impatient, or intolerant, or hoodwinked, or shut in to a petty view, shall have no part in carrying men forward to a true humanity, shall never stand as examples of the true human-kind. What is truly human has always upon it the broad light of what is genial, fit to support life, cordial, and of a catholic spirit of helpfulness. Your true human being has eyes and keeps his balance in the world; deems nothing uninteresting that comes from life; clarifies his vision and gives health to his eyes by using them upon things near and things far. The brute beast has but a single neighborhood, a single, narrow round of existence; the gain of being human accrues in the choice of change and variety and of experience far and wide, with all the world for stage—a stage set and appointed by this very art of choice—all future generations for witnesses and audience. When you talk with a man who has in his nature and acquirements that freedom from constraint which goes with the full franchise of humanity, he turns easily from topic to topic; does not fall silent or dull when you leave some single field of thought such as unwise men make a prison of. The men who will not be broken from a little set of subjects, who talk earnestly, hotly, with a sort of fierceness, of certain special schemes of conduct, and look coldly upon everything else, render you infinitely uneasy, as if there were in them a force abnormal and which rocked toward an upset of the mind; but from the man whose interest swings from thought to thought with the zest and poise and pleasure of the old traveller, eager for what is new, glad to look again upon what is old, you come away with faculties warmed and heartened—with the feeling of having been comrade for a little with a genuine human being. It is a large world and a round world, and men grow human by seeing all its play of force and folly.

Let no one suppose that efficiency is lost by such breadth and catholicity of view. We deceive ourselves with instances, look at sharp crises in the world's affairs, and imagine that intense and narrow men have made history for us. Poise, balance, a nice and equable exercise of force, are not, it is true, the things the world ordinarily seeks for or most applauds in its heroes. It is apt to esteem that man most human who has his qualities in a certain exaggeration, whose courage is passionate, whose generosity is without deliberation, whose just action is without premeditation, whose spirit runs towards its favorite objects with an infectious and reckless ardor, whose wisdom is no child of slow prudence. We love Achilles more than Diomedes, and Ulysses not at all. But these are standards left over from a ruder state of society: we should have passed by this time the Homeric stage of mind—should have heroes suited to our age. Nay, we have erected different standards, and do make a different choice, when we see in any man fulfilment of our real ideals. Let a modern instance serve as test. Could any man hesitate to say that Abraham Lincoln was more human than William Lloyd Garrison? Does not everyone know that it was the practical Free-Soilers who made emancipation possible, and not the hot, impracticable Abolitionists; that the country was infinitely more moved by Lincoln's temperate sagacity than by any man's enthusiasm, instinctively trusted the man who saw the whole situation and kept his balance, instinctively held off from those who refused to see more than one thing? We know how serviceable the intense and headlong agitator was in bringing to their feet men fit for action; but we feel uneasy while he lives, and vouchsafe him our full sympathy only when he is dead. We know that the genial forces of nature which work daily, equably, and without violence are infinitely more serviceable, infinitely more admirable, than the rude violence of the storm, however necessary or excellent the purification it may have wrought. Should we seek to name the most human man among those who led the nation to its struggle with slavery, and yet was no statesman, we should, of course, name Lowell. We know that his humor went further than any man's passion towards setting tolerant men a-tingle with the new impulses of the day. We naturally hold back from those who are intemperate and can never stop to smile, and are deeply reassured to see a twinkle in a reformer's eye. We are glad to see earnest men laugh. It breaks the strain. If it be wholesome laughter, it dispels all suspicion of spite, and is like the gleam of light upon running water, lifting sullen shadows, suggesting clear depths.

Surely it is this soundness of nature, this broad and genial quality, this full-blooded, full-orbed sanity of spirit, which gives the men we love that wide-eyed sympathy which gives hope and power to humanity, which gives range to every good quality and is so excellent a credential of genuine manhood. Let your life and your thought be narrow, and your sympathy will shrink to a like scale. It is a quality which follows the seeing mind afield, which waits on experience. It is not a mere sentiment. It goes not with pity so much as with a penetrative understanding of other men's lives and hopes and temptations. Ignorance of these things makes it worthless. Its best tutors are observation and experience, and these serve only those who keep clear eyes and a wide field of vision.

It is exercise and discipline upon such a scale, too, which strengthen, which for ordinary men come near to creating, that capacity to reason upon affairs and to plan for action which we always reckon upon finding in every man who has studied to perfect his native force. This new day in which we live cries a challenge to us. Steam and electricity have reduced nations to neighborhoods; have made travel pastime, and news a thing for everybody. Cheap printing has made knowledge a vulgar commodity. Our eyes look, almost without choice, upon the very world itself, and the word "human" is filled with a new meaning. Our ideals broaden to suit the wide day in which we live. We crave, not cloistered virtue—it is impossible any longer to keep to the cloister—but a robust spirit that shall take the air in the great world, know men in all their kinds, choose its way amidst the bustle with all self-possession, with wise genuineness, in calmness, and yet with the quick eye of interest and the quick pulse of power. It is again a day for Shakespeare's spirit—a day more various, more ardent, more provoking to valor and every large design even than "the spacious times of great Elizabeth," when all the world seemed new; and if we cannot find another bard, come out of a new Warwickshire, to hold once more the mirror up to nature, it will not be because the stage is not set for him. The time is such an one as he might rejoice to look upon; and if we would serve it as it should be served, we should seek to be human after his wide-eyed sort. The serenity of power; the naturalness that is nature's poise and mark of genuineness; the unsleeping interest in all affairs, all fancies, all things believed or done; the catholic understanding, tolerance, enjoyment, of all classes and conditions of men; the conceiving imagination, the planning purpose, the creating thought, the wholesome, laughing humor, the quiet insight, the universal coinage of the brain—are not these the marvellous gifts and qualities we mark in Shakespeare when we call him the greatest among men? And shall not these rounded and perfect powers serve us as our ideal of what it is to be a finished human being?

We live for our own age—an age like Shakespeare's, when an old world is passing away, a new world coming in—an age of new speculation and every new adventure of the mind; a full stage, an intricate plot, a universal play of passion, an outcome no man can foresee. It is to this world, this sweep of action, that our understandings must be stretched and fitted; it is in this age we must show our human quality. We must measure ourselves by the task, accept the pace set for us, make shift to know what we are about. How free and liberal should be the scale of our sympathy, how catholic our understanding of the world in which we live, how poised and masterful our action in the midst of so great affairs! We should school our ears to know the voices that are genuine, our thought to take the truth when it is spoken, our spirits to feel the zest of the day. It is within our choice to be with mean company or with great, to consort with the wise or with the foolish, now that the great world has spoken to us in the literature of all tongues and voices. The best selected human nature will tell in the making of the future, and the art of being human is the art of freedom and of force.—*Atlantic Monthly.*

The heavens forbid
But that our loves and comforts should increase,
Even as our days do grow.—*Othello, ii, 1.*

From lowest place when virtuous things proceed,
The place is dignified by th' doer's deed.
All's Well that Ends Well, ii, 3.

WHAT IS TO BE ADMIRED?

It is easy to plan work for the children on formal lines—so easy to collate sets of words for them to spell, as busy work and otherwise—so easy to fill the "practical" pages of an educational journal with suggestions of this cheap type. But this is not to be admired or sought after. All of the work given the children to do should be in the line of utilizing their life experiences for better culture of body, mind and soul. Read the article, "Learning Together" in this issue.

LEARNING TOGETHER.

By Ellen E. Kenyon Warner.

"What can your children spell?" asked the Superintendent in the first room. The teacher glibly answered, "The Primer words to page 47, the days of the week, the months of the year, the twelve most common first names in the class, the seven colors, the four seasons, and this list of opposites—sweet, sour, hot, cold."

The examiner tried them. They popped up in rows and jerked out their letters and syllables with such startling celerity that the examiner was beset by nervous doubt of his ability to give out words fast enough for them. He put on his best galop, however, and in an incredibly short time, the last little speller had dropped into his seat. Only six out of the fifty children had "missed," and in four of these cases the "next" had caught up the word and rattled off its orthography before the examiner could be quite sure it had been misspelled. Mentally out of breath, but seeing in the gaze of the self-satisfied class that immediate and complimentary comment upon their performance was expected, he said under his breath, "H'm! military discipline all day long. Too much of it." Then he turned to the teacher and faced the difficulty of criticising without wounding a faithful worker.

He knew that in the next room the teacher would have but a few words upon which she could safely promise ninety per cent. of success in an exercise such as this. Besides those few, the children would be able to write many more in dictated sentences, some knowing familiarly words whose orthography others would ask for before attempting to write them. Indefinite are such results as this, and he had always felt dissatisfied with them because it was impossible to fit them justly to the examination blank in which he semi-annually framed the status of each teacher. He was an old education man, with a secret approval for that sort of teaching which would measure up in neat squares, and thus enable him to keep his records in ship-shape for ready reference.

But this morning, he was stricken with sympathy for the children. The sensation, as excited by excellent scholastic achievement, was a new one, and he hardly knew what to make of it. This teacher had taken his cue, but had followed it to an extreme in which he dimly felt lay a lesson that might lead to a reversal of his theory of teaching. Feeling that the blame was chiefly his own, he said to the brightly confident little woman waiting before him for expected praise, "I'll talk this over with you when there's more time. Just now, I will only say that I fear you are giving too much thought to the formal side of your work. You have done superlatively well in what you have attempted, but the aim is narrow and narrowing."

The children saw the teacher's face fall as the examiner left the room, and knew that he had not admired her work as fully as she had expected he would. They saw it grow thoughtful, too, and to their surprise she sat down at her desk, dropped her hands in her lap, and looked at them silently, as if revolving some problem. She had never wasted so many moments in all their knowledge of her. They almost held their breath in anticipation of the next wonder.

Through the stillness there came to that energetic little woman a sense she had never given herself time to feel before—a sense of the great dependence of those little ones upon her leadership, and of her own responsibility toward them. "Have I worked for them or for myself?" she asked, and her conscience smote her in the answer. To score a high mark as their teacher had been her aim. No teaching ideal of her own had she cherished. The Superintendent's theory she had tried to serve, working as his subordinate. Neither conscience nor intellect had stirred in question of his infallibility until now that she had failed to please him. Self-accused and humbled, she sat before the children whose souls, she believed, would some day call hers to account for whatever wrong she might have done them. What harm *was* she doing them?

With a sudden sense of the children's sympathy, she sat forward in an attitude of consultation. Who could tell her "what harm," if not the little ones themselves? She would get the clue to educational reform from them.

"Children," she began, "Mr. Jennings thinks you spell wonderfully well. I am wondering if we could have done anything that would have pleased him better. He is a kind-hearted man and loves children. If you were to meet him out of school, you would have real good times with him. What would you tell him if he were to visit your parents in their homes—if he were your uncle, say? Come! let us imagine that Mr. Jennings is our uncle. What shall we do to please him most? Spell words for him?"

"I'd tell him a story," said one child timidly.

The teacher turned her thoughtful eyes upon Julie and smiled encouragingly as she asked, "What story would you tell him, dear?"

Unaccustomed to such "drawing out" as this, and feeling herself the incarnation for the moment of the general scare that pervaded the ranks in consciousness of the precious school minutes that were flying by "unimproved," Julie answered rather gaspingly, trying to say as much in as little time as possible, "The story of the Ugly Duckling. It wasn't ugly when it was a swan."

The teacher's gaze remained fixed upon Julie, and became absent as the effort to define the lesson of the moment abstracted her thought. Story telling! The children would revel in it, but how would that prosper their "studies"? She had heard of myth study and biographical incident as a foundation for history, but had never given much attention to these fanciful theories. Her class must learn to spell.

"Children, we are going to take a few minutes to talk this over—perhaps half an hour, perhaps until lunch time. Do not let us feel hurried. We'll talk slowly for once. I want you to tell me just what is in your minds. Why do you think Mr. Jennings was not so pleased with us as we wanted him to be?"

A look of relief settled upon the class as they relaxed to the feeling that they might give their thoughts time to "come out right end first," as an older pupil of Miss Lamb's had once said.

"I think he didn't like it because some of us missed our words," said one child after a pause.

"I don't," rejoined another promptly. "I think he was mad because I took up Leonard's word so quick."

"We raced too much," ventured a third, evidently in echo of his predecessor's thought. The pondering eyes were turned upon the last speaker.

"Perhaps we did, Bertie. But do you not think we ought to be praised for doing our work quickly?"

Emboldened by the air of receptivity which had suddenly transformed his teacher, Bertie answered: "My mamma says I hurry too much in school, and then I come home and eat too fast at lunch time."

"I'm afraid you do, Bertie," said Miss Lamb slowly, "I do myself, sometimes, and it is not good for either of us. But you and I must both learn that we must do some things quickly and some things slowly." As she spoke, Miss Lamb wrote at the top of a pad that happened to lie before her, "Learning together." It was borne in upon her that there were lessons for her to learn in association with these children—lessons of whose necessity she had been quite unconscious.

"But I forget," said Bertie.

"Yes, you forget," repeated the teacher musingly. "You reach the table in a nervous tremor from overpush during the morning at school, and are not wise enough to know that you must relax before you can digest your meal. I 'forget' myself. I need to practice relaxation and I must teach you the same art. Children, I am going to write something over here in this corner of the black board that is very important. I want all of you who can tell time to watch the clock toward the close of every morning session from now until promotion, and when it says a quarter of twelve to point to this writing. That will remind me that I must spend the last few minutes of the morning in getting you rested up for luncheon and in talking with you about how to take care of your bodies."

1. Work rapidly.
2. Rest before eating.
3. Eat slowly.

"But now about the spelling. How can we learn so many words unless we give every spare minute to it, as we have done?"

"My cousin Nellie doesn't learn so many words, but she can write little letters," suggested a pupil.

"How can she write letters without knowing how to spell a great many words?"

"If she doesn't know a word she asks her teacher."

"But if I should help you by telling you the words, as Nellie's teacher does, you would not remember them as you do after hard study."

"My big brother looks in the dictionary when he don't know a word," ventured one upon whom it was dawning that somehow or other big people got along without carrying everything in their heads.

"Yes," admitted Miss Lamb, "that is an advantage that grown folks have. And you want me to be your dictionary until that time comes for you."

The little brains were grasping the question sufficiently to feel that this would be a great relief from drudgery and not altogether wrong. A few faces showed distinct assent to the proposition.

"I've a good mind to try it," thought the teacher. "What an amount of labor it would save—and time, too, for something that is perhaps better worth while than the everlasting spelling drill. To be able to write little letters—how delighted the midgets would be!"

"But, children," she continued, "it is surely a fine thing to know things yourself, and not to have to ask other people. Suppose you wanted to write a letter out of school—you would be glad to know how to spell the names of the days and months."

"That's what I said to Nellie, but she says, 'What's the use of knowing how to write November when it's only May?'"

"Timeliness! Teach for present use." Where had Miss Lamb heard those words? It did not matter. She would try to what extent she could apply them in her next term's work. Meantime she would ask Mr. Jennings if he thought the hint they contained at all practical. Perhaps he could help her in interpreting them. Or had he lessons to learn himself? She strongly suspected that she would find him a little vague as to what he wanted her to do next term. Some change would be encouraged—of that she felt convinced, and perhaps she (and the children) could help him to know what direction he would best like the change to take.

A PRAYER.

Teach me, Father, how to go
Softly as the grasses grow;
Hush my soul to meet the shock
Of the wild world as a rock;
But my spirit, propt with power,
Make as simple as a flower.
Let the dry heart fill its cup,
Like a poppy looking up;
Let life lightly wear her crown,
Like a poppy looking down,
When its heart is filled with dew,
And its life begins anew.

Teach me, Father, how to be
Kind and patient as a tree.
Joyfully the crickets croon
Under shady oak at noon;
Beetle, on his mission bent,
Tarries in that cooling tent.
Let me, also, cheer a spot,
Hidden field or garden grot,
Place where passing souls can rest
On their way and be their best.

CHARLES EDWIN MARKHAM.
Scribner's Magazine.

EDITORIAL NOTES.

"Deliver not the tasks of might
To weakness, neither hide the ray
From those, not blind, who wait for day,
Tho' sitting girt with doubtful light.

"That from Discussion's lips may fall
With Life, that, working strongly binds—
Set in all lights by many minds,
So close the interests of all."

THE Jubilee of the Normal School, Toronto, and its celebration, which occurred at the end of October, was an event of more than ordinary interest. The re-union of those who graduated from the school prior to 1875, was made pleasant by the recalling of former days and work, and no doubt an important impetus is given to ther ecognition of the fact that teachers are members of a "learned profession." Very appropriately divine service was held in the Metropolitan Church on 31st Oct., where the late Chief Superintendent of Education worshipped for many a day. The sermon was preached by the Rev. Dr. Dewart, who was a member of the 1st class in 1847.

On Monday, Nov. 1st, at 2 p.m., the unveiling of the portraits of past principals of the Normal School, and past head masters and head mistresses of the Model School took place. Hon. G. W. Ross presided, and briefly explained the cause of their being together.

The portrait of Thomas Jaffray Robertson, first principal, was unveiled by David Fotheringham, B.A., I.P.S., South York; that of John Herbert Sangster, M.A., M.D., second principal, by Rev. R. P. McKay, M. A., Toronto; that of Henry W. Davies, M.A., M.D., third principal, by Charles A. Barnes, B.A., I.P.S. for Lambton. These gentlemen spoke in the highest terms of their old teachers as the highest type of manhood, and told of the influence for good that characterized the actions and instruction of the principals.

The portraits of Mrs. Dorcas Clark, M.D. (1852-1865), and that of Miss Adam (1865-1866), were unveiled by Mrs. Nasmith, a former pupil of theirs. Miss Caven unveiled that of Mrs. Cullen (1867-1884). Mr. David Ormiston, M.A., of Whitby, and Dr. Hodgetts, of this city, gave accounts of past headmasters. They were Archibald McCallum, M.A. (1848-1858), David Fotheringham (1858), James Carlyle, M.D. (1858-1871), James L. Hughes (1871-1874), William Scott, B.A. (1874-1882), Charles Clarkson, B.A. (1882 1886).

The reminiscences of student life at the Normal and Model from 1847 to 1875, by Mrs. Catherine Fish; William Carlyle, I.P.S., Oxford; David Ormiston, Whitby; Rev. Mungo Fraser, D. D., Hamilton; Mrs. Georgina Riches, Toronto; Joseph H. Smith, and A. S. Allan, were listened to with much pleasure.

In the evening a conversazione was held in the public hall and museum of the Education Department. This was very largely attended, and proved to be a brilliant social event. Hon. Dr. Ross and Mrs. Ross received the visitors at the entrance to the amphitheatre. The musical part of the program was skilfully conducted by S. H. Preston, music master of the Normal School. The graduates of the various years congregated in little groups here and there throughout the building, and lived over again their happy Normal days.

On Tuesday, November 2nd, at 2 p.m., the celebration was continued by the delivery of four addresses. Mr. Thomas Kirkland, M.A., present principal of the Normal School, reviewed "*The History of the Toronto Normal School.*" Mr. James L. Hughes presented "*The Schools of the Twentieth Century.*" "*Protestant Education in Quebec*" was dealt with by Mr. S. P. Robins, M.A., LL.D., principal of the McGill Normal School, and formerly assistant master of the Toronto Normal School. Mr. John Herbert Sangster, M.A., M.D., took as the subject of his address "*Where do we stand educationally as compared with fifty years ago?*" It was remarked by many that these were the best addresses that have been delivered on educational subjects for many years.

In the evening about one hundred of the visitors and the leading educationists of the city sat down to a banquet in the Rossin House. Hon. Dr. Ross was in the chair, the vice-chairs being occupied by Principal MacMurchy, Jarvis Street Collegiate Institute, and Prof. Hume, Toronto University. "The Dominion Parliament" was responded to by Dr. Platt, ex-M.P.; "The Legislature" by Dr. G. S. Ryerson; "The Army, Navy and Volunteers" by Col. Sam Hughes, M.P. "Higher Education" was responded to by President Loudon; Dr. Reynar, of Victoria University; Provost Welch, of Trinity University; and Dr. Parkin, of Upper Canada College. "Sister Institutions" was proposed by Prof. Hume and responded to by Dr. Robins, of

McGill Normal School, and Dr. McCabe, of Ottawa Normal School. "The Learned Professions" was ably responded to by Dr. McPhedran and Dr. Hellems. "The Graduates of the Normal School" was proposed by Dr. J. H. Sangster and responded to by several visiting teachers and inspectors. The banquet and celebration was brought to a close by singing "God Save the Queen."

Much praise is due to the President, the Hon the Minister of Education; the Vice President, Principal Thomas Kirkland, M.A.; the chairman of the ex-Committee, Inspector Jas. L, Hughes; and the secretary, Wm. Scott, B.A., Normal School, and Mr. Angus McIntosh, Head Master Model School, Toronto, for the skill and energy and time given to bring to so successful an issue an event which we believe will have an important influence on education in Canada. The first fifty years of the Toronto Normal is now a part of past history.

There seems to have arisen some misunderstanding among the teachers of the Province of Quebec over the morality or immorality of influencing votes at an election, and after investigating the circumstances, one is at a loss to know how any such difference of opinion could have arisen. Canvassing for votes may or may not be a wrong thing in itself, but coercing people to vote through an influence that can harm is one of the greatest iniquities that can be perpetrated in an age of freedom. Among politicians, canvassing for votes has come to be recognized as a necessary thing to do, but we have yet to find the politician, sound or unsound, who has ever openly declared that it was a right and proper thing to do—anything but an immoral act—to exercise this *seemingly* necessary function over those whom he has the power to injure should they fail to take his advice. Employers of labor continue to exercise the function of using their influence at an election, but any conduct of theirs that can be construed into coercion, is ever met with condemnation even among the politicians themselves, and is continually being frowned upon by the press. And if such be the case, there can be no question as to the morality of canvassing in a society such as a synod of clergymen or a convention of teachers. The introduction of canvassing and coercing is alike iniquitous in the abstract and subversive of the best interests of the institution where such practices are tolerated.

Whether the teachers of Quebec are likely to confess to the unseemliness of conduct lately practised by one or two of the leading spirits of their convention, who have evidently been taking it sore to heart that any act of theirs should be impugned, it is not for us to say. By way of vindication we see that an attempt is to be made to raise a laugh over the offence, and to claim that it is a question of no moment who shall be the officers of any teachers' association no matter how important its functions may be. At the best, it is a mere family arrangement, and if the members of the family interested in it quarrel over the matter it is no concern of the public to take cognizance of the storm-in-a-tea-kettle strife. But is it of no public moment that men who claim to be the representatives of the higher moralities should indulge in practices that are condemned even by those who think that canvassing before an election has come to be only a seeming necessity. The offence of coercion, direct or indirect, is surely not to be placed upon those offended by the offence, or upon those who have been brave enough to direct public opinion towards the offence. Besides, the offence has repeatedly been defined, we are told by the gentlemen who have just committed it, and this with the loudest indignation against the practice of canvassing and coercing. But, perhaps inconsistency, not to call it by a severer name, is a "two-penny halfpenny affair" also.

In this connection, as the letter of Mr. Hewton, who has been throwing light on this matter, has been inserted in our correspondence section, it cannot be out of place to report what such an honest authority in the Eastern Townships as the *St. John's News*, has said on the subject:

"Mr. R. J. Hewton never does anything by halves. If he has anything to say he says it, and calls a spade a spade, regardless of consequences. At the recent teachers' convention in Montreal he denounced in unmeasured terms the private caucussing and pre-arrangement of ballots by a few city teachers. While nearly every one admitted Mr. Hewton's pluck and indomitable energy, some, even among his best friends, thought he was a little too severe. He might, these contended, have attained greater results by a more moderate course, and evidently this was Bystander's opinion. But Mr. Hewton did not stop to consider the question of expediency. He was confronted with what he conceived to be a gross injustice and he exposed it and spared no one connected with it. Now he replies to Bystander and abates not one jot or tittle of his original position. He has nailed his colors to the mast and will stand by them. Whether one may or may not entirely agree with Mr. Hewton in this matter, there is one thing very certain, if there were no Hewtons in the Teachers' Association it would become an organization to register the opinions and serve the purposes of a few city educationists."

The New Brunswickers become a little restless now and again over their University, though at the bottom they are generally loyal to the higher education, and are proud of their college at Fredericton. The feeling has sometimes arisen in certain ultra-economical quarters that the institution cost a little too much, but it has always subsided in presence of the efforts put forth to improve its organization and curriculum. There is sometimes a revival of the "anti-classics" movement, but it never reaches a compass beyond one or two who have had no experience of the benefits a classical education confers upon the student. Then there is the reformer who never has a platform of his own to substitute for the platform he would overwhelm. The curriculum is a poor affair. There is little or no harmony in the organization. There is no enthusiasm in the deliberations of the administration. And so the would-be reformer runs on in the abstract, with no suggestion as to a remedy. When the reformer becomes somewhat iconoclastic, and would sweep Latin and Greek into the dust-bin of effete curricula, and claims that he knows all about it, he only gives point to the laugh which every educationist enjoys when he reads a paragraph like this, even if it comes all the way from Germany:

"The German newspapers," says the *Educational Journal* "record some frank expressions of opinion on the part of members of the reactionary agrarian party in Prussia in regard to elementary education. It is said that one of the sons of Prince Bismarck will not hear of the school teacher on his estate having a better house than an agricultural laborer. Herr von Below-Saleske declared that 'people don't need much school learning in order to grub potatoes.' Herr von Helldorf thus summarised his educational programme: 'I am not for teaching arithmetic to the agricultural labourer. It will only spoil him. He has got to lead horses and to handle the plough, not figures.' No wonder that there are rumors of hostility in these quarters against the educational zeal of Dr. Bosse."

We think, however, that there is one defect in the organization of the New Brunswick University, which could be slightly improved in order that the *esprit de corps* of its *alumni* and *alumnal* may be developed into something broader and more spirited. The University has produced many local men of standing and some of remarkable outside prominence, and yet for some reason or other, when a degree comes to these as a reward for their genius and culture and industry, it has generally been obtained from some outer institution, simply because, as it has been alleged, somebody in the Alumni Society, remembering certain idiosyncrasies of their student days, blocks the way to the conferring of the well-merited honor. It would be invidious for us to mention the names of those who have been thus overlooked. The members of the Alumni Society can easily recall them, if they will only run away for a moment from local prejudice and less important university matters. In a word, the institution has made itself too local. It has been burying itself away for years from the world of letters and science. It is not in touch with Canadian affairs, and if we have by any chance laid bare the secret of its sequestration, it is to be hoped that the discovery will not give any offence, but encourage the men who have the best interests of the institution at heart to make more of its honor-conferring powers and thus bring it in line with our other Canadian collegiate corporations, as fundamental elements of our nationality.

It would appear that Prince Edward Island is not free from the influence that would provoke another "school question" in its capital. The settlement of the various difficulties at the time of the passing of the Free School Act of 1877 was happily concluded by Bishop McIntyre and Dr. Harper, now of Quebec. The settlement, naturally enough, did not give universal satisfaction at the time, but it formed a basis for peaceable operations which have continued ever since, and was loyally adhered to by the good old philanthropist who induced his people to accept the terms of the Board of School Commissioners. There have been recent changes on that Board, however, which have led to a restlessness in the community, though, let us hope, not anything very serious. The city schools continue under very much the same organization that was inaugurated in 1877, and if any difficulty occurs it will be in connection with the transfer, support and supervision of a new school which is being conducted under the Bishop's direct supervision in the Pownal Street district of Charlottetown. There are two institutions for the higher education on the Island, St. Dunstan College, a Roman Catholic institution, and The Prince of Wales' College, an institution supported by the province, but beyond this there is no separating of the schools, which are in every district under the supervision of one Board of Commissioners and one Board of Education.

The appointments to the Educational Council should have been made by the 15th Oct. last. The nominees of the Senate of the University of Toronto are President Loudon, Chancellor Burwash, Rev. Father Teefy, and Professors Baker, Alexander and Hutton. The nominees (six) of the Government of Ontario are not yet known.

In cities the great majority of children leave school at or before 14 years of age, in the country the age may be a little higher. The problem which faces the educator is how to teach the little knowledge that these children have acquired so that they will, after leaving school, continue the work begun in the school. That is, that each one will make a continuous effort for self-improvement. How can the teacher inspire the young learner with such a love of knowledge as will make him forego other pleasures in order to gratify that for useful learning? For the schoolmaster this is the question of the age.

And yet, until this is accomplished, the teacher's work is unfinished. Every recourse of modern life is required for this purpose; the hearty co-operation of parents and teachers: the active support of all churches: the best efforts of all publishers: and the wise strengthening of all these by school trustees. May Canada soon see this combination at work for the proper education of our people. The good time is coming.

CURRENT EVENTS AND COMMENTS.

WHILE the "Manitoba School Question" still continues to trouble some people in their sleep, the people of Manitoba themselves continue to develop the system of schools inaugurated by the Greenway Government. Among the later staff changes is to be mentioned the appointment of Mr. Alexander McIntyre, B.A., science master in the Brandon Collegiate Institute, to the position of Inspector of the eastern division of the province. There is a colony of educationists in that city now of the clan McIntyre, which is likely to lead to confusion in the Winnipeg Post Office, but the members of that colony are all good and tried men, and the confusion of name will have to be surmounted, for it is the desire of all who know the McIntyres of Manitoba to see them flourish as they continue to use their energies in the development of the Manitoba School System. Mr. Alexander McIntyre's appointment has given evident satisfaction. He will begin his new duties at the beginning of the new year.

There are few who will not be satisfied at the decision come to lately in regard to the keeping of the Theological Department of Bishop's College at Lennoxville. It was proposed that it should be removed to Quebec, though the proposal never seemed to have much of an argument behind it. A special committee of the corporation of the institution has settled the matter by the drawing up of the following report:—

"The committee to whom was referred the question of the desirability of the removal of the Theological Department of Bishop's College from Lennoxville to Quebec, beg leave to report that after very full statements of the position by the Bishop, the chancellor, and other members of the committee, in view of the conditions of the establishment of the University, and its present successful position, they recommend that it is not desirable that any change be made in the direction suggested. The committee adjourned to meet at Lennoxville at the call of the Bishop to consider the question of providing increased accommodation for students, now said to be urgently needed."

It is reported that the authorities of the University of New Brunswick have all but decided to have a three year's course for the B.A. instead of a four years' course as it has been. The step is discussed in the following way by a student writing to the *Educational Review* :

"Whatever may be urged against it there is also something to be said in its favor, among other things that the president of one of the largest and most influential seats of learning in the United States has come out in favor of a three years' course. In a young country where the field for specialists is limited, four years seems a long time and a large slice of a man's years of usefulness to devote to an Arts Course, and if it be possible to limit the time consistently with thoroughness it is most desirable that it should be done, especially from the standpoint of the young man or woman who has to work his or her own way.

"The colleges having a four years' course cease work in the spring and do not resume until autumn, taking four months or more summer vacation. Why should this be done? Are the labors of students or professors more arduous than those say of the schools? If not, why should they require a longer rest? With the students of the leisure classes these long recesses may be popular, but with those of less means, and having less time, they are the reverse. Some studying and reading may be done in the time, but in the case of most of the students and professors they pass their time as other people, having nothing particular to do. It is true that it affords opportunity to some to earn a little toward expenses, but the field for such is curtailed save in the direction of book agencies. There is no chance now open for teaching, and take it all in all the average student would prefer attendance at college during much of the long vacation if it would insure graduation one year earlier. After all the value of an Arts degree does not so much depend upon time as application. If length of time in attendance at lectures is to be the criterion, by shortening the vacations as much time can be put in in three years as with the existing ones in four years."

What with the assimilation of the matriculation examination, which is now one and the same for all colleges affiliated with McGill University, and the regulations of the Protestant Committee of the Council of Public Instruction, the union colleges of the Province of Quebec are likely to become extinct. The first to give way to the pressure is Stanstead College, and it is more, than likely that St. Francis College will not be able to come up to the standard next year. The only institution of the kind left then will be Morrin College, and though the numbers attending the latter institution fall somewhat short of the requirements, this year, a generous consideration of its affairs may lead to its continuance.

In connection with the discussion in our columns on religious instruction, the following from a headmaster at a conference in England: The effect, said he, of the new methods was not so much in the things taught as in the way they were taught, and he was quite convinced that a large proportion of the difficulties in the elementary and secondary schools depended entirely upon the character of the teachers. The main thing, however, he wished to say was that he hoped Mr. Rutty's friends would not try to force their views forward in the form of definite regulations, for he was quite sure that if they tried to bring it into Parliament, and thereby to the public notice, they would not get what they wanted; they must take the masters and influence them. At present the masters were trusted, and allowed to do what they thought best, and the main thing was to see that they got the right men in the right place, and trust them to carry on what they tried to do at present.

The *Pall Mall Gazette* says that the Rev. Charles L. Dodgson, of Christchurch, is a sort of Dr. Jekyll and Mr. Hyde. He is a mathematician not unknown to fame. As Lewis Carroll he is one of the best known story-tellers. The two existences overlap in that attractive work, "The Tangled Tale," which is a series of arithmetical puzzles conveyed in the form of amusing narratives. In *Nature* Mr. Dodgson comes out stronger than ever in the arithmetical puzzle line, and has produced for the edification of schoolboys two new rules.

Here is a rule for finding the quotient and remainder produced by dividing a given number by 9, the process being no severer than subtraction: "To find the 9-*remainder*, sum the digits; then sum the digits of the result; and so on, till you get a single digit. If this be less than 9 it is the required remainder; if it be 9, the required remainder is 0."

To find the 9-*quotient* you draw a line under the given number, and put its 9-remainder (found as above) under its unit-digit, then subtract downwards, putting the remainder under the next digit, and so on. If the left-hand end digit of the given number be less than 9, its subtraction ought to give the remainder 0; if it be 9, it ought to give the remainder 1, to be put in the lower line and 1 carried, when the next subtraction will give 0. Now mark off the 9-remainder at the end of the right-hand end of the lower line, and the rest of it will be the 9-quotient. The following is an example of the process: Divide 736,907 by 9.

736907
———
81878,5

the remainder is 5, the quotient 81878.

Mr. Dodgson gives a corresponding rule for dividing by 11. His discovery, he explains, arose out of the odd fact which he once remarked, that if you put 0 over the unit-digit of a given number which happens to be a multiple of 9, and subtract all along, always putting the remainder over the next digit, the final subtraction gives the remainder 0, and the upper line, omitting its final 0, is the 9-quotient of the given number. Mr. Dodgson's rules are really a simplification, and will probably be adopted by many teachers of arithmetic. It is with pardonable pride, therefore, that he gives the date (September 28, 1897) on which he brought them to completion, just as though they had been patented in order to forestall competition.

St. John, New Brunswick, says the *Review*, appears to be the only city in Canada in which University Extension lectures have been maintained with any degree of permanence. The course this year was opened by Prof. Davidson, who is giving a series of lectures on the Commercial Relations between Great Britain and her Colonies. The subject is of great interest, and Dr. Davidson, who has devoted special attention to this and kindred subjects for many years, has already enlisted the keenest interest on the part of his class by the clear presentation of his facts and the force and precision of his argument. Miss M. E. Knowlton, of the St. John High School, who makes her début as a University Extension lecturer this year, is giving lectures—or, as she modestly calls them, "talks,"—on Browning, to the evident enjoyment of those who would obtain a clearer insight into the masterpieces of this poet. The second course in January and February will be awaited with great interest from the fact that three St. John editors—J. V. Ellis, M.P., of the *Globe*, Jas. Hannay of the *Telegraph*, and S. D. Scott of the *Sun*—will, in two lectures each, deal with important epochs of Canadian history, and Prof. Stockley will deliver a course of eight lectures on Molière.

At Syracuse, N. Y., the police have arrested five boys, all under sixteen, and all of respectable families, accused of a number of petty burglaries. It seems that the further aspiration of these lads was to go West and become train robbers. No doubt they had all received a good literary education, probably in the Public Schools. Instances of juvenile crime multiply in the United States, and if we are comparatively free from them here, we are not by any means free from juvenile faults which betray a want of moral discipline in the schools. It is a serious drawback from the advantages of our system of public education that it weakens the sense of responsibility in parents and leads to a neglect of home training, without which character cannot well be formed. A school teacher has enough to do in imparting literary instruction to his class, without undertaking to form the characters of individual pupils. The evils of parental indifference consequent on the transfer of responsibility to the state have been strikingly set forth by Dr. J. M. Rice in a work on the American Public Schools, which everyone concerned in popular education ought to read. Meantime, if any citizens caring, above all things, for the formation of character, choose to send their children to schools of their own, where they think character is better formed, there seems to be no reason why they should be crushed. As taxpayers, they are all the time contributing their full share to the maintenance of the Public School system, though they cannot conscientiously send their children to the Public School. Nor do they fail to impart the literary instruction which the policy of the state requires. This is a free country, let us have the full advantages of freedom, that of free experiment in education among the rest.—*Witness, Montreal.*

ASTRONOMICAL NOTES—DECEMBER.

THOS. LINDSAY, TORONTO.

OBSERVERS who had been expecting to see the advance guard of the Leonid meteors were quite disappointed during Novembe The night of Sunday, Nov. 14th, wa the time when the earth plunge into the thickest of the stream, but dense clouds obscured the heavens, and even had it been clear, the meteors would have been lost in the bright moonlight. We must wait another year for an opportunity to see a great display.

As we near the close of the year the planets become more favorably situated for observation. Mercury is evening star, and may be seen at greatest elongation east on the evening of Dec. 20th. The planet will be in close conjunction with the new moon on the evening of Dec. 24th. Venus, still morning star, will be seen in the same field of the telescope, with Mars on the morning of Dec. 30th. The observation will be of interest only on account of the positions of the planets, as their discs are quite small.

Jupiter is slowly coming into good position, and increasing in angular diameter. Towards the end of December the giant planet rises about midnight. Early morning observers may see satellite I. and its shadow on the disc of Jupiter, on December 20th, at 3 o'clock a.m. Again on the morning of Dec. 20th, at 5 o'clock, we may see the shadows of sats. I. and III. on the disc. It may be noted that a good two-inch telescope will show these shadows as little round black dots. The moons themselves, when in transit over Jupiter, are not so easily seen. It requires at least three-inch aperture to show these easily.

Saturn must be looked for before sunrise, and far south among the stars of Scorpio. We may expect to hear of some original work being done in planetary study during the coming year, as Prof. J. E. Keeler, of Allegheny, has announced his intention of bringing spectroscopic analysis to bear on the question of the rotation periods of the planets. With everything favorable, and with such instruments as have been employed in determining the velocity of stars in the line of sight, it is proposed to note the shifting of the lines in the spectrum of a planet, directing the spectroscope first upon the hemisphere approaching us and then upon the receding. The varying velocity of the outer and inner edges of Saturn's rings were determined in this way and by Prof. Keeler. There is every reason to believe that the positive proof as to the rotation of Venus may be given by the same authority.

There will be one interesting occultation during December. On the evening of the 27th, about 6 o'clock, the dark limb of the moon occults the 4th mag. star Theta in the constellation of Aquarius.

SCHOOL WORK.

ONTARIO NORMAL COLLEGE NOTES.

The examinations for students leaving in December begin on the 7th inst.

The following time-table has been issued:

9—12.

Dec. 7. Science of Education.
" 8. Psychology.
" 9. Methods in Mathematics (Pass).
" 10. Methods in English (Pass).
" 11. Methods in French and German (Pass).
" 13. Methods in Science (Pass Chemistry, Physics and Biology).
" 14. Methods in English (Specialists).
Dec. 15. Methods in Mathematics (Specialists).

1.30—4.30.

" 7. Methods in Latin (Pass).
" 8. School Management.
" 9. History of Education.
" 10. Methods in Elementary Science (Physics and Botany)
" 11. Methods in Greek (Pass).
" 13. Methods in Classics (Specialists).
" 14. Methods in French and German (Specialists).
Dec. 15. Methods in Science (Specialists).

The sessional examinations start on the 16th.

A branch of the Y.M.C.A. has been formed, with a prospective membership of 40. The following officers were elected: Pres., W. A. Hamilton; Vice-Pres., R. W. Anglin, B.A.; Secretary, D. Craig, B.A. Mr. J. L. Murray, late General Secretary of the Canadian College Missions, addressed a large audience of students in the Assembly Hall, Mr. E. S. Hogarth, B.A., presiding. The objects of the Society were explained to the students and their financial support and prayers requested.

On Friday evening, Nov. 12th, Mr. Frank Yeigh, of Toronto, gave a Musical Picture Travel Talk on British Land and Letters, illustrated by stereoptican views. Invitations were extended to the students of the College, the Collegiate and the Model School. Music was furnished by the ladies of the College.

The Literary Society meets every Friday afternoon in the Assembly Hall. Dr. McLellan has made this a part of the course, and students have the choice of attending and taking part in the proceedings or "grinding" in a class-room set apart for the purpose.

A source of great pleasure is the reading of the *O. N. C. Jottings*, a paper devoted to college items. Judging from the number of poems, spring cannot be far distant.

A football match between teams selected from the graduates and 1st C.'s resulted in a victory for the latter. Score, 4—1.

The college team have finished their series. The following is their record for the season: Games won, 1; games drawn, 1; games lost, 4.

CORRESPONDENCE.

MR. HEWTON REPLIES TO BYSTANDER.

A Spirited Letter from a Fearless Man.

To the Editor of *The News*:

DEAR SIR,—May I ask for space in the columns of *The News* for a few remarks prompted by "Bystander's" last letter? First, however, I would like to give expression to the pleasure I always feel in reading his able articles. Whether we agree with his views of matters or not, we must admit that he presents them in a readable manner.

The part of his letter to which I wish to draw attention is that in which he dismisses the grave charges, which from evidence placed in my hands, I felt it my duty to make at convention, and the storm of passion these charges evoked, as a "two penny half penny matter." That depends altogether on the standpoint from which you view it. If it be only a question of who shall fill the offices of the association, then I quite agree with "Bystander," for it would be impossible to select a bad list from its membership; but the question is a broader and greater one than this. The Provincial Association has been hitherto regarded as the teachers' parliament, where all could meet on a common footing and express their thoughts without fear or favor; it has assumed the right, and the assumption has been concurred in, of expressing its views on various public matters; these views have received the consideration due, not to the opinions of an individual, or of a clique, but to those of representatives of every section of the province. The association has been instrumental in introducing needed reform into the Protestant school system of the province. Anything, therefore, tending to reduce its representative character, or to throw it into the hands of a clique, however able and respectable, must be injurious to the association in particular, and to public education in general. It cannot add to the prestige or dignity of the association to have its members openly adopt the methods of the ward politician. A few men should not be allowed to trail its fair reputation in the dust, rob it of its best characteristics, kill the free exchange of thought at its meetings, and block the only channel our teachers at large have for giving expression to a common opinion.

Well did "Bystander" write in the letter referred to, and well may it be applied to the actions of those who manipulated the ticket elected at the last convention. "Plain honesty is no match for professional skill . . . virtue is admirable, but it is cunning that triumphs."

Plainly then if my charges were true it is a grave matter, and, indeed, it would be a grave matter to make such charges were they not true.

In connection with this there is

ONE SIGNIFICANT FACT

that cannot have escaped the notice of so astute an observer as "Bystander," viz., that no attempt was made to refute my statements. No ember rose in his place and stated that these things could not be so. What! was there not a storm of disapproval from a certain part of the hall? Did not certain gentlemen try to howl the speaker down? Yea, truly, but that did not commit them to anything, and be it noted that not one of the gentlemen who had raised such an outcry, rose to say that he at least had not convened a meeting of his subordinate teachers or laid the printed ticket before them. I wonder why! Well, but did not Dr. Robins and Mr. Rexford reply? Dr. Robins and Mr. Rexford, it is true, both spoke after I did, presumably in reply to me, but while I have no desire to add to or take away from anything these estimable friends of mine said, I cannot remember and the reporters do not seem to have discovered, that either of them attempted to controvert my statements. Dr. Robins stated a fact patent to all—that I am a taller man than he is—he then as usual referred to his skill as an educationist, but had not one word of condemnation for the open lobbying, while Mr. Rexford's reply consisted of a bitter attack on Mr. Truell. Neither of these gentlemen said that if their names had been used as I publicly stated they had been, it had been done without their knowledge or consent. Surely this was a fitting time and place for such denials.

A circumstance which makes

THE CAUCUS STILL MORE REPREHENSIBLE

is the nature of the relation existing between the subordinate teachers and the headmasters of the city schools on the one hand, and the superintendent of schools for Montreal on the other. The headmasters each year send to the superintendent a report regarding their subordinate teachers; these reports, the teachers believe to have no little influence on their tenure of office. What liberty of action then was left them when they were told by the headmasters that the superintendent, in company with the Principal of the Normal School and the Rector of the High School, had been concerned in concocting the ticket that was laid before them. When we consider this in connection with the fact that ballot papers were secured before the convention took place, it ceases to be a small matter. Do these gentlemen think us simple enough to believe that this "slate" was heaven-born, and heaven-printed, that they received it from, they knew not where, but were so struck with its surpassing excellence (possibly because their own names were on it) that they rushed from railway station to railway station, from boarding house to boarding-house, from member to member distributing the same? If so, they would indeed have us believe that they are wise as doves and harmless as——, well turtle doves! What shall be said of the manliness of officers of the association who made use of their position as officers to conspire against other officers—their equals in standing and experience? What effect can we expect the adoption of such a mode of action to have on the public morality of the rising generation? If this be the code of the present day, then must my standard of measurement be an old-fashioned one, but I have not lost faith in the old saying, "Magna est veritas, prevalebit," and so shall raise my voice, though none other be raised, in protest against the introduction of anything that tends to reduce the liberty of thought and action enjoyed in the past by the members of the Provincial Association of Protestant Teachers.

Pardon me for trespassing so extensively on your valuable space.

R. J. HEWTON.

Richmond, Que., Oct. 30th, 1897.

CONTEMPORARY LITERATURE.

A new serial, "With all her Heart," has lately been begun in the *Littell's Living Age.*

The housekeeper is fully instructed as to the Thanksgiving Turkey in the November number of *Table-Talk*, also there are "A Few Words about Mincemeat," and "Some Ways of Using Cranberries," all of which sounds very sensible and hunger-inspiring.

Those who are in the teaching profession will turn with more than usual interest to an article in the November *Scribner's*, entitled "Confessions of a College Professor." It is necessary for even highly educated people of more than average ability to come to the conclusion that in the ultimate they are not going to create much of a sensation in the world. This would be both annoying and depressing if it were not for something else that is even more true, "Is not the life more than meat?" One can be happy and even great in character and yet quite insignificant. The magazine is specially valuable as containing six full-page drawings by A. B. Frost.

There is a little story in a recent issue of *The Youth's Companion*, called "The Unsuccessful Teacher," which points out again to the doubting mind that after we have gone away and can't see things any more for ourselves, it is possible that good work may become evident. W were n): told everything when we were children, and afterwards found that there was some sense in that; there may be in this too.

In the *Bookman* some like one thing, some another; but one person at least prefers the poetry. The fact that occasionally selections are made from books of verse recently issued, insures a more felicitous choice than if the editor made a desperate point of printing only the best that had been offered to him, although that is often very good. It has been a great pleasure to find in a few successive numbers, such poetry as "The Ships of St. John," by Bliss Carman, "Resurgam," by Virginia Woodward Cloud, and "Within the Walls," by Alice Wardwell.

"Tommy, the Foot-Ball, and the Toy-Balloon," drawn by E. W. Kemble, and reproduced in the November number of *St. Nicholas*, must have come very near to the heart of the boy. "A Funny Little School," by Ruth McEnery Stuart, is the tale of an educational dilemma, and contains many valuable points on human nature while it is being taught. A new serial, "With the Black Prince," by W. O. Stoddart, is begun in the November number.

John Strange Winter is a good name on the front page of a magazine for an agreeable novelette. The lady contributes the complete novel to *Lippencott's* for November, and the name she has chosen for it is "The Price of a Wife." Among the articles may be mentioned "The Day of Dialect," a very sensible statement of the case, by T. C. DeLeon; and "Novelists as Costumers," by Eva A. Madden.

The Christmas number of the *Toronto Saturday Night* has been issued and merits more than a usually large sale. The short stories, of which there are a number, are lively and interesting and are well illustrated, this is particularly the case with Miss Sullivan's. Many will be glad to see in the Christmas Number a department devoted to the record and explanation of Canadian sport. There is a great opportunity for some publication to help to keep wholesome, elevate and encourage this important part of the life of our country, and this opportunity *Saturday Night* is rapidly making its own. It is a pleasure, as great as it is rare, to read an account of any contest which is a true report of fact, and not either an angry reprisal or a partizan rejoicing.

The Littell's Living Age for September 18th contains the sequel to "Gibbon's Love-Story" by Edith Lyttelton, taken from the *National Review*.

In *Heath's Modern Language Series* "Der Bibliothekar," by Gustav Von Moser, edited by B. W. Wells, has recently been issued.

"The True Story of Eugene Aram," by H. B. Irving, taken from *The Nineteenth Century*, will be found in *Littell's Living Age* for October 9th.

Referring to a recent report prepared by Mr. De la Bruere, Superintendent of Public Instruction, an article in the *Signal*, signed "Progrès," expresses indignation, at the small salaries paid teachers in French schools as compared with those given in the English schools. The report referred to shows that the average salary paid to teachers in the French Catholic primary schools is $233 a year, while the same class of teachers in English Protestant schools get $516. In the model schools and acadamies, French Catholic teachers get $442, while the English Protestant schools give $805. As regards female teachers, the average salary of those holding diplomas is, in the French Catholic schools, $103, and in the English Protestant schsols, $177, and those having no diplomas get $77 in the French schools and $142 in the English schools. Lady teachers in French model schools and academies get an average of $133, while the same class of teachers get $304 in the English Protestant schools. Commenting on the above, the writer says:—

"Why do we pay less than the English people for our male and female teachers? Is it with a view to get education at a rebate? Is it simply with a view to secure the luxury of placing our children in the hands of ignorant and incompetent persons? There is nothing to be wondered at if the English people give their children a practical education, since they pay to have good teachers. I trust that in the plan of school reform which the Hon. Mr. Robidoux is preparing, there will be a few clauses to regulate the salary of our teachers, and force our school-boards, against their own will, to pay the teaching staff decent salaries."

"Round the Year in Myth and Song," by Florence Holbrook. American Book Company, New York. A pretty and entertaining school reader intended for the third and fourth grades. The illustrations are particularly good, attention having been specially directed to Greek and Roman story.

"The Story of Jean Valjean," edited by Sarah E. Wiltse. Ginn & Company, Boston. No mistake can be made in attempting to gain attention for Victor Hugo's great masterpiece. It is extremely hard to make up one's mind about the advisibility of editing, that is making extracts from a whole which has been given to the public in that shape first by the author, but at least it invites attention to the original.

The University of Toronto has recently placed certain chapters from Dr. Bourinot's "Parliamentary Practice and Procedure in Canada," on the list of books it requires for the study of Political Science. The author has accordingly prepared some additions and alterations to this part of his work, and it has been published in a separate and convenient volume by Dawson Brothers, of Montreal. It is to be hoped that this will lead to the more general study and understanding of the Constitution of Canada.

We have received from the University Press, Oxford, a copy of the new "Presbyterian Book of Praise" for the use of the Church in Canada. To the members of the committee too much praise cannot be given for the way in which they have concluded their arduous undertaking. The benefit that they have bestowed upon the Church cannot be fully estimated for years, but it is to be hoped that the knowledge and pleasure they have themselves gained will be an immediate compensation. It now remains for the members of the Presbyterian Church, particularly for its ministers, to make themselves familiar with the music and the meaning of these psalms and hymns and spiritual songs, so that ignorance or indifference may not prevent the power of the book. The type, binding and paper are all most excellent.

"The Federal Judge," a novel by Charles K. Lush. Houghton, Mifflin & Company, Boston and New York.

This is a story relating to conditions, many of which are peculiar to the States. Judges are there subject to popular elections, a circumstance which is likely to produce complications from which we are happily free. But we are not altogether free from speculation and "rush," and a very rapid man of affairs with his eyes open might see some strange things about himself in this novel. The characters developed are interesting and vivid, but a great deal that most readers would like to hear about them has been left out, another speedy western way. The book, however, is well worth reading.

"King Lear," in the Pitt Press Shakespeare for Schools, edited by A. W. Verity. University Press, Cambridge. Among other valuable assistance collected for the study of this play will be found Charles Lamb's notable criticism of it.

From the Cambridge University Press we have received, also, "The First Book of Maccabees," edited by W. Fairweather and J. Sutherland Black, and "Quand j'Etais Petit," part 2, by Lucien Biart, edited by James Boielle.

Other books received are:—"A School History of the United States," by John Bach McMaster. The American Book Company, New York. "Histoire de la Premiere Croisade," edited by A. V. Houghton. Macmillan & Co., through their Toronto agents the Copp, Clark Co. "Little Lessons in Plant Life for Little Children," by H. H. Richardson, B. F. Johnson Publishing Co., Richmond. "The Natural System of Vertical Writing," by A. F. Newlands and R. K. Row. D. C. Heath & Co., Boston.

"An Elementary Course of Infinitesimal Calculus," by Horace Lamb. The University Press, Cambridge.

"This book attempts to teach those portions of the Calculus which are of primary importance in the application of such subjects as Physics and Engineering." The students at our Colleges, etc., reading with the intention of taking honors in Mathematics and Physics will find in this book much to aid them in their course of preparation.

"Gems of School Song," selected and edited by Carl Betz. American Book Company, New York. There is always an opening for good songs prepared for school use, and in the present text-book many will be found admirably adapted for that purpose. Selections have been made from the songs in use in Germany, many of which have not been before set to English words.

"Higher Arithmetic," by W. W. Beman and D. E. Smith. Ginn & Company, Boston. This text-book is intended more particularly for review work and deals with arithmetic as a science and not as a commercial convnience.

Eldredge and Brother, Philadelphia, have recently published a revised edition of Dr. Hart's "Manual of Composition and Rhetoric." The revision, which includes a new division on Invention, is the work of the author's son, and is modern in its character.

A book which will be of interest to Canadian educationists is "The Universities of Canada, their history and organization, with an outline of British and American University Systems." It has been prepared as an appendix to the report of the Minister of Education for 1896.

THANKFULNESS.

When gratitude o'erflows the swelling
heart,
And breathes in free and uncorrupted
praise,
For benefits received, propitious
heaven
Takes such acknowledgment as fragrant
incense,
And doubles all its blessings.

—*Lillo.*

Or any ill escaped, or good attained,
Let us remember still Heaven chalked
the way
That brought us thither.

—*Shakespeare.*

Lightning Source UK Ltd.
Milton Keynes UK
UKHW011619160119
335572UK00012B/1061/P